Product Management

McGraw-Hill/Irwin Series in Marketing

Product Management

Fourth Edition

Donald R. Lehmann
Columbia University

Russell S. Winer
New York University

McGraw-Hill Irwin

Boston   Burr Ridge, IL   Dubuque, IA   Madison, WI   New York   San Francisco   St. Louis
Bangkok   Bogotá   Caracas   Kuala Lumpur   Lisbon   London   Madrid   Mexico City
Milan   Montreal   New Delhi   Santiago   Seoul   Singapore   Sydney   Taipei   Toronto

**McGraw-Hill
Irwin**

PRODUCT MANAGEMENT

Published by McGraw-Hill/Irwin, a business unit of The McGraw-Hill Companies, Inc., 1221 Avenue of the Americas, New York, NY, 10020. Copyright © 2005, 2002, 1997, 1994 by The McGraw-Hill Companies, Inc. All rights reserved. No part of this publication may be reproduced or distributed in any form or by any means, or stored in a database or retrieval system, without the prior written consent of The McGraw-Hill Companies, Inc., including, but not limited to, in any network or other electronic storage or transmission, or broadcast for distance learning.

Some ancillaries, including electronic and print components, may not be available to customers outside the United States.

This book is printed on acid-free paper.

2 3 4 5 6 7 8 9 0 FGR/FGR 0 9 8 7 6 5

ISBN 0-07-286598-9

Editorial director: *John E. Biernat*
Sponsoring editor: *Barrett Koger*
Editorial coordinator: *Scott Becker*
Executive marketing manager: *Dan Silverburg*
Media producer: *Craig Atkins*
Project manager: *Kristin Puscas*
Senior production supervisor: *Sesha Bolisetty*
Coordinator freelance design: *Artemio Ortiz Jr.*
Lead supplement producer: *Cathy L. Tepper*
Senior digital content specialist: *Brian Nacik*
Cover design: *Artemio Ortiz Jr.*
Typeface: *10/12 TimesNewRoman*
Compositor: *GTS—New Delhi, India Campus*
Printer: *Quebecor World Fairfield Inc.*

Library of Congress Cataloging-in-Publication Data

Lehmann, Donald R.
    Product management / Donald R. Lehmann, Russell S. Winer.—4th ed.
        p. cm.—(McGraw-Hill/Irwin series in marketing)
    Includes bibliographical references and indexes.
    ISBN 0-07-286598-9 (alk. paper)
    1. Product management. I. Winer, Russell S. II. Title. III. Series.
HF5415.15.L44 2005
658.5′6—dc22
                                                                    2004053060

www.mhhe.com

To our families,
  colleagues,
  and students

Brief Contents

Contents

Chapter 4
Category Attractiveness Analysis   74

Chapter 5
Competitor Analysis   97

Chapter 6
Customer Analysis   139

Preface

One of the, if not *the,* basic tasks of a company, is the marketing of its products and services. This book focuses on those individuals who have the primary responsibility for the market success of the company's products and services. In many companies, particularly packaged goods companies, the person in charge of this activity has the title *product manager.* Although, as we note in Chapter 1, the title is not always the same, there are always individuals in the company who are, or should be, the "expert" for the product, someone to whom senior managers can assign responsibility for the execution of marketing plans and someone who advances or fails as a result of the product's performance.

The product manager's job is becoming increasingly complex. Due to, among other things, changes in information technology, the increased diffusion and improvement in the Internet, increasing global competition, and changing customer needs and wants, the job of the product manager involves continually collecting and synthesizing information, forecasting changes in competition and market conditions, revising market strategies, and adapting decisions such as price and communications to changing market conditions. In addition, cooperating with other parts of the organization (e.g., sales, operations) and outside parties (e.g., suppliers and channels) is critical. The purpose of this book is to provide a basic approach for dealing with these issues.

The fourth edition of *Product Management,* covers three major tasks facing marketers in general and product managers in particular:

1. Analyzing the market.
2. Developing objectives and strategies for the product or service in question.
3. Making decisions about price, advertising, promotion, channels of distribution, and service.

We use the development of a marketing plan as a unifying framework, a process that integrates the three tasks and provides a written record of the brand's history, prospects, and hopes.

WHY WE WROTE THE BOOK

Many fine textbooks deal with marketing management and strategy issues. These books either are general introductions to marketing management or focus more exclusively on strategic issues. One way to look at the existing set of textbooks is to relate them to job responsibilities. The general marketing management texts are excellent devices for introducing marketing concepts to all employees in an organization. The strategy books are more advanced and fit well with the jobs of senior marketing managers such as group product managers, vice presidents of marketing, and the like. These people usually manage "portfolios" of products and, sometimes, many product managers.

We have found that most existing textbooks do not adequately cover marketing managers who have day-to-day responsibilities for managing either a single product or service or a closely related product line. These managers know what the marketing concept is and understand the general pros and cons of basic strategy decisions (e.g., Which segment should I pursue?). What they need to know is how to write product marketing plans, how to select specific marketing strategies, and how to implement those strategies by making decisions regarding so-called marketing mix instruments. That is the focus of this book.

A second reason for writing this book is our belief that much of the research that marketing academics have produced has great relevance for practicing managers but is generally inaccessible to them. In this book, we attempt to bridge this gap. Particularly in the chapters on marketing decision making, we have attempted to integrate findings from academic research in the marketing management, consumer behavior, and marketing science literature.

The differences, then, between *Product Management* and other marketing textbooks are (1) its hands-on approach, (2) the focus on decision making, and (3) the attempt to simulate what the product manager's job is actually like.

As a result, we do not aim to be comprehensive; rather, we focus on the key tasks facing product managers. For example, there is no chapter on sales force management because typically the product manager has little influence on sales force size, compensation, territory design, reward systems, and so on. We also omit a very important part of any managerial position: interpersonal skills. Clearly, a large part of a product manager's success is usually related to an overall ability to get things done in a complex and often political organizational setting. We leave discussions of these issues to the appropriate experts.

WHAT IS NEW IN THE FOURTH EDITION

The most important changes in the fourth edition are as follows:

- We have expanded the chapter on customer analysis (Chapter 6). Since customers are both the key to a successful business and at the core of marketing, we felt some additional material was warranted. This includes some newer material such as the lifetime value of a customer.

- We also expanded the discussion of marketing strategy (Chapter 8). We present a measure of brand equity based on sales and prices and discuss customer-based strategy (acquisition, retention, expansion, and deletion).

- Of course, in the year 2004, any marketing book has to include the Internet. Although the core of a product manager's job has not changed, the Internet has certainly affected a number of activities. The outline of the marketing plan, for example, now has sections for website design. In addition, the pricing chapter (Chapter 10) features a discussion on issues such as online auctions.

- We have expanded Chapter 14 on Customer Relationship Management and Chapter 16 on Marketing Metrics. We feel that this is warranted given the increased attention being paid to both CRM and the measurement of the effectiveness of marketing expenditures, i.e. marketing ROI.

- One of the features readers liked best about earlier editions is the pair of running examples. The two examples in the fourth edition are energy bars and personal digital assistants (PDAs).

The basic outline of the book is the same, so past users and readers should be comfortable with the new edition.

THE STRUCTURE OF THE BOOK

As noted previously, the book covers three major areas of product manager responsibilities. The structure of the book uses the operating product marketing plan as a unifying theme. The marketing plan guide, given in the appendix to Chapter 2, is also an outline for the book:

Part 1 (Chapters 2 through 7) describes the marketing planning process and the background analyses necessary for constructing a successful marketing plan. Rather than taking a checklist or fill-in-the-blank approach as do many books on marketing planning, we attempt to keep the process as simple as possible while giving a sound rationale for answering the major questions.

Part 2 (Chapters 8 and 9) describes how to set sound product objectives and develop a product strategy as a result of the market analysis conducted in Part 1. Chapter 9 presents this material in the context of new products.

Part 3 (Chapters 10 through 14) covers the marketing mix with an emphasis on decisions. While Customer Relationship Management (Chapter 14) is not a classic marketing mix topic, it has become critical for product managers over the last decade.

Part 4 (Chapters 15 and 16) covers important ancillary topics such as financial analysis and marketing metrics, different measures product managers can use to assess the success of the plan.

INTENDED AUDIENCE FOR THIS BOOK

This book can be used at both the undergraduate and graduate levels. At the undergraduate level, the book can be used in a capstone course for seniors who have had several other marketing courses. At the MBA level, the book works best in a course positioned between the core marketing course and an advanced marketing strategy course. Those three courses make a very nice three-course sequence for marketing majors or those with a serious interest in marketing.

We also planned for the book to have a practitioner audience. As we have noted, *Product Management* is meant to be a practical, "hands-on" book based on actual product manager experiences across a wide variety of product categories. As a result, the book is not purely academic but attempts to integrate practical results from academic research that are not otherwise easily available to practicing managers. A product manager could read this book and immediately apply the concepts to his or her situation. Positive feedback from participants in executive education courses and other practicing managers support this contention.

We chose to title the book *Product Management* to connote the applicability of the concepts to high-tech, low-tech, and no-tech manufacturing, and to service situations. Our examples are purposefully diverse and, we hope, make the book useful to a toothpaste brand manager, a computer software product manager, and a product manager in the financial services sector.

We always appreciate feedback (of course especially so when it is positive). We invite you to send us e-mail with comments, suggestions, and questions.

Donald R. Lehmann
drl2@columbia.edu

Russell S. Winer
winer@stern.nyu.edu

About the Authors

Donald R. Lehmann

Donald R. Lehmann is George E. Warren Professor of Business at the Columbia University Graduate School of Business. He has a BS degree in mathematics from Union College, Schenectady, New York, and an MSIA and PhD from the Krannert School of Purdue University.

His research interests include modeling individual and group choice and decision making, empirical generalizations and meta-analysis, the introduction and adoption of new products and innovations, and measuring the value of marketing assets such as brands and customers. He has taught courses in marketing, management, and statistics at Columbia, and has also taught at Cornell, Dartmouth, New York University, and the University of Pennsylvania. He has published in and served on the editorial boards of *Journal of Consumer Research, Journal of Marketing, Journal of Marketing Research, Management Science,* and *Marketing Science,* and was founding editor of *Marketing Letters.* In addition to numerous journal articles, he has published several books including *Market Research and Analysis, Analysis for Marketing Planning, Product Management,* and *Meta Analysis in Marketing.* Professor Lehmann has served as Executive Director of the Marketing Science Institute and as President of the Association for Consumer Research.

Russell S. Winer

Russell S. Winer is the Deputy Dean and William Joyce Professor of Marketing at the Stern School of Business, New York University. He received a B.A. in Economics from Union College and an M.S. and Ph.D. in Industrial Administration from Carnegie Mellon University. He has been on the faculties of Columbia and Vanderbilt universities and, most recently, the University of California at Berkeley. He has been a visiting faculty member at M.I.T., Stanford University, New York University, Cranfield School of Management (U.K.), the Helsinki School of Economics, the University of Tokyo, and École Nationale des Ponts et Chausées. He has written three books, *Marketing Management, Analysis for Marketing Planning* and *Product Management,* and has authored over 60 papers in marketing on a variety of topics including consumer choice, marketing research methodology, marketing planning, advertising, and pricing. He is a past editor of the *Journal of Marketing Research,* the current co-editor of the *Journal of Interactive Marketing,* and is on the editorial boards of the *Journal of Marketing,* the *Journal of Marketing Research,* and *Marketing Science.* He has participated in executive education programs around the world, and is currently an advisor to a number of startup companies.

Chapter One

Introduction to Product Management

Overview

This book focuses on the job of managing a product. Not every marketing organization has a person with that exact title "product manager"; while many such jobs exist, the people who fill them could be called "brand managers," "marketing managers," or the like. We intend the generic title *product manager* to apply to different kinds of organizational structures and different kinds of companies, whether they provide consumer goods, industrial products, or services.

What makes this book different from the large number of books on "marketing management" or "marketing strategy"? We take the perspective of a manager whose primary responsibility is a product or a closely related product line. Broadly speaking, the product manager has two responsibilities. First, the product manager is responsible for the planning activities related to the product or product line.[1] Thus, the product manager's job involves analyzing the market, including customers, competitors, and the external environment, and turning this information into marketing objectives and strategies for the product. Second, the product manager must get the organization to support the marketing programs recommended in the plan. This may involve coordinating with other areas of the firm, such as research and development for product-line extensions, manufacturing, marketing research, and finance. It also involves internal marketing of the product to obtain the assistance and support of more senior managers in the firm. Figure 1.1 gives a perspective on a product manager's interactions within and outside the firm.

What, then, are the differences between a focus on the product manager and a more general marketing management perspective? Figure 1.2 indicates what separates the two. One key difference is that marketing managers in charge of a division or strategic business unit have more concerns about managing "portfolios" of products and about the long-term strategic direction of their business groups. Because product managers in our sense are in charge of a single product or a closely related product line, they are not

[1] When we use the term *product* throughout the book, we are referring to all kinds of products, including services. *Product* is simpler to use than *product/service*. While there are well-documented differences between marketing manufactured goods and services, the structure we present in this book is meant to be a template that can be used for all products.

1

FIGURE 1.1 **A Product Manager's Potential Interactions**

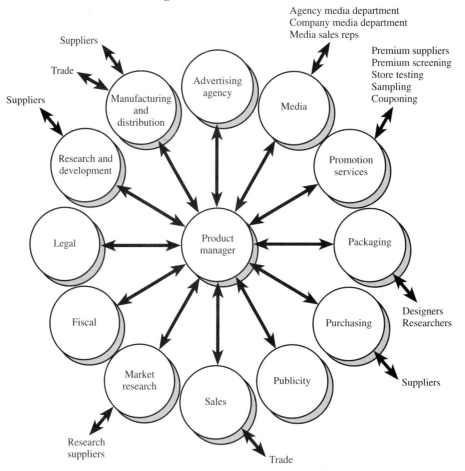

Source: Philip Kotler, *Marketing Management: Analysis, Planning, Implementation, & Control.* 11th ed., Prentice-Hall, 2003, p. 672. Reprinted with permission of Prentice-Hall, Inc., Upper Saddle River, New Jersey.

concerned on a day-to-day basis about the health of the general business area in which they operate.[2] A second key contrast is in the nature of decision making. Divisional marketing managers typically make strategic decisions about which products to add or drop and manage to meet an overall divisional financial objective. While product managers are involved with developing marketing objectives and strategies for their products, their key decisions are tactical and revolve around the marketing mix: how much to spend on advertising, how to react to a competitor's coupon promotion, which channels of distribution are appropriate, and similar questions. Finally, product managers and marketing managers face different time horizons. Product managers face substantial pressure to attain and hence focus on short-run market share, volume, or profit targets. Marketing

[2] The problem with the traditional product management structure is discussed later in this chapter. The narrow product or brand focus at the expense of the product category as a whole has given rise to a new position at many packaged goods companies: the category manager.

FIGURE 1.2   **Product versus General Marketing Management**

	Product Management	General Marketing Management
Scope of responsibility	Narrow: Single product or product line	Broad: Portfolio of products
Nature of decision making	Mainly tactical	Mainly strategic
Time horizon	Short-run (often annual or shorter)	Long-run

managers are also concerned with short-run targets, but they more often take a longer-term perspective of where the business is going.

Thus, this book focuses on the product manager's tasks of marketing planning, developing product strategy, and implementing that strategy through various marketing tools. The intended audience includes those who manage individual products and services or want to know how this is done. This book is not intended for senior managers whose responsibilities include managing groups of products. Excellent books for higher-level marketing managers include those by Aaker (2001), Day (1990), and Rao and Steckel (1998). *Product Management* also focuses largely on existing products, although we devote a chapter, Chapter 9, to the management of new products.

MARKETING ORGANIZATION

Although we briefly described the tasks of the "typical" product manager, they vary quite widely from organization to organization. The kinds of tasks product managers perform are highly related to how marketing is organized.[3] Three organizational structures for marketing have been identified: organizing by product, by market, and by function.

Product-Focused Organizations

Figure 1.3 provides a general view of this form of marketing organization. This is the classic "brand" management structure that Procter & Gamble developed in the 1930s. It is most often found in packaged goods industries, but it also exists in other industries. It is commonly used where different products use the same channels of distribution.

In this structure, the product manager acts as a "mini-CEO," taking responsibility for the overall health of the brand. Over time, a well-defined hierarchy within the product management system has developed, with key roles assigned to assistant and associate product managers. Often these jobs are entry-level positions for individuals who want careers in product management.

The tasks of these elements of the hierarchy are typically the following. The assistant product manager's job includes market and share forecasting, budgeting, coordinating

[3] Note that we resist referring to the marketing "function" within an organization. Referring to marketing as a functional area of the firm implies that only people in the marketing function perform marketing tasks. Nothing could be further from the truth; as service and other businesses are discovering, in today's business environment, with its growing emphasis on customer service, marketing is often looked at as everybody's job. More will be said about this in Chapter 14.

FIGURE 1.3   **Product-Focused Structure**

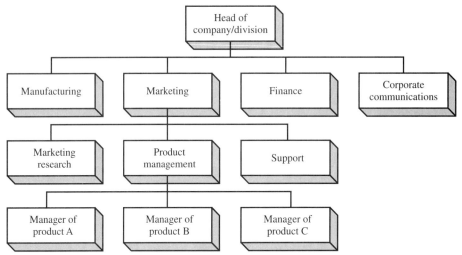

with production, executing promotions, and packaging. In general, the brand assistant's tasks involve becoming more familiar with the category within which the brand competes. Associate product managers have more freedom to develop brand extensions, and sometimes even manage a small brand. The product manager, of course, has the ultimate responsibility for the brand. Figure 1.4 shows an illustration of a "classic"

FIGURE 1.4   **General Foods Corporation (ca. 1984): Desserts Division Organizational Chart**

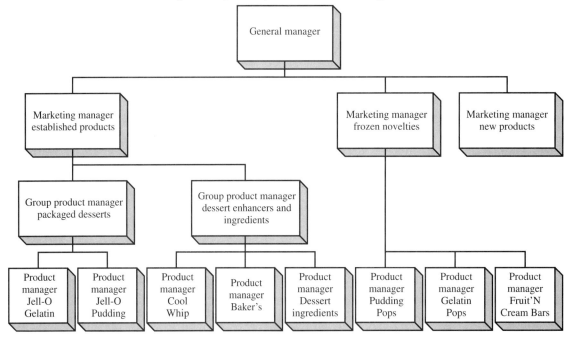

product-focused organization from General Foods Corporation's Desserts Division (from around 1984).[4]

As previously noted, this structure is not limited to packaged goods companies. Figure 1.5 illustrates the organizational structure of Adobe Systems Inc., a computer software company. The product marketing group has product managers whose responsibility is to put together marketing strategies and programs for their products such as Acrobat, Photoshop, and PageMaker. In this organization, product marketing differs from "marketing" in that the latter is more tactical in nature; that is, marketing offers support to product managers in the form of designing promotional events, trade show displays, and so forth. Also, note that the sales organization is responsible for all promotional programs oriented toward the channels.

The product management system has several advantages. The locus of responsibility is clear because the person responsible for the success of the product is the product manager and no one else. Because of this, it is also clear to whom the organization can turn for information about the product. Product managers' training and experience are invaluable; they develop the ability to work with other areas of the organization and the persuasion and communication skills necessary to be an advocate for the product. In fact, companies with product-focused marketing organizations are often breeding grounds for senior executives of other companies that highly value the training received.

The product management system also has its weaknesses. The narrow focus on one product can lead to an inability to step back and ask more fundamental questions about customer needs. It can also be a very centralized structure in which the product manager is somewhat removed from "where the action is" in the field. One of the changes in marketing organizations we will discuss later is an attempt to flatten the organization and decentralize product management, particularly when significant differences exist in regional tastes for a product. In addition, some people complain that product managers are too myopic in their quest for quarterly or even shorter-term sales and market share goals. One result of this perspective has been the dramatic increase in the use of short-term marketing tools, such as sales promotions, for consumer packaged goods. A final risk in a product-focused organization, particularly for industrial products, is that it could result in several salespeople representing different products from the same company calling on the same customer. This problem is most likely to occur when the sales force is organized by product specialties and is not necessarily a general characteristic of product management organizations. In companies that use "family" brands (brand names that have a common component such as "Kraft"), the separation of brand managers' activities can result in inefficient use of marketing funds to build that brand name.

These and other problems that product managers face have led some to predict the "death" of the product management system and widespread "burnout" among product managers (see, for example, Berthon, Hulbert, and Pitt, 1999; Reyes, 2003). Some of the factors leading to burnout are senior managers who have a short-term focus that stifles innovation, an explosion of marketing data leading to information overload, corporate downsizing, and more responsibility and pressure with less autonomy.

---

[4] Since then, of course, General Foods has merged with Kraft and become part of the Altria Group, Inc. (formerly, Philip Morris).

FIGURE 1.5   Adobe Systems Marketing Organization

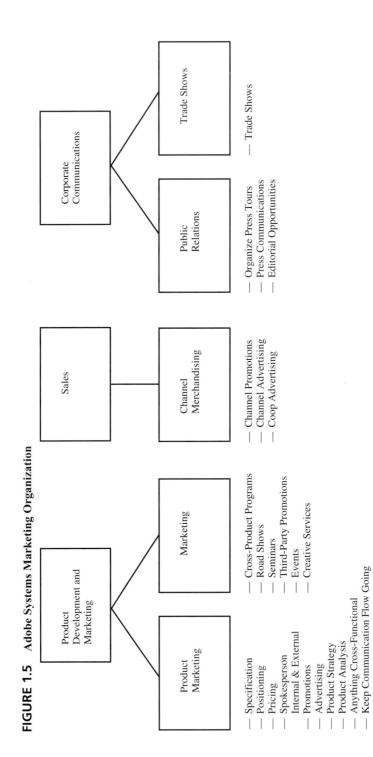

FIGURE 1.6 GM's New Organizational Structure

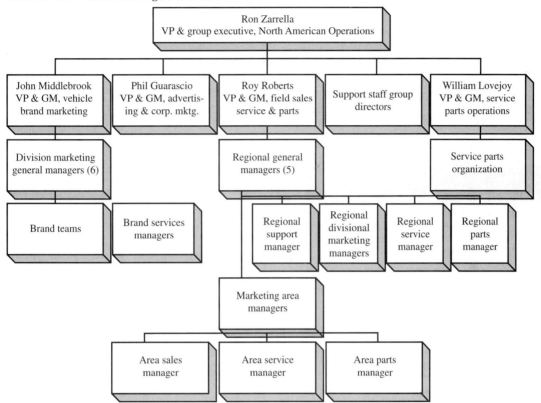

Perhaps the biggest "black eye" for the product/brand management system was its implementation at General Motors. In a massive reorganization in the mid-1990s (Figure 1.6), GM's marketing organization (the left side of the chart) had division marketing general managers (e.g., Cadillac) as well as brand teams (e.g., DeVille). The job of the brand team was to pay special attention to a particular model and attempt to develop a unique positioning for that model among the myriad number of GM brands. However, in 2002, new vice chairman for product development, Bob Lutz, quietly sent a number of brand managers to new assignments or to early retirement and the remaining received new job titles.

At the same time, the product management system continues to flourish in many consumer and industrial product companies. One study (Gorchels, 1995) reported that hospitals with a product management organization outperformed those without it on nearly all performance indicators, including occupancy rate, gross patient-revenue per bed, average profit margin, and return on assets. In addition, companies continue to adopt the organizational structure. Several major automobile manufacturers such as Ford and Mitsubishi have adopted the focus on individual brands and products that the product management system brings, despite GM's problems.

Market-Focused Organizations

Figure 1.7 describes the market-focused organization. This structure defines marketing authority by market segment. Segments can be defined by industry, channel, regions of the country or the world, or customer size. The market-focused structure is clearly useful when there are significant differences in buyer behavior among the market segments that lead to differences in the marketing strategies and tactics used to appeal to them. For example, banks often define their activities in terms of corporate versus consumer business, and within the corporate business they often define market segments in terms of customer size.

Figure 1.8 shows the marketing organization of one of the regional Bell Telephone operating companies (often referred to as RBOCs). This organizational chart divides marketing into three large groups: consumer, business, and interindustry (business with other carriers, such as Sprint). Within each business market are different operational functions and product management. For example, within the consumer sector are product managers for custom-calling features such as call waiting and special phone directory listings. Within the business sector are product managers for pay telephones, central office phone services, local area network planning services, and many other services. This type of organization, however, does not give managers full responsibility for their services and products. Product managers are instead more like coordinators who implement marketing programs developed by the staffs of the three business managers.

Clearly the big advantage of this market-based structure is its focus on the customer. This focus on customers as assets makes it easier to consider changes in customer tastes and when necessary modify or eliminate some of the products currently being marketed. It is particularly useful when the product being marketed is a system that bundles a number of products made by the company or when the customer purchases many different products from the company. A product management structure offers insufficient motivation to spend time on a system sale, which may involve little revenue for a particular product. The market-based structure makes it easier to get the product managers to pull together. These managers often have better knowledge about the company's lines of products than do the product managers in a product-focused company.

FIGURE 1.7 **Market-Focused Organization**

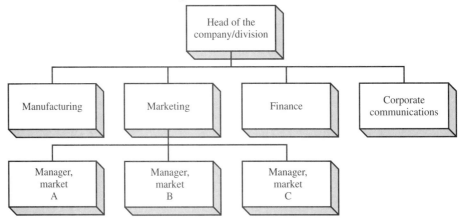

FIGURE 1.8 Marketing Organization: Regional Bell Operating Company

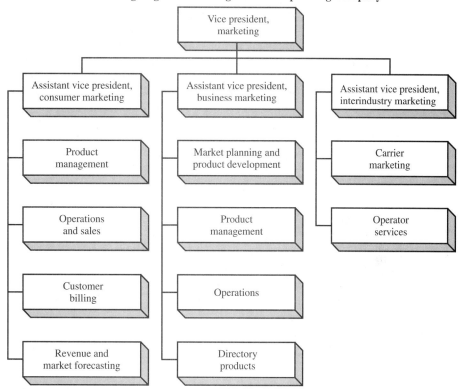

A drawback of this structure is the potential conflict with the product management structure that may lie beneath it. In addition, some of the mini-CEO training and experience of traditional product managers is lost. Importantly, however, most of the skills, procedures, and activities required to be a good product manager are critical for market-focused management as well.

Levi Strauss reorganized its marketing organization in 1998 in order to focus on customer segments (the former organization was functional; see the next section). As part of their reorganization, the company named marketing managers in charge of 15- to 24-year-olds (all Levi-branded products), and young adults (24–35; Dockers and Slates brands) (Cuneo, 1998).

Functionally Focused Organizations

As opposed to the product-focused and market-focused organizations, functionally focused organizations align themselves by marketing functions such as advertising and sales promotion. A general illustration of this type of structure appears in Figure 1.9. Most marketing organizations have some aspect of this structure; it is common, for example, for sales and marketing research to be separate functions. However, in functionally focused structures, no single person is responsible for the day-to-day health of a product. Marketing strategies are designed and implemented through the coordinated activities.

FIGURE 1.9 **Functionally Focused Organization**

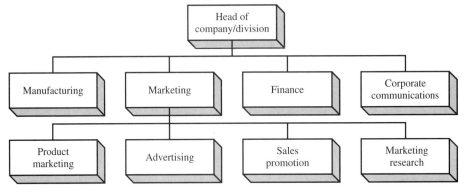

Figure 1.10 represents the organizational structure of a well-known toy manufacturer that markets three different products. Reporting to the vice president of marketing are marketing support, advertising and public relations, publications (a magazine targeted toward product users), and merchandising, which deals with retailers and point-of-purchase displays. In this company, the CEO and the vice presidents make marketing strategy decisions. Strategies are implemented through discussion and coordination

FIGURE 1.10 **Marketing Organization: Toy Manufacturer**

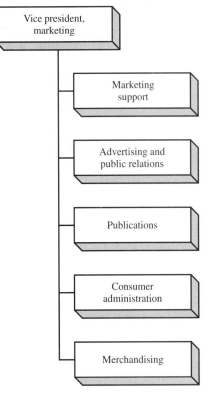

among the functional areas. This structure serves the company well when it is producing only two products. As the company adds products, however, the increased coordination needed raises the potential for confusion and makes it questionable whether the company can continue to sustain its success.

This highlights one of the drawbacks of the functionally oriented structure: Who is responsible for the product? Someone must take day-to-day responsibility for each product or service marketed by the organization. Conflicts between product marketing strategies can be resolved only by spending substantial time in meetings. The management training aspect of the structure also focuses on functional rather than general management education.

However, this kind of structure has some advantages. It is administratively simple: The groups are designed to be parallel to normal marketing activities. Functional training is better; for example, a person whose sole responsibility is to develop sales promotions will bring better skills to that area. Also, it may be desirable that the marketing vice president does much of the planning because of that person's broader business perspective.

THE ROLE OF THE SALES FORCE

The previous discussion focused on the organizational structure of marketing management within companies. Although sales is an element of the marketing mix, most companies have separate sales organizations with their own structures and coordinating relationship with marketing organizations (see, for example, the Adobe marketing organization chart in Figure 1.5).

Briefly, there are three kinds of sales organizational structures. One structure is organized around product lines. This product/product structure sells a product or product line to all markets and often coexists with a product-focused organization. The second structure, product/market, has a product-oriented marketing structure, but each salesperson sells all products marketed by a division to a single market. Finally, the market/market structure has a market-based marketing organization and a sales force that sells a complete product line to a single market.

These structures have different advantages and disadvantages, with the product/product and the market/market structures exhibiting the most extreme characteristics. Advantages often cited for the product/product structure are easy administration, clear communications with manufacturing and operations, and effective cost control of product expenses. As in the product management system, a disadvantage is lack of concern with and communication about customer needs as well as duplication of effort. In the market/market structure, customer needs may be better served by both existing and new products. However, lines of responsibility for individual products are blurry.

MARKETING ORGANIZATION IMPLICATIONS OF GLOBAL MARKETING

Global marketing is the attempt to market a product or service using a common strategy around the world with only minor tactical changes in packaging, advertising, and the like. Some companies, most often producers of consumer products, have been successful global marketers. These include Coca-Cola, McDonald's, British Airways, Nike, Unilever, Procter & Gamble, and Tambrands.

Unfortunately, global marketing often conflicts with companies' organizational structures. Most companies do not become global overnight. Usually they begin by exporting their products to some countries outside the domestic market, often using local agents for distribution. These evolve into rather strong local organizations that can have substantial power in making decisions involving pricing, packaging, and even brand names. Of course, these regional managers are most familiar with local customs, institutions, and customer needs.

In the mid-1990s, many companies reduced the clout of these country or regional managers. Strategic questions about brands were often handled by global divisions. Companies like Dow Chemical and Oracle reorganized to centralize decision making about their products. With respect to the latter, human resources personnel found that each country had a different employment contract, so the legal department had to handle each country separately. Oracle France had a different logo than Oracle U.K., and the customer support organizations in the different countries did not speak to each other (*The Economist,* 2002). The typical international marketing structure with powerful country heads limits the ability to market globally or even market a product using a similar strategy in a specific region of the world. For example, in 2000, the battery maker Exide had 10 separate country organizations. In this structure, the European country managers were actually undercutting each other in price as they were trying to maximize their own results to meet their targets (Lublin, 2001). This clearly does not help build even a consistent regional brand, much less a global one.

In the 21st century, the traditional role of the country manager is changing due to global competition, global customers, global integration, regional trading blocs, and strategic alliances. The role of the country manager as "king" or "queen" in his or her region is shifting to multinational companies using sales managers who report to either regional managers or centralized product managers. However, some kind of local management will always be necessary to allow a company to stay close to local customers and government authorities.

As has historically been the case, Procter & Gamble has been a leader in providing a new model for global marketing organizational structure. Their new model draws a distinction between high- and low-income markets. In richer countries, the centralized business unit has responsibility for allocating resources; in poorer areas such as China and Eastern Europe, the country or regional managers make the key decisions. The company has found that in less wealthy areas, it is important to have local knowledge about channels, raw materials, and the like. However, it is even more complex as P&G also allocates decision making depending upon the product. When consumers use an identical product in similar ways all over the world (e.g., shampoo), decisions are made through global headquarters. With products such as laundry detergents that have varied usage by country, business teams have been created by product line within individual countries. An example is Germany, where a local team works with the division responsible for laundry products in Western Europe (*The Economist,* 2002).

PRODUCT MANAGEMENT: FACT VERSUS FICTION

Much of the preceding description of the product manager's job and the types of organizational structures that affect the role of product managers was general. As is always the case, there are exceptions to the rules. Even within a specific organization type, the product manager's job varies among industries and among products.

A survey of 25 product managers at a wide variety of firms sheds some light on the product manager's job (Amin, Lee, and Sirotzky, 2003). To get a flavor for the responses to the survey, summaries from four of the interviews are provided in the appendix to this chapter. Although the sample is not large or randomly selected, we can draw some general implications.

Backgrounds

The only common trait appearing in the sample of product managers was that there is no single background that predicts success. Even within the same industry, companies exhibited a high degree of variability in their product managers' education and experience. The only consistent factors are that (1) they had proven themselves as managers in roles prior to their current positions, and (2) they all had at least a bachelor's degree. An MBA is common but not required.

In high-tech companies, many managers had undergraduate degrees and some experience in engineering. In these companies, value is placed on understanding the technological possibilities of the products as well as the ability to market and sell them. This is especially true when the position requires coordinating with engineering to modify a product based on customer feedback. In this situation, the product manager's role combines marketing expertise with product knowledge. An engineering background can also lend credibility to the product manager when dealing with a high-tech company composed mainly of engineers.

Critical Skills

Negotiation

The skill that is mentioned the most among the managers interviewed was some type of negotiations, persuasion, or influence management. Product/brand managers often find themselves managing teams of functional partners who are essentially players involved with reaching the end goal but over whom they hold no direct authority. Thus, these managers find themselves in a constant state of persuasion or influence management, always looking for the best win-win scenarios where all goals can be obtained.

Teamwork

The other skill that seemed common to most individuals is the ability to work in and lead teams of individuals from all parts of an organization. Because the product manager must synthesize information from a variety of departments, the role requires managers to coordinate, organize, and facilitate workers from many groups both inside and outside the organizations. For example, at Colgate-Palmolive, a brand manager needs to work with the new products group when developing a brand extension of an existing product in his or her line. At the same time, the manager must coordinate development of a line extension with suppliers and distributors to ensure that the product will reach the right locations, in the right quantities, and at the right time. In another example, in the financial services sector, an American Express brand manager works with customer service and people in more financially driven functional areas such as risk and corporate finance.

When managing not only a brand but also a group of either peers or junior level managers, the product manager must foster harmony among these individuals. When the manager is responsible for the development of junior staff as well as a product, she or he must ensure that these individuals are in the right role for them, allowing them to feel challenged and involved. This means that the brand manager must ensure that the associate and assistant brand managers are contributing up to their potential and that they feel challenged and rewarded by the work.

Communications Skills

A large part of the role of any product manager is communicating the successes and challenges of the product or brand to upper management and the company as a whole. In addition, product managers may be called upon to communicate the benefits of their product to the outside world in the form of advertising or promotional materials. Both of these tasks require the manager to be an excellent communicator, in both written and oral forms, as they are in effect the ambassadors of their product.

Analytical Ability

In some organizations, the product manager's job requires a great deal of quantitative analysis, interpretation, and general number crunching, particularly in companies that position marketing as a source of strategic information. For example, at consumer package goods and beauty/health care companies, the product managers are measured against the sales performance of their brands and the perceived brand position in the marketplace. Analytical skills are critical to ensure that constant analysis of sales targets, share versus competition, and impact of promotions is taking place. At DoubleClick, the Internet advertising media firm, there is also a heavy emphasis on analytical ability, although in a different way. In this case, the product managers are involved in brainstorming meetings to discuss new products. If the product is deemed viable, then the manager must develop an overall business plan and a "4Ps" (product, price, promotion, place) analysis before seeking approval from senior management. This is done in conjunction with more traditional pricing analysis for each existing product and modeling to determine sales targets.

The Marketing Plan

The importance, name, role, authors, and even existence of marketing plans in companies vary across a wide range. Surprisingly, size is not always an indicator of importance; while some large, established companies "live and breathe" a marketing plan, others such as software companies place little or no importance on the plan. Further, while one would expect smaller companies to have fewer resources to devote to developing a plan, some devote substantial time to one.

Plans could be called anything from marketing requirements documents (MRDs) to merchandising plans (for retailers like The Gap). However, they typically contain product definitions, features, target markets, timelines, and resources needed to develop a marketing strategy for the product or service. Most often, product managers write marketing plans with input from other functions such as finance, operations, and marketing communications. The time needed to write a plan averages two to three months with some variance in how often they are written. For example, managers at the fashion company Ann Taylor write plans according to the season.

Variance across Industry/Company Size

A number of differences were observed in the product management function across industries and different-sized companies.[5] These include the following:

- In high-tech companies, new product development is commonly a substantial component of a product manager's job. In fact, the line is sometimes "gray" as to whether a product manager belongs to the marketing or new products group in the organizational chart.

- The smaller the company, the more hands-on responsibilities the product manager has while, interestingly, some common product management responsibilities such as pricing and marketing strategy are shifted to upper management.

- Due to the nature of high-tech products and their Internet-savvy customers, the Internet is a more valuable tool for direct customer feedback in such companies than for traditional consumer product companies and is often relied upon for the generation of new product ideas. This also results in a much faster job pace.

- Traditional consumer products companies have the luxury of standardized secondary research due to the maturity of their industries, while market research for high-tech companies is a looser concept and is invariably less comprehensive and less formal.

- Performance evaluations at consumer products companies tend to incorporate profit-and-loss-related criteria while high-tech companies tend to focus more on successfully completing new product projects on time and meeting launch goals.

CHANGES AFFECTING PRODUCT MANAGEMENT

It is often said that the only constant is change. Product managers such as those in the study described in the previous section face many challenges in adapting to the changes in the marketing environment. Some of the key changes are as follows:

1. *The Web.* Clearly, since the birth of the World Wide Web (WWW) in the mid-1990s, the nature of marketing has changed dramatically. The Web is a new channel of distribution, a new communications medium, and a new way of creating a community around a brand. It can be used for both customer acquisition and customer retention purposes. The Web is part of brand building, and it affects many other facets of the product manager's job. This is true for consumer products and services and even more for business-to-business products. One key impact of the Web is that it has changed the format of the marketing plan we will describe in Chapter 2. All plans must now have a section devoted to how the product manager plans to integrate the Web into his or her plan.

2. *The data explosion.* As the product managers interviewed for this book noted, effective marketing today requires sophisticated information management. For consumer packaged-goods companies, this means better and more timely information on market shares, sales, and distribution due to the proliferation of scanners in supermarkets. Almost all products sold through the retail system are more effectively tracked by

---

[5] These results are accumulated over the four sets of interviews that have been conducted for the four editions of the textbook.

both the retailer and the manufacturer due to increased use of information technology. The use of laptop computers and fax machines means quicker transmission of competitor information and sales call reports from the field. Database marketing—launching marketing programs from computerized customer lists—is becoming a key approach for obtaining and keeping customers. Websites routinely use "data mining" software to plumb the depths of the transaction and traffic data in order to better place advertisements and make unique offers to site visitors.

3. *The increased emphasis on brands.* The 1980s was clearly the era of sales promotion and price discounts. These activities may increase short-term volume, but they have negative long-term effects on how consumers see the brand. A brand once associated with quality becomes associated with low price and discounting. A major trend that started in the 1990s was the realization that one of the greatest assets a company has is its set of brands and the image and confidence customers have in them. This has continued into the 21st century as product managers worry about the proliferation of channels and media and the impact of the introduction of price comparison websites. A key term used by product managers is *brand equity,* the value of the brand name. Brand names such as Coke, Mercedes, IBM, Amazon, and Federal Express are not just descriptive labels but are product attributes that require consistent investment for maintenance and enhancement. We expand on this issue in Chapter 8.

4. *Changes in the balance of market power.* Prior to the mid-1980s, manufacturers held the upper hand in dealing with retailers due to asymmetry in information: Manufacturers had a better idea of what was selling than retailers because of better data collection methods. Today improvements in information technology and partnerships between manufacturers and sellers in developing measurement systems have given both parties equal access to sales and market share data. As a result, the balance of power in distribution channels has shifted from the manufacturer to the retailer. This has created more manufacturer awareness, even among manufacturers with powerful brand names, that retailers must be treated as key customers (indeed, Procter & Gamble refers to retailers as its customers) and that it is as important to be close to them as it is to the end customer. This is the so-called Wal-Mart effect, as that company has become the largest in the world through the pricing power it can deliver to customers from the pressure it puts on its suppliers. A countervailing force in some product categories such as books and CDs is that end customers hold increasing power due to the Web. Customers can demand what they want, when they want it, and the price they are willing to pay with a few clicks of the mouse.

5. *Increased importance of customer retention programs.* Companies are becoming very attuned to the lifetime-value-of-a-customer concept, whereby one measures the value of a customer by the discounted stream of income from future purchases. By focusing more on keeping customers than on attracting brand switchers, who have a greater overall propensity to switch to someone else eventually, product managers are paying more attention to customer service and satisfaction programs, database marketing, and advertising and promotion programs aimed at satisfying current customers and/or getting them to buy more of the product. It may even make sense to have different managers in charge of customer acquisition and customer retention.

6. *Increased global competition.* Unquestionably, product managers have to be equipped to deal with worldwide competition—not only by having appropriate organizational structures, as discussed earlier in this chapter, but also by obtaining experience and knowledge about how a variety of cultures conduct business. Countries in different parts of the world are forming trading blocs (e.g., the European Union, MERCOSUR in South America) and economic free-trade zones that are changing the "rules of the game."

CHANGES IN MARKETING ORGANIZATIONS

As noted previously, companies have used a variety of organizational forms for their marketing function. Most of the changes in the environment noted earlier have led to important shifts in resource allocation within the firm rather than to massive shifts in the organizational structure. These include investments in the new interactive methods for reaching customers, data processing capabilities, and so on.

As the developer of the brand management system, Procter & Gamble is often benchmarked for its marketing organization changes. Thus, when the company announced in 1999 that it was changing its brand management system toward a "market development" organization (MDO), many companies took notice (Neff, 1999a). The new MDO system reorganized brand managers into geographically and ethnically based "customer business" or sales teams in order to develop comarketing programs with retailers, redesigning stores, establishing partnerships with other companies, and generally looking more broadly on a multibrand, household basis. The result is a kind of hybrid between the brand- and market-focused organizations described earlier in this chapter. For example, an MDO project in the Philippines attempted to boost the sales of several P&G brands by putting washing machines into more homes. In a joint venture with a manufacturer and a bank, P&G gave consumers low-interest credit cards they could use to buy the washers. Similarly, a group focusing on low-income U.S. consumers developed a lower-priced, nonconcentrated version of Dawn dishwashing detergent for sale in a particular retail chain, Dollar General stores (Neff, 1999b).

P&G also recognized that its brand management structure was ill-suited to handle the fast-paced Internet marketing environment. The company established an independent organization, Reflect.com, offering customized beauty care products with the intention of transferring the learning into the parent company. Today, Reflect.com is thriving (see Figure 1.11). This is another good illustration of the fact that marketing organizations should adapt to the changing business environment as any good marketing strategy should.

One change mentioned earlier that has had a strong impact on marketing organizations is the increased power of the retailer in the distribution system channel, particularly for consumer products. The perspectives of manufacturers and retailers are quite different. Retailers' scarce resource is their selling space, and they care less about how a particular brand is selling than what is happening to the sales of a product category, department, or store as a whole. In other words, retailers are more interested in a category perspective than a brand perspective. Of course, the reverse is often true for manufacturers.

This category perspective can be coupled with the data explosion that has given retailers, manufacturers, and data suppliers a microscope under which to analyze the

FIGURE 1.11 **Reflect.com**

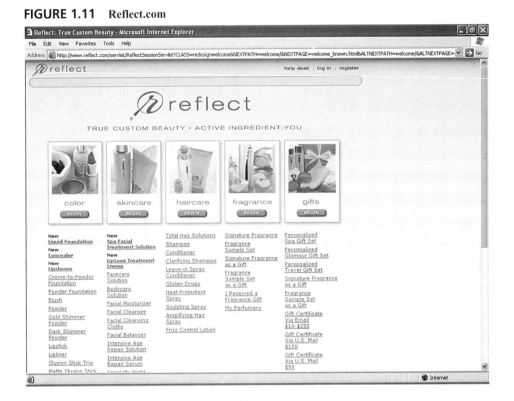

performance of different product categories in different parts of the country, different parts of a state, and different areas within a city. To optimize their product mix, retailers not only want to offer the appropriate brands in a category, they want the mix of brands and product varieties to be appropriate for the ethnic and socioeconomic composition of the shopping areas in which particular stores are located.

Thus, in the early 1990s, a concept called category management was introduced into the product manager's lexicon (A. C. Nielsen, 1992; *Progressive Grocer,* 1999). Category management has been defined as a process that considers product categories to be business units that should be customized on a store-by-store basis in a way that satisfies customer needs. Retailers have category managers who, like product managers and their brands, are empowered to operate their categories as separate businesses.

The category management phenomenon has had an important impact on product management organizations from the perspective of the responsibilities of product managers and the sales force. This is highlighted in Figure 1.12. Under the traditional approach (that is, when manufacturers had information about which products were selling and which were not), the sales force focused on gaining distribution, getting retailers to promote their brands, and pushing the product managers for trade-oriented promotions to increase short-run volume. As noted earlier in this chapter, the product manager's job has traditionally been to develop the marketing strategies and programs for his or her product.

More recently, however, marketing organizations have begun to view the retailer as a partner in the effort to provide a mix of products that best satisfy customer needs. Under

FIGURE 1.12 Changing Organization Structures

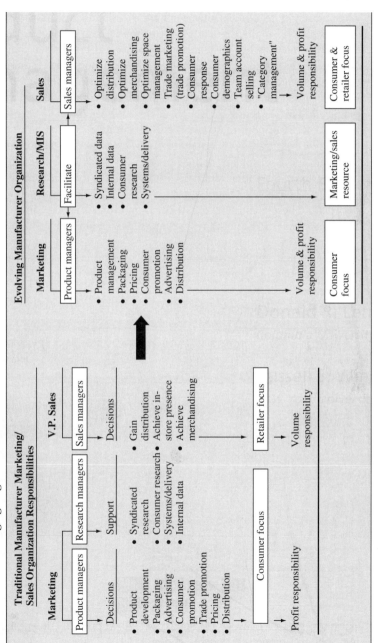

Source: A. C. Nielsen, *Category Management: Positioning Your Organization to Win*, NTC Business Books, 1992, pp. 106–107.

a category management system, manufacturers have to be concerned about meeting not only their objectives but also the retailer's. This has meant that within the manufacturer, the product management, sales, and marketing research organizations also have to work together as a team, since typically a salesperson sells a large number of a company's products managed by an equivalently large number of product managers. Salespeople work closely with product managers and marketing research management information systems (MIS) people to provide information to both product managers and salespeople, the former interested in customer behavior toward brands and the latter concerned with customer behavior toward the whole product category. Interestingly, in this era of category management, the salesperson is really the key person since she or he is the link between product managers interested primarily in their brands and retailers interested mainly in their categories. The job of the salesperson is to become intimately familiar with the needs of both the retailer and the customer so that he or she can configure the company's offerings appropriately to a particular store. The pressure on the salesperson to understand both retailer and customer is expanding; a new acronym, CMAR, stands for "consumer marketing at retail." Under CMAR, the salesperson will not only have to understand how his/her brand of, say, cereal fits into the ready-to-eat cereal category but how it fits into the entire breakfast occasion (Turcsik, 2002). Interestingly, some Internet companies have also found the category organization format to their liking. Figure 1.13 shows the home page from eBay. As can be seen, the well-known auction site organizes its products by categories and has category managers to oversee their activity. We will return to this category management phenomenon in Chapter 13.

FIGURE 1.13   eBay Home Page

FIGURE 1.14   **Restructuring the Adaptive Marketing Organization**

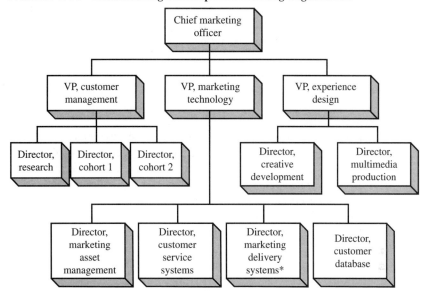

*Includes the management of ad-serving, e-mail, and affiliate-program systems.

Some feel that the new, interactive environment of the early 21st century will place more emphasis on developing strategies and brand messages reflecting millions of customer interactions. The impact of this new environment could result in what has been termed the "adaptive" marketing organization (Nail, Charron, and Parr, 2000) with a chief marketing officer (CMO) and three direct reports (see Figure 1.14):

1. VP, customer management, who is in charge of customer "cohorts."
2. VP, marketing technology, who develops the information technology structure for the company's databases, customer relationship management, and other information-intensive activities.
3. VP, experience design, who translates customer understanding into technical requirements.

Many similar ideas have been generated by other marketing writers and thinkers. However, while it is clear that organizational changes will occur, the basic problem of having to develop successful marketing programs for individual products and services will never disappear.

OVERVIEW OF THE BOOK

Marketing Planning

The first seven chapters of the book cover the background analysis for developing marketing plans. A distinctive feature of the marketing-planning chapters is the use of two running illustrations of the material presented, energy snack bars and personal digital assistants (PDAs). These illustrations are introduced in Chapter 2. Chapter 2 also presents an overview of marketing planning, including a rationale for developing marketing plans. An important part of this chapter is a comprehensive outline of a marketing plan. One of the key changes in the marketing environment facing product managers is the shifting nature of competition. Chapter 3 discusses the importance of looking at competition from a broad perspective, one beyond the narrowly defined product category. Chapters 4, 5, and 6 describe the core background analyses for marketing plans: category, competitor, and customer analysis. Chapter 7 discusses how to develop estimates of both market potential and future sales or market share, at either the brand or product level.

Marketing Strategy

Chapter 8 discusses how objectives and a complete marketing strategy are developed based on the background analyses from Chapters 4 through 7. While this book is intended to be a template for all kinds of products and services, there are some aspects of being a product manager on a new product that are different and need additional discussion. Chapter 9 covers the marketing planning and strategy process from the perspective of new products.

Marketing Program Decisions

The rest of the book focuses on decisions product managers typically have to make as part of their jobs. Our approach to this section is unusual in two ways. First, we do not attempt to cover all aspects of an area. As a result, for example, we do not cover the creative aspects of advertising in depth. Instead, we discuss the issues we believe are most critical to product managers, such as setting budgets and evaluating advertising effectiveness. Second, where appropriate, we discuss recent results from the academic marketing research literature and make them accessible to practicing product managers.

We cover key marketing mix variables, including pricing (Chapter 10), advertising (Chapter 11), and sales promotion (Chapter 12). We do not cover sales management in this book. While the sales force is a key resource and, as the discussion about category management illustrated, is increasingly becoming a partner with product management in working with retail and end customers, the survey discussed earlier indicated that most product managers do not have authority over decisions about its size, allocation of resources, and other functions. In fact, as we noted in this chapter, sales and marketing are usually separate organizations.

The last four decision-oriented chapters of the book cover some topics not usually discussed in other marketing management texts that are extremely important for product management in the early 21st century. In Chapter 13, we discuss how decisions about channels of distribution and the general problem of reaching customers have become more complex. For example, substantially increased spending on direct marketing is one new way companies are reaching customers. In Chapter 14, we focus on developing a framework for customer relationship management, or CRM as it is called. Customer retention has become as important as customer acquisition in today's competitive environment. In Chapter 15, we discuss financial analysis and profit planning. Many marketing students underestimate the importance of a solid background in financial analysis and cost accounting in a product management career. We pay particular attention to alternative definitions of profit. Finally, in Chapter 16 we describe a set of marketing "metrics," standards by which you can judge the effectiveness of the marketing plan.

In sum, this book is intended to give the reader background and knowledge essential to being a successful product manager. At the same time, we try to communicate the excitement of being involved with the day-to-day decisions that determine the success of products, brands, and services.

SUMMARY

We characterize the product manager's job by three distinct activities: (1) collecting and analyzing background product category data, (2) utilizing the background analysis for marketing strategy development, and (3) implementing the marketing strategy through marketing mix and related decisions. Doing an excellent job at these activities, however, does not guarantee a successful career in product management. As indicated in Figure 1.1 and supported by the interviews with product managers described earlier in the chapter, the interpersonal activities of leadership, coordination, team building, and communications are becoming increasingly critical aspects of the job and often determine a person's rate of advancement in the company. In this book, we do not attempt to prescribe how an existing or aspiring product manager can become successful at those activities; we leave that to other books and courses. Rather we concentrate on monitoring the marketing environment and the planning, strategy, and decision-making aspects of the job.

References

Aaker, David A. (2001) *Strategic Market Management,* 6th ed. New York: John Wiley & Sons.

A. C. Nielsen (1992) *Category Management: Positioning Your Organization to Win.* Chicago: NTC Business Books.

Amin, Malini, Deborah Lee, and Liliana Sirotzky (2003) *A Comparison of Product Management Across Industries*, unpublished independent study, Stern School of Business, New York University.

Berthon, Pierre, James M. Hulbert, and Leyland F. Pitt (1999) "Brand Management Prognostications," *Sloan Management Review,* Winter, 53–65.

Cuneo, Alice Z. (1998) "Levi Strauss Reorganizes U.S. Division," *Advertising Age,* August 24, 1.

Day, George S. (1990) *Market Driven Strategy.* New York: The Free Press.

The Economist (2002) "From Baron to Hotelier," May 11, 55–56.

Gorchels, Linda M. (1995) "Traditional Product Management Evolves," *Marketing News,* January 30, 4.

Lublin, Joann S. (2001) "Place vs. Product: It's Tough to Choose A Management Model," *The Wall Street Journal,* June 27, A1.

Nail, Jim, Chris Charron, and Jennifer Parr (2000) "Branding Divorces Advertising," *The Forrester Report,* Cambridge, Massachusetts: Forrester Research.

Neff, Jack (1999a) "P&G Redefines Brand Manager for MDO Days," *Advertising Age,* April 26, 4.

Neff, Jack (1999b) "The New Brand Management," *Advertising Age,* November 8, S2.

Progressive Grocer (1999) "Category Management 2000," September.

Rao, Vithala R., and Joel H. Steckel (1998) *Analysis for Strategic Marketing.* Reading, Massachusetts: Addison-Wesley.

Reyes, Sonia (2003) "End of the Brand Manager," *BRANDWEEK,* May 19, 4.

Turcsik, Richard (2002) "Dawn of the CMAR Era?" *Progressive Grocer,* April 15, 40–42.

Appendix

SAMPLE RESPONSES FROM PRODUCT MANAGERS

1. *Company:* Large consumer health care company

   Title: Brand manager

   Background: Undergraduate degree from a large state university, MBA with a marketing major from a top-15 school. Worked for several health care companies before her current position. Current position as brand manager for one of the company's leading growth brands.

   Responsibilities/evaluation: She is responsible for defining the strategic direction of the brand, developing advertising to ensure that the product claims and strategic platform are maintained, managing the profit/loss in its entirety, and coaching and developing her direct reports. She is evaluated by the quality of her strategic thinking, communication skills, leadership, and analytical thinking as well as the P&L performance.

   Marketing mix: She is responsible for all multiple areas including pricing, promotion, advertising, distribution, and interfacing with the sales force.

   Typical day: Makes sure that channels of communication are open to all parties with whom she works. Works with the sales, forecasting, marketing research, and promotion teams. With the latter, makes sure that the FSI (free standing insert) promotions reflect the brand strategy.

   How the job is changing: The brand manager job at this company has not changed in the last few years. The main goal is to think faster and better than the competition. Her job has changed somewhat to be more of a manager in terms of developing her people.

2. *Company:* Large financial services company.

   Title: VP product portfolio (credit cards)

   Background: Social science undergraduate degree from an Ivy League university, MBA with a concentration in marketing from a top-15 business school.

   Responsibilities/evaluation: Managing the relationships and separate positioning of the different credit cards in the portfolio. This includes management of the P&L involving the acquisition of new card members and increasing the spending and amount of revolement of existing card members. Evaluation is based on the overall performance of her portfolio.

   Marketing mix: She is involved with price, promotion, advertising, sales force, and customer service.

Typical day: She works with marketing, direct mail, and the Internet programs. She is constantly conducting analyses to see how she can make the portfolio more profitable through segmentation and better customer service.

How the job is changing: Her job requires the basic skills of multitasking, analytics, negotiating, public speaking, and influence management. In addition, she has both tactical and strategic responsibilities. These have not changed significantly recently.

3. *Company:* Large beauty products company.

   Title: Director, global marketing.

   Background: BA from a large state university and an MBA from a well-known regional program. Previous background is in investment banking.

   Responsibilities/evaluation: Responsible for the development of new products to be launched globally, including the formula and the packaging as well as the overall strategy. She develops the global strategy and then leaves the local execution to the country managers. She is evaluated by the sales growth for her category and the performance of the key brand launches.

   Marketing mix: Her main responsibilities are to develop frameworks for local managers to make the key decisions in their countries. For example, she recommends price based upon competitive analyses and global advertising themes. The promotion, channels, sales force, and customer service functions are performed locally.

   Typical day: Meeting with people on the new product development team such as engineering for packaging and formula development, product testing, and marketing research.

   How the job is changing: The focus today is on what is likely to happen over the next several years. Because the beauty markets are changing so rapidly, the bar is continually being raised on what is a successful innovation. Also, with a more sensitive economic climate, she has to pay more attention today to customer willingness-to-pay for new beauty products.

4. *Company:* Large high-technology company.

   Title: Product manager.

   Background: Liberal arts undergraduate degree followed by service in the Marine Corps. Has an MBA focused on operations and supply chain management from a top-50 school. Worked for a large consulting company before joining the current firm.

   Responsibilities/evaluation: Responsible for product strategy, product specifications, business requirements, product design. He also sets sales targets and gathers customer feedback from the field. He is evaluated in terms of the size of the market, product penetration, market share, number of licensing agreements.

   Marketing mix: Main responsibilities include pricing, channel management, sales management, and some customer service activities.

   Typical day: Tasks include working with product engineers on specifications; talking to sales for feedback on pricing, competition, and sales success; working with marketing to develop marketing plans and marketing materials. Much of what he does is coordination and communication across groups to ensure deadlines are met.

   How the job is changing: The company is moving toward more of a marketing focus to incorporate more sophisticated analysis of customer preferences and market drivers. The product managers will therefore spend more time with customers attempting to build their needs and wants into new products earlier than has been done before.

Chapter Two

Marketing Planning

Overview

Definition and Objectives of Plans

The discussion in Chapter 1 about the product manager's job noted that developing a marketing plan is a key responsibility. In fact, some people believe the development of the annual marketing plan is the single most important activity of the product manager (Stasch and Lanktree 1980).

Marketing planning has become a major activity in most firms. A survey by Hulbert, Lehmann, and Hoenig (1987) found that over 90 percent of marketing executives engaged in formal planning. These executives spent, on average, 45 days each year on planning, relying most heavily on information from the sales force, management information systems, and internal marketing research. The development of marketing plans, which are generally annual and focus on a product or one or more product lines, is thus an important function for marketers, one that is believed to improve both coordination and performance.

The marketing plan can be divided into two general parts: the situation analysis, which analyzes the background of the market for the product, and the objectives, strategy, and programs based on the background analysis that direct the product manager's actions. While most books and the popular press concentrate on the latter, incorrect or inadequate analysis often leads to poor decisions about pricing, advertising, and the like. The next few chapters of this book are devoted to the critical task of providing the analysis on which to base an action plan—in short, the marketing homework.

What is a marketing plan? A working definition is:

> A **marketing plan** is a *written* document containing the guidelines for the *business center's* marketing programs and allocations over the *planning period.*

Several parts of this definition have been emphasized and merit further explanation.

First, note that the plan is a *written* document, not something stored in a product manager's head. This characteristic of marketing plans produces multiple benefits. Requiring that the plan be written calls for disciplined thinking. It also ensures that prior strategies that succeeded or failed are not forgotten. In addition, a written plan provides a vehicle for communications between functional areas of the firm, such as manufacturing, finance, and sales, which is vital to the successful implementation of the plan. Also, a written marketing plan pinpoints responsibility for achieving results by a specified date.

FIGURE 2.1 Time Horizons for Marketing Plans

Time Period	Consumer Products	Industrial Products	Services
1 year	62%	45%	65%
3 years	5	5	8
5 years	15	17	3
Long term	4	3	6
Indefinite	0	2	2
Other	14	28	16

Source: Howard Sutton, *The Marketing Plan in the 1990s* (New York: The Conference Board, 1990), p. 25.

Finally, a written plan provides continuity when management turnover occurs (a significant issue for the product manager position) and quickly introduces new employees to the situation facing the business.

A second aspect of the marketing plan definition to note is that it is usually written at the *business center* level. This is purposely vague because the precise level at which plans are written varies from organization to organization. For example, in a company using a brand management organizational structure, a marketing plan is written for each brand that is (at least nominally) a profit center. Alternatively, some companies write plans for groups of brands or products, particularly when fixed costs are difficult to allocate by individual product. Thus, while marketing planning is common, it occurs at different organizational levels. In this book, we focus on specific products or closely related product lines.

For example, Kraft develops a separate marketing plan for each brand of cereal marketed by the Post Division, such as Raisin Bran. Alternatively, the medical equipment company referred to in Chapter 1 develops an overall marketing plan for reagents, the chemicals added to blood before it is analyzed, despite the fact that many different reagents exist. The reagents are grouped by application type, and parts of the overall reagent marketing plan are devoted to each group.

A final item to note from the definition of a marketing plan is that the *planning period* or horizon varies from product to product. Retailing, for example, traditionally has short planning cycles to match seasonality and the vagaries of fashion trends. Industrial firms and firms manufacturing consumer durables tend, more so than frequently purchased consumer product or service firms, to have longer than annual marketing plans. Automobiles, for example, have longer planning cycles because lead times for product development or modifications are longer. With such long lead times, the plan would cover several years with annual updates and would focus on tactical issues such as promotion.[1] Other factors contributing to variation in the length of planning horizons are rates of technological change, intensity of competition, and frequency of shifts in the tastes of relevant groups of customers. The typical horizon, however, is annual, as the data in Figure 2.1 indicate.

The Internet has had a substantial impact on the planning cycle times. "Internet time" has come to mean that planning assumptions are often voided quickly by changes in the

---

[1] For the auto companies with brand management systems, the planning horizons could be shorter. In addition, cycle times for new models are diminishing as well.

FIGURE 2.2 **Hierarchy of Planning**

Corporate
strategic
planning

Group or
sector
planning

SBU
planning

Annual
marketing
(business)
plan

economic environment (e.g., how much venture capital is available), the number of competitors, regulatory shifts (e.g., privacy, Napster-type disputes on copyright protection), and technological change. Thus, the data in Figure 2.1 are perhaps somewhat out-of-date (no new survey is available). Even if plans have similar horizons today, there is a substantial need for frequent updates.

Often there is confusion between *strategic* planning and *marketing* planning, which are distinct in two ways. First, strategic planning usually takes place at a higher level in the organization than marketing planning. As Figure 2.2 shows, strategic planning takes place at the corporate, group, or strategic business unit levels. At these levels, objectives are broad (e.g., return on investment or assets) and strategies are general (e.g., Westinghouse divesting of manufacturing nuclear power generating plants and Disney purchasing the television network ABC). Marketing planning takes place at the business center level and has specific objectives (e.g., market share) and strategies (e.g., pursuing the small-business segment). A second difference is that due to the long-term nature of strategic plans, they usually have a longer time horizon than marketing plans; a horizon of three to five years or more with annual updates is not uncommon.

In summary, the marketing plan is an operational document. It contains strategies for a product, but it focuses on a shorter time span than the strategic plan. Marketing plans are specific statements of how to achieve short-term, usually annual, results.

The objectives of a marketing plan can be stated concisely as follows:

1. To define the current situation facing the product (and how we got there).
2. To define problems and opportunities facing the business.
3. To establish objectives.
4. To define the strategies and programs necessary to achieve the objectives.
5. To pinpoint responsibility for achieving product objectives.
6. To encourage careful and disciplined thinking.
7. To establish a customer–competitor orientation.

The last objective is particularly important. Today most product managers are aware of the *marketing concept* popularized in the 1960s, dictating that marketers must develop strategies that maintain a customer orientation. This customer orientation was reinforced in the 1980s by Peters and Waterman's book *In Search of Excellence* and the total quality management (TQM) movement. Today the marketing concept has been translated into a strong focus on customer retention and service (an issue we explore in Chapter 15). Less commonly acknowledged is the fact that a *competitor* orientation, especially in today's business environment of more competitors and shorter life cycles, is equally important. In recent years, a few books with the word *warfare* in their titles have focused on the competitive nature of marketing (see, for example, Ries and Trout, 1986). The vast majority of products and services are not monopolies; competitors often determine a brand's profits as much as any action taken by the product manager does. In addition, in fast-moving Web-based product categories, the competitors' actions change virtually daily and need to be monitored. By emphasizing the importance of having both a customer orientation and a competitor orientation, the marketing plan focuses on the two most important components of the strategy development process. This is consistent with recent research at the firm level showing that a significant and positive relationship exists between a firm's degree of market orientation (as measured by customer and competitor orientation, and interfunctional coordination) and performance (see Deshpandé, 1999). One would think that at this point in time, all companies would be interested in researching their customers and competitors. However, a study by Day and Nedungadi (1994) suggested that a large percentage of companies do not study either customers or competitors. In their sample, 41 percent of the companies admitted to paying little attention to what customers believe or what competitors are doing. Another 30 percent studied only customers and 13 percent studied only competitors. Thus, only 16 percent of the companies in their sample analyzed both customers and competitors.

Frequent Mistakes in the Planning Process

Unfortunately, not all organizations attempting to develop marketing plans have been pleased with the process. The Strategic Planning Institute and the authors have identified the most common mistakes in planning (generally defined) that are relevant to marketing planning as well.

The Speed of the Process   The planning process can either be so slow that it seems to go on forever or so fast that managers rush out a plan in a burst of activity. In the former case, managers required to constantly complete forms that distract them from operational tasks burn out. In the latter case, a hastily developed plan can easily lead to critical oversights that impede the strategies developed.

The Amount of Data Collected It is important to collect sufficient data to properly estimate customer needs and competitive trends. However, as in many other situations, the economic law of diminishing marginal returns quickly sets in on data collection. Usually a small percentage of all the data available produces a large percentage of the insights obtainable. What is the "right" amount of information? Although we could say that product managers ought to collect about 10 pounds of magazine articles or visit 187 websites, no prescription for data collection effort would be sensible. One of the purposes of this book is to point product managers toward the most important areas for data collection to avoid both under- and over-collecting information.

Who Does the Planning? In the late 1960s, strategic planning models developed by the Boston Consulting Group, McKinsey & Company, General Electric, Shell Petroleum, and others led to the formation of formal strategic planning groups in many major corporations. Essentially the planning process was delegated to professional planners, while implementation of the plans was left to line managers. Naturally, line managers resented the process. They thought the planners had no "feel" for the markets for which they were planning, and were managing by the numbers rather than considering market intuition gleaned from experience. As a result, hostility between the staff planners and line managers led to strategies that were either poorly implemented or ignored. Presently, poor results from staff-directed planning and recent economic recessions have led to cuts in non revenue-producing jobs, making line managers get more involved with planning, both strategic and marketing. At many successful companies, such as Emerson Electric, "the people who plan are the people who execute" (Knight, 1992). Besides leaving planning to those who will implement the plans, it is important to involve managers from other functions in the firm. This helps to ensure buy-in from all relevant parties.

The Structure Any formal planning effort involves some structure. The advantage of structure is that it forces discipline on the planners; that is, certain data must be collected and analyzed. Interestingly, many firms believe the most important result of planning is not the plan itself but the necessity of structuring thought about the strategic issues facing the business. However, an apparent danger is that the structure can take precedence over the content so that planning becomes mere form filling or number crunching with little thought for its purposes. Thus, although there must be enough structure, the process should not be too bureaucratic. A good solution to this dilemma is to use the plan format shown in the appendix to this chapter as a guide but to set a rigid timetable. A flexible format helps to prevent the plan from deteriorating into mindless paper shuffling.

Length of the Plan The length of a marketing plan must be balanced, neither so long that both line and senior managers ignore it nor so brief that it omits key details. Many organizations have formal guidelines for the optimal length of plans (similar to Procter & Gamble's dreaded one-page limit on memos), so what is long for one firm is optimal for another.

FIGURE 2.3 **Lengths of Marketing Plans**

Length	Consumer Products	Industrial Products	Services
10 pages or fewer	28%	23%	26%
11–20	17	22	22
21–30	18	11	15
31–50	21	17	12
51 or more	16	27	24

Source: Howard Sutton, *The Marketing Plan in the 1990s* (New York: The Conference Board, 1990), p. 25.

Figure 2.3 provides some data on lengths of plans. The data show an interesting U-shaped pattern: Many plans are 20 pages or fewer, and many are 51 pages or more. However, the median lengths are 30 pages for industrial products, 25 for consumer products, and 21 for service businesses. Thus, typical marketing plans are between 20 and 30 pages in length.

Frequency of Planning A potential problem occurs if the product manager plans either more or less frequently than necessary. Frequent reevaluation of strategies can lead to erratic firm behavior and make the planning process more burdensome. However, if plans are not revised as needed, the product's marketing strategies may not adapt quickly enough to changes in the environment, and its competitive position may deteriorate. This has become increasingly apparent in the Internet age. Often a company adopts its fiscal year as its planning cycle. Sometimes it is difficult to determine the appropriate planning interval with precision. However, after several planning cycles and some experimentation, the appropriate amount of time becomes apparent.

Number of Courses of Action Considered Too few alternatives may be discussed, thus raising the likelihood of failure, or too many, which increases the time and cost of the planning effort. It is important to have diverse strategic options (e.g., both growth and hold strategies) because discarded strategies often prove useful as contingency plans. In fact, one job of the product manager is to prioritize possible marketing strategies at a given point in time. The most appropriate strategy clearly should be implemented first, and the others should become contingency plans.

Who Sees the Plan The successful implementation of a marketing plan requires a broad consensus from as many corporate departments as possible. Increasing the "buy-in" to the marketing plan increases its likelihood of success. For example, a strategy emphasizing high quality is difficult to implement if manufacturing does not simultaneously emphasize quality control. Growth objectives may be achievable only by relaxing credit policies. A common mistake is to view the plan as the proprietary possession of the marketing department.

Not Using the Plan as a Sales Document A major but often overlooked purpose of a plan is to generate funds from either internal sources (e.g., to gain budget approval) or external sources (e.g., to gain a partner for a joint venture or to secure venture capital financing). The plan and its proponents compete with other plans and their proponents for scarce resources. Therefore, the more appealing the plan and the better the product managers' track records, the better the chance of budget approval.

Insufficient Senior Management Leadership As with many intrafirm programs, commitment from senior management is essential to the success of a marketing planning effort. Mere training is insufficient. One organization with which we are familiar did and said all the right things about implementing a marketing planning process, but frequent turnover of marketing vice presidents with different backgrounds, values, and attitudes toward the development of marketing plans prevented a successful planning effort.

Not Tying Compensation to Successful Planning Efforts Managers are usually driven by their compensation plans. Product managers' compensation should be oriented toward the achievements of the objectives stated in the plan. If the organization rewards profit margins and the negotiated objective of the plan is market share, a fundamental conflict will arise that will lead to a concentration on margins rather than on what is best for the product at that time.

What Makes a Good Planning System: Some Empirical Results

Although few systematic studies of marketing planning systems have been published, some useful guidelines for improving planning have appeared in the marketing literature. A major component of a good marketing planning system is its thoroughness. A marketing planning process is considered to be thorough if it does the following (Stasch and Lanktree, 1980):

1. Utilizes experience from several managerial levels rather than just from product managers. Particularly in organizations in which senior marketing managers have risen through the ranks, considerable knowledge exists of past successful and unsuccessful product marketing strategies.
2. Employs a variety of both internal and external sources of information rather than just internal information. For example, the advertising agency working on the product account can often be a valuable source of information.
3. Extends over a period of time sufficient to collect and analyze the data necessary for developing the marketing strategies.
4. Employs a number of incentives for the product managers in addition to employment security or advancement.

Is Planning Worthwhile?

Again, few studies empirically link the quality of planning systems to performance as measured in terms of higher profitability or increased market share. One study found that strategic planning in general is not positively related to levels of performance, but firms with formal planning systems have less variation in profitability than those without them (Capon, Farley and Hulbert, 1988). Using a sample of six firms, another study found a generally positive relationship between the thoroughness of the marketing planning effort and various performance measures (Stasch and Lanktree, 1980). Although it is difficult to directly relate marketing planning to improved market performance, most managers believe planning provides intangible benefits such as a disciplined approach to strategy development and the assurance that the external environment is considered at all times.

THE PLANNING PROCESS

Approaches to Planning

In general, the planning process works as shown in Figure 2.4. Whereas the collection and analysis of data and the development of product strategies take place over a limited time frame, there is no beginning or ending to the planning process as a whole. The formal part of the process is followed by implementation, during which programs such as distribution, promotion, advertising, and the like are executed. Monitoring and evaluating both the performance of the plan and changes in competition or customers in the external environment are also continuous tasks. This information feeds back into the formal planning part of the process. This circular aspect of marketing planning ensures that the plan is not "cast in stone" and can be revised as necessary. It also guarantees that information obtained from the market concerning the performance of the plan is integrated into next year's plan.

Two general approaches to planning have been developed. In *top-down* planning, the marketing plans are formulated by either senior or middle management with the aid of staff and product management and then implemented by the latter. In *bottom-up* planning, the lower ranks down to field salespeople are actively involved in the planning process through collecting competitor and customer information and making forecasts. The information is subject to higher-level review, but lower management personnel play key roles in the process.

Both systems have some commendable characteristics. The rationale often used for top-down planning is that the higher the level the person occupies in the organization, the better the perspective on the problems facing the business. Field salespeople, for example, tend to consider the competitive battleground as their sales territories and not necessarily the national or even international market. Bottom-up planning systems are often characterized by better implementation than top-down approaches, since the people primarily charged with executing the plan are involved in its development.

FIGURE 2.4 **The Planning Process**

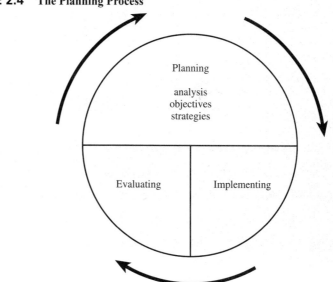

Source: Mary Ann Pezzullo, *Marketing for Bankers* (American Bankers Association, 1982), Washington, D.C. p. 32.

Steps in the Planning Process

In most organizations, collecting information and structuring the marketing plan require a sequential planning process. This process generally includes eight steps, as shown in Figure 2.5.

Step 1: Update the facts about the past. Data collected for marketing planning purposes are often provisional or estimated. For example, planning for 2002 takes place in 2001. At that time, annual data on market sales or share would be available only for 2000 at best and often only for 1999 or even earlier due to delays in the data collection process. As a result, planners often use forecasts or extrapolations of partial results. However, when new data become available, they should replace figures that were estimated or forecasted.

Step 2: Collect background data. Data collection focuses on information available about the current situation, which forms the situation analysis part of the plan. Again, lags in collecting data about an industry or product category mean that the time period of the data often does not match the period of analysis.

FIGURE 2.5 **Marketing Planning Sequence**

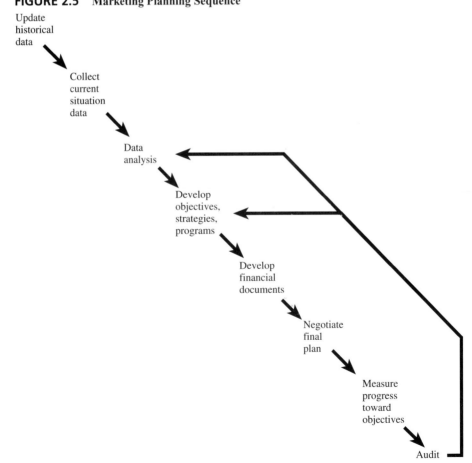

Update historical data

Collect current situation data

Data analysis

Develop objectives, strategies, programs

Develop financial documents

Negotiate final plan

Measure progress toward objectives

Audit

Step 3: Analyze historical and background data. Analyze the existing data to forecast competitors' actions, the behavior of customers, economic conditions, and so forth. Such an analysis need not be quantitative; in fact, as later chapters show, much of the analysis is qualitative and draws implications from non-numerical data. This analysis leads to delineating key opportunities and threats to the business.

Step 4: Develop objectives, strategies, and action programs. Use the implications drawn from the background data (see step 3) to formulate objectives, strategies, and marketing mix decisions. This is, in fact, the critical activity of the planning process because it outlines in detail what will be done with the product during the year (or the appropriate planning period). However, the order of the steps indicates that logical strategic thinking cannot be done without considering the facts at hand.

Objectives, strategies, and mix decisions are constrained by the company's mission, objectives and strategy, policies, resources, and legal considerations, among other factors. Thus, this part of the process generally involves (1) setting product objectives, (2) developing strategies and programs to achieve the objectives, (3) comparing programs in terms of their abilities to achieve objectives (e.g., market share) within the terms of company policies and legal constraints, and (4) selecting a basic objective, strategy, and program combination.

Step 5: Develop pro forma financial statements. Such statements typically include budgets and profit-and-loss figures.

Step 6: Negotiate. Rarely, if ever, is the marketing plan generated from steps 1 to 5 implemented without several rounds of negotiations with senior management. In a brand management organizational structure, the plans themselves must be marketed both inside and outside marketing as managers compete for their desired portions of corporate or divisional resources. In large organizations, this negotiation process can last as long as all the prior steps.

Step 7: Measure progress. To correct the plan if the environment changes within the planning period, progress toward stated objectives must be monitored. This implies that marketing research and other information relevant to measuring the quantities stated as objectives (e.g., market share or sales) must continue to be collected.

Step 8: Audit. After a planning period, it is customary to determine variances of planned versus actual results and sources of the variances. This audit provides important diagnostic information for both current and future planning efforts and thus acts as a source of feedback on the planning effort.

The planning sequence is therefore a logical flow of events leading from data collection and analysis to strategy formulation to auditing the performance of the plan. It implies that sound strategic thinking cannot occur until the product manager has used all available information to draw implications about future market conditions.

COMPONENTS OF THE MARKETING PLAN

Although nearly every firm has its own format (see Hopkins, 1981, and Sutton, 1990, for examples), most marketing plans do have a common set of elements. The appendix to this chapter provides a sample marketing plan outline, which is summarized in Figure 2.6. This outline describes the major areas of analysis and data collection required for a "typical"

FIGURE 2.6 **Marketing Plan Summary**

I. Executive Summary
II. Situation Analysis
   A. Category/competitor definition
   B. Category analysis
   C. Company and competitor analysis
   D. Customer analysis
   E. Planning assumptions
III. Objectives
IV. Product/Brand Strategy
V. Supporting Marketing Programs
VI. Financial Documents
VII. Monitors and Controls
VIII. Contingency Plans

marketing plan. The rationale and a brief description of each major component of the plan follow, giving an overview of the plan and a context for the planning chapters of the book.[2]

The Executive Summary

A senior manager often must review many marketing plans, so a brief summary of the marketing plan focusing on the objectives, strategies, and expected financial performance is necessary. This brief overview is useful for quickly reviewing the major elements of the plan and easily comparing product plans.

If the plan is being used as a business plan for a new product or service (e.g., an Internet-based service), the Executive Summary is crucial. In this case, other relevant information includes the business model (that is, how revenues will be generated), the amount of money needed from investors, how the money will be spent, key management, and a summary of the financial projections.

Situation Analysis

The Situation Analysis contains the data and concomitant analysis so vital to developing sound marketing strategies. It is the "homework" part of the marketing plan; no strategy should be developed without first analyzing the product category in which the product competes. The Situation Analysis is composed of six major parts.

The first major section of the Situation Analysis is the definition of the competitor set or *category definition.* In this part, the product manager considers both close and distant competitors and prioritizes them. This is an excellent place to start because the definition of your competitors impacts much of what follows.

The *category analysis* identifies factors that can be used to assess the attractiveness of a product category (or industry if more appropriate) in which the product competes at a given point in time. Since all markets are dynamic in that competitors, customers, technology, and sales growth rates change, the underlying attractiveness of a product category as a target for investment can also change.

Given the definition of the category, *competitor analysis* asks who the key competitors are in the market and what their likely future strategies are. Competitor analysis is

---

[2] Marketing planning software with predesigned planning formats is also available from Business Resource Software (*www.brs-inc.com*) and Palo Alto Software (*www.palo-alto.com*).

becoming an increasingly important activity. A critical section of the competitor analysis component is what is often termed a *resource analysis* or self-assessment. By comparing the product to its key competitors the strengths and weaknesses become clear.

The aim of the *customer analysis* is to guarantee that the product manager retains a customer focus at all times. This customer focus is critical to success in today's competitive marketplace. It is vital to understand not only who the customers are but also how and why they behave the way they do. As can be seen from the outline, quite a number of issues have to be resolved here.

The fifth part of the background assessment deals with a wide variety of *planning assumptions*. First, the product's market potential is a key number in making decisions about expected future category growth, resource allocation, and many other areas. Market and product forecasts and assumptions about uncontrollable factors, such as raw materials or labor supply, are also relevant.

As noted earlier, the background assessment is the homework to be done before formulating marketing objectives and strategies. It may be more enjoyable to develop the marketing strategy for a product during the next planning horizon, but the preliminary data collection and analysis are more vital because drawing implications from the background data often makes the optimal strategies apparent.

Marketing Objectives/Strategy

It is logical to follow the background assessment by the strategy portion of the plan, which includes two sections: a statement of marketing objectives (where do we want to go?) and the marketing strategy itself (how are we going to get there?).

Supporting Marketing Programs

This is the implementation part of the plan. Decisions about pricing, channels of distribution, customer service programs, advertising, and other relevant marketing programs are described in this section.

An important new part of the programs part of the plan is the product manager's Internet plans. Unless the plan is being developed for a stand-alone Web business, all companies today need to think about their Internet strategy. In particular, some questions need to be addressed: How will a website integrate with our existing business? Who are the targets of the site? How can we use the website for customer retention purposes?

The Rest of the Plan

The final three parts of the marketing plan do not form a cohesive unit, but they are nevertheless important components. The financial documents report the budgets and pro forma profit-and-loss (P&L) or income statements. Senior managers, naturally, inspect the expected financial outcome carefully. In fact, the P&L statements are often the key element in securing approval for the plan. The monitors and controls section specifies the type of marketing research and other information necessary to measure progress toward achieving the stated objectives. The kind of information collected depends on the objectives; for example, if a market share increase is the objective, information must be collected in time to check for possible shortfalls. Finally, contingency plans are helpful, particularly in dynamic markets where either new products or new competitors create the need for changes in strategy before the end of the plan's horizon. These contingencies are often previously considered strategies that were discarded.

FIGURE 2.7 **Sonesta Hotels Marketing Plan Outline**

***Note: Please keep the plan concise—Maximum of 20 pages plus summary pages. Include title page and table of contents. Number all pages.

I. *Introduction.* Set the stage for the plan. Specifically identify marketing objectives such as "increase average rate," "more group business," "greater occupancy," or "penetrate new markets." Identify particular problems.

II. *Marketing Position.* Begin with a single statement that presents a consumer benefit in a way that distinguishes us from the competition.

III. *The Product.* Identify all facility and service changes that occurred last year and are planned for next year.

IV. *Marketplace Overview.* Briefly describe what is occurring in your marketplace that might impact your business or marketing strategy, such as the economy, the competitive situation, etc.

V. *The Competition.* Briefly identify your primary competition (3 or fewer) specifying number of rooms, what is new in their facilities, and marketing and pricing strategy.

VI. *Marketing Data*
   A. Identify top 5 geographic areas for transient business, with percentages of total room nights compared to the previous year.
   B. Briefly describe the guests at your hotel, considering age, sex, occupation, what they want, why they come, etc.
   C. Identify market segments with percentage of business achieved in each segment in current years (actual and projected) and project for next year.

VII. *Strategy by Market Segment*
   A. Group
      1. *Objectives:* Identify what you specifically wish to achieve in this segment. (For example, more high-rated businesses, more weekend business, larger groups).
      2. *Strategy:* Identify how sales, advertising and public relations will work together to reach the objectives.
      3. *Sales Activities:* Divide by specific market segments.
         a. Corporate
         b. Association
         c. Incentives
         d. Travel agent
         e. Tours
         f. Other
         Under each category include a narrative description of specific sales activities geared toward each market segment, including geographically targeted areas, travel plans, group site inspections, correspondence, telephone solicitation and trade shows. Be specific on action plans, and designate responsibility and target months.
      4. *Sales Materials:* Identify all items, so they will be budgeted.
      5. *Direct Mail:* Briefly describe the direct mail program planned, including objectives, message, and content. Identify whether we will use existing material or create a new piece.
      6. *Research:* Indicate any research projects you plan to conduct next year, identifying what you wish to learn.
   B. Transient (The format here should be the same as group throughout)
      1. *Objective*
      2. *Strategy*

FIGURE 2.7   Sonesta Hotels Marketing Plan Outline—*continued*

3. *Sales Activities:* Divide by specific segments.
   a. Consumer (rack rate)
   b. Corporate (prime and other)
   c. Travel Agent: business, leisure, consortia
   d. Wholesale/Airline/Tour (foreign & domestic)
   e. Packages (specify names of packages)
   f. Government/Military/Education
   g. Special Interest/Other
4. *Sales Materials*
5. *Direct Mail*
6. *Research*

C. Other Sonesta Hotels
D. Local/Food & Beverage
1. *Objectives*
2. *Strategy*
3. *Sales Activities:* Divide by specific market segments.
   a. Restaurant and Lounge, external promotion
   b. Restaurant and Lounge, internal promotion
   c. Catering
   d. Community Relation/Other
4. *Sales Materials* (e.g., banquet menus, signage, etc.)
5. *Direct Mail*
6. *Research*

VIII. *Advertising*
A. Subdivide advertising by market segment and campaign, paralleling the sales activities (group, transient, F&B).
B. Describe objectives of each advertising campaign, identifying whether it should be promotional (immediate bookings) or image (long-term awareness).
C. Briefly describe contents of advertising, identifying key benefits to promote.
D. Identify target media by location and type (e.g., newspaper, magazine, radio, etc.).
E. Indicate percent of the advertising budget to be allocated to each market segment.

IX. *Public Relations*
A. Describe objectives of public relations as it supports the sales and marketing priorities.
B. Write a brief statement of overall goals by market segment paralleling the sales activities. Identify what proportion on your effort will be spent on each segment.

X. *Summary:* Close the plan with general statement concerning the major challenges you will face in upcoming year and how you will overcome these challenges.

Source: Howard Sutton, *The Marketing Plan in the 1990s*, The Conference Board, 1990, pp. 34–35.

Example

Figure 2.7 shows the planning form for Sonesta Hotels.[3] As can be seen, this company limits the plan to 20 pages, excluding exhibits. Sections IV, V, and VI cover the situation analysis. The rest of the plan describes the marketing objectives, strategies, and action

[3] Other examples of marketing plans appear in Willam A. Cohen, *The Marketing Plan,* 2nd ed. (New York: John Wiley & Sons, 1997).

FIGURE 2.8   **Official Website of Sonesta Hotels**

programs. Note the separate objective, strategy, and program sections for different market segments (group and transient customers) and products (food and beverage). Clearly, advertising and public relations are viewed as very important to the hotel industry because they merit distinct sections of the plan. In general, the two major parts of the plan—the situation analysis and the objectives, strategies, and programs—are covered well by this structure. This company's plan differs from the general format previously described in several ways. For example, the company prefers an initial description of its differential advantage over competitors (Section II), as opposed to discussing this as part of the product positioning. In addition, as can be seen from the home page of the company's website (Figure 2.8), Sonesta has integrated an Internet strategy (Section V of the plan) into its marketing plans by establishing a "Web Club" for building a community around the brand. This would not be unusual today, of course.

TWO CASE STUDIES

In Chapters 3 through 7, we illustrate the concepts presented with two running examples. In these examples, objectives and strategies will be developed from background analyses. Because most product strategies, particularly those in high-technology industries, are subject to considerable change, the two examples are meant to illustrate the use of background analyses for developing the marketing plan; they do not necessarily provide current data about the products and brands involved.

Energy Bars (ca. 2002)[4]

One of the segments of the broad snack bar category is energy bars. Snack bars include such items as granola bars while health bars include, for example, cereal or diet bars. Energy bars are defined as vitamin-enriched, nutritious bars intended either to boost performance or replenish nutrients following exercise or as a complete snack or meal replacement. The energy bar category is highly fragmented with over 100 competitors and 700 brands. There are several sub-categories such as energy/endurance, functional/ nutritional, diet/weight loss, and high protein/body building. PowerBar, Balance Bar, Luna Bar, and Clif Bar are major competitors in the energy bar category.

Overall snack bar sales were over $1.4 billion in 2002; of this, energy bars were nearly $300 million with a 28 percent growth rate over 2001. Industry experts expect the energy bar category to continue to grow in the 25–30 percent range annually.

Some marketing mix information about the energy bar category is the following. Price ranges between $1 and $3 per bar. The typical price in the grocery and drugstore channel is $1.39. More specialized bars such as Ultra Low Carb and high protein tend to be priced at the higher end of the range. Promotion in this category has been the primary form of communications with sponsorships, sampling, and in-store activities being favored. Distribution for the category has expanded significantly over the last five years with the largest players in the market gaining national distribution in grocery, natural foods, drug, mass, and even club stores.

Due to the high growth rate in the category, established companies such as Nestlé, Kraft, and Kellogg's recognized the potential and acquired PowerBar, Balance Bar, and Kashi, respectively, in 2000. Coca-Cola/Minute Maid acquired Odwalla at the end of 2001, primarily for its juice business rather than for the energy bar brand. Clif Bar has decided to remain independent.

Our analyses will be conducted from the perspective of Odwalla Bar. The brand's website is shown in Figure 2.9. Odwalla Inc. was founded in 1980 to create socially responsible products that nourished the body with natural ingredients. After establishing a popular line of natural juices and juice-based drinks, Odwalla introduced the brand extension in the energy bar category in 1998. Although market share is difficult to determine since many energy bars are sold by retailers such as REI which sells outdoor and related enthusiast products, as of late 2002, Odwalla was the sixth-best selling bar. Sources of information used for this illustration are shown in Figure 2.10.

Personal Digital Assistants (ca. 1999)[5]

A growing need for smaller and lighter mobile computing devices to organize and store personal data and to communicate while on the road has created a market for a class of electronic devices known as personal digital assistants (PDAs). Often called by other

---

[4] This illustration is based on Monica Brown, Eleanor Huang, Jennifer Okanes, and Jennifer Wickland, "Odwalla Bar Marketing Plan," Haas School of Business, University of California at Berkeley, 2002.

[5] This illustration is based on Caroline Chi, Juan Eraso, Jennifer Lee, Mei Mei, and Frederik Pettersson, "VISOR 2000: Marketing Plan for the Year 2000," Haas School of Business, University of California at Berkeley, 1999, and Joe Conley, "Handspring Visor," Graduate School of Business, Stanford University, 2000.

FIGURE 2.9   Odwalla Bar Website

names such as high-end electronic organizers, palmtop computers, and personal communicators, PDAs are handheld computers that combine communications, personal organization, and word processing capabilities.

PDAs generally weigh less than one pound, measure less than four inches by seven inches by one inch, and display less than one-fourth the number of pixels of a subnotebook personal computer (PC) (they have much smaller screens and less brightness). Device navigation and data entry are accomplished by using either a built-in miniature keyboard or a penlike stylus. Some PDAs support both methods of input. The well-publicized introduction in 1993 of the Apple Newton MessagePad essentially marked the beginning of the PDA product category (electronic personal organizers existed prior to

FIGURE 2.10   Reference Sources for the Energy Bar Category

AC Nielsen SPINS 2000
Advertising Age
Confectioner magazine
Consumer focus groups
Information Resources Incorporated
Interviews with category brand managers
Mintel International Group

FIGURE 2.11   PDA Sales Growth

Source: *Computer Reseller News,* May 31, 1999.

1993). However, the Newton failed in the marketplace from a combination of high price and a set of features that did not match needs of any particular segment. Similar products by Sharp, Casio, and AT&T met the same fate.

In 1996, the market was changed dramatically by the introduction of the Palm Pilot from the Palm division of 3Com Corporation. The Pilot's designers were determined to keep the device small, light, and inexpensive—even if that meant giving up advanced features such as e-mail and faxes. The product was designed to do the following:

• Fit in a shirt pocket.
• Perform instantly.
• Synchronize its calendar and database seamlessly with a desktop computer by pushing just one button.
• Be useful right out of the box.

To keep the price down, the product was also designed for easy manufacturing. For example, while organizers from Sharp and Casio would use between 8 and 15 screws of different sizes, the Palm Pilot used only 3—reducing part costs and complexity.

The success of the Palm Pilot was instantaneous. While Newton sales reached a total of 150,000 units by the end of 1995, Palm Pilot sales were 360,000 units in 1996 and increased to 1.2 million in 1998. The sales growth of the total PDA category through 1999 is shown in Figure 2.11. PDAs use two competing operating system platforms: the Palm OS and PocketPC (formerly Windows CE) made by Microsoft. Market shares (as of 1997) of the leading brands are shown in Figure 2.12.

In July 1998, the original Palm Pilot creators left 3Com and formed a company called Handspring. Handspring was in the business of designing and marketing PDAs that utilize attachable modules to expand, enhance, and personalize the functionality and experience that a customer has with the PDA.[6] Our analysis will take the perspective of

---

[6] In this context, a module is a piece of hardware that is attached to a PDA and contains software that enables some specific functionality such as a modem or a game.

FIGURE 2.12   **Market Share for U.S. Palmtop Market (1997)**

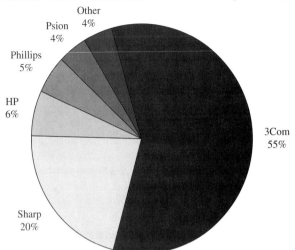

Source: Dataquest in article from *Forbes,* July 5, 1999, p. 122.

Handspring's first product, the Visor, which was introduced in 1999. Sources used in this illustration are shown in Figure 2.13.

Clearly, the market for PDAs has changed significantly since 1999. In 2003, Handspring was acquired by its original parent, Palm, to form PalmOne. PalmOne sells the most popular PDA brand, the Tungsten, as well as the Treo, which was originally developed by Handspring. Other popular models are Hewlett-Packard's iPaq and Sony's Clié. More than 9 million PDAs are estimated to have been sold by 2004. Innovations such as smaller size and better functionality have led to a blurring of the product category

FIGURE 2.13   **Reference Sources for the PDA Category**

Brandweek
Business Week
CNET News.com
CNN.com
Computer Reseller News
Electronic News
Forbes
Forrester Research reports
Fortune
Frost & Sullivan reports
Gartner Group reports
Handspring: *www.handspring.com*
The Industry Standard
International Data Corporation reports
OneSource Information Services
Pen Computing
San Francisco Chronicle

FIGURE 2.14 **PalmOne/Handspring Website**

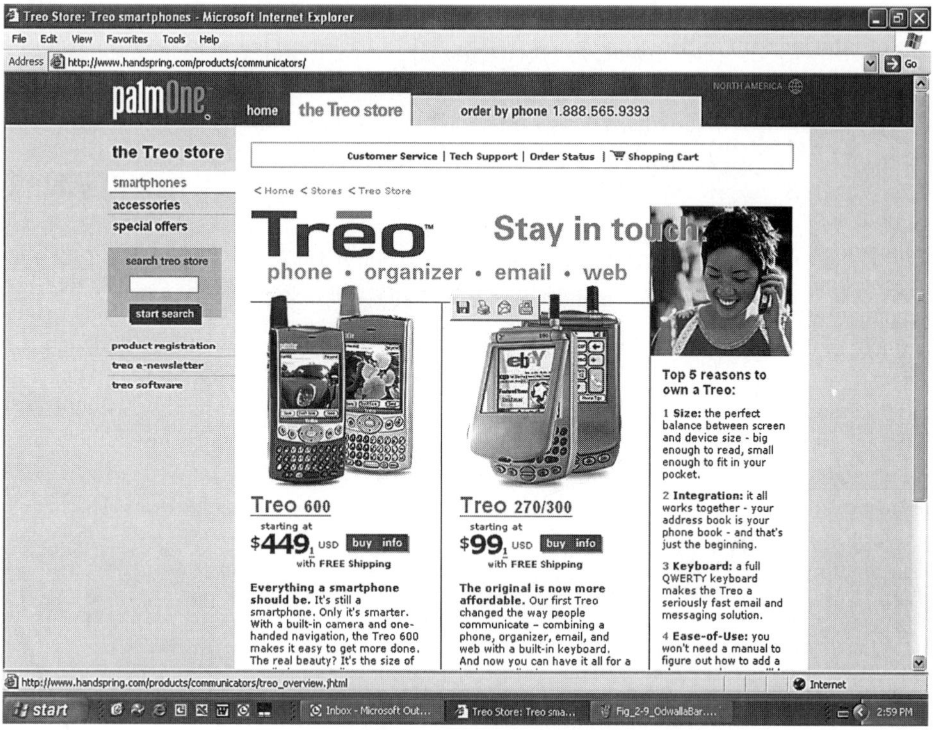

lines between cellular phones and PDAs. In fact, as can be seen from the website shown in Figure 2.14, the term PDA is beginning to disappear in favor of "Smartphone." However, despite these changes, the extant category characteristics in 1999 are sufficiently similar to those currently that make the somewhat older data still amenable to an excellent illustration of the marketing planning tasks described in this book.

SUMMARY

The marketing plan provides a unifying theme for the job of the product manager. While product managers have responsibility for many tasks, such as arranging trade shows, checking print advertising copy, and managing distribution channel members, day-to-day tasks should have the marketing strategy as a guiding theme. This theme emanates from a careful analysis of the market, giving the product manager ideas on how to differentiate his or her product from the others from which customers can choose. The tasks (marketing tactics), guiding theme (marketing strategy), and analysis (situation or background analysis) are what marketing plans and planning are about.

References   Capon, Noel, John U. Farley, and James M. Hulbert (1988) *Corporate Strategic Planning.* New York: Columbia University Press.

Cohen, William A. (1997) *The Marketing Plan,* 2nd ed. New York: John Wiley & Sons.

Day, George S., and Prakash Nedungadi (1994) "Managerial Representations of Competitive Advantage." *Journal of Marketing,* April, 31–44.

Deshpandé, Robit (1999) *Developing a Market Orientation.* Thousand Oaks, CA: Sage Publications.

Hopkins, David (1981) *The Marketing Plan.* New York: The Conference Board.

Hubert, James, Donald R. Lehmann, and Scott Hoenig (1987) "Practices and Impacts of Marketing Planning." Unpublished working paper, Columbia University.

Knight, Charles (1992) "Emerson Electric: Consistent Profits, Consistently." *Harvard Business Review,* January–February, 1992, 57–70.

Ries, Al, and Jack Trout (1986) *Marketing Warfare.* New York: McGraw-Hill.

Stasch, Stanley, and Patricia Lanktree (1980) "Can Your Marketing Planning Procedures Be Improved?" *Journal of Marketing,* Summer, 79–90.

Sutton, Howard (1990) *The Marketing Plan in the 1990s.* New York: The Conference Board.

Appendix

MARKETING PLAN OUTLINE

I. *Executive Summary.* A one- to three-page synopsis of the plan providing highlights of the current situation, objectives, strategies, principal actions programs, and financial expectations.

II. *Situation Analysis*
   A. Category/competitor definition.
   B. Category analysis.
      1. Aggregate market factors.
         a. Category size.
         b. Category growth.
         c. Stage in the product life cycle.
         d. Sales cyclicity.
         e. Seasonality.
         f. Profits.
      2. Category factors.
         a. Threat of new entrants/exits.
         b. Bargaining power of buyers.
         c. Bargaining power of suppliers.
         d. Pressure from substitutes.
         e. Category capacity.
         f. Current category rivalry.
      3. Environmental factors.
         a. Technological.
         b. Political.
         c. Economic.

         d. Regulatory.

         e. Social.

    C. Company and competitor analysis.

       1. Product features matrix.

       2. Objectives.

       3. Strategies.

       4. Marketing mix.

       5. Profits.

       6. Value chain.

       7. Differential advantage/resource analysis.

         a. Ability to conceive and design new products.

         b. Ability to produce/manufacture or deliver the service.

         c. Ability to market.

         d. Ability to finance.

         e. Ability to manage.

         f. Will to succeed in this category.

       8. Expected future strategies.

    D. Customer analysis.

       1. Who are the customers?

       2. What do they buy and how do they use it?

       3. Where do they buy?

       4. When do they buy?

       5. How do they choose?

       6. Why they prefer a product.

       7. How they respond to marketing programs.

       8. Will they buy it again?

       9. Long-term value of customers.

      10. Segmentation.

    E. Planning assumptions.

       1. Market potential.

       2. Category and product sales forecasts.

       3. Other assumptions.

III. *Objectives*

    A. Corporate objectives (if appropriate).

    B. Divisional objectives (if appropriate).

    C. Marketing objective(s).

       1. Volume and profit.

       2. Time frame.

       3. Secondary objectives (e.g., brand equity, customer, new product).

       4. Program (marketing mix).

IV. *Product/Brand Strategy*

    A. Customer target(s).

    B. Competitor target(s).

    C. Product/service features.

    D. Core strategy.

       1. Value proposition.

       2. Product positioning.

V. *Supporting Marketing Programs*

    A. Integrated marketing communications plan.

    B. Advertising.

C. Promotion.
D. Sales.
E. Price.
F. Channels.
G. Customer management activities.
H. Website.
I. Marketing research.
J. Partnerships/joint ventures.

VI. *Financial Documents*
A. Budgets.
B. Pro forma statements.

VII. *Monitors and Controls*
A. Marketing metrics.
B. Secondary data.
C. Primary data.

VIII. *Contingency Plans*

## Chapter Three

Defining the Competitive Set

Overview

In Chapter 2, we presented an overview of marketing planning and an outline of a marketing plan that can be used in virtually any product management situation. Of particular importance to the marketing plan is the background analysis of "homework," which focuses on the existing category and the competitive and customer situations. However, before beginning the analysis, the product manager must have a good conceptual definition of the product category to serve as the focus for data collection and analysis. This chapter provides tools to develop that category definition. In particular, we point out several possible ways to define the competition for a product or product line.

In our view, product managers tend to view competition too narrowly. For example, a product manager for a line of notebook computers would likely view other notebook computers as the major competitors. This is a natural outgrowth of the short-term orientation discussed earlier that pervades product management; competitor products or services that are most similar receive the most attention. However, as we argue in more detail later in this chapter, a myopic view of competition can be dangerous. For example, a parent thinking of purchasing a personal computer for a child going to college might be debating between the higher portability of a laptop versus the lower price and higher security characterizing a desktop. In this case, the two subcategories of PCs obviously compete. Other possibilities today include advanced personal digital assistants and tablet PCs. Thus, many different products compete for the same needs the student has for doing his or her work.

In some sense, everything competes with everything else for scarce resources, usually money. Since this concept of competition is not useful to the product manager, the key question in defining competition is not whether two products compete but the extent to which they compete. The degree of competition is a continuum, not a discrete *yes* or *no*. Defining competition therefore requires a balance between identifying too many competitors (and therefore complicating instead of simplifying decision making) and identifying too few (and thus overlooking a key competitor).

This chapter focuses on customer-based competition; in other words, a competitor is defined as one competing for the same customers. Competitors tangle on other bases

FIGURE 3.1   **Bases of Competition**

1. Customer oriented
     Who they are: competition for the same budget
     When they use it
     Why they use it: benefits sought
2. Marketing oriented: advertising and promotion
     Theme/copy strategy
     Media
     Distribution
     Price
3. Resource-oriented
     Raw materials
     Employees
     Financial resources
4. Geographic

as well. For example, Sun Microsystems and Amazon.com, although noncompetitors in terms of customers, compete for computer programmers—the same labor supply. Kodak and jewelers compete for silver—raw materials. Suppliers are also a basis for competition; in 1990, hard disk drive manufacturer Conner Peripherals sued rival Seagate Technology on the grounds that Seagate blocked Conner's supplies of a critical component. In 2000, Palm Inc. could not make enough units to meet demand because it was fighting with cell-phone makers like Nokia and Motorola for a limited supply of memory chips and liquid-crystal screens. Avon and Tupperware compete for home demonstration sales—the same channel of distribution. Similarly, frozen food manufacturers that use the freezer cabinets in supermarkets compete for shelf space. Geographically based competition is important for local retailers—for example, hardware stores—and multinational firms in the market for telecommunications equipment such as Ericsson (Sweden), NEC (Japan), and Nortel (Canada). In other words, competition exists across many dimensions. Figure 3.1 summarizes these different bases of competition.

As Figure 3.1 suggests, competitors can be defined using several criteria. Competition can exist for customers in terms of their budgets (disposable income: vacations versus financial products), when they use a product (evenings: a basketball game versus a movie), and benefits sought (cancer treatments: bioengineered drugs versus chemotherapy). Competition is also related to marketing activities such as advertising (time on network television programs) and distribution (shelf space). The battle for shelf facings in supermarkets has led to a variety of manufacturer concessions to retailers to obtain desirable shelf positions, and the struggle for shelf space occurs across as well as within traditional product category boundaries. Examples of resource-based and geographic-based competition have already been mentioned.

Another crucial competition occurs *within* a company, when different units in an organization request funds for their marketing plans. In this form of competition, the plan serves mainly as a sales document, and its financial projections often become the key to the "sale." This competition is often intentional; it puts pressure on product managers to develop sound marketing plans.

Misidentification of the competitive set can have a serious impact on the success of a marketing plan, especially in the long run. Overlooking an important competitive threat can be disastrous. For example, for many years the Swiss controlled the market for premium watches and Timex dominated the market for inexpensive watches. When Japanese firms such as Casio developed electronic watches in the 1970s, they were not viewed as a threat or serious competition in either business. Today both Timex and Swiss firms offer electronic models, and only the strong success of the Swatch brand of inexpensive fashion watches saved the Swiss watch industry.

A second illustration comes from the U.S. coffee industry (Yip and Williams, 1986). Coffee manufacturers traditionally felt free to pass along increased costs to consumers when a freeze in Colombia or another coffee-producing country restricted the supply of coffee beans. However, during 1977 and 1978, retail coffee sales dropped nearly 20 percent due to price increases. Much of this decrease can be accounted for by the concurrent rapid increase in demand for soft drinks and juices. Witness also the recent attempt by Pepsi to compete with coffee manufacturers by introducing a morning cola, Pepsi A.M. (which, unfortunately, failed). In fact, share of occasion and so-called share of stomach competition is a major consideration of food and drink producers.

Pity the owner of a small "mom and pop" video store in 2004. Strong retail competitors such as Blockbuster exist with greater selection and considerably more marketing muscle due to national advertising and direct-mail campaigns. Netflix allows you to receive DVDs in the mail. Moreover, the video store owner competes against another giant, Sony, which sells the small satellite dishes that, when combined with a home entertainment service, can deliver video on demand. In addition, every telephone and cable company wants to get into the video-on-demand business shipping video images over telephone lines (DSL) and cable modems.

Finally, the automobile industry has had to be dragged kicking and screaming into the Internet age. In 2002, over 80 percent of Acura, Audi, Porsche, and BMW buyers used the Web to research their car purchase before buying.[1] Before Ford, Chrysler, General Motors, and other car companies started developing their online businesses, companies like Autobytel, CarPoint, and CarsDirect were selling automobiles through their Internet sites. The bigger companies ignored the smaller upstarts as they thought that they would not be serious competitors. Although these Internet sellers are either defunct or have developed a different business model (e.g., referrals to dealers), the new competition certainly caught the attention of the major manufacturers.

Ambiguous definition of the competition creates uncertainty in market definition and therefore ambiguity in market-related statistics such as market share. This leaves open the possible manipulation of market boundaries, particularly when compensation or allocation decisions are at stake. For example, assume an objective for a notebook computer weighing four pounds with a hard disk drive but no floppy disk drive is to gain 10 percent market share. The ability to achieve this objective depends on whether the "market"

---

[1] Josef Federman (2003), "In the Driver's Seat," *The New York Times*, May 19, p. R12.

is defined as all notebook products, including floppy and CD-ROM drives, all portable Windows-based computers, all desktop computers plus portables, and so on. A chocolate-covered granola bar could have a large share if measured in the snack bar category or a very small share if considered in the snack food category. Recently, to combat complacency, General Electric required redefining the markets in which they compete so their share was 15 percent or less.

Data from the travel industry provide an additional example of how market shares do not tell the whole story. As of late 2003, Expedia held 36 percent of the online travel booking business, with Travelocity at 24 percent and Orbitz at 13 percent (Federman, 2003; Thomaselli, 2003). However, it is estimated that just under 50 percent of the total travel market is Web based. Thus, the Internet companies face serious competition not only within their narrowly defined set but outside as well, indicating that the high market share owned by Expedia.com is only part of the story of their performance.

In this chapter, therefore, we take the view that the definition of the competitive set ultimately affects what strategy is pursued, and the definition can be too narrow or too broad for the market conditions at the time. Not all authors subscribe to this approach (see, for example, Abell, 1980) as some believe the corporate mission or business definition selected affects the set of competitors for a firm. In other words, the definition of competition is a decision made by the product manager. Unfortunately, competitors usually do not care how a company chooses to define itself or how a product manager defines competition, and they are thus free to compete against a firm's products even if that firm does not define itself to include them as competitors.

In this chapter, we describe several levels of competition that can be useful for conceptualizing the competitive set. In addition, we discuss methods that can help determine the competition at the various levels. Finally, we describe the notion of enterprise competition.

LEVELS OF MARKET COMPETITION

Definitions

One way to delineate the set of competitors facing a brand is to consider the proximity of other products to the physical attributes of the product in question.[2] As Figure 3.2 shows, the problem of defining competition can be viewed as defining a set of concentric circles with the product or brand in question at the center.

A product's features are defined as the presence (or absence) of a characteristic or attribute (e.g., calories, weight). The *value* of a feature is the level of the characteristic (e.g., 0 calories, 5 pounds). Thus, Coke and Diet Coke share the same features—carbonation, cola taste, sweetness, and the like—but have different values of some of the features since Diet Coke has fewer calories and is artificially sweetened.

---

[2] Again, the use of the term *physical* does not preclude services from utilizing the proposed method for identifying competitors. Services can also be described in terms of their actual characteristics, for example, interest rate for a mortgage.

FIGURE 3.2 **Example of Levels of Competition**

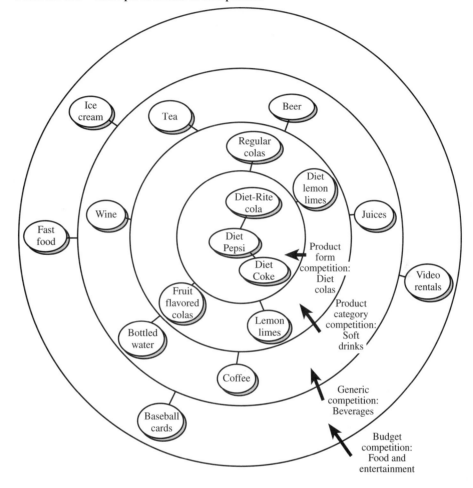

The narrowest perspective one can take of competition is called *product form*. These products typically pursue the same market segment, and their features therefore have similar values. As Figure 3.2 shows, from Diet Coke's perspective, a narrow view of competition would include only diet colas, such as Diet-Rite and Diet Pepsi. These brands appeal to similar consumers: those seeking a cola taste with low calories. Similarly, Compaq, Gateway, Dell, IBM, Toshiba, and others compete in the Windows-based notebook/laptop computer category. Again, although the brands differ slightly on some characteristics, they use the same operating system and are fairly similar in weight. Apple's Ibook might not be included in this product form competition, since it has a different operating system. Interestingly, competition in the notebook market could be asymmetrical in that companies that produce Windows machines may not view Apple as a competitor, but Apple might be interested in selling machines to customers who currently have Windows-based desktop computers. To further clarify the definition of product form competition, subnotebook and tablet products would comprise totally different sets of product form competitors.

Thus, product form competition is a narrow view of competition because it considers only those products that "look" the same as the product or service in question. This might be an acceptable perspective in the short run, as these would be the most serious competitors on a day-to-day basis. It is also a convenient definition of competition because it mimics the way commercial data services often measure market shares. For example, A. C. Nielsen, a major provider of market share information to consumer packaged goods companies (along with its main competitor, Information Resources, Inc., or IRI), provides market share information not only on the entire soft-drink category but also on the diet product segment alone. This narrow definition of the market supplied by a data collection service can have the unfortunate effect of setting an industry standard for looking at competition and market shares in a way that does not represent the true underlying competitive dynamics in the industry. Thus, the product form view, while perhaps providing the set of the closest competitors in a product feature sense, is too narrow for a longer-run view of competition.

The second level of competition is based on those products or services with similar features. This type of competition, called *product category,* is what product managers naturally think of as the industry. For example, personal computers, fast food, televisions, and the like describe sets of competitors that are aggregates, or composites, of narrower product forms. All soft drinks (Figure 3.2) form a market as well. This is, in fact, the traditional way to determine the composition of a competitive set. While somewhat broader than product form competition, this product category definition of competition still takes a short-run view of market definition. To recall an earlier example, the video store "industry" faces critical competition from the telecommunications "industry."

The third level of competition is longer term and focuses on substitutable product categories. At this level, termed *generic competition,* competition, and therefore the market, is defined as consisting of those products and services fulfilling the same customer need. Thus, soft drinks compete with orange juice in the "thirst-quenching" market, fast-food outlets compete against frozen entries in the "convenience" eating market, and so on.

This need based perspective is essential if a manager wishes to avoid both overlooking threats and ignoring opportunities. This perspective is well described in Levitt's classic article (1960) that admonishes several industries for defining their businesses too narrowly. Railroads viewed themselves as providing rail-based rather than general transportation services and lost much of their business to trucks and airlines. Steel companies thought they were providing steel rather than general structural material. Some firms, on the other hand, do take a generic perspective in defining themselves and their competitors. For example, the world's largest business-to-business e-commerce network is GE Global Exchange Services. With over 100,000 trading partners and 1 billion transactions annually worth $1 trillion in goods and services, the CEO Harvey Seegers views his competitors as the post office, telephone companies, and facsimile makers since they are also in the business of moving things from the physical to the digital world (Claburn, 2002). Brunswick, the maker of billiard tables, views itself as being in the furniture business, competing for fashionable products to fit in the home. As a result, it is developing new contemporary-styled tables that can be customized with felt of different colors (Fitch, 2003).

Benefits do not have to be defined at the product level. For example, in Japan, the large banks have new competition for consumer financial products from nonfinancial institutions with significant brand names that provide consumer confidence or extensive retail systems that supply convenience and availability (Dvorak, 2000). Examples of the former are Sony and BMW, which have both applied to Japanese regulators for permission to make consumer loans. An example of the retail availability benefit is Ito-Yokado, best known as the operator of the 7-Eleven convenience store chain.

A critical difference between generically defined competitors and either product form or product category competition is that the former is *outward* oriented while the latter two are *inward*. Product form and product category competitors are defined by products that look like those we are producing. Generic competitors are defined by looking outside the firm to the customers. After all, who really defines competition, the firm or the customer? It is the customer who determines what alternative products and services solve the problem at hand. Although in some cases there may be a limited number of ways to solve the same problem or provide the same benefit, in most instances focusing on the physical product alone ignores viable competitors.

Southwest Airlines has used this outward perspective on competition to build what is generally considered to be the most successful U.S. airline. The reasons for its success are well-documented: it focuses on short-haul flights, it does not serve meals or offer in-flight films, but it does offer extraordinary value with fares often 60 percent below those of the competition, on-time flights, and airports with less congestion. When developing its concept, instead of focusing on rivals in the airline industry, Southwest realized that for short-haul destinations, surface transportation like cars and trains were substitutes for flying. By concentrating on the factors that lead people to choose to drive versus fly and eliminating or reducing everything else, the company's value proposition was established (Kim and Mauborgne, 1999). While some airlines such as JetBlue and Song are challenging its domination in the low-price segment, Southwest is expected to fight strongly to maintain its position.

Procter & Gamble has also viewed an outward perspective on competition as key to the development of new products. In particular, the company reexamined the laundry detergent market to enter the home dry cleaning product business (Parker-Pope, 1998). Instead of looking at the $4 billion U.S. laundry detergent market, of which P&G held a 51 percent share, the company wanted to pursue the $10 billion that U.S. consumers spend annually to clean their clothes, including $6 billion for dry cleaning. They realized that the 50 percent share was just 20 percent of a much larger market. The company therefore introduced Dryel, a home dry-cleaning kit.

An even more general level of competition is *budget* competition. This is the broadest view of competition: It considers all products and services competing for the same customer dollar as forming a market. For example, a consumer who has $500 in discretionary disposable income could spend it on a vacation, a ring, a money market instrument, or a variety of other things. That this is the case can be seen in the advertisement shown in Figure 3.3 for De Beers diamonds. Clearly, the company realizes that the money spent on a diamond could be spent fixing up a kitchen, among a variety of other options. A purchasing manager may have a fixed budget for office equipment that includes copy machines, word processing software upgrades, or a new water cooler service. While this view of competition is conceptually useful, it is very difficult to implement strategically since it implies an enormous number of competitors.

FIGURE 3.3 De Beers Advertisement

FIGURE 3.4 Defining Competition Using Customer Segments

	Market Segments		
Generic Competitors	**Business Travelers**	**Tourists**	**Students**
Airline	X	X	
Bus		X	X
Train		X	X
Automobile (own)		X	
Automobile (rent)		X	

Overlapping Market Segments

An additional and valuable way to conceptualize the definition of competitors is based on market segments. Consider the market for travel services shown in Figure 3.4. The modes of travel listed on the left are generic competitors in that they satisfy the benefits of providing transportation. The market segments across the top could be defined in many ways, depending on the benefit being analyzed. The generic competitors in the first column indicate how a customer would look at the travel problem. Consider the route between San Francisco and Los Angeles (a nine-hour drive or one-hour flight). For the business traveler, the major competitors would be airlines, primarily Southwest and United. For tourists, airlines, trains, car rental agencies, or their own cars would be substitutes if time is not critical. Students on a budget might consider buses and trains as competitors.

The Impact of Metamediaries

It should be noted that the growth of websites that perform multiple functions and offer a number of services has created a broad group of competitors. These sites, often called *metamediaries,* seek to bundle disparate services that fulfill a customer's needs for a particular transaction. For example, Figure 3.5 shows the home page from Autobytel.com. This company's most direct competitors are automobile retailers (product category competition). However, it can be seen that the site offers links to financing, insurance, warranties, maintenance, and other services bringing in competitors from other categories. This is of great concern to companies in those other categories that are more "vertically" positioned in that they can only handle one aspect of the transaction.

Product Strategy Implications

The four-level model of competition just described has significant implications for developing product strategy and for a product manager's marketing problems. A different set of tasks must be accomplished at each level of competition for a product to be successful in the market. Figure 3.6 shows these tasks in conjunction with the appropriate level of competition.

At each level of competition, part of the job of the product manager is fairly clear, and marketing managers are trained to handle it: Convince the customer that your company's version of the product, your brand, is better than others available. In other words, your most direct competitors are other brands of like product form. What differs at each level is how much additional marketing has to be done beyond touting your own brand's advantages. At the product form level, none is required. Clearly, when the competition is viewed as consisting only of other products with similar levels of features, marketing

FIGURE 3.5 **Autobytel.com Website**

activities directly aimed at the similar competitors are all that is required (e.g., Toshiba is a better laptop computer than IBM). However, the problem becomes more complex as the competitor set widens. At the product category level, the product manager must also convince customers that the product form is best in the product category (e.g., tablets are better than notebook/laptop computers). At the generic competition level, the product manager must also convince customers that the product category solution to the customer's problem (the benefit derived from the product category) is superior to the solution provided by other product categories (e.g., taking an airplane is superior to taking a train). This is critical when a totally new product category is introduced. For example, when Procter & Gamble introduced disposable diapers in the 1970s, the main marketing job was to convince mothers to switch from the generic competitors, cloth diapers and diaper services. Finally, it might also be necessary to convince customers that the generic

FIGURE 3.6 **Levels of Competition: Implications for Product Strategy**

Competitive Level	Product Management Task
Product form	Convince customers that the brand is better than others in the product form
Product category	Convince customers that the product form is the best in the category
Generic	Convince customers that the product category is the best way to satisfy needs
Budget	Convince customers that the generic benefits are the most appropriate way to spend the discretionary budget

benefit of the product is better than other ways to spend discretionary money (e.g., taking a cruise versus putting a down payment on a new car).

Consider the problem facing the marketing manager for a line of low-priced stereo components such as Pioneer. What competition does this product manager face? First, competitors are fighting for the same segment of the stereo market (product form competitors), so the manager must show that Pioneer is superior to others competing in the low-priced segment. Second, there are other, higher-priced component manufacturers (product category competitors), and the Pioneer manager must communicate to customers the advantages of low-priced components over more expensive alternatives (e.g., Bang and Olufsen). Third, the manager must consider generic competitors. These could include all-in-one systems ("boom boxes") or lower-priced rack stereo systems as well as the manufacturers of other entertainment consumer durables such as TVs, video game systems, and DVD players (Sony, Nintendo, Panasonic, Sanyo). Customers must be convinced to buy stereos rather than these other products. Finally, alternative ways to spend the money could be relevant (budget competition). As a result, customers need to be convinced about the benefits of buying stereos instead of taking a vacation or buying stocks. While this latter problem may seem a little farfetched, it is undoubtedly true that stockbrokers, retail jewelers, travel agents, and many other businesspeople worry about customer alternatives for spending money.

It is also important to note that as one moves from product form toward budget competition, customer targets also begin to change. Product form competition suggests battling for exactly the same customers in terms of who they are and why they buy, although not necessarily where or when they buy: One soft-drink manufacturer (Coca-Cola) may concentrate on fountain sales and another (Pepsi) on grocery store sales. As the company moves toward budget competition, both who its customers are and why they buy begin to differ as the need to be satisfied becomes more general. Because the key to success in business is obtaining and keeping customers, the most crucial form of competition will generally be product form and category, in which competition occurs for the same customers. On the other hand, generic competition can destroy entire product categories when a major innovation occurs, and thus it too requires attention, especially for long-run planning.

Note that products thought of as substitutes, and therefore generic or budget competitors, may also be viewed as complements. For example, a customer might be trying to decide between purchasing word processing or spreadsheet software (budget competition). These potential competitors could be turned into allies through joint ventures or cobranding (e.g., Dreyer's Ice Cream and M&Ms) or bundling (Microsoft's Office suite of applications). Thus, this delineation of competitive levels defines *potential* competitors and not necessarily mortal foes.

Illustrations

The two illustrations introduced in Chapter 2 were energy bars and personal digital assistants (PDAs). Let's look at competitor definitions in light of the information provided in that chapter and some use of "managerial judgment."

Energy Bars

Figure 3.7 shows the competitive structure of the energy bar category. As can be seen, the narrowest definition of competition, product form, is at the center of the diagram and lists the main competitors in the energy bar product segment, including Odwalla.

FIGURE 3.7 **Energy Bar Competition**

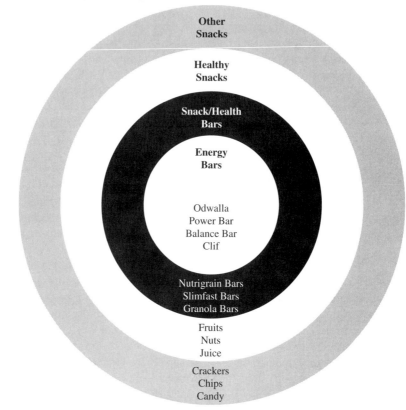

The next level out, product category competition, consists of the other bars that are positioned as either snacks or healthy food. The two circles combined comprise the snack bar "industry." The other two levels, healthy snacks and other snacks would be generic competition because they fulfill some of the same needs as the energy bars. There is no budget competition shown here as it would consist of any other product priced between $1 and $3 and is, therefore, not very useful to the product manager.

Personal Digital Assistants

Figure 3.8 indicates the different levels of competition for the PDA category. The closest competitors were those PDAs that offered address/telephone/fax record keeping, calculators, financial calculations, and optional links to personal computers and modems via wireless communications (referred to as PIMs, or Personal Information Mangers). The major competitors to Handspring's Visor were products from Palm, Casio, and Compaq. These products were marketed as offering many of the functions needed by businesspeople away from the office at a moderate price. The product category consists of these plus lower-end PDAs with more limited communications capabilities, smaller screens, less software, and a lower price. One job of the Visor product manager, then, was to differentiate it from these lower-end models, primarily on the basis

FIGURE 3.8 **PDA Competition**

Level of Competition	Definition	Competitors	Need Satisfied

Product form PDAs	Full-featured PDAs	Palm Pilot VII
		Compaq AERO
		Casioplus integrate
		  communication
			Personal information
			  management

Product category	PIMs	Palm III Royal Casio PV-100	PIM only

Generic	Notebook/subnotebook
	  computers
		IBM
		Toshiba
		Many others
			Other solutions to the
			  above

	Paper-based solutions	Rolodex Day Timer	

Budget	Business items costing
	  $100–$1,000
		Fax machines
		Personal copiers
		Cellular phones
		Furniture
		  (e.g. Steelcase)	

of price but perhaps also by indicating that a simpler product may be all that is needed, particularly if the user also has a notebook computer. The generic competition consists of two quite different kinds of products. First, as is the case today, notebook and sub-notebook computers can provide all the benefits of PDAs at a larger size, a higher price, and slower access to the information. However, manual, paper-based solutions still exist. One can still use a Rolodex, a Day-Timer, or just paper files to obtain many of the benefits of the PDAs. Add a cellular phone and this combination matches the full-featured PDAs as well. There are many serious budget competitors. If we consider other business-related personal productivity items, we see that portable printers, home fax machines, and similar items compete with PDAs. Of course, other durable goods may also compete for the same dollar as well.

METHODS FOR DETERMINING COMPETITORS

The easiest way to define competition is to let someone else do it for you. For example, you can use the predefined categories provided by a commercial data service as the definition of the competitive set. A second example of an external definition of markets is the Standard Industrial Classification (SIC) code used by the U.S. government.[3] This system assigns products to two-digit major groups (e.g., 34, Fabricated Metal), three-digit groups (e.g., 342, Cutlery and Hand Tools), four-digit industries (e.g., 3423, Hand and Edge Tools), and five- or more digit representations of products (e.g., 34231,11 Pliers). Clearly, both of these external sources of information define competition based on

[3] Since 1997, the SIC code system has been replaced by the NAICS (North American Industrial Classification System), which updated the SIC industry categories. However, SIC data are still used worldwide.

physical product similarities (product form or category definitions). As a result, relying exclusively on these categorizations will overlook both generic and budget competitors.

Two alternative approaches to assessing the set of competitors facing a brand permit a broader definition advocated in this chapter: managerial judgment and customer-based evaluation.

Managerial Judgment

Through experience, salesperson call reports, distributors, or other company sources, product managers can often develop judgments about the sources of present and future competition.

One way to structure the thought process is to use a tabular structure such as that shown in Figure 3.9 (a variant of Ansoff's [1965] well-known growth matrix). Box A represents product form competition, that is, those products or services that are basically the same and are pursuing the same customers. Box C represents product form competitors that target other customers.

The most interesting cell of Figure 3.9 is B. This cell represents potential future competitors that already have a franchise with our customers but do not offer the same product or service. In this case, the product manager might try to forecast which firms in B are likely to become more direct competitors. Examples of companies capitalizing on prior customer familiarity are numerous. In telecommunications, IBM had a considerable franchise with large business customers through its mainframe computer business. IBM easily moved to cell A through its investments in MCI and Rolm. In the orange juice category, Procter & Gamble had perhaps the best franchise of any consumer product manufacturer with both supermarkets and consumers, which it used to develop the Citrus Hill brand. Disney's purchase of Capital Cities/ABC is consistent with its entertainment franchise. Both Dell and Hewlett-Packard have started selling flat-panel TVs. This type of movement into new product areas is common; companies often try to leverage their brand equity in one category to grab sales in others that serve the same customers. Managers should assess the likelihood of such horizontal movements as well as their chances of success, although some moves, such as Dell's, will always be difficult to predict.

Cell D competitors are the most difficult to predict, as they currently sell different products to different customers. One example of the impact of such a competitor in consumer durables was Litton Industries' commercialization of microwave technology, which created a new competitor for General Electric in the kitchen appliance market.

Perhaps the least scientific but most useful way to see what a product or service might compete with is to imagine the item as a "prop" for a stand-up comedian. The comedian, unencumbered by convention (and sometimes good taste), can create many uses for a product, therefore suggesting different competitive products.

FIGURE 3.9 **Managerial Judgment of Competition**

Markets	Product/Services	
	Same	Different
Same	A	B
Different	C	D

Technology substitution is particularly relevant for technological products. Judgments by engineers, marketing managers, and other experts may suggest other products or technologies that substitute for current ones. For example, in many telecommunications and computer networking applications, infrared or wireless communications are substituting for optical fiber, which in turn substituted for wire or "twisted pair," thus producing successive technological generations of competitors.

A study by Clark and Montgomery (1999) attempted to characterize how managers use judgment in identifying competitors. They found that three major factors are positively related to whether a company is perceived as a competitor:

- Size
- Success
- Threatening behavior

Interestingly, they also found that when using judgment alone, managers named relatively few competitors. Thus, due to their day-to-day experiences of competing with product form and category competitors, managers using judgment to define their competitive set run the risk of creating a set that is too small relative to the reality of market conditions.

Customer-Based Measures

Two types of customer data are commonly used to assess market structures: actual purchase or usage data and judgments (Day, Shocker, and Srivastava, 1979). The former are particularly useful for understanding product form and category competition; because it is difficult to understand what alternatives were considered when purchases were actually made, the usual assumption is that purchases are made within a narrow definition of competition. However, what customers have actually done does not necessarily indicate what they would have preferred to do in the past or are likely to do in the future. Judgmental data are needed to understand broader definitions of competition as well as to estimate how a new product affects the structure of competition.

Using Behavioral Data

A key source of purchase data used in consumer packaged goods applications is data collected from electronic scanners. Households enroll with a commercial firm, either A. C. Nielsen or Information Resources, Inc. (IRI). Before scanning in their purchases at the cash register, the cashier scans an identification code indicating that the purchases to follow are for a particular household. The brands and package sizes are coded by Universal Product Code (UPC, or bar codes). Alternatively, since many products have substantial purchase volume outside supermarkets (e.g., convenience stores, vending machines), A. C. Nielsen has developed an in-home scanning system called Homescan in which the panel member scans the UPC codes at home with an infrared "wand" and the data are dumped into a computer and downloaded via modem. While most of the data collected from consumers using these technologies are aggregated to estimate sales and market shares for brands, the household-level data are very useful for identifying patterns of repeat purchasing of brands and brand switching.

Figure 3.10 shows a common way to organize the data from scanners. The figure is a brand-switching matrix for a specific product category. Because most of these analyses concern predetermined product categories, patterns of competition within categories

FIGURE 3.10 **Brand-Switching Matrix**

		Time $t + 1$				
		A	B	C	D	E
	A	.6	.2	.2	0	0
Time t	B	.2	.3	.4	.1	0
	C	.2	.3	.5	0	0
	D	0	.1	.1	.5	.3
	E	.1	0	0	.4	.5

or subcategories (product form) but not across categories (generic) can be determined. This approach is usually best applied to frequently purchased goods or services. The numbers in the table represent purchase probabilities calculated across panel households from one purchase occasion (time t) to the next (time $t + 1$) for a set of brands, A through E. Probabilities of brand switching have been proposed as measures of customers' perceived similarities, and therefore substitutability, among brands (see, for example, Kalwani and Morrison, 1977, and Lehmann, 1972). High brand-switching probabilities suggest a high degree of competition.

The diagonal elements in Figure 3.10 represent the degree of brand loyalty; for example, 60 percent of the households buying brand A on one occasion repurchased it on the next purchase occasion. The off-diagonal elements represent brand-switching behavior; for example, 20 percent of the time purchases of brand A were followed by a purchase of B. The row numbers must sum to 1, as a household must buy one of the five brands.

While sophisticated methods are available for analyzing large brand-switching matrices, simple observation of Figure 3.10 indicates that there are clearly two main groups of brands, A-B-C and D-E. In addition, within the A-B-C cluster, B and C seem to form another group. We could conclude that within the market for this product, there are two principal product forms and an even narrower set of two within one of the clusters.

An example of this kind of analysis on real consumer purchasing data for soft drinks appears in Figure 3.11 (Rao and Sabavala, 1981). These analyses typically create a tree-like diagram with the branch structure indicating the competition implied by consumer purchasing patterns. As the figure indicates, the competition for a national brand is other national brands, while the major competition for a regional brand is the other regional or family brand. Within the national brand competition, the regular brands compete against one another, as do the diet brands. Finally, there is competition within national diet colas and national diet noncolas.

A problem with using purchase data to understand product form and category competition is that brand switches occur across complements as well as substitutes. Consumers might purchase complements when they want variety (McAlister and Lattin, 1985). For example, consider a consumer who views Coke and Pepsi as direct substitutes but sometimes likes a lemon-lime drink such as 7UP as a break from Coke/Pepsi. Now suppose a recording of purchases shows a purchase sequence of Coke–Coke–7UP–Coke. A researcher might analyze the brand switch from Coke to 7UP for that consumer and mistakenly infer it was due to substitutability reasons rather than to the desire for a change. If this were true for a large number of consumers, the product manager would believe that

FIGURE 3.11   **Defining Competition with Brand Choice Data**

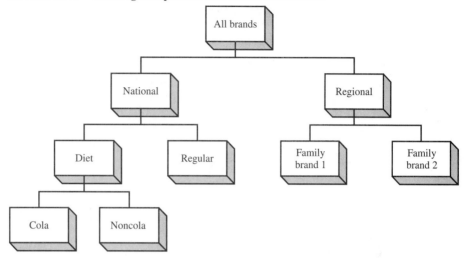

Source: Reprinted by permission from Vithela Rao and Darius Sabavala, "Inference of Hierarchical Choice Processes from Panel Data," in *Journal of Consumer Research,* June 1981, published by the University of Chicago Press. © 1981 by the University of Chicago.

Coke and 7UP were competitors and might design his or her strategy with that in mind when the truth is that 7UP is not a competitive threat in the usual sense.

One problem with using purchase data is that the data are often at the household level. Observed switching between two brands could be due to different household members' preferences rather than to any substitutability reasons. For example, purchases of Coke and Pepsi could be for two different people or a true switch of brands by one individual. The difference is crucial.

Panel or sales data can be used to calculate cross-elasticities of demand, another basis for estimating patterns of competition. A cross-elasticity is the percentage change in one brand's sales compared to a percentage change in a marketing variable for another brand, such as price. If a cross-elasticity with respect to price is positive (a brand's sales decline when another brand's price drops), the two brands or products in question are considered to be competitive (Cooper, 1988).

The major problem with this approach is estimating the cross-elasticities: It is assumed there is no competitive reaction to the price cut and the market is static with respect to new entrants, product design, and so forth. In addition, a positive cross-elasticity does not guarantee cause and effect, that is, that the price decline (increase) of the brand in question actually caused the other brand's sales to decline (increase). And, as with measuring brand switching, the set of brands or products usually must be defined a priori.

In today's e-commerce environment, it is relatively easy for Internet-based companies to obtain site-switching data. Comscore Media Metrix, for example, tracks site navigation behavior (*clickstream* data) for a panel of Web surfers so an Internet retailer can determine from which sites a person has come and to which sites she or he is going after visiting or purchasing. These kinds of data are much more difficult to interpret, of course, as Web surfers can visit many sites in one session and skip around with low cost.

In summary, the estimates of competition using actual behavior are useful because they represent what consumers *actually* do, not what they *might* do, which surveys indicate.

For the most part, however, without specially designed and expensive data collection, these estimates apply primarily to frequently purchased, nondurable goods. In addition, they tend to be most appropriate when a product class is defined a priori and when competition within product form or category is sought.

Using Customer Judgments

Several methods have been proposed for estimating competition from customer judgments. All are essentially paper-and-pencil exercises in which customers are surveyed in focus groups, shopping mall intercepts, or other environments. Although not based on actual customer behavior, they have the advantages of providing insight into potential future market structures, producing broader definitions of current structures, and being applicable to all types of products and services, including industrial products and consumer durables.

Judged overall similarity measures between pairs of products or brands, and it can be used to create geometric representations in multidimensional spaces called *perceptual maps.* The brands or products are represented by points in the space, while the dimensions represent the attributes customers use to make the similarity judgments. Brands located close to one another are judged to be similar and thus form a defined market.[4] If brands are the objects of the mapping exercise, only product category or product form competition can be assessed. However, if a larger set of products is used, more interesting generic competition can be identified.

As an example, Figure 3.12 presents a perceptual map from the generic category of desserts. The analysis must begin with a prespecified set of the relevant alternatives, which can be developed through focus group research that identifies products satisfying a given need. The points not attached to the vectors represent the various products the focus group identified as filling the need for dessert. The vectors help determine attributes for defining the space, but are not relevant to the market competition issue. Information about the competitive sets is obtained by examining clusters of points. The upper-right quadrant would be very useful to, say, the brand manager for Jell-O. From the map, it is clear that Jell-O is perceived to be quite similar to custard, pudding, tapioca, Lo-Cal mix, and Dzerta, a mixture of gelatin and other products.

Similarity within consideration sets is an approach developed by Bourgeois, Haines, and Sommers (1979) that asks customers to take a large set of products and divide them into groups of items that can be substituted for one another, that is, items that would be considered together on a purchase occasion. The customers are then asked to judge the similarity of the products within each group. By accumulating similarity judgments across the customers, a perceptual map can be developed. Thus, this approach is somewhat similar to the preceding one, but it collects the similarity judgments after consideration sets have been formed. Other variants of this approach use verbal protocol data gathered as customers think aloud while considering a purchase decision.

The consideration set concept itself has been extensively explored (see, for example, Hauser and Wernerfelt, 1990, and Andrews and Srinivasan, 1995). When making a purchase decision, customers often simplify the process by reducing the number of available products and brands that can satisfy a need to a smaller set from which they make

---

[4] There are other methods for constructing perceptual maps besides similarity ratings, for example, factor and discriminant analysis of attribute ratings.

FIGURE 3.12 **Defining Competition with Perceptual Mapping**

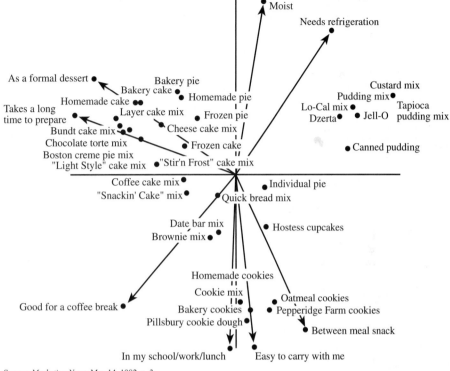

Source: *Marketing News,* May 14, 1982, p. 3.

the ultimate decision. Clearly, the options in this smaller set closely compete against one another. However, the usefulness of the consideration set concept is limited by the sets' variability across customers and across distribution channels and by the fact that they are dynamic: Consideration sets change from one purchase occasion to another.

Product deletion is an interesting approach to defining competition based on customer reaction to product unavailability (Urban, Johnson, and Hauser, 1984). Products or brands in a set are presumed to be substitutes and consequently form a market if, when one of them is deleted from the choice set, customers are more likely to buy from the remaining products than from products outside the original set. For example, suppose a choice set of Internet websites for purchasing books is Amazon.com, BiggerBooks.com, Barnesandnoble.com, and others. If, when BiggerBooks.com is eliminated from the set, customers are more likely to choose Amazon or Barnesandnoble than any other site, the three brands are presumed to be competitors.

Although its authors describe product deletion as useful primarily to partition product form markets into submarkets, there is no reason the approach could not be used in a more general setting. For example, if milk is unavailable and orange juice and soft drinks are subsequently chosen more often than tea or coffee, then milk, juice, and soft drinks apparently compete at the generic level.

Substitution in use estimates degree of competitiveness through judged similarities of products in usage contexts (Stefflre, 1972, Ratneshwar and Shocker, 1991). First, customers list all possible uses and contexts (e.g., a party or one's own use) for a target product or brand. Next, either the original sample or a fresh sample of respondents list other products or brands that provide the same benefits or uses and rate their appropriateness for the different contexts or use occasions. This method clearly has the potential to produce a large number of generic competitors or even budget competitors.

As an illustration, suppose the target product of interest is a baseball game. A brief sketch of the analysis is as follows:

Target: Baseball game.

Uses: Sports event, entertainment.

Substitutes: Horse racing, movies, dinner at a restaurant, visiting a sports bar.

Thus, substitution in use can produce a fairly diverse set of competitors.

Summary

Figure 3.13 summarizes the methods for determining competition along two dimensions: (1) the usefulness of each method for determining competition at a certain level and (2) the kind of research data typically used to implement the method. With respect to the latter, information is divided into primary sources (data collected specifically to determine competitors) and secondary sources (data collected for some purpose other than to determine the structure of the market).

As Figure 3.13 indicates, all the methods are useful for determining product form competition. Managerial judgment and behavior-based customer data are useful mainly for developing product form and product category markets. Customer information that is judgment based, however, can also be used to assess generic competition. Since cross-elasticities, judged similarity, technology substitution, product deletion, and substitution in use either start with an a priori market definition (which could be very broad) or are usage based, they cannot really be used to define budget competition, that is, those

FIGURE 3.13   **Methods versus Competition Levels and Information Required**

	Level of Competition				Typical Data Sources	
Approach	**Product Form**	**Product Category**	**Generic**	**Budget**	**Primary**	**Secondary**
Existing definitions	X	X				X
Technology substitution	X	X	X		X	
Managerial judgment	X	X			X	X
Customer behavior based:						
Brand switching	X	X				X
Interpurchase times	X	X				X
Cross-elasticities	X	X	X			X
Customer evaluation based:						
Overall similarity	X	X	X		X	
Similarity of consideration sets	X	X	X	X	X	
Product deletion	X	X	X		X	
Substitution in use	X	X	X		X	

Note: An *X* indicates that either the method is useful for determining competition at that level or it employs data of a certain type.

products fighting for the same customer dollar. Since the consideration set approach has no such restrictions, it can be used to assess budget competition.

With respect to data requirements, judgment-based customer evaluations require primary data, while behavior-based methods can use secondary data. When applied to consumer packaged goods, behavior-based methods utilize commercially available scanner panel data. Consumer judgments might supplement purchase data with primary data, for example, from interviews focusing on motivations for brand switching. Managerial judgment can (and at least implicitly does) utilize both primary data (e.g., discussions with distributors) and secondary data (e.g., salesperson call reports).

COMPETITOR SELECTION

Examining competition at four levels makes intuitive sense, and the practical implications for a product manager are substantial. One implication already mentioned is that marketing strategy must be developed with an eye toward four different problems: (1) convincing customers in your market segment that your brand is best (product form competition); (2) convincing buyers that your product form is best (product category competition); (3) convincing buyers that your product category is best (generic competition); and, occasionally, (4) convincing buyers that the basic need your product fulfills is an important one. A product manager must decide what percentage of his or her budget to spend on each problem.

A second implication of the four levels of competition is that product managers must choose a selective competitor focus. A product manager cannot focus either analysis or strategy on every product in the market perceived to be a competitor due to limited available resources. Choosing whom to compete against has major implications for both performance standards (e.g., determining share of what) and strategy (e.g., competitive advertising). For example, the Odwalla brand manager must select whether to compete against only other energy bars or against the broader snack bar category.

The product manager can decide which competitors to focus on by examining three factors: (1) the time horizon of the marketing plan being developed, (2) the stage of the product life cycle relevant for the product, and (3) the rate of change in the technological base of the product.

In the one-year operating marketing plan most common for product managers, competition *must* be defined primarily on a product form basis and secondarily using any other appropriate bases. Clearly, the brands that compete with the one in question on a day-to-day basis are in the product form or a subcategory. For these brands, the product manager must have intimate knowledge of the customers, the competitors, and the effects of environmental changes such as demographics. For example, in an annual planning cycle, Sanka's major competitors are primarily other decaffeinated instant coffees. What about other decaffeinated or regular coffees? The selection of other competitors in the product category (coffee) or generic group is a judgment call based on where the product manager sees potential growth opportunities or whether a category or a generic competitor is attacking the product form. In this example, Sanka also competes more against other decaffeinated coffee brands than regular brands. As we mentioned earlier, competition such as soft drinks and juices is a serious issue for the category, and efforts to compete are funded by the coffee trade association. For longer-term plans, all four levels of competition are relevant, with special emphasis placed on the generic level to identify important competitive threats.

The stage of the product life cycle may be relevant to defining competition because the breadth of view of the industry varies over time. In the early growth stages of a product, particularly a new technology, competition must be broadly defined (generic competition) since a large part of the marketing task is to convince customers to substitute a new product for an existing one that was previously satisfying their needs. On the other hand, in mature markets, the focus should generally be on product form and category competitors to best assess whether or not to stay in a market.

Finally, where the rate of technological change is rapid, competition should be conceived as broadly as possible. This is characteristic of the communications field, in which such diverse products as word processors, fax machines, the Internet, home computers, cable TV, and satellites compete for certain services. Alternatively, narrow definitions are sufficient for fields in which new technical advances occur less frequently, as is the case with food products.

Given that the appropriate levels of competition have been selected, that is, that the "market" has been defined by the product manager, attention shifts to choosing relevant competitors. This assessment may require preparing a preliminary competitor analysis or at least updating the previous plan's competitor analysis. The factors determining which competitors are relevant relate to forecasts of competitors' likely strategies, which the competitor analysis should provide. However, the resources the competitors can bring to bear in the market are also critical. This focus on resources highlights a final perspective on competition called *enterprise competition.*

ENTERPRISE COMPETITION

Ultimately products and services do not compete against one another; companies do. The resources a company has to support the product are a key determinant of its ability to successfully implement a marketing strategy. Thus, while we have examined competition in this chapter from the perspective of a brand or product, it is important to note that enterprise competition (firm versus firm) involves a higher-level perspective in developing strategies.

For example, in the computer workstation market, the Hewlett-Packard product line competes against Sun, IBM, and Silicon Graphics, among others. However, not all competitors are created equal. When HP develops a marketing strategy against IBM, it competes not only in terms of product features and benefits communicated but also against IBM's resources: its financial support, sales force, and image. HP must develop different strategies to compete against IBM than those it uses to compete against Sun, which is many times smaller than IBM.

Figure 3.14 shows the diverse set of companies competing in the financial services industry. This could easily be expanded to include companies such as Fidelity, Vanguard, Citibank, and the like and products such as IRAs and annuities. As a traditional financial services company, American Express is used to competing against Merrill Lynch and Prudential in insurance, commercial lending, and securities. However, General Motors,

FIGURE 3.14 Enterprise Competition in Financial Services

	FDIC-Insured Depository	Consumer Loans	Credit/Debit Cards	Mortgage Banking	Commercial Lending	Mutual Funds	Securities	Insurance
American Express	X	X	X			X	X	X
Food		X	X	X	X			X
General Electric	X	X	X	X	X	X		X
General Motors		X	X	X	X			X
Merrill Lynch	X		X	X	X	X	X	X
Prudential	X	X	X	X	X	X	X	X
NetBank	X	X	X	X	X	X	X	X

General Electric, and Ford, typically thought of as industrial powers, also compete with American Express for consumer loans, credit/debit cards, commercial lending, and insurance. In addition, the "bricks and mortar" world of American Express is quite different from the Internet-only bank, NetBank. Thus, the American Express green card product manager competes against products with a very diverse set of corporate parents and some of the deepest pockets in the world.

It is often difficult to understand brand-level competition without understanding the broader context in which it occurs. For example, the Bic versus Cricket cigarette lighter battle may make little sense without recognizing the general competition between Bic and Gillette, which includes razors and pens as well as lighters. In addition, Kimberly Clark, a fierce competitor with Procter & Gamble (P&G) in the disposable diaper market, acquired Scott Paper with the intention of using the Scott brands (e.g., toilet tissue) to compete against P&G (Charmin) and therefore help dilute P&G's resources available to compete in the more lucrative diaper category.

Enterprise competition is often characterized by asymmetries in competitive perspectives. For example, Odwalla probably views PowerBar and Balance Bar as more serious competitors than Clif Bar because the former are owned by major companies (Nestlé and Kraft). Companies with large resources have to be monitored more carefully due to their abilities to disrupt the marketplace with large advertising and promotion campaigns. Since Clif Bar is independent, it is not as likely to pose large problems for Odwalla, at least in the short term. Conversely, Clif Bar certainly views the others as major competitors.

SUMMARY

In this chapter, we argued that the set of competitors that pose a threat to a product can be highly varied and can come from a variety of what have traditionally been referred to as industries. Therefore, a "market" or an "industry" is often dynamic and difficult to define; often the labels are used more for convenience than to accurately describe the underlying patterns of competition. We presented a framework to conceptualize competition and methods to help form ideas about the competitive set. Finally, we discussed approaches to selecting competitors by choosing the relevant levels and specific brands.

Essentially, we suggest that competitors are those companies whose products or services compete for the same customers either directly through offering similar products or services (product form or category competition), indirectly through satisfying similar basic needs (generic competition), or in terms of budget. The product manager in charge of an existing product in an established category would generally be most interested in product form or category competition, since those are the products that immediately threaten his or her "livelihood." However, for new product plans, a generic perspective is very important since the new product is substituting for another category satisfying similar customer needs.

References

Abell, Derek (1980) *Defining the Business*. Englewood Cliffs, NJ: Prentice-Hall.

Andrews, Rick L., and T. C. Srinivasan (1995) "Studying Consideration Effects in Empirical Choice Models Using Scanner Panel Data," *Journal of Marketing Research*, February, 30–41.

Ansoff, H. Igor (1965) *Corporate Strategy*. New York: McGraw-Hill.

Bourgeois, Jacques, George Haines, and Montrose Summers (1979) "Defining An Industry," paper presented at the ORSA/TIMS Market Measurement Conference, Stanford University.

Claburn, Thomas (2002) "Inside Line," *Smartbusinessmag.com*, April, 28.

Clark, Bruce H., and David B. Montgomery (1999) "Managerial Identification of Competitors," *Journal of Marketing*, July, 67–83.

Cooper, Lee (1988) "Competitive Maps: The Structure Underlying Asymmetric Cross-elasticities," *Management Science*, June, 707–23.

Day, George S., Allan D. Shocker, and Rajendra V. Srivastava (1979) "Customer-Oriented Approaches to Identifying Product Markets," *Journal of Marketing*, Fall, 8–19.

Dvorak, Phred (2000) "Japanese Banks Face New Competitors," *The Wall Street Journal*, May 17, A22.

Federman, Josef (2003) "In the Driver's Seat," *The New York Times*, May 19, R12.

Fitch, Stephane (2003) "Pocketing a New Market," *Forbes*, October 13, 125.

Hauser, John R., and Birger Wernerfelt (1990) "An Evaluation Cost Model of Consideration Sets," *Journal of Consumer Research*, March, 391–405.

Kalwani, Manohar, and Donald Morrison (1977) "A Parsimonious Description of the Hendry System," *Management Science*, January, 467–77.

Kim, W. Chan, and Renée Mauborgne (1999) "How Southwest Airlines Found a Route to Success," *Financial Times*, May 13, 20.

Lehmann, Donald R. (1972) "Judged Similarity and Brand-Switching Data as Similarity Measures," *Journal of Marketing Research*, August, 331–34.

Levitt, Theodore (1960) "Marketing Myopia," *Harvard Business Review*, July–August, 45–56.

McAlister, Leigh, and James Lattin (1985) "Using a Variety-Seeking Model to Identify Substitute and Complementary Relationships among Competing Products," *Journal of Marketing Research*, August, 330–39.

Parker-Pope, Tara (1998) "P&G Targets Textiles Tide Can't Clean," *The Wall Street Journal,* April 29, B1.

Rao, Vithala, and Darius Sabavala (1981) "Inference of Hierarchical Choice Processes from Panel Data," *Journal of Consumer Research,* June, 85–96.

Ratneshwar, S., and Allan D. Shocker (1991) "Substitution in Use and the Role of Usage Context in Product Category Structures," *Journal of Marketing Research,* August, 281–95.

Stefflre, Volney (1972) "Some Applications of Multidimensional Scaling to Social Science Problems," in *Multidimensional Scaling: Theory and Applications in the Behavioral Sciences,* Vol. III, A. K. Romney, R. N. Shepard, and S. B. Nerlove, eds. New York: Seminar Press.

Thomaselli, Rich (2003) "Travelocity Hands McKinney $30M Biz," *Advertising Age,* October 27, 6.

Urban, Glen, Philip Johnson, and John R. Hauser (1984) "Testing Competitive Market Structures," *Marketing Science,* Spring, 83–112.

Yip, George, and Jeffrey Williams (1986) "U.S. Retail Coffee Market (A)," Harvard Business School case #9-586-134.

Chapter **Four**

Category Attractiveness Analysis

Overview

For either new or existing products, product managers must ask whether the category of interest is sufficiently attractive to warrant new or continued investment—by their company, current competitors, or potential new entrants. The product portfolio approach popularized by the Boston Consulting Group uses the market growth rate to indicate attractiveness. Other models utilize a two-dimensional strategic grid consisting of market attractiveness and business position (see Cravens, 1994).

The kind of analysis described in this chapter is often characterized as "industry" or "market" analysis. Because the focus of this book is on product management, we focus on the product category, which defines the set of competitors against which one most often competes on a daily basis. While this may seem to be a narrow definition, particularly after the discussion in the preceding chapter, a product manager can adapt the analysis presented in this chapter to the definition of product category or industry most appropriate for the circumstances.

An essential component of the marketing planning process is an analysis of a product's potential to achieve a desired level of return on the company's investment. An analysis of this type not only assesses financial opportunities but also provides ideas about how to compete better given structural characteristics of the category.

The characteristics of a product category rarely all point in the same direction. As a result, categories that some firms find attractive will be of little interest to others. For example, most food categories are characterized by low but steady sales volume growth. A growth rate of 4.5 percent in the frozen potato category would probably seem high to the Ore-Ida product manager but quite low to a Cisco Systems marketer. In the automobile market, most observers consider the luxury car segment (over $40,000) overpopulated with models from every major car manufacturer in the world. However, Ford chose to purchase Jaguar because of the considerable brand equity in the name and because Ford management believed the brand gave the company an instant entry into the luxury car field.

Besides the product manager for the manufacturer or service provider, another interested party to this analysis is the distribution channel. As noted in Chapter 1, more channel members, particularly retailers, are interested in category management, the profitable management of entire product categories. Clearly, retailers will give

FIGURE 4.1   Category Attractiveness Summary

Aggregate category factors:
   Category size
   Category growth
   Stage in product life cycle
   Sales cyclicity
   Seasonality
   Profits
Category factors:
   Threat of new entrants
   Bargaining power of buyers
   Bargaining power of suppliers
   Current category rivalry
   Pressure from substitutes
   Category capacity
Environmental factors:
   Technological
   Political
   Economic
   Regulatory
   Social

more space and/or selling time to those categories that are "attractive," which means faster inventory turnover, greater total profits, and less space for categories that are "unattractive." Thus, the kind of analysis described in this chapter is also relevant to (and probably is also being performed by) the channel members in the distribution system.

In this chapter, we examine the important factors (summarized in Figure 4.1) in assessing the underlying attractiveness of a product category. The three main areas of inquiry include basic aggregate factors, category factors related to the major participants, and environmental factors. We also discuss sources of information for the attractiveness analysis components and apply the concepts to the energy bar and PDA categories.

AGGREGATE MARKET FACTORS

Six major market factors impact market attractiveness (Figure 4.2).

Category Size

Category size (measured in both units and monetary value) is an important piece of data about any market. It is clearly an important determinant of the likelihood that a product will generate revenues to support a given investment. In general, larger markets are better than smaller ones. Besides having more market potential, large categories usually offer more opportunities for segmentation than small ones (see Chapter 6). Therefore, both large firms and entrepreneurial organizations might find large markets attractive. Large

FIGURE 4.2 **Attractiveness of Market Variables**

	Attractiveness	
	High	Low
Market size	+	−
Market growth	+	−
Sales cyclicity	−	+
Sales seasonality	−	+
Profit level	+	−
Profit variability	−	+

markets, however, tend to draw competitors with considerable resources, thus making them unattractive for small firms. Witness the soft-drink category. Coca-Cola and PepsiCo spent $240 million in the first six months of 2003 on advertising alone supporting Coke, Diet Coke, Pepsi, and Diet Pepsi, and this did not include money spent on promotion (*Advertising Age*, 2003). Thus, absolute size by itself is not sufficient to warrant new or continuing investment.

Market Growth

As mentioned previously, market growth is a key market factor advocated by various planning models. Not only is current growth important, but growth projections over the horizon of the plan are also critical. Fast-growing categories are almost universally desired due to their abilities to support high margins and sustain profits in future years. However, like large categories, fast-growing ones also attract competitors. For example, while Procter & Gamble developed the U.S. market for disposable diapers, the high growth rate supported the entry of other firms such as Johnson & Johnson and Kimberly Clark. In technology-based markets, fast growth often means dramatic shifts in market shares and the virtual disappearance of rival products. In the Internet browser market, Netscape had 13 percent of the market and Mosaic had 60 percent in 1994. However, by 2002, Netscape had 8 percent of the market, Mosaic had disappeared, and Microsoft's Internet Explorer held 91 percent (Angwin and Sandberg, 2002). Thus, growth brings the prospects of increasing revenues but also dynamic market structures in terms of competitors.

Product Life Cycle

Category size and category growth are often portrayed simultaneously in the form of the product life cycle (see Figure 4.3). Usually presumed to be S-shaped, this curve breaks down product sales into four segments: introduction, growth, maturity, and decline. The introduction and growth phases are the early phases of the life cycle when sales are growing rapidly, maturity represents a leveling off in sales, and the decline phase represents the end of the life cycle.

Figure 4.3 also presents a general assessment of the attractiveness of a category at each stage of the life cycle. In the introductory phase, both the growth rate and the size of the market are low, thus making it unattractive for most prospective participants, who would rather wait on the sidelines for a period of time. When market growth and sales start to take off, the market becomes more attractive. In the maturity phase, the assessment is unclear; while the growth rate is low, the market size could be at its peak. This

FIGURE 4.3 **Category Attractiveness over the Product Life Cycle**

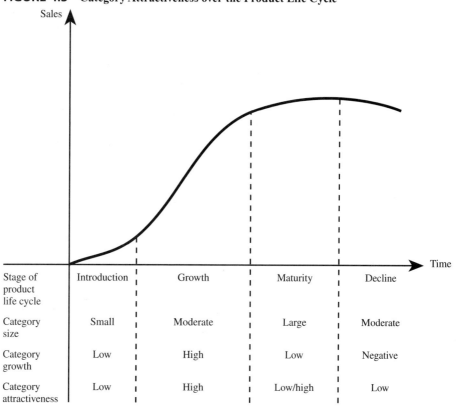

Stage of product life cycle	Introduction	Growth	Maturity	Decline
Category size	Small	Moderate	Large	Moderate
Category growth	Low	High	Low	Negative
Category attractiveness	Low	High	Low/high	Low

is the classic pattern for soft drinks, fast food, and many other consumer packaged goods: large dollar volume with slow growth. Finally, the decline phase usually is so unattractive that most competitors flee the category.

However, the attractiveness of products in different phases of the life cycle is not always clear. While the introductory phase has low growth and sales volume, it can be attractive to be the pioneer from a long-run market share perspective (Kalyanaram, Robinson, and Urban 1995; Urban et al., 1986). Products in the growth phase are not ensured success—witness the failures of Osborne and Commodore in the early days of personal computers and the well-documented difficulties that even "big name" companies such as AT&T and Hewlett-Packard have had in the home segment of the personal computer market. Even products in the decline phase, the "last ice man," can be very profitable. Lansdale Semiconductor and Rochester Electronics are the last companies to manufacture the 8080 microprocessor introduced by Intel in 1974. Some companies in the toy, defense, and telecommunications industries make products or need spare parts that use these old chips.

Sales Cyclicity

Many categories experience substantial interyear variation in demand. Highly capital-intensive businesses such as automobiles, steel, and machine tools are often tied to general business conditions and therefore suffer through peaks and valleys of sales as gross domestic product (GDP) varies. Similarly, businesses tied to interest rates, such as real estate and other financial services, are susceptible to cycles. Products based on agricultural commodities are affected by yearly climactic conditions. This is clearly not an attractive characteristic of a category, as these sales swings affect profits, employment levels, and cash available for new product development. Many firms attempt to develop products and acquire other businesses to eliminate interyear sales cyclicity.

Seasonality

Seasonality—intrayear cycles in sales—is generally not viewed positively. For example, in the last few years, the toy industry has reduced its reliance on the Christmas period to generate most of its sales. Such seasonal business tends to generate price wars because there may be few other opportunities to make substantial sales. However, most products are seasonal to some extent. Some, such as cold remedies, lawn mowers, fuel oil, and ice cream, are very seasonal.

Profits

While profits vary across products or brands in a category, large interindustry differences also exist. For example, the average profit margins for footwear, personal care, and biotechnology were 5.7, 20.9, and 49.3 percent, respectively, in 2002.[1]

These differences in profitability across industries are actually based on a variety of underlying factors. Differences can be due to factors of production (e.g., labor versus capital intensity, raw materials), manufacturing technology, and competitive rivalry, to name a few. Suffice it to say that product categories that are chronically low in profitability are less attractive than those that offer higher returns.

A second aspect of profitability is that it varies over time. Variance in profitability is often used as a measure of industry risk. Semiconductors offer abnormally high returns when demand is good but concomitant poor returns when demand slumps. Food-related businesses, on the other hand, produce relatively steady, if unspectacular, profits. As is usually the case, product managers must make a risk–return trade-off, evaluating the expected returns against the variability in those returns.

CATEGORY FACTORS

Although the aggregate factors just described are important indicators of the attractiveness of a product category, they do not provide information about underlying structural factors affecting the category. A classic model developed by Porter (1980) considers five factors in assessing the structure of industries:

The threat of new entrants.

The bargaining power of buyers.

The bargaining power of suppliers.

The amount of intracategory rivalry.

The threat of substitute products or services.

---

[1] *S&P Analysts' Handbook,* 2002 Annual Edition (New York: Standard & Poor's).

We adapt these factors to the category analysis and add a sixth factor, production or service capacity.

Threat of New Entrants

If the threat of new entrants into the product category is high, the attractiveness of the category is diminished. Except for the early stages of market development, when new entrants can help a market to expand, new entrants bring additional capacity and resources that usually heighten the competitiveness of the market and diminish profit margins. Even at early stages of market growth, the enthusiasm with which new entrants are greeted is tempered by who the competitor is. For example, while online investment companies like E*Trade publicly welcomed Charles Schwab's entry into the market, it is unlikely that they were as happy in private.

The barriers to entry erected by the existing competition are key to the likelihood that new competitors will enter the market. This sounds anticompetitive and illegal, but it is only definitely anticompetitive; making it difficult for new competitors through legal means is a common strategic weapon of product managers. Some of the potential barriers to entry follow.

Economies of Scale

An important barrier to entry in the automobile industry is the large plant size needed to operate efficiently, obtain quantity discounts on raw materials, and so on. Small manufacturers (e.g., Rolex) are normally content with serving the high-priced market segment. Economies of scale are obtainable in areas other than manufacturing. For example, in the hospital supply business, profit margins are better on larger orders because the costs of taking and fulfilling an order are largely fixed. Service costs are also subject to economies of scale because it costs about the same to set up a service center to service many customers or retailers as it does to service a few. Large advertisers usually get quantity discounts when buying blocks of media time on TV, radio, and other media.

Product Differentiation

Well-established brand names or company reputations can make it difficult for new competitors to enter. In the ready-to-eat breakfast cereal industry, the big four—Kellogg, Kraft/General Foods, General Mills, and Quaker Oats—have such long-established reputations that a new branded competitor would find it difficult to establish a brand franchise. The high barriers in the cereal industry were the subject of a lawsuit (ultimately unsuccessful) by the U.S. government.

Capital Requirements

Large amounts of capital may be necessary to establish manufacturing facilities, chain store locations, or marketing programs. It is easy to think of very capital-intensive industries, such as chemicals and aircraft, which require enormous amounts of money to set up plants. However, many categories are much more marketing intensive, through either advertising or distribution. For example, some mail-order computer companies buy their machines from other companies and spend most of their money on advertising, distribution, and service. Thus, capital barriers are clearly not confined to plant and equipment.

The fast-food category has enormous fixed costs for marketing (advertising and promotion) and distribution.

Switching Costs

These are the costs of switching from one supplier to another. *Supplier* can be interpreted in a business-to-business sense or in an end-customer context. If switching costs are high, as they are in the mainframe computer and computer software businesses, it is difficult to convert a competitor's existing customers. Federal Express has given its business customers software that enables them to monitor the status of their own packages in the FedEx system. This creates a barrier to potential new entrants as well as making it difficult for competitors to get FedEx customers to switch package delivery firms. It is more difficult to build in switching costs into consumer products, particularly supermarket items, as consumers can simply change brands the next time they shop. However, a notable exception is Gillette, which tries to sell the notion of a shaving "system" and thus promotes the use of its blades with its razors. Another example is home video game manufacturers such as Sony and Nintendo, which have security devices in their game cartridges and proprietary hardware that allow only games made by each company or their licensees to be used with the system.

In the information technology arena, building such barriers to switching is often referred to as *lock-in* (Shapiro and Varian, 1999). Loyalty programs are good examples of building switching costs from lock-in. If you are a member of United Airlines' Mileage Plus program, you tend to choose United when possible in order to increase the accumulated mileage in your account.

Distribution

New products can find it difficult to obtain shelf space. Coca-Cola and PepsiCo have created so many varieties of their basic colas that branded rivals such as 7Up have found it more difficult to gain shelf space, particularly since private labels have made significant inroads into the soft-drink category. Supermarkets, drugstores, and other chain retailers often charge *slotting allowances,* payments from manufacturers for placing their goods on shelves. This practice obviously creates a barrier to entry, particularly for smaller firms that find it difficult to pay the fees.

The willingness of the competitors in the category to vigorously retaliate against newcomers can also act as a barrier. When small Minnetonka, Inc., innovated with a pump for hand soap, both Colgate-Palmolive and Procter & Gamble immediately copied the package and outspent Minnetonka in promotion. That story has been repeated in the toothpaste category.

Barriers change over time. When Xerox's patent on its basic copying process expired, the number of competitors in the copier market expanded dramatically. Likewise, when a prescription drug's patent protection ends, a generic with a much lower price is invariably introduced.

It is important not only that product managers note the likelihood of a new entrant based on the above factors, but that they also assess the ability of a product to heighten entry barriers. Again, although raising barriers to entry has a negative connotation, particularly to a company's lawyers, there are legal means of inhibiting competition in a product category. Thus, a product manager could ask: Is there anything I can do to make it more difficult for a new entrant or even a current competitor to compete against me? The answers are related to the factors noted above. For example, if threat of entry is easy (a negative for the category), then (1) differentiate more; (2) raise the stakes (capital) required to compete effectively; (3) build in switching costs, thus making it harder for customers to switch brands; (4) lock up distribution and/or supply to the extent it is legal; or (5) if appropriate, signal your intention to strongly retaliate. Product managers commonly attempt most of these tactics. Note that brand extensions occupy shelf space, and many companies spend money to limit brand switching through database marketing and loyalty programs, that is, tracking individual customer buying habits and offering promotions via direct mail or telemarketing.

Bargaining Power of Buyers

Buyers are any people or organizations that receive finished goods or services from the organizations in the category being analyzed. Buyers can be distributors, original equipment manufacturers (OEMs), or end customers. Suppliers are any institutions that supply the category of concern with factors of production such as labor, capital, raw materials, and machinery.

High buyer bargaining power is negatively related to industry attractiveness. In such circumstances, buyers can force down prices and play competitors off against one another for benefits such as service. Some conditions that occur when buyer bargaining power is high include the following:

1. *When the product bought is a large percentage of the buyer's costs.* Historically, the automobile industry (the buyer) had little buying power over the steel industry (the industry of concern) because steel has been so important to car manufacturing. This power, however, is increasing as car manufacturers replace steel with plastics and reduce the number of suppliers they use to gain price concessions and productivity improvements.
2. *When the product bought is undifferentiated.* If product managers in the category of concern view what they sell as a commodity, buyers will have a great deal of power. Good examples of this include the leverage held by customers of commodity chemicals or bulk semiconductors. In such situations, buyers view the offerings as indistinguishable and bear down on price.
3. *When the buyers earn low profits.* Ailing industries such as farm equipment can generally extract better terms from supplier industries than can healthy industries.
4. *When the buyer threatens to backward integrate.* Among other pressures felt by semiconductor manufacturers is the constant threat by computer companies to make their own chips. IBM's purchase of part of Intel is such an example. Consumers also backward integrate, as the growth of do-it-yourself hardware and furniture stores indicates.
5. *When the buyer has full information.* Consumers can exert more power in retail stores if they are fully aware of competitive offerings. For example, car dealers are more willing to negotiate on price when a buyer demonstrates he or she has collected dealer cost information from a source such as *Consumer Reports* or Edmunds.com.
6. *When substitutes exist for the seller's product or service.* Although this is a separate category factor, described below, it also clearly affects buyer power.

In general, consumers wield their buyer power only on an individual and generally limited basis. This is not true in industrial businesses in which customers such as the U.S. government can wield large amounts of power. However, if consumers can be organized as a group, they become a more important customer and thus exert more power than would otherwise be the case. For example, the large population of retired consumers are powerfully linked through the American Association of Retired Persons (AARP). Similarly, buying cooperatives have increased power. For example, major U.S. hospitals have banded together to demand better terms of purchasing routine supplies such as tongue depressors, bandages, etc.

Again, the product manager's objective is to decrease buyer power. This is accomplished, for example, by increasing product differentiation (e.g., making your product an essential component), helping customers become more profitable through services such as technical assistance or manufacturing-related consulting, and building in switching costs.

Bargaining Power of Suppliers

This assessment is really the mirror image of the buyer power analysis. High supplier power is clearly not an attractive situation because it allows suppliers to dictate price and other terms, such as delivery dates, to the buying category. Supplier bargaining power is generally higher under the following circumstances:

1. *Suppliers are highly concentrated, that is, dominated by a few firms.* Organizations in need of supercomputers face strong suppliers because very few exist worldwide (IBM, Cray, NEC, and a few others).

2. *There is no substitute for the product supplied.* The supercomputer falls in this category, although this power is diminishing with the increased computing speed offered by workstations. In contrast, the power of the Organization of Petroleum Exporting Countries (OPEC) diminished in the 1970's as industries converted plants to use oil and coal, and is currently rising again.

3. *The supplier has differentiated its product or built in switching costs.* AK Steel Inc. increased its power with the automobile industry by offering General Motors a delayed payment plan, a guarantee of no work stoppages, a demonstration of how cheaper steel could be substituted in certain areas, and extra service such as supplying steel already prepared with adhesives for some applications.

4. *Supply is limited.* Clearly when capacity and output are limited, buyers have little opportunity to extract special terms.

Product managers can reduce supplier power by looking for new sources of supply, substitute materials, and other strategies.

Category Rivalry

Product categories characterized by intense competition among the major participants are not as attractive as those in which the rivalry is more sedate. A high degree of rivalry can result in escalated marketing expenditures, price wars, employee raids, and related activities. Such actions can exceed what is considered "normal" market competition and can result in decreased welfare for both consumers and competitors.[2]

Several examples highlight the negative aspects of rivalry. In the cell phone category, four of the top six service providers (Verizon, Cingular, AT&T, and Sprint) spent over $1.5 billion on advertising in the first half of 2003. What did this accomplish? The four companies have customer "churn" (loss) rates of 1.9, 2.8, 2.7, and 2.7 percent *monthly*. Compaq (prior to its acquisition by Hewlett-Packard) and Dell were well known to be bitter rivals in the personal computer industry; situated 200 miles apart in Texas, they stole each other's employees, traded vicious attacks in the press, and hired focus groups to find holes in the rival's strategies (Pope, 1993). Other well-known intense rivals are Oracle and Siebel in the software industry, chipmakers Intel and AMD, amusement park operators Six Flags and Disney, and giant Japanese trading companies Matsushita and Sony in consumer electronics.

These are some of the major characteristics of categories exhibiting intensive rivalries:

1. *Many or balanced competitors.* The fast-food, automobile, and personal computer industries each have several large, well-endowed competitors. At one time, the commercial aircraft manufacturing industry had one strong company, Boeing, and two weaker companies, McDonnell Douglas and Airbus. With Boeing's acquisition of McDonnell Douglas and Airbus's string of successes in landing customers, the two are now quite even and bitter competitors.

2. *Slow growth.* The relevant issue here, of course, is that in mature markets, growth can come only from a competitor.

3. *High fixed costs.* In such categories, there is intense pressure to keep operations running at full capacity to lower average unit costs. For this reason, capital-intensive industries such as paper and chemicals are highly competitive.

4. *Lack of product differentiation.* When little differentiation exists, products and services look like commodities to customers and price warfare erupts.

5. *Personal rivalries.* In some industries, personal rivalries develop around strong personalities who exhibit strong competitive instincts. Sun's Scott McNealey and Microsoft's Bill Gates frequently snipe at each other in speeches and articles. Oracle and Siebel are competitors in the customer relationship management (CRM) category. Even though he used to work for Oracle, Tom Siebel and Larry Ellison (Oracle's CEO) bring the corporate competitiveness into the personal arena.

Overall, it is difficult for the product manager to have an impact on category rivalry.

Pressure from Substitutes

Categories making products or delivering services for which there are a large number of substitutes are less attractive than those that deliver a relatively proprietary product, one that uniquely fills a customer need or solves a problem. Since almost all categories suffer from the availability of substitutes (recall the discussion from Chapter 3), this may

---

[2] *New York Times,* November 24, 2003, p. C4.

FIGURE 4.4 Impact of Category Factors on Attractiveness

	High	Low
Threat of new entrants	−	+
Power of buyers	−	+
Power of suppliers	−	+
Rivalry	−	+
Pressure from substitutes	−	+
Unused capacity	−	+

not be a determinant of an unattractive product category. However, some of the highest rates of return are earned in categories in which the range of substitutes is small. For example, the broadcast media industry, which had few substitutes (although that is changing rapidly), earned much higher margins (nearly 30 percent) than coal (under 10 percent), which definitely has available alternatives.

Determining the degree to which substitutes exist relates to the definition of the category. However, as noted in Chapter 2, some products, such as soft drinks, clearly have more generic competitors, whereas others, such as farm tractors, find their main competition within the category.

Capacity

Chronic overcapacity is not a positive sign for long-term profitability. When a category is operating at capacity, its costs stay low and its bargaining power with buyers is normally high. Thus, a key indicator of the health of a category is whether there is a consistent tendency toward operating at or under capacity. For example, during recessions, consumer spending on travel services is low, resulting in overcapacity at many worldwide resorts. This leads to low bargaining power with buyers, who can bargain down rates on cruises and other vacations.

Figure 4.4 summarizes the category analysis. For an actual marketing plan, each of the major categories in the figure should be expanded to include the factors discussed in this chapter. In addition, the implications of the analysis should be stated, not just whether or not the category is attractive. Since, as a product manager, you are in the category whether you like it or not, the important output of the category analysis is what the product manager learns about how to better compete in the product category.

ENVIRONMENTAL ANALYSIS

A definition of *environment* would be those factors outside the control of both the firm and its industry, or, stated another way, the external factors unrelated to the product's customers and competitors that affect marketing strategies. The vulnerability of a product category to changes in the environment is an unattractive characteristic, but virtually all product managers must deal with it. As mentioned earlier in the chapter, if a category's sales are tied to the domestic economic situation, cyclicity can result. Alternatively, categories that are well positioned to take advantage of environmental changes may prosper, as can product managers who view these changes as opportunities to gain competitive advantage.

Environmental factors fall into five groups: technological, political, economic, regulatory, and social. These factors should be examined to assess category attractiveness and to determine if any forecasted changes dictate changes in strategy.

Technological Factors

Figure 4.5 displays a model of the technological environment that is useful for conceptualizing sources of technological change in an industry (adapted from Thomas, 1974, for a product category). The "technology" and "impetus" dimensions are self-explanatory. The "process" dimension draws a distinction between the development of a new product (invention), the introduction of the product (innovation), and the spread of the product through the population (diffusion).

The two key dimensions used to assess a category's attractiveness are technology and process. Major changes are occurring in the energy, materials, transportation, information, and genetic (bioengineering) areas. With respect to information, for example, electronic scanning systems installed at supermarket cash registers enable retailers to closely monitor sales of different items for both inventory and shelf space allocation decisions. Bioengineering research is being used to both improve crop yields and find cures for various diseases such as cancer.

Product categories that are weaker on the technology dimension are particularly vulnerable to competition both from new products and from foreign competitors that have made

FIGURE 4.5   **Typology of Technical Developments**

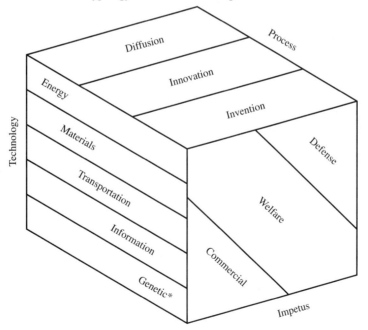

*Includes agronomic and biomedical developments.

Source: Philip S. Thomas, "Environmental Analysis for Corporate Planning," *Business Horizons* 17 (October 1974), p. 27.

the necessary investment. For example, in the 1980s most major U.S. steel firms used blast furnace technology developed in the 1800s. Foreign steel firms and domestic companies that invested in modern manufacturing technology have been highly successful in the past decade. On the positive side, U.S. strength has been computer software. Thus, an attractive product category is one that is well positioned to take advantage of technological changes that may be necessary to remain competitive against new, substitute technologies.

There is, however, a point beyond which technology can create a backlash, particularly among consumers. This has been referred to by John Naisbitt (1984) as "high tech versus high touch." For example, automatic teller machines have depersonalized banking to the point where some consumers yearn for the human contact afforded by tellers. Several years ago, Citibank in New York proposed to allow only its wealthiest customers to make transactions through personal contact; other customers would have been forced to use machines. Consumers protested so vehemently that Citibank scrapped the idea. Although frequently touted as a wave of the future, home banking through personal computers has never really caught on with consumers in a big way. Similarly, although grocery shopping through the Web has grown significantly due to the efforts of companies like Freshdirect, Peapod, and some other small companies, it still accounts for less than 1 percent of the $400 billion U.S. retail grocery market (Lee, 2003).

Attractive product categories are strong in invention, innovation, or diffusion of new products or services. Most technologically based companies must continually innovate because the life cycles for their products are extremely short. In contrast, success in frequently purchased packaged goods, while often continuously upgraded in various ways (e.g., packaging, flavor), is determined more by the quality of the marketing programs such as promotion, advertising, etc.

Political Factors

A second environmental factor relates to the category's sensitivity to political factors. These are particularly relevant for products with substantial foreign markets. Figure 4.6 conceptualizes the sources of political risk, the groups that generate political risk, and political problems in operating the business (Robock, 1971).

For example, many multinational companies are either actively marketing or considering marketing products in China and other countries experiencing economic reform, such as Vietnam, Cambodia, and even Iraq in the post-Saddam era. Following Figure 4.6, the sources of political risk are competing political philosophies (the risk that communism or some form of autocracy hostile to market reforms could return) and possible social unrest and disorder. The results of these risks could be a halt to conducting business, damage to property, and personal risk to employees.

Such analysis aids in evaluating geographically defined market segments for the line. If a sufficient percentage of a product's sales came from risky foreign markets, the product could in fact look unattractive relative to others.

Domestic U.S. political risk is generally not as great, but it is still important. Domestic risk is usually related to which political party is in power. Republicans tend to favor free market economies. Therefore, products hard hit by foreign competition (e.g., shoes, commodity semiconductors, automobiles) would probably receive no relief through quotas or increased tariffs. With Democrats, defense spending has historically been a target, and hence the fortunes of defense-related products are at risk. However, these political

FIGURE 4.6 Conceptualizing Political Risks

Sources of Political Risk	Groups through Which Political Risk Can Be Generated	Effects on International Business Operations
Competing political philosophies (nationalism, socialism, communism)	Government in power and its operating agencies	Confiscation: loss of assets without compensation
Social unrest and disorder	Parliamentary opposition groups	Expropriation with compensation: loss of freedom to operate
Vested interests of local business groups	Nonparliamentary opposition groups (Algerian "FLN," guerrilla movements working within or outside country)	Operational restrictions: market shares, product characteristics, employment policies, locally shared ownership, etc.
Recent and impending political independence	Nonorganized common interest groups: students, workers, peasants, minorities, etc.	Loss of transfer freedom: financial (dividends, interest payments, goods, personnel, or ownership rights, for example)
Armed conflicts and internal rebellions for political power	Foreign governments or inter-governmental agencies such as the EEC	Breaches or unilateral revisions in contracts and agreements
New international alliances	Foreign governments willing to enter into armed conflict or to support internal rebellion	Discrimination such as taxes or compulsory subcontractings
		Damage to property or personnel from riots, insurrections, revolutions, and wars

Source: Stefan H. Robock, "Political Risk: Identification and Assessment," *Columbia Journal of World Business,* July–August 1971, p. 7.

risks are dynamic. With the lowering of world tensions following the demise of the Soviet Union and the Eastern European communist bloc, defense spending declined. However, after the events of September 11, 2001, industries supplying defense and security-related products have done very well.

Economic Factors

Almost all capital goods industries (machine tools, farm equipment, mainframe computers) are sensitive to *interest rate fluctuations,* since their high costs to buyers are often financed at short-term interest rates. Consumer durables such as homes, cars, and stereos are also sensitive to interest rates, although consumer credit card rates do not react as much to changes in the prime lending rate as do commercial rates. Inflation rates, of course, are tied to interest rate fluctuations.

The financial impact of having foreign markets or producing in other countries can vary widely over time depending on *currency exchange rates.*

Since service businesses often hire relatively unskilled labor at low wage rates, they are highly dependent on *employment conditions.* When employment rates are high, for example, fast-food employees are hard to find and it is necessary to pay them more because higher-paying jobs are available. Demand and supply of labor for each industry must be considered as well. The supply of engineers is cyclical. When supply is down, many firms in technically related businesses suffer from a shortage of skilled labor.

Products such as automobiles and other consumer durables that have broad customer bases are often sensitive to *fluctuations in GDP growth.* When the country is in a recession, the sales of these products decline.

Regulatory Factors

Government and other agencies have an impact on category attractiveness through regulations. Some product categories have become less attractive over time because of laws that restrict product managers' abilities to market or that raise the overall cost of doing business. Government regulations, for example, restrict the media the tobacco industry can use for advertising. Pharmaceutical companies and many companies that make medical products are subject to stringent testing requirements that can change over time. Alternatively, government intervention can help some product categories. The U.S. government's restrictions on Japanese auto exports is an example, as is the subsidy given to certain agricultural commodities.

A good example of the impact of regulation on a pharmaceutical product is Genentech's tPA, an anticlotting drug. The company was so confident that the drug would succeed that it invested a considerable amount of money in manufacturing equipment, employees, premarketing, and product inventory. However, the Food and Drug Administration rejected the drug in May 1987, and within a week Genentech's market value dropped by nearly $1 billion.

It is not possible to generalize about the sources of regulatory impact because each product category is affected by different regulatory bodies. As a result, this part of the analysis must be highly category specific.

Social Factors

Trends in demographics, lifestyles, attitudes, and personal values among the general population are of particular concern for consumer product manufacturers and services. First, new products have been developed to fit into today's lifestyles. The growth of the size of the section in many supermarkets devoted to freshly prepared entrees is a direct result of the increase in dual-career and busy households with a need for convenience and easy preparation. Second, new features have been added to existing products. Upper-income consumers can have global positioning system (GPS) mapping systems in their cars and telephones with which they can surf the Web and snap digital pictures. Finally, promotion has changed. The aging "baby boomer" (reportedly similar in age to the clearly youthful authors) is commonplace today in television ads, as is the mysterious "Generation X" (young adults) consumer and "Gen Y" youths.

What is not as generally recognized is the importance of understanding trends in lifestyles and demographics for business-to-business products. Because the demand for such products is often derived demand, that is, ultimately generated by consumers, changes in the source of that demand can clearly affect demand for an industrial product. For example, the chemical manufacturer making polymers used in paints is affected by the amount of money consumers spend in fixing up houses and in new construction. For companies that provide business-to-business products, the key question to ask in assessing attractiveness is whether the *customers* of the product being considered are in the "right" industries. Unsurprisingly, firms supplying the "hot" categories tend to do well, and those that are heavily tied to declining consumer products do not.

For consumer products, a key question is whether the product category under consideration is well positioned to take advantage of current trends. Some products are "hot" because they appeal to the large and increasingly affluent baby boomer group; these include furniture and electronic appliances, upscale fast-food chains, clothing, and financial and travel services. Other products have been developed for consumers at the older end of the baby boom generation (those now reaching their late-50s). For example, a large part of the market for the Audi TT, Porsche Boxster, BMW Z3/4, and other sports cars introduced in the late 1990s through the early 2000s are people over 40 who wish to reduce their psychological age. Products having trouble, on the other hand, include coffee, cigarettes, and brown alcohol (except for high-end scotch whiskey), which are being buffeted by demographic and taste trends.

Because of the rise of the Internet globally, many pundits forecast that the 21st century will be the age of the customer. The shift of power from the seller to the customer is facilitated by both the increase in the information that customers have available to them and the lowering of shopping costs, which makes it easier for customers to compare options in terms of features and price. It has been said that today, customers can pretty much have what they want when they want it and at the price they wish to pay.

At least in the early part of the 21st century, the major demographic changes in the United States that will underlie consumer demand are the following (Miller, 1999):

- The aging of the baby-boom generation (those born between 1945 and 1964); Figure 4.7 shows the change in the U.S. population over the years 1995–2005. Witness the growth in the 40- to 59-year-old age bracket. Clearly, this has tremendous implications for products and services targeting more mature consumers.

FIGURE 4.7   **Projected Change in U.S. Population 1995–2005**

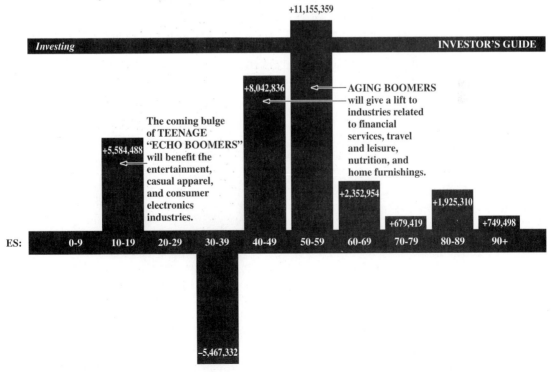

Source: "Betting on the Boomers," by Erick Schonfeld, *Fortune,* December 2, 1995. © 1995 TIME INC. REPRINTED BY PERMISSION.

FIGURE 4.8   The 10 Themes of N-Gen Culture

The Net Generation: Youth between 4 and 20 who are computer and Internet literate.

1. *Fierce independence:* A strong sense of independence and autonomy.
2. *Emotional and intellectual openness:* When N-Geners go online, they expose themselves.
3. *Inclusion:* A global orientation in their search for information, activity, and communication.
4. *Free expression and strong view:* The Internet has exposed them to a much greater range of ideas, opinions, and arguments than they would have experienced without it.
5. *Innovation:* A constant search for ways to do things better.
6. *Preoccupation with maturity:* N-Geners insist that they are more mature than adults expect.
7. *Investigation:* A strong ethos of curiosity, investigation, and the empowerment to change things.
8. *Immediacy:* The children of the digital age expect things to happen fast, because in their world, things *do* happen fast.
9. *Sensitivity to corporate interest:* They believe that too many perspectives are being left out of the broadcast images and they believe corporate agendas play a role in this shortfall.
10. *Authentication and trust:* Because of the anonymity, accessibility, diversity, and ubiquity of the Internet, N-Geners must continually authenticate what they see or hear on the Web.

Source: Don Tapscott, *Growing Up Digital,* McGraw Hill, New York, New York, 1998.

- The increasing importance of children as consumers; see Figure 4.8 for one writer's conceptualization of how today's children, or N-Geners (for the net generation), can be characterized. It is undoubtedly the case that children growing up in today's technology-charged society will be different consumers when they reach their prime spending years than their parents.

- A growing gap between society's haves and have-nots. Figure 4.9 shows that despite overall increased prosperity, the differences between the wealthier U.S. households and the poorer is increasing, particularly comparing the top 10 percent to the bottom. On

FIGURE 4.9   U.S. Income Inequality

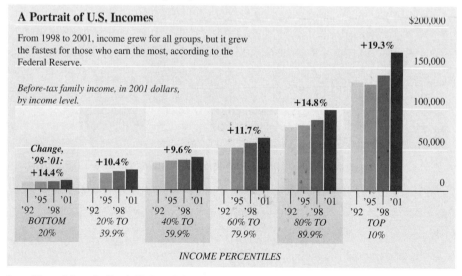

Source: "Economic Inequality Grew in 90's Boom, Fed Reports," *New York Times,* January 23, 2003, p. C1.

a net worth basis, the differences are even greater. The net worth of families in the top 10 percent jumped 69 percent, to $833,600, in 2001 from $492,400 in 1998. By contrast, the net worth of families in the lowest fifth of income earners rose only 24 percent, to $7,900 (Andrews, 2003).

- An increasingly diverse population; by 2025, non-Hispanic whites will comprise 62.4 percent of the U.S. population, down from 72.5 percent in 1998.

Given this as a backdrop, some key forces driving the era of the consumer are the following:

1. *The shrinking day.* More time spent working and committing to family-related activities means less time doing things they do not want to do like housework and cooking. This latter phenomenon is manifested in the growth of the share of food purchases in restaurants versus supermarkets. As can be seen in Figure 4.10, the share of purchases in restaurants passed the supermarket share in 1992 and the gap is widening. What consumers increasingly value in terms of products and services is time and convenience.

2. *Connectedness.* It is predicted that the Web will be where people turn to for a sense of community—between buyers and sellers, information suppliers and consumers, friends and family. While it is perhaps premature to say that all of this exists today (2004), clearly the trends point in that direction. It is commonplace for college students to chat with their friends for hours using an Instant Messenger service, and even for family members in the same house to communicate with each other.

3. *Body versus soul.* Some forecast that the new consumers will increasingly stay home to shop, meditate, and pamper their bodies but that they will also expect more in terms of entertainment (e.g., big screen plasma TVs). An example of this trend is what has been termed the "entertainmentization" of retailing where stores stage events, show videos on big screens, and attempt to add entertainment to everyday shopping experiences. The shrinking day also leads to consumers placing higher value on the spiritual. Witness Campbell Soup's motto: "M'm! M'm! Good for the Body. Good for the Soul." Investments in personal fitness will remain strong as will expenditures on expensive junk food (e.g., super-premium ice cream).

4. *Individualism.* Consistent with the trend toward individualism is an increase in products and services tailored to small groups, called *mass customization.* From Nike's custom-designed running shoes to Dell's made-to-order personal computers, customers want products built for them (or at least, they want the impression that they are). This

FIGURE 4.10 **Share of Food Purchases**

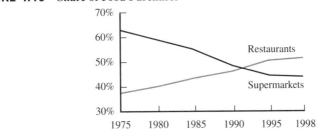

Source: *Nation's Restaurant News,* 1999.

trend toward the individual has also led to a dramatic growth in the small office, home office (SOHO) market to about 4 million workers who now claim their main offices in their homes. Accompanying mass customized products are marketing programs tailored to individuals, or *1–1 marketing.*

Any attempt to project these kinds of trends is fraught with difficulties, of course; the landscape is littered with forecasts that have gone awry (see, for example, Schnaars's 1989 book describing a number of such erroneous forecasts). In addition, many books continue to be produced that attempt such forecasts (books by Popcorn and Marigold, 1998, and Wacker, Taylor, and Means, 2000, are examples). However, the fundamental demographic and socioeconomic factors that underlie the forecasts provide incontrovertible evidence that change will occur. It is essential the product managers think about the impact of these changes on their businesses.

ILLUSTRATIONS

Energy Bars

Figure 4.11 summarizes a category attractiveness analysis for the energy snack bar category. Sources of information for this and the PDA illustration are listed in Chapter 2 in Figures 2.10 and 2.13. The aggregate market factors overall are very positive. The total market size for energy bars is not that large but it has a significant growth rate, and the profit margins are very high. A particularly positive factor is that the product is not seasonal due to the year-round use of exercise (i.e. running, skiing, gym workouts). The category factors are not so positive. Since it is a food product that is relatively easy to make, the threat of entrants is quite high, particularly from companies already in the food business. Switching costs are low and differentiation is difficult. There are also many substitutes and a considerable amount of competition. The environmental factors are generally positive, particularly the social factors which have helped to grow the category.

The purpose of this analysis is to enable the product manager to focus on aspects that expose weaknesses of the category and the brand. These are, of course, those factors with minus signs next to them. While the energy bar category has some significant positive factors (e.g., growth), there are some problems that product managers have to deal with. Obviously, key issues are in the areas of product differentiation and barriers to entry. Building strong brand names is one activity that accomplishes both objectives. This could also happen as the large companies involved with the category (Nestlé, Kraft, and Kellog's) raise their advertising and promotion spending and put more money into distribution. This raises the barriers to entry from a financial perspective and makes it more difficult for the smaller, independent brands to compete.

Personal Digital Assistants

Figure 4.12 shows a category attractiveness analysis for PDAs (recall that this is circa 1999). The aggregate market factors showed a market that was in the growth stage of the product life cycle. The factors here were all positive. The Palm Pilot created a market out of one thought dead by many observers. The market size, growth, and profitability of this category were all very positive factors that led to increased competition. With little cyclicity or seasonality, it is easy to see why. The category factors were a

FIGURE 4.11   Energy Bars: Category Attractiveness Summary

Factors	Analysis	Assessment Market Attractiveness
Aggregate Market		
Category size	• $504 million energy bars in 2001. • Energy bar category contains four primary brands, plus their sub-brands and over a hundred smaller players.	++
Category growth	• Average annual growth rate of 57% between 1997 and 2001. • U.S. energy bar category sales forecasted at $750 million in 2003 for a continued expected growth of 22%. • Industry reports suggest current annual growth for the energy bar market at 25%–30%. • Category expanding: new competitors are entering, existing brands are expanding with new products and flavors, market penetration and usage occasion is increasing.	++
Product life cycle	• Both the category and Odwalla Bars specifically are both securely in early stages of the growth phase.	++
Sales cyclicity	• While energy bars are premium-priced for their convenience and nutrient level, the base dollar point of $1–$3 per bar is low such that they are not directly impacted by GDP variations.	+
Seasonality	• Year-round sales. • Category overall may experience a slight sales increase in the spring and summer months during "race season" and as users are engaged in more outdoor activities and desire quick, portable energy.	++
Profits	• As most major competitors are within the product portfolios of larger consumer goods companies, it is difficult to benchmark profitability within the energy bar category specifically. Nevertheless, the recent acquisition of the leading competitors reflects an expectation for strong profit potential. • Increased category competitiveness may lead to lower pricing and profits.	+
Category		
Threat of new entrants/exits	• Strong potential for new competitors given that the category is profitable, fairly easy to enter, and increasingly relevant to consumers. • Further, with the "big three" brands strongly in place (PowerBar, Clif (including Luna), and Balance), it is most likely that small competitors will enter through the natural foods channel, creating more direct competition with Odwalla bars.	−
Economies of scale	• Competitors within the broader category of snack bars would likely experience economies of scale with a relatively easy entry into the energy bar market.	−
Product differentiation	• Within the mainstream energy bars, differentiation is largely through brand, taste, and flavor variety. With the exception of targeted nutrition products like protein- or carbohydrate-specific products, nutritional levels are largely at parity.	−
Capital requirements	• Capital requirements are relatively low, increasing the threat of new entrants.	−
Switching costs	• Switching costs are very low, opening the door to potential competitors.	−

continued

FIGURE 4.11 Energy Bars: Category Attractiveness Summary—*continued*

Factors	Analysis	Assessment Market Attractiveness
Category (contd.)		
Distribution	• As there are not specialty requirements for distribution (refrigeration, etc.), it would be very easy for any of the "center of the store" consumer food companies to enter the category and add on to their existing distribution structure. This is particularly true for companies that have an established relationship with the category buyer. • Shelf life	–
Bargaining power of buyers	• Lots of competitors with relatively similar options distinguished by brand and taste keeps retailer power strong.	–
Bargaining power of suppliers	• As the suppliers of raw inputs for energy bars are largely agricultural, the commodity nature of agriculture keeps prices and supplier power low. While still relatively low, supplier power will be higher for nutrient supplement suppliers.	+
Pressure from substitutes	• Considerable. • Fresh fruit, cereal bars, smoothies, candy bars, etc. are all suitable portable substitutes for the mainstream energy bar consumer. True athletes are most likely to substitute with higher nutrient level energy bars.	–
Category capacity	• Appears to be high given current scenario of more than 100 manufacturers and many more products. But, still, it is too early to determine true capacity.	+
Current category rivalry	• Very high. Differentiation largely by taste and flavor variety, and by targeting unique market segments.	–
Environmental		
Technological	• Technology could play a significant role with respect to manufacturing efficiencies and taste profiles.	+
Economic	• While premium priced, energy bars have so far seemed to fare the recession well. Still, however, if economic conditions persist, consumers may opt for less expensive alternatives like fresh fruit or non-energy snack bars.	+
Political/regulatory	• The energy bar category is regulated by the FDA as are other food products. There are not to our knowledge, however, additional regulations directed toward the energy bar category.	0
Social	• As lives get busier and mealtimes shrink, energy bars will continue to be an acceptable meal replacement.	+ +

mixed bag. On the plus side, the bargaining power of buyers was low due to strong brand names (Palm, Casio) and switching costs to changing brands due to different interfaces, file formats, and the like. Supplier components were relatively standard but on occasion, semiconductor supplies become tight. On the downside, the rivalry between brands was becoming intense and there was increasing price competition. Perhaps more importantly, there were significant substitutes on the horizon in the form of wireless cellular phones that could perform many functions (which we see today). Of course, the old standard, Day-Timers, are still very popular. The environmental factors were mixed.

FIGURE 4.12 Category Attractiveness Analysis: Personal Digital Assistants

Factor		Attractiveness
Aggregate Market Factors:		
Market size	$2.3 billion	+
Market growth	30%–40%	+
Product life cycle	Growth	+
Profits	Good	+/0
Sales cyclicity	None	+
Sales seasonality	None	+
Category factors:		
Threat of new entrants	Moderate; R&D required, distribution	0
Bargaining power of buyers	Low; high switching costs	+
Bargaining power of suppliers	Moderate; PCs use similar components	0
Category rivalry	Intense	−
Pressure from substitutes	High	−
Category capacity	Not a problem for now	+
Environmental factors:		
Technological	Very sensitive	−
Political/regulatory	Telecommunications deregulation	+
Economic	Relatively inexpensive	+
Social	More work done on the road	+

Further deregulation of the telecommunications industry will help the high-end PDAs due to their extensive communications capabilities. The main plus for the product category from this set of factors was that it was right in step with the way work is changing: More work out of the office and on the road increases the need for quick, convenient ways to take notes and keep records of phone numbers and appointments. The main negative factor was technology. Continued miniaturizing of components and product innovation could make the PDA category obsolete if the functions were transferred to phones, watches, or "wearable" computers such as those that have come out of MIT's Media Lab. While the basic customer benefits provided will not change, the form factor certainly could.

Again, the objective is to seek out the negatives in this analysis and try to develop programs to turn them around. In this case, the main negatives, category rivalry, pressure from substitutes, and sensitivity to technological change, are difficult to handle. Perhaps the main message was that Handspring should not have been wedded to its existing form factor (i.e., the handheld PDA) but should have leveraged its brand into new forms as the technology evolved. This, of course, happened with the revolutionary Treo.

SUMMARY

As we went through the three major groups of factors for assessing category attractiveness, we stressed the importance of qualitative assessment: indicating whether the factor had a positive or negative (or possibly neutral) impact on product management in that category of analysis. Clearly, certain factors have the potential to affect some products in a category more than others. For example, a product with a strong brand name is better able than one without strong brand identification to create a barrier to entry as a potential limit to brand switching. Thus, the purpose of this analysis is to develop a general perspective on the effects of the major factors on product managers in the category.

References

Advertising Age (2003) October 13, 26.

Andrews, Edmund L. (2003) "Economic Inequality Grew in the 90's Boom, Fed Reports," *The New York Times,* January 23, C1.

Angwin, Julia, and Jared Sandberg (2002) "Netscape Goes One More Round," *The Wall Street Journal,* January 24, B1.

Cravens, David W. (1994) *Strategic Marketing,* 4th ed. Burr Ridge, IL: Richard D. Irwin, Chap. 2.

Kalyanaram, Gurumurthy, William T. Robinson, and Glen L. Urban (1995) "Order of Market Entry: Established Empirical Generalizations, Emerging Empirical Generalizations, and Future Research," *Marketing Science,* Part 2 of 2, G212–21.

Lee, Louis (2003) "Online Grocers: Finally Delivering the Lettuce," *Business Week,* April 28, 67.

Miller, Annetta (1999) "The Millennial Mind-Set," *American Demographics,* January, 60–65.

Naisbitt, John (1984) *Megatrends: Ten New Directions for Transforming Our Lives.* New York: Warner Books.

Petersen, Laurie (1992) "Pepsi Buys the Month of April, But Will It Sell?" *Marketing Week,* February 24, 9.

Popcorn, Faith, and Lys Marigold (1998) *Clicking: 17 Trends That Drive Your Business— And Your Life.* New York: Harperbusiness.

Pope, Kyle (1993) "For Compaq and Dell, Accent Is on Personal in the Computer Wars," *The Wall Street Journal,* July 2, A1.

Porter, Michael E. (1980) *Competitive Strategy.* New York: The Free Press.

Robock, Stefan H. (1971) "Political Risk: Identification and Assessment," *Columbia Journal of World Business,* July–August, 7.

Schnaars, Steven P. (1989) *Megamistakes.* New York: The Free Press.

Shapiro, Carl, and Hal R. Varian (1999) *Information Rules.* Boston: Harvard Business School Press.

Thomas, Philip (1974) "Environmental Analysis for Corporate Planning," *Business Horizons,* 17, October, 27.

Urban, Glen L., Theresa Carter, Steven Gaskin, and Zofia Mucha (1986) "Market Share Rewards to Pioneering Brands: An Empirical Analysis and Strategic Implications," *Management Science,* June, 645–59.

Wacker, Watts, Jim Taylor, and Howard B. Means (2000) *The Visionary's Handbook: Nine Paradoxes That Will Shape the Future of Your Business,* New York: Harperbusiness.

Chapter **Five**

Competitor Analysis

Overview

Consider the following scenario (Green, 1998). A dozen students descend on Disney's Paradise Island in Orlando, Florida. They have been assigned to interact with strangers and extract secrets from them. One student targets a Philadelphia landscaper. Within minutes, she has discovered that he makes $1,500 per week, has lost his savings in a divorce settlement, and owns a house worth $150,000. Another student finds from an Arkansas businessman that he keeps at least $1,000 in his checking account. While the reader might think that this is an "unofficial" school for thieves and scam artists, it is actually a course sponsored by the Centre for Operational Business Intelligence. Their teachers are former counterintelligence agents experienced in uncovering secret information and training others to do the same. The students have been sponsored by companies to help their employers gather competitive intelligence.

The collection of competitor intelligence is of course not limited to domestic companies or ethical behavior. Consider this quote from a 50-year veteran of Japan's corporate industrial "spy wars" on how he obtains information from corporate employees (Fulford, 1995): "We follow our targets to their favorite bars, make friends with them and find out what their weak spots are. If they don't have any, we make them." These examples highlight the often negative view many have of competitive analysis. Here we take a different approach and emphasize that useful competitor analysis does not require illegal or unethical activities.

For most of the reasons mentioned in Chapter 1 concerning the difficulties of the product manager's job, competitor analysis has received more attention in recent years. In slow-growth markets, sales growth must come from the competitors. With shorter product life cycles, product managers must recoup investments in a shorter period of time, which makes errors of judgment about competition difficult to overcome. Technology available to managers makes collecting and disseminating information within the organization easier as well as quicker. Finally, given the generally high level of turbulence product managers face from increased foreign competition, dramatically changing technology and rates of innovation, large shifts in interest rates and stock valuations (both up and down), and changing customer tastes, it is more important than ever to keep abreast of changes in all factors exogenous to the firm, including competition. As Figure 5.1 shows, the manager of competitor intelligence has become an important figure in many multinational corporations.

In fact, given the number of marketing books with the term *warfare* in the title (see, for example, Ries and Trout, 1985), the recent history of marketing strategy has been as

FIGURE 5.1 Advertisement for Competitor Intelligence Manager

International Competitive Intelligence Manager

McGraw-Hill Higher Education – Sales/Marketing Division

McGraw-Hill/Irwin has an opening for an International Competitive Intelligence Manager in our Sales & Marketing Division. Through online learning and multimedia tools McGraw-Hill Higher Education, Professional and International group, is a leading global provider of educational materials and professional information.

Tasks:

- Collect, process and report competitive data and intelligence.
- Coordinate, improve and develop information systems in our Sales & Marketing Division.
- Supply analyses of competitors for the numerous divisions in Higher Education.

The Manager will be part of the Sales & Marketing Information team and will report to the V.P of Sales & Marketing Information. The office location is in Hightstown, New Jersey.

Qualifications:

- Bachelor's Degree and at least three years of International Marketing/ Sales, preferably in a business-to-business market.
- Experience in international competitive intelligence and college textbook publishing.
- Effective communication and interpersonal skills.
- Ability to set priorities; to plan, organize and control workflow; and analyze the situations and the marketing environment.
- Thorough understanding of information systems, information technology and the role of systems in processing and communicating competitive data and intelligence.

We offer a challenging career in an exciting international environment with good opportunities for advancement.
For further information, please contact the Human Resource Director for Higher Education Margaret Hanover at 609-789-5221 or by e-mail marg_hanover@McGraw-Hill.com
Please send your application with attention to Human Resource Director-MHHE, 148 Princeton/Hightstown Road, Hightstown, NJ 08520-1450

McGraw-Hill Higher Education is a world leader in educational and professional information in a variety of formats including web-publications, technology and textbooks. Headquartered in Hightstown, NJ. More information can be obtained by visiting our website at www.McGraw-Hill.com

McGraw-Hill Higher Education
A Division of The McGraw-Hill Companies

oriented toward competitors as the 1960s were toward the customer. The traditional view of the marketing concept is a focus on the needs and wants of the customer. Since the 1980s, however, it has become increasingly clear that meeting customer needs is not enough for success. What is critical to a product's success is meeting customer needs *better* than a competitor can, often at a lower cost. This implies an equally strong focus on understanding competitors' marketing strategies and capabilities.

Many companies have, of course, discovered the importance of competitor analysis. Here are some examples:[1]

- Microsoft deployed a team of engineers and marketers specifically to track Linux, the fast-growing, free operating system that is becoming more popular. The team has attempted to convince potential corporate users that Linux is not a real competitor to Windows.
- Frontier Airlines competes head-to-head with United on many routes in the western United States. To try to anticipate United's moves, Frontier hired a former United planning executive as its planning director to get "inside" United's corporate head. For example, instead of swamping a market with flights, Frontier learned that if it flew only twice a day to a city, United was not likely to increase its capacity there.
- Every week, Tom Sternburg, founder and CEO of Staples, the office supply superstore, drops by one of his stores and a competitor's. He focuses mainly on what the competitor is doing well rather than simply criticizing the competitor for its weaknesses. He looks at customer service, store visibility, displays, and how easy the prices are to read.
- Palm Computing has a chief competitive officer whose job is to predict competitors' likely future strategies. His main job is to follow Microsoft and its Windows CE operating system. His methods include talking with customers, sales staff, and suppliers.

An annual survey of the best American players in the intelligence game found the following rank ordering (Green, 1998):

1. Microsoft
2. Motorola
3. IBM
4. Procter & Gamble
5. General Electric, Hewlett-Packard (tied)
6. Coca-Cola, Intel (tied)

It would be a mistake to assume that competitor intelligence gathering is only for large companies. An example illustrates that small companies can profit from such activity as

---

[1] Sources for these examples are Lee Gomes (1999), "Upstart Linux Draws a Microsoft Attack Team," *The Wall Street Journal*, May 21, p. B1; Stephanie Gruner (1998), "Spies Like Us," *Inc.*; Scott McCartney (1999), "Upstart's Tactics Allow It to Fly in Friendly Skies of a Big Rival," *The Wall Street Journal*, June 29, p. B1; Todd Wasserman (2000), "Spy or Spinmeister?" *Marketing Computers*, May, pp. 53–58.

well (*The Wall Street Journal,* 1989). The CEO of a small company turned a discussion with a customer into a problem for a competitor. The company, an importer of lamps and office furniture, had recently faced increased competition. The CEO learned from a retailer that one of the company's competitors had just raised the prices of some expensive lamps. The executive quickly relayed the information to the firm's salespeople, who used the information to win new business. Given the amount of information that is available on the Internet for free and for anyone who searches, there is no reason that a small company cannot be almost as sophisticated as a large one in understanding its competitors.

It is a fact that competitors, both large and small, constantly provide information to the marketplace, what economists refer to as *signals* (see, for example, Schelling, 1960). Signals can be of two varieties. *Costly* signals are actual actions taken by a competitor such as the construction of a new plant, the introduction of a new product, a change in price, and so forth. The other variety is communications through the media, with customers, and with other marketplace actors. These have been referred to as *cheap talk* signals as they are costless, nonbinding, nonverifiable communications.[2] An example of this kind of signal is the marketing manager who announces in an interview that she intends to match a competitor's price if it is lowered. The job of the product manager is to collect both kinds of information and be wary about cheap talk signals that may be less than truthful.

Why don't all firms have a formal reporting system designed to collect and analyze information about competitors? After all, in some companies (e.g., Japanese firms), managers are trained to make competitive intelligence gathering everyone's business. Yet the Conference Board estimates that fewer than 5 percent of U.S. companies have sophisticated intelligence systems.

Overconfidence about a product's continued success can reduce willingness to collect competitor information. An impressive list of companies (General Motors, Coca-Cola, McDonald's) that were somewhat overconfident at one time can be produced, along with a list of competitors that were ignored until they made significant inroads into the markets (Toyota, Pepsi, Burger King). A second reason for insensitivity to competition is uncertainty about where to collect the necessary information and how to analyze it. This excuse grows weaker all the time as consultants specializing in competitive intelligence gathering, articles and books containing tips on where to collect information, and computerized databases containing articles about companies proliferate, and as the Web is increasingly and easily used for obtaining information. A final reason for not collecting competitive intelligence is an ethical consideration: the fear that either illegal methods or otherwise "dirty tricks" have to be used to obtain such information. Many examples of such approaches to collecting information exist, and some of these are mentioned later in the chapter. However, information can almost always be obtained ethically.

At the very minimum, firms should view methods for collecting information about competitors from a defensive perspective, that is, how they can prevent information about themselves from landing in the laps of important competitors. John Sculley, the former

---

[2] Actually, they are not entirely costless. Some companies such as Apple have been sued by stockholders for not delivering on new products that the company has announced.

CEO of Apple, became so alarmed at the number of leaks of important secrets that he had a six-minute video made for new employees warning them about the implications of "loose lips" (Zachary, 1989). This is becoming increasingly problematic for companies as improved technology for "eavesdropping" and decreased employee loyalty from corporate downsizings increase competitors' ability to obtain corporate secrets. A 1995 survey of Fortune 1000 companies showed that about 75 percent believe theft or attempted theft by computer of customer information, trade secrets, and new product plans increased over the previous five years (Geyelin, 1995).

To analyze competitors, a commitment to developing a competitive strategy that includes a willingness to expend resources on collecting data is necessary. However, the data themselves are usually not the major problem product managers face. There are many sources of competitive intelligence. What is often lacking is a structure to guide the collection and analysis of the data, that is, a clear idea of what questions the data should address.

Figure 5.2 shows the competitor analysis model used in this chapter. At the top of the figure, the key inputs to the model are, of course, data. The first part of this chapter describes data sources available for competitor analysis. It may seem to make more

FIGURE 5.2   **Competitor Analysis System**

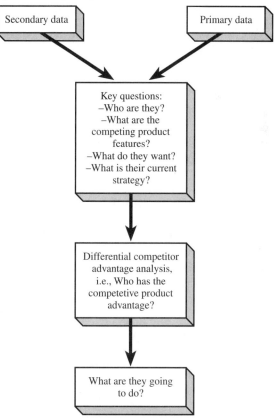

sense to first identify the questions to be answered, but the data collection process for understanding competitor behavior is somewhat unstructured, and information is continually being received and processed. It is thus useful to first understand the major sources of information and then apply them to the important questions that must be addressed. The two kinds of data described are *secondary* data, or data that have already been collected by someone else for some other purpose (i.e., "library" data), and *primary* data, or information derived from studies specially designed to answer a particular set of questions.

The data analysis portion of the process is the second major area of this chapter and is represented by the three questions in Figure 5.2. These cover six major areas of interest:

Who are the major competitors?

How do the competing products/services stack up against each other?

What are the objectives of the major competitor products?

What is the current strategy being employed to achieve the objectives?

Who has the competitive edge?

What are they likely to do in the future?

We addressed the first question in Chapter 3. Even though an attribute advantage (e.g., faster processing speed) does not necessarily translate into product success, a matrix featuring the attributes of the competing products/services is a useful exercise simply to compare the offerings. The next two parts of the analysis assess the current objectives and strategy of the competing products. Differential competitor advantage analysis assesses the strengths and weaknesses of competing products based on information about the competitors' capabilities along a set of dimensions. An important output of this analysis assesses key strengths and weaknesses. The final element of the competitor analysis could be called the "bottom line." The purpose of examining the competitors is to be able to forecast what they are likely to do over the next planning cycle so we can then incorporate that forecast into our own strategies. Taken together, the issues shown in Figure 5.2 comprise a fairly complete picture of the activities of competing products.

A caveat to this chapter is that an intensive analysis of competition cannot substitute for a customer focus. In the end, it is better for a product manager to satisfy customer needs and ignore competition than do the reverse. Placing too much importance on keeping up with competitors can result in inadequately monitoring shifts in customer tastes. One benefit of the systematic approach to marketing planning advocated in this book is that it does not favor or ignore either customers or competitors.

SOURCES OF INFORMATION

Secondary Sources of Information

As with marketing research in general, product managers should always begin a competitor analysis with a search of secondary sources of information. Secondary sources are generally less expensive and easier to obtain than primary data and often cover most

FIGURE 5.3 **Secondary Sources of Competitor Information**

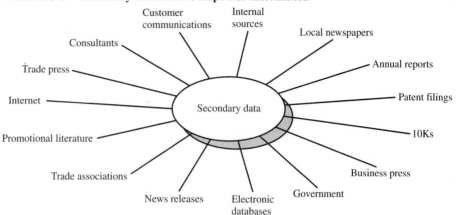

of the important questions we need to ask about competitors. Figure 5.3 identifies popular secondary sources companies can use. An exhaustive listing of all secondary sources of information is beyond the scope of this book; however, many good listings of these sources exist (see, for example, Lehmann, Gupta, and Steckel, 1998; Patzer, 1995). Many of these sources are also useful for tracking foreign companies doing business in the United States or other markets. Fortunately, with the explosive growth of the Internet, many of these sources are available from your desktop, rendering obsolete the former term for secondary sources of information, "library" sources.

Internal Sources

Good information about competing products probably already exists within the company or division. Data can be found in past marketing plans, special studies commissioned by strategic planning groups, or simply in someone's office. As noted at the beginning of the chapter, some companies establish competitor hot lines or databases that can be accessed easily.

Local Newspapers

An excellent inexpensive source of information about competitors is local newspapers. For example, if a key competitor's product is manufactured in a small town, subscribing to the local newspaper is an excellent way to keep tabs on hirings and other changes. A U.S. medical supply manufacturer was shocked when a Japanese competitor significantly increased output at a new plant in Kentucky. The U.S. company had to reduce prices to maintain market share. What is interesting is that many details about the new plant—cost, number of employees, the products to be produced—were reported in the *Lexington Herald-Leader* in 1987, three years before the plant opened (Teitelbaum, 1992).

Annual Reports

Much of the information in an annual report is for public relations value, and the discussion is at the corporate, not product, level. However, careful analysis of annual reports can produce some interesting insights even at the product level, particularly by examining the product areas the report does *not* mention. Often one can get useful information about areas of corporate emphasis from the message from the chairman or the text. Annual reports sometimes mention locations of manufacturing facilities and the names of key corporate decision makers. Although the financial information is aggregate, some data on cost of goods sold can be useful. These reports are, of course, available only for publicly held companies. For private companies, Dun & Bradstreet publishes its famous D&B reports, which estimate the financial performance of those firms.

10K Statements

Another reporting requirement for publicly held corporations is the 10K statement. Often this is more useful than the annual report because it is broken down by line of business and does not have the "gloss" of the annual report.

One clear implication of these two sources of information is that a cheap way to keep up with the corporate parent of a competitor is to become a shareholder (preferably a small one!). Shareholders receive the annual reports and 10Ks as well as admission to the annual shareholder meetings, which can be another useful resource.

Financial documents, including annual reports and 10Ks, are also available at most business libraries and stockbrokerage offices, where other useful financial documents such as new business prospectuses can be found.

Patent/Trademark Filings

Within the last decade, commercially available data networks such as CompuServe have made patent filings available. Obviously, patents give some notion of the manufacturing process and technology underlying the product. However, companies have been known to apply for patents on mistakes or on products that they have no intention to market. A company called MicroPatent (see Figure 5.4) permits the downloading of patents and technical diagrams via its Web-based service.

General Business Publications

Excellent sources of information about products and companies are general business publications such as *Business Week, Fortune, Forbes,* and *The Wall Street Journal.* One might wonder why companies are often willing to disclose what should be proprietary information concerning, for example, future marketing strategies. Some potential audiences are investors, employees, and perhaps even competitors who might be the target for strategic warnings. To get information from these publications, product managers can subscribe to clipping services and electronic databases or clip appropriate articles themselves.

News Releases

Companies usually retain public relations firms to release information to the press concerning new products, senior management appointments, and the like. These releases often show up in newspapers and trade publications, but it is possible to get on a direct distribution list.

Promotional Literature

Sales brochures (often referred to as *collateral material*) or other promotional literature focusing on a competing product or product line are extraordinarily valuable. Sales literature is a rich source of information concerning the product's strategy, since it usually has details about how the product is being positioned and differentiated versus those of

FIGURE 5.4 **Micropatent**

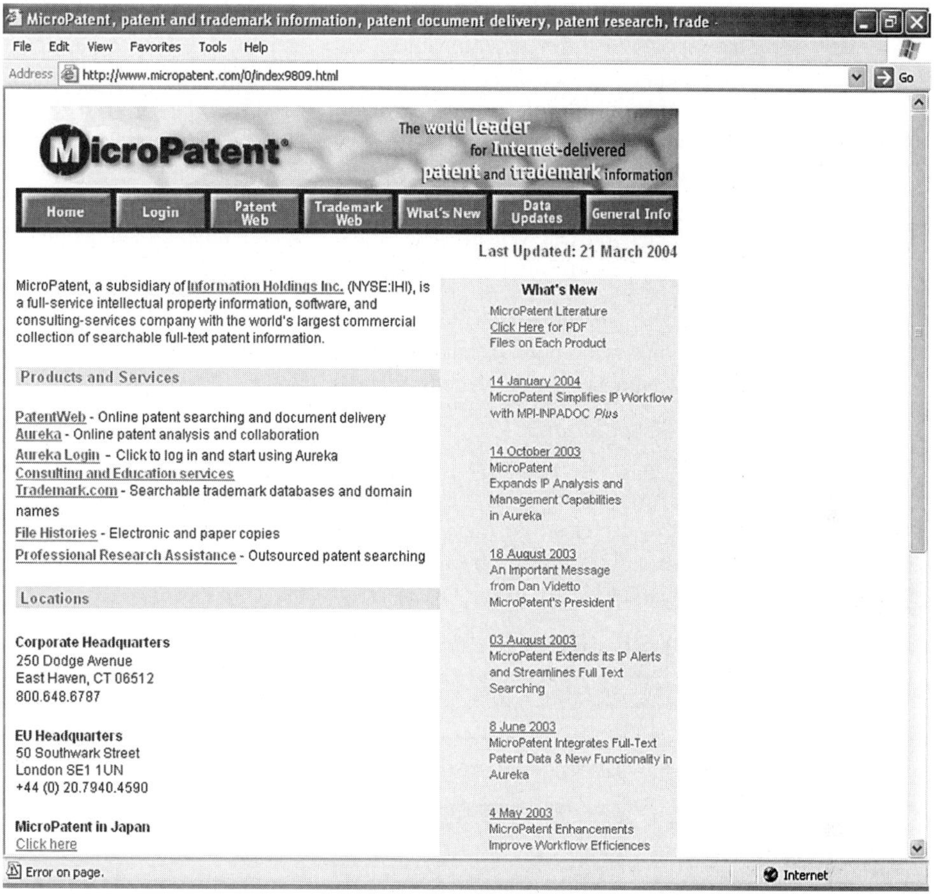

Source: MicroPatent's PatentWeb Services, *http://www.micropatent.com/o/patentweb9809.html,* March 31, 2000.

competitors (including your product), product attribute and performance data, key phone numbers, and even personnel to contact.

Trade Press

These periodicals narrowly focus on a particular industry or product category. Representing this class of literature is *Women's Wear Daily* for the retail clothing trade, *Billboard* for the record and video industry, *Rubber Age* and *Chemical Week* for their respective industries, and *Test and Measurement World* for semiconductor testing equipment. This class of publications is obviously a rich source of information concerning new product announcements, personnel shifts, advertisements for products, and industry or category data on sales and market shares. Somewhat broader are "new economy" magazines such as *Wired* and *Business 2.0* which followed companies with a technology orientation. Some "e"-zines such as *Colloquy* deliver information about new loyalty/frequency programs. It is safe to say that virtually every product category and business sector has its own set of publications.

Consultants

Competitor analysis is a fertile area for consulting services. Many of these firms sell industry reports to different companies. They usually develop these reports from secondary sources and thus sell a service that substitutes for the firm's own efforts. One type of company services all industries. For example, New York–based FIND/SVP offers a variety of industry research reports through its website, *www.findsvp.com.* In 2004, the company offered a 234 page report on "Chinese Markets for Baby Care Products" for $3,500. The report covers consumption trends, primary competitors, distribution channels, and consumer behavior. The website, *www.marketresearch.com,* brokers competitor analysis reports from a number of different companies. (See Figure 5.5).

Employee Communications

Companies often publish internal newsletters targeted toward employees. These newsletters may report on new vendors, new employees, and so forth.

Trade Associations

Most companies are members of trade associations (a listing of such associations is available in business libraries). These associations are usually formed for public relations or lobbying purposes, but they also often perform market research for the member firms. While usually focused on customers, this research may also provide some information about market shares, price levels, and so on.

FIGURE 5.5 **Market Research**

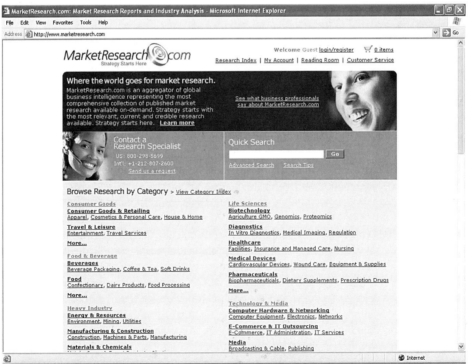

Source: Market Research.com, *http://www.marketresearch.com/.* Copyright © 2000, All Rights Reserved, Market Research, Inc.

Government Sources

The U.S. government collects a considerable amount of information about industries. However, as noted in Chapter 3, the data are usually at the NAIC (North American Industrial Classification) level and therefore are not very useful for understanding specific product competitors. More useful information is collected by agencies such as the Federal Communications Commission, the Food and Drug Administration, and state agencies. For example, if Pacific Bell submits a request for a rate increase, competitors such as Sprint and MCI can obtain cost information from the filing since the request is public information.

Electronic Data Services

The Web has a number of sites that are of particular interest for this kind of analysis. Some of them offer free information and others are subscription based:

- Hoover's Online: Income statement and balance sheet numbers for public companies.
- Dun & Bradstreet's Online Access: Short reports on 10 million U.S. companies, many of them privately held.
- NewDirectory's 24-Hour Newsstand: Links to the websites of more than 14,000 English newspapers, business journals, magazines, and computer publications around the world.
- American Demographics: Provides demographic data as well as a directory of marketing consultants.
- Competitive Intelligence Guide (*www.fuld.com*): Sleuthing tips along with an "Internet Intelligence Index."

The biggest of all of these services is DIALOG, which offers access to such databases as Port Import Export Reporting Service (PIERS), the *Financial Times,* Moody's, and press releases by more than 10,000 U.S. corporations.

A number of specialized Web-based services exist that perform a variety of competitive intelligence activities. Here is a sampling:

- Strategy Software (*www.strategy-software.com*) takes the data you have collected about competitors and organizes it into reports.
- C4U is a download that scans the Web for any changes in a predefined set of sites and reports the changes.
- AdRelevance offers a Web advertising tracking service that, among a number of services, can help you determine if a competitor is increasing/changing its advertising.
- Company Sleuth has an e-mail alert system that notifies you via e-mail if information about a new SEC filing, new release, patent, and so on from a competitor has been published on the Internet.

A convenient way to search through the Web is with a search engine such as Google. The user can type a company name, such as "Sony," and (eventually) reach Sony's home page and other pages linked to Sony. At Hewlett-Packard's page (*www.hp.com*), a browser can find product information and news about HP (see Figure 5.6). Information seekers can determine HP's resellers, extent of technical support, and a large amount of other data.

FIGURE 5.6 **Hewlett-Packard Website**

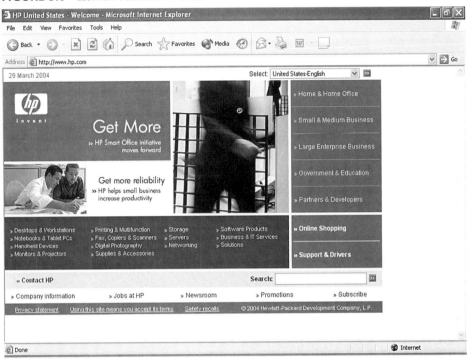

Source: ©1994–2004 Hewlett Packard Company.

Primary Sources of Information

Figure 5.7 lists the most important primary sources of information about competitors. Many of these are also sources of secondary information, depending on when the information was originally collected.

FIGURE 5.7 **Primary Sources of Competitor Information**

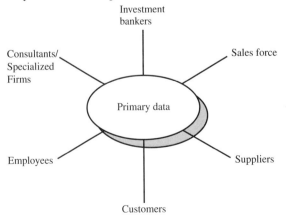

Sales Force/Customers

One of the most underutilized sources of information in companies is the sales force. Salespeople are trained to sell, but how many are trained to be part of a competitor intelligence force? Since they interact with customers on a regular basis, salespeople are in an excellent position to find out about recent competitor sales pitches, pricing, and many other dimensions. Depending on the product, salespeople are often in a position to collect information merely by being trained observers. Xerox salespeople, for example, are trained to note competitor copiers. Forward-looking companies use information from salespeople for quick updates on competition. With notebook computers, salespeople can make their calls, fill out call reports electronically, and send the information back to the local office or headquarters via modem. For competitor tracking, the call report should have a section related to noting anything new or different picked up during the call.

Of course, the salespeople must get the information from customers. Every attempt by suppliers and vendors to cultivate a potential customer involves the transmission of information. Unfortunately, customers may be reluctant to give away such information, believing it means playing "dirty tricks" on the competition. To aid in overcoming this reluctance, the data collection can be positioned as giving the vendor an opportunity to provide better service or products to the customer; that is, the salesperson can clearly show that the customer will benefit by passing along the information. Usually the data can be obtained from public sources anyway; it is just quicker for the vendor to obtain it from the customer (Yovovich, 1995).

Employees

Generalizing from the use of salespeople to collect competitor intelligence, much can be learned about competition from observation in the marketplace by any company employee. If the product category in question is sold in the supermarket, an employee can easily observe changes in price, packaging, and shelf display.

Suppliers

Often competitors' suppliers are willing to give information about shipments to impress potential buyers. Imprints on packaging cartons can provide useful information because they often disclose the name and address of the carton's maker. Following up with the carton manufacturer may lead to estimates of sales volume.

Consultants/Specialized Firms

Consultants can often be used to develop special-purpose reports, as opposed to the off-the-shelf variety referred to under secondary sources. For example, tns media intelligence/cmr is one of the leading firms developing reports on media spending by brand.

Investment Bankers

Investment bank reports are excellent sources of both secondary and primary data on competitors, particularly if a bank wishes to gain the firm as a new client. Analysts employed by the investment banks develop detailed analyses of the prospects of different firms and products in an industry. While their perspective is financial performance, much of the information is useful to product managers.

Other Sources

Help-Wanted Ads

Often help-wanted ads contain valuable information, such as job requirements and salary levels. Other information is available as well; sometimes the purpose of the ad is to fill positions opened by an expansion of business or a new plant opening. Although many ads disclose only a box number for a reply, many provide information about the organization paying for the ad. This can be done online as well, through searches of help-wanted ads from Monster (*www.monster.com*), craig's list (*www.craigslist.com*) and other similar sources.

Trade Shows

Company representatives often attempt to obtain information at the booths of competitors. This is becoming more difficult, however, as companies increasingly try to screen the people to whom they provide information to avoid revealing too much to competitors. In addition, spying is now so common at trade shows that hot new products are usually displayed only in hotel suites open to major customers, joint venture partners, and industry reporters who agree not to disclose information until product release dates. This is particularly true at large trade shows such as Comdex, the computer industry trade show, where industry players like Michael Dell, founder of Dell Computer Corporation, roam through the aisles trying to pick up information quickly before they are recognized. Even if some information is gained, however, about as much is lost from your own company, so usually the net gain is small.

Plant Tours

This is a rapidly disappearing phenomenon, largely because companies are becoming skittish about giving away valuable information. The most popular tourist destination in Battle Creek, Michigan was Kellogg's cereal plant until the company stopped giving tours several years ago, citing competitor information gathering as the reason. Gerber stopped its Fremont, Michigan plant tours in 1990 after spotting sales representatives from competitor firms taking the tour. Although there are some exceptions, most tours today are like the amusement park–like tour at Hershey Foods' facility in Hershey, Pennsylvania, which offer little to be learned about how the products are really made.[3]

Reverse Engineering

A common way to analyze a competitor's product is to purchase it and take it apart. This is referred to as *reverse engineering* in high-technology industries and sometimes as *benchmarking* in service markets.[4] In general, it is wise to become a customer of a competitor by, for example, purchasing a computer or software, opening a small bank account, etc. One important reason to do so is to estimate the competitor's costs of manufacturing or assembly. Another objective is to assess the product's strengths and weaknesses. Companies such as Emerson Electric, General Motors, and Xerox perform this kind of analysis routinely. For example, in the late 1970s, Xerox benchmarked Canon's copiers and tried to

---

[3] A good article on how to analyze the data obtained from a plant tour is David M. Upton and Stephen E. Macadam (1997), "Why (and How) to Take a Plant Tour," *Harvard Business Review,* May–June, pp. 97–106.

[4] The term *benchmarking* is also used more generally to refer to the tracking and analysis of any process such as manufacturing, billing, customer service, and so on, in both competing and noncompeting organizations.

beat each component of the latter's machines on cost and quality. In designing the Lexus, Toyota bought competitors' cars, including four Mercedes, a Jaguar XJ6, and two BMWs, put them through performance tests, and then took them apart (Main, 1992).

Monitoring Test Markets

Some companies test market products in limited areas of the country or the world to better understand decisions about pricing, advertising, and distribution. While this is often useful, test markets can be fertile grounds for competitors to get an early view of the product and how it will eventually be marketed after rollout to the larger market.

Hiring Key Employees

This practice obviously provides a considerable amount of information. However, new employees may not legally transmit what are considered to be trade secrets to new employers. Trade secrets can have a narrow interpretation, however, that does not cover marketing strategies or complete plans. Some companies attempt to hinder employees, particularly senior managers, from jumping to a competitor by including a special clause in the employment contract. At Hewlett-Packard, new employees are asked to sign nondisclosure agreements and attend a training program, complete with video, that defines how HP interprets "trade secrets" (Guthrie, 1993).

Ethically Questionable Sources

Our purpose in describing some of the unethical approaches to collecting competitor information is not to encourage readers to use them but to point out that such activities do occur. As mentioned earlier in the chapter, a key reason to learn about the various approaches to collecting information about competitors is to become more defensive minded. Of course, it is virtually impossible to completely defend against lying and cheating. However, on a hopeful note, these approaches rarely uncover something an ethical approach cannot; there are usually several ways to collect a key piece of information.

Aerial Reconnaissance

It is illegal in the United States for a company to hire an airplane or a helicopter to take aerial photographs of a competitor's facilities as they are being constructed, because this action is interpreted as trespassing. Procter & Gamble won a lawsuit against Keebler for spying on a new soft-cookie-making facility being constructed in Tennessee in 1984. Companies can, apparently legally, purchase photographs taken from satellites: Sweden and France are partners in a satellite joint venture that sets aside a limited percentage of the transponder time for commercial purposes (usually map making and municipal planning). In 1994, Lockheed Missiles & Space Company, a subsidiary of Lockheed Corporation, received the first license from the U.S. government to sell spy-quality satellite pictures for commercial use. Lockheed has the technology to photograph a car from 400 miles in space.

Buying/Stealing Trash

It is not illegal to take a company's trash after it leaves the firm's facility. However, companies have been known to either bribe employees or otherwise obtain access to discarded documents. Recently, Avon admitted it had hired private detectives to run through rival Mary Kay's trash to attempt to defend against a takeover attempt by the latter. The maneuver was not illegal because Mary Kay's dumpster was in a public parking lot (Zellner and Hager,

1991). In a highly publicized 2000 incident, Oracle hired a firm to sift through the trash of the Independent Institute, a think tank Oracle accused of having a tie to Microsoft after it ran a high-profile ad criticizing the U.S. government's antitrust case against the software company. Even the highly-regarded Procter & Gamble has been involved with "dumpster diving"; in 2001, it was found guilty of stealing Unilever's trash. Simple defensive mechanisms include shredders and incinerators. Unfortunately, in today's online world, "trash" also means electronic mail that was thought to be discarded when it actually was not.

Bribing Printers

Some companies attempt to obtain predistribution copies of catalogs and other material.

Running Phony Want Ads

Not all help-wanted ads are for actual positions. Some companies run ads in an attempt to get disgruntled employees from competitors to apply. These applicants then can be probed for information.

Snooping on Airplanes

The continuous process of squeezing more seats into airplanes and the proliferation of laptops provide ample opportunity for business travelers to collect information from screens. Some flights are notoriously packed with executives from particular industries; for example, the flights from San Jose to Austin are generally filled with computer industry people.

One executive was creative in deterring such activity. On a flight from San Francisco, he detected a pair of eyes intently looking at his computer screen. Having experienced this before, with a few keystrokes he opened a file called READTHIS.doc which produced a single sentence on the screen: "If you can read this, you ought to be ashamed of yourself." The passenger in the next seat retreated (De Lisser, 1999).

The ethics of various data collection methods is a continuum from methods that are clearly illegal (stealing a competitor's marketing plans) to obviously legal (reading an article in a trade magazine). Today there is more pressure than ever to uncover information about competitors. The Society of Competitive Intelligence Professionals, now numbering over 7,000 members, has established an ethical code that requires members to comply with the law, identify themselves when seeking information about competitors, and respect requests for confidentiality. However, those bent on violating legal and ethical standards do not tend to join such societies. It is therefore incumbent on companies to develop policy statements that clearly define the standards expected from employees in this area of competitor intelligence gathering and to strongly enforce them.[5]

CREATING A PRODUCT FEATURES MATRIX

Although product features do not translate into benefits sought by customers, a very useful graphic is to simply chart the differences between the main products or services offered in the category. The basic structure of the matrix is shown in Figure 5.8. A useful

---

[5] For further reading on the ethical aspects of competitor analysis, see U. Srinivasa Rangan and Michael E. Porter, "Ethical Dimensions of Competitive Analysis," Harvard Business School case study number 9-792-088, 1992.

FIGURE 5.8   **Product Features Matrix**

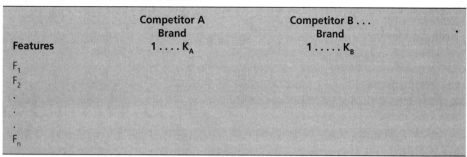

Features	Competitor A Brand 1 . . . . K_A	Competitor B . . . Brand 1 . . . . . K_B
F_1		
F_2		
.		
.		
.		
F_n		

complement to the features matrix is a set of importance weights (see Chapter 6) or at least some indicator of the relative importance of the different features. Taking the basic feature information together with the relative importance weights gives you a very good idea of the strengths and weakness of your product relative to the competition.

ASSESSING COMPETITORS' CURRENT OBJECTIVES

A critical step in a competitor analysis is to assess what the current objectives are for the major competitor products. An assessment of current objectives provides valuable information concerning the intended aggressiveness of the competitors in the market in the future. It also provides a context for assessing the capabilities of competitors; that is, does the firm marketing brand A have the resources to successfully pursue such an objective?

When discussing objectives, it is important to define the term precisely, for many different types of objectives exist. In the context of marketing planning, three basic product objectives can be identified. A *growth* objective usually implies increasing the brand's units or market share, with profit conditions being secondary. The *hold* objective could also be termed a *consolidation* objective. A hold scenario might be logical for a brand that is losing market share in that a reasonable first step in reversing its fortunes is to stop the slide. Finally, a *harvest* objective, also referred to as *milking,* describes a situation in which profit is paramount relative to market share. In other words, at the product level, objectives are typically stated in terms of either market share or profits. At the corporate level, return on investment or other, more aggregate, statistics becomes more relevant.

Determination of Competitor Objectives

While a brand's objective determines, to a great extent, what strategies will be pursued and hence what actions will be taken in the marketplace, usually it does not take a substantial amount of research to uncover it. What is required is sensitivity to competitors' actions through observation, salesperson call reports, and the other resources mentioned in the previous section of this chapter. For example, in 1998, Boeing announced in a major business publication that it was going to emphasize profits over market share—good news for Airbus (Browder, 1998).

Let us consider two major options outlined above: the growth versus harvest choice. If a competitor's brand is being pushed to improve its market position at the expense of short-term profits, some of the following are likely to occur: a cut in price, increased advertising expenditures, increased promotional activity to both consumers and distributors, or increased distribution expenses.

In other words, a product manager who is trying to expand a brand's market share will spend money on market-related activities and/or reducing price. Such actions can be easily monitored by brand managers, advertising account representatives, and other parties with access to information about the rival brand's actions.

Brands being harvested would be marketed in the opposite way. An increase in a competitor's price, decreases in marketing budgets, and so on can be interpreted as a retreat (perhaps only temporary) from active and aggressive competition in the market. While the product manager cannot exactly estimate the size of the share loss expected, it is not difficult to establish the direction of the objective, which is the most important competitor information.

Two other factors are relevant to the assessment of competitors' objectives. First, the product objectives of a firm with a foreign-based parent are often affected by the country of origin. In many cases, such firms have financial backing from a government or major banks and are not as concerned with short-term losses as they are with establishing a viable market position or obtaining foreign currency. Although at one time Japanese firms were the ones usually referred to in this context, other countries, such as Korea and Singapore, are also homes to firms that are strongly interested in building market share in the United States. Thus, depending on the competitor, cues concerning the competitor brand's objectives can be obtained from the geographical home of the parent firm. A second relevant factor is whether the ownership of the competitor firm is private, public, or government. Since private firms do not have to account to stock analysts, long-term profits may be more important than showing consistent positive quarterly returns. On the other hand, if a family depends on a firm it controls for current income, profits may be more important than market share. Finally, government-controlled firms may have objectives such as maintaining employment, providing service, or currency exchange.

An interesting variant of the impact of private ownership on objectives occurs if the privatization resulted from a leveraged buyout (LBO). In these cases, even though the company is private, it is often more interested in profits and cash flow to pay down debt than it is in plowing money into market share gains. An excellent example is the well-publicized LBO by Kohlberg Kravis Roberts & Company (KKR) of RJR Nabisco in 1988. Because of the large load of debt the firm took on, many of RJR's brands became vulnerable to competitors that took advantage of the opportunity to go for market share gains. These included Philip Morris in tobacco products because RJR was reluctant to enter the low-price cigarette category, and competitors in snack foods, which took advantage of large cuts in advertising and promotion expenditures for Ritz crackers and Planters products. As of 1995, RJR was free of KKR, and began to attempt to regain the market share lost to Philip Morris, particularly for its flagship Winston brand (Teinowitz, 1995). A similar result often occurs as a result of mergers (Lorge, 1999).

A less apparent level of objectives can be deduced from a firm's operating philosophy and procedures. For example, a firm that seeks to minimize capital investment will be slow to respond to a competitor that makes a heavy capital outlay (for example, Emery

Air Freight when Federal Express bought its own airplanes in the mid-1970s). Similarly, firms that compensate sales staffs with commissions based on a percentage of sales indicate that volume rather than profitability is a key objective. In fact, the key performance measure by which employees are judged has a distinct influence on a firm's performance.

Estimates of the objectives pursued by competitors provide important information for the development of strategy. Certainly a brand that is aggressive in its pursuit of market share must be viewed as a different type of competitor than one that is attempting primarily to maximize profits. The latter would clearly be more vulnerable to an attack on its customers, whereas a confrontation with the former brand might be avoided. In other words, a study of the brands' objectives provides a first-level analysis of the competitor brand's likely strategy.

This type of analysis has been profitably applied. During the late 1970s, Coca-Cola was concerned primarily with holding market share and improving profits. PepsiCo, on the other hand, viewed its rival's drowsiness as an opportunity and became more aggressive, gaining share points and improving its position versus Coca-Cola in store sales. Miller Brewing's successful attack on Budweiser during the 1970s was prompted by a similar observation.

ASSESSING COMPETITORS' CURRENT STRATEGIES

The second stage in competitor analysis is to determine how competitors are attempting to achieve their objectives. This question is addressed by examining their past and current marketing strategies.

MARKETING STRATEGY

Many authors have attempted to define the concept of strategy. At the product level, a marketing strategy can be thought of in terms of three major components: target market selection, core strategy (i.e., positioning and differential advantage), and implementation (i.e., supporting marketing mix). These components are described in more detail in Chapter 8; we will briefly discuss them here in the context of understanding a competitor's product strategy.

The first major component is the description of the market segment(s) to which competing brands are being marketed. Market segments can be described in various ways, as shown in Chapter 6 (Figures 6.5 and 6.6). Since few brands are truly mass marketed, that is, marketed equally to all potential customers, the key is to determine which group(s) each competitor has targeted. This helps to avoid segments in which there may be intense competition and to determine under- or nontargeted segments that may represent opportunities.

The second strategy component is what is called the *core strategy*. This is the basis on which the rival is competing, that is, its key claimed differential advantage(s). Differential advantage is a critical component of strategy because it usually forms the basic selling proposition around which the brand's communications are formed. It is also called the brand's *positioning* or *value proposition.*

Product managers essentially have a choice between two types of differential advantage: advantage based on price/cost or on product features. In other words, products are usually positioned on price or quality dimensions, although some marketers choose a "value" positioning with midrange price and quality. Concentration on price often follows the classic approach developed by the Boston Consulting Group in the 1970s, which advocates taking advantage of the experience curve that assumes costs are driven down with increases in cumulative production volume, thus allowing the product manager to cut prices and maintain margins over time. The quality differential advantage is superiority on some other product dimension (real or psychological) such as service, packaging, or delivery terms. Necessary conditions for such a core strategy to be successful are that customers value the characteristics claimed as advantages and that the differential can be maintained for a significant period of time without being copied.

An important characteristic of quality differential advantages is that they can be perceived, rather than actual, differences. For example, IBM's core strategy since its inception has been service based. This advantage can be supported by hard data (e.g., number of field service representatives, mean response time, and so on). On the other hand, Reebok's claimed differential advantage during its "U B U" campaign was related to individuality. Such positioning is clearly outside the domain of physical product differences, but it can still be effective in differentiating Reebok from Nike. Physical product differences are often stressed in industrial, durable, or new frequently purchased product strategies. Companies producing mature frequently purchased products that are physically similar or "commodities" often emphasize perceptual differences.

Comparing Value Chains

Porter (1985) developed a concept called the *value chain* that can be used to compare a brand or company's strengths and weakness against another. The basic value chain is shown in Figure 5.9. An important point made by the value chain is that differentiation can be obtained through efforts of the whole corporation, not just through marketing. One way to differentiate is through *inbound logistics,* that is, through the selection of the highest-quality raw materials and other inputs including

FIGURE 5.9 **Value Chain**

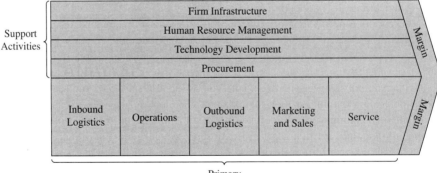

Source: Michael Porter, *Competitive Advantage* (New York: Free Press, 1980), p. 37.

technology. A reason that Steinway has consistently built the best pianos in the world is through the use of the best wood that can be found. For years, the supercomputer company Cray had a significant technological edge on other companies. A second way to gain competitive advantages is through *operations* advantages. One of the ways that McDonald's has been the fast food market leader throughout the world is by significant investments in training programs that produce consistency in service and product quality. *Outbound logistics* provides a third basis for differentiation. This can be through speedy and on-time delivery such as the Federal Express promise and fulfillment of the promise during its earlier days of being there "absolutely and positively overnight." A company called Premier Industrial Corporation distributes nuts and bolts, seemingly a commodity, but differentiates itself from competition (and has higher margins) by agreeing to ship in any quantity desired by the customer. *Marketing and sales* also serve to differentiate. The IBM sales force has historically been a major advantage to the company in terms of its ability to satisfy customer needs better than competitors. Finally, *service* can be an important differentiator, as the retailer Nordstrom has found. The product manager can use the value chain concept to check at each step of the process if and how a competitor is gaining competitive advantage in the category.

Marketing Mix

The final strategy component of competitors that must be assessed is the supporting marketing mix. The mix provides insight into the basic strategy of the competitor and specific tactical decisions. These decisions are what customers actually see in the marketplace; neither are they exposed to nor do they particularly care about a product's marketing strategy. However, customers are exposed to price, advertising, and other marketing mix elements. The areas to consider and some questions to address follow.[6]

Pricing

Pricing is a highly visible element of a competitor's marketing mix; therefore, it raises several questions. For example, if a brand's differential advantage is price based, is the list price uniform in all markets? If the strategy is quality based, what is the price differential claimed? Are discounts being offered? What is the pattern of price changes over time? In general, any price-related information pertaining to the implementation of strategy is relevant.

Promotion

With respect to sales management, what kinds of selling approaches are being employed? Are the salespeople aggressive in obtaining new accounts? What are their commission rates? In terms of advertising, what media are being used? What creative activities? Are competitors referred to either directly or indirectly? Sales promotion activities—for example, which types and how often—are also important.

---

[6] For a more complete description of the components of a marketing strategy, see Russell S. Winer (2004), *Marketing Management,* 2nd ed., Upper Saddle River, New Jersey: Prentice-Hall.

Distribution

Have the channels of distribution shifted? Is the brand being emphasized in certain channels? Is the manufacturer of the competing product changing the entire system, for example, by opening its own retail outlets or putting more emphasis on direct marketing?

Product/Service Capabilities

A major determinant of a company's capabilities, at least in the short run, is the physical makeup of its product or service, which in general is less easily changed than, say, price or advertising. A product filled with expensive parts is unlikely to be positioned as a low-end product. Similarly, physical properties (e.g., stability under high temperatures) go a long way toward dictating target market uses and hence strategy. Many engineering plastics categories are segmented on the basis of physical properties, for example, DuPont's Delrin versus Celanese's Celcon. Different applications can be dominated by a different company's offerings. Therefore, a comparison of the competitive product offerings, the physical product or service, and how it is presented and sold should be performed.

How to Assess Competitors' Strategies

Recall that the two key elements of a strategy are the segments it appeals to and the core strategy. For industrial products, both can be easily determined by examining three sources of information: product sales literature, the company's own sales force, and trade advertising. The former provides information about the core strategy because brochures usually detail the points of difference the competitor wants to emphasize. Even if the sales literature does not present a product features chart, it should indicate the brand's major strengths. Physical brochures are not often needed today; most industrial firms' websites provide a wealth of technical and positioning information that helps to determine the core strategy. A firm's own sales force can provide some data concerning targeted companies or industries, much of it resulting from informal contacts, trade show discussions, and the like. Finally, trade advertising is useful because it reveals the segments being targeted and the differential advantage being touted. One can determine the differential advantage directly from the ad copy and the target segments at least partially by the publication (location) in which the ad appears.

For consumer goods or other products targeted toward a large audience, simply tracking competitors' ads, either yourself or by using one of the services such as those mentioned earlier in this chapter, provides most of the necessary information. Television ads can be examined for their messages (differential advantage) and for the programs in which they appear (target segment[s]). TV advertising is quite useful for determining the core strategy because the nature of the medium prohibits communicating all but the most important messages. Similarly, print advertising can provide equivalent information, but with greater elaboration of the core strategy.

For example, consider the copy for a print ad in *Forbes* for Rolex watches, shown in Figure 5.10. From data obtained from Mediamark Research's *Magazine Total Audiences Report, Spring 2003,* we know that 73.8 percent of the readers are 18 to 49 years old, 38.8 percent have household income over $75,000, and 83.3 percent either attended or

FIGURE 5.10 Detecting a Competitor's Strategy

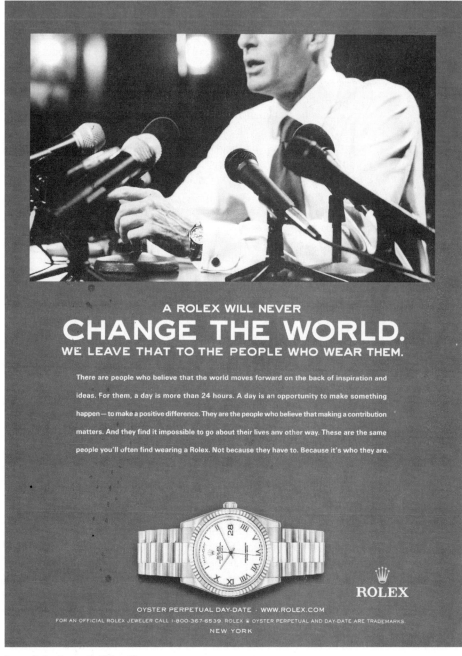

Source: *Forbes,* January 12, 2004, p. 17.

graduated from college (among many other variables measured by Mediamark Research). It is probably not a surprise that readers are businesspeople with high incomes. Looking at the copy itself, the ad copy says nothing about the physical characteristics of the watch, only the people who wear them: people in (or who aspire to) leadership positions. Note that there is no explicit mention of the competition. The product manager might also be interested in the price of the ad; these data are obtainable from publications such as *Marketer's Guide to Media.*

Information about implementing current strategies is also easily found. Pricing information can be obtained from basic market observation: Distributors, salespeople, customers, advertising agencies, or even a firm's own employees acting as customers on their own behalf can be the sources of pricing data. Promotion, distribution, and product information can be obtained from similar sources. In other words, as in determining competitors' objectives, it takes market sensitivity rather than sophisticated management information systems to assess much of the competitive activity.

One apparent but often overlooked source of information mentioned earlier in this chapter is being a customer or stockholder of competitors. Both customers and stockholders get special mailings and information that make strategy assessment easier. Furthermore, personal use of competitors' products often gives one a feeling for them that does not come through even the best-prepared research. Thus, policies that forbid or discourage the use of competitive products are usually foolish.

Technology Strategy

An important task is to assess the technological strategies of the major competitors. This can be done using the following framework of six criteria (Maidique and Patch, 1978):

1. Technology selection or specialization.
2. Level of competence.
3. Sources of capability: internal versus external.
4. R&D investment level.
5. Competitive timing: initiate versus respond.
6. R&D organization and policies.

These decisions generally lead to four basic strategies, each of which has different requirements for success, listed in Figure 5.11. Consider the blank audiocassette market in the early 1970s. This was the early stage of the product life cycle, with no major competitors. Gillette's Safety Razor Division was considering entering this market, as was Memorex, a manufacturer of computer tape and related products. Gillette had competitive advantages over Memorex in marketing and finance, but it was decidedly at a disadvantage in terms of R&D, manufacturing, and the apparent match of its skills and image to the cassette category in the minds of customers. The end result was a success for Memorex and a failure for Gillette in test marketing.

At this point in the analysis, it is often useful to summarize the products of the major competitors. Figure 5.12 provides a general format that is useful for both summarizing the results and for communicating them.

FIGURE 5.11 Typical Functional Requirements of Alternative Technological Strategies

	R&D	Manufacturing	Marketing	Finance	Organization	Timing
First to market	State-of-the-art R&D	Pilot and medium-scale manufacturing	Stimulating primary demand	Access to risk capital	Flexibility over efficiency; encourage risk taking	Early-entry inaugurates the product life cycle
Second to market	Flexible, responsive, and advanced R&D capability	Agility in setting up manufacturing medium scale	Differentiating the product; stimulating secondary demand	Rapid commitment of medium to large quantities of capital	Flexibility and efficiency	Entry early in growth stage
Late to market or cost minimization	Skill in process development and cost-effective production	Efficiency and automation for large-scale production	Minimizing selling and distribution costs	Access to capital in large amounts	Efficiency and hierarchical control; procedures rigidly enforced	Entry during late growth or early maturity
Market segmentation	Ability in applications, custom engineering, and advanced product design	Flexibility on short to medium runs	Identifying and reaching favorable segments	Access to capital in medium or large amounts	Flexibility and control required in serving different customers' requirements	Entry during growth stage

FIGURE 5.12 Format for Competitive Product Analysis

	Competitor A Brand 1 . . . K_A	Competitor B Brand 1 . . . K_B
Product:		
Quality		
Value chain		
Benefits		
Target segment:		
Who		
Where		
When		
Why		
Place:		
Distribution method		
Distribution coverage		
Promotion:		
Total effort ($)		
Methods		
Advertising:		
Strategy/copy		
Media		
Timing		
Total effort ($)		
Price:		
Retail		
To trade		
Technological strategy		

DIFFERENTIAL ADVANTAGE ANALYSIS

Several frameworks have been proposed to indicate what information to collect about competitors. A useful way to examine competitors' capabilities is to divide the necessary information into five categories that include the competitors' abilities to conceive and design, to produce, to market, to finance, and to manage (Figure 5.13). You might need information from both the corporate and product levels. For example, the financial capabilities of a corporate parent are important in determining the amount of money that could support a specific product.

Ability to Conceive and Design

This category measures the quality of competitors' new product development efforts. Clearly, a firm with the ability to develop new products is a serious long-term threat in a product category. The use of such procedures as total quality management generally improves product design capabilities.

FIGURE 5.13   **Examples of Competitor Information to Collect**

A. Ability to conceive and design
  1. Technical resources:
    a. Concepts
    b. Patents and copyrights
    c. Technological sophistication
    d. Technical integration
  2. Human resources:
    a. Key people and skills
    b. Use of external technical groups
  3. R&D funding:
    a. Total
    b. Percentage of sales
    c. Consistency over time
    d. Internally generated
    e. Government supplied
  4. Technological strategy:
    a. Specialization
    b. Competence
    c. Source of capability
    d. Timing: initiate versus imitate
  5. Management processes:
    a. TQM
    b. House of Quality
B. Ability to produce:
  1. Physical resources:
    a. Capacity
    b. Plant
      (1) Size
      (2) Location
      (3) Age
    c. Equipment
      (1) Automation
      (2) Maintenance
      (3) Flexibility
    d. Processes
      (1) Uniqueness
      (2) Flexibility
    e. Degree of integration
  2. Human resources:
    a. Key people and skills
    b. Workforce
      (1) Skills mix
      (2) Union
  3. Suppliers
    a. Capacity
    b. Quality
    c. Commitment
C. Ability to market:
  1. Sales force:
    a. Skills
    b. Size
    c. Type
    d. Location
  2. Distribution network:
    a. Skills
    b. Type

  3. Service and sales policies
  4. Advertising:
    a. Skills
    b. Type
  5. Human resources:
    a. Key people and skills
    b. Turnover
  6. Funding:
    a. Total
    b. Consistency over time
    c. Percentage
    d. Reward system
D. Ability to finance:
  1. Long term:
    a. Debt/equity ratio
    b. Cost of debt
  2. Short term:
    a. Cash or equivalent
    b. Line of credit
    c. Type of debt
    d. Cost of debt
  3. Liquidity
  4. Cash flow:
    a. Days of receivables
    b. Inventory turnover
    c. Accounting practices
  5. Human resources:
    a. Key people and skills
    b. Turnover
  6. System:
    a. Budgeting
    b. Forecasting
    c. Controlling
E. Ability to manage:
  1. Key people:
    a. Objectives and priorities
    b. Values
    c. Reward systems
  2. Decision making:
    a. Location
    b. Type
    c. Speed
  3. Planning:
    a. Type
    b. Emphasis
    c. Time span
  4. Staffing:
    a. Longevity and turnover
    b. Experience
    c. Replacement policies
  5. Organization:
    a. Centralization
    b. Functions
    c. Use of staff

Ability to Produce

This category concerns the production capabilities of the firm. For a service firm, it is the ability to deliver the service. A firm operating at capacity to produce a product is not as much of a threat to increase sales or share in the short run as is a firm that has slack capacity, assuming a substantial period of time is required to bring new capacity online. Product quality issues are important here.

Ability to Market

How aggressive, inventive, and so on are the firms in marketing their products? Do they have access to distribution channels? A competitor could have strong product development capabilities and slack capacity but be ineffective at marketing.

Ability to Finance

Limited financial resources hamper effective competition. Companies with highly publicized financial problems (such as the now defunct airlines Eastern, Pan Am, and Braniff), firms going through LBOs, and companies or divisions for sale (which have limited marketing expenditures) become vulnerable to competitors in their product lines. For example, when Procter & Gamble announced in 2001 that it was selling its Jif peanut butter and Folgers coffee brands, competitors took notice (Bittar, 2001). While financial ratios are key pieces of information, how the competitor allocates its resources among products is also critical.

Ability to Manage

In the mid-1980s, Procter & Gamble replaced the manager of its U.S. coffee business with the coffee general manager from the United Kingdom. This new manager had a reputation for developing new products; in a 15-month period, for example, he oversaw the launch of four new brands, above average for the company. The message to competitors such as General Foods was clear: New products were likely to be a focus of the Folgers division. A stronger emphasis on marketing at RJR Nabisco's tobacco division emerged in 1989 when a former senior manager who had a reputation for building brands was named CEO. He was in charge when the controversial but successful "Joe Camel" advertising campaign was developed.

What to Do with the Information

This is the stage at which many competitor analysis efforts fall flat. What do we do with all the information we collected? We need a useful format for synthesizing this information.

A first step toward making sense out of the data is to construct a table patterned after Figure 5.14. This forces the product manager to boil down the information to its essential parts and provides a quick summary of a large amount of data.

A critical part of the analysis is including the product for which the plan is written. This would be done in the column of Figure 5.14 labeled "Our Product." Detecting the strengths and weaknesses of the company's product is sometimes referred to as an *internal* or *resource* analysis. However, in our context, this comparison forms the basis of the differential competitor advantage analysis shown in Figure 5.1. One outcome of this analysis could be a structured comparison of the competing firms and products on a small set

FIGURE 5.14 Competitor Capabilities Matrix

	Firm/Product				Our Product
	A	B	C	D	
Conceive and design:					
• Technical resources					
• Human resources					
• Funding					
•					
•					
•					
•					
Produce:					
• Physical resources					
• Human resources					
•					
•					
•					
•					
•					
Market:					
• Sales force					
• Distribution					
• Service and sales policies					
• Advertising					
• Human resources					
• Funding					
•					
Finance:					
• Debt					
• Liquidity					
• Cash flow					
• Budget system					
•					
•					
•					
Manage:					
• Key people					
• Decision process					
• Planning					
• Staffing					
• Organization structure					
•					
•					

FIGURE 5.15 **Differential Competitor Advantage Analysis**

Critical Success Factors	Firm/Product					
	A	B	C	D	E	Our Product
1						
2						
3						
4						
5						
Overall Rating						

(5 to 10) of factors that are critical to success in the relevant product category. Such a comparison could be structured along the lines of Figure 5.15. In this figure, the entries in the cells of the tables can be rated from, say, 1 to 10 to evaluate each firm or product on the critical success factor. This by itself forces the product manager of "our" product to evaluate (as honestly as possible) his or her product's capabilities versus those of competitors on a factor-by-factor basis. In addition, an overall rating gives the product manager a more global feel for the toughest competitors in the market, which may not necessarily be reflected in market shares or profits.

ASSESSING A COMPETITOR'S WILL

Even the strongest competitor can be overcome if it is not committed to the market. Similarly, a weak competitor can cause massive damage if it is fanatically committed. At some point, it is crucial to assess competitors' strength of will or commitment. This requires going beyond objectives (what do they want?) to assess the intensity with which they approach the task (how badly do they want it?). Most competitions involve several key times when each competitor has the choice of backing down or continuing the fight. In assessing the likelihood that a competitor will continue the fight (an act that sometimes is not rational in a profit sense), one should assess the following factors.

1. *How crucial is this product to the firm?* The more crucial the product is in terms of sales and profits, number of employees, or strategic thrust, the more committed most companies will be to it. This helps explain why efforts to unseat a market leader by attacking the heart of the market provoke violent reactions, whereas a strategy that nibbles away at secondary markets is more likely to go unmatched. For example, eBay's key product is its online auction. Attempts by Amazon.com and others to develop similar auctions are considered to be a strong threat to eBay's viability and are met with increased promotions and advertising and expansions in the number of auction categories.

2. *How visible is the commitment to the market?* It may be difficult for companies to admit they are wrong once they are publicly committed. A good example of this is Exxon's Office Systems Division, which was clearly in trouble for a long time before it was sold in 1985. Also, Coca-Cola held on to New Coke and repositioned it several times even though it did not sell well after its introduction.

3. *How aggressive are the managers?* Personality differences exist, and some individuals are more combative than others. This aspect of management may not be detected in the management analysis in Figure 5.14. Only by knowing how badly a competitor "wants it" can one successfully approach the next task: predicting future competitor strategies.

PREDICTING FUTURE STRATEGIES

We now have three sets of information about the competitors in the product category. First, we have assessed what their likely objectives are, that is, for what reward they are currently playing the game. Second, we have made a judgment about their current product marketing strategy. We also have some idea about their resources and how they compare to ours. The final step is to put it all together and answer the question: What are they likely to do in the future? In particular, we are interested in their likely strategies over the subsequent planning horizon, usually a year.

This is a critical activity, particularly for firms that are vulnerable to a major new competitor encroaching on their turf. Charles Schwab & Company was very concerned about how Merrill Lynch's move to the Internet would affect its very successful eSchwab business. Of the $15 trillion in individual assets in the United States, about $5 trillion is managed by full-service firms like Merrill, Prudential, and PaineWebber. About $1 trillion is managed by discount brokers, and much of that goes to Schwab. Merrill Lynch's strategy involved many brokers and retail locations, a largely "bricks and mortar" approach. Schwab had taken a "clicks and mortar" approach by combining the Internet and retail locations, but relatively few of the latter. For months, Schwab executives pondered how Merrill would enter the Web-based business.

Sometimes competitors will actually signal their likely future strategies through sources previously discussed. For example, in an article in a major newspaper, MCI gave six-months' notice to the regional Bell operating companies (RBOCs) by specifying the 10 U.S. cities where it was going to begin offering local phone service to businesses. While a major target of the article was the investment analyst community, we are sure the RBOCs were also quite interested in the announcement (*San Francisco Chronicle,* 1995). Of course, the product manager must be aware that such signals could be of the "cheap talk" variety mentioned at the beginning of the chapter.

Often, however, the competition does not come right out and indicate what strategies they will pursue. In that case, subjective estimates can be based on the information previously collected and analyzed. One way to approach the problem is to emulate what forecasters do with historical data. With historical observations on both a dependent variable (in our context, a competitor's strategy) and independent variables useful to predict the dependent variable (in our context, the resource variables), the forecaster might do one of two things. First, the forecaster might assume the trend will continue, that is, suppose that the only relevant information is the historical pattern of past strategies. For example, if the brand has a track record of positioning with a high-quality, high-price program, one could extrapolate into the future and assume the trend will continue. Similarly, if a brand has been appealing to increasingly mature consumers, a manager might assume it will continue to do so. An alternative way for the forecaster to proceed is to try to establish a cause-and-effect relationship between the resource variables and the strategy, in other words, to link changes in resources or abilities to the strategies to be pursued.

Some examples will help clarify this approach. Several years ago, Merrill Lynch spent heavily to bring in managers with packaged goods experience to develop the markets for its financial services. Competitors (Dean Witter, E. F. Hutton) could forecast that this would result in an emphasis on market segmentation (pursuing high-potential customers) and increased spending on marketing-related activities such as advertising. Similarly, Bethlehem Steel invested billions of dollars to upgrade its flat-rolled steel facilities. Competitors could forecast that this investment in highly efficient capacity would improve Bethlehem's ability to simultaneously cut price and protect margins. A third approach to strategy forecasting does not explicitly employ historical data but rather makes use of data in a different way. Corning Glass's highly profitable Corning Ware line was coming off patent. At the same time, it was well known that several companies (Libby-Owens-Ford, Anchor Hocking) were looking at that business. Corning was interested in finding out how a competitor would enter to preempt the entry strategy. To forecast the probable entry strategy, it asked senior managers to role-play (i.e., simulate) a competitor and determine how, if they were managing the entry, they would attack Corning Ware. This exercise provided useful defensive information for Corning.

Thus, a third approach to forecasting competitors' possible actions is to simulate them. One can take the existing data already collected, have different managers play the roles of the product managers for the competitors, and develop competitor action scenarios. SmithKline Beecham (now GlaxoSmithKline), the pharmaceutical company, did exactly that when Tagamet (an antiulcer drug), then the largest-selling prescription drug in the world, was coming off patent. In this case, it knew who the competitor was going to be: Glaxo Holdings. SmithKline prepared its salespeople for Glaxo's anticipated promotion of its drug, Zantac, in terms of differential advantage (fewer doses needed per day) and for counteracting arguments against Tagamet. Although Zantac eventually replaced Tagamet as the category leader, SmithKline believed the simulation helped dampen the impact of Zantac. Another company using the simulation approach is Intel, which has a full-time group within the company that develops strategies that competitors may follow. To complete the Merrill Lynch–Schwab story started above, Schwab managers concluded that their company stood for "full service" on the Internet the way Merrill stood for that strategy in the offline world. Thus, to be proactive, Schwab increased the amount of guidance its employees offered customers and provided more high-quality research on the Schwab site (Kirsner, 1999).

In general, there has been little systematic study of how to predict competitor moves. Using the airline industry as a case history, some recent research has studied how competitors react to a competitive move (Chen, Smith, and Grimm, 1992). The main empirical findings were:

The greater the competitive impact, the greater the number of responses made.

The greater the intensity of the move, the greater the number of counteractions.

The greater the implementation requirement, the smaller the number of responses.

The more tactical the move, the greater the competitive response.

FIGURE 5.16   **A Competitive Conjecture Process**

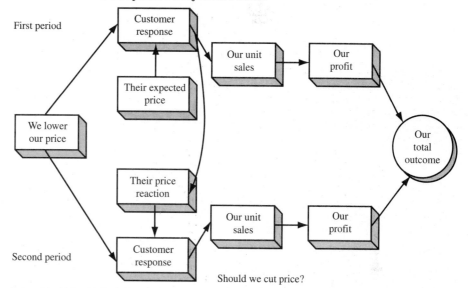

Source: Adapted from Marian C. Moore and Joel E. Urbany, "Blinders, Fuzzy Lenses, and the Wrong Shoes, Pitfalls in Competitive Conjecture," *Marketing Letters,* July 1994.

An approach similar to simulation uses economic game theory. While game theory is theoretically elegant, it is limited in its ability to model real-world situations involving large numbers of competitors and many possible moves. However, the basic principles can be shown in the illustration highlighted by Figure 5.16 (Clark, 1998; Moore and Urbany, 1994). Suppose "our" firm ("we") is thinking about lowering its price on a product. In the time period of the price cut (first period), we would expect customers to compare our new, lower price to the competitor's ("their") price and that this would increase our unit sales and perhaps profits (depending upon the price elasticity of demand). However, where most managers fail is that they do not anticipate the competitor's reaction in the second or next period after our price cut. If they cut their price as well, the customer response will be more complicated but it will probably result in lower sales and profits for us. If we anticipate that the competitor will lower price, it does not make much sense for us to do so in the first period since the resulting "equilibrium" will be the same sales levels before we cut price but at lower prices, margins, and profits. The key here is the concept of thinking ahead, anticipating competitor's moves, and integrating them into the *current* decision.

ILLUSTRATIONS

Energy Bars

The major competing brands to the Odwalla bar are PowerBar, Balance Bar, and Clif Bar and their variants. An additional competitor, Kashi GoLean, comes from the natural food/energy bar category. A product feature matrix is shown in Figure 5.17. A summary of the strategies, differential advantage analysis, and expected future strategies, abbreviated

FIGURE 5.17 **Energy Bars: Competitor Feature/Strategy Matrix**

Features	Odwalla	Kashi Go Lean	Clif Bar	Power Bar	Balance
Bar Weight	2.4 oz	2.8 oz	2.4 oz	2.3 oz	1.8 oz
# Bars/Box	12	12	12	12	15
Calories	240	290	230	240	200
Fat	6 g	6 g	4 g	3.5 g	6 g
Protein	6 g	13 g	10 g	10 g	14 g
Carbohydrates	40 g	49 g	41 g	45 g	22 g
# Flavors	7	8	12	11	7
# Chocolate	2	4	5	3	4
# Salty	0	0	0	0	0
# Other	5	4	7	8	3
Taste (scale 1–5, 5-best)	3	2	3	1	3
Dipped (Y/N)	No	Yes	No	No	Yes
Price (Bar/Box)	$1.35/$14.25*	$1.69/**$20.00**	$1.35/**$14.25**	**$1.35**/$14.25	$1.35/**$16.49**
Product Claims	Nourishing food bar, ingredients you can pronounce	Taste so decadent, but they are a healthy alternative, high protein and fiber	Nutrition, energy, natural ingredients	Energy for optimum performance	40-30-30 nutritional philosophy, nutrition and taste
Target Consumer	Natural food and health enthusiast	Health enthusiast/ dieter	Athletes, general consumer	Athletes	Health conscious, general consumer
Distribution	Natural food and some grocery, drug, and mass	Natural food, grocery, some drug, and mass	Grocery, drug, mass, natural food, club	Grocery, drug, mass, natural food, club	Grocery, drug, mass, natural food, club
Brand Positioning	Nutrition and health	Health and diet	Energy and nutrition	Energy	Energy and nutrition

*Prices in bold are confirmed from company websites. Alternate prices are taken from REI, Whole Foods, and Safeway.

to conserve space, is shown in Figures 5.18 and 5.19. Information is shown only for the main brands, not the sub-brands (e.g., Clif Luna).

Brand Objectives

All four brands appear to be pursuing market share growth strategies. The category is at a relatively early stage in the product life cycle, so it is too early to be going exclusively for profits. The smallest brand, Kashi, also seeks to increase its presence in the channels.

Brand Strategies

PowerBar: This brand invented the energy bar category. While it has maintained a loyal following of athletes, it lost ground to competitors as the market expanded to include more mainstream consumers. As a result, the brand has launched a number of extensions, including PowerBar Pria targeting women and a breakfast bar, Harvest.

FIGURE 5.18 Energy Bars: Differential Competitor Analysis

	PowerBar	Balance Bar	Clif Bar	Kashi	Odwalla
Parent company	Nestle (2000)	Kraft Foods (Feb 2000)—a division of Philip Morris Company	Independent	Kellogg's (2000)	Coca-Cola Company (2001)
Deal amount	Not Disclosed	$268 million	N/A	$33 million	$181 million
Total sales before merger	1999—$135 million	1999—$100.9 million	N/A	1999—$25 million	$128.3 million (Less than 5% is from food bar)
Founder	Founded in 1986 by former Olympic marathon runner Brian Maxwell and chemist Jennifer Biddulph	Founded in 1992, became a publicly traded company in 1998	Gary Erickson was a competitive cyclist who made his living designing bike saddles—owner and CEO	Founded by Philip and Gayle Tauber	Founded in 1980 by longtime friends Greg Steltenpohl, Gerry Percy, and Bonnie Bassett to fund musical and multi-media presentations they wanted to create for local schools and events to educate about cultural diversity issues and the environment
Products	Energy for sports—Performance, Power Gel, Protein Plus. Everyday energy—Harvest and Pria	Balance Original (1992), Balance Plus (1998), Balance Outdoor (1999), Balance Gold (2000), Balance Oasis (2001), Balance Satisfaction (2002)	Clif Bar, Shot, Mojo bar, Luca and Clif Ice Series	Cereal—Kashi Pilaf, Kashi to Good Friends, Puffed, Medley, Honey Puffed, Pillows; Portable Meals—Kashi go; Others—Kashi Baby & Me and Kashi GoLEAN Cereal Slimming System soy-based cereal, shakes, and bars.	Drinks—100% Essential Juices, Odwalla organics, Nutritionals, Smoothies, Quenchers, Future Shake, Natural Spring water. Food Bars—Odwalla Bars
Management		James Wolfe, President and Chief Executive Officer of Balance Bar	Gary Erickson, CEO and Founder	Philip and Gayle Tauber, founders, signed a 2-year deal to continue managing the Kashi line	

continued

FIGURE 5.18 Energy Bars: Differential Competitor Analysis—*continued*

	PowerBar	Balance Bar	Clif Bar	Kashi	Odwalla
Latest product	Pria—energy bar for women—2002	Balance Satisfaction—meal replacement bar	Season's Eatings—Spiced Pumpkin Pie-and Caramel Apple Cobbler (limited time only)	New flavors—Mocha Java and Oatmeal Raisin Cookie	Odwalla Bars and Spring water; Fresh Samantha acquisition in 2001
Distribution	54 distributors worldwide with very strong presence in Europe	Balance Bar is sold through retail grocery, mass merchandise and club stores, and natural foods stores nationwide.	Clif and Luna are sold through grocery, mass, club, and natural food stores.	With Kellogg's acquisition of Keebler in 2001, the company now has a strong DSD system for faster distribution. At this point, it doesn't appear to be used for Kashi bars.	Odwalla products are currently sold in over 30 states. Odwalla Bars are available in additional states and can also be purchased through the Web. Minute Maid has very strong distribution.
Sponsorship	Lance Armstrong Foundation, colleges, 2004 Olympics, athletes and events sponsor.	Golf and adventure racing	Sponsors sports and athletics as well as nonprofit organizations and events	No sponsorships listed	Art and music
Production		Manufactures products through copacking agreements.			
Employment		90 employees primarily at its Carpinteria, CA, headquarters.		20 employees at its La Jolla, CA headquarters.	
Other		Markets a full range of energy/nutrition bars under the Balance Bar name as well as a line of bars under the Jenny Craig brand through a license arrangement.		Kellogg's recently launched Krave, a new high-protein bar brand.	Strong sales on the West Coast, particularly Northern California; weaker distribution in the middle of the country

FIGURE 5.19 **Energy Bar: Current and Future Strategy Matrix**

	Clif Bar Inc.	PowerBar Inc.	Balance Bar Inc.	Kashi Co.
Objectives	Grow market share and volume.	Grow market share and volume.	Grow market share and volume.	Grow revenue and distribution.
Current strategies	Product innovation.	Product introductions in new segments, increased advertising spend.	Products launching and expanding in multiple segments of category.	Product line extensions (new flavors) and distribution focus.
Expected future strategies	Focus on product innovation and grassroots marketing.	Focus on product development, increased advertising, and promotions.	Focus on product line and brand extensions to fill category.	Focus on expanding distribution to gain shelf space nationally in grocery, drug, and mass channels.

Balance Bar: This brand does not appear to have a strong focus. Like PowerBar, it has focused on brand extensions funded by its parent, Kraft, and is attempting to fill as many segments as possible.

Clif Bar: This is the only independent company among the top brands. It is looking to hold on to its top market position in the face of competition with much greater resources. To lure athletes, the brand launched an extension, Ice Bar, and a salty Mojo Bar straddling the health and snack categories.

Kashi: Its marketing focus has been to expand its distribution. It has used its parent, Kellogg's, to accomplish this.

Differential Competitor Advantage Analysis

PowerBar: This company has been very successful at differentiating itself by targeting hardcore athletes and positioning itself solidly in the energy bar category. This tradition is from its founder, Brian Maxwell, who was a former Olympic marathon runner.

Balance Bar: Their main competitive advantage is a solid distribution system as it is marketed in natural foods, mass merchandise, club, grocery, and a number of other channels of distribution.

Clif Bar: This is the most customer-oriented brand as its managers do the best job interacting with customers and listening and responding to their needs. It is perceived by consumers to be the most innovative and creative of the major brands.

Kashi: Kashi is a natural cereal and convenience foods company. The company's products are made with a blend of sesame and seven whole grains. The brand is strongly associated with grain and fiber.

Expected Future Strategies

PowerBar: This brand is likely to continue to be more aggressive in targeting mainstream markets and thus continue to launch more brand extensions. The brand's managers will also invest heavily in advertising and promotions.

Balance Bar: With the assistance of Kraft's resources, the brand will continue to introduce more extensions.

FIGURE 5.20 PDA Product Features Matrix

	Visor	Visor Deluxe	Palm III	Palm IIIe	Palm Pilot PE	PV-100	PV-200	Cassiopoeia E-100	Cassiopoeia E-11
Price suggested retail price	$179 ($149++)	$249	$216	$205	$235	$123	$100	$499	$276
Physical Properties									
Form	Pad	Pad	Pad	Pad	Pad	Pad	Pad	Pad	Pad
Size	4.8 × 3.0 × 0.7	4.8 × 3.0 × 0.7	4.7 × 3.6 × 0.7	4.7 × 3.2 × 0.7	4.6 × 3.2 × 0.7	4.9 × 3.2 × 0.6	4.9 × 3.2 × 0.6	5.1 × 3.3 × .8	4.9 × 3.3 × 0.8
Weight, oz	5.4	5.4	6.4	5.8, 6.0 with battery	5.1	4.8	4.8	9	6.7
Memory and Processor Speed									
RAM, processor speed	2 MB	8 MB	2 MB, 16 MHz	2 MB	1 MB, 16 MHz	1 MB	2 MB	16 MB, 131 MHz	8 MB, 100 MHz
Expandable RAM	No	No	No	No	No	No	No	Yes	No
Display									
Diagonal screen size	3 in	3 in	4.1	4.1 in	4.1 in	4 in	4 in	3.9 in	3.9 in
Resolution			160 × 160		160 × 160	128 × 128	128 × 128	240 × 320	240 × 320
Color (If no, gray shades)	No	No, 16 shades	No, 4 shades	No	No, 4 shades	No, 4 shades	No, 4 shades	Yes	No, 4 shades
Touch screen	Yes	Yes	Yes	Yes	Yes	Yes	Yes	Yes	Yes
Backlight	Yes	Yes	Yes	Yes	Yes	Yes	Yes	Yes	Yes
Other									
Interfaces									
Total # of serial ports	0	0	1	1	1	1	1	1	1
Number of type II PC cards	0	0	0	0	0	0	0	0	1
IR port	Yes	Yes	Yes	yes	No	Yes	Yes	Yes	Yes
Other ports	USB, Springboard Slot								

Clif Bar: Like the others, the emphasis for this brand will be on extensions. Its goal is to remain ahead of both Balance Bar and PowerBar.

Kashi: This brand will focus on new flavors and expand distribution to gain shelf space in grocery, drug, and mass channels.

Personal Digital Assistants

In this category, there are many competitors and product features. A sampling of the features matrix is shown in Figure 5.20 (again, circa 1999). The analysis will focus on the offerings from Handspring's two major competitors, representing different operating system platforms, Palm (Palm OS) and Casio (PocketPC/Windows CE).

Brand Objectives

Since the PDA was in the growth stage of the life cycle, all of the products were trying to gain volume to bring down costs and establish market positions. This resulted in a price drop of the major competitors (e.g., Palm) following the usual early skimming approach to grab those who need to be the first with the latest technology (at the highest price).

Brand Strategies

Palm: This company decreased price on the low-end models (Palm III) and introduced higher-end models (Palm V) with advanced features and color screens. The strategy was clear: Offer different product options for different target segments. Of particular interest to Palm was the nonbusiness user, that is, an expansion into the "average" or home user segment.

Casio: Differentiating on the basis of the operating system was not working as, despite Microsoft's feelings to the contrary, users did not see the advantages of PocketPC/Windows CE over Palm's operating system. Therefore, Casio attempted to differentiate on the basis of product features and not price.

Differential Competitor Advantage Analysis

Figure 5.21 shows a competitive capabilities matrix. The main implications are the following:

Palm:

Strengths: Market leader, cash availability, large number of software developers, large and strong community of users, strong brand equity.

Weaknesses: Lost key managers to Handspring, uncertainty from the spin-off from 3Com.

Casio:

Strengths: Economies of scale in production, creativity, good brand name (though weaker than Palm in this category).

Weaknesses: Dilution of resources into 61 different businesses run by the corporation.

Expected Future Strategies

Palm:

Continued licensing of its operating system and establish the Palm OS as the industry standard. If the Palm III does not work with the low-end, nonbusiness

FIGURE 5.21 **Comparison of Competitor Resources: PDAs**

Company's Ability to . . .	Palm Pilot	Casio (Windows CE Platform)	Handspring
1. **Conceive and design** (technical and human resources, funding, etc.)	Loss of talent (many original Palm founders have left) may negatively impact its ability to create new products.	Casio is a Japanese company and given the way Japanese companies normally operate, we assume it has plenty of resources, both human and capital.	• Handspring has a great ability to conceive and design products since its founders created the Palm Pilot. They have a lot of experience, vision, and creativity. • Due to the founders' success, they have a lot of funding available to them since investors are confident with their ability to succeed. • Again, due to the founders' prior success and high-profile careers, Handspring has attracted the best talent to work here.
2. **Produce** (physical and human resources)	Palm relies on contract manufacturers to produce its products. Given the volume produced by Palm, its leadership position, and the abundance of electronic contract manufacturers, Palm probably has no problem with production.	Great economies of scale. Plants worldwide.	• Depends on contract manufacturers to make the PDAs. Upside: many contract manufacturers so there is flexibility and we make what we need. Downside: depends on someone else so cannot entirely control quality and also in times when demand is great, may not demand what we want. Also have lower bargaining power relative to Palm due to smaller production volumes. • Handspring has good contacts with manufacturers since founders previously transacted with them. • Handspring depends on the module producers to make the modules. But again, due to the abundance of consumer electronic manufacturers, the production of modules will not be difficult or too risky.
3. **Market** (sales force, distribution, service/sales policies, advertising, human resources, funding)	Palm is the leader and has been in the industry for several years. As such, it will have very good and strong relations with retailers. Retailers know that Palm sells and they will give Palm a relatively higher portion of the shelf space.	Strong marketing experience of electronics products to the channels.	• Because of start-up status, Handspring has limited overworked resources. Limited in how many PDAs they can sell and distribute over year 2000. • Need to market the most strategically attractive segments since we are resource constrained (human and financial). • Limited sales force. • New and not very strong relationships with distribution channels, so may be harder to get Handspring in the door. • Internet is a good resource.
4. **Finance** (debt, liquidity, cash flow, budget system, etc.)	Hard to separate from 3Com. Presumed to have growing sales with a 70+% market share.	Decreasing growth in sales and losses in FY99.	Financially, limited to how much they can spend so can't be as aggressive as would like. For example, cannot target every segment in full force. Must focus on the most strategically attractive segment and will not be able to target all over the next year.

market, they will probably develop a new product just for this market. Possible venture into non-PDA products and applications that use the Palm OS (e.g., home Web appliances).

Casio:

Continue to develop its head-to-head rivalry with Palm and build a brand around advanced and creative product innovation. Unlike Palm, Casio was already a known brand with the consumer market. Thus, like Palm, they will probably introduce a product into this segment soon.

SUMMARY

Competitive analysis is an important component of strategy development. Many approaches have been followed and this chapter provides a framework that integrates several of these. Like most other analyses, however, the key ingredient is not clever devices, unethical behavior, or elegant presentation. Rather, the quality of competitor analysis depends heavily on the effort devoted to it.

References

Bittar, Christine (2001) "Balancing Act: P&G Shuffles Brands, People," *Brandweek,* March 26, 8.

Browder, Seanna (1998) "Course Change at Boeing," *Business Week,* July 27, 34.

Chen, Ming-Jer, Ken G. Smith, and Curtis M. Grimm (1992) "Action Characteristics as Predictors of Competitive Responses," *Management Science,* March, 439–55.

Clark, Bruce H. (1998) "Managing Competitive Interactions," *Marketing Management,* Fall/Winter, 9–20.

De Lisser, Eleena (1999) "Hearing and Seeing Business Travel Blab and Laptop Lapses," *The Wall Street Journal,* November 8, A1.

Fulford, Benjamin (1995) "Spy Biz Thrives on Sex, Lies, Audiotapes," *The Nikkei Weekly,* December 23, 1995, p. 1.

Geyelin, Milo (1995) "Why Many Businesses Can't Keep Their Secrets," *The Wall Street Journal,* November 20, B1.

Green, William (1998) "I Spy," *Forbes,* April 20, 90–96.

Guthrie, Julian (1993) "Brain Drain," *San Francisco Focus,* October, 24.

Kirsner, Scott (1999) "Charles Schwab & Company," *Wired,* November, 135–44.

Lehmann, Donald R., Sunil Gupta, and Joel H. Steckel (1998) *Marketing Research.* Reading, MA: Addison-Wesley.

Lorge, Sarah (1999) "Attacking at a Moment of Weakness," *Sales & Marketing Management,* April, 13.

Maidique, Modesto A., and Peter Patch (1978) "Corporate Strategy and Technological Policy," unpublished working paper, Harvard Business School.

Main, Jeremy (1992) "How to Steal the Best Ideas Around," *Fortune,* October 19, 102–6.

Moore, Marian C., and Joel E. Urbany (1994) "Blinders, Fuzzy Lenses, and the Wrong Shoes: Pitfalls in Competitive Conjecture," *Marketing Letters,* July, 247–58.

Patzer, Gordon L. (1995) *Using Secondary Data in Marketing Research: United States and Worldwide.* Westport, CT: Quorum Books.

Porter, Michael E. (1985) *Competitive Advantage.* New York: The Free Press.

Ries, Al and Jack Trout (1985) *Marketing Warfare.* New York: McGraw-Hill.

San Francisco Chronicle (1995) "MCI Details Assault on the Baby Bells," March 7, D-2.

Schelling, Thomas C. (1960) *The Strategy of Conflict.* Cambridge, MA: Harvard University Press.

Teinowitz, Ira (1995) "Marketing, Ad Woes Choking RJR Brands," *Advertising Age,* June 26, 3.

Teitelbaum, Richard S. (1992) "The New Race for Intelligence," *Fortune,* November 2, 104–7.

The Wall Street Journal (1989) "'Competitor Intelligence': A New Grapevine," April 12, B2.

Yovovich, B. G. (1995) "Customers Can Offer Competitive Insights," *Business Marketing,* March, 13.

Zachary, Pascal (1989) "At Apple Computer Proper Office Attire Includes a Muzzle," *The Wall Street Journal,* October 6, A1.

Zellner, Wendy and Bruce Hager (1991) "Dumpster Raids? That's Not Very Ladylike, Avon," *Business Week,* April 1, 32.

Chapter Six

Customer Analysis

Overview

Since businesses run on revenue and revenue comes from customers, it is critical to understand them. It is thus no accident that this is the longest chapter. Customers, not products, are the ultimate source of operating income. Companies increasingly at least espouse being customer-centric and a large and increasing number have created the position of customer insights managers or the equivalent to assemble and disseminate the customers' "voice" throughout the organization. Further, increased emphasis is being placed on customer "touch points," places where the customer comes in contact with the company or its products and services. How these encounters turn out determines in large measure future sales and the success (or failure) of a product. However, before deciding how to satisfy or even delight customers, you first need to identify them: who they are, where they are, what they want, etc. This chapter provides some guidance on how to approach this critical task.

By *customer* we mean not only current customers of a given product but also both customers of competitors and current noncustomers of the product category (i.e., potential customers). The term *customer* also refers both to immediate customers (i.e., supermarkets and discount stores and critically Wal-Mart for consumer product companies such as P&G and manufacturers for component manufacturers such as Intel) and to final customers (i.e., individuals and businesses). Similarly, while many firms have recently made huge ($100 million) investments in customer relationship management (CRM) systems that emphasize IT (information technology), few feel the investment has paid off. Hence, our focus here is on understanding customers rather than data collection and warehousing.

In this chapter, we do three things. First, we suggest an approach to systematically analyzing customers. Figure 6.1 suggests that product managers need to answer eight questions. Who are the customers for this product or service? What are customers buying and how do they use it? (Customers buy benefits rather than simply product features or characteristics.) Where do customers buy products? When are purchase decisions made? How do customers make purchase decisions? Why do customers choose a particular product? In other words, how do they value one option over another? How do they respond to marketing programs such as advertising and promotions? And finally, will they buy it again? Second, we introduce the concept of long-term value of customers. This is an essential concept which guides the amount of effort

FIGURE 6.1 What We Need to Know about Current and Potential Customers

Who buys and uses the product
What customers buy and how they use it
Where customers buy
When customers buy
How customers choose
Why they prefer a product
How they respond to marketing programs
Will they buy it (again)?

to direct to specific customers. Finally, we discuss market segmentation, that is, how to efficiently and effectively group customers to simplify strategic and tactical thinking and decisions.

WHAT WE NEED TO KNOW ABOUT CUSTOMERS

Who Buys and Uses the Products

Buyers versus Users

For most industrial goods and many consumer products, the *who* must be broken into several different entities within the organization or household, including the following:

1. Initiator (who identifies the need for product).
2. Influencer (who has informational or preference input to the decision).
3. Decider (who makes the final decision through budget authorization).
4. Purchaser (who makes the actual purchase).
5. User.

The identities of the above individuals can differ widely. For example, in an industrial market, the end user may be an engineer who is concerned mainly with technical features, whereas the purchasing agent emphasizes cost and reliability of delivery. One reason for the success of Federal Express was its ability to take the decision on how to send overnight packages away from the shipping clerk by making the user the purchaser. Similarly, adults often purchase cereal, toys, or fast-food meals even though the user of the product is a child. Products targeted toward gift givers (e.g., silverware as a wedding gift) also highlight the difference between the buyer and the user.

This distinction between buyer, user, and other purchase influencers is particularly important for industrial products. The mark of a top salesperson is the ability to identify the different people involved in making a decision, understand the relative power over the purchase each person holds, and learn what they value. For example, in selling word processing software to a law firm, the needs of the secretaries (ease of use, support, readable screen) differ from those of the office manager (high productivity, no bugs in the software, good service) and from the person approving the purchase (low cost, reliable delivery). Figure 6.2 provides a template for this kind of analysis.

FIGURE 6.2 Buying Roles and Needs/Benefits Sought

Needs/Benefits Sought	Buying Roles				
	Initiator(s)	Influencer(s)	Decider(s)	Purchaser(s)	User(s)
A					
B					
C					
D					

Descriptive Variables: Consumer Products

The most obvious and popular basis for describing consumers is their general characteristics (Figure 6.3). The key categories are:

1. *Demographic.* The most commonly used demographics are age, sex, geographic location, and stage in the life cycle. These characteristics have the advantage of being relatively easy to ascertain. Unfortunately, in many cases segments based on demographics are not clearly differentiated in their behavior toward the product.

2. *Socioeconomic.* Socioeconomic variables include income and such related variables as education, occupation, and social class, with income and education generally being more useful. As in the case of demographics, the relationship between these variables and purchase behavior can be weak.

3. *Personality.* Given the relatively limited predictive power of demographic and socioeconomic variables, the fact that many marketing people are trained in psychology, and the natural desire to find a general basis for profiling consumers that will be useful across many situations, it is not surprising that marketers have attempted to use personality traits as a basis for segmentation. Unfortunately, general personality variables have proven even less useful than demographic or socioeconomic variables in predicting purchasing behavior.

4. *Psychographics and values.* Psychographics represent an evolution from general personality variables to attitudes and behaviors more closely related to consumption of goods and services. Also known as lifestyle variables, psychographics generally fall into three categories: activities (cooking, sports, traveling, etc.), interests (e.g., art, music), and opinions. They are thus, not surprisingly, often referred to as AIO variables. These have been widely used as bases for segmentation and for the creation of advertising themes. Many researchers have used the VALS (Values and Lifestyles) typology and its updated version, VALS2, (see Figure 6.4) developed by SRI International, as a basis for defining segments. Figure 6.4 also shows a lifestyle typology, GLOBALSCAN, which was developed by the advertising agency Backer Spielvogel Bates Worldwide based on a survey of 15,000 adults in 14 countries.

FIGURE 6.3 **Major Segmentation Variables for Consumer Markets**

Variable	Typical Breakdown
Geographic	
Region	Pacific, Mountain, West North Central, West South Central, East North Central, East South Central, South Atlantic, Middle Atlantic, New England
City or metro size	Under 5,000; 5,000–20,000; 20,000–50,000; 50,000–100,000; 100,000–250,000; 250,000–500,000; 500,000–1,000,000; 1,000,000–4,000,000; 4,000,000 or over
Density	Urban, suburban, rural
Climate	Northern, southern
Demographic	
Age	Under 6, 6–11, 12–19, 20–34, 35–49, 50–64, 65+
Gender	Male, female
Family size	1–2, 3–4, 5+
Family life cycle	Young, single; young, married, no children; young, married, youngest child under 6; young, married, youngest child 6 or over; older, married, with children; older, married, no children under 18; older, single; other
Income	Under $10,000; $10,000–$15,000; $15,000–$20,000; $20,000–$30,000; $30,000–$50,000; $50,000–$100,000; $100,000 and over
Occupation	Professional and technical; managers, officials, and proprietors; clerical, sales; craftspeople, foremen; operatives; farmers; retired; students; homemakers; unemployed
Education	Grade school or less; some high school; high school graduate; some college; college graduate
Religion	Catholic, Protestant, Jewish, Muslim, Hindu, other
Race	White, black, Asian
Nationality	American, British, French, German, Italian, Japanese
Psychographic	
Social class	Lower lowers, upper lowers, working class, middle class, upper middles, lower uppers, upper uppers
Lifestyle	Straights, swingers, longhairs
Personality	Compulsive, gregarious, authoritarian, ambitious
Behavioral	
Occasions	Regular occasion, special occasion
Benefits	Quality, service, economy, speed
User status	Nonuser, ex-user, potential user, first-time user, regular user
Usage rate	Light user, medium user, heavy user
Loyalty status	None, medium, strong, absolute
Readiness stage	Unaware, aware, informed, interested, desirous, intending to buy
Attitude toward product	Enthusiastic, positive, indifferent, negative, hostile

Source: Philip Kotler, *Marketing Management*, 8th ed., 1994, p. 271. Adapted with permission of Prentice Hall, Inc. Upper Saddle, NJ.

FIGURE 6.4   Lifestyle Typologies

VALS	VALS2	GLOBALSCAN
Inner-directed consumers	Principle-oriented consumers	Strivers
Societally conscious	Fulfilleds	
Experientials	Believers	Achievers
I-am-me consumers		
Outer-directed consumers	Status-oriented consumers	Pressured
Achievers	Achievers	
Emulators	Strivers	Adapters
Belongers		
Need-driven consumers	Action-oriented consumers	Traditionals
Sustainers	Experiencers	
Survivors	Makers	
	Strugglers	

Another typology, the List of Values (LOV) Scale (Kahle, Beatty, and Homer, 1986), delineates nine basic values:

1. Self-respect.
2. Security.
3. Warm relationship with others.
4. Sense of accomplishment.
5. Self-fulfillment.
6. Sense of belonging.
7. Respect from others.
8. Fun and enjoyment.
9. Excitement.

These typologies are often related to purchasing patterns and afford the product manager the opportunity to match potential buyers with the appropriate media and message to communicate with them (Corfman, Lehmann, and Narayanan, 1991).

Descriptive Variables: Industrial Products

The same type of variables used to describe consumers can also be used to describe organizations (see Figure 6.5 for a list of some popular variables). For industrial-product customers, the traditional focus has been on firm characteristics such as size (e.g., number of beds in a hospital), industry, and location; that is, the demographic variables appropriate for describing companies. However, a variety of other kinds of variables can be used, such as operating variables (e.g., customer technology), purchasing approaches (e.g., centralized versus decentralized), situational factors (e.g., order size, physician specialty), and "personal" characteristics (e.g., attitude toward risk).

Concepts of personality and psychographics can also be applied to organizations. Although it may be unusual to think of a firm as having a personality, one important segmentation variable in technologically oriented industries is innovativeness. The innovators, organizations that adopt new technologies earlier than others in their industry,

FIGURE 6.5 Major Segmentation Variables for Business Markets

Demographic
- *Industry:* Which industries should we focus on?
- *Company size:* What size companies should we focus on?
- *Location:* What geographical areas should we focus on?

Operating Variables
- *Technology:* What customer technologies should we focus on?
- *User/nonuser status:* Should we focus on heavy, medium, light users or nonusers?
- *Customer capabilities:* Should we focus on customers needing many or few services?

Purchasing Approaches
- *Purchasing-function organization:* Should we focus on companies with highly centralized or decentralized purchasing organizations?
- *Power structure:* Should we focus on companies that are engineering dominated, financially dominated, etc.?
- *Nature of existing relationships:* Should we focus on companies with which we have strong relationships or simply go after the most desirable companies?
- *General purchase policies.* Should we focus on companies that prefer leasing? Service contracts? Systems purchases? Sealed bidding?
- *Purchasing criteria:* Should we focus on companies that are seeking quality? Service? Price?

Situational Factors
- *Urgency:* Should we focus on companies that need quick and sudden delivery or service?
- *Specific application:* Should we focus on certain applications of our product rather than all applications?
- *Size of order:* Should we focus on large or small orders?

Personal Characteristics
- *Buyer–seller similarity:* Should we focus on companies whose people and values are similar to ours?
- *Attitudes toward risk:* Should we focus on risk-taking or risk avoiding customers?
- *Loyalty:* Should we focus on companies that show high loyalty to their suppliers?

Source: Philip Kolter, *Marketing Management,* 8th ed., 1994, p. 278. Adapted with permission of Prentice Hall, Inc. Upper Saddle River, NJ.

are often referred to as "lead users." Lead users have two charactcristics: (1) they face general needs before the bulk of the industry does, and (2) they can benefit significantly by obtaining an early solution to those needs (Urban and von Hippel, 1988). These are obviously valuable customers, as they not only provide early sales and spread (hopefully) favorable word of mouth information, but also help the company make necessary product modifications and improvements.

Many of the same variables used to segment markets for consumer and industrial goods are used to segment markets internationally. Figure 6.6 lists key segmentation variables used in direct marketing campaigns in Europe.

What Customers Buy and How They Use It

The most obvious answer to the "what" question revolves around the identity of the items or services purchased (including brand, purchase amounts, and benefits and features chosen). Any product manager who doesn't have such basic data is generally not long employed.

Benefits

The firm produces features but customers purchase benefits. Recognizing this distinction is a problem in technology-driven companies that tend to focus on the development of new

FIGURE 6.6 Key Segmentation Variables Used in Direct Marketing Campaigns in Europe

	Belgium	Denmark	France	Germany	Greece	Ireland	Italy	Netherlands	Portugal	Spain	UK
Most commonly used consumer segmentation criteria	Social class Nielsen zones Geographic Database	Demographic from census Database	Sociodemo-graphic Database	Age Profession Income Family status Lifestyle	Urban/rural Profession Database	Age Income Profession Family status Database	Age Sex Profession Housing types	Age Sex Geographic Lifestyle Database	Income Urban/rural Education Political bias Database	Age Sex Education Urban/rural Geographic proximity Database	Age Sex Profession Lifestyle Database
Most commonly used business segmentation criteria	SIC* Size VAT	SIC Size Turnover Decision	SIC Size Turnover	SIC Turnover Size	Size Turnover SIC	Size Turnover Location Liquidity	SIC Size Turnover Number of telephone lines	Size/SIC Turnover Branches Credit rating Decision makers	Size SIC	Size Turnover	SIC Size

*SIC: Standard Industrial Classification.

Source: *Marketing Director International*, 1991.

technologies and complex products without adequate concern about whether the benefits the technology provides solve customers' problems better than the old products do. Focusing on benefits is also important in understanding the competitive set. The old story about the drill manufacturer that recognized it was selling holes, not drills, not only indicates that benefits are more important than the physical product but also helps to define the competition based on the benefit (referred to in Chapter 3 as *generic competition*). Thus, a key problem facing the product manager is to understand what benefits different customer groups or market segments are seeking. As Figure 6.2 shows, the needs or benefits sought can vary with the buying role in the decision-making unit as well as by customer segment.

For example, consider a Cadillac Seville. The following distinction can be drawn between features and benefits:

Feature	Benefit
300-horsepower engine	The ability to pull away quickly from potentially dangerous situations. With the increased traffic, you'll feel much safer in this car.
Northstar engine	Will not need a tuneup for the first 100,000 miles. You'll enjoy a smooth-running engine with fewer trips to the dealer for service.
Adjustable seats	Controls allow you to make easy adjustments to your seating position so you'll stay fit, alert, and comfortable throughout your trip.
ABS brakes	Your wheels won't lock up and skid. This means you have an extra margin of safety.

This kind of description appeals both to the features-hungry customer and to the customer who needs the features translated into terms he or she can understand.

Purchase Pattern (Two-Product Assortment)

As mentioned in Chapter 1, there is increased use of customer databases for target marketing and customer retention programs. Database marketers often use three criteria for evaluating and segmenting customers in their databases:

1. *Recency:* How recently has the customer bought from you?
2. *Frequency:* How many different products does the customer buy, and what are the time intervals?
3. *Monetary value:* What is the value of the customer's purchases in terms of profits?

The RFM approach is used to rate each customer in the database on a scale, perhaps by multiplying the three criteria and then rank ordering customers in terms of attractiveness. When prospecting for new customers, top-ranked customers can be profiled using the descriptors noted earlier, and then potential customers can be matched against these descriptors.

The ultimate customer profile is based on their lifetime value. Decisions about customer acquisition and retention (i.e., will they buy it again?) as well as the level of effort to direct toward each customer depend on the future net revenues expected from them. While measures such as size, wealth, and past purchases provide crude estimates of worth, the value of a customer is the discounted sum of future net revenue of the customer. The net revenue depends on the amount and type of transactions (i.e., volume and margin) as well as the cost to service (retain) the customer.

On a direct-cost basis, not all customers are profitable. Often small accounts do not generate sufficient revenue to cover the cost of servicing them, although the cost of dealing with large accounts often makes them unprofitable as well. In fact, some companies estimate that 80 to 90 percent of their customers are nonprofitable, leading to such contested practices as "slamming" (transferring accounts to other companies without their consent). Credit card holders who pay off their balances on time, cable subscribers in remote areas, and "high service" customers who heavily use toll-free numbers are common examples of unprofitable customers.

On the other hand, customers that are unprofitable in the short run may be very profitable in the long run. While the cost of acquiring a customer (solicitation plus special deals) is typically greater than first-year profits for life insurance, magazine subscriptions, and many other businesses, lower long-run maintenance costs (due to high repeat rates) lead to strong positive returns in subsequent years. Calculating the value of a customer is straightforward, although heavily influenced by assumption. We discuss this concept in detail in Chapter 14.

A useful way of quickly summarizing potential customers is to describe where they are (and plan to be) in terms of relating to the product. Potential customers fall on a continuum from unaware to enthusiastic advocates. The stages include:

1. Unaware
2. Aware
3. Accepting (i.e., willing to use the product)
4. Attracted (i.e., have a positive attitude toward the product)
5. Active (i.e., buy and/or plan to buy the product)
6. Advocates (i.e., not only buy but actively encourage others to do so)

Delineating which, and how many, customers fall in each stage provides an important basis for strategy formulation (e.g., how much unmet potential is there?).

Product Assortment

Another useful piece of information related to the "what" question involves the number of different brands purchased by customers in the segments (i.e., what else). For many frequently purchased consumer goods, panel or similar data are available that provide purchase histories for individual consumers (e.g., brands purchased were A, A, A, B, A, A, C, A, A, A), which when aggregated produce switching tables such as Figure 3.10. For industrial products, it is useful to understand how many different vendors a customer employs and the assortment of models, quality levels, and the like from which the customer chooses. For example customers may also use Emery, DHL, UPS, the U.S. Postal Service, fax, and e-mail.

Share of Wallet is another key characteristic of customers. Knowing what fraction of spending is on your particular product has clear implications for strategy. (Hint: It is hard to get more than 100 percent.)

Use

How customers use a product is fairly straightforward, including when, where (e.g., at home or in the office), how, and with what else they use it. In essence this gets at the key concept of product experience. For example, cranberry sauce is widely used at

Thanksgiving in the United States out of a sense of tradition and to provide color to the meal, which is very different from for nutritional value or to fill up.

Arm & Hammer found out about putting a box in the refrigerator and using baking soda to deodorize drains from customer suggestions. Often customers find uses for a product that the company never dreamed of. Interestingly, the way a product is used may or may not be related to why customers originally bought it.

Where Customers Buy

Where customers make purchase decisions is a critical input into decisions about the channels of distribution (see Chapter 13). Many product managers think of channels as being fixed and traditional, but customers migrate to other channels as their information needs and other market conditions change.

Take, for example, the home stereo market. During the 1960s, consumers started replacing consoles (the turntable, tuner, and amplifier housed in what looks like a piece of furniture) with stereo components. The locus of purchase was mainly small stereo stores and some mail-order firms. In the 1990s most of these purchases occurred in electronics superstores such as Best Buy. Recently the Internet has emerged as an important source of both product information and purchases.

Why did this happen? First, consumers' need for information diminished over time. The component system is no longer a novelty; most people are not buying their first system but upgrading an old one. Media such as *Consumer Reports* provide excellent information on features and quality. Thus, whereas customers relied on salespeople for technical information and product comparisons in the 1960s, Best Buy merely indicates what is on sale and whether it is in stock. In addition, more products are available, which has brought down margins. Large-volume retailers (e.g., Best Buy, Wal-Mart) typically dominate in such an environment.

A similar picture emerged in personal computers. The small computer retailers gave way to large hardware and software superstores such as CompUSA, specialized software discounters such as Egghead, mail-order firms such as Dell and Gateway 2000, and eventually Internet sites. The phenomenon of moving from specialty retailer to discounter is often repeated and predictable.

When Customers Buy

A relevant dimension to understanding customers is the timing issue. When they buy encompasses time of year, time of month, and even time of day. Fast-food operators, for example, segment by "daypart," that is, breakfast, lunch, dinner, and snacking times. *When* also includes when customers buy in terms of sales or price breaks and rebates, on the assumption that those who buy because of a special deal (i.e., deal-prone consumers) may be different than those who pay full price.

Some sales variation is predictable due to the nature of the product. Snowblower sales to end users are most likely to be highest during winter or in late fall; sales to channels occur earlier. Capital equipment sales are often made near the end of a fiscal year to spend money that may not be there next year. However, as noted in Chapter 4, highly seasonal categories are less attractive due to the pressures placed on manufacturing, personnel, and cash flow. Thus, competitors in such categories look for ways to even out demand as much as possible. For example, cold remedies are marketed well before the major cold seasons to get households to stock up and lock out competing brands.

How Customers Choose

One major focus is on how customers collect (or are exposed to) information about products (e.g., advertisements, in-store personnel, brochures, magazines, or, increasingly, the Internet). In addition to defining information sources, the process used to make decisions is relevant. Often the decision process is emotional, holistic, automatic, and/or spontaneous. (Responses to the question "How did you choose it?" include "I just wanted it," "It was in stock," "The old one broke/ran out," or "I just grabbed something.") Knowing the manner in which choice is made is relevant to strategy decisions even when the decision process is not very deliberate. Frequently, however, the process is, or can be, described as "rational." For this type of decision, customers essentially compare alternatives on features via a multiattribute model.

Consideration

Being in the consideration set (akin to an approved supplier list for business-to-business purchases) is critical. Understanding who is willing to use the product (finds it acceptable) goes a long way toward forecasting sales and formulating strategy.

The Multiattribute Model

The process of how customers make decisions has been extensively studied (Wilkie, 1990). In addition, comprehensive models have been developed that focus on consumer decision processes (Howard, 1989), information processing (Bettman, 1979), and organizational buying behavior (Johnston and Lewin, 1996). While it is impossible to provide a comprehensive discussion here of how customers make choices, the multiattribute model offers a concise and practical conceptualization of customer decision making that is useful in both consumer and industrial contexts. The multiattribute model of decision making is composed of four parts. First, the products or alternatives in a product category are assumed to be collections of attributes. Attributes can be defined in terms of physical characteristics or, as described earlier, benefits sought. Second, each customer is assumed to have a perception about how much of each attribute the alternatives in a product category contain. Third, each customer is assumed to place an importance value, or weight, on obtaining each attribute when making a choice in the category. Finally, customers are assumed to combine the attribute and importance weight information using some process, or *rule,* to develop their most preferred option in the product category. We therefore address four questions:

1. Which attributes do customers use to define a product?
2. How do customers determine how much of each attribute a brand possesses?
3. How are the importance weights determined?
4. What decision rule is used to combine the information?

Attributes Identifying the set of relevant attributes is not easy; using managerial judgment alone can seriously misestimate the number and types of attributes used in making decisions. One way to collect information is through focus group research. Participants in the focus group are first selected from the relevant segment(s). The moderator of the focus group then elicits from the set of respondents what characteristics or benefits the customers want to see in a product.

A second approach is through survey-based methods, using open-ended and/or fixed-response questions. For example, to determine the set of attributes for a notebook computer, the product manager could ask the respondent to list (open-ended) or check off (closed-ended) those used in making a decision.

Perceptions Once the attributes have been identified, the next step is to determine customers' perceptions of the amount of each attribute possessed by each brand or product option in the category. This is often done by direct questioning. Suppose that weight is a key attribute of a notebook computer. Then the following question could be asked: "On a 1 to 7 scale where 1 is the lightest and 7 is the heaviest, how heavy is the _____ brand of laptop computer?" This question would be asked for the brands or models of interest to the product manager (often restricted to those the customer is familiar with or willing to consider buying). Similar questions would be used for other attributes.

An indirect approach to determining perceptions uses a marketing research methodology called *multidimensional scaling* (also referred to as *perceptual mapping*). This method provides a spatial representation of the brands in a product category based on customers' perceptions of similarity (or dissimilarity) among products. The characteristics used to differentiate customers' perceptions of the brands are inferred from their relative locations in the product space. The perceptions of the characteristics are inferred from their positions along the axes in the space (see Figure 3.12 for an example). Suppose a bank manager is interested in understanding customers' perceptions of the five retail (consumer) banks in a city. One approach is to take all the possible pairs of the five banks (10) and ask respondents to rate on some scale—say, 1 to 10, with 10 being the most similar—how similar each pair is. A computer program (e.g., SAS) would then be used to locate the banks in a multidimensional space such that the number of dimensions was as small as possible but that the implied perceptual distances between the banks were replicated. Figure 6.7 shows a representative output of such a program.

Each bank is represented by a point in the two-dimensional space. The distances between the points closely replicate the information given by the respondents. For example, banks

FIGURE 6.7 **Bank Perceptual Map**

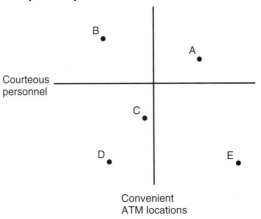

B and E are the farthest apart in the space. This means that those two banks were perceived to be the most dissimilar. The labels on the two axes (the attributes) can be determined by two methods: judgmentally based on the manager's knowledge of the market, or estimated based on other information collected from the respondents. The map leads to two major implications. First, the two key characteristics used by bank customers in this city are the courtesy of the personnel and the convenience of the locations of the automated teller machines (ATMs). Second, the perceived performance of the banks on those attributes differs. Bank E is perceived to have the surliest personnel, and bank D has the most convenient ATM locations. Thus, perceptual mapping can give useful information about both the characteristics being used in assessing perceived similarities and dissimilarities among products and the perceptions of the products on those characteristics. While not generally thought of as a substitute for direct questioning, which has largely supplanted it in practice, it can provide useful supplemental information.

Importance Weights   Like product attribute ratings, attribute importance weights can be assessed through direct questioning. Returning to the notebook computer example, a sample question could be the following: "On a 1-to-7 scale with 7 being very important, how important is weight in your purchase decision?" The same question would then be asked on the other attributes, such as speed of the microprocessor, screen viewing characteristics, and so on. The respondent could also be asked to rank order the attributes in terms of importance.

An alternative approach uses *conjoint analysis* (Green and Wind, 1975). This method permits the product manager to infer the importance of different product attributes from customer rank orderings of alternative product bundles of attributes.

As an example, assume there are three important attributes in a notebook/subnotebook computer purchase decision: weight, battery life, and brand. Assume also that each characteristic can have two different levels or values, as shown in Figure 6.8. The respondent's task is to rate on some scale or rank order the eight combinations from most to least preferred.

In Figure 6.8, a hypothetical response to the rank ordering task gives a 1 to the most preferred combination and an 8 to the least preferred. One combination (three pounds, four hours, and a Dell) clearly dominates, and another (five pounds, two hours, and a

FIGURE 6.8   **Conjoint Analysis: Notebook Computers**

Three attributes of laptop computers:
  Weight (3 pounds or 5 pounds)
  Battery life (2 hours or 4 hours)
  Brand name (HP, Dell)
Task: Rank order the following combinations of these characteristics from 1 = Most preferred to 8 = Least preferred

Combination	Rank
3 pounds, 2 hours, HP	4
5 pounds, 4 hours, Dell	5
5 pounds, 2 hours, HP	8
3 pounds, 4 hours, HP	3
3 pounds, 2 hours, Dell	2
5 pounds, 4 hours, HP	7
5 pounds, 2 hours, Dell	6
3 pounds, 4 hours, Dell	1

FIGURE 6.9 **Importance Weight Variation by Segment**

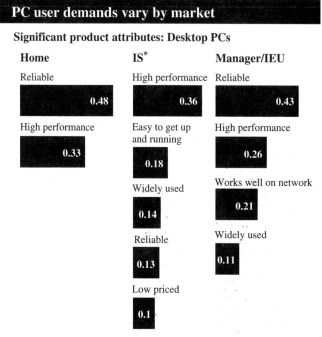

*Information Systems Professionals

Source: *Brandweek,* December 5, 1994, p. 21. © 1994 ASM Communications, Inc. Used with permission.

Hewlett Packard) is clearly the least preferred. However, trade-offs must be made for the combinations of attributes between those two options. In this case, the average ranking for the three-pound options is 2.5 ([1 + 2 + 3 + 4]/4); for the five-pound options, 6.5; for the four-hour options, 4.0; for the two-hour options, 5.0; for the Dell, 3.5; and for HP, 5.5. Looking at the differences in the average ranks, the most important characteristic to this respondent is weight (difference = 4.0), followed by the brand name (2.0) and finally battery life (1.0). While the actual analysis and design of conjoint studies are more complicated than this, the basic ideas are the same.

An example of how importance weights can vary by market segment is shown in Figure 6.9. There is a dramatic difference in the rankings of the attributes when comparing personal computer attributes/benefits among home users, information systems (IS) professionals, and managers. Note also how price, commonly thought to be the most important attribute, was way down the list for IS professionals and not even on the lists for the home users and managers.

Combining the Information The most common way to combine attribute information is to use a *compensatory* rule, which simply multiplies each attribute importance weight by the attribute value and sums these terms for each person and product, as in Figure 6.10. The product of importance weight times rating is simply summed down each column of the table to get a score for each segment. A separate score is constructed for each competing brand.

A compensatory rule such as the multiattribute model implies that all attributes are considered and that weakness in one can be compensated for (hence the name) by

FIGURE 6.10 **Multiattribute Decision Making: Compensatory Rule**

	Segment 1	Segment 2	Segment 3
Attribute A	Weight $\times$ Rating = $Score_{1a}$		
Attribute B	$Score_{1b}$		
Attribute C	$Score_{1c}$		
Attribute D	$Score_{1d}$		
Attribute E	$Score_{1e}$		
Segment Score	$Score_{1a} + \ldots + Score_{1e}$		

strength in another. Of course other rules may be in effect, many of which are easier for the purchaser to implement.[1] For example, a *lexicographic* rule first compares all products on the most important characteristic alone and eliminates those which are not at the top. A *conjunctive* rule assumes the customer sets minimum cutoffs on each dimension and rejects a product if it has any characteristic below the cutoff.

Customers as Problem Solvers

Customers can be described in terms of the difficulty of the problem they are attempting to solve (Howard, 1989). In extensive problem-solving (EPS) situations, customers are concerned mainly with understanding how the product works, what it competes with, and how they would use it. EPS is generally found among first-time purchasers and with products that are technologically new. Limited problem solving (LPS) occurs when the customer understands the basic functioning of the product and what it competes with, and is concerned with evaluating the alternatives on a small number of attributes. This is generally the approach to most large-ticket purchases when the customer has made purchases in the category before (e.g., consumer durables). The third basic type of purchase is routinized response behavior (RRB), where customers essentially follow a predetermined rule for making decisions. Most routine order purchases fall into this category, but so do many big-ticket items (e.g., some people always buy a Volvo). Since customers who follow this approach can be expected to ignore most information, the implications for marketing strategy are dramatic. Product managers with a product that is bought routinely should make it easy for the customer to keep buying. If a product has little market share and the objective is to increase it, the product manager must "shock" the customer into considering the product to break him or her of the routine. Promotions, significant price breaks, and free samples are useful shock devices.

Why They Prefer a Product

The fourth, and in some ways the most critical, component of customer analysis examines why customers make purchase decisions. Central to this question is the concept of *customer value:* what the product is worth to the customer. Customer value depends on the benefits offered (from the customer's perspective) and the costs involved (price, maintenance, etc.). Value is very different from cost: An item costing only pennies to produce may be worth thousands of dollars if it solves an important problem in a timely and efficient manner, and

---

[1] Of course, there are other explanations, such as a dominated brand being a more effective marketer in terms of distribution. Many of the brands rated highly by *Consumer Reports* do not have the highest market shares in their categories.

a product that is costly to produce may have little value. Knowing the value customers place on a product makes it much easier to make key decisions such as setting price.

The customer value of a brand is composed of three basic elements:

1. Importance of the usage situation.
2. Effectiveness of the product category in the situation.
3. Relative effectiveness of the brand in the situation.

Thus, customer value involves two basic notions of value: *category* value, which essentially assumes no competing brand exists (points 1 and 2 above) and *relative* (brand) value, which involves comparison of the product with other products. Because new markets eventually attract competitors, relative effectiveness determines eventual share and profitability (e.g., most chemical product categories in which formulations vary eventually are chosen based on physical properties such as rigidity and stability under different temperatures).

Sources of Customer Value

Sources of value (benefits) can be classified into three broad categories: economic, functional, and psychological.

Economic   A fundamental source of value is the economic benefit a customer derives from using a product. This is a particularly relevant aspect in business-to-business situations and is often formalized as the economic value to the customer (see Appendix 6A). Essentially it is the net financial benefit to the customer from using one product versus another.

Functional   Functional value is defined by those aspects of a product that provide functional or utilitarian benefits to customers. In other words, value is provided by the performance features of a product (e.g., luggage capacity, fuel economy).

A particularly important category of functional characteristics involves service. Customers derive value from three kinds of service. Before-sales service involves providing information. Time-of-sales service facilitates purchase, such as reliable and fast delivery, installation and start-up, and convenient financial terms. After-sales service involves providing both routine and emergency maintenance. Even when a product is involved, service often plays a critical role (e.g., when a water heater breaks, most people call a plumber rather than search for low prices on the Internet). Nothing is more likely to cement a long-term customer relationship than speedy and effective reaction to a problem or more apt to destroy one than a slow and bureaucratic response. Monitoring service quality has (appropriately) become a much more important activity, as discussed in Chapter 14.

Psychological   This source of value is basically the image of the product, including how the product "feels" (e.g., sporty, luxurious, high-tech) and whether that feeling matches the image the customer wants to project. Price is clearly part of product image; some customers may prefer a high price (either because they view price as a signal of quality or engage in conspicuous consumption), whereas others prefer a low price. The importance of image (as opposed to functional attributes) was highlighted by adverse reaction to Coke's formula change (even though it was preferred in blind taste tests) and the strong positive reaction to the reintroduction of Classic Coca-Cola.

Partly inspired by a wave of corporate takeovers, the value of the brand name per se has received much attention (Aaker, 1991, 1996). To a customer, *brand equity* is the value of a product *beyond* that explainable by economic and functional attributes. (Brand equity also represents value to the manufacturer, as discussed in Chapter 8.) It can be represented by the premium a customer would pay for one product over another when the economic and functional attributes are identical.

A number of methods exist for measuring brand equity at the customer level including Y&R's Brand Asset Valuator, Research International's Equity Engine, and Millward-Brown's Brand Z. Basically they break down into five broad categories (see also Aaker, 1996; Keller, 2002):

1. *Awareness.* Being aware of a brand is usually a requirement for its purchase (at least for sober customers). It also leads to more favorable opinions due to the reduced risk associated with a familiar option.
2. *Associations.* Images related to overall quality as well as specific product attributes and user characteristics (e.g., young, hip) impact the reaction to a brand.
3. *Attitude.* Overall favorability toward a brand is a critical part of brand equity. A special form of this is inclusion in the consideration set (i.e., the willingness to consider buying the brand, similar to being on an approved supplier list in business-to-business marketing) or, put differently, acceptability.
4. *Attachment.* Loyalty to a brand is the strongest type of equity (although in the extreme case of addiction it has some undesirable consequences), and the most beneficial for sellers. In the extreme (100 percent retention), it guarantees a nonending stream of income. It also may pass from one generation to the next (Moore, Wilkie, and Lutz, 2002).
5. *Activity.* The strongest fans of a brand become advocates, spreading positive word of mouth and encouraging channels to stock the brand as well as participating in brand communities (Muniz and O'Guinn, 2001; McAlexander, Schouten, and Koenig, 2002).

We discuss brand equity and its implications in more detail in Chapter 8.

Manifestations of Customer Value

A variety of signs of the value of a product are evident even without special efforts to measure them:

Price. Price is the company's assessment of the product's value.

Price sensitivity. A product with constant sales when prices increase generally is of greater value than one for which demand slumps.

Satisfaction. Survey-based satisfaction measures are standard practice (e.g., course evaluations).

Complaints and compliments. The number of complaints or compliments the company receives indicates the product's value.

Word-of-mouth. Although often difficult to track, spoken and written comments provide a useful subjective assessment of a product's value. Monitoring chat rooms and bulletin boards on the Web is one way to track word-of-mouth.

Margin/profit contribution. Generally, higher margins indicate partially monopolistic positions due to greater communicated value.

Dollar sales. Total dollar sales provide an aggregate measure of the value of a product as assessed by the market.

Competitive activity. Competitive activity such as new-product introductions indicates that the total gap between customer value and company costs is sufficiently large to allow for profits even when more companies divide the market.

Repeat purchase rate. High loyalty indicates high brand value.

Assessing the Value of the Product Category

Many ways can be devised to estimate the value of a product category. One particularly useful method focuses on the value of different uses or applications of a product.

1. Determine the uses of the product. Like the substitution-in-use approach discussed in Chapter 3 for generating generic competitors, a first step is to determine the present and potential uses to which a particular product category can be put.
2. Estimate the importance of the uses. This estimate could focus on individual customers or market segments and may simply be projected sales to the segment.
3. List competing products for the uses.
4. Determine the relative effectiveness of the product category in each usage situation.

A hypothetical example of this approach, based on the personal computer category, appears in Figure 6.11. Rather than using numbers, this scale uses adjectives since, typically, some of the entries are hard to quantify. However, the main value of the exercise is to generate broad indicators toward which particular uses of the microcomputer should be targeted.

Assessing the Value of the Brand/Product/Service

Assessing the total value of a brand can be done indirectly. A high-value brand has high share, high repeat purchase rate, low elasticity with respect to price, and limited competitive brand shopping.

FIGURE 6.11 Personal Computer Product Category Value

Use	(IMP) Importance	Competitive Products	(REL) Relative Effectiveness	Category Value (IMP) × (REL)
Video games	Some 20	TV attachments, board games	Very good	High
Bookkeeping	None 1	Accountant, service bureau, "books"	Marginal	Low
Learning skills	Very low 4	Books, school	Inferior	Low
Data analysis	Large 65	Large-scale computer, time sharing, consultant, calculator	Good	High
Report preparation	A little 10 $\overline{100}$	Typewriter, word processor, secretarial service	OK	Fairly low

Using customer responses to estimate the value of a brand generally involves direct ratings. This includes several approaches:

1. *Ratings* (e.g., "How good is *X* for use *Y*?") for competing products. Remember we are generally interested in relative and not absolute value. Therefore, an average of 4 on a 5-point scale indicates good value if the other products are getting 2s and 3s, but little value if the other products are getting averages of 4.5 and 4.8.

2. *Constant sum ratings across brands,* such as "Please rate the following brands by dividing 10 points among them":

   Brand A _____

   Brand B _____

   Brand C _____

   Brand D _____

   Total   <u>10</u>

3. *Graded paired comparisons,* which require customers to indicate which of a pair of products they prefer and by how much. This is often done in terms of dollar amounts (Pessemier, 1963), as shown in Figure 6.12.

4. *Conjoint analysis* of customer ratings of products described in terms of attributes, including price and brand name. Through analysis (basically regression analysis), the relative importances of the attributes, as well as the values of different levels of these attributes, are determined.

FIGURE 6.12 **Dollar Metric Example: Soft Drink Preference**

Pair of Brands (more preferred brand circled)	Amount Extra Willing to Pay to Get a Six-Pack of the More Preferred Brand (cents)
Data	
(Coke) Pepsi	2
(Coke) 7UP	8
(Coke) Dr. Pepper	5
(Coke) Fresca	12
(Pepsi) 7UP	6
(Pepsi) Dr. Pepper	3
(Pepsi) Fresca	10
7UP, (Dr. Pepper)	3
(7UP) Fresca	4
(Dr. Pepper) Fresca	7

	Analysis		
Coke:	+ 2 (versus Pepsi) + 8 (versus 7UP) + 5 (versus Dr. Pepper) + 12 (versus Fresca)	=	27
Pepsi	− 2 + 6 + 3 + 10	=	17
7UP	− 8 − 6 − 3 − 4	=	−13
Dr. Pepper	− 5 − 3 + 3 + 7	=	2
Fresca	− 12 − 10 − 4 − 7	=	−33

Emotions, Metaphors, and Conceptual Understanding

Of course, not all approaches are as cognitive/rational as implied by the previous discussion. Advances in cognitive science and neuroscience provide both methods and insights into behavior (e.g., Wells, 2003). One approach (Zaltman, 2003) summarizes what products mean to consumers in a collage of pictures, capturing emotional as well as cognitive processes. Such work is increasingly common in practice. Other authors go into considerable detail to demonstrate and interpret the use of emotion/feelings (e.g., O'Shaughnessy and O'Shaughnessy, 2003) and overall experience (e.g., Schmitt, 1999). Nonetheless, it is still useful to conduct some of the systematic analyses suggested in this chapter if for no other reason than to quantify the potential of different customer types revealed by more qualitative analysis.

Indeed, much effort is being expended to hear "the voice of the customer" (Baraba and Zaltman, 1990). Such efforts not only provide qualitative insight but also a means for communicating the findings of more standard approaches.

How They Respond to Marketing Programs

In addition to the product itself, sensitivity to and preference for prices (and means of payment), distribution and availability (including the effect of direct marketing), advertising, promotion, and service are fundamental aspects of a market. Moreover, sensitivity typically varies by customer and at least a segment-level analysis is usually called for. Methods for assessing sensitivity include:

1. *Expert judgment,* using the knowledge of managers, the salesforce, etc.
2. *Customer survey-based methods,* including both direct questioning (e.g., "How important is . . . ?") and more subtle approaches such as conjoint analysis.
3. *Experiments,* in both controlled settings (e.g., in shopping malls or specially designed stores or labs) and actual markets.
4. *Analyses of past data,* comparing results across markets, or where individual customer record data are available (e.g., scanner data) at the individual level. Such analysis often uses techniques such as regression analysis to predict sales as a function of mix elements or logit analysis (basically a type of regression) to assess the impact of mix elements on market share or individual choice probabilities.

Assessing sensitivity to elements of the marketing mix is a large, ongoing task. The output of this assessment has implications primarily for the tactical/programmatic elements of marketing (e.g., how much to spend on advertising). Since this assessment requires specialized data not readily available outside the company, we do not discuss mix assessment in detail here.

Will They Buy It (Again)?

A critical issue involves whether customers will purchase the product in the future, which for current users depends heavily on their satisfaction with past purchases.

Satisfaction

Perhaps the most obvious trend in business in the late 1980s and early 1990s was the religious zeal with which quality programs were promoted, especially in the United States. Providing quality in order to satisfy current customers and retain them in the future is a logical consequence of the basic principle of marketing, to create and maintain customers. So-called relationship marketing also stresses the long-term value of a customer where a single transaction (sale) is not the ultimate goal.

Quality is ultimately measured in terms of customer satisfaction. Further, satisfaction has a strong relative component to it. (Are customers of a certain product category more or less satisfied than those of a different but potentially substitutable one? Are customers of my company's product more or less satisfied than customers of a competitor's?)

Measurement of satisfaction has three key aspects:

1. Expectations of performance/quality.
2. Perceived performance/quality.
3. The gap between expectations and performance.

Much of the early work on satisfaction focused on the gap between expectations and performance, and a widely used scale called SERVQUAL (Parasuraman, Zeithaml, and Berry, 1988) was developed based on it. Subsequently, emphasis has also been placed on the direct impact of expectations and performance on satisfaction as well as the effect of expectations on perceived performance (Anderson and Sullivan, 1993; Boulding, Staelin, Kalra, and Zeithaml, 1992). Thus satisfaction is now typically modeled as a function of (1) expectations, (2) performance, and (3) the difference between expectations and performance (with "negative disconfirmation," when performance falls short of expectations, aka service failure, having a stronger impact than positive disconfirmation).

Of course, indirect measures of satisfaction abound, including word-of-mouth comments, complaints, and, perhaps most importantly, repeat purchase (or lack thereof). The basic reason for caring about satisfaction is that it leads to loyalty and customer retention. Hence, measures of intended or actual repeat purchasing provide a useful way to simultaneously measure satisfaction and its impact. Note that it is possible for customers to be satisfied but not repurchase due to, among other things, poor product supply, variety seeking or multiple sourcing, and large promotional deals. Similarly they may be unsatisfied but continue to purchase, for example, when dealing with a monopoly. Several authors have assembled satisfaction data across industries and demonstrated its link to retention (Fornell, 1992) and profitability (Anderson, Fornell, and Lehmann, 1994).

Intentions

Intentions are imprecise predictors of future purchase (as in he or she "had good intentions but . . ."). Still they provide early signs of future sales. In fact, surveys of customers (asking "Would you buy _____ ?" and/or "How much _____ will you buy?") are a staple input to sales forecasts, especially for industrial products, and we discuss them in greater detail in Chapter 7.

SEGMENTATION

Each customer is unique to some degree. As a consequence, mass marketing (one marketing program for all customers) is typically inefficient. Since it is time-consuming and not very profitable to develop a separate strategy for each customer, some grouping of customers into segments is often useful. Some categories have so few customers that each can be treated as a separate segment and analyzed separately. Examples are passenger aircraft, military products (e.g., battle tanks), and nuclear generators. In addition, there is a trend toward *mass customization,* or one-to-one marketing, which focuses on marketing products and services to individuals rather than to segments. Examples are Levis custom-tailored jeans for women and Internet-based services that the user can customize (Pine, Victor, and Boynton, 1993). Segmentation is a compromise between treating each customer as unique and assuming all customers are equal. Segmentation programs provide insights about different kinds of customer behavior and make marketing programs more efficient. As information technology has advanced and as small retail operators have always known, so-called one-to-one marketing has become a more viable approach, but segmentation is still the norm.

Desirable Criteria for Segments

What makes a good basis for segmentation? While there is no single way to say what is best (anyone suggesting there is probably doesn't understand the problem or is selling a particular method), the following six criteria provide a useful standard for evaluation:

1. *Sizable.* Segments must be of sufficient size in terms of potential sales. While some customers may be large enough to consider on their own, as a rule, billion-dollar companies don't care much about J. R. Smith at 1188 Maple Street, or all the people on Maple Street for that matter.

2. *Identifiable.* Segments should be identifiable so that they can be referred to by more pleasing titles than segment A and segment B (e.g., the 35-to-50 segment, the sports-minded, companies in New York). More importantly, the identity of the segments provides an aid to strategic and tactical decisions.

3. *Reachable.* It may be sufficient for strategic purposes to identify a segment. For purposes of planning the marketing mix (e.g., advertising), however, it is useful to be able to target efforts on a segment. A sports-minded segment tends to be reachable through specific media (e.g., *Sports Illustrated,* ESPN), whereas people who prefer the color blue, though identified, may be harder to reach efficiently (except by labels on blue towels, or by copy that employs the color blue).

4. *Respond differently.* Ideally, segments should respond differently to at least some of the elements of the offering. If all segments respond the same, then no specialized programs can be used. For example, some customers may be sensitive to advertising but not price, whereas others are concerned about price but unaffected by advertising, and still others care about a single attribute such as downtime. The sensitivity to changes in market offering forms a useful basis for both describing the overall market and defining segments. It also makes the "why they buy" part of the analysis particularly crucial.

5. *Coherent.* When interpreting a segment, it is implicitly assumed that all members are homogeneous. This is always violated to some extent. What is important is that the average member of a segment be reasonably close to the rest of the members. Hence, an important conceptual requirement of a segment is that the within-segment variation in behavior be smaller than between-segment variation. (This desired condition is

often operationalized as the basis for statistical tests for determining the number of segments.)

6. *Stable.* Since future plans are based on past data, segments (and hopefully but not necessarily the members of those segments) should be fairly stable over time.

Methods for Market Segmentation

Many of the methods developed for market segmentation, particularly by marketing academics, are highly technical and not in widespread use. In this section, we focus on three that are simple to apply and for which there is easy-to-use computer software: (1) cluster analysis, (2) tabular analysis, and (3) regression analysis. We also briefly describe a fourth approach, latent class analysis. We assume the product manager has customer data from surveys or other sources measuring both descriptive information and information about behavior toward the product in question. Again, we interpret the term *customer* broadly to imply that data should be collected from former and potential as well as current customers.

A useful approach to segmentation analyses relates information about the two kinds of segmentation variables: descriptors and behavioral variables. Neither type by itself is very useful. We know that approximately 50 percent of the population is men and 50 percent women. This information alone is not helpful because it does not indicate whether men or women have a greater propensity to buy our product. Alternatively, suppose we know that 20 percent of the population consists of heavy buyers, 40 percent of medium buyers, and 40 percent of light buyers. Again, this information is not very useful if we do not know who these buyers are (in terms of income, geography, and so forth); that is, we have no way to reach any of the groups. As a result, the methods on which we focus relate descriptor and behavioral data about customers in different ways to form market segments.

Cluster Analysis

One way to generate segments is to collect data about the descriptor and behavioral variables from a sample of customers and then form groups by means of cluster analysis. Cluster analysis examines the values of the variables for each respondent (from a sample of customers) and then groups respondents with similar values. Consider Figure 6.13. Each dot represents a combination of factors, say, age (X_1) and purchase quantity (X_2). In this case, three obvious clusters emerge. These clusters are appealing in that the members of each cluster are similar to one another and different from members of other clusters in terms of age and purchase quantity. A product manager would conclude from this analysis that the youngest customers purchase the most, oldest customers the second most, and middle-aged people are not interested. Cluster analysis programs are widely available in commercial computer software packages such as SAS and SPSS. (Unfortunately, such clear clusters rarely emerge.)

For example, a regional phone company employed cluster analysis to understand its residential customers. The company collected information on descriptors, attitudes, and behavior (usage was measured in dollars) and formed six segments based on clustering those households that "looked the same" based on the variables:

1. Low income/blue collar: "Fledglings."
2. Frugal/retired: "Thrifties."
3. Contented middle class: "Contenteds."

FIGURE 6.13 **Cluster Analysis Illustration**

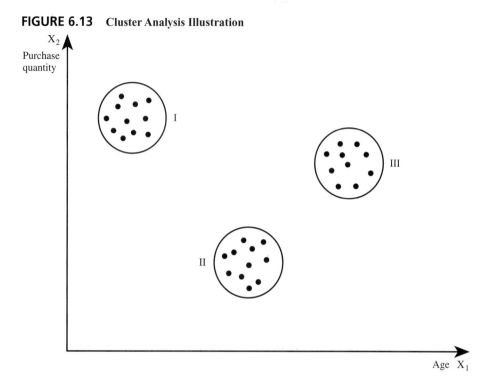

4. Aspiring middle-class status seekers: "Climbers."
5. Technology-driven strivers: "Techies."
6. Contented upper middle class: "Executives."

A more detailed profile of the segments is shown in Figure 6.14.

Mobil also applied cluster analysis to gasoline buyers to tailor different stations to neighborhoods with different profiles and needs (Sullivan, 1995). The company identified five segments of gasoline buyers:

1. Road warriors: higher-income, middle-aged men who drive 25,000 to 50,000 miles per year, buy premium gas with a credit card, and buy sandwiches and drinks from the convenience store (16 percent of buyers).
2. True blues: men and women with moderate to high incomes who are loyal to a brand and sometimes to a particular station (16 percent).
3. Generation F3 (fuel, food, and fast): upwardly mobile men and women, half under 25 years old, who are constantly on the go; drive and snack a lot (27 percent).
4. Homebodies: usually homemakers who shuttle their kids around during the day and buy gas from whatever station is along the way (21 percent).
5. Price shoppers: not loyal to a brand or station, rarely buy premium (20 percent).

Many gas companies have targeted the last group. However, Mobil emphasized better service and amenities to customers in the first two segments and was able to charge 2 cents more per gallon than competitors in some markets.

FIGURE 6.14 **Cluster Analysis: Phone Company Market Segmentation Scheme**

	Fledglings	Thrifties	Contenteds	Climbers	Techies	Executives
Mean age	37	51	44	43	38	40
Mean income	$26k	$27	$37k	$31k	$40k	$48k
Occupation	Blue collar	Retired/blue collar	Administrative/ professionals	Administrative/ sales	White collar	White collar
Education	14	12	14	16	18	18
Married	60%	72%	76%	65%	33%	72%
Children	44%	38%	51%	54%	75%	33%
Mobility	High	Low	Medium	Medium	High	Low
Home value	$70–85k	$60–80k	$70–85k	$60–80k	$80k+	$90k+
Dual income	Low	Medium	Medium	High	Highest	Medium
Number of phones	Low	Low	Medium	Medium	High	High
Type of phones	Basic/standard	Basic/standard	Medium mix	Medium mix	All types	All types
Monthly bill	Low	Low	Medium	Very high	Very high	Very high
Technology adoption	Late adopters	Laggards	Late adopter	Early adopter	Innovator	Early adopter
Purchase criteria	Value/money	Security	Convenience	Status	Environmental control	Quality
Application	Social interaction	Safety and protection	Social interacton	Social interaction	Personalized systems	Time saving

A third example highlights the use of a geodemographic system called PRIZM (Potential Rating Index by Zip Market), marketed by Claritas Corporation. PRIZM's basic analysis is performed on U.S. ZIP codes. Based on the 1990 census, the PRIZM system examined the means of a set of demographic variables for all of the nearly 40,000 U.S. ZIP codes. Using the demographic variables, the ZIP codes were then clustered into 62 different groups. These 62 groups are given catchy names based on the mean levels of the variables, such as "Norma Rae–ville," "Cashmere & Country Clubs," and "American Dreams." The final crucial step, of course, is to relate membership in the geodemographic clusters to purchasing of various products and services (the behavior variable).

One approach uses census data to break neighborhoods into 62 clusters. These are then both profiled and related to specific category usage. Figure 16.15 shows a sample of clusters as well as the number of "wild things members" who reside in each cluster. Figure 6.16 provides another example from Strategic Mapping, Inc.'s Cluster-PLUS 2000 for the disposable diaper market. This analysis developed 60 segments using data similar to that used by PRIZM. Figure 6.16 provides the number of households in each segment, the percentage of U.S. households in the segment (% Base), the estimated number of disposable diapers used in one day in the segment (Usage), the percentage of U.S. daily disposable diaper use (% Usage), the average number of diapers used per household in that segment (Avg. Use), and an index that is the ratio of % Usage ÷ % Base and gives some idea about the usage rate of that segment relative

FIGURE 6.15 PRIZM Profile Report by Social Group

PRIZM Clusters Grp	PRIZM Clusters #	PRIZM Clusters Nickname	Households Count	Households % Comp	Wild Things Members Count	Wild Things Members % Comp	Wild Things Members % Pen	Wild Things Members Index
S1	01	Blue Blood Estates	1,238,206	1.20	8,050	3.00	0.70	250
S1	02	Winner's Circle	2,334,557	2.26	12,112	4.51	0.50	200
S1	03	Executive Suites	1,285,478	1.25	3,950	1.47	0.30	118
S1	04	Pools & Patios	1,925,199	1.87	8,326	3.10	0.40	166
S1	05	Kids & Cul-de-Sacs	3,071,716	2.98	12,340	4.60	0.40	154
U1	06	Urban Gold Coast	584,328	0.57	1,271	0.47	0.20	84
U1	07	Money & Brains	1,129,180	1.09	4,768	1.78	0.40	162
U1	08	Young Literati	951,439	0.92	2,251	0.84	0.20	91
U1	09	American Dreams	1,506,981	1.46	4,068	1.52	0.30	104
U1	10	Bohemian Mix	1,516,622	1.47	1,961	0.73	0.10	50
C1	11	Second City Elite	1,948,380	1.89	8,934	3.33	0.50	176
C1	12	Upward Bound	1,871,373	1.81	6,459	2.41	0.30	133
C1	13	Gray Power	2,190,352	2.12	6,384	2.38	0.30	112
T1	14	Country Squires	1,441,183	1.40	8,012	2.99	0.60	214
T1	15	God's Country	2,772,759	2.69	12,126	4.52	0.40	168
T1	16	Big Fish, Small Pond	1,409,739	1.37	5,201	1.94	0.40	142
T1	17	Greenbelt Families	1,569,283	1.52	5,575	2.08	0.40	137
S2	18	Young Influentials	1,360,848	1.32	3,198	1.19	0.20	90
S2	19	New Empty Nests	2,246,499	2.18	8,020	2.99	0.40	137
S2	20	Boomers & Babies	1,047,008	1.01	2,865	1.07	0.30	105
S2	21	Suburban Sprawl	1,452,512	1.41	2,835	1.06	0.20	75
S2	22	Blue-Chip Blues	2,128,142	2.06	5,633	2.10	0.30	102
S3	23	Upstarts & Seniors	1,397,561	1.35	3,207	1.20	0.20	88
S3	24	New Beginnings	1,216,509	1.18	1,431	0.53	0.10	45
S3	25	Mobility Blues	1,516,782	1.47	2,329	0.87	0.20	59
S3	26	Gray Collars	2,002,749	1.94	4,262	1.59	0.20	82
U2	27	Urban Achievers	1,638,535	1.59	3,347	1.25	0.20	79
U2	28	Big City Blend	1,104,724	1.07	2,576	0.96	0.20	90
U2	29	Old Yankee Rows	1,368,473	1.33	1,868	0.70	0.10	52
U2	30	Mid-City Mix	1,120,686	1.09	997	0.37	0.10	34
U2	31	Latino America	1,308,097	1.27	1,460	0.54	0.10	43
C2	32	Middleburg Managers	1,863,879	1.81	5,655	2.11	0.30	117
C2	33	Boomtown Singles	939,270	0.91	1,530	0.57	0.20	63
C2	34	Starter Families	1,572,732	1.52	2,910	1.08	0.20	71
C2	35	Sunset City Blues	1,809,532	1.75	4,150	1.55	0.20	88
C2	36	Towns & Gowns	1,395,701	1.35	1,984	0.74	0.10	55
T2	37	New Homesteaders	1,739,259	1.69	5,623	2.10	0.30	124
T2	38	Middle America	2,358,753	2.29	6,413	2.39	0.30	105
T2	39	Red, White & Blues	1,850,258	1.79	4,549	1.70	0.20	95
T2	40	Military Quarters	437,797	0.42	1,180	0.44	0.30	104
R1	41	Big Sky Families	1,563,136	1.51	6,168	2.30	0.40	152
R1	42	New Eco-topia	919,723	0.89	3,482	1.30	0.40	146
R1	43	River City, USA	1,853,803	1.80	5,618	2.09	0.30	117
R1	44	Shotguns & Pickups	1,991,232	1.93	4,743	1.77	0.20	92
.	.	.						
.	.	.						
R3	62	Hard Scrabble	2,037,936	1.97	4,140	1.54	0.20	78
Total			103,192,375	100.00	268,337	100.00	0.30	100

Note: Not all 62 clusters are listed above. Copyright © 2000 by Claritas Inc.

FIGURE 6.16 ClusterPLUS 2000 Product Potential Report

Item: S1150 Number of Disposal Diapers Used in HH on Avg Day
Market: U.S.
Demographic Base: Households
Group Set: Clusters

Description	Base Count	% Base	Usage	% Usage	Avg Use	Index
Totals: U.S.	96,976,894	100.00	44,435,425	100.00	0.46	100
C54: Young Blacks with Kids	796,378	0.82	656,588	1.48	0.82	180
S45: Low Income Younger Blacks	794,712	0.82	623,785	1.40	0.78	171
C40: Younger Mobile Singles	1,551,509	1.60	1,072,648	2.41	0.69	151
U10: New Families, New Homes	1,794,370	1.85	1,208,366	2.72	0.67	147
S22: Young Families Dual Income	2,545,890	2.63	1,696,654	3.82	0.67	145
S07: High Inc, Young Families	1,582,765	1.63	1,026,304	2.31	0.65	142
T53: Low Income Ethnic Mix	2,408,568	2.48	1,532,643	3.45	0.64	139
U44: Young Black Families	1,097,859	1.13	694,500	1.56	0.63	138
U48: VYng BCollar Hispanic Fams	887,710	0.92	544,265	1.22	0.61	134
C57: Black Lowest Inc Fem Hd HH	1,102,997	1.14	670,655	1.51	0.61	133
S35: Avg Age/Inc Flue Collars	3,111,554	3.21	1,831,753	4.12	0.59	128
C27: Yng Avg Inc, Hispanics Apts	1,606,595	1.66	922,631	2.08	0.57	125
R26: Yngr Settld BCollar Fams	2,202,399	2.27	1,224,826	2.76	0.56	121
U30: Yngr Homeowners L Val Home	1,777,653	1.83	946,531	2.13	0.53	116
R47: Below Avg Inc Work Couples	3,295,708	3.40	1,732,530	3.90	0.53	115
U18: Yngr Hisp/Asian Homeowners	1,336,855	1.38	696,558	1.57	0.52	114
U23: Yngr Families Lo Val Homes	2,342,629	2.42	1,195,549	2.69	0.51	111
C52: Mid-Age Old Apts	1,111,753	1.15	562,416	1.27	0.51	110
T37: Below Avg Inc Blue Collar	2,726,056	2.81	1,343,793	3.02	0.49	108
R28: Settld Couples Lo Val Homes	5,259,551	5.42	2,547,153	5.73	0.48	106
U46: Above Avg Age Low Inc/Rent	1,281,639	1.32	597,541	1.34	0.47	102
C55: Low Inc Mobile Hispanics	1,725,271	1.78	800,347	1.80	0.46	101
R43: Below Avg Inc Blue Collars	3,991,458	4.12	1,802,116	4.06	0.45	99
S03: Well Educated Professional	1,972,176	2.03	877,473	1.97	0.44	97
S50: Very Young Hispanics	560,158	0.58	243,992	0.55	0.44	95
S12: High Inc Settled Families	2,208,503	2.28	960,122	2.16	0.43	95
U08: Hi Inc Urban Professionals	1,390,450	1.43	593,088	1.33	0.43	93
U04: Upscale Urban Couples	1,635,493	1.69	671,429	1.51	0.41	90
C29: Avg Age & Inc Few Kids	1,731,043	1.79	700,570	1.58	0.40	88
C25: Young WCollar Singles Apts	2,472,066	2.55	954,393	2.15	0.39	84
U31: Very Young Apt Dwellers	3,196,517	3.30	1,202,506	2.71	0.38	82
S05: Younger Affluent w/Kids	1,812,746	1.87	676,769	1.52	0.37	81
T19: Above Avg Age White Collar	2,141,629	2.21	793,668	1.79	0.37	81
U24: Avg Inc Apts Fewer Kids	1,728,593	1.78	611,974	1.38	0.35	77
U36: Avg Income Hispanics	1,098,132	1.13	380,782	0.86	0.35	76
U14: High Inc WCollar Apt/Condo	2,741,736	2.83	945,426	2.13	0.34	75
C34: Younger, Hispanics/Asians	2,031,995	2.10	699,422	1.57	0.34	75
S13: WCollar High Value Homes	1,539,106	1.59	519,431	1.17	0.34	74
S21: Suburban Married Couples	1,989,228	2.05	619,096	1.39	0.31	68
S38: Retired Homeowners	1,187,663	1.22	368,475	0.83	0.31	68
R06: Rural Affluents, New Homes	919,158	0.95	281,294	0.63	0.31	67
C15: Single Prof High Rent Apts	2,159,119	2.23	634,909	1.43	0.29	64
S09: Mature Couples Profs	1,139,545	1.18	321,101	0.72	0.28	61
R16: Younger Couples with Kids	2,509,079	2.59	681,097	1.53	0.27	59
S02: Mid-Age Affluent w/Kids	718,314	0.74	194,525	0.44	0.27	59
S01: Established Wealthy	543,731	0.56	135,722	0.31	0.25	54
C17: Prof & Retirees Apt/Condo	1,266,237	1.31	274,325	0.62	0.22	47
C11: Ctr City Affluent Few Kids	968,301	1.00	185,212	0.42	0.19	42
*G59: GQtrs: Military	45,649	0.05	29,083	0.07	0.64	39

*Results should be viewed with caution—insufficient sample size.   Note: Calculations are based on Source Market Usage.

Source: Strategic Mapping, Inc. based upon Simmons Market Research Bureau data.

to the size of the segment. While this index obviously is not the only criterion for choosing a target segment (e.g., no data by brand are shown), the information is a useful part of an overall picture of consumer behavior in the disposable diaper category.

Industrial customers can also be segmented on the basis of reactions to marketing mix variables (Rangan, Moriarty, and Swartz, 1992). For example, a large industrial-product company segmented its national accounts based on the trade-offs made between price and service to form four segments:

Programmed buyers: small customers that do not consider the product important and make routine purchases.

Relationship buyers: small buyers, loyal to the supplier, that pay low prices and obtain high service levels.

Transaction buyers: large buyers for which the product is important and that obtain price discounts, expect high service levels, and switch suppliers.

Bargain hunters: large buyers that get the lowest prices and the highest service.

Using electronic scanner data, product managers can segment by store. For example, Kraft can alter the mix of flavors of cream cheeses sold by supermarkets across different neighborhoods. Retailers also use this analysis. Target's store on Phoenix's eastern edge sells prayer candles (the area is heavily populated by Catholic Hispanics) but no child-toting bicycle trailers. The Target 15 minutes away in affluent Scottsdale sells the trailers but no portable heaters. Heaters can be found 20 minutes south in Mesa, which has a cooler climate (Patterson, 1995).

Of course segmentation is not a new topic. In February 1949 critic Russell Lynes produced a conceptual segmentation of American consumers that was both insightful and led to a Broadway show (Figure 6.17).

Tabular Analysis

The simplest analysis uses categorical variables based on customer responses. For example, surveys usually ask respondents to identify the range in which their incomes fall, such as "$20,000–$29,999," "$30,000–$39,999," and so on, or what their favorite brand is. Sometimes surveys ask questions that are continuously "scaled," for example, "How many times did you go to the movies last month?" The answers can then either be analyzed as given or be placed in categories (e.g., 0–2 times, 3–5 times, 6 or more).

As an illustration, consider the data in Figure 6.18. These data were taken from a survey of 1,004 users of cranberry sauce (DeBruicker, 1974). The descriptor variables, located in the leftmost column, are based on some prior analyses of data concerning attitudes toward cooking. These four categories are "convenience oriented," "enthusiastic cook," "disinterested," and "decorator." The descriptor variable is sometimes referred to as the *independent* variable. The behavioral categories, located across the top, are divided into three groups based on self-reported usage: heavy, medium, and light. This variable is referred to as the *dependent* variable. Entries in the table or cells indicate the number of consumers who simultaneously satisfy both a descriptor group and a behavioral group. In other words, 81 people were both heavy users of cranberry sauce and convenience oriented. The row sums and the column sums are called *marginals*.

FIGURE 6.17   Taste Segmentation

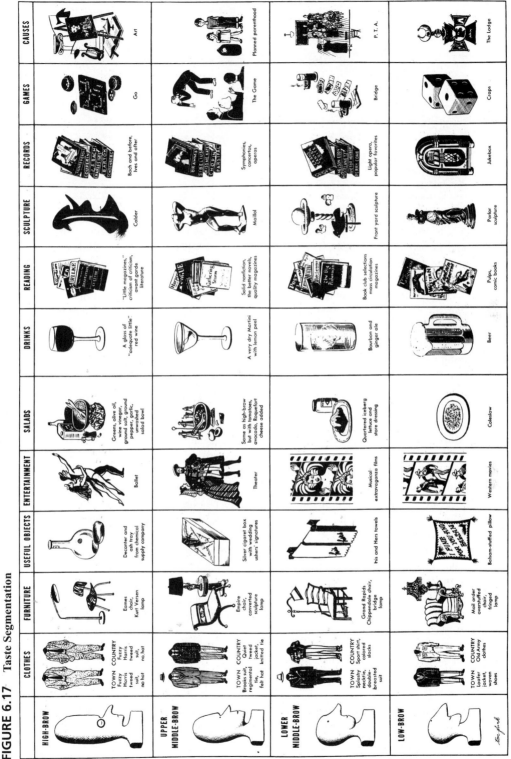

Source: *American Heritage* magazine, December 1999, p. 64.

FIGURE 6.18 Raw Data: Cranberry Sauce Usage

Cooking Attitude	Heavy Users	Medium Users	Light Users	Total (row marginal)
Convenience oriented	81	144	74	299
Enthusiastic cook	97	115	45	257
Disinterested	35	108	127	270
Decorator	45	96	37	178
Column total (marginal)	258	463	283	1,004

Product managers have many descriptor variables to choose from, not to mention several behavioral variables. An important task is to sift through the candidate descriptors to find some that are useful to describe the heavy, medium, and light buyers. Is cooking attitude such a variable?

Before analyzing the results in great detail, it is useful to determine if there is a *statistically significant* relationship between the independent variable, cooking attitude, and the dependent variable, usage quantity. The most common and simplest approach is a *chi-square* test. In this test, each cell based on the survey results (e.g., Figure 6.18) is compared to an *expected* cell size or the number of people that would be expected in that cell if attitude toward cooking were independent of usage quantity. The expected cell size can be calculated by multiplying the marginal for the row in which the cell is located by the marginal for the column in which the cell is located and dividing by the total sample size. For example, the expected cell size for the convenience-oriented–heavy-usage cell is $(299 \times 258)/1,004 = 77$. Then the chi-square value is determined by taking the sum over all cells of the (Observed − Expected)^2/Expected. For Figure 6.18, the chi-square value is 86. Combined with the number of degrees of freedom of the table (the number of rows minus 1 times the number of columns minus 1) and the significance level of the test, it is compared to a table of chi-square values found in any statistics book. In this example, the chi-square value of 86 with 6 degrees of freedom exceeds the table value of 12.6 at the 95 percent confidence level. Thus, there is a significant relationship between consumers' attitudes toward cooking and their reported cranberry sauce usage levels.[2]

A second step in the analysis is to better understand the nature of the relationship between the two variables[3] by calculating percentages. The two most common ways to calculate percentages are to divide each cell by its row marginal to obtain row

[2] The chi-square tests from different descriptor variables can be compared to see which of these the product manager should consider further in the segmentation analysis. This is more complicated than it sounds, as the chi-square values of tables with different numbers of rows and/or columns (degrees of freedom) cannot be directly compared. One alternative is to standardize all the tables to the same size. A second alternative is to use a computer program such as SAS that prints out the exact level of significance of each chi-square result and rank orders the descriptors by this number.

[3] Cross-tabular analysis can easily be extended to tables with more than one independent variable. The same logic for the chi-square test holds.

FIGURE 6.19 Cranberry Sauce Usage Percentages

Cooking Attitude	Heavy Users	Medium Users	Light Users
Convenience oriented:			
Row %	27%	48%	25%
Column %	31	31	26
Enthusiastic cook:			
Row %	38	45	18
Column %	38	25	16
Disinterested:			
Row %	13	40	47
Column %	14	23	45
Decorater:			
Row %	25	54	21
Column %	17	21	13

percentages or to divide each cell by its column marginal to obtain column percentages. Figure 6.19 shows the row and column percentages for the cranberry sauce data.

The row percentage indicates what percentage of the row category customers are in the column group. In the example, 27 percent of convenience-oriented consumers are heavy users. The column percentage indicates what percentage of the column category are in the row group. In the example, 31 percent of heavy users are convenience oriented. Of course, the product manager must interpret these two types of percentages differently.[4]

Assume the manager is interested in medium users because heavy users are saturated and light users probably cannot be convinced to consume more cranberry sauce. Which customers should the product manager pursue? One obvious group is convenience-oriented cooks, as this group has the largest number of medium buyers (31 percent) and is the second most "concentrated" (48 percent of them are medium users). Enthusiastic cooks might also be targeted, as they are the largest group of heavy users (38 percent).

Regression Analysis

Like cross-tabular analysis, regression analysis is used when the product manager can specify an explicit relationship between a dependent (behavioral) variable and one or more descriptor (independent) variables.[5] However, unlike cross-tabular analysis, regression theoretically assumes a continuously measured dependent variable. Using the cranberry sauce illustration, if the dependent variable is reported usage in number of cans rather than categories of consumption, then regression will be more appropriate.

Suppose that income and family size are key segmentation variables in addition to the four categories of cooking attitudes. Assume three categories of income (low, medium,

---

[4] To see this more clearly, consider the descriptor "men" and the behavioral variable "reads *Playboy* magazine." In this case, a large percentage of *Playboy* readers are men, but a small percentage of men are *Playboy* readers.

[5] We assume in this section that the reader has some working knowledge of regression analysis.

FIGURE 6.20 Cranberry Usage Data by Person

Person	Cranberry Sauce Usage (number of cans)	Cooking Attitudes				Income			Family Size
		CO	EC	DI	DEC	LO	MED	HI	
1	5	0	1	0	0	0	1	0	4
2	2	1	0	0	0	0	0	1	3
3	0	0	0	1	0	1	0	0	5
4	6	0	0	0	1	0	1	0	4
5	3	1	0	0	0	1	0	0	3

and high) are reported on the survey as well as the actual number of people in the family. We can then specify a *model* of the following form:

$$\text{Usage} = f(\text{CO, EC, DI, DE, LOWY, MEDY, HIGHY, FAMSIZE}),$$

where the dependent variable is the reported usage rate of cranberry sauce and the independent variables are the descriptors: convenience oriented, enthusiastic cooks, disinterested, decorator, low income, medium income, high income, and family size, respectively.

Generally, a person can be in only one category of cooking attitude and one category of income. In addition, assume these two variables cannot be represented by continuously measured numbers such as reported usage (number of cans) and family size (number of people). Therefore, we need to create *dummy variables* to represent the cooking attitude and income variables. These variables are simply 0 or 1, indicating membership in one of the categories.

Figure 6.20 provides hypothetical survey responses of five individuals. The first column contains values of the dependent variable, usage of cranberry sauce in number of cans. The next four columns represent cooking attitude. However, each respondent can have 1 in only one of the columns and must have a 1 in one of them because the categories are mutually exclusive and collectively exhaustive. The next three columns represent the income variable. Finally, family size is reported as the actual number.

Due to statistical (and logical) restrictions, if a dummy variable has n categories, only $n - 1$ are needed in the regression. Therefore, rewriting the regression model in equation form, we obtain

$$\text{Usage} = a + b\text{CO} + c\text{EC} + d\text{DI} + e\text{LOWY} + f\text{MEDY} + g\text{FAMSIZE},$$

where a to f are regression coefficients estimated using the data in Figure 6.20 and some computer software (e.g., Excel).

The coefficient g is interpreted in the usual way: For a one-person change in family size, usage changes by g units. For example, if g is positive, a one-person increase (decrease) in family size is predicted to increase (decrease) usage by g units. The coefficients b, c, d, e, and f, however, are interpreted differently. Recall that these variables are measured as either 0 or 1 depending on membership in that category. For each set of dummies, a coefficient is interpreted as the *contrast* from the omitted category. For example, b, the coefficient of the dummy variable "convenience oriented," is interpreted as the estimated difference in cranberry sauce usage between a person who is convenience oriented versus one who is a decorator (the omitted category). Likewise, f, the coefficient of "medium income," is the estimated difference in usage between a person who reports having medium income versus one who has high income. (It is irrelevant which category is dropped, as the estimated differences would be the same even though the coefficients themselves would change.)

Suppose we obtained the following results in which all coefficients are statistically significant:

$$\text{Usage} = 10.3 + 2.1 \times \text{CO} - 1.9 \times \text{EC} - 3.5 \times \text{DI}$$
$$- 2.5 \times \text{LOWY} - 1.1 \times \text{MEDY} + 0.9 \times \text{FAMSIZE}.$$

What would be the market segmentation implications? In this case, convenience-oriented cooks have the highest usage rate: 2.1 units more, on average, than the omitted category, decorators. Both of the other categories of cooking attitude use less than decorators, as the negative signs on their coefficients indicate. In terms of income, high-income consumers are estimated to have the highest usage rate (signs on the other income variables are negative). Finally, for every one-person increase in family size, reported usage increases an estimated .9 units (i.e., cans). Thus, the profile of the largest cranberry sauce users is (hypothetically) high-income, convenience-oriented cooks with large families.

One statistic produced with regression is R^2, which measures the degree to which the equation "fits" the data on a 0 to 1 scale, with 1 being a perfect fit. Unfortunately, for frequently purchased products, these kinds of equations tend to have low R^2 values. However, despite the poor fits, these regressions often point to useful bases for segmentation. Figure 6.21 shows that large and significant differences in product consumption can exist even when the R^2 values are low.

Regression approaches also povide information about the response to marketing mix variables. For example, Bolton and Myers (2003) found that price sensitivity depends on various service characteristics (e.g., quality, support). More important, segments in terms of price responsiveness exist across countries and continents, suggesting that segmentation schemes based on responsiveness rather than country boundaries are often useful for global marketing (TerHofstede, Steenkamp, and Wedel, 1999).

Latent Class Analysis

The previous methods begin with individual customers and then aggregate them. Latent class methods, by contrast, begin with the market as a whole and then determine what segmentation pattern best trades off parsimony (few segments) and the ability to explain behavior. This relatively recent approach (see Appendix 6B) is intriguing but requires considerable sophistication, and so it is not yet widely employed. (What this means is you can either (1) ignore it, (2) use it for competitive advantage, or (3) drop the term in conversation to either impress or mystify others.)

A simple kind of latent structure analysis focuses on brand switching data. However, rather than estimating share at the individual level and then grouping similar individuals together (e.g., via cluster analysis), this method simply derives segment-level probabilities and market shares. Grover and Srinivasan (1987) provide an example of such segmentation for the instant coffee market. Subjects who always bought the same brand were classified as loyals while the rest (switchers) were then broken into various segments. Figure 6.22 shows the four-segment solution, which appeared to be the best

FIGURE 6.21 Light and Heavy Buyers by Mean Purchase Rates for Different Socioeconomic Cells

R^2	Product	Description		Mean Consumption Rate Ranges		Ratio of Highest to Lowest Rate
		Light Buyers	Heavy Buyers	Light Buyers	Heavy Buyers	
.08	Catsup	Unmarried or married over age 50 without children	Under 50, three or more children	.74–1.82	2.73–5.79	7.8
.07	Frozen orange juice	Under 35 or over 65, income less than $10,000, not college grads, two or less children	College grads, income over $10,000, between 35 and 65	1.12–2.24	3.53–9.00	8.0
.04	Pancake mix	Some college, two or less children	Three or more children, high school or less education	.48–.52	1.10–1.51	3.3
.08	Candy bars	Under 35, no children	35 or over, three or more children	1.01–4.31	6.65–22.29	21.9
.08	Cake mix	Not married or under 35, no children, income under $10,000, TV less than 3½ hours	35 or over, three or more children, income over $10,000	.55–1.10	2.22–3.80	6.9
.09	Beer	Under 25 or over 50, college education, nonprofessional, TV less than 2 hours	Between 25 and 50, not college graduate, TV more than 3½ hours	0–12.33	17.26–40.30	—
.02	Cream shampoo	Income less than $8,000, at least some college, less than five children	Income $10,000 or over with high school or less education	.16–.35	.44–.87	5.5
.06	Hair spray	Over 65, under $8,000 income	Under 65, over $10,000 income, not college graduate	0–.41	.52–1.68	—
.09	Toothpaste	Over 50, less than three children, income less than $8,000	Under 50, three or more children, over $10,000 income	1.41–2.01	2.22–4.39	3.1
.03	Mouthwash	Under 35 or over 65, less than $8,000 income, some college	Between 35 and 65, income over $8,000, high school or less education	.46–.85	.98–1.17	2.5

Source: Frank Bass, Douglas Tigert, and Ronald Lonsdale, "Market Segmentation—Group versus Individual Behavior," Reprinted from *Journal of Marketing Research 5*, published by the American Marketing Association, (August 1968), p. 267.

FIGURE 6.22 Four-Segment Solution for the Instant-Coffee Market

Brand[a]	Caffeine[b]	Process[c]	Manufacturer[d]	Aggregate Market Share (MS)	Loyal Segment Size	Switching Segments			
						1	2	3	4
						.19*	.22*	.18*	.06*
							Size (total = .65)		
							.22*	.18*	.06*
						Within-Segment Market Shares (ρ)[e]			
HP	D	R	PG	.13	.05*	.09*	.20*	.13*	.08
TC	C	FD	N	.10	.04*	.07	.03	.18*	.03
TC	D	FD	N	.07	.01	[f]	—	.32*	.12*
FL	C	R	PG	.12	.04*	.20*	.16*	.04*	—
MH	C	R	GF	.21	.08*	.42*	.15*	.07*	.06
S	D	R	GF	.16	.07*	.04*	.22*	.11*	.15*
S	D	FD	GF	.03	.01*	—	.05*	.03*	—
MX	C	FD	GF	.04	.01*	.04*	.03*	.04*	—
N	C	R	N	.06	.01*	.14*	—	—	.27*
N	D	R	N	.03	.01	—	.07*	—	.27*
B	D	FD	GF	.05	.02*	—	.09*	.08*	.02
Total				1.00	.35	1.00	1.00	1.00	1.00

*Parameter estimate/standard error > 2.

[a]Brand names: HP = High Point; TC = Taster's Choice, FL = Folgers, MH = Maxwell House, S = Sanka, MX = Maxim, N = Nescafé, B = Brim.

[b]D = decaffeinated, C = caffeinated.

[c]FD = freeze dried, R = regular (spray dried).

[d]PG = Proctor & Gamble, GF = General Foods, N = Nestlé.

[e]Underlined numbers denote the two largest choice probabilities within the segment.

[f]Probabilities constrained to zero for model identification.

Source: Rajiv Grover and V. Srinivasan, "A Simultaneous Approach to Market Segmentation and Market Structuring," *Journal of Marketing Research 24* (May 1987), p. 147.

FIGURE 6.23 Preference Segmentation and Price Sensitivity

	Loyal Segments				Switching Segments*				
	A	B	C	P	1	2	3	4	5
Choice probabilities									
A	1				.790	.219	.152	.095	.192
B		1			.089	.646	.259	.238	.332
C			1		.069	.092	.520	301	.133
P				1	.052	.043	.065	.367	.343
Segment size (% of all households)									
	19.0	5.8	3.9	2.7	9.3	9.7	25.8	16.4	7.4
Price sensitivity									
β					−1.87	−1.44	−3.07	−5.42	.37†

*For switching segments 1 through 4, purchase probabilities greater than .10 are underlined.
†Price coefficient statistically *insignificant* at the .05 level.

Source: Wagner A. Kamakura and Gary J. Russell, "A Probabilistic Choice Model for Market Segmentation and Elasticity Structure," *Journal of Marketing Research 26* (November 1989), p. 385.

compromise between explanation and parsimony. The results suggest very small hard-core loyal segments (which in total account for 35 percent of the market) and four switching segments with tendencies to favor two or more brands.

Kamakura and Russell (1989) extend this approach to include price sensitivity. They analyze 78 weeks of purchases of a refrigerated (once opened) food product with a 10-week average purchase cycle. The four brands (A, B, C, P) were average priced at $4.29, $3.54, $3.38, and $3.09 and had choice shares of 35.8, 27.8, 23.8, and 12.6 percent, respectively. The resulting segments appear in Figure 6.23. Interestingly, these results also suggest that about one-third (31.4 percent) of the customers are hard-core loyal. In addition, the segments differ in terms of price sensitivity. Segments 1 and 2 (which account for 19 percent of the market) appear to be relatively insensitive to price and fairly brand loyal. By contrast, segments 3 and 4 (which account for 42.2 percent of the market) are quite price sensitive and tend to spread purchases across several brands. Segment 5 appears not to respond to price or be very brand loyal; perhaps this small (7.4 percent) segment represents customers for whom the product is low involvement and who simply pick a brand by reaching for the most readily available one.

Judgment-Based Segmentation

There is a strong tendency to derive segments by examining data. Still, some of the most useful segmentation schemes are simply descriptors on bases selected by managers, such as customer usage rate (heavy users, light users, nonusers) or product preference. While these are not elegant and are unlikely to suggest a new approach, they are often more useful than so-called natural clusters because the segments are readily identifiable and reachable and obviously have responded differently to the product offering. In fact, it is always advisable to use such a segmentation strategy as at least a basis for comparison with the results of more "data mining" oriented approaches.

No simple way exists to tell how to get the best segmentation scheme. In that respect it's a lot like art—you can tell whether you like it or not but never prove it's the best. The problem when segmenting based on intuition, of course, is that given faulty memory and perceptions, it may produce segments for a market that exists only in the mind of a manager.

Summary

The approaches discussed here can be applied to any product, consumer or industrial, low-tech or high-tech, as long as the required data are available. Many other methods have been used. Two methods discussed earlier in this chapter, conjoint analysis and multi-dimensional scaling, are good examples. In addition, other multivariate techniques (e.g., logit/probit, Automatic Interaction Detector, and CHAID, as well as Bayesian methods) can be applied to obtain information about existing market segments.

ILLUSTRATIONS

Energy Bars

Who the Customers Are

According to SPIN (A.C. Nielsen Consumer Reports),

> 63.7 percent of volume is from households with greater than $40,000 income.
>
> 32.4 percent of volume is from households with greater than $60,000 income.
>
> 72.8 percent of volume is from households with no kids.
>
> 65.8 percent of volume is from households where the Head has some college education.
>
> 39.4 percent of volume is from households with the Head under 35 years old.

Eaten by about 1 in 5 people (Figure 6.24).

Customer segments:

> "Hard-core athletes": the original consumer target, who use energy bars, gels, and other portable food products to maintain a high level of strenuous activity.
>
> "Musclemen": individuals trying to maximize their muscle mass through use of energy bars, protein powders, and other dietary supplements.
>
> "Dieters": individuals using energy bars as a meal replacement or snack alternative in an effort to lose or maintain weight.
>
> "Health purists": individuals who insist on the nutritional benefits of organic and all-natural foods.
>
> "Health conscious and on-the-go": individuals with busy lifestyles who seek a healthier alternative to traditionally available fast foods.
>
> "Sports enthusiasts": active individuals seeking sustained energy for less strenuous activity than hard-core athletes.

FIGURE 6.24 **Percent Who Have Eaten Energy Bars in the Last Six Months**

Female	20%
Male	18%
65 and over	12%
55–64	10%
45–54	20%
36–44	21%
25–34	21%
18–24	27%

Source: Mintel International Group's March 2002 Survey of 2,026 Adults

"Specialty segments": such as women and minorities, who desire specific nutritional formulations geared to their unique health requirements.

"Nutrition-seeking families": households that actively seek to promote healthier eating habits among all members of the family, both adults and children.

Overall
Relatively educated, well-off, all ages and genders.

What They Buy
Convenience

Taste

Texture

Health benefits

Performance/energy

Hunger satisfaction

Price (expect to pay $1.00 to $1.50 per bar)

Packaging/buy in bulk

Availability

What Use For
Meal replacements

Snacks

Athletic energy booster

Where They Buy
Health food stores

Outdoor retailers (e.g., REI)

Grocery stores

Drug stores

Convenience stores

Mass merchandizers

Club stores

Odwalla Customers

Tried Odwalla juice first.

Prefer: lighter, fruiter flavors and chewier, whole-grain texture.

Taste matters more than performance.

Personal Digital Assistants

Who the Customers Are

In 2000, the customers for PDAs were primarily upscale mobile professionals. Users were predominantly male, analytical and quantitative in nature, well educated, and over 21 years of age.

Mobile professionals, the key target market, can be segmented as in Figure 6.25. These labels do not help the product manager locate these people, of course. However,

FIGURE 6.25 PDA Market Segments

Segment	Size	Characteristics	Distinctive Attribute
Wide Area Travelers:			
Globetrotters	10%	Age 45–54; mostly male Employed in senior positions	Innovators, have modems installed in their portable PCs
Road Warriors	20%	Mostly in corporate management and sales, property management and real estate	High cellular phone usage Overall compuer usage lower than for other mobile pros
Corporate Wanderers	12%	Travel less than Globetrotters or Road Warriors; spend most time visiting employees within their own companies	Employ portable PCs least Heaviest fax users (on PCs) High e-mail users Longest owners of cellular phones
Local Area Travelers:			
Collaborators	8%	Age 25–44 Well-educated young professionals, tend to hold advanced degrees Team leaders, project managers	Innovators High use of pagers (20% of segment) Not very mobile but need mobile products
Corridor Cruisers	15%	Similar profile to Collaborators	Not as likely to adopt new products as Collaborators
Hermits	8%	Least mobile Youngest segment (many under 35) Seldom work with others Mostly finance and telemarketing	Heavy e-mail users Virtually all are PC users but not portable users
Solo Practitioners	16%	Like Hermits but older Diverse collection of technical professionals in small to medium-size companies	Typically connect to corporate network when traveling Highest connect times of any group
Small-Site Bosses	11%	Run small businesses	Highest portable PC purchase intention in next 12 months; shifting to portable PC as primary computer

early adopters of PDAs have a high incidence of purchasing other high-tech consumer products such as personal and laptop computers, home fax machines, cellular phones, and so forth.

What They Buy

Buyers and potential buyers of PDAs seek the following features in decreasing order of importance:

Small size/light weight.

PC connectivity.

E-mail communications capability.

Phone/address book.

Appointment book/calendar/alarm.

One-way paging.

PDAs were initially valued primarily as organizers and less as communications devices by current users (Figure 6.26). This implies that two benefit segments are emerging: (1) those who value PDAs solely for their organizer features and (2) a smaller but growing group who value them for communications. According to a *Forrester Brief,* 63 percent of buyers use PDAs both at home and at work, 31 percent only for personal use, and 6 percent solely for work. As communications capabilities improve, this latter group will grow. At the present time, demand drops to essentially zero when the price of a PDA exceeds $500 and appears to increase steeply as it drops below $500. Also, the Palm operating system still has a greater share than Windows CE.

How They Buy

Advertising and marketing have not been key influencers in PDA purchase decisions to this point. Current users sought out the devices themselves. Again, this is not unusual for a product at the early stage of the product life cycle. Later users, however, will rely more on information-based advertising and recommendations from colleagues and friends.

FIGURE 6.26 **Important PDA Functions**

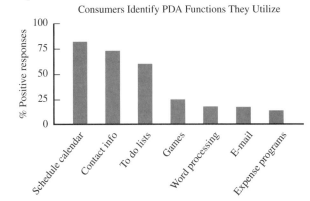

Source: Forrester Research Inc., July 1999.

Where They Buy

Customers buy lower-priced, low-feature devices from consumer electronics stores and office supply superstores (e.g., Office Max, Office Depot). Higher-end PDAs are purchased from computer stores or through mail order or via the Internet.

Motorcycles

For those readers who find ice cream and PDAs too tame to be interesting, Figures 6.27 and 6.28 show a segmentation scheme for motorcycle riders.

FIGURE 6.27 **Motorcycle Segment Lifestyle Descriptors**

Segment	Description
Tour Gliders (13.8%)	I like long-distance touring bikes. I use my bike for touring. My bike is made more for comfort than for speed. I love to ride long distances . . . to me, 500 miles is a short trip. I like bikes with plastic farings and engine covers.
Dream Riders (39.8%)	Most of the time, my motorcycle is just parked. I like wearing a helmet when I ride. I don't know many other people that ride motorcycles. My bike is pretty much stock. I mainly use my bike for short trips around town.
Hard Core (9.7%)	Some people would call me and my friends "outlaws." I have spent lots on speed modifications for my bike. Sometimes I feel like an "outlaw." Some people would call me a "dirty biker." I think it's true that "real men wear black."
Hog Heaven (8.7%)	When I'm on my bike, people seem to be admiring me. I really believe that cars are confining, like a "cage." Women admire my motorcycle. When I ride I feel like an Old Wild West cowboy. I feel close to other motorcyclists I see on the road.
Zen Riders (20.3%)	I like dirt bikes. When I'm on my bike, people seem to be admiring me. I like the attention I get when I'm on my bike. Most of the time, my motorcycle is just parked. I get excited about motocross or scrambling.
Live to Ride (7.6%)	I love to ride long distances . . . to me, 500 miles is a short trip. Motorcycles are a total lifestyle to me. Riding, to me, is often a magical experience. It's true that "I live to ride and ride to live." My bike is everything to me.

Source: William R. Swinyard, "The Hard Core and Zen Riders of Harley Davidson: A Market-Driven Segmentation Analysis," *Journal of Targeting, Measurement and Analysis for Marketing* 4, June 1996, pp. 349–50.

FIGURE 6.28 Summary of Demographic and Motorcycle Ownership Characteristics, by Segment

	Tour Gliders	Dream Riders	Hard Core	Hog Heaven	Zen Riders	Live to Ride
Demographics						
Average owner age	42.6	42.9	36.2	39.2	36.9	36.6
Sex male	93.8%	95.1%	93.5%	85.4%	94.7%	91.7%
Married	60.0%	68.5%	51.1%	56.1%	75.0%	58.3%
Number of children at home	1.3	1.2	1.0	1.2	1.2	1.2
Education: college graduate	15.4%	24.7%	8.7%	7.3%	19.8%	25.0%
Income of $50,000 and over . . .						
Personal	29.7%	30.2%	4.4%	31.7%	26.3%	25.0%
Household	50.8%	52.0%	26.6%	41.0%	55.4%	55.5%
Average income:						
Personal	$40,438	$40,087	$27,389	$34,744	$38,816	$33,667
Household	$46,563	$46,500	$34,944	$40,397	$47,435	$44,222
Occupation: Professional/ managerial	21.5%	30.1%	0.0%	26.8%	19.8%	29.4%
Motorcycle Ownership						
Motorcycle is 1991 or newer	24.6%	30.7%	7.3%	22.0%	28.7%	15.2%
Owned motorcycle under 2 years	16.7%	22.7%	10.3%	35.5%	30.4%	30.3%
Brought motorcycle new	40.0%	50.0%	15.2%	45.0%	33.0%	55.9%
Model year of principal Harley	1985.9	1985.8	1980.5	1986.2	1983.6	1985.7
This is their first motorcycle	1.5%	9.0%	15.9%	19.5%	9.4%	2.8%
No. of motorcycles owned	9.06	5.34	6.3	6.82	5.7	9.77
No. of Harleys owned	4.74	1.63	2.85	2.13	1.44	2.12
Money spent on motorcycle for . . .						
Purchase of motorcycle	$9,048	$7,460	$5,082	$6,631	$6,966	$8,976
Parts/accessories this year	$ 690	$ 322	$1,260	$ 321	$ 767	$ 860
Parts/accessories in total	$1,571	$1,426	$3,233	$2,419	$1,734	$2,483
Estimated value of motorcycle today	$10,066	$8,414	$8,062	$8,591	$8,827	$10,342
Riding per year . . .						
Number of miles	7351	3675	7099	5051	4169	9662
Number of days	188	109	187	148	112	214
Number years riding	24.1	20.2	16.5	16.9	18	17.7
Type of motorcycle they ride:						
Touring	39.0%	16.4%	0.0%	7.9%	12.6%	31.3%
Full Dress	18.6%	18.6%	11.4%	10.5%	14.9%	18.9%
Cruiser	23.8%	26.0%	36.4%	29.0%	28.7%	31.3%
Sportster	5.1%	30.5%	29.5%	52.6%	35.6%	0.0%
Other type	13.6%	8.5%	22.7%	0.0%	8.0%	18.8%

Source: William R. Swinyard, "The Hard Core and Zen Riders of Harley Davidson: A Market-Driven Segmentation Analysis," *Journal of Targeting, Measurement and Analysis for Marketing* 4, June 1996, p. 351.

SUMMARY

All phases of customer analysis provide potentially useful information. However, a tremendous amount of this information can be summarized in a figure that includes segments across the top and the various aspects of customer analysis as the rows (Figure 6.29). The process of arriving at a useful version of Figure 6.29 is likely to be messy, imprecise, and involve trial and error. The best approach is to try several different schemes for defining segments (e.g., versions of who or why, possibly in combination). The choice of which segmentation scheme to use often depends on the insight gained and the potential for the segmentation scheme to lead to useful strategies (e.g., selecting which segments to serve) and efficient program (e.g., advertising, distribution) determination.

In analyzing customers, it is both natural and useful to look at history. Nonetheless, the reason for doing so is not to be a good historian, but to be a good forecaster. Put differently, one needs to make judgments about what might cause behavior to change (including both your actions and outside influences such as culture, competition, economic conditions, and regulation, as well as natural aging of customers). In addition, some assessment is needed of the likelihood these causal influences will in fact change. Finally, the impact of likely changes on customer behavior, and consequently on sales, must be analyzed. Then and only then will customer analysis be useful for deciding what to do in the future and what trends to monitor most closely.

FIGURE 6.29   **Summarizing Customer Analysis**

	Segment			
	A	B	C	D
Descriptors				
Who they are				
What they buy				
Where they buy				
When they buy				
How they buy				
Why they buy				
How they respond to marketing				
Will they buy in the future?				
Customer Relationship Stage				
Unaware				
Aware				
Accepting (considering)				
Attracted (like it)				
Active (current customers)				
Advocating (recommend it)				
Lifetime Value				

References

Aaker David A. (1996) *Building Strong Brands.* New York: The Free Press.

Aaker, David A. (1991) *Managing Brand Equity.* New York: The Free Press.

Anderson, Eugene, Claes Fornell, and Donald R. Lehmann (1994) "Customer Satisfaction, Market Share, and Profitability," *Journal of Marketing* 58, July, 53–66.

Anderson, Eugene W. and Mary W. Sullivan (1993) "The Antecedents and Consequences of Customer Satisfaction for Firms," *Marketing Science* 12, Spring, 125–43.

Baraba, Vincent P., and Gerald Zaltman (1990) *Hearing the Voice of the Market.* Boston, MA: Harvard Business School Press.

Bettman, James R. (1979) *An Information Processing Theory of Consumer Choice.* Reading, MA: Addison-Wesley.

Bolton, Ruth N., and Matthew B. Myers (2003) "Price-Based Global Market Segmentation for Services," *Journal of Marketing* 67, July, 108–28.

Boulding, William, Richard Staelin, Ajay Kalra, and Valerie A. Zeithaml (1992) "Conceptualizing and Testing a Dynamic Process Model of Service Quality." Cambridge, MA: Marketing Science Institute Working Paper, 92–127.

Corfman, Kim P., Donald R. Lehmann, and Sundar Narayanan (1991) "The Role of Consumer Values in the Utility and Ownership of Durables," *Journal of Retailing,* Summer, 184–204.

DeBruicker, F. Steward (1974) "Ocean Spray Cranberries (A)" and "Ocean Spray Cranberries (B)," Harvard Business School case studies 9-575-039 and 9-575-040.

Fornell, Claes (1992) "A National Customer Satisfaction Barometer: The Swedish Experience," *Journal of Marketing* 56, January, 6–21.

Green, Paul E., and Yoram Wind (1975) "New Way to Measure Consumers' Judgments," *Harvard Business Review,* July–August, 107–17.

Grover, Rajiv, and V. Srinivasan (1987) "A Simultaneous Approach to Market Segmentation and Market Structuring," *Journal of Marketing Research,* 24, May, 139–52.

Howard, John A. (1989) *Consumer Behavior in Marketing Strategy.* Englewood Cliffs, NJ: Prentice Hall.

Johnston, Wesley J. and Jeffrey E. Lewin (1996) "Organizational Buying Behavior: Toward an Integrative Framework," *Journal of Business Research* 35, 1–15.

Kahle, Lynn P., Sharon E. Beatty, and Pamela Homer (1986) "Alternative Measurement Approaches to Customer Values: The List of Values (LOV) and Values and Life Styles (VALS)," *Journal of Consumer Research,* December, 405–9.

Kamakura, Wagner A., and Gary J. Russell (1989) "A Probabilistic Choice Model for Market Segmentation and Elasticity Structure," *Journal of Marketing Research* 26, November, 379–90.

Keller, Kevin L. (2002) *Strategic Brand Management,* 2nd ed. Upper Saddle River, NJ: Prentice Hall.

Lehmann, Donald R., Sunil Gupta, and Joel Steckel (1998) *Marketing Research.* Boston: Addison-Wesley.

Lovelock, Christopher H. (1979) "Federal Express (B)," HBS Case Services, case # 9-579-040, Harvard Business School, Boston, MA 02163.

Lynes, Russell (1949) "Highbrow, Lowbrow, Middlebrow," February, *Harper's.*

McAlexander, James H., John W. Schouten, and Harold F. Koenig (2002) "Building Brand Community," *Journal of Marketing* 66, January, 38–54.

Martin, Justin (1994) "Make Them Drink Beer," *FORECAST,* July–August, 34–40.

Moore, Elizabeth S., William L. Wilkie, and Richard J. Lutz (2002) "Passing the Torch: Intergenerational Influences as a Source of Brand Equity," *Journal of Marketing* 66, April, 17–37.

Muniz, Albert M., Jr., and Thomas C. O'Guinn (2001) "Brand Community," *Journal of Consumer Research* 27, March, 412–32.

O'Shaughnessy, John, and Nicholas Jackson O'Shaughnessy (2003) *The Marketing Power of Emotion.* New York: Oxford University Press.

Parasuraman, A., Valerie A. Zeithaml, and Leonard L. Berry (1988) "SERVQUAL: A Multiple-Item Scale for Measuring Consumer Perceptions of Service Quality," *Journal of Retailing* 64, Spring, 12–37.

Patterson, Gregory A. (1995) "Target 'Micromarkets' Its Way to Success: No 2 Stores Are Alike," *The Wall Street Journal,* May 31, A1.

Pessemier, Edgar A. (1963) *Experimental Methods of Analyzing Demand for Branded Consumer Goods with Applications to Problems in Marketing Strategy,* Bulletin #39, Pullman, WA: Washington State University Bureau of Economic and Business Research, June.

Pine, B. Joseph II, Bart Victor, and Andrew C. Boynton (1993) "Making Mass Customization Work," *Harvard Business Review,* September–October, 108–19.

Rangan, Kasturi, Rowland R. Moriarty, and Gordon S. Swartz (1992) "Segmenting Customers in Mature Industrial Markets," *Journal of Marketing,* October, 72–82.

Schmitt, Bernd (1999) *Experimental Marketing.* New York: The Free Press.

Sullivan, Allanna (1995) "Mobil Bets Drivers Pick Cappuccino over Low Prices," *The Wall Street Journal,* January 30, B1.

TerHofstede, Frankel, J. B. Steenkamp, and Michel Wedel (1999) "International Market Segmentation Based on Consumer-Product Relations," *Journal of Marketing Research* 36, February, 1–17.

Urban, Glen L., and Eric von Hippel (1988) "Lead User Analyses for the Development of New Industrial Products," *Management Science,* May, 569–82.

Wells, Melanie (2003) "In Search of the Buy Button," *Forbes* 172, September 1, 62–70.

Wilkie, William L. (1990) *Consumer Behavior,* 2d ed. New York: John Wiley & Sons.

Zaltman, Gerald (2003) *How Customers Think.* Boston, MA: Harvard Business School Press.

Appendix 6A   Economic Value to the Customer (EVC)

BASIC CONCEPT

The economic value to the customer is the net dollar value (savings) from using a particular product (often a new one) instead of a relevant substitute (often the one currently used). That is, it is the difference in the total direct cost of using two competing products. Total cost is measured either for a particular time period (e.g., month, year) or activity (job). Since it is frequently used as a means to set price for a new product, it is often computed using the price of the comparison/old product as part of its cost but no price for the new product. At the most general level, the calculation looks like Figure 6A.1 where the difference in Total Costs ($TC_A - TC_N$) is the economic (cash) value of switching from the old to the new product for the time period or activity level used as a basis of calculation. (For example, if the monthly EVC is $10,000, then the yearly savings is $120,000; similarly, if the EVC is $5,000 per job and the firm completes 40 jobs per year, the yearly EVC is $200,000.)

EXAMPLE

A new synthetic motor oil is about to be introduced with the primary benefit that it needs to be changed less frequently, specifically once every two years regardless of mileage. Assume current oils need to be changed every 6,000 miles at a cost of $30 per change (oil at a dollar a quart or a total of $5, labor $20, disposal of oil $5) for an average car. What is the EVC of the new oil to a driver who drives 15,000 miles per year?

This is a straightforward problem where it is relatively easy to get the EVC for a given mileage. First set up Figure 6A.2 similar to Figure 6A.1. We use a two-year basis because it makes the calculation easy. The key distinction between the old and the new is the number of oil changes needed in the two year period: 1 for the new product and $(2)(15,000/6,000) = 5$ for the old product.

Therefore the economic value (benefit) to using the new product versus the old is $150 − $25 = $125 over the two-year period. Converting this to a per-quart basis means the value of the new oil is $125/5 = $25 per quart.

FIGURE 6A.1   Total Cost Comparison

	(New) Product N	Current (Old) Product A	EVC for New Product
Product (part) price	?	P_A	
Labor costs			
Related (e.g., parts) costs			
TOTAL COST	TC_N	TC_A	$TC_A - TC_N$

FIGURE 6A.2 Total Cost: Two Years

	New Synthetic Oil	Old Oil
Product price	?	5 changes × $5/change = $25
Labor costs	1 change × $20 = $20	5 changes × $20/change = $100
Other costs (oil disposal)	$5	5 change × $5 = $25
TOTAL	$25	$150

IMPLICATIONS

One of the major implications of an EVC calculation is for setting prices. For example, consider the improved lubricant example of Figure 6A.2. For such an "industrial" product (i.e., one without important functional/performance or psychological benefits), the maximum price the rational average driver would be willing to pay would be $25 per quart. However, at that price drivers have no incentive to switch to the synthetic (i.e., they are indifferent). In order to give them an incentive to switch, therefore, you must pick a price below $25 (but hopefully above cost). If direct costs are $8 per quart, one then selects a price between $8 and $25. Generally the greater the competition (i.e., number of producers of synthetic oil), the need to quickly capture customers, and available production capacity, the lower the price.

ISSUES

First, the calculation assumes that customers believe the benefits exist, optimally use the new product, and perform the calculation correctly. One can deal with the calculation aspect by providing it to potential customers (in ads, sales pitches, etc.). In terms of beliefs, anyone "trained" to change oil frequently will doubt that the synthetic oil can go two years without changing. If they change it more frequently, the EVC drops. Therefore, educating customers is a relevant activity so they both believe the claims and use the product correctly.

Second, EVC depends on the usage rate. In this example, heavy users will find the product much more valuable. Consider two drivers, one who drives 3,000 miles per year and one who drives 45,000. The low-mileage (3,000 miles) driver needs only one change every two years anyway, while the high-mileage driver would need 15. As Figure 6A.3 shows, the low-mileage driver should be willing to pay at most $1 per quart (the same as for regular oil), whereas the high-mileage driver might pay up to $85. The point of this is that economic value to the customer depends on the particular customer in question.

FIGURE 6A.3 The Relation of EVC of Usage Rate

	New Product	Old Product		
		Low Mileage (3,000)	Average Mileage (15,000)	High Mileage (45,000)
Product price	?	1 × $5 = $5	$25	15 × $5 = $75
Labor costs	$20	1 × $20 = $20	$100	15 × $20 = $300
Other costs	$5	1 × $5 = $5	$25	15 × $5 = $75
TOTAL COSTS	$25	$30	$150	$450
EVC		$5	$125	$425
EVC/Quart of new product		$1	$5	$85

Appendix 6B Latent Class Methods

Advances in both computer power and methods have made feasible a different approach to segment construction and interpreting. Most methods discussed in the chapter basically attempt to take individuals and aggregate them into segments. By contrast, latent class methods simultaneously estimate segment sizes and their behavior. These methods make use of the simple fact that aggregate market behavior is the sum of individual or segment level behavior:

$$\text{Total Market Behavior} = \sum_{segments} \left(\begin{array}{c} \text{Size of} \\ \text{Segment } i \end{array} \right)\left(\begin{array}{c} \text{Behavior of} \\ \text{Segment } i \end{array} \right)$$

$$= \sum_{segments} W_i B_i$$

The latent class approach *simultaneously* estimates segment sizes (W_i s) and segment behavior (B_i s). Segment membership is not known in advance (i.e., there is not a high income or nonresponsive-to-promotion segment specified in advance) and individual customers are not assigned to particular segments.

A key issue involves deciding on the number of segments. Basically this decision involves trading off between better describing a market (which allowing for more segments always does since it increases the number of parameters estimated) and keeping only important or "significant" segments. This trade-off is often accomplished with statistical tests on results of allowing for an additional segment (e.g., five versus four segments) or by comparing the abilities of the more and less parsimonious models to forecast behavior of a holdout sample (that is, customers who were not used to estimate the parameters).

When there is enough data to get an estimate of behavior at the individual customer level, latent class methods often incorporate probabilities of segment membership for each customer:

$$\text{Market Behavior} = \sum_{customers} \sum_{segments} P_{ij} B_i$$

where P_{ij} – probability person j is a member of segment i.

In interpreting such analyses, it is desirable to describe segments in terms of descriptor variables (demographics, firm characteristics). This can be done separately from the latent class analysis by relating individuals' estimated probabilities of being in each segment to other characteristics; that is, letting $P_{ij} = f$(characteristics of Customer j). This two-step approach then becomes:

$$\text{Step 1: Market Behavior} = \sum_{customers} \sum_{segments} P_{ij} B_i$$

$$\text{Step 2: } P_{ij} = \sum_{characteristics} C_{li} X_{li}$$

Occasionally the two steps are combined in a single step:

$$\text{Market Behavior} = \sum_{customers} \sum_{segments} \sum_{characteristics} (C_{li} X_{lj} B_i)$$

Currently latent class methods have not been widely applied in commercial settings. It is a good bet, however, that their use will increase substantially.

Chapter Seven

Market Potential and Sales Forecasting

Overview

The key document that outsiders (read those in finance and top management) look for first in evaluating a product plan is the P&L statement. In turn, the key element of the P&L is the top line, revenue. In other words, the revenue (or sales) forecast is the critical element on which the justification for a plan is built. Surprisingly, however, often remarkably little effort is spent scrutinizing this versus, say, the advertising budget, much less considering how the ad budget relates to sales. Therefore, understanding how forecasts are constructed, and how much uncertainty is in them, is critical for both constructing and evaluating marketing plans.

In this chapter, we describe methods for forecasting future sales or market share. Of course, other forecasts such as costs are also required. Fortunately most of the methods described here (e.g., time series extrapolation) apply to other types of forecasts as well.

A critical part of forecasting is the specification of key assumptions. Often product managers make assumptions about factors beyond their control. Most of these are environmentally related factors, such as those covered in Chapter 4. For example, the product manager for Healthy Choice must make assumptions about the likelihood of continued interest in low-calorie entrées and the reaction to carbohydrates. The product manager for Fuji film must make assumptions about the supply of silver as well as the demand for digital photography. Marketing personnel in the home construction business make assumptions about future interest rates. These assumptions both summarize earlier analyses and establish the basis for potential estimates and forecasts.

DEFINITIONS

The terms *potential* and *forecast* are used in many contexts, and are frequently confused. We use the following definitions:

Potential: The maximum sales reasonably attainable under a given set of conditions within a specified period of time (i.e., what you might or could achieve).

187

FIGURE 7.1 Forecasts versus Potential

	Expectations	**Possibilities**
Firm/brand	Sales forecast	Sales potential
Category	Market forecast	Market potential

Forecast: The amount of sales expected to be achieved under a set of conditions within a specified period of time (i.e., what you probably will achieve).

Quota: A related concept, quotas are typically set by senior managers and are what an individual in the company, for example, a salesperson, is expected to achieve (i.e., what you should achieve).

Figure 7.1 shows the distinction between potential and forecast in a sales context. The key difference between the concepts is that *potential* represents what *could* happen in a category if the product in question had full distribution and heavy advertising and promotion, and appealed to all the customers who could possibly purchase the product. Alternatively, *forecasts* represent *expectations,* which (usually) fall far below the potential in a market. Both potentials and forecasts depend on a set of conditions. These conditions can be divided into the four major categories of what customers do, what the firm does, what competitors do, and what occurs in the general environment (economy, culture).

Potentials and forecasts are time dependent. Stated differently, what may not be possible in the short run may be quite attainable in the longer term. While strategic plans depend on long-term potentials, annual plans focus primarily on short-run potentials and forecasts. This suggests a firm can fall into a trap: by optimizing short-run decisions, the firm may make what in the long run is a less than optimal series of decisions. That is one reason why products are often assigned different objectives, such as increasing sales (when the long-term potential seems large and increasing) or maximizing cash flow (when the long-term potential appears low).

MARKET POTENTIAL

Overview

It is hard to estimate the upper limit or maximum of sales. In addition, although managers may perceive potential as a fixed number, it is in fact dynamic and can change dramatically over time. The key to understanding this point is the clause "under a given set of conditions within a specified period of time." In other words, market or sales potential change depending on market factors such as average category price or general economic conditions.

For example, when Texas Instruments introduced its first handheld calculator, the SR10, which made slide rules largely obsolete, it had four functions (add, subtract, multiply, divide), no memory, and cost over $100. Now calculators and even computers far better than the SR10 are given away as promotions. The market potential of the original calculator was limited to those individuals, usually scientists or college students, who needed to make math calculations and could afford the price. When the number of functions offered dramatically increased and the price rapidly fell, more people could both use and afford one. Consequently both market potential and sales increased.

What They Are Used For

There are five major uses of potential estimates:

1. *To make entry/exit decisions.* Potentials (both market and sales) are key numbers in the strategic decisions of what markets to be in.

2. *To make resource level decisions.* One key aspect of allocation decisions relates to stage in the life cycle. Generally firms are more willing to allocate resources during growth phases. Of course, just because sales have plateaued does not mean they have reached potential. An interesting illustration of the differences between conventional product life cycle thinking and market potential thinking can be found in the running shoe category. In the 1960s, a buyer could get sneakers cut either high or low and in either black or white. The major brands were Keds and Converse. The product life cycle indicated maturity. In the 1970s, the market shot up with the introduction of performance shoes such as Nike, Adidas, and Puma. It became commonplace to wear running shoes to work and then change into work shoes. However, the market again became mature. What happened in the 1980s? Brands such as Reebok and L.A. Gear appealed to segments (e.g., aerobics) and fashion, and again the market jumped. Now a stupefying array of walking shoes, running shoes (for different mileages, degree of pronation, etc.), trail running shoes, cross-trainers, and court shoes are available. One manager's mature market is another's growth market. Thus, as many writers have warned (Dhalla and Yuspeh, 1976), the product life cycle concept must be used carefully.

3. *To make location and other resource allocation decisions.* Both manufacturing plants and distribution facilities tend to be located based on potential estimates, as do retail stores. Similarly sales force efforts and advertising are often allocated across products or regions based on potential.

4. *To set objectives and evaluate performance.* Potentials provide a standard to try to achieve. When actual sales fall below potential, a key question is "Why is there such a difference?" Examining this often leads to changes in market strategy and programs. For example, sales managers use market (or more accurately, area) potential in two ways. First, sales territories are often designed to have equal market potential so that different salespersons can be better judged on the basis of actual sales. Second, sales quotas are often set based on the potential sales in a territory.

5. *As an input to forecasts.* A major use of potentials in annual planning is as a basis for the sales forecast. In this case, a forecast is viewed as the product of potential times the percent of potential expected to be achieved.

Information Sources

Market potential may be estimated in a variety of ways. While the details involved depend on the particular industry and product under consideration, this section suggests some general approaches to assessing potential. Past sales data are useful, and for a stable market provide the key information for both a potential estimate and a sales forecast. In new markets, however, such data may be unavailable, inaccurate, or unduly

FIGURE 7.2 **Deriving Potential Estimates**

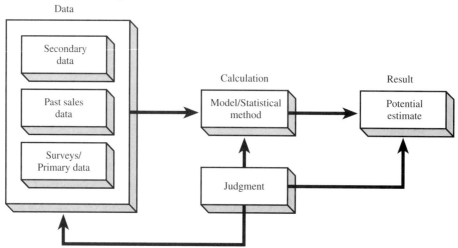

influenced by isolated events. Even when such data are available, other data should *not* be ignored. Figure 7.2 summarizes a process for deriving potential estimates (which is also useful for forecast development). It is useful to recognize the important role played by judgment not just in directly influencing estimates but also indirectly through data collection and model selection. The exact data and calculations used depend on the situation. Some of the sources useful for potential estimates (and forecasts) are already familiar to readers.

Government Sources

Market size estimates are available for many industries from sources such as the U.S. Department of Commerce and the Bureau of the Census (e.g., *Survey of Current Business, Current Industrial Reports*). Even when specific size estimates for an industry or a product are not available, government data may be useful as inputs to the potential estimate. Examples include breakdowns of industry by location, size, and Standard Industrial Classification (SIC) code, and forecasts of general economic conditions.

Trade Associations

These groups are a good source of information for particular industries or product categories, although they may be a bit optimistic.

Private Companies

A number of private companies track and forecast sales for various industries (e.g., FIND/ SVP, mentioned in Chapter 5). Some also survey capital spending plans (e.g., McGraw-Hill), consumer sentiment, and durable purchasing plans (e.g., the Survey Research Center at the University of Michigan).

Financial and Industry Analysts

Industry specialists often provide forecasts or potential estimates for various industries (e.g., Forrester and Gartner for computers).

Popular Press

A substantial amount of material finds its way into the business press (e.g., *Fortune, Forbes, Business Week*) or specialty publications.

The Internet

As in most areas, the Internet provides access to a wide and increasing pool of information.

While many sources exist, their competency and accuracy may not be very high. (It is comforting to assume that published potential estimates and forecasts are accurate and done by experts, but both the accuracy and expertise are often suspect. Think of it this way: The person who prepared the forecast may have been a classmate of yours!) To understand or assess the value of a forecast (whether provided by an outsider or a sub-ordinate), it is important to have at least a rudimentary knowledge of how forecasts are constructed. This chapter therefore goes into some detail on forecasting methods in the hope that the reader will become a more intelligent consumer of forecasts.

New or Growing Product Potential

In considering both the saturation level (ultimate potential) and the time pattern of market development, it is useful to compare the product to its major (and typically older) competitors. This can be accomplished by considering three major dimensions: relative advantage, compatibility, and risk.

Relative Advantage

In terms of benefits provided, is the new product superior in key respects and, if so, to what degree? Noticeably superior benefits increase both the saturation level and the rate at which the level is achieved. Also, in general, the relative advantage of a new product usually increases over time as various modifications and line extensions appear.

Compatibility

The fewer and less important the changes required to understand and use a new product, the faster it will be adopted. Compatibility issues relate not only to customers but also to intermediaries, the company itself (e.g., sales staff), and, if customers use a certain product as a component in another product, their customers as well. Therefore, if a chemical company is planning to manufacture a new product, issues of manufacturing compatibility and sales staff effort arise within the company along with potential problems regarding the behavior of wholesalers (assuming the product is sold through that channel), and customer problems (is retooling required?). Incompatibility tends to decrease over time. Finally, while incompatibility may be primarily psychological (i.e., "We just don't do things that way here"), failure to consider psychological barriers to adoption is often disastrous, at least in the short run.

Risk

The greater the risk involved (financial, possible impact on product quality if a new component fails, and so on), the lower the probability that someone will buy the new product. Typically, risk—at least in terms of price—tends to drop over time, thus increasing potential.

Overall, the higher the relative advantage (benefits) and the lower the costs (incompatibility, risk), the greater the potential and the faster it is likely to be achieved.

Role of Analogous Products

Examining the pattern of use and adoption of analogous products or services is often quite useful, especially for growing or new products. For either, the previous adoption patterns of similar products provide a clue to the likely pattern and rate of adoption and the eventual saturation level. As will be seen later in this chapter, analogies are also useful for sales forecasting.

The problem with using analogies is that two products are rarely perfectly comparable. To be reasonably comparable, both the newer product and its older analogue should be targeted to a similar market; be similar in perceived value, both in toto and in terms of the major benefits provided; and be similar in price. Under these criteria, a microwave oven could be compared to a dishwasher in that both are targeted at households, stress convenience and time savings, and cost about the same. In contrast, a mainframe computer from 1960, a microcomputer from 1984, and a wireless device linked to the Internet are not analogous, even though one is a direct descendant of the other, because the target market (companies versus individuals), perceived value (number crunching and billing versus convenience and word processing or entertainment and information), and price (a million dollars versus a few hundred) all differ dramatically.

Mature Product Potentials

The more mature products are, the more sales come from reorders from past customers. Reorders in a mature market are of two types. For a consumable product, repurchasing will be in proportion to the market need (if an industrial product) or usage rate (if a consumer product). For a durable product, repurchasing will occur to replace a worn-out product, to upgrade to get new features, or, importantly, to add an additional model (e.g., a second TV; Bayus, Hong, and Labe, 1989).

METHODS OF ESTIMATING MARKET AND SALES POTENTIAL

The role of managerial judgment in deriving potential is crucial and ubiquitous. It influences the type of data examined, the model used to derive the estimate, and often the estimate itself. Although statistical knowledge is useful, logic or common sense is much more important. Therefore, after estimating market potential, the product manager should step back and ask, "Does this estimate make sense?"

Analysis-Based Estimates

A formula-based method can be developed based largely on the potential users or buyers of the product in question in a three-step process.

1. *Determine the potential buyers or users of the product.* Buyers should be interpreted broadly as customers who have the need, the resources necessary to use the product, and the ability to pay. This often results in the product manager assessing that almost all customers are in the potential market (and maybe they are). An alternative approach is to work backward: Who *cannot* qualify as a potential customer? This might include apartment dwellers for lawn mowers, diabetics for regular ice cream, and so on. The product manager can determine potential customers judgmentally. In addition, other

data sources that could be useful are surveys, commercial sources such as data from Simmons Market Research Bureau or MRI, and government documents.

As an example, consider the problem of estimating the market potential for laptop computers. One judgmental approach for determining the number of potential adult employed users is to divide the market into categories such as: (1) "fleet workers" who are not in an office but need portable computing capabilities in a warehouse or manufacturing line, (2) "road warriors" who are on the road full time and need a virtual office, (3) "office functionalists" who work mainly out of the office but sometimes from home, (4) "corridor cruisers" who need their office computers when they go to business meetings, and (5) "road runners" who need a second office but less intensively than "road warriors" do (Beeh, 1994).

2. *Determine how many are in each potential group of buyers defined by step 1.* Often steps 1 and 2 are done simultaneously. If defined in terms of a particular demographic group, for example, people above age 60, sources such as the *Statistical Abstract of the United States* help determine how many people are in the group. For the previous example of laptop computers, the estimated group sizes were 15 million "fleet workers," 10 million "road warriors," 8 million "office functionalists," 6 million "corridor cruisers," and 5 million "road runners."

   The potential U.S. market for ice cream includes most individuals. If we start with a population of 280 million, we might remove diabetics and individuals with lactose intolerance or other reasons not to consume dairy products. Considering the percent who have these conditions would eliminate approximately 16 million diabetics and 30 million with lactose intolerance, leaving about 234 million as the potential market. Of course, many of these are young children, so the size of the buying market is smaller.

3. *Estimate the purchasing or usage rate.* This can be done by taking either the average purchasing rate determined by surveys or other research or by assuming that the potential usage rate is characterized by the heaviest buyers. The latter notion would be based on the assumption that all buyers could be convinced to purchase at that heavy rate. Market potential is then calculated by simply multiplying the number obtained from step 2 by the number from step 3, that is, the number of potential customers times their potential usage rate. For example, if we assume one laptop computer per potential user, the U.S. installed base market potential is simply 44 million units. The market potential estimate derived in this manner usually results in a large number compared to current industry sales. To get annual potential, the installed base potential of 44 million must be multiplied by the percent who buy each year. Assuming purchases are made every four years, this leads to an annual potential of 11 million. This method is often referred to as the successive ratio or chain ratio method. However, the number itself is often not as important as the process of trying to get the number. Estimating market potential using this kind of analysis forces the product manager to think about who the potential customers for the product are, which can often result in new thinking about untapped segments. A second impact of the market potential estimate is that it usually reveals a significant amount of untapped purchasing power in the market that is waiting for a new strategy, a new product formulation, or perhaps a new competitor.

Two examples help illustrate this method. The first illustration is from the infant/toddler disposable diaper category. The potential users are rather obvious in this case.

FIGURE 7.3 Market Potential: Electric Coil

SIC	Industry	Purchases of Product	Number of Workers	Average Purchase/ Worker	National Number of Workers	Estimated Potential
3611	Electrical measuring	$160	3,200	$.05	34,913	$1,746
3612	Power transformers	5,015	4,616	1.09	42,587	46,249
3621	Motors and generators	2,840	10,896	.26	119,330	31,145
3622	Electrical industry controls	4,010	4,678	.86	46,805	40,112
		$12,025				$119,252

During the 1990s, an average 4 million babies were born annually in the United States. The average child goes through 7,800 diapers in the first 130 weeks of life (2.5 years) until toilet training, or 60 per week (Deveny, 1990). Thus, the annual market potential for disposable diapers [(2.3)(4 million) babies][60 diapers/week][52 weeks/year] is 28.7 billion. This figure includes babies who are allergic to the diapers as well as households using cloth diapers or diaper services. Importantly, households using cloth diapers are still potential customers.

A second application shown in Figure 7.3 is typical of estimates of market potential for industrial products (Cox, 1979, Chapter 7). In this case, the potential customers are identified by SIC code. How much they can buy is extrapolated from an activity measure, in this case dollars of purchases per employee. A defect of this approach, however, is that current nonbuying SIC codes that are potential buyers are not included in the analysis.

Now consider again U.S. consumption of ice cream. In 1999, the population was 273,401,000. Of these, 16 million suffer from diabetes (and hence cannot consume regular ice cream) and 30 million are lactose intolerant. Removing these leaves 227,401,000 potential customers (plus those who are both diabetic and lactose intolerant). On average, consumption per person is 46.6 pints per year. This means potential is 10.5 billion pints per year which, at an average price per pint of $3.19, translates into a $33.5 billion dollar market.

For handheld devices (PDAs), market potential in 2000 was based on a total population of 278.1 million. From this we eliminate children under 13 (56.2 million) and those who live below the poverty level (21.1 million) for a potential market size of 200.8 million. Note that this potential assumes each person buys only one and that purchases occur annually, so potential can vary widely as these assumptions are altered. Notice also that it changes each year and hence is not a static concept.

This method has to be used carefully for durable consumer products or industrial products with long interpurchase cycles. In those cases, buyers not in the market because they recently purchased the good must be subtracted from the total. However, sometimes multiple purchases of such products occur; for example, many households have two or three VCRs, DVD players, or even PCs.

This approach to estimating market potential has implications for increasing the sales volume in a category or for a brand. There are two ways to increase sales. First, the product manager can increase the number of customers—by pursuing new segments, developing new products, or just getting more customers in existing segments (see Chapter 8). Second, the purchase rate can be increased; that is, the product manager can attempt to get customers to buy more through promotions, package size changes, and other tactics. These approaches have been used successfully at General Mills, which has a large number of mature products (e.g., Hamburger Helper, Betty Crocker cake mixes; Sellers, 1991).

Area Potential

Potential is often derived by breaking down total sales by area. When sales data are available for a variety of regions, along with some data on characteristics of the regions, it is common to use a weighted index that combines these characteristics to indicate the relative potential in the area. Many consumer goods companies use the general *Sales and Marketing Management* buying power index, which is 0.2 × (percentage of the population of the area compared to the United States) + 0.3 × (percentage of retail sales of the area of the United States total) + 0.5 × (percentage of disposable income of the area of the United States total). When population, retail sales, and disposable income are input as a percentage of the total United States, this index projects the percentage of the product sold in the various regions. For established products, these weights may be estimated from the actual sales data by, for example, running a regression of sales versus various factors such as the number of schools in the region. Product-related data, such as sales of analogous products, might also be used. In fact, as noted earlier in this chapter, sales of truly analogous products are often the best indicators of potential. An index approach for a hypothetical new copying system might be as follows:

Bases: Percent population in the region (P)

Percent schools in the region (S)

Percent retail businesses in the region (RB)

Percent banks in the region (B)

Percent offices in the region (O)

Percent warehouses in the region (WH)

Percent manufacturing facilities in the region (MF)

Percent other businesses in the region (OB)

Percent Xerox sales in the region (XS)

Percent other copier sales in the region (CS)

$$\text{Index} = W_1 P + W_2 S + W_3 RB + W_4 B + W_5 O + W_6 WH + W_7 MF + W_8 OB + W_9 XS + W_{10} CS$$

Here the *W*s are the weights assigned to each factor.

Sales Potential

Sales potential is the firm-level analogy to market potential. An obvious approach to calculating sales potential is to multiply the estimated potential of the market by some market share figure. This share figure should represent potential share, which the firm could achieve under optimal conditions (but usually not 100 percent).

SALES FORECASTING

Overview

As noted earlier, forecasting deals with expectations of the future, that is, what will happen. The most obvious things for a product manager to be concerned about, and the focus of this chapter, are sales, market share, and profits.

Other quantities are of course important to forecast as well. *Resources* used as a factor of production must be forecast (note the earlier discussion about general planning assumptions). Sometimes the key resources are human, making it important to forecast the needed labor pool. *Costs* are also an important factor to forecast. If the product is manufactured and follows the experience curve, costs are somewhat more predictable than in other situations. For many product managers, accurate forecasts of the rate of change of *technology* are critical to keeping an edge on competitors. General *economic conditions* have important effects on many types of businesses. Finally, in global businesses currency exchange rates have a major impact on profits.

Forecasts are used in several ways.

1. *To answer "what if" questions.* In considering which strategy and tactics to follow, the key is an estimate of the outcomes of the various strategies and tactics, typically the sales and profit levels. The simplest "what if" question is what will happen next year if everything remains as it has been in the past, which makes the forecast basically an extrapolation.

2. *To help set budgets.* Sales forecasts become the basis of a budget because they specify both sales levels to be attained and, by implication, the resources needed. All pro forma income statements are based on a sales forecast.

3. *To provide a basis for a monitoring system.* Deviations from forecasts serve as warnings to product management to reexamine a market and their strategy in it. Both positive and negative deviations from forecasts can lead to a better understanding of the marketplace through an examination of the underlying causes.

4. *To aid in production planning.* With more companies and their channels moving to just-in-time production and distribution systems with low levels of inventory, accurate forecasting is becoming even more critical. This is particularly important in the personal computer industry. Mistakes in forecasting demand for personal computers cost Compaq $50 million and IBM much more in 1994 (McWilliams, 1995). For several years Apple Computer underestimated the demand for its Powerbook laptop computers, which exacerbated its financial problems.

5. *By financial analysts to value a company.* The huge valuations of the "dot.com" companies at the end of 1999 could be justified only on the basis of large growth rates. Further, deviations from forecasts have a major impact on stock prices (e.g., missing sales or earnings targets).

A good forecast takes into account four major categories of variables, all of which either have been or will be discussed in this book: customer behavior (Chapter 6), past and planned product strategies (Chapter 8), competitor actions (Chapter 5), and the environment (Chapter 4). Company actions are predictable and/or under the control of the product manager, although, as noted in Chapter 1, many decisions such as pricing and advertising may be made in other parts of the company. In contrast, customer and competitive actions are much harder to forecast. The general environment consists of such elements as the state of

FIGURE 7.4 **Scenario-Based Forecasts**

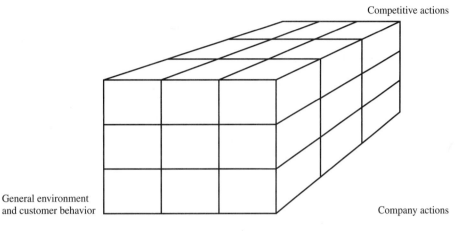

General environment
and customer behavior

Competitive actions

Company actions

the economy, key industries in it, demographic changes in the population, and costs of basic resources. Although some of these elements can be forecast by the product manager, they are generally derived from secondary sources, such as government projections, and appear in the category analysis or the planning assumptions section of a marketing plan. While environmental changes affect the plan mainly through their impact on competitor and customer behavior, they can be so crucial that we treat them separately here.

Forecasting can be thought of as the process of assessing the possible outcomes under reasonably likely combinations (sometimes called scenarios) of the four basic determinants of outcome. This suggests that forecasting without considering competitive reactions is, unless the competitors are asleep, insufficient. The forecasting process can be viewed as a process of filling out a three-dimensional grid such as that shown in Figure 7.4, with the likely outcomes contingent on values of the three sets of independent variables.

The forecast in each cell should not be a single number but rather a range of possible outcomes. While a forecast of 787.51 may sound better than 800 ± 50, it is likely to be misleading and an example of foolish precision (which puts you out on a limb with your boss). Do not expect forecasts to six decimal places, especially when such precision is not crucial to making a sound decision.

Knowing the range of likely results is crucial for strategy selection. A product manager may be unwilling to undertake a strategy with a high expected result (e.g., a profit of $8 million) that also has a reasonably likely disastrous result (e.g., a loss of $5 million). Conversely, a product manager may be willing to gamble on a possible large return even if the likely result is a small profit or even a loss. It is also useful to know the likely range of outcomes for purposes of monitoring and control. For example, in one situation, a drop of 30 percent below the forecast may be well within the expected range and therefore not necessarily be a cause for a major reanalysis, whereas in a different situation, a 15 percent drop below the forecast may signal a serious problem.

At this point, it should be clear that producing a forecast for each possible combination of factors is a tedious task at best. Consequently, it is desirable to limit the task to, say, three environments (expected, benign, and hostile) and a limited number of competitive postures (e.g., status quo, more/less aggressive). This limitation should, however,

FIGURE 7.5 Summary of Forecasting Methods

	Judgment				Counting	
	Naive		**Executive**			
Dimensions	**Extrapolation**	**Sales Force**	**Opinion**	**Delphi**	**Market Testing**	**Market Survey**
1. Time span	Short/medium term	Short/medium term	Short/medium term	Medium/long	Medium	Medium
2. Urgency	Rapid turnaround	Fast turnaround	Depends on whether inside or outside company	Needs time	Needs time	Needs time
3. Quantitative skills needed	Minimal	Minimal	Minimal	Minimal	Moderate level	Yes
4. Financial resources needed	Very low	Low	Could be high if outside experts used	Could get high	High	High
5. Past data needed	Some	Not necessary	Not necessary	Not necessary	Not necessary	Not necessary
6. Accuracy	Limited	Highly variable	Poor if one individual; better if a group	Best under dynamic conditions	Good for new products	Limited

Source: David M. Georgoff and Robert G. Murdick, "Manager's Guide to Forecasting," *Harvard Business Review,* January–February, 1986, pp. 110–20.

be made with two points in mind. First, the initial forecasts may suggest a promising avenue or a potential disaster that may lead to refining the scenarios. Second, the assumptions made in forecasting are crucial; therefore, it is desirable to designate them formally as *planning assumptions.*

Level of Accuracy Needed

Obviously, more accuracy in a forecast is better than less. Also, assuming a reasonably intelligent forecasting procedure is being employed (something one should *not* generally assume), then the only way to get a better forecast is to spend more time, effort, and money. Since increasing forecast accuracy has severely diminishing marginal returns (to make the range of a forecast half as large will generally at least quadruple its cost), at some point the cost of improving the forecast will exceed the benefit.

The benefit of a better forecast usually is greater when (1) the price of the product is high in either absolute or relative terms ($40,000 may not be much to IBM but it is to the authors); (2) product demand is relatively volatile; and (3) the cost of an error in forecasting (including reorder cost and the cost of being out of stock—which may include the long-term loss of a disenchanted customer) is high. The cost of a better forecast increases as (1) the number of items or product forms increases (e.g., machine tool A with feature X, with features X and Z, and so on); (2) the method becomes more complicated to use; and (3) the forecast (and its basis) is difficult to communicate to others

Time Series			Association/Causal			
Moving Average	**Exponential Smoothing**	**Extrapolation**	**Correlation**	**Regression**	**Leading Indicators**	**Econometric**
Short/medium	Short/medium	Short/medium/ long	Short/medium/ long	Short/medium/ long	Short/medium/ long	Short/medium/ long
Fast turnaround	Fast turnaround	Fast turnaround	Fast turnaround	Moderately fast	Moderately/ fast	Needs time
Minimal	Minimal	Basic skills	Basic skills	Basic skills	Basic skills	High level
Low	Low	Low	Moderate	Moderate/high	Moderate	High
Necessary	Necessary	Necessary	Necessary	Necessary	Necessary	Necessary
Good only in stable environment	Good in short run	Good for trends, stable time series	Highly variable	Can be accurate if explained variance is high	Moderately accurate at best	Best in stable environment

in the organization. (Generally speaking, review committees prefer not to hear about Fourier series, correlated errors, and so on.)

Judgment-Based Methods

A large number of methods have been developed for forecasting (Chambers, Mullick, and Smith, 1971; Georgoff and Murdick, 1986; Wheelwright and Makridakis, 1985). Figure 7.5 compares a number of methods. Here we discuss four basic approaches: judgment based, customer based, sales extrapolation, and model based. The first set of methods is referred to as *judgment-based* methods because, unsurprisingly, they rely solely on judgments.

Naive Extrapolation

One method of naive extrapolation uses the last-period sales level and adds x percent, the estimated percentage change in sales. For example, dishwasher sales could be forecast to be last year's plus 6 percent. A related approach might be termed "graphical eyeball." This requires plotting the past sales series and then "eyeballing" the next value to match the past pattern (see Figure 7.6).

Sales Force Composite

Salespeople are often asked to make sales forecasts. Their forecasts can then be aggregated to create a sales forecast for the product or product line. The advantage of this

FIGURE 7.6 Graphical Eyeball Forecasting

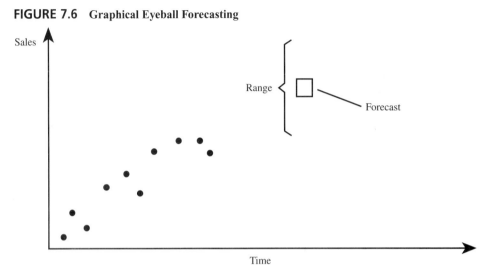

approach is that salespeople are close to customers and thus in an excellent position to understand their purchasing plans. Unfortunately, when the forecast is used to set quotas, such forecasts are naturally on the low side. Alternatively, salespeople can be overly optimistic in an attempt to impress the sales manager.

Jury of Expert Opinion

An extreme example of this method relies on a single expert's opinion. If the expert happens to know the Delphic oracle or be a mystic, the forecast can be excellent. Unfortunately, it is hard to know ahead of time whether someone can predict the future.

Many studies have been published deriding expert forecasts. Consider the following business-related predictions made by "experts" (Cerf and Navasky, 1984):

> With over 50 foreign cars already on sale here, the Japanese auto industry isn't likely to carve out a big slice of the U.S. market for itself. (*Business Week,* August 2, 1968)
>
> A severe depression like that of 1920–1921 is outside the range of probability. (Harvard Economic Society, November 16, 1929)
>
> The phonograph . . . is not of any commercial value. (Thomas Edison, ca. 1880)

TRW sponsored a major technological forecasting project back in the mid-1960s. Some of their predictions were:

- A manned lunar base by 1977.
- Commercial passenger rockets by 1980.
- Undersea mining and farming by 1981.

Despite examples like these, expert forecasts can be useful. The key to the value of expert judgment is the ability of the expert to recall and assimilate relevant data in making a guess. While judgment is often unsystematic, it is an important supplement to other methods and can overcome some of the limitations of quantitative techniques.

The jury approach collects forecasts from a number of experts. The forecasts are then combined in a particular manner, such as a simple or weighted average, in which the weights can be the level of expertise. A variant of the jury approach is the panel consensus method, in which a group of experts is put in a room where they attempt to develop a forecast. Unfortunately a strong, vocal member of the group often drives the result.

An example of the jury approach was provided every month by *Wired* magazine. In each issue, a group of experts in an area were asked for the year in which certain phenomena were likely to occur. For example, in 1995 five experts were asked about the year in which we could expect to be able to purchase custom clothing overnight. The average of the experts was 1999 (*Wired,* 1995).

Delphi Method

The *Delphi method* is a variation of the panel consensus. The process begins by asking a number of individuals to independently produce a forecast. An outside person then collects the forecasts and calculates the average. Next, the outside person returns to each participant both the original forecast and the average and asks the participants to reconsider their initial forecasts. Typically, the participants then change their forecasts to more nearly conform to the average. If the process is repeated several times, consensus is generally achieved. Delphi panels are often established to forecast sales of new technologies (e.g., videotext) for which historical data do not exist.

Customer-Based Methods

A second set of methods relies on customer data.

Market Testing

This category includes a large set of methods involving primary market research. The methods include mall intercept surveys, focus groups, and at-home or at-work situations in which potential customers are asked to respond to a product concept. Methods such as conjoint analysis, discussed in Chapter 6, are widely used to assess desired product features and ultimate market share.

Market Surveys

Market surveys are a specific form of primary market research in which potential customers are asked to give some indication of their likelihood of purchasing the product. A common approach is to use a 1-to-10 scale, with a 10 implying certainty of purchase. Customers frequently overstate their likelihood of purchase (although for really new products they often underestimate their eventual purchase likelihood). Researchers often use either a "top box" approach (i.e., count only the 10s as purchasing) or some other method based on the past relation between intent and purchase as the basis for the forecast. Alternatively, respondents are asked to indicate the quantity of a product they expect to purchase. These purchase intention surveys are then extrapolated to the population to form demand forecasts. Purchasing agents, for example, are often surveyed to determine demand for industrial products. Standard survey problems, such as nonresponse bias (are the people who do not respond to the survey different from those who do?) and inaccurate responses, exist with this method.

Whom to Survey

When conducting surveys for industrial products, it is not clear whom to talk to within a company even if the company is known. For example, when the Federal Communications

Commission (FCC) invited bids for cellular mobile phone licenses in various cities, it required a study of market potential as part of the application. Most applicants attempted to address this by phone surveys, contacting the manager of telecommunications (or someone having a similar title) and asking about how many phones the company would use. However, it is not clear that these managers knew how many were needed or had much authority over such acquisitions.

To determine which companies to survey, first specify the potential segments and then ensure there are enough of each type included to get a reasonable estimate. Unfortunately, if there are 10 target groups and five size variations per group, this leads to a large sample size.

Consider Figure 7.7, which shows the number of firms by employee number in several SIC codes. How would you apportion the sample and still be able to represent each segment accurately? The answer requires a balance between a stratified sample based on assumed variability of demand and getting a reasonable number in each cell.

How to Deal with the Results

It would be preferable if the results "made sense," but sometimes they are inconsistent. For example, assume that the average firm sales for the five size categories in Figure 7.7 were as follows: 192, 181, 490, 360, and 2,000. Do you treat these figures as "truth," or do you smooth them so bigger firms spend more? Moreover, what do you do if total demand comes out three times expected? Do you scale every estimate down by one-third?

In summary, then, while surveys may produce a useful number, they are equally likely to produce numbers that, without "creative" manipulation, appear on the surface to be wrong.

Sales Extrapolation Methods

A third set of methods utilizes historical sales data and is referred to as *time-series* methods.

Moving Averages

Moving averages, an old forecasting standby, are widely used to reduce the "noise" in data to uncover the underlying pattern. In doing so, it is important to recognize that past data have at least four major components:

1. Base value
2. Trend
3. Cycle(s) (seasonality)
4. Randomness

Moving averages essentially smooth out random variations to make the patterns (trends and cycles) more apparent.

For purposes of introduction, consider the simple moving-average approach. A three-period moving average of sales at time t is given by

$$\bar{S}_t = (S_{t-1} + S_t + S_{t+1})/3$$

Note that (1) each data point used is weighted equally and (2) no trend or cycle is accounted for. To see how this method works, consider the three-month moving average

FIGURE 7.7 Potential Customers by Industry and Size

SIC	Industry	Percent of 1981 Demand Accounted For	Total Number of Firms	Number of Employees				
				50–99	100–249	250–499	500–999	1,000 or More
28	Chemical	20	7,012	754	610	293	193	123
29	Petroleum	20	444	57	73	53	42	22
33	Primary metals	10	1,889	266	352	181	74	108
12	Bituminous	2	4,050	295	272	166	80	11
20	Food	5	10,032	1,114	957	393	153	57
22	Textile	2	1,786	207	229	187	160	50
26	Paper and allied products	10	1,314	184	235	116	104	58
34	Fabricated metal	3	4,568	310	111	16	2	—
36	Electrical equipment	3	942	90	109	94	43	35
49	Electricity, gas	25	5,250	766	588	214	97	69
	Total		37,287	4,043	3,536	1,713	948	533

Expected Maximum Spending by Size Category

Employee Size	Maximum Spending
50 to 99	$ 100,000
100 to 249	200,000
250 to 499	500,000
500 to 999	750,000
1,000 or more	1,000,000

FIGURE 7.8 Sample Data

Period	Sales	Three-Period Moving Average	Raw Changes	Average Change
1	100	—	—	—
2	110	105	+10	—
3	105	115	−5	10
4	130	125	+25	10
5	140	130	+10	5
6	120	140	−20	10
7	160	152	+40	11.33
8	175	—	+15	—

for the eight periods of sales given in Figure 7.8. The moving average for the first three periods of data is 105, the simple average of 100, 110, and 105. The moving average for periods 2 through 4 is 115, the average of 110, 105, and 130. As can be readily seen by comparing the moving averages to the "Raw Changes" column, the fluctuation in values is much less in moving averages than in the raw data, and a consistent trend of increase of about 10 units per period becomes quite apparent. Forecasts can now be based on the pattern of moving averages rather than on the raw data.

The basic moving-average method just described can be extended to track trends and seasonal patterns as well. For example, to smooth a trend, simply calculate the period-to-period changes and average them as in Figure 7.8. While other methods, such as regression, are more sophisticated means of developing forecasts, moving averages remain a popular approach.

Exponential Smoothing

A second time-series approach is called *exponential smoothing*. The formula for a simple exponentially smoothed forecast is

$$\hat{S}_{t+1} = aS_t + (1 - a)\hat{S}_t$$

where "^" refers to a forecast. In other words, an exponentially smoothed forecast for period $t + 1$ is a combination of the current period's sales and the current period's forecast. The parameter a is between 0 and 1 and can be determined from historical sales data. In reality, exponentially smoothed forecasts are close relatives to moving-average forecasts in that the former weight past sales using exponentially declining weights.[1] As in the case of moving averages, this approach literally smooths out the random variation in period-to-period values. Trends and cycles are estimated separately.

Regression Analysis

A simple and popular form of extrapolation uses regression analysis with time (period) as the independent variable and is easily accomplished by using Excel or similar programs. Time series regression produces estimates of the base level (intercept) and the trend (slope). Seasonal patterns can either be removed a priori from the data or estimated

---

[1] To see this, simply rewrite the equation in terms of period t, that is, $\hat{S}_t = aS_{t-1} + (1 - a)\hat{S}_{t-1}$, and substitute repeatedly for S_t in the equation in the text.

FIGURE 7.9   Times-Series Extrapolation

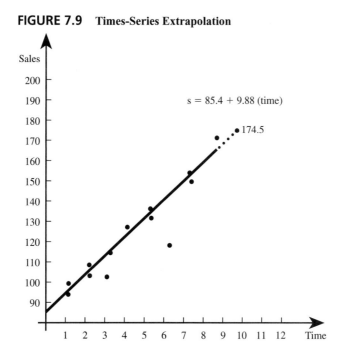

in the model using dummy variables (see Chapter 6). If we ignore seasonality, the model is simply

$$Sales = a + b(time)$$

Addressing the same eight-period example from Figure 7.8 produces the graph in Figure 7.9 and the predicted results in Figure 7.10. The forecast for period 9 based on this model would be

$$S_9 = 85.4 + 9.9(9) = 174.5$$

This is represented by the dotted extension to the fitted line in Figure 7.9. Two other useful statistics produced are the R^2, a measure of fit that is the percentage variance in the dependent variable (sales) explained by the independent variable (time), and the standard error of the estimate, which is a measure of the variance of the errors (the differences

FIGURE 7.10   Time-Series Regression Example

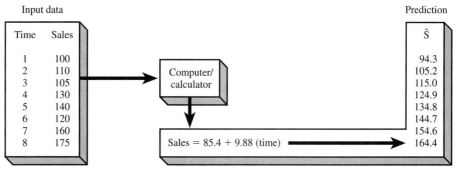

FIGURE 7.11 Trial over Time for a New Product

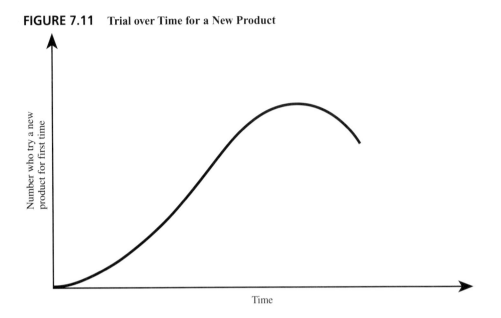

between the predicted values of sales based on the preceding equation and the actual values) about the line. Rather than just using the point forecast, 174.5, a confidence interval or a range of likely outcomes should be placed around it. For a one-period-out forecast, this is done by multiplying the standard error of the estimate (in this case, 12.3) by 2 to approximate a 95 percent confidence interval. The forecast then becomes 174.5 ± 24.6. Longer-term forecasts can be developed simply by plugging in values for time periods later than 9, extending the line farther out in time, although the confidence interval also grows wider.

Sometimes sales data are highly nonlinear, as in Figure 7.11. This product life cycle curve is clearly not a straight regression line. Figure 7.11 can be estimated using a variety of functional forms. We discuss one, the Bass model (Bass, 1969), later in this chapter.

Model-Based Methods

The fourth category of forecasting methods is often termed *association* or *causal* because the techniques utilize one or more variables other than time to predict sales (e.g., advertising).

Regression Analysis

This method is a generalization of the time-series model: Instead of having only time as the independent variable, other variables that could affect sales are included. For example, a regression model to predict sales of Pepsi might be the following:

$$\text{Sales} = a + b(\text{advertising}) + c(\text{price}) + d(\text{population age 13–25})$$

Given historical data on sales, advertising, price, and population, the coefficients *a, b, c,* and *d* can be estimated and used to develop a forecast.

Leading Indicators

Economists use certain macroeconomic variables to forecast changes in the economy. When changes in these variables occur before changes in the economy, they are termed *leading indicators.* For example, changes in employment, housing starts, interest rates, and retail sales are often associated with changes in the economy. The construction and real estate industries use leading indicators to forecast demand. Industry-specific leading indicators also exist, such as retail auto dealer inventories for the automobile industry.

Econometric Models

These are essentially large-scale, multiple-equation regression models. During the 1970s they were extremely popular, and companies such as Data Resources, Inc. (subsequently bought by McGraw-Hill) sold these models to companies seeking to develop better forecasts of industry sales. They are less popular today as companies strive to keep their expenditures down. In addition, they never forecasted as well as advertised. A noteworthy failure came during the Arab oil embargo of the early 1970s when the models predicted less damage to the U.S. economy than actually occurred.

What Methods Are Used?

Figure 7.12 shows the results of a survey of 96 companies examining which forecasting methods are actually used in practice (Sanders and Manrodt, 1994). For the short and medium term, judgmental approaches are heavily used. The most frequently used quantitative method is a moving average. The general nature of these results were confirmed by a Product Development Management Association sponsored study based on 168 respondents (Kahn, 2002; Figure 7.13). This is rather discouraging given the length of time more sophisticated methods have been available. However, regression is used quite frequently, particularly for long-run forecasts. Since regression is sufficient for most situations and widely available (e.g., in Excel), we concentrate on it.

FIGURE 7.12 Forecasting Method Usage

	Forecast Period			
Forecasting Technique	**Immediate (<1 month)**	**Short (1 month–<6 months)**	**Medium (6 months–1 year)**	**Long (>1 year)**
Judgmental				
Manager's opinion	27.9%	39.8	37.1	9.3
Jury of executive opinion	17.5	28.9	40.1	26.2
Sales force composite	28.6	17.5	33.1	8.7
Quantitative				
Moving average	17.7	33.5	28.3	8.7
Straight-line projection	7.6	13.2	12.5	8.2
Naive	16.0	18.5	13.8	0
Exponential smoothing	12.9	19.6	16.8	4.2
Regression	13.4	25.1	26.4	16.5
Simulation	3.4	7.8	11.2	8.3
Classical decomposition	0	6.8	11.9	9.3
Box-Jenkins	2.4	2.4	4.9	3.4

Source: Reprinted by permission, Nada R. Sanders and Kari B. Manrodt, "Forecasting Practices in the U.S. Corporations: Survey Results," *Interfaces*, March–April, 1994. Copyright 1994. The Institute of Management Sciences and the Operations Research Society of America (currently *Informs*), 2 Charles Street, Suite 300, Providence, RI 02904 USA.

FIGURE 7.13   **Use of New Product Forecasting Techniques by All Responding Firms**

Forecasting Technique	Average Use Across All Types of New Products (%)
Customer/market research	57%
Jury of executive opinion	44
Sales force composite	39
Looks-like analysis	30
Trend line analysis	19
Moving average	15
Scenario analysis	14
Exponential smoothing techniques	10
Experience curves	10
Market analysis model (including the ATAR model)	10
Delphi method	8
Linear regression	7
Decision trees	7
Simulation	5
Expert systems	4
Other	3
Nonlinear regression	2
Diffusion models	2
Precursor curves (correlation method)	1
Box-Jenkins techniques (ARMA/ARIMA)	1
Neural networks	0

Source: Kahn, Kenneth B. (2002) "An Exploratory Investigation of New Product Forecasting Practices," *The Journal of Product Innovation Management* 19, 133–43.

Using Regression Models for Forecasting

Given the results from Figure 7.12 and the wide applicability of regression to other marketing contexts (see segmentation research in Chapter 6), we devote significant space in this chapter to show how it is used in forecasting contexts. Regression models are generally developed in three stages. First, the variables assumed to affect dependent variables are specified. For a prediction of unit sales, the variables selected might be

Sales = f(our price, competitors' prices, our advertising, competitors' advertising, disposable income)

Next, a model is specified indicating the form of the relation between the independent variables and sales. Most often the nature of the relationship is linear, such as

Sales = $b_0 + b_1$ (our price) + b_2 (competitors' prices) + b_3 (our advertising) + b_4 (competitors' advertising) + b_5 (disposable income)

Finally, the model is estimated by means of regression analysis, using commonly available computer programs:

Sales = $1.2 - .3$ (our price) + $.4$ (competitors' prices) + 1.1 (our advertising) $- .3$ (competitors' advertising) + $.2$ (disposable income)

The estimated model serves two primary purposes. First, the model can be used to forecast sales. Notice that to use this regression model to forecast, one must first forecast the values of the independent variables. This is because all the variables are *contemporaneous;* that is, current (say, 2005) sales are determined by current (2005) prices, advertising, and disposable income. We use data from some point in the past through 2003 to estimate the model. However, to forecast sales for 2005, we need 2005 values for the independent variables. While some of the variables may be under the product manager's control (price, advertising), several others must be forecasted. If this is difficult, regression becomes less useful as a forecasting device. Put differently, try to use predictor variables that are themselves easy to forecast.

Second, a regression model can answer "what if" questions. In the preceding example, b_1 is the marginal effect of changing our price and b_3 is the marginal effect of changing our advertising. If we are willing to assume the relationships between price, advertising, and sales are causal rather than just correlational, the product manager can answer a question such as "What if I increase my price by \$5?" In this case, based on the model, an increase in price would be predicted to lead to a change in sales of: $(5)(-.3) = -1.5$.

Developing Regression Models

While developing regression forecasting models is largely a trial-and-error process, certain steps can make the process more systematic and efficient.

1. *Plot sales over time.* It is useful to get a feel for the sales series by simply plotting sales versus time. An important use of this plot is as an aid for identifying key variables that might be useful in predicting changes in sales. Any peaks or valleys in the sales series can prompt the product manager to try to uncover the factor that may have caused that sharp change.

   Figure 7.14 shows the (deseasonalized) monthly sales series from 1973 to 1975 of presweetened breakfast cereal purchases made by a sample of households on a dairy panel (Neslin and Shoemaker, 1983). A significant price increase for sugar occurred during 1974 and resulted in a sharp increase in cereal prices. It is difficult to pick out the effect of price alone from the graph. However, it is clear that an overall positive trend in purchases occurred over the three-year period. Some variable accounting for that trend should be included in the regression model.

2. *Consider the variables that are relevant to predicting sales.* The product manager or a team of managers familiar with the product category should brainstorm to develop a set of factors that affect sales. At this stage, the list of variables should be long, allowing for as much creativity as possible. In terms of the type of variables to include, it is generally useful to consider which variables in each of the following categories might be most appropriate:

   a. Customer status and traits (e.g., the size of the population in a particular age category).
   b. "Our" marketing programs (e.g., advertising).
   c. Competitive behavior (e.g., new product introductions).
   d. General environment (e.g., gross domestic product).

   In the case of presweetened cereals, two major factors affecting sales are price and advertising. As noted above, the data are already deseasonalized, so any winter-versus-summer consumption factors for cold cereals have already been eliminated from the sales series. For simplicity, the upward trend of the data can be accounted for by a trend variable that assumes the values 1 through 36. Finally, advertising may have what is called a lagged effect on sales. In other words, not only may current

FIGURE 7.14 **Cereal Sales Data (monthly)**

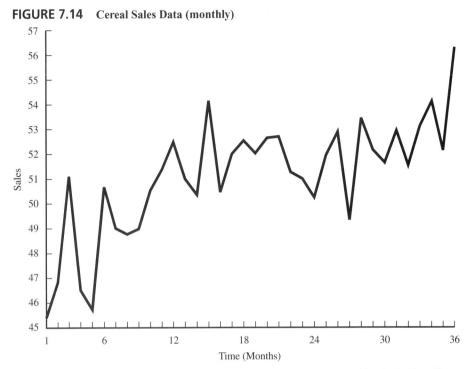

Source: Scott A. Neslin and Robert W. Shoemaker, "Using a Natural Experiment to Estimate Price Elasticity: The 1974 Sugar Shortage and the Ready-to-Eat Cereal Market," *Journal of Marketing,* Winter 1983, pp. 44–57.

advertising affect current sales but last month's advertising may also affect current sales through consumer recall. Thus, the general form of the model is

$$\text{Cereal sales} = f(\text{price, advertising, lagged advertising, trend})$$

3. *Collect data.* Once the variables have been specified, historical values for those variables must be collected. There must be as many historical values for the independent variables as there are for the sales variable. Here, since there are 36 observations on cereal sales, the analyst needs 36 observations on price and advertising (lagged advertising can be computed directly from the advertising series). Figure 7.15 shows the data for this example.

4. *Analyze the data.* There are several aspects to the data analysis step of the model-building process.

First, it is important to examine the *correlations among the independent variables.* Many time series variables are highly correlated because they tend to change over time at the same rate. For example, if the economy is expanding, employment and GDP are highly correlated. If a product is being rolled out nationally, the number of distribution outlets and advertising may be highly correlated. If two or more independent variables are highly correlated, computational and interpretation problems can arise. Therefore, an important first step after the data have been collected is to construct a correlation matrix among the variables (remember, we want high correlations between the independent variables and sales, the dependent variable). Note that the diagonal of the matrix (Figure 7.16) contains 1s; the correlation of a variable with itself is obviously 1. The analyst should be on guard against correlations with high

FIGURE 7.15 Cereal Data

Sales	Price	Advertising	Time	Lagged Advertising
45.4	29.0	6803	1	—
46.8	28.7	6136	2	6803
51.1	28.1	8850	3	6136
46.5	27.9	6689	4	8850
45.7	27.9	7004	5	6689
50.7	27.6	7801	6	7004
49.0	27.0	7091	7	7801
48.8	26.7	6958	8	7091
49.0	26.6	7357	9	6958
50.6	26.7	7010	10	7357
51.4	26.7	6627	11	7010
52.5	26.7	7350	12	6627
51.0	26.6	6952	13	7350
50.4	26.6	7441	14	6952
54.2	26.8	7519	15	7441
50.5	27.1	8409	16	7519
52.0	27.6	8084	17	8409
52.6	28.3	7830	18	8084
52.1	28.6	7399	19	7830
52.7	28.9	7566	20	7399
52.7	29.3	7076	21	7566
51.3	29.8	7310	22	7076
51.0	30.9	7604	23	7310
50.3	31.6	6793	24	7604
52.0	31.6	7038	25	6793
52.9	31.6	6514	26	7038
49.4	31.7	6439	27	6514
53.5	31.7	6056	28	6439
52.2	31.7	6148	29	6056
51.7	31.1	5787	30	6148
53.0	30.9	6043	31	5787
51.6	30.5	6191	32	6043
53.2	30.3	8034	33	6191
54.2	29.7	8404	34	8034
52.2	29.8	9524	35	8404
56.4	29.9	8973	36	9524

absolute values (i.e., above .90, although this number should not be considered a rigid threshold). More generally, you want the correlations between the independent and dependent variables to be larger than the correlations among the independent variables. High negative correlations, which are as harmful as positive ones, are not a major problem here, although time and price are closely related.

Second, *run the regression.* The regression results from the cereal illustration are shown in Figure 7.17, assuming a simple linear form of the model.

Third, determine the *significant predictors* of the dependent variable (i.e., sales). Even when care is taken to choose only those variables thought to be excellent predictors of sales, some often turn out to have little effect. To assess the strength of the effect of an independent variable on sales, look at the ratio of the absolute value of the regression

FIGURE 7.16 **Cereal Data Correlation Matrix***

	Price	Advertising	Time	Lagged Advertising
Price	1.0	−.28	.76	−.26
	(35)	(35)	(35)	(35)
	.00	.10	.00	.13
Advertising	−.28	1.00	.05	.55
	(35)	(35)	(35)	(35)
	.10	.00	.76	.00
Time	.76	.05	1.00	−.02
	(35)	(35)	(35)	(35)
	.00	.76	.00	.90
Lagged advertising	−.26	.55	−.02	1.00
	(35)	(35)	(35)	(35)
	.13	.00	.90	.00

*The numbers in each cell are presented as: correlation, (sample size), significant level.

coefficient to its standard error (given on all regression printouts), otherwise known as the t statistic. Generally speaking, if this ratio is greater than 2, the variable is referred to as a significant predictor of sales. Examining the first results in Figure 7.17, we can see that price is marginally significant ($t = 1.92$), advertising is insignificant ($t = 1.21$), time is very significant ($t = 5.02$), and lagged advertising is not significant ($t = .41$) at the 5 percent significance level. A decision to be made here is whether to rerun the regression after dropping insignificant variables. *Parsimony* is important in forecasting models, because fewer independent variables must be predicted to develop the ultimate forecast for a "smaller" model. Since lagged advertising is relatively unimportant, regression 2 in Figure 7.17 repeats the regression with that variable eliminated. Price is now significant ($t = 2.45$), as is the time trend, although advertising is still insignificant.

Fourth, check the *signs* of the significant independent variables. This is a logic check and is perhaps the most important test of all. The product manager *must* ensure

FIGURE 7.17 **Regression Results: Cereal Data***

1. Model: Sales = 58.528 − .461 (price) + .00044 (advertising) − .00015 (lagged advertising) + .211 (time)
   (.242)   (.00037)   (.00037)   (.042)
   Standard error of the estimate = 1.479
   Adjusted R^2 = .60

2. Model: Sales = 60.041 − .538 (price) + .00033 (advertising) + .230 (time)
   (.244)   (.00032)   (.038)
   Standard error of the estimate = 1.468
   Adjusted R^2 = .65

3. Model: In Sales = 3.193 − .053 (In price) + .090 (In advertising) + .044 (In time)
   (.095)   (.043)   (.007)
   Standard error of the estimate = .028
   Adjusted R^2 = .68

*Numbers in parentheses are standard errors.

that the signs on the regression coefficients make sense. For example, a significant positive sign on a price coefficient is a problem; most of the time, these kinds of sign flip-flops are due to what is called *specification error,* the omission of one or more key variables from the model. In the breakfast cereal example, the signs are all in the appropriate direction for the significant variables.

Fifth, check the R^2 of the equation. This is what most analysts gravitate toward first. However, a high R^2 does not guarantee a good forecasting model. This is due to the fact that regression is basically a correlational procedure and it is possible to choose variables that are nonsensical but do explain variance in sales. That is why we stress the combination of spending time a priori in choosing independent variables, checking the signs on the coefficients, *and* looking at the R^2. The R^2 of the breakfast cereal model is .65, as shown in Figure 7.17. This is not particularly high for a time-series model and implies that the forecast confidence interval will be relatively wide.

Finally, develop the forecast and confidence interval. As noted earlier, the forecast is developed by plugging in the appropriate values of the independent variables. In addition, a confidence interval can be constructed using the standard error of the estimate. This produces three forecasts: best guess (the point forecast), optimistic (the high end of the confidence interval), and pessimistic (the low end of the confidence interval).

Taking the results of the second cereal regression from Figure 7.17, we can develop a forecast for the first out-of-sample period, January 1976. If we assume the price will be 30 cents per 10 ounces (remember, this is over 28 years ago) and category advertising will be $9 million, then, given that the value of the time is 37, the forecast is 55,400 ounces purchased for the panel members (55.4 in the units of Figure 7.15). Given a standard error of the estimate of 1.47, a 95 percent confidence interval around the forecast is ±2,940 ounces, or a range of 52,460 to 58,340 ounces. Thus, 55,400 becomes the best guess, 52,460 the pessimistic and 58,340 the optimistic forecast. Note that this process can and generally should be repeated for different scenarios (e.g., assumptions about price), as we discuss later.

Recognizing Uncertainty

In order to make forecasts with a regression model, it is necessary to know or forecast the values of the predictor variables (e.g., GDP, advertising) in the next period. When these are known, a reasonable forecast includes a best guess obtained by substituting the known values, a pessimistic forecast (typically the best guess minus two standard errors of estimate), and an optimistic forecast (the best guess plus two standard errors of estimate). Since the predictor variables are rarely known with certainty, it is useful to construct both optimistic and pessimistic scenarios and to generate forecasts based on them. The resulting 3-by-3 table (see Figure 7.18) gives a much clearer picture of the uncertainty inherent in the market (and what it depends on). While managers like to have *the* forecast, they *should* be given information like that in Figure 7.18. (Of course, that is easier for the authors, both of whom have tenure, to say than it is for a junior person facing a demanding boss.)

The impact of uncertainty about predictor variables can be shown more dramatically graphically (Figure 7.19). Notice here that the true range is considerably larger than the range implied by using the standard error of the regression as a basis for estimating uncertainty. What this means is that unless you are fairly certain of what the value of

FIGURE 7.18   Format for Reporting a Regression Model Based Forecast

Scenario	Forecast		
	Pessimistic Forecast − 2S_{YX}	**Best Guess** Forecast	**Optimistic** Forecast + 2S_{YX}
Pessimistic: No change in GDP Advertising down 10 percent			
Best guess: GDP up 3 percent Advertising up 10 percent			
Optimistic: GDP up 5 percent Advertising up 25 percent			

the predictor variable will be, it doesn't help forecast very much. Hence, variables that are easy to predict (e.g., year, GDP) are, *ceteris paribus,* more useful as predictors than variables that are themselves unpredictable (e.g., consumer sentiment, commodity prices).

Nonlinear Relations

Most regression forecasting models are linear; that is, they are of the form

$$\text{Sales} = b_0 + b_1 X_1 + b_2 X_2 + \ldots,$$

where X_1 and X_2 are the independent or predictor variables and the sales total is the dependent variable.

FIGURE 7.19   The Impact of Uncertain Predictors on Forecasting

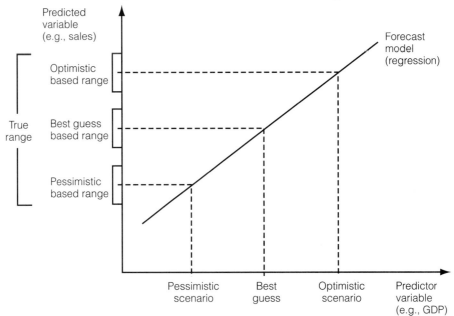

In some cases, there is a nonlinear relationship between the Xs and sales. For example, there may be diminishing returns to advertising. In the linear framework, each dollar of advertising is equally effective. If there are diminishing returns to advertising, the impact of the millionth dollar is less than the tenth. This can be handled in the regression framework by, for example, using a logarithmic function:

$$\text{Sales} = b_0 + b_1 (\log \text{advertising})$$

One model, which has been used fairly extensively, is a multiplicative model (in economics, referred to as a Cobb-Douglas function):

$$\text{Sales} = b_0 X_1^{b_1} X_2^{b_2}$$

which can be written and estimated with a standard regression program by using a logarithmic transformation of the variables:

$$\log \text{Sales} = \log b_0 + b_1 (\log X_1) + b_2 (\log X_2)$$

An interesting implication of this formula is that the coefficients are interpreted as *elasticities* rather than slopes. Thus, b_1 would be interpreted as the percentage change in sales due to a 1 percent change in X_1.

The results of a logarithmic model of the breakfast cereal data appear in Figure 7.17 (regression number 3). It is interesting that the results differ from those of the linear model. Here the price elasticity is insignificant ($t = .56$), whereas the advertising elasticity is significant ($t = 2.09$), as is the trend. The slope results for price and advertising from the linear model were the opposite. This can happen when two different theories about how sales are created are specified. It also suggests that a third model, using a linear function of price and a logarithmic one for advertising, might be the best.

Share Forecasts

To this point we have focused on volume forecasts. In stable markets, share is critical. Share forecasts are typically based largely on the impact of marketing mix components (price, promotion, advertising) on sales or share. For share modeling, the so-called logit model is now widely applied. Its basic form is:

$$\text{Share Brand } i = \frac{\exp(BX_i)}{\sum_{\text{all brands}} \exp(BX_j)}$$

where $\exp(BX)$ means e to the power BX, and BX is a function such as $B_0 + B_1$ (Advertising $) + B_2$ (Price). Logit models can be used to answer "what if?" questions such as, What will happen if I increase advertising 20 percent and competitors don't match the increase?

Forecasting Really New Products

For many products, the requirement that regression models have a large number of years (or other time period) of data is unrealistic. This is particularly the case for technological innovations or new durable goods. In addition, the demand in the early stages of the product life cycle does not necessarily look very linear. Figure 7.11 demonstrates such a sales curve. For example, the product manager for a PDA in 1995 did not face the same forecasting environment as the product manager for Quaker Oatmeal. PDAs had not been for sale for many years (mainly since 1992), and were in the early growth stage of the product life cycle.

To handle such situations, models have been developed to forecast first purchases of products. The most popular model in marketing is the Bass model (1969). The model assumes two kinds of customers: innovators, who purchase the product early in the life cycle, and imitators, who rely on word of mouth from other purchasers. This results in what is called a *diffusion* process. The model used by Bass has the following form:

$$P_t = p + [q/M]Y(t - 1)$$

where

P_t = Probability of purchase given no previous purchase.

$Y(t - 1)$ = Total number who have purchased the product through period $t - 1$.

M = The market potential (saturation level).

q = Parameter representing the rate of diffusion of the product reflecting the influence of others (also called the *coefficient of imitation*).

p = Initial probability of purchase (also called the *coefficient of innovation*).

Sales in period t is

$$S(t) = [M - Y(t - 1)] P_t,$$

Substituting P_t from the first equation into the sales equation, we obtain

$$S(t) = pM + [q - p]Y(t - 1) - q/M[Y(t - 1)]^2$$

If q is greater than p (the rate of imitation is greater than the rate of innovation), the sales curve will rise and then fall. If q is less than p (the rate of imitation is less than the rate of innovation), the sales curve will fall from its initial level.

The model can be estimated running a regression of the form

$$\text{Sales} = c_0 + c_1 Y(t - 1) + c_2[Y(t - 1)]^2$$

that is simply using sales as the dependent variable, with the independent variables being the cumulative number of previous adopters and that quantity squared. In other words, all that is needed are historical sales data. Once the c coefficients are estimated, the quantities p, q, and M can be solved for by the following identities:

$$c_0 = pM, c_1 = [q - p], \text{ and } c_2 = -q/M$$

There are three equations and three unknowns, so p, q, and M have unique solutions.[2] Forecasts of sales can also be developed directly from the sales equation.

The Bass model has fit past adoption patterns well. For example, it correctly forecast a downturn in sales of color TVs in the late 1960s, something the "expert" forecasts at the major manufacturers failed to do because they used essentially linear extrapolation. Unfortunately, the model is sensitive to the number of periods of data that are available and can be unreliable when only four or five years of data exist.[3] Also, for example, the

---

[2] If c_2 is less than zero, p must be solved for using the quadratic formula. It has two solutions, one negative and the positive one that is used.

[3] Reasonable forecasts are obtainable when the results of past studies—essentially the average values of p and q—are combined with data (Sultan, Farley, and Lehmann, 1990).

market saturation level, M, is probably affected by price, and the imitation parameter, q, is affected by advertising (Horsky and Simon, 1983; Jones and Ritz, 1991). While the preceding model includes no marketing variables, an extended model incorporating these variables has been developed (Bass, Krishnan, and Jain, 1994).

ILLUSTRATIONS

Energy Bar Potential

We assume (optimistically) that consumers eat an average of one bar per day (a real "saturation" level). We then examine how many people are potential customers. Here we start with the entire population and then subtract those we consider not to be consumers due to age, allergies, or income level. (Note in doing this we over-adjust since some consumers fall in multiple categories, i.e., are over 74 and poor). The resulting potential number of customers is 215,430 (Figure 7.20).
Therefore

$$\text{Potential} = (215 \text{ million})(365 \text{ bars/year}) = 78.5 \text{ billion bars per year}$$

Notice here how critical the usage assumption (bars consumed per week) is to this estimate; if we assume a more realistic 1 bar per week average, the potential estimate drops to a more reasonable, but still hard to attain, 11.2 billion bars per year, a far cry from current levels.

Forecasting Energy Bar Sales via Regression

Forecasting U.S. sales of energy bars is difficult for several reasons. First, there are relatively few years of data to go on (here we use five years, 1997–2001, to forecast 2002). Second, many of the macroeconomic variables one might use (e.g., household income, CPI) are highly correlated, forcing a choice of one (here number of households). Third, causal variables such as price and new product entries are difficult to forecast. For the sake of the example, we use advertising spending of Power Bar, the category creator, partly because it was available. (Note we need to forecast this for 2002, which introduces more uncertainty in the forecast.) The data appear in Figure 7.20. The resulting regression model produced an R^2 of .998, inflated because of the scarcity of data points. The model was

$$\text{Dollar sales} = -7{,}130{,}000{,}000 + 71.29 \text{ (number of households)} + 9{,}557{,}467 \text{ (Power Bar Advertising)}$$

with a standard error of 9,314,701.

FIGURE 7.20 **Potential Energy Bar Customers**

	2003 Potential Consumers (000s)
U.S. population	284,332
Minus children under 5 years old	18,602
Minus 70% of adults over 74 years old	18,014
Minus population allergic to wheat	3,000
Minus population allergic to nuts	3,128
Minus population below poverty level (9.2%)	26,159
Total potential consumers in 2003	**215,430**

FIGURE 7.21 Power Bar Data

Year	$ Sales	Number of Households	Power Bar Advertising in Millions
1997	85,506,530	99,965,175	9.72
1998	158,197,712	101,042,864	8.36
1999	217,109,706	102,118,600	7.00
2000	353,108,889	103,245,963	14.00
2001	504,000,000	104,344,445	20.00

Households are fairly easy to forecast; here we use 105,458,124 (admittedly ridiculous precision). Power Bar advertising is harder to forecast, so we use three scenarios: an optimistic 26 million, a best guess of 24 million, and a pessimistic 18 million, a decrease from 2001. (Notice how sensitive the forecast is to this assumption.) The resulting forecasts, with ±2 standard errors, equal to 18,600,000, used as a conservative estimate of the uncertainty, are the following:

	Power Bar	
Advertising Level	Forecast	Range
18 million	558,100,000	539,500,000 to 576,700,000
24 million	615,600,000	597,000,000 to 634,200,000
26 million	634,600,000	616,000,000 to 653,200,000

Note that, even with R^2 above .99, there is significant uncertainty stemming mostly from uncertainty about the causal market factors (here Power Bar advertising) which drive sales. Notice also how much less this is than the potential estimate, suggesting the result is feasibly attainable.

PDA Sales

Consider the problem of forecasting PDA sales in 1995. The four years of data available at that time (Figure 7.22) provide a limited basis for illustrating the basic Bass model. The results of running the Bass model are

$$\text{Sales} = 78.123 + .783Y(t) - .0007Y(t)^2$$

FIGURE 7.22 Bass Model: PDA Actual versus Predicted

Year	PDA Sales (000s)	Predicted	Percent Error
1992	63	·78.123	24.0%
1993	150	124.674	16.9
1994	200	213.144	6.6
1995	285	282.104	1.1
1996	?	283.614	?

The model predicts historical sales quite well. In addition, q is much greater than p ($q = .798$ and $p = .065$), indicating that the product has favorable word of mouth. The forecast for 1996 is for 284,000 units, or essentially no growth. As we now know, sales have continued to grow. However, a large part of this growth is due to decreased prices and increased quality (i.e., communication capabilities) as well as the explosion of the Internet. In particular, the Palm Pilot was introduced in 1996. This emphasizes the difficulty in forecasting sales early in a life cycle; clearly estimating the Bass model using all data to the present would produce a much higher forecast for future sales.

Forecasts made in early 2000 were much more bullish:

- IDC (via CNETNews.com) suggests sales will increase from 5.4 million in 1999 to 18.9 million in 2000.
- Industry Standard (using analysis by Forrester Research) suggested that by 2000 there could be 15 million PDAs in use and that by 2002 handhelds will outsell PCs.
- Mobile Insights (via Field Force Automation) suggested sales of "mobile information appliances" would be over 25 million and surpass sales of notebooks.

Still upgrades, the influence of Blackberry, technology convergence, wireless features, and mergers, make even these forecasts seem dated. The point is that in fast-changing markets, forecasts rarely age gracefully.

USING FORECASTS

As noted earlier in this chapter, it is difficult to say which techniques are good and which are bad because success often depends on the circumstances. Accuracy depends on factors such as time horizon, how much money is spent on the forecast, how much time was spent developing the forecast, the volatility of the category, and the like.

Although using quantitative procedures may at times seem tedious, two major reasons encourage their use: (1) they simplify routine, repetitive situations, and (2) they force explicit statements of assumptions. When using quantitative methods, it is best to take the following supplementary steps:

1. *Do sensitivity analysis.* Only when a result seems to be stable over method and data points (e.g., drop one or two years of data and rerun the analysis) can the forecast be advanced with much conviction.
2. *Examine large residuals.* Residuals are individual forecasting errors made for each period. By examining the characteristics of those periods when the forecast was inaccurate, you can often uncover omitted variables.
3. *Avoid silly precision.* This means round off the forecast and give an honest plus or minus range.
4. *Be tolerant of errors.* Expect the methods to improve one's odds of making a good forecast, not guarantee them. Be suspicious of forecasts with very narrow ranges.
5. *Remember that you will generally miss the turning points.* Quantitative (as well as qualitative) forecasting methods work well as long as the patterns that occurred in the

past extend into the future. Whenever a major change occurs, however, most forecasts will be way off. Stated another way, most forecasting methods are relatively useless for predicting major changes in the way the world operates, and consequently most forecasts do not include the effects of these changes.

Combining Forecasts

So far this chapter has described a number of forecasting methods and their strengths and weaknesses. When you are making an important forecast, it is both common and prudent to make several forecasts and then combine them, perhaps using some averaging method. An average of a set of forecasts using disparate methods will tend to be better than a forecast using only one method that is susceptible to its own particular weaknesses.

The results of several methods can be summarized in a table such as that in Figure 7.23. The range of these forecasts provides a useful indication of the uncertainty faced. Moreover, deciding how to combine these forecasts forces one to make explicit assumptions. In Figure 7.23, a simple average is used as the combination rule (that is, equal weighting), but weights could also be assigned, for example, in inverse proportion to the size of the confidence interval (Wilton and Gupta, 1987).

Gaining Agreement

The previous discussion implies that only one person is involved with developing a forecast. Sometimes forecasts are "top down": A higher level manager develops a forecast for each product's sales. Alternatively, forecasts can be "bottom up," an aggregation of several forecasts made by regional salespeople, country managers, or others. Unfortunately, top-down and bottom-up forecasts rarely agree with either each other or growth targets established for the product. The process of reaching agreement is both useful and frustrating.

In understanding bottom-up forecasts, you should recognize that both personal incomes and budgets depend on the forecast. Personal incomes, especially salespeople's,

FIGURE 7.23 Sample Format for Summarizing Forecasts

	Forecast		
Method	**Pessimistic**	**Best Guess**	**Optimistic**
1. Time series extrapolation			
2. Regression model:			
Version A			
Version B			
3. Expert judgment:			
Expert A			
Expert B			
4. Own judgment			
5. Bottom-up forecast			
Average			

are tied to quotas, which in turn are derived from forecasts. Therefore, a salesperson will tend to be conservative in his or her forecast to make the sales goal or quota easier to attain. In contrast, certain managers may overstate sales potential to gain a larger budget. Thus, the bottom-up process, though based on the knowledge of those closest to the customer, may well produce a biased estimate. Total reliance on either bottom-up or top-down methods is generally a mistake.

Why Not Just Go to the Web?

An increasingly common approach to forecasting is to search the Internet for forecasts and then combine them, typified by averaging the estimates. This is expeditious but somewhat naive. First, ask yourself where their forecasts came from. Chances are they are influenced by earlier forecasts, creating a snowball or cascade effect where early forecasts have a big impact. Second, consider who did the forecasts and how: Often the person has less training than you do as a result of reading this chapter. If that makes you uneasy, good. The point is that, if the forecast is important, you need to understand the process used to make it and either make it yourself or find a reliable (as opposed to convenient) source.

SUMMARY

Market potential is generally poorly understood, yet very important for different reasons. Low estimates of market potential result in marketing managers declaring categories mature too soon. This tends to create opportunities for ambitious competitors who have different views on the amount of untapped potential. The mere act of trying to calculate potential market size often gives the product manager ideas about how to extend the product or service into new segments, a topic we consider further in the next two chapters.

Forecasting is one of the most important jobs facing the product manager. The forecast is an input to aspects of marketing strategy. It is also critical to production planning. When forecasts are substantially off on the high side, objectives are overly ambitious; inventories are too large; and senior managers, production personnel, and channel members become upset. When the forecast is much lower than actual, the losses are opportunity costs: lost sales. Multiple methods and logic, plus some knowledge of regression analysis, provides a good basis for forecasts. Luck helps also.

References   Bass, Frank M. (1969) "A New Product Growth Model for Consumer Durables," *Management Science,* January, 215–27.

Bass, Frank M., Trichy V. Krishnan, and Deepak C. Jain (1994) "Why the Bass Model Fits without Decision Variables," *Marketing Science* 13 (Summer), 203–23.

Bayus, Barry L., Saman Hong, and Russell P. Labe, Jr. (1989) "Developing and Using Forecasting Models of Consumer Durables: The Case of Color Television," *Journal of Product Innovation Management* 6, 5–19.

Beeh, Jenny E. (1994) "PCs Are Taking to the Streets," *Advertising Age,* October 31, 28.

Cerf, C., and V. Navasky (1984) *The Experts Speak.* New York: Pantheon Books.

Chambers, John C., Satinder K. Mullick, and Donald D. Smith (1971) "How to Choose the Right Forecasting Technique," *Harvard Business Review,* July–August.

Cox, William E. (1979) *Industrial Marketing Research.* New York: John Wiley & Sons.

Deveny, Kathleen (1990) "States Mull Rash of Diaper Regulations," *The Wall Street Journal,* June 15, B1.

Dhalla, Nariman K., and Sonia Yuspeh (1976) "Forget the Product Life Cycle Concept!" *Harvard Business Review,* January–February, 102–12.

Georgoff, David M., and Robert G. Murdick (1986) "Manager's Guide to Forecasting," *Harvard Business Review,* January–February.

Horsky, Dan, and Leonard S. Simon (1983) "Advertising and the Diffusion of New Products," *Marketing Science,* Winter, 1–18.

Jones, J. Morgan, and Christopher J. Ritz (1991) "Incorporating Distribution into New Product Diffusion Models," *International Journal of Research in Marketing,* June, 91–112.

Kahn, Kenneth B. (2002) "An Exploratory Investigation of New Product Forecasting Practices," *The Journal of Product Innovation Management* 19, 133–43.

McWilliams, Gary (1995) "At Compaq, a Desktop Crystal Ball," *Business Week,* March 20, 96.

Neslin, Scott A., and Robert W. Shoemaker (1983) "Using a Natural Experiment to Estimate Price Elasticity: The 1974 Sugar Shortage and the Ready-to-Eat Cereal Market," *Journal of Marketing,* Winter, 44–57.

Sanders, Nada R., and Karl B. Manrodt (1994) "Forecasting Practices in US Corporations: Survey Results," *Interfaces,* March–April, 92–100.

Sellers, Patricia (1991) "A Boring Brand Can Be Beautiful," *Fortune,* November 18, 169.

Sultan, Fareena, John U. Farley, and Donald R. Lehmann (1990) "A Meta-Analysis of Applications of Diffusion Models," *Journal of Marketing Research,* February, 70–77.

Wheelwright, Steven C., and Spyros Makridakis (1985) *Forecasting Methods for Management.* New York: John Wiley & Sons.

Wilton, Peter C., and Sunil Gupta (1987) "Combination of Forecasts: An Extension," *Management Science,* March, 356–72.

Wired, November 1995, p. 76.

Appendix 7   Time Series Regression with Seasonal Factors

Consider the following data on quarterly fuel oil shipments to the United Kingdom in 1964–66 (Figure 7A.1). In plotting these data, we see that there is, as expected, a very strong seasonal effect (Figure 7A.2). Clearly, ignoring the seasonal component would be a major error. (It would also produce significant autocorrelation.) Running four separate regressions is impractical because there would only be three observations per regression. It would be possible to deseasonalize the data before performing the regression, using an adjustment factor for each quarter such as

$$\frac{\text{Average sales for the particular quarter}}{\text{Average sales for all quarters}}$$

Possibly the most appealing approach, however, is to employ dummy variables. This would consist of first creating ("dummying up") a variable for each of the four quarters (Figure 7A.3). The following equation would then be estimated by regression:

$$\text{Shipments} = B_0 + B_1\,(\text{Time}) + B_2\,(\text{Winter}) + B_3\,(\text{Spring}) + B_4\,(\text{Summer})$$

Note that one of the possible dummy variables must be left out so the computer program will run. If all the independent variables are included, the independent variables are perfectly multicollinear. In this case it is impossible to invert a key matrix, and the program will bomb. (Alternatively, we could drop the constant B_0 and retain all four dummy variables if that were an option of the computer program being used.) In general, if a categorical variable has c categories, $c - 1$

FIGURE 7A.1   **Fuel Oil Shipments to the United Kingdom**

Quarter	Year	Sales
1	1964	210
2		120
3		140
4		260
1	1965	220
2		125
3		145
4		270
1	1966	225
2		128
3		149
4		275

FIGURE 7A.2 **Graph of Fuel Oil Shipments**

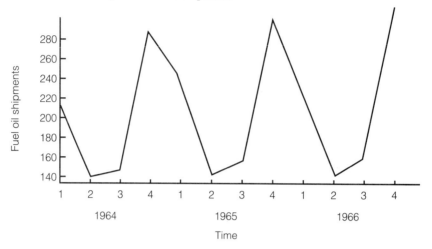

dummy variables must be employed. Here, fall was excluded. This does not affect the forecasts, which are independent of the variable deleted. The results were:

$$B_0 = 256.5$$
$$B_1 = 1.468$$
$$B_2 = -45.6$$
$$B_3 = -141.1$$
$$B_4 = -122.2$$

FIGURE 7A.3 **Seasonal Dummy Variables**

Shipments	Time	Dummy Variables			
		Winter	Spring	Summer	Fall
210	1	1	0	0	0
120	2	0	1	0	0
140	3	0	0	1	0
260	4	0	0	0	1
220	5	1	0	0	0
125	6	0	1	0	0
145	7	0	0	1	0
270	8	0	0	0	1
225	9	1	0	0	0
128	10	0	1	0	0
149	11	0	0	1	0
275	12	0	0	0	1

FIGURE 7A.4 **Predicted Shipments by Season**

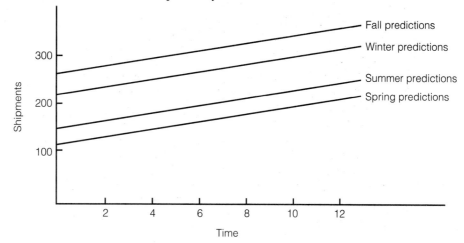

Predictions for each of the quarters are thus:

Winter: Shipments $= B_0 + B_1 \,(\text{Time}) + B_2(1) + B_3(0) + B_4(0)$
$= (B_0 + B_2) + B_1 \,(\text{Time})$
$= 210 + 1.468 \,(\text{Time})$

Spring: Shipments $= (B_0 + B_3) + B_1 \,(\text{Time})$
$= 115.5 + 1.468 \,(\text{Time})$

Summer: Shipments $= (B_0 + B_4) + B_1 \,(\text{Time})$
$= 134.4 + 1.468 \,(\text{Time})$

Fall: Shipments $= B_0 + B_1 \,(\text{Time})$
$= 256.6 + 1.468 \,(\text{Time})$

The results are shown graphically as Figure 7A.4. The coefficients of the dummy variables are interpreted as the difference in the average value of the dependent variable between the category of the dummy variable and the category of the variable that has no dummy variable (in this example, fall). Thus,

$$B_2 = \frac{210 + 220 + 225}{3} - \frac{260 + 270 + 275}{3} + 3(1.468)$$
$$= -50 + 3(1.468) = -45.6$$

If this model were used to predict shipments in the second quarter of 1968, the "best guess" prediction would then be

$$\text{Predicted shipments} = 155.5 + 1.468(18) = 142$$

Chapter **Eight**

Developing Product Strategy

Overview

The previous chapters gave a detailed view of the background analysis homework helpful to developing a marketing plan.[1] This chapter addresses the reason for doing all the analysis, the selection of product strategy (i.e., the action plan for the product). That action plan should address three related questions:

1. *Where are we headed?* Here the focus is on basic objectives such as growth versus profits.
2. *How will we get there?* This is the core of marketing/product strategy that addresses issues such as whether to focus on existing versus new customers. It is summarized in a Targeting and Positioning statement defining (*a*) customer targets, (*b*) competitive targets, and (*c*) the proposition (general offering) that will enable the firm to succeed in capturing the targeted customers in the face of competition.
3. *What will we do?* This addresses specific programs or tactics to be employed in order to implement the core strategy. Basically it entails describing the marketing mix (product, pricing, promotion, distribution, service).

This chapter focuses primarily on number (2), targeting and positioning. Specific programs are covered in the following chapters.

Benefits of Strategy

A successful strategy leads to at least three key outcomes:

First, it *enhances coordination* among functional areas of the organization as well as within marketing. Different areas of the organization have different perspectives on how to make a product successful. Product managers often like to increase advertising spending. Sales managers favor (more) flexible pricing policies. Production personnel typically advocate longer production runs and fewer products. Financial/accounting analysts require quantitative justification of expenditures and favor quick results.

---

[1] Much of our thinking about marketing strategy has been influenced by James "Mac" Hulbert, Columbia Business School; William Brandt, Impact Planning Group; and Abraham Schuchman, long-time marketing professor at Columbia.

For example, suppose a computer manufacturer wishes to target a specific industry with unique product features. The image or "positioning" of the product is high quality and technological superiority. In such a case, a sales manager's flexible pricing orientation is inconsistent with the strategy. The production people may be upset with the approach because it means lower volume and more customization. The brand-building activities of the advertising agency are difficult to evaluate in financial terms for the accounting personnel. One purpose of strategy is to ensure that all members of the team are working together (i.e., on the same proverbial page). Of course, a strategy that is not accepted, poorly articulated, or not well understood cannot provide the necessary coordination.

Second, strategy *defines how resources will be allocated.* Resources are limited. Typically some resources, such as manufacturing or service capacity, sales force time, money, and so forth, will be more limited than others. In addition, these resources are often shared. For example, a single sales force often sells many products. The lower the level of the organization, the more resources are typically shared. Therefore, at the product level it is essential that the strategy provide clear guidance for the allocation of resources across activities.

Third, strategy should *lead to a superior market position.* Chapter 3 showed how the definition of competitors is critical to market success. A good strategy takes cognizance of existing and potential competitors and their strengths and weaknesses (see Chapter 5). A *competitively sensible* marketing strategy has at least one of four main characteristics:

1. It is something a competitor *cannot* do. A competitor's inability could be based on patent protection (e.g., the pharmaceutical industry), extra capacity, or some other proprietary or technological advantage. For example, until the release of Windows 95, Apple Computer was the only personal computer supplier with a truly easy-to-use graphical user interface. Other operating systems, notably DOS and earlier versions of Windows, could not match the Apple interface. Note, however, that cannot do does not mean forever, as Apple found out as Windows 98, NT, etc., eroded its position.

2. It is something a competitor *will choose not to do.* Often smaller companies pursue small segments of the market in the hope that large companies will ignore them due to financial criteria. For example, Silicon Graphics, Inc., a manufacturer of computer workstations, specialized in computers that manipulate three-dimensional images on screen for jet design, movie special effects, and other applications. The other major suppliers of workstations, Sun, IBM, and Hewlett-Packard, built more general-purpose computers that did not perform as well as those made by Silicon Graphics for the segment's needs.

3. Competitors *would be at a disadvantage if they do it.* Sears's marketing strategy of "everyday low pricing" (see Chapter 10) was an unsuccessful attempt to emulate the success of Wal-Mart because the company was not prepared to fully integrate a low-cost and low-price orientation in the entire organization.

4. *It causes us to gain if the competitor does it.* Campbell Soup Company ran an advertising campaign around the theme "Soup is good food." Such a theme is clearly generic and is aimed at increasing soup consumption in general. Since Campbell has

a dominant position in the market, it benefits from such generic promotion. However, Heinz or Lipton could not afford such a strategy because it would likely primarily cause Campbell's sales to increase.

In sum, a good marketing strategy coordinates functional areas of the organization, helps allocate resources efficiently, and helps the product attain the market position management desires. It also identifies an advantage over the other products and services pursuing the same customers.

ELEMENTS OF A PRODUCT STRATEGY

A more complete statement of marketing strategy for a product consists of seven parts (Hulbert, 1985):

1. Statement of the objective(s) the product should attain.
2. Selection of strategic alternative(s).
3. Selection of customer targets.
4. Choice of competitor targets.
5. Statement of the core strategy.
6. Description of supporting marketing mix.
7. Description of supporting functional programs.

The first two elements, objectives and strategic alternatives, establish the general direction of the strategy. The next three elements, selection of customer and competitor targets and description of the core strategy, are the essence of marketing strategy.[2] Taken together, they are often referred to as positioning, that is, how the product is to be differentiated from the competition in the minds of the target customers. Finally, the supporting marketing mix and functional programs relate to the implementation of the strategy.

A systematic approach to developing strategy helps achieve the coordination and integration referred to earlier. There is a logical order to the aspects of the strategy: It is clear that marketing mix decisions such as price and advertising logically depend on the basic strategy. For example, the strategy of a high-quality positioning to upscale customers, such as Ralph Lauren's Polo clothing line, is logically implemented by high price, exclusive distribution, and classy advertising to obtain consistency between the strategy and implementation.

SETTING OBJECTIVES

An organization has a variety of objectives, beginning with mission or vision and ranging from corporate to product. The type of objective that is our concern addresses the question "Where do we want to go?" Clearly, the answer to such a question will differ

---

[2] Product selection is also part of the marketing strategy as well, that is, "which products" to "which markets?" Because we assume the role of a product manager in this book, the basic product choice is taken as given. Modifications of the product are discussed in Chapter 9.

FIGURE 8.1 **Hierarchy of Objectives**

Level 0   Company Mission/Vision

↓

— — — — — — — — — — — — — Corporate objectives — — — — — — — — — —

Level I

↓

Corporate strategies

↓

— — — — — — — — — — — — — Divisional objectives — — — — — — — — — —

Level II

↓

Divisional strategies

↓

— — — — — — — — — — — — — Product/Brand objectives — — — — — — — — —

Level III

↓

Brand strategies

↓

— — — — — — — — — — — — — Program objectives — — — — — — — — — — —

Level IV

↓

Tactics

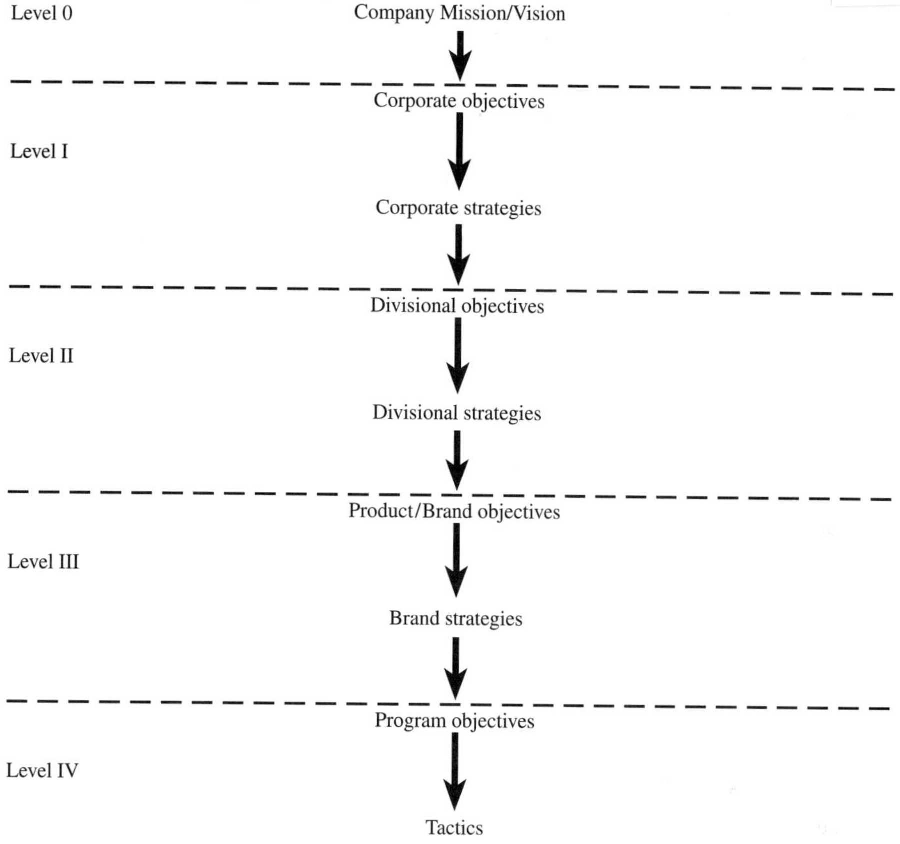

depending on the level of the organization. At the corporate level, objectives related to return on investment, stock share price, and business mix are common. However, they are not very useful for the marketing manager because they give little guidance at the product level for how to proceed.

Figure 8.1 represents the different levels of objectives and strategies in an organization, that is, a *hierarchy of objectives.* Objectives at different levels of the organization should mesh to achieve overall corporate objectives. The job of ensuring that individual product objectives add up to the organization objective usually falls to corporate personnel who are responsible for negotiating both business unit and product objectives to achieve the overall objective.

In this chapter, we are concerned primarily with level III, product objectives. The two objectives most commonly set for specific products or services are growth—in terms of sales revenues or market share—and profitability. It is usually not possible to optimize both simultaneously during the time span of an annual marketing plan. The kinds of activities necessary to achieve an ambitious market share objective work against satisfying an ambitious profit objective.

For example, to reach a market share objective, the usual actions include price reductions, increased spending on advertising, increasing the size of the sales force, and so forth. Significant growth in share is, at the margin, achievable only by increasing expenditures or lowering profit margins per unit. The trade-off between profits and share is exemplified by Japanese auto manufacturers that shifted to a profit orientation from a share objective, partly due to losses suffered when the yen rose to 80 to the dollar in 1995. The result was the introduction of upscale cars (e.g., Lexus) and SUVs (*Business Week,* 1996).

Few managers employ a growth objective without some consideration of its impact on the product's profits (although several Internet firms did so, disastrously in many cases). Likewise, profitability may be the main goal but subject to share maintenance or controlled decline (i.e., harvesting). The objective to be maximized might be called the *primary* objective and the objective acting as the constraint the *secondary* objective. A third objective that can be set for a product is cash flow. When a company is bought through a leveraged buyout (as was the rage in the 1980s), cash flow to pay down debt is a primary concern, and thus the company's products are often charged with generating cash.

Other characteristics of good objectives are the following:

1. They should have *quantified standards* of performance. In other words, every objective statement should include a metric on which to evaluate performance such as "increase market share two share points."
2. They should be ambitious enough to be *challenging,* but not unrealistic. Objectives act as motivators. If regularly set too high, employees treat them as meaningless. Unrealistic objectives also lead to missed earnings targets, an event punished fairly harshly by the stock market. If set too low, the organization is not sufficiently challenged to reach its potential.
3. They should have a *time frame* within which to achieve the objectives. For annual planning purposes, the year serves as the primary time frame, with perhaps quarterly checkpoints.

Two key questions for the product manager with respect to objectives are (1) which one should be pursued and (2) how high a target should I set?

To answer the first question, product managers should consider industry, competitor, and customer analyses and the company's current and anticipated financial resources. For growth objectives to be feasible, there must be some competitor vulnerabilities that can be exploited (competitor analysis), a customer segment with remaining potential (customer analysis), or general category growth anticipated (industry analysis).

Some industries have traditional objectives. For example, in consumer products, the focus for many years was market share and sales volume. Product managers have been under constant pressure to "move cases" of products. However, a recent trend emphasizes profits over traditional volume targets. This is difficult to implement for two reasons. First, information systems at most companies do a good job of measuring share and sales volume on a regular basis but not of measuring profits. Second, and perhaps more important, companies do not always reward product managers on the basis of profits; the key to fast-track careers has been to increase volume and share.

The second issue is how ambitious to be: If a manager is pursuing increased market share, how much increase is appropriate? In some cases, no growth in share is challenging enough: If a product has had declining share, halting the decline could be considered ambitious. The size of the gain to be expected depends on the market size forecasts and the anticipated activities of competitors. If the competitors are going for profits, it can be a good time to gain significant share. Still, if all companies plan to increase share (i.e., share goals total 130 percent), some will clearly be disappointed.

A number of noneconomic or nonquantitative objectives are also pursued, although not necessarily as primary product objectives. For example, it is difficult to find a U.S. company that has not made a major push for quality, and many firms have specific customer satisfaction objectives (e.g., to increase satisfaction from 70 to 75 on a 100-point scale). Similarly, maintenance of brand equity is a concern in a growing number of companies. There is an obvious link between these "enabling" objectives and economic objectives: Achieving the former should eventually lead to reaching the latter.

In sum, the task of setting objectives involves choosing the appropriate objective, quantifying the objective, and setting a time frame for its achievement.

SELECTION OF STRATEGIC ALTERNATIVES

The choice of strategic alternatives follows the selection of the primary objective. This is the first step in developing the marketing strategy for the product or service that provides broad guidelines for the ultimate strategy selected. Figure 8.2 presents alternative strategies in a treelike structure. The diagram assumes the long-run objective of any product manager is to maximize the product's long-run profits (which in turn should maximize shareholder value). We link the description of the alternatives to the selection of whether the primary objective is growth in sales/share and hence long-run profits or short-term profitability. The options available depend on the objective. If a manager chooses growth, the two main ways to achieve it are market development and market penetration, often via the introduction of new products or extensions. Market development strategies are directed toward selling the current product to current noncustomers; market penetration aims at current or past customers of the product category. If the manager chooses the profitability path, the primary focus is on either decreasing inputs (basically cutting costs, also known as denominator management) or increasing outputs (sales revenue).

Increasing Sales/Market Share

Market Development Strategies

These strategies are aimed at noncustomers of the product (i.e., customer acquisition). One approach is to pursue nonusers in segments already targeted. For example, if an Internet service is targeted to law firms, a development strategy would pursue those law firms that have not yet purchased the product (as well as pursuing current customers with value-added). Essentially, this approach tries to tap remaining market potential from those segments identified as prime prospects. One example is the increased attention small business owners have received from large banks such as Wells Fargo. While the banks already have customers from that segment, the lack of growth from lending to larger clients gives the banks more incentive to expand their marketing efforts to get more customers from entrepreneurial companies.

FIGURE 8.2 **Strategic Alternatives**

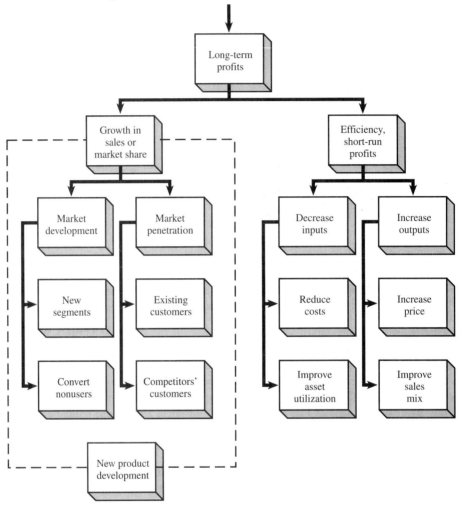

A second approach is to enter new markets, developing segments previously ignored by the product category. An example of this strategy is the attempt by Kodak and Fuji to attract children to photography using a variety of promotions and special programs (Bounds, 1994). Another example is the seed company that put small containers of vegetable seeds in plastic wheelbarrows at garden supply stores to try to get children to begin gardening at a young age. Similarly, antacids such as Tums have been positioned as not only solving stomach acid problems but also as a calcium additive. The classic example is Arm & Hammer baking soda, which has been marketed as useful for several purposes.

Market Penetration Strategies

An alternative, and often overlooked, way to increase market share or sales volume is to increase the usage rate of the brand's existing customers (i.e., customer expansion). The biggest asset a company has is its customer base, and it should be leveraged as much as possible. Product managers can obtain more volume from existing customers by, for example, using larger package sizes, promoting more frequent use, or getting a larger share of the business if the customer uses several vendors (i.e., share of wallet).

Many firms have successfully taken this track. Banks try to get a larger share of commercial customers' business by cross-selling other services, such as cash management and annuities. Coupons are often used to induce customers to buy larger package sizes in the hope of increasing the consumption rate (Wansink, 1996; Chandon and Wansink, 2002). Product managers should always ask themselves: Is the actual consumption rate equal to the *potential* rate?

A second route to increasing sales or market share is to attract competitors' customers (i.e., customer acquisition), that is, to induce brand switching. This is a difficult strategy when the switching costs are high (e.g., mainframe computers, nuclear generators). In addition, the strategy could be risky. First, it can incur the wrath of a larger, more formidable competitor. Second, it may involve substantial use of sales promotion, which could make the strategy unprofitable. Third, a strategy inducing brand switching may call for comparative advertising, which is not only expensive but also risky; if poorly executed, it may call attention to the competitor's brand, particularly if the brand is the market leader. Because of the increase in credit card issuers (e.g., AT&T, General Electric, "affinity" cards), category participants resorted to stealing the best customers from one another (Pae, 1992). AT&T was heavily involved in defending its long-distance phone calling business from MCI, which developed new services (e.g., "Friends and Family") and launched price comparison ads to steal AT&T customers, as well as the Baby Bells, Sprint, and other newer entrants. The 2002 "churn" (switching) rate in cell phone customers was 20 percent a year *before* it became possible to keep your same phone number when switching companies.

Increasing Profitability

Decreasing Inputs

One way to increase profits is cost reduction. Obvious candidates for reduction are costs of marketing such as advertising, promotion, selling expenses, marketing research, and so forth. Unfortunately, reducing these inputs may have adverse long-run effects. A possible danger in stressing variable cost reduction is that a reduction in the inputs can cause a commensurate reduction in the outputs. Aluminum Company of America (Alcoa) restructured its operations in 1992 and reduced its workforce; the result was a rejection rate at one of its can manufacturing facilities of 25 percent and a drop in customer satisfaction to below 50 percent (Milbank, 1992). At the same time, some minor product changes can save a substantial amount of money. For example, Ford reduced its costs $8 million to $9 million per year by decreasing the number of carpeting options from nine to three and saved $750,000 by using black screws rather than color-matched screws on Mustang side mirrors (Schwartz, 1996).

A second way to decrease inputs is to improve the utilization of the assets. This might mean keeping down accounts receivable and, for a manufactured product, the costs of inventories. Other, related activities include running production equipment more efficiently and, at a more aggregate level, investing idle cash on hand in overnight interest-bearing securities.

Product managers choosing the profit branch of the tree must, of course, also choose customer targets. The probable approach for this objective would be to concentrate on current customers. In fact, one of the most obvious ways to improve profits is to reduce customer turnover/churn, (i.e., increase customer retention).

Increasing Outputs

The easiest way to increase revenues from existing unit sales is to improve prices. This can be done in a variety of ways, including increasing the list price, reducing discounts (think rebates on car purchases), reducing trade allowances, and so forth. Of course this can lead to a substantial drop in unit sales and hence lost revenue. There is also the issue of competitive reaction, which has doomed many airline price increases and hurt P&G's attempt to institute everyday low pricing (EDLP; Ailawadi, Lehmann, and Neslin, 2001).

The other way to increase revenues is to improve the sales mix. The 80/20 rule often holds: 20 percent of the product variants (sizes, colors, etc.) produce 80 percent of the sales or profits. In such an instance, it may make sense to emphasize selling more of the profitable items. Alternatively, if we apply the rule to customers, the product manager may want to de-emphasize unprofitable customers and concentrate resources on those producing 80 percent of the profits (i.e., customer deletion).

Summary

We have presented two broad strategic options available to a marketing manager in terms of strategic alternatives.[3] This does not mean that a manager is limited to either growth or profits. For example, it is common to seek reductions in variable costs while pursuing market share gains. In addition, a product manager may choose both to increase the consumption rate of current customers and to introduce product-line extensions.

The marketing manager's dilemma is that while several of the options may appear to be equally attractive, it is very difficult and expensive to successfully implement multiple strategic alternatives. Part of the difficulty arises from the multiple positionings different alternatives may require. For example, to simultaneously obtain new customers and get current customers to buy more, different advertising campaigns may have to be run, projecting different images and confusing customers. Multiple strategies prevent economies of scale from advertising copy, increase the use of more expensive media (i.e., spot versus national TV), and so forth, thus increasing expenses. It also creates confusion within the organization about what the goals really are. Hence, there is pressure on the product manager to select a subset of the options available and concentrate resources on them.

POSITIONING: CHOICE OF CUSTOMER TARGETS

In selecting a customer target, three key considerations are critical:

1. *Size/growth of the segment.* An important part of customer analysis focuses on which customer groups are growing and how fast.
2. *Opportunities for obtaining competitive advantage.* Competitor analysis assesses which market segments competitors are pursuing and their claimed competitive

---

[3] A similar view of the alternatives in a high-tech context is provided by Kadanoff (1995), pp. 24–26. She labels current customers in the installed base as "Low-hanging fruit," new customers in current segments as "Juicy fruit," new customers in "adjacent" markets as "Ripe fruit," new customers in new segments as "Fruit on the vine," and new customers in developing segments as "Seedlings."

advantages, the resources they can put into the market, and their likely future marketing strategies.

3. *Resources available.* This is covered in the self-analysis part of the assessment of competition analysis.

As mentioned earlier, positioning entails a specific statement of how the product differs from the competition in the minds of a specific set of customers, and encompasses (1) customer targets, (2) competitor targets, and (3) some attribute(s) by which the differentiation will occur. The choice of which customer group(s) to target follows immediately from specification of the strategic alternatives and the segments developed in the customer analysis. If the profit route is taken, the customer targets are generally current ones, for example, "men 18 to 25" or "banks with assets between $100 million and $1 billion." The task is similar for any of the growth alternatives. For a market penetration strategy aimed at the product's own customers or a market development strategy aimed at nonusers, the customers of the current strategy would again be selected. For the market penetration strategy aimed at stealing competitors' customers, the specific descriptors of those customers would be used. Finally, for the market development strategy aimed at new segments, the descriptors from the new segments chosen would be specified.

Consider Handspring's strategy in the PDA market in 2000. Given that their basic product was strong on convenience and low in price, their target segments differ from the traditional PDA customer: upscale, price-insensitive business professionals. One can identify three segments worth pursuing (Figure 8.3). Why choose to serve customers

FIGURE 8.3 **Target Segments for Handspring**

Factor	Price-Sensitive Business Professionals	Nonbusiness Professionals	Nonprofessionals
Benefits, key attributes of PDA	• Functionality, expandability • Status • Design, sleek, small, nice screen • Price • Memory, speed	• Ease of use, convenience • Design, sleek, small, nice screen • Price • Functionality, expandability • Status • Durability	• Ease of use, convenience • Price • Fun/Enjoyment (music, games) • Design, nice screen • Battery life • Status, sense of belonging (cool product)
Main factors affecting PDA purchase	• Price • Functionality • Memory	• Ease of use • Functionality • Price	• Ease of use • Price • Design, sleek, small, nice screen
Where do they purchase?	• Through company, possibly buy themselves at consumer electronics retailers • Over Internet	• Through company, possibly buy themselves at consumer electronics retailers • Over Internet	• Consumer electronics retailers • Over Internet
When do they buy?	• When colleagues buy	• When colleagues buy	• When friends, neighbors, or classmates buy • Receive or purchase as gift

who currently provide little profit? In the case of such acquisition strategies, this means ensuring that the value of acquired customers is greater than their acquisition cost (see Chapter 14).

POSITIONING: CHOICE OF COMPETITOR TARGETS

Even if the competition is not explicitly mentioned in any of the product's communications programs, it is still important to consider which competitors are the primary targets of the strategy. For a penetration strategy that involves stealing competitors' customers, the targeted customers should be identified based on an analysis of which competitor's customers are both valuable and the most easily pried away. However, all strategic alternatives at least implicitly involve competition because of the necessity to position the product *against* major competitors.

Positioning involves some prioritization of the competitors, both direct and indirect. Again, the chief source of information about this choice is the situation analysis in Chapter 5, which details the strengths and weaknesses of the competition. The hope is to identify a weak or docile company with significant sales that can be easily overcome. Unfortunately such targets are not always available (Ries and Trout, 1986; Czepiel, 1992). Market leaders often take defensive steps and therefore focus on the strong second competitor and perhaps the third one. The followers in the market take different competitor stances depending on their market share relative to the leader. A strong second might focus on offensive warfare and target the leader. Weak followers often try to avoid the major competitors and seek market niches that have either few or weak rivals. For example, in banking they might be a "boutique," offering customized services targeted at individuals with high net worth, thus avoiding full-scale competition with large banks.

POSITIONING: CORE STRATEGY

The core strategy defines the differential advantage to be communicated to the target customers, often referred to as *product positioning*. The advantages that can be employed fall into two basic categories: (1) cost/price (economic) differential advantage and (2) differentiation based on product offering or service features.[4] (Note that differentiation can include psychological as well as functional benefits.) In other words, you either have to have a lower price that can be supported in the long run only with lower costs or be better on some element of the product offering customers recognize as a benefit.

As several examples show, being "stuck in the middle" can be disastrous. In 1991, Compaq Computer was in deep trouble. The previously high-flying computer company, known for its high-priced, high-quality personal computers, showed its first-ever quarterly loss. The loss occurred because it was neither the low-price nor the quality/performance

---

[4] See, for example, Porter (1985). Porter actually advocates a third basic strategy, market segmentation. However, we believe market segmentation is a necessary part of any strategy.

leader in an increasingly competitive market. United Airlines' shuttle ("express") service failed to significantly affect Southwest Airlines in the large California market since it was not lower priced nor perceived to be of higher quality.

In general, the positioning decision has four steps (Day, 1990, Chapter 7):

1. Identify alternative positioning themes by consulting the advertising account team, the product team, and past marketing plans.

2. Screen the alternatives according to whether each is (*a*) meaningful to customers, (*b*) feasible given the firm and product resources and customer perceptions, (*c*) competitively sensible (see the definition in the overview of this chapter), or (*d*) helpful for meeting the product objective.

3. Select the position that best satisfies these criteria *and* can be sold to the marketing organization.

4. Implement programs (e.g., advertising) consistent with the product position selected.

This systematic approach ensures that alternative positionings are considered and diverse constituents consulted.

The core strategy should be easy to summarize and communicate in paragraph form. Sometimes this statement of the core strategy is referred to as the *value proposition*. The value proposition for Southwest Airlines, for example, could be the following:

To provide travelers with the lowest-cost air transportation with an enjoyable, fun atmosphere.

This clearly states that Southwest's differential advantage is price and fun, not food, frills, and nonstop routes.

Cost/Price (Value) Strategy

Almost every product category has a competitor that focuses on price or "value," as opposed to product features or on some aspect of the product other than price. Wal-Mart made Sam Walton the richest man in the United States. Charles Schwab invented the discount brokerage business. Private labels have become very popular in many supermarket product categories, and are often the number one brands in their categories (e.g., frozen juices, drinks, and cookies). Mail-order personal computers stressing price constitute a huge business, and for a time Packard-Bell (now aligned with NEC) was the largest vendor of personal computers in the United States largely through its low-price, mass distribution channel approach.

Not all products can be the low-price leader. Many firms lack the required size, capital, or other resources. First, a high volume of a single product or family of products should be produced or sold. Focused production hastens cost reduction, which must be continuously pursued. Second, investment should focus on efficient facilities and market share. Again, efficiency does not apply just to production equipment. The lowest-cost companies pay strict attention to corporate overhead, including size of staff, perks such as jets and limousines, fancy offices, and so on. Finally, control should focus on cost in manufacturing products and delivering services, as well as activities such as advertising and promotion.

In pursuing lower costs, the product manager should focus on important activities in which their cost is high. The important costs involved vary widely over different products.

For a personal computer, decreased cost of semiconductors, microchip boards, video screens, and the like, all bring the cost of the product down significantly. However, for a laundry detergent, the major cost items might be the thickness of the plastic package and the size of the label.

The low-price core strategy poses real risks. One is that customer tastes shift, and the product being produced in large quantities may no longer be desired (e.g., Atari and other video games before the Nintendo era). A second is that technological shifts can either make it easier for competitors to have the same costs or make the product obsolete. Competitors can also leapfrog in cost cutting, which eliminates the cost differential advantage. One advantage of a low-price strategy is that there is probably always room in a product category for a low-priced, "value" option because some segment of customers will always be price sensitive. The key question, of course, is how large the price-sensitive segment is, how many competitors will target it, and, therefore, whether it is worth the investments necessary to be a cost leader.

Nonprice Strategy

One way to think about the nonprice differential advantage is as a product characteristic, not necessarily tangible, that allows the product manager to obtain a price higher than the price that would be allowed under perfect competition. As every student of microeconomics (and, it is hoped, every reader of this book) knows, with many suppliers of undifferentiated commodities, the market price tends to approach marginal cost. Therefore, a differential advantage that creates added value in the minds of customers enables the producer to obtain a higher price than the pure competition case; with a significant differential advantage, customers focus on product benefits other than price.

From where can a differential advantage be obtained? Figure 8.4 portrays what is called the *total product concept* (Levitt, 1986). The *generic* product is the bundle of characteristics—the functional aspects of a product. For example, an automobile could be described by quality of tires, miles per gallon, engine size, and so forth. The *expected* product is described by other benefits delivered by the product that customers have come to take as routine. For cars, the expected product includes some degree of reliability and warranty coverage. The *augmented* and *potential* products are often what give rise to differential advantage. The augmented product includes features or benefits that can be delivered now to go beyond expectations—for example, a satellite-based global positioning system (GPS) for tracking. The potential product contains those features or benefits that can be added to a product or service some time in the future. Customers remember restaurants that offer free meals when a customer is dissatisfied or the retail clerk who pays special attention to a customer when the store is busy. Actions which enhance the customer's purchasing and consumption experience generally lead to repeat buying.

The point here is that differential advantages are often obtained by going beyond what customers expect, to provide unanticipated product benefits. It may take some creative thinking, but one important aspect of providing differential advantages is to move away from asking, "How can I make this product different?" to asking, "What am I selling?" By focusing on what customers are buying—that is, benefits, and more broadly, customer experience—product managers can better determine how to make their products or services different from the competition.

FIGURE 8.4 Total Product Concept

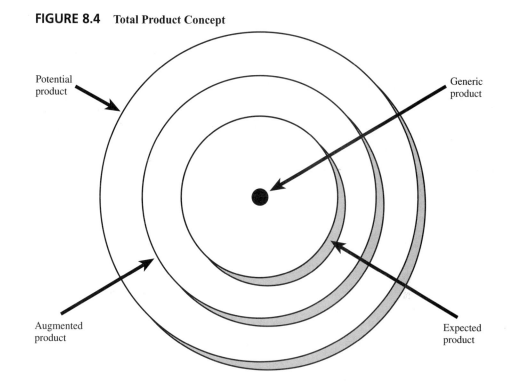

Product managers typically use five areas for differentiation (Schnaars, 1991).

1. *Quality.* Product quality has many dimensions. For example, particularly for technologically based products, enhanced quality can mean improved performance. Intel originally differentiated its products by being technologically ahead of other semiconductor
   companies. Quality can also mean superior design. Automobile brands such as Lexus,
   computers such as Apple, stereo manufacturer Bang & Olufsen, and consumer product companies such as Sony emphasize superior design in their products. Customer
   service is also an area for differentiation based on quality (we expand on this in Chapter 14). Manufacturers such as Timken (bearings) and Caterpillar (farm equipment) are
   well known for their customer service. For service businesses, product quality and customer service are virtually synonymous. Airlines such as Singapore and retailers such
   as Nordstrom differentiate on this basis. For manufactured products, quality can also
   mean reliability and durability. Brands marketed by the appliance manufacturer Maytag,
   for example, are advertised on this dimension (the "lonely repairman").

2. *Status and image.* In the bottled water category, brands such as Evian and Perrier have
   claimed this point of differentiation from other bottled waters. Many consumer fashion
   brands, such as Rolex watches and Polo clothing, use this approach.

3. *Branding.* A particular aspect of image involves brands. Brand names and their values communicated to customers, brand equity, can serve as a point of differentiation.
   IBM, McDonald's, and Nestlé are leading brands worldwide. It is particularly interesting when a product that had previously been considered a commodity is differentiated

FIGURE 8.5 **Joint Space for Colas**

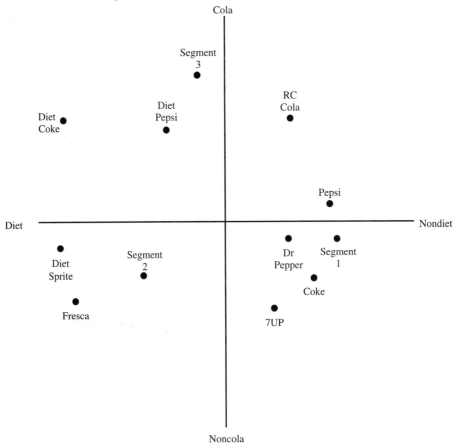

and becomes successful after branding, such as Perdue chickens. A more recent illustration is the campaign by Intel using ads touting "Intel Inside."

Perceptual mapping, described in Chapter 6, has been extensively used by product managers to assess the current perceptual positions of brands among customer and competitor targets and to help determine if the current positioning is effective or whether repositioning can help. Figure 8.5 shows what is called a *joint space* because it not only indicates brand locations versus competition on the two axes but also displays *ideal points,* the preferred bundle of attributes of clusters of households. Note that the map incorporates all three aspects of positioning. Customers are represented by the ideal points (the segments are numbered according to size), competitors are located on the map, and the differential advantage can be assessed using the brand attributes represented by the axes.

Consider the joint space figure from the perspective of RC Cola. RC is perceived as a nondiet cola, but it is equidistant from segment 1, which is close to Coke and Pepsi, and segment 3, which seems to want a lower-calorie cola. RC can position itself more within the mainstream, where it would encounter heavy competition from Coke and

Pepsi. Alternatively, it can pursue segment 3 with a "lighter" image where it would find fewer competitors, but also fewer potential customers.

4. *Convenience and service.* Many consumer products are differentiated on the basis of convenience. Lexus and Infiniti differentiated themselves from other luxury car brands by making it easier for customers to have their cars serviced, giving free loaner cars, and sometimes making arrangements to pick up the car at the customer's home. Home shopping grocery services focus on convenience to entice people with home computers and modems to change their buying habits and purchase their weekly supermarket orders from home.

5. *Distribution.* The product manager can sometimes gain differential advantage by reaching customers more efficiently and effectively than competitors (see Chapter 13 for more on this topic). Federal Express, through its Powership terminals, allowed its customers to determine for themselves where their packages are in the system and to order the "product." Thus, Federal Express becomes, in effect, the customers' shipping department.

The requirements for a nonprice differential advantage core strategy are naturally quite different from those for a cost/price strategy. First, the strategy requires searching for continuous product improvements (or improvements in perceptions) to maintain the differential advantage. Second, a differential advantage core strategy requires flexibility in both production and management to keep up with changes in customer tastes and competition.

The risks involved in the differential advantage core strategy are also considerable. First, the cost/price differential may become so great that customers are willing to pay less to get less. Perhaps the biggest problem is that the differential can often disappear due to imitation. Witness the quick adoption of frequent-flier programs by almost all the major airlines. Who remembers—or cares—that American was the first with such a program?

MANAGING BRAND EQUITY

Managing a product's reputation is one of the most important strategic jobs facing the product manager. Like objects owned by a firm such as manufacturing equipment and buildings, a brand name is an asset, and a potentially valuable one.

For several years, the growth of private label brands and higher spending on price-oriented promotions led pundits to predict the "death" of national and international brands. This belief was given further credence when "Marlboro Friday," the Friday in April 1993 on which Philip Morris reduced the price of its venerable Marlboro brand by 40 cents per pack to combat private label cigarettes, caused sharp drops in the stock prices of manufacturers of national brands. This action was replicated by the cereal manufacturers, led by Post (also owned by Philip Morris) and Kellogg's in April 1996.

There is no question that many private labels have in effect become brands (as President's Choice, originally a house brand of Loblaw's, formally did). Yet many brands remain powerful and profitable. Several companies have decided that the best way to combat lower-priced competitors, whether private labels for supermarket products or clones for computers, is to reemphasize their brand names. Companies such as Coca-Cola, Hewlett-Packard, and P&G invest in advertising and attempt to reduce harmful price-oriented promotions. Such efforts caused the sales of private labels to plateau and made 12 out of the 15 *Fortune* most admired companies household brand names (Morris, 1996). Of course, branding alone is not enough: during 1999 and 2000, new Internet companies poured massive dollars into ads designed to attract customers and build brand recognition (the first level of brand equity), with at best mixed success.

Brands are also engaged in global warfare against counterfeiters and "knockoffs," products that are almost identical to the originals with very similar (or the same) brand names and packaging but substantially lower prices. Knockoffs mislead customers into thinking that the product is the well-known global brand. Counterfeiting is particularly prevalent in the music CD, computer software, and clothing industries (the U.S. government has sent numerous trade missions to China to try to persuade them to crack down on these activities to little effect). The problem is not just the lost revenues but the potential for the reputations of the global brands to be damaged by poorly made substitutes.

In Chapter 6 we described brand equity in terms of awareness, associations (image), attitude (overall quality), attachment (loyalty), and activity (e.g., word of mouth). A slightly different version developed by Aaker (1996) appears in Figure 8.6 and includes five categories:

1. *Brand loyalty.* The strongest measure of a brand's value is the loyalty (repeat buying, word of mouth) it engenders among customers. Sometimes the loyalty is circumstantial: Repeat buying comes from a lack of reasonable alternatives. Circumstantial loyalty includes what are called *proprietary* assets (e.g., patents, copyrights, trademarks, control of an airport) that give a firm at least a temporary monopoly position (the impact of generic drugs when an ethical drug comes off patent suggests that much of the advantage is in fact circumstantial and hence temporary). In other situations, loyalty reflects an *efficiency* motive: The brand is good, so we automatically select it to minimize effort. Notice that an important special case of efficiency loyalty occurs when a customer relies on an "expert" (e.g., a dealer) to make the choice for her or him and the expert has a preferred alternative. In this case, loyalty is really channel-created loyalty.

    The strongest form of loyalty is *attachment.* In this case, the customer doggedly seeks out a product, often out of deference to its role in a previous situation (e.g., "They were there when I needed them") and sometimes in an almost ritualistic manner (e.g., stopping at a certain ice cream store as a rite of summer). This level of loyalty insulates a brand from competitive pressures such as advertising and price promotion and leads to higher margins and profits.

2. *Brand awareness.* The simplest form of brand equity is familiarity. A familiar brand gives the customer a feeling of *confidence* (risk reduction), and hence it is more likely to be both considered and chosen. There is also convincing evidence that, on average, customers *prefer* brands with which they are familiar. Finally, choosing a known brand gives the customer a *justification* for the decision, an explanation for his or her actions. This justification also serves a *social* role, indicating that the person has bought something of value.

3. *Perceived quality.* A known brand often conveys an aura of quality (good or bad). A quality association can be of the general halo type; for example, Levi Strauss for years had an outstanding reputation both for its products and as a place to work. Associations can also be attribute or category specific: Gillette makes fine-quality razors,

FIGURE 8.6 **Brand Equity**

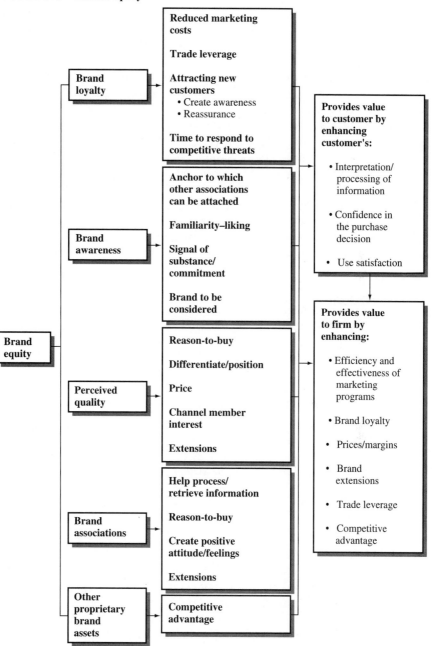

Source: Reprinted with permission of The Free Press, a division of Macmillian, Inc. from *Building Strong Brands* by David A. Aaker. Copyright 1996 by David A. Aaker.

Apple produces user-friendly products, and Samsonite products last forever. In some cases, a brand becomes synonymous with a category (e.g., Xerox, Kleenex, FedEx). Further, a brand often has strong price associations that influence quality perceptions (e.g., a Kmart brand product is expected to be low in price and probably low in quality as well).

4. *Brand associations.* More subjective and emotional associations are also an important part of brand value. These include *personal* associations; Gatorade's "Be Like Mike" campaign was a blatant example, but every celebrity endorsement contains elements of it. Other associations are more emotional, relating to such lifestyle or personality characteristics as *stability* (see many Kodak ads, as well as Prudential's "A piece of the rock"), being *"hip"* or *"with it"* (a standard appeal of fashionable clothing companies, soft drinks, beer, and liquor), and being *responsible* (e.g., environmentally conscious, currently both an important issue and the subject of much hype). Other strong associations may be with the type of customer or user of the product (e.g., white shirts and bald heads with business executives) or geographic region (e.g., country of origin for Japanese cars, Swiss watches). Figure 8.7 provides a general list of both product attribute and user images. Taken together, these associations form a *brand personality* that suggests situations for which a brand is (and is not) suitable (Aaker, 1997).

FIGURE 8.7 **Some Brand Attribute and Image Dimensions**

Attributes	Image Dimensions
Flavor/taste	Reliable—unreliable
Caffeine content	Old—young
Price	Technical—nontechnical
Packaging	Sensible—rash
Size	Interesting—boring
Calories	Creative—noncreative
Brand name	Sentimental—nonsentimental
Sweetness	Impulsive—deliberate
Weight	Trustworthy—untrustworthy
Warranty	Conforming—rebellious
Durability	Daring—cautious
Convenience	Forceful—submissive
Color	Bold—timid
Style	Sociable—unsociable
Comfort	
Freshness	
Construction material	
Availability	
Serviceability	
Compatibility	
Energy efficiency	
Instructions	
Automation	
Ease of use	

Source: Rajeev Batra, Donald R. Lehmann, and Dipinder Singh. "The Brand Personality Component of Brand Goodwill: Some Antecedents and Consequences," in David A. Aaker and Alexander L. Biel, eds., *Brand Equity and Advertising: Advertising's Role in Building Strong Brands* (Hillsdale, N.J.: Lawrence Erlbaum Associates, 1993), pp. 83–96.

5. *Other brand assets.* Other assets, such as patents and trademarks, are clearly valuable. However, we exclude these from brand equity since they are tied to the physical product or process and not to the brand *per se.*

Brand equity creates value for both customers and the firm. Customers can use brand names as simplifying heuristics for processing large amounts of information: Awareness of the brand name Lexus and the brand associations generated can act as a substitute for reading *Consumer Reports,* talking to friends, and other information sources. Dannon introduced its brand of bottled water under the assumption that consumers who view its yogurt positively will transfer that good feeling to the new product. Over-the-counter cold and headache remedies by well-known companies such as Bayer and Johnson & Johnson command significantly higher prices than their private label counterparts because of the trust customers have in those companies. Thus, firms benefit enormously from having strong brand names. Investment in a brand name can be leveraged through brand extensions and increased distribution. High brand equity often means less price sensitivity, which allows higher prices to be charged, a significant competitive advantage. Similar effectiveness can exist for other marketing activities such as advertising and promotion.

An example of the power of brand names is the ill-fated Audi 5000, which was accused on a widely viewed edition of TV's *60 Minutes* of having a problem with sudden acceleration. The program claimed the car suddenly lurched forward although the driver's foot was not on the gas pedal. Audi failed to view protecting the brand name as one of its chief marketing jobs. As a result, the company handled the problem by accusing U.S. drivers of making mistakes and stepping on the accelerator rather than the brake. Regardless of the truth (it was eventually concluded that the cars did not have a problem), protecting the asset—the company's brand name—should have been Audi's priority. The sales of *all* Audi products dropped two-thirds between 1985 and 1989. As a consequence, the manufacturer introduced new models (Quattro, 100, etc.) and eliminated the problem-ridden 4000 and 5000 lines. This problem of how to handle disasters and their impact on the brand name continues to surface. Consider the problems faced by Ford and Firestone over tread separation in their tires. Another example is Intel's initial reaction to problems with its Pentium processor.

The importance of brand equity raises three important issues for product managers. First, it is particularly important for packaged goods manufacturers that face increasing competition from supermarkets' "own label" brands. The price difference a national brand can support relative to a private label is a direct function of the level of brand equity of the national brand. Even more basic, high brand equity helps get the brand into distribution channels, an obviously critical step in selling the product.

A second question is: How far can a successful brand name be stretched? Clearly Toyota, Nissan, and Honda believed luxury cars could not be sold with cars with a cheaper image; hence, the development of Lexus, Infiniti, and Acura, respectively. Not only are the brand names different but the cars are sold in separate dealerships. Mitsubishi believed otherwise. It marketed a new luxury coupe, the Diamante, along with the rest of its product line, to limited success.

Third, the product manager must view the management and sustenance of brand equity as an important task. This suggests the desirability of both measuring and setting objectives for brand equity. Aaker (1996) provides 10 guidelines for building strong brands:

1. *Brand identity.* Each brand should have an identity, a personality. It can be modified for different segments.
2. *Value proposition.* Each brand should have a unique value proposition.
3. *Brand position.* The brand's position should provide clear guidance to those implementing a communications program.
4. *Execution.* The communications program needs to implement the identity and position, and it should be durable as well.
5. *Consistency over time.* Product managers should have a goal of maintaining a consistent identity, position, and execution over time. Changes should be resisted.
6. *Brand system.* The brands in the portfolio should be consistent and synergistic.
7. *Brand leverage.* Extend brands and develop cobranding opportunities only if the brand identity will be both used and reinforced.
8. *Tracking.* The brand's equity should be tracked over time, including awareness, perceived quality, brand loyalty, and brand associations.
9. *Brand responsibility.* Someone should be in charge of the brand who will create the identity and positions and coordinate the execution.
10. *Invest.* Continue investing in brands even when the financial goals are not being met.

Measuring Brand Value

In order to manage brand equity, it is helpful to measure it. Such measurement is not only the concern of product managers, however. The board of governors of the United Kingdom's Accounting Standards Board held public hearings on rules to require all companies to value their brands, and some companies in the United Kingdom and the United States carry brands on their balance sheets. Grand Metropolitan, for example, carried specific brand equities for Smirnoff, Pillsbury, and Burger King.

Given the large amount of attention paid to brand equity in the last few years, it is not surprising that a variety of consulting firms, advertising agencies, and other interested parties have developed their own approaches to measuring the value of brands and, as a result, rankings of relative brand equities (e.g., Research International's Equity Engine, Milward-Brown's Brand Z, and Y&R's Brand Asset Evaluator). These measures focus on the image of brands (i.e., the customer's view). For example, Y&R's BAV assesses a brand in terms of stature (knowledge and esteem) and strength (differentiation and relevance) and has shown, along with Stern, Stewart & Co., that the ratings are related to profits, specifically EVA.

Interbrand assesses the financial value of a brand in two steps. First, it computes the revenue premium vs. a generic competitor. It then adjusts this with a multiple which attempts to account for differences in industry growth and other factors. Based on this, Coca-Cola was the most valuable brand in 2002, worth about $70 million followed by Microsoft ($65 million), IBM ($52 million), GE ($42 million), and Intel ($31 million). (For more, see its website, *Interbrand.com*.)

An example of a survey-based approach is Landor's ImagePower. The 1999 study on consumer perceptions of technology brands was based on over 6,000 respondents from a mailing to 50,000 Internet users. Each respondent had to provide information for at least 50 of the 250 brands evaluated. Landor used four primary measures: appropriateness (how relevant the brand is to everyday life), share of heart (how highly the person regards the brand), distinctiveness (how unique and different the brand is from competition), and share of mind (how familiar the person is with the brand). Based on its survey, the top five technology brands in 1999 were the following:

1. Windows
2. Microsoft
3. Yahoo!
4. Pentium
5. Microsoft Word

Obviously, Microsoft has been an effective marketer.

An example from the technology area is a quarterly survey conducted by Techtel Corporation. The firm surveys business buyers of computer equipment including software and hardware on measures such as awareness, trial, purchase, and repurchase intention. The survey also measures the percentage of the buyers who have a positive opinion about a brand. An illustration of the results is shown in Figure 8.8 for IBM notebook computers. The squares represent the opinion measure while the vertical bars represent those who bought recently (within the previous quarter). The obviously high correlation between positive opinion and purchasing measures gives some assurance that brand strength converts into actual buying behavior. Further, opinions such as these turn out to be predictors of stock price movements (Aaker and Jacobsen, 2001).

Product managers can measure overall brand value through a variety of means. Basically, measuring brand value requires answering the question "How much more value does the product have with the brand name attached?" Methods such as those discussed in Chapter 10 can be used to measure brand value. One other method already discussed, conjoint analysis, can also be used. By simply using brand name as an attribute and using the different brand names in the market or fictitious brand names being considered for a new product, the part-worths estimated are quantitative measures of the value of a brand name relative to the others used in the experimental design. (Recall that in the example in Chapter 6 we found different values for Dell and HP.)

A related method relies on so-called hedonic regression. This technique regresses market price (or the amount customers say they are willing to pay for various products) against product features and brand name:

$$\text{Price} = B_0 + B_1 (\text{Feature 1}) + B_2 (\text{Feature 2}) + \cdots$$
$$+ C_1 (\text{Brand A}) + C_2 (\text{Brand B}) + \cdots$$

The output gives a dollar value for each brand. (Of course, when actual prices are used, this analysis ignores the sales volume of each brand, so it may present a somewhat distorted view of the value to those customers who choose to buy each product.)

The various components of brand value can also be assessed in relatively straightforward ways. Different levels of awareness measurement (e.g., aided or unaided) are possible. Attribute associations can be directly assessed ("If ABC Inc. made a product with X amount of attribute A, how much of attribute B would you expect it to have?").

FIGURE 8.8 IBM Notebook Computers: Purchase versus Positive Opinion

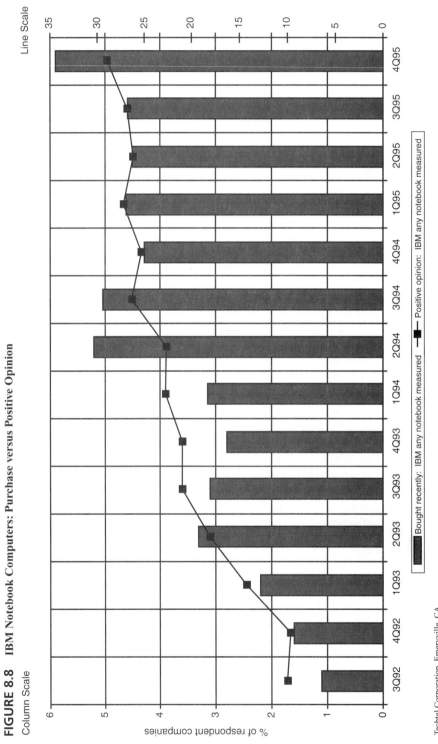

Techtel Corporation, Emeryville, CA.
Source: Developed by Techtel Corp. T-MAS™ © 1992–1996 and data © 1987–1996 by Techtel Corp. and others.

A simple product-market level measure is the extra revenue a brand receives vis-à-vis a private label product of equal quality, which is driven by two components: price premium and share premium. Brand equity realized in a particular year is thus simply the additional revenue the brand received, assuming both its share and price are greater than those of the private label (Ailawadi, Lehmann, and Neslin, 2003). For example, according to IRI's 1997 Marketing Fact Book, Dreyer's price premium versus private label was $0.90 - 0.53 = 0.37$ and its volume was approximately (14.29%)(36.83)(100 million households), so an estimate of its realized equity in 1997 is ($0.37)(526.3 million) = $194 million. This measure does not explicitly include additional costs—variable and fixed—associated with the brand or its growth and extension potential (i.e., future value). Still, it provides a simple measure that is easy to calculate and hence monitor (and serves as the core of the Interbrand method).

RELATION TO CUSTOMER STRATEGY

As suggested earlier, different product strategies suggest different approaches to customers. Four basic customer strategies are available:

1. Customer acquisition (i.e., getting new customers by market development or market penetration by capturing competitors' customers).
2. Customer retention (i.e., keeping current customers satisfied via enhancing brand loyalty or through superior service).
3. Customer expansion, either getting customers to buy more of what they are currently buying (increasing usage) or "cross-selling" other products (i.e., market potential via increasing business with existing customers).
4. Customer deletion, dropping customers that are not profitable (both now and potentially in the future) in such a way as to not generate legal problems or public relations disasters.

Taken together, the results of these activities determine sales and form a high-level implementation of basic strategy (i.e., growth versus profit). We discuss these in more detail in Chapter 14.

PRODUCT STRATEGY OVER THE LIFE CYCLE

We have repeatedly mentioned the importance (and weaknesses) of the product life cycle concept. One way the life cycle can be used is to conceptualize different general approaches to developing core strategies and tactics.

Introduction Strategies

Up to this point, this book has focused mainly on existing products, but the introductory phase of the life cycle is a useful place to begin this analysis (more will be said about new products in the next chapter). This stage in the life cycle has several characteristics. First, there are often few competitors, perhaps only one. Second, sales volume increases slowly due to the small number of firms marketing the product and the reluctance on the part of customers to purchase it. Early on, selling and advertising focus on selling the generic product; the effort is on product form benefits. Distributors also have the power in the relationship because the product is still unproven with customers, so securing distribution is a major issue. (In the Internet world this means developing links from other sites, etc.) Prices can be high or low depending on the entry strategy of the firm(s) marketing the product.

What are the core strategy options at this stage? There are two well-known options: *skimming* and *penetration*. The skimming strategy assumes a product feature–based differential advantage that allows the product manager to enter and stay in the market during the introductory period with a high price. Target customers are the least price sensitive, that is, the pioneers or early adopters of the product. A penetration strategy is just the opposite: The product manager uses a low-price core strategy and attempts to get as many customers and establish a significant market share position as quickly as possible. This is particularly beneficial if purchase by one customer makes the product more attractive to others.

A skimming strategy is useful when the cost structure of the product is largely variable costs, usually the case when the product is a manufactured good. A high margin can be sustained because the product manager is not under intense pressure to cover large fixed costs. Distribution outlets should be limited to protect the high price. This strategy is most effective when high entry barriers exist because the high price and high margins make the category very attractive to potential competitors. The margins can then be used to fund investment in research and development, leading to new products which can be skim priced when the inevitable competition arrives in the current product category.

A penetration strategy is more appropriate when fixed costs are high (e.g., many services, general purpose computer software). When a broad segment is being pursued, it is important to obtain wide distribution and thus spend heavily on trade-oriented promotion. The product manager is also under pressure to make the market as large as possible, which involves generic or product category marketing. This is a more expensive strategy due to the lower margins and higher marketing costs. The product manager should use a penetration strategy when the lead in the market will likely be short-lived.

There are strategic advantages to being first in a market and establishing a strong position early, consistent with a penetration strategy. Much empirical research shows that the first "mover" (or, more precisely, the first to achieve substantial market position) in a category has an advantage (called, not surprisingly, the *first-mover advantage*) in that it tends to maintain its lead through the product life cycle (Urban et al., 1986). Some of this advantage is obvious: Early movers get first access to distribution channels, establish awareness, and have the first opportunity to establish brand loyalty and create preferences (Carpenter and Nakamoto, 1989). However, followers often overtake leaders, so first movement itself is no guarantee of success (Golder and Tellis, 1993).

Several examples illustrate the different core strategies available. Consumer electronics and industrial product companies almost always pursue a skimming strategy. When VCRs, camcorders, flat screen TVs, and similar products were introduced, they were priced high initially and then fell in price over time. Since usually only one brand was on the market for some months and the early customers for such products (electronics nuts) are generally price insensitive, there was little rationale for pricing low initially. In addition, the products needed word of mouth to help spread information about their utility. Alternatively, penetration pricing is often used for consumer packaged goods because market share is very important for retaining shelf space in supermarkets. This is clearly evident in Internet strategies that give away the product for free, hoping (often unreasonably) to recoup costs with advertising revenues and future sales.

Growth Strategies

The growth phase of the product life cycle encompasses two different kinds of market behavior: early growth—the phase just following the introductory phase—and late growth—the phase in which the rapid increase in sales begins to flatten out. The growth phase has several features beyond the obvious fact that product category sales are growing. First, the number of competitors increases. This puts pressure on product managers to hold distribution channels and changes the focus of sales and communications to the superiority of the product over others in the category. As customers become more knowledgeable about the product and the available options, this puts pressure on price. Finally, with the increased competition, market segmentation begins to be a key issue facing product managers.

The general strategic options relate to the product's position in the market: whether it is a leader (the brand with the leading market share) or a follower. The leader can choose either to fight, that is, keep the leadership position, or to flee, which cedes market leadership to another product. If the leader chooses to fight, it can attempt to either simply maintain the current position (a dangerous approach, since it is difficult to know exactly what it takes to maintain the position) or keep enhancing the product or service. Why would the leader flee? It is possible that the new entrants in the market are just too strong (as indicated by the competitive analysis) and raise the stakes for competing to a level the incumbent cannot sustain. Witness Minnetonka, which established the liquid soap category. When Lever Brothers and Procter & Gamble jumped in, Minnetonka sold out. Exit is always an option. Other options are to attempt to reposition the product so it can be a strong number two or three brand, which can be accomplished through resegmenting the market, or to retreat to a specific niche.

The follower also has a number of options, the choice of which depends on the strength of the leader, its own strength, and market conditions. One option is to exit quickly and invest in some product that has better long-term potential. A follower can also be content to be a strong number two or three by fortifying its position. The riskiest move is to try to leapfrog the competition. Some companies do this successfully through pure marketing muscle and an imitative product. For example, Johnson & Johnson often allows another company to establish the market and then becomes number one through superior marketing. Specifically, in over-the-counter yeast infection drugs: Schering-Plough established the market and J&J followed with its Monistat 7 brand, which quickly obtained more than half of the market (Weber, 1992).

Other companies attempt to leapfrog through technological innovation. A good example is Docutel Corporation in the 1970s (Abel, 1977). Docutel was the first company to develop and market automated teller machines (ATMs) to banks in the United States. The company was very small at the time, with only $25 million in sales in 1974. The market for ATMs grew rapidly during the 1970s as banks discovered they could use ATMs to differentiate themselves from other banks in a geographical area. However, new competitors entered the market, including mainframe computer manufacturers IBM, Burroughs, and NCR, as well as two firms in the bank vault and security information business, Diebold and Mosler. In addition, customers became more concerned about cost savings from the machines as opposed to marketing advantages. Thus, Docutel, the market leader, had to make a fight-or-flight decision. Fighting would mean making substantial investments in marketing and product development, particularly in developing software compatible with banks' computer systems. In addition, the company would have to decide which market segments to target. Alternatively, the company could be a strong number two or three given the potential size of the market. Unfortunately, Docutel did not make a clear decision to pursue any strategy and was ultimately surpassed in the market by Diebold.

Maturity Strategies

The maturity stage of the life cycle is characteristic of most products, particularly consumer products. Product categories exhibiting fierce battles for market share and access to distribution channels, large amounts of money spent on trade and customer promotion, and aggressive pricing are often in this stage of the product life cycle.

In maturity, the sales curve has flattened out and relatively few new buyers enter the market. While some untapped market potential usually remains, it is difficult and/or expensive to reach. Buyers are sophisticated and well versed in product features and benefits. Where differential advantage can be obtained, it is usually through intangible benefits such as image or through the extended product concept discussed earlier (e.g., service, distribution). Market segments are also well defined, and finding new ones that are untapped is a struggle.

The general strategies in mature markets are similar to those in growth markets, and depend on the relative market position of the product in question. A focus on key products and brands has been the hallmark of P&G's rejuvenation at the beginning of the 21st century. However, leaders sometimes look at the time horizon for "cashing out" the product. If the product manager is committed to a product for an extended time period, the objective is usually to invest just enough money to maintain share. An alternative objective is to "harvest" the product, that is, set an objective of gradual share decline with minimal investment to maximize short-run profits. Other firms have alternatives that depend on the leader's strategy. If the leader is harvesting the product, the number one position may be left open for an aggressive number two brand. If the leader is intent on maintaining that position for a long time (many leading consumer packaged goods brands have been number one for over 50 years!), the follower may choose to be a profitable number two or to exit the category.

Strategies for the Decline Stage

In the decline stage of the life cycle, sales of the category are dropping. So is the number of competitors. Markets reach the decline stage for a variety of reasons. Perhaps the most obvious is technological obsolescence. The demise of the buggy whip is such a case. However, shifts in customer tastes also can create declining categories. The decline of brown alcohol consumption can be related to changing tastes for "white" alcohol such as gin and vodka, and subsequently, for wine and microbrewed beer.

Perhaps the clearest strategy is to try to be the last in the market. By being last, a product gains monopoly rights to the few customers left. This, of course, results in

FIGURE 8.9   **Strategy over the Life Cycle**

	Life Cycle Stage			
	Introduction	**Growth**	**Maturity**	**Decline**
Competitive Position: Leader/Follower				
Objective				

Positioning
  Customer targets
  Competitor targets
  Differential advantage				

the ability to charge commensurately high prices. For example, Lansdale Semiconductor was the last firm making the 8080 computer chip introduced by Intel in 1974. While most applications of computer chips are well beyond the 8080, the 8080 was still used in military systems that were typically built to last 20 to 25 years, such as the Hellfire and Pershing 2 missiles and the Aegis radar system for battleships. Where did the Department of Defense go when it needed 8080s? There was only one supplier: Lansdale.

Summary

A useful way to think about strategic issues over the life cycle is to use a table such as Figure 8.9 which encourages both an audit of current position (share; leader–follower) and change in objectives, positioning, and programs as the industry situation changes.

ILLUSTRATIONS

Odwalla Energy Bar

Objective

Grow 10 percent faster than the category.

Customer Targets

  Existing juice customers

  Health conscious and on-the-go

  Sports enthusiasts

  Health purists

  Nutrition-seeking families

Competitive Targets

  Clif Bars and Clif Luna

  Kashi Go LEAN

  Balance (Outdoor, Plus, Oasis)

Core Strategy

Increase distribution to 80 percent ACV in mainstream grocery stores.

Focus on natural health.

Leverage brand name, Minute Maid resources.

Handspring

Objective

To capture 15 percent of the PDA market by the end of year 2.

Customer Targets

As in Figure 8.3, there are three main targets:

Price-conscious professionals (including buyers for company salesforces, etc.).

Nonbusiness professionals (e.g., teachers).

Nonprofessionals (e.g., stay-at-home spouses, students, retired people).

Competitive Targets

Palm

Sharp

Core Strategy

Simplicity/convenience.

Low price.

Expandability (via expansion slot).

SUMMARY

This chapter provides the reason for doing the background analyses described in Chapters 3 through 7. The central component of the marketing plan is objectives and strategies for the product that synthesize the current market situation into a recommended plan of action. The strategy, which can be summarized as in Figure 8.9, then leads to specific marketing programs, such as pricing and advertising. The success of a strategy is largely dependent on the integration of the situation analysis and programs in providing a coherent direction for the product.

Strategy can be organized in multiple ways. Here the focus was on a key strategic alternative, growth versus efficiency. Other perspectives include customer strategy, brand equity, new products, and stage in the life cycle. While at first this may be confusing, closer inspection reveals a close relationship among them. Growth strategies tend to be preferred during growth states of markets, require new products, focus on customer acquisition and expansion, and involve building brand equity. Efficiency strategies, by contrast, tend to be preferred later in life cycles and involve focusing on retaining and/or expanding current customers, making minimal or simple product changes, and leveraging brand equity, often through licensing or selling the name. Figure 8.10 describes these likely contingencies.

FIGURE 8.10 Linked Strategic Issues

		Strategic Alternatives	
		Growth	**Efficiency**
Customer Strategy	Acquire	✓	
	Retain		✓
	Expand	✓	
	Delete		✓
Brand Strategy	Build	✓	
	Leverage	Brand Extensions	Line Extensions
	Milk		License
Product Strategy		New Products	Prune Product Line
Life Cycle Stage	Introduction	✓	
	Growth	✓	
	Maturity		✓

References

Aaker, David A. (1996) *Building Strong Brands.* New York: The Free Press.

Aaker, David A. (1991) *Brand Equity.* New York: The Free Press.

Aaker, David A., and Robert Jacobsen (2001) "The Value Relevance of Brand Attitude in High Technology Markets," *Journal of Marketing Research* 38, November, 485–93.

Aaker, Jennifer (1997) "Dimensions of Brand Personality," *Journal of Marketing Research* 34, August, 347–56.

Abel, Derek F. (1977) "Docutel Corporation," Harvard Business School case study 9-578-073, 1977.

Ailawadi, Kusum, Scott Neslin, and Donald R. Lehmann (2001) "Market Response to a Major Policy Change in the Marketing Mix: Learning from Procter & Gamble's Value Pricing Strategy," *Journal of Marketing* 65, January, 44–61.

Ailawadi, Kusum L., Donald R. Lehmann, and Scott A. Neslin (2003) "Revenue Premium as an Outcome Measure of Brand Equity," *Journal of Marketing* 67, October, 1–17.

Batra, Rajeev, Donald R. Lehmann, and Dipinder Singh (1993) "The Brand Personality Component of Brand Goodwill: Some Antecedents and Consequences," in David A. Aaker and Alexander L. Biel, eds., *Brand Equity and Advertising: Advertising's Role in Building Strong Brands.* Hillsdale, NJ: Lawrence Erlbaum Associates, 83–96.

Bounds, Wendy (1994) "Photography Companies Try to Click with Children," *The Wall Street Journal,* January 31, B1.

Business Week (1996) "Japan Turns a Corner," February 26, 108–9.

Carpenter, Gregory S., and Kent Nakamoto (1989) "Consumer Preference Formation and Pioneering Advantage," *Journal of Marketing Research,* August, 285–98.

Chandon, Pierre, and Brian Wansink (2002) "When Are Stockpiled Products Consumed Faster? A Convenience-Salience Framework of Postpurchase Consumption Incidence and Quantity," *Journal of Marketing Research* 39, August, 321–35.

Czepiel, John A. (1992) *Competitive Marketing Strategy.* Englewood Cliffs, NJ: Prentice Hall, Chapter 1.

Day, George S. (1990) *Market Driven Strategy.* New York: The Free Press, Chapter 7.

Golder, Peter N., and Gerard J. Tellis (1993) "Pioneering Advantage: Marketing Logic or Marketing Legend," *Journal of Marketing Research* 30, May, 158–70.

Hulbert, James M. (1985) *Marketing: A Strategic Perspective.* Katonah, NY: Impact Planning Group.

Kadanoff, Marcia (1995) "Customers Who Are Ripe for the Picking," *Marketing Computers,* December, 24B26.

Keller, Kevin L. (2002) *Strategic Brand Management.* Upper Saddle River, NJ: Prentice Hall.

Lefton, Terry and Weston Anson (1996) "How Much Is Your Brand Worth?" *Brandweek,* January 29, 43–44.

Levitt, Theodore (1986) *The Marketing Imagination.* New York: The Free Press.

Mehegan, Sean (1996) "A Picture of Quality," *Brandweek,* April 8, 38–40.

Milbank, Dana (1992) "Restructured Alcoa Seeks to Juggle Cost and Quality," *The Wall Street Journal,* August 25, B4.

Morris, Betsy (1996) "The Brand's the Thing," *Fortune,* March 4, 72–86.

Pae, Peter (1992) "Card Issuers Turn to Stealing Customers," *The Wall Street Journal,* August 18, B1.

Porter, Michael E. (1985) *Competitive Advantage.* New York: Free Press.

Ries, Al, and Jack Trout (1992) *Marketing Warfare.* New York: McGraw-Hill.

Schnaars, Steven P. (1991) *Marketing Strategy: A Customer-Driven Approach.* New York: The Free Press.

Schwartz, Karen (1996) "Pennies Saved, Millions Earned," *San Francisco Chronicle,* March 24, D1.

Urban, Glen L., Theresa Carter, Steven Gaskin, and Zofia Mucha (1986) "Market Share Rewards to Pioneering Brands: An Empirical Analysis and Strategic Implications," *Management Science,* June, 645–59.

Wansink, Brian (1996) "Does Package Size Accelerate Usage Volume?" *Journal of Marketing* 60, July, 1–14.

Weber, Joseph (1992) "A Big Company That Works," *Business Week,* May 4, 124–29.

Chapter Nine

New Products

Overview

This book has intentionally focused on existing products, partly because unless they are successful, an organization has no internal resources to develop and launch new products. In addition, as you will see, much of the same logic behind marketing existing products applies to new products. However, because of their importance, we focus on new products in this chapter from the perspective of an existing brand and/or product manager. Readers interested in an in-depth treatment should consult one of the many excellent books on the subject (Cooper, 1993; Moore and Pessemier, 1993; and Urban and Hauser, 1993).

Most new products are new in limited ways. New colors here, an added ingredient there, a 30 percent upgrade in capacity, etc., are not earth-shattering innovations. Yet these "slightly new" products account for a tremendous amount of sales volume and profits. They are also often the responsibility of a product, brand, or category manager and an integral part of the marketing plan. By contrast, really new products are rare (one packaged goods manufacturer has a database of 5,000 product launches, of which none may be really new). However, their impact can be substantial, greatly expanding or creating new product categories (e.g., PCs). For these reasons we focus on slightly new products first. Later in the chapter we discuss the development and marketing of "really new" products.

Each year thousands of new products are introduced in U.S. supermarkets alone. Most are not very new, however. Rather, the "slightly new" products consist of minor variations on existing products through (1) changing ingredients (e.g., to reduce the fat content of foods), (2) adding features, or (3) "me-too" entrants that closely resemble existing (competitors') products. These products are the type generally introduced by existing product managers and account for substantial sales and profits and for that reason are very important. Further, the production process involved may be quite sophisticated. Still, these are essentially "lemon-scented" products (named for the first new product, a lemon-scented soap, studied by one of the authors), also known as *continuous innovations*. Most of their sales are drawn from existing products in the category. In general, customers readily understand what these products are used for and what they compete with (e.g., lemon-scented soap competes with lime-scented soap).

New products can be introduced for either offensive (e.g., to gain sales or share) or defensive (to match or block competitors) purposes. To simplify discussion (and because offensive is more exciting than defense in general), we primarily focus the discussion

FIGURE 9.1 Considerations in Adding or Dropping a Variant

Adding	Dropping
Customer based	
New customers attracted	Old customers lost
Old customer cannibalization	Customer switching
Confusion and dilution of brand equity	Signal of weakness
Operations based	
Loss of economies of scale	Impaired efficiency
Problems in gaining additional distribution	Maintaining distribution
Additional servicing needs	Servicing old versions

on offensive (i.e., optional) new products. The decision about the product or services offered is closely linked to two others, namely, what brand (existing vs. new) will be attached to the product, and which customers (old vs. new) will be the target for the product.

The development of new products typically occurs in stages. At each stage, the product is evaluated to determine whether it makes sense to proceed to the next stage. Most products follow a pattern such as Figure 9.1.

While this (systematic) approach works fairly well for slightly new products, it is difficult to apply to really new ones. Not surprisingly, the development and marketing of lemon-scented and really new products differ markedly. For that reason, we first describe key aspects of the approach for most new products and then discuss special considerations for really new products.

PRODUCT MODIFICATIONS

Phrases such as *continuous quality improvement, redesign,* and *updated styling* all point toward modifying the product. Such modification can be of three types: clearly better (e.g., an upgrade), different (e.g., a styling or ingredient change that is likely to appeal more to some customers and less to others), and inferior (e.g., the substitution of a less expensive ingredient or aspect of the offering). In assessing the desirability of a product change, the reactions of three groups are crucial: loyal customers, occasional customers, and current noncustomers. Obviously, the ideal situation is for all three groups to try the new version, prefer it, and buy it more often. Because this almost never occurs, however, results involve the changes in behavior in the different groups. Based on this plus cost considerations, a decision can be made.

The basic dilemma can be considered by using the typology in Figure 9.2. The task begins by assessing the number of loyal customers, occasional customers, and noncustomers who might consider trying a new version of a product. Next, the trial rates for each group must be assessed. Consider the now famous New Coke introduction. One unforeseen problem with the introduction was that loyal Coke buyers would not even try the new version: Coke was a prisoner of its past success and brand equity to the point where many loyal Coke drinkers viewed any change as undesirable. Thus, an interesting

FIGURE 9.2 **Product Stages**

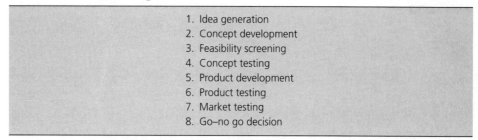

1. Idea generation
2. Concept development
3. Feasibility screening
4. Concept testing
5. Product development
6. Product testing
7. Market testing
8. Go–no go decision

trade-off appears at the trial stage: Big changes may induce noncustomers to try but cost you loyal customers; small changes may retain loyals but not attract new customers. Consequently, we could expect more dramatic changes from smaller-share products that risk losing fewer loyal customers.

After trial, reactions can (somewhat arbitrarily) be divided into three categories: those who prefer the new version, those who like the new version about the same as the old (essentially indifference), or those who do not like the new version (prefer the old).

The final information needed is the profit implications of each combination of customer type, decision to try or not try, and reaction to trial. Some profit implications are relatively clear: Nontrial by loyal or occasional customers means the loss of these customers and hence whatever lifetime value they represent. Similarly, if loyal or occasional customers try the new product and are indifferent between the new and old versions, there is no profit implication other than the change in margin resulting from price and cost differences between the new and old formulations. Triers among either occasional customers or noncustomers who find the product "good but not great" essentially contribute whatever profits (or losses) result from their trial sale and then return to their traditional buying patterns. In considering new variants, then, the impact of customers can be structured via a decision tree, which shows that the big plus is occasional users or nonusers who increase their usage and the big minus is loyal customers who decrease or cease usage.

Of course, noncustomer considerations are also relevant. The most obvious is cost. This includes both the raw material cost and any other costs of the offering (e.g., the amount of the deductible on insurance policies, the interest rate on money market accounts, the amount of training offered). Other considerations include the impact on employees (in terms of morale) and the overall image of the company.

It is important to recognize that modifications can occur not just in the physical product but in any aspect of the offering. Changing channels of distribution (e.g., by selling a product previously available in specialty stores through discount stores) can either increase or decrease the potential market and can also affect the quality image of the product and hence its brand equity and sales. Similarly, lowering price or changing the advertising focus can both open new markets (customer segments) and reduce or cut off old ones. Perhaps the most interesting type of product modification involves the service experience. A fairly ordinary flower becomes special when it is personally delivered; a simple oil change for a car becomes an event if the garage provides a comfortable waiting area.

FIGURE 9.3 Assessing the Impact of Product Redesign on Customers

Current Customers	Reaction	Response after Trial	Impact on Sales/Profits
1. Loyal	A. Try	Prefer	Gain
		Like	Neutral
		Not like	Loss
	B. Not try		Loss
2. Occasional	A. Try	Prefer	Gain
		Like	Trial sales gain
		Not like	Loss
	B. Not try		Loss
3. Noncustomers	A. Try	Prefer	Gain
		Like	Trial sales gain
		Not like	Trial sales gain
	B. Not try		Neutral

For many products, packaging is an integral part of the product (e.g., styling in cars). For others, the package is also a dispensing mechanism with appeal of its own (e.g., Smuckers wide-mouth jam jars, squeezable ketchup bottles, pump toothpaste, liquid soap containers). For some, the container is merely a covering. Even for mere coverings, however, the package presents an opportunity for advertising and image building. McDonald's change in packaging from plastic to biodegradable paper earned the company positive reactions. Packaging changes have contributed to a surge in sales for many products, including Kaytee bird seed and Ray-O-Vac batteries (Morgenson, 1992). Sutter Home's white zinfandel wine sales were reported to have increased 15 percent in six weeks following a label redesign. Of course, not all packaging innovations are successful (e.g., Benedicta's mayonnaise in a tube).

Changing a package is not cheap; often a few hundred thousand dollars are spent on design and retooling for a simple label change. Relative to advertising and promotion, however, a package change is fairly inexpensive. Remember that packaging is inherently part of the product and should be treated—and potentially altered—as any other attribute would be.

Although all these modifications have specialized aspects, they can be evaluated using a version of the framework in Figure 9.3, combined with cost and profit data. Notice that many modifications have both a fixed-cost component (the cost of the changeover) and a variable-cost-per-unit impact.

LINE EXTENSIONS

Introducing additional product variants that use the existing brand name, also known as line extensions, is a popular way to capitalize on the original brand's equity. Many products actually are product families with a number of close relatives designed to appeal to various segments. Lemon-scented soaps and carbide-tipped drill bits are variations on a basic product. Some variants that simply add a small amount of a new ingredient to a basic product have been wildly successful (e.g., seltzer with fruit flavor); others have been flops (e.g., Clairol's Touch of Yogurt Shampoo).

A more general question that arises is how many different Tides, Jell-Os, or Honda Civics there should be. Considerable evidence exists that, after a point, more options are neither desired by customers nor cost-effective (Broniarczyk, Hoyer, and McAlister, 1998).

The reason for using multiple versions is simple: They can appeal to multiple segments, either increasing potential sales (the customer base) or allowing for price discrimination among users with slightly different needs and preferences (e.g., the multiple fares and conditions for airline seats). They also allow for the provision of a full line of products under a single name, making shopping easier and hence potentially building customer loyalty and brand equity. The reasons for not using multiple versions are likewise straightforward: Efficiency of operation (production, inventory, distribution) is enhanced when there are fewer versions to worry about. For example, Toyota found it better to introduce Lexus rather than try to sell a luxury-priced Toyota. Similarly Listerine, which for years advertised that its effectiveness was related to its taste, resisted selling sweet-flavored versions. Further, overuse of a brand may dilute and weaken brand equity, especially when the line elements differ in important ways (e.g., quality). Finally, too many options confuse customers.

Basically, the choice of number of product variations involves the trade-off between two strategies that have both at times been highly successful: Henry Ford's Model T ("any color as long as it is black") and Alfred Sloan's multiple nameplates (Chevy, Pontiac, Oldsmobile, Buick, Cadillac). The efficient (Model T) strategy failed when the market began to develop distinct segments. The multiple nameplate strategy proved unsuccessful when model proliferation and overlap (including the now infamous use of Chevy engines in Cadillacs) created customer confusion, and the lack of an integrated manufacturing strategy (i.e., a common "platform" across models, which had successfully been implemented by Japanese automakers) led to increased costs. The choice of number of versions of a basic product to offer follows the "Goldilocks" principle: not too few, not too many, but just the right number. The car example also points out another fundamental principle: Involving operations thinking in designing variants, not just bringing them in after the product is designed, will save money and potentially improve customer acceptance.

Of course, the ultimate form of product variants is customized marketing (also known as mass customization and one-to-one marketing). Here customers are allowed to choose from a large number of options, typically on a feature-by-feature basis. This strategy, combined with an efficient build-to-order manufacturing system, enabled Dell to gain leadership in the PC business and is the standard approach at Chinese restaurants. Downsides to the approach include operational inefficiency and confusion or frustration for less-expert customers who prefer a reduced choice set.

Assuming a number of versions exist, the more relevant question is whether to increase or decrease the number on the margin. Should a variant be added or deleted? Beyond saying it depends on the long-run incremental profit, it is often useful to break down the consideration of adding or dropping a variant into customer-oriented and operations-oriented concerns (see Figure 9.1).

Adding a Product Variant

One reason to add a product variant is to attract new customers (i.e., market development or penetration; see Chapter 8). One concern in doing so is current customer switching (cannibalization), which can be either beneficial (e.g., going from a lower-margin to a higher-margin version) or detrimental. Also, obviously, there is concern over customer defections. These possibilities require good estimates of profit implications, which in this case place a value on a customer, typically a value much greater than that of the initial sale (see Chapter 14) and the contribution margins of the different versions before and after addition of the new version. In other words, you need both customer and cost data to evaluate the effect of adding a product variant. A final, and unfortunately even harder to assess, aspect of adding versions is customer confusion and dilution of brand equity. Customer confusion is a special problem when the new version differs in quality level. In the automobile industry, levels of options (DE/DX, LE/LX) are essentially appended to the same basic vehicle and seem to be well received and understood. However, when the intended quality spread gets wide enough, even car manufacturers tend to create a new name (e.g., Honda introduced the Acura). Black & Decker essentially gave up trying to sell its regular line of power tools to professional users; instead, it bought and promoted a separate line, DeWalt, to the professional market.

It is generally easier to gain customer acceptance by producing a variant of similar quality than to create one of substantially higher quality. Of course, it is relatively easy to sell a lower-quality (or at least lower-priced) version of a product, but doing so tends to decrease loyalty and equity, sometimes dramatically.

There is also something to be said for maintaining a relatively streamlined set of product variants from the customer's viewpoint. Assuming customers do not view choosing a product as their life's work, they may appreciate a limited choice with clear distinctions among versions. As a corollary, customers may avoid products for which an overabundance of versions makes choosing the best one more trouble than it is worth. The information overload facing a purchaser of snow skis or tennis rackets sometimes makes customers postpone a decision because of confusion and the desire not to make the wrong choice.

Operational issues also influence the decision to add a variant. An obvious impact is on efficiency through economies of scale. Although flexible manufacturing can cut the cost penalty for offering different versions, labeling, stocking and inventory, and demand forecasting still add costs. Each version has the potential to be misforecast, leading to problems of understocking (and hence customer disenchantment) or overstocking (which results in additional carrying costs and distress sales). Just-in-time manufacturing reduces inventory cost to the manufacturer, but also often passes it on to suppliers who then account for it in the prices they charge. Another issue is distribution. Many distribution channels (or customers in the case of direct sales) like to be able to obtain multiple items from the same supplier (which argues for a large number of variants), but not to face such a broad array of options that their own inventory and purchasing tasks become too complicated (which argues for a limited number of versions). A manufacturing company is often allotted a fixed amount of product space (shelf facings) for its products, meaning any increase in one version (e.g., cherry flavored) means a decrease in the retail support of another (e.g., lemon-lime). The sales staff must also be able to allocate time and effort across variants.

Dropping a Product Variant

The decision to drop a variant (product deletion), typically one with slow sales or low profits, is in many ways just the opposite of the decision to add a variant. Considerations include how customers of the old version will react, as well as cost and operational issues. One difference is that dropping a variant means there is one less product version to contribute to (absorb) overhead costs. If any allocated costing system is used, dropping one version will adversely affect the costs, and hence the profits, of other versions. Another and more important consideration is the signal that dropping a version can send. Dropping a variant is an admission of failure and may be seen by customers or distribution channels as an indication of reduced commitment to the product category.

GETTING IDEAS FOR NEW PRODUCTS

Ideas for product modifications and extensions come from many sources, both proactive and reactive. Sources that rely on active efforts of the company utilize many aspects of the situation analysis:

1. *Customer analysis,* in particular, usage/needs analyses and surveys of attitudes and attribute importance, including both unstructured (e.g., focus groups) and structured (e.g., conjoint analysis) approaches. Also, many companies maintain facilities where customers are less obtrusively observed using company products or product mock-ups (e.g., Sony on Michigan Avenue in Chicago, Whirlpool at its headquarters).

2. *Competitor analysis,* specifically studying what competitors sell or are working on. Most new products are copies of competitors' products (e.g., RC, not Coke or Pepsi, first introduced diet cola).

3. *Active search,* particularly of new products and processes in other areas with an eye toward incorporating them in the company's own product.

4. *Category analysis,* examining changing social trends and technologies (often through various media and trade associations).

5. *Brainstorming.* Generating ideas for new products can be difficult. For that reason, a number of structured procedures have been generated such as Tauber's (1972) HIT method, the noun-verb word-pair approach of Durge, O'Connor, and Veryzer (1996), and so-called creativity templates (Goldenberg, Mazursky, and Solomon, 1999). A variation on this is what we call "grammatical tinkering." This approach first requires a detailed description of a current product in terms of current customers (who, what, how, why, etc., as in Chapter 6, which is essentially the customer target component of strategy in Chapter 8) plus the product offering (product benefits, features, and composition) as well as marketing programs such as distribution, service, pricing, and advertised use. Once constructed, creativity simply consists of breaking these "rules,"

first one at a time and then in combination. This approach generates multiple types of new products such as:

New market/customer acquisition: Who else can we sell it to?

Customer expansion: What else can we sell them?

Product variants and line extensions: What different features can we add, replace, or displace?

Value chain changes: How else can we get it to the customer?

In addition, a number of sources often present ideas, suggestions, and complaints that lead to new products:

1. Customers, and often more importantly, ex- or noncustomers who reject current products.
2. Employees, especially the sales force.
3. Suppliers, who are also a good source of information about competitors.
4. Distribution channels.
5. Operations people, who often suggest ways to simplify a process.
6. Internal and External R&D, including technological breakthroughs.
7. Design, a field which has recently taken on increased importance in many categories.
8. Entrepreneurs, who often approach larger companies with ideas or products. (Unfortunately, this raises a number of legal and ethical issues about ownership of the idea.)

Of course one can also use outside help (i.e., companies such as IDEO) to generate new products. When such sources are combined with intuition (managerial judgment), there should be no shortage of sources for new product ideas. The real issue is how to recognize a good idea (and a bad one) when confronted with it. Remember, Teflon and Post-it Notes were basically mistakes that a "prepared mind" saw as having value.

TESTING SLIGHTLY NEW PRODUCTS

While general guidelines exist for new product success (Cooper, 1994; Goldenberg, Lehmann, and Mazursky, 2001; Henard and Szymanski, 2001; Montoya-Weiss and Calantone, 1994), it is prudent to test each new product separately. This section discusses some of the most common tests.

Concept Testing

The initial test for most new products involves getting customer reactions to the product concept. The main purposes of a concept test are to (1) choose the most promising from a set of alternatives, (2) get an initial notion of the commercial prospects of a concept, (3) find out who is most interested in the concept, and (4) indicate what direction further development work should take. Samples are often convenience oriented. Common sample sources include community groups, employees, and central locations (e.g., shopping centers and trade shows). The typical approach presents customers with a verbal or written statement of the product idea and then records their reactions. Many researchers include physical mock-ups and advertising statements in the concept test. (These are technically prototype or prototype/concept tests.) The data gathered are both diagnostic (Why do you like/not like the product?) and predictive (Would you buy it if it cost x dollars?). Including a concrete "would you buy" question is crucial if the results are to be at all useful predictively. The data collection procedures fall into the following three major categories.

Surveys

Surveys are useful for getting large samples for projection purposes. On the other hand, it is often difficult to effectively convey a concept in a survey, especially an impersonal one. Appendix 9A shows some different mail concept tests taken from a National Family Opinion (NFO) brochure from 1975. Basically they gather four types of reactions:

1. Attitude (Is the product good/bad?).
2. Uniqueness/differentiation (How unique is this product?).
3. Relevance (How relevant is the product to you?).
4. Intention (Will you buy the product?).

Focus Groups

The strength of focus groups is their diagnostic power in that they can be used to get detailed discussions of various aspects of the concept. As predictors of actual sales, they are fairly inaccurate due to their small sample sizes.

Demonstrations

A popular way to present a concept is to gather a group of consumers, present them with a "story" about the new product (often including an ad or personal demonstration), and record their reactions. Questions asked typically relate to the following:

1. Do they understand the concept?
2. Do they believe the concept?
3. Is the concept different from other products in an important way?
4. If different, is the difference beneficial?
5. Do they like or dislike the concept? Why?
6. What could be done to make the product more acceptable?
7. How would they like to see the product (color, size, etc.)?
8. Would they buy it?
9. What price would they expect to pay for it?
10. What would their usage be in terms of volume, purpose, source of purchase, and so forth?
11. Where would they shop for it?

Concept tests are often sequential. In the first stage, a concept screening test, several concepts are briefly described and subjects asked for an overall evaluation (e.g., intention to buy). Screening tests are used to reduce the concepts under consideration to a manageable number. Next, concept generation/refinement studies (often involving focus groups) are used to refine the concept statements. This is typically followed by concept evaluation tests. These tests are based on larger samples and attempt to quantitatively assess demand for the concept based on samples of 200 to 300. Such tests are typically done competitively in the sense that other new concepts and/or existing products are evaluated at the same time (Moore, 1982).

Product Testing

Product Tests

Assuming initial concept screening results are positive, the next step often involves physically producing the product[1] and then getting consumers to use it. The purpose of a product test is to (1) uncover product shortcomings, (2) evaluate commercial prospects, (3) evaluate alternative formulations, (4) uncover the appeal of the product to various market segments, and (5) if lucky, gain ideas for other elements of the marketing program. Such tests may be either branded (best for estimating sales) or unbranded/blind (best for focusing directly on physical formulation).

There are three major types of product use tests. Initially such tests are usually conducted with small samples (often using convenience samples, such as employees). These initial tests are diagnostic and are directed toward eliminating serious problems with the product (e.g., the jar won't fit in the door of a refrigerator), as well as getting a rough idea of how good it is vis-à-vis competitive products. This phase also allows the company to find out how the product is actually used and, potentially, to change the target appeal.

The second type of use test includes a limited-time-horizon forced-trial situation where customers are given the product to use and asked for their reactions to it. At the end, a simulated purchase occasion is also used. This may consist of a hypothetical "would you buy" type of question or, better, an actual choice situation where the customer either chooses one of a set of products, including the new product (usually at a reduced price), or simply chooses to "buy" or not buy the new product. To get a meaningful result, many researchers use a stratified sample. The strata are usually either product category usage rate (heavy, medium, light, none) or brand usually used. This stratification ensures adequate sample size to predict the effect of the product on key market segments.

The most elaborate form of product use test requires placement of the product in homes (or business settings for industrial products) for an extended period. For packaged goods, this period is usually about two months. The advantage of this extended period is that the results allow both for initial expectations to wear out and for problems that manifest themselves only over time to develop (e.g., food that goes stale). Subjects complete "before" and "after" questionnaires, as well as maintain a diary of actual use of the new and competitive products over the period of the test. Here, again, the inclusion at the end of the test of an actual choice situation helps give the results a bottom-line orientation.

---

[1] Note that the product used in this phase is typically specially produced and may not match the quality of the product under mass production. For example, Knorr soup product test samples were produced in Europe, while the actual mass-produced product was made in a new, computerized plant in Argo, Illinois, which produced a product of different quality. Hence, the success or failure of the test product does not necessarily imply success or failure of the actual product.

Product tests are common in business-to-business markets as well. Often these involve use of early ("beta") versions by so-called lead users. For example, in 2000 Microsoft distributed a test version of a software to Barnes and Noble just before the new, and much hyped and anticipated, Harry Potter book came out. The version both worked well enough to aid Barnes and Noble and allowed Microsoft to fine-tune the product before launching it in the broader market.

Discrimination and Preference Testing

When a product formulation is changed, a crucial issue is the customer reaction (see Figure 9.3). Reaction has three aspects: discrimination (Can they tell the difference?), preference (Which version do they prefer, and by how much?), and reaction to change per se (Are they basically pro change, or is any change upsetting?). Here we focus on the ability of customers to actually tell the differences among products.

Discrimination is the ability to correctly identify differences from the product alone, without cues such as brand name and ingredients. Industrial goods sold to or given to engineers and chemists are often subjected to testing to determine their makeup, which makes discrimination fairly precise. In many cases, however, customers cannot distinguish among versions of a product without labels attached. Most people cannot distinguish among brands of beer, soda, or wine based on taste alone or among insurance policies based on the fine print. The inability to discriminate has two main consequences. First, it suggests that within a range it is possible to alter a product without customers noticing the difference. This ability often disappears when labels are included, however. For example, when some ingredients in food are assumed to be good (e.g., soluble fiber) or bad (e.g., cholesterol, nonbiodegradable ingredients, or toxic components), including the good ones becomes a plus whereas including the bad ones may disqualify a product from further consideration, even when the foods are indistinguishable in taste and appearance.

The second consequence of customers' inability to discriminate is its impact on the interpretation of preference judgments. Stated preference can be the result of true discrimination or of random guessing. This means single preference judgments cannot be unambiguously interpreted. Assume, for example, that 60 percent of a sample say they prefer brand A over brand B. This result could be because all subjects could discriminate and 60 percent actually prefer brand A. On the other hand, perhaps only 20 percent could discriminate and preferred brand A and 80 percent randomly guessed to arrive at their preference ($20\% + [80\%(50\%)] = 60\%$). Or it could mean that 50 percent could discriminate and among them 35 percent preferred A and 15 percent preferred B ($35\% + [50\%(50\%)] = 60\%$). Fortunately methods exist for separating these conditions (Appendix 9B).

Market Tests

The ultimate in realism is a market test. The purpose of such a test is to (1) predict sales and profits from a major product launch and (2) "practice" so that marketing, distribution, and production skills are developed before entering full-scale operations. (Note that this precludes test marketing products with high initial fixed cost or investment requirements.) Projections are typically made for both share and actual sales, appropriately adjusted to national levels. When a market test is designed, it is important to clearly delineate what information is to be gathered and why before proceeding. Several decisions must be made.

Action Standards

Standards for evaluating the results should be set up in advance. These standards should specify when the various possible decisions (e.g., stop the test, continue the test, revamp the product, go national) will be implemented.

Where to Test

The choice of where to test market is a serious problem. For consumer products, most market tests are done in two to three cities. (This further emphasizes that the "test" is not designed to try out numerous strategies; at most, two to three alternatives can be used.) Locations (typically cities) are chosen on the basis of representativeness of the population, the ability of the firm to gain distribution and media exposure in the area, and availability of good research suppliers in the area. Also, areas that are self-contained in terms of media (especially TV) are preferred. Of course, cable TV and the Internet make this more difficult. The result is that certain medium-size cities are often chosen, such as Syracuse, New York; Fresno, California; and Fort Wayne, Indiana.

What to Do

The best test market designers are careful to make the effort in the area proportional to what would reasonably be expected in a national launch. Notice that here we mean effort, not budget. If a city has particularly expensive (the usual case when buying spot TV ads) or inexpensive media costs, allocating budget on a population basis would result in a media schedule with either too few or too many exposures. The goal is to make distribution, price to consumers (price breaks to retailers and wholesalers are needed to gain distribution), and so forth as representative as possible. What typically happens, however, is that the effort afforded the product (including the human talent) is somewhat greater than the comparable national effort.

How Long

The question of how long to run a test is not easily answered. Obviously, a longer run gives more information, but it also costs more and gives competitors more time to formulate a counterattack. Consumer packaged goods may stay in test markets for six months or more in order to include several purchase cycles, so repeat usage as well as trial can be accurately assessed. (It is not uncommon for a product to gain a big initial share, due to trial, and then lose share as repeat business fails to live up to trial.)

Cost

For a consumer packaged good, test marketing costs run well over $1 million. Advertising and promotion often account for 65 to 70 percent of the budget, with the rest of the budget divided between information gathering and analysis and miscellaneous administrative and other expenses.

Information Gathering

During a test market, a variety of information is gathered, most of it related to actual sales. When monitoring sales, it is important to recognize that a large percentage of first-year factory sales (e.g., 30 percent) often represent a one-time stocking up by the channels of distribution, not sales to final consumers. The three major data sources are (1) actual sales (typically measured in at least 40 stores per area) plus distribution, promotion, and so forth; (2) surveys that measure awareness, attitude, and so forth; and (3) panels that report actual purchase and allow monitoring of trial and repeat rates.

Quasi-Market Tests

Market tests tend to be expensive. In addition, they take time and tip off competitors to your plans. For those reasons, a number of simulated testing methods have been developed. Silk and Urban's (1978) ASSESOR, BASES (currently the most prominent approach for consumer products), and Blackburn and Clancy's (1980) LITMUS model estimate sales using pretest market data plus a large database of past new products (to calibrate the results). Specifically, ASSESOR uses a simulated shopping trip following advertising exposure and an in-home use period. In most cases, the market share estimates are within one share point of the share observed in the market. With LITMUS, movement from awareness to trial and trial to repeat is estimated based on a laboratory experiment. These are, not surprisingly, both less expensive and somewhat less reliable than models based on actual market experience. Nevertheless, they grew substantially in popularity during the 1980s and 1990s.

FORECASTING

Forecasting sales is always difficult. (If it weren't, all products that went national after test marketing would succeed.) However, at least for frequently purchased consumer products, some fairly widely used procedures have been developed. It is possible to simply wait and see at what levels sales stabilize. Unfortunately, this takes a fairly long period (years) and hence a lot of money. What is really desired is an early warning system that forecasts the eventual sales level of a new product before it is attained. Four basic factors are the keys to eventual sales:

1. Awareness.
2. The eventual proportion of consumers who try the product (trial).
3. The proportion of triers who remain with the brand (repeat).
4. The usage rate of the product category among eventual users.

Notice that for durable goods, trial is basically first purchase, which may be the only purchase for several years (e.g., a household's car, a company's computer system). For frequently purchased products for which trial is relatively easy to induce, repeat rates are the key to success. Many models exist that attempt to project these factors early in the introduction. Models continue to be developed for forecasting new product sales (Urban, Hulland, and Weinberg, 1993), and most research suppliers have their own versions. Still, the models follow a structure that has been around for at least 40 years.

Awareness

As in all the stages of the model, one can simply introduce the product, monitor awareness, and, by plotting awareness versus time, observe (or formally forecast) where the product is headed. Alternatively, one can relate awareness to its underlying causes. Awareness is usually modeled as a function of advertising. For example, the awareness stage of Blattberg and Golanty's (1978) TRACKER model is as follows:

$$Awareness: \ln\left(\frac{1 - A_t}{1 - A_{t-1}}\right) = a - bG_t$$

where

A_t = Cumulative awareness in period t.

G_t = Gross rating points in period t.

N. W. Ayer (an ad agency that in 2000 became part of Bcom3) studied several introductions and, based on this research, modeled awareness in a more complex fashion as follows (Claycamp and Liddy, 1969):

$$Awareness = a_1 + b_1 \text{ (product positioning)}$$
$$+ b_2 \text{ (media impressions)(copy execution)}$$
$$+ b_3 \text{ (ad messages containing consumer promotions)}$$
$$+ b_4 \text{ (category interest)} + e_1$$

Trial

Like awareness, initial purchase is often tracked across time, with the objective of forecasting its eventual level. This can be done graphically as in Figure 9.4. Alternatively, the saturation level can be estimated by running a regression of cumulative trial versus exp $(-t)$:

$$\text{Cumulative trial } (t) = S(f) = a + be^{-t}$$

Here a is the eventual penetration level.

FIGURE 9.4 Typical Penetration for New Brand Over Time

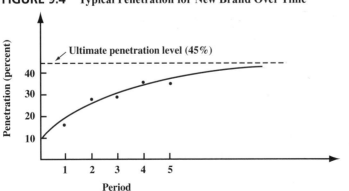

When trial is forecast based on market factors, advertising, distribution, and promotion are often used. The Ayer model was:

$$
\begin{aligned}
\text{Initial purchase} = a_2 &+ b_1 \text{ (estimated awareness)} \\
&+ c_2 \{(\text{distribution})(\text{packaging})\} \\
&+ c_3 \text{ (if a family brand)} \\
&+ c_4 \text{ (consumer promotion)} \\
&+ c_5 \text{ (satisfaction with product samples)} \\
&+ c_6 \text{ (category usage)} + e_2
\end{aligned}
$$

Similarly, the trial stage of the TRACKER model is:

$$
T_t - T_{t-1} = a(A_t - A_{t-1}) + b(A_{t-1} - T_{t-1})
$$

where

T_t = Cumulative trial in period t.

A_t = Awareness in period t.

Repeat Rate

The eventual repeat rate can be deduced graphically by plotting repeat versus either time (Figure 9.5) or purchase occasion. As Figure 9.6, based on 120 products studied by NPD Research demonstrates, repeat rate is a good predictor of success.

Usage Rate

The relative product category usage rate of buyers of the new brand is obtained either by using purchase panel data to estimate it or judgmentally.

Other Models

The earliest of the new product models that attained widespread interest was that of Fourt and Woodlock (1960; see also Bass, Krishnan, and Jain, 1994). This model was intended to predict the market success of grocery products.

FIGURE 9.5   **Typical Repeat Rate for New Brand Over Time**

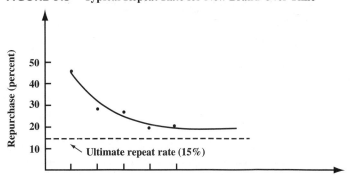

FIGURE 9.6 Repeat Rates and Product Performance

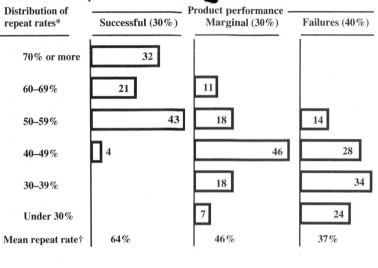

Distribution of repeat rates*	Successful (30%)	Marginal (30%)	Failures (40%)
70% or more	32		
60–69%	21	11	
50–59%	43	18	14
40–49%	4	46	28
30–39%		18	34
Under 30%		7	24
Mean repeat rate†	64%	46%	37%

* Based upon 120 new products.
† Percent of triers who will ever repeat.

Source: "We Make the Answers to Your Marketing Questions Perfectly Clear" (New York: NPD Research, 1982).

The first stage of the model attempts to predict penetration (eventual level of trial). It assumes (1) there is an eventual penetration level (P) and (2) each period some percentage of the nonbuyers who eventually will buy the product buy it. The second stage of the model focuses on repeat purchase. Specifically, it focuses on the repeat ratios, the portion of initial buyers who repeat purchase once (N_1/N_0), the portion of first repeat purchasers who repeat purchase a second time (N_2/N_1), and so forth. This stage is used for forecasting sales in the next period as the sum of new buyers, plus first repeaters, second repeaters, and so forth. This model proved to be somewhat cumbersome in application. It also implicitly assumes the market is constant in terms of advertising, distribution, pricing, and so forth, a troublesome albeit useful assumption. Parfitt and Collins (1968) produced a simpler model than Fourt and Woodlock's. Their approach focuses on predicting market share rather than actual sales. The three key elements in using their model are to (1) estimate eventual penetration (P), (2) estimate the ultimate share of their purchases that buyers will make of the new brand (M), and (3) estimate the relative product category usage rate of buyers of the new brand (U). The estimated eventual share is thus simply the product of $P \cdot M \cdot U$.

Continuing with the example represented in Figures 9.4 and 9.5 and assuming eventual users of the product buy 80 percent as much as an average product category user, we estimate the ultimate share to be $P \cdot M \cdot U = (45\%)(15\%)(.8) = 5.4\%$.

Numerous other models also exist, such as ESP, the NEWS Model (Pringle, Wilson, and Brody, 1982) and Assmus's (1975) NEWPROD. Experience with these models has been quite good, with predicted share generally within 1 percent of actual share when test market data are used as input and within 2 percent when only pretest market data are used.

BRAND EXTENSIONS

Extending brands beyond their original category (e.g., Levi's into dress clothing, Nike into sportswear) has been increasingly popular. These decisions are generally both riskier than adding variants (line extensions) and beyond the control of a product manager. Nonetheless, because they are likely to influence the original brand and are also interesting to consider, we discuss them briefly.

A considerable amount of attention has been paid to brand extensions across categories (Aaker and Keller, 1990; Tauber, 1988). Consider the following possible brand extensions:

H & R Block estate settlements.

Pepsi tofu patties.

Minute Maid cranberry juice.

IBM pens.

Levi's suits.

Tide facial cleanser

McDonald's film processing

If you are "typical" (that is, similar to others to whom we have shown this list), your reaction may be something like the following:

H & R Block estate settlements: Sounds reasonable; they're pretty good at preparing tax forms (a big part of estate work).

Pepsi tofu patties: Pepsi can sure market food products, but somehow a dark, sugar-filled drink doesn't seem to go with a natural food.

Minute Maid cranberry juice: An obvious extension; don't they do this already?

IBM pens: Why would they bother? Besides, what do they know about making pens?

Levi's suits: I remember this—it didn't work, did it?

Tide facial cleanser: Makes me think of sandpaper rubbing on my skin.

McDonald's film processing: I see chemicals in my food and ketchup on my film in a bun.

From these kinds of reactions, plus more extensive survey research (Bottomley and Holden, 2002; Keller, 2002; Park, Milberg, and Lawson, 1991), it appears that brand extension value depends on the value of the original brand (e.g., the extension value of Lehmann-Winer, Inc., is pretty limited) and the fit in the new category. Fit, in turn, focuses heavily on two issues:

1. Technical competence sharing or transfer: Do the skills and quality and service levels of the original brand and its attributes transfer productively to the extension category?

2. Image match: Are the products consistent in terms of image on such dimensions as young-old, serious-fun, etc. (Batra, Lehmann, and Singh, 1993)?

Based on these considerations, the H & R Block estate settlement concept seems to match on both, as does Minute Maid cranberry juice. But Minute Maid cranberry juice, unfortunately, is less matched operationally. Because oranges grow on trees in Florida and cranberries in bogs in Massachusetts, different growers are needed, different machines are needed to extract the juice, etc. The issue of operational efficiency is important but separate from the issue of how well brand value (equity) transfers from the customer's perspective. In contrast, Pepsi tofu patties and Levi's suits fail to match in terms of image and personality, and IBM pens seem not to involve technology sharing. While at some level Tide facial cleanser (P&G does know how to get things clean and sells personal care products) and McDonald's film processing (convenience) make sense, at least the initial reaction is visual and negative.

The success of an extension also seems to depend on the order in which extensions occur (Keller and Aaker, 1992). One study found that brand extensions work best in more mature markets (e.g., as a later entrant) for frequently purchased consumer goods and generally outperform new products (Sullivan, 1992).

Another interesting study evaluated the impact of brand extensions on market share and advertising efficiency as measured by the advertising/sales ratio. Smith and Park (1992) collected data from 188 product/brand managers in consumer goods companies and from 1,383 consumers. The managers provided data on

1. Products offered ("focal" products) and whether or not they were extensions.
2. Other products using the same brand name or company logo as the focal product.
3. Age of the focal product.
4. Number of competitors of the focal products and extensions.
5. Advertising/sales ratio of the focal products and extensions.
6. Market shares of the focal products and extensions.

Consumers provided measures of brand strength (the average of seven-point quality and value scales), extension similarity to focal product (both extrinsic and intrinsic), whether the product could be evaluated through inspection as opposed to actual use, and general product class knowledge. Not surprisingly, parent brand strength related to extension brand share but not to the advertising/sales ratio. Neither extension share nor the advertising/sales ratio was related to the number of products associated with a brand. Similarity of the extension, extensions that are experience goods, and the presence of few competitors increase the market share. These effects decrease as the extension ages or when customers have considerable product knowledge. Although our focus has been mainly on the success of the new product, a key issue regarding extensions is the impact of the extension on the original brand. One study examined the impact of extensions on beliefs about the original brand (Loken and Roedder-John, 1993). Dilution effects occurred for both within-category extensions (i.e., adding product variants) and across-category extensions. Dilutions were greater for specific attributes (e.g., gentleness) than for more general attributes (e.g., quality). Perhaps most interesting, dilution was greater for moderately consistent extensions than for clearly different extensions. However, other research has shown that successful extensions can enhance brand equity (Ahluwalia and Gürhan-Canli, 2000; Balachander and Ghose, 2003; Swaminathan, Fox, and Reddy, 2001).

REALLY NEW PRODUCTS

Really new products really are different. They

1. Create or expand a new category, thereby making cross-category competition the key (e.g., fruit teas versus soft drinks).
2. Are new to customers for whom substantial learning is often required (i.e., what it can be used for, what it competes with, why it is useful).
3. Raise broad issues such as the appropriate channels of distribution and organizational responsibility.
4. Create (sometimes) a need for infrastructure, software, and add-ons.

Figure 9.7 gives some examples of really new products. While slightly to really new products form a continuum, notice how these differ from lemon-scented soaps or printers that produce six instead of five pages of output per minute.

Clearly, the less new the new product, the more analysis of and decisions for it resemble those for existing products. To highlight the differences, we contrast four situations: (1) existing product, mature market; (2) existing product, dynamic/growing market (basically a new product that has been around for awhile); (3) a slightly new product; and (4) a really new product. As Figure 9.8 shows, the task becomes increasingly complex

FIGURE 9.7   **Examples of Really New Products**

Packaged Goods	
	Bottled tea
	Light beer
	Frozen vegetables
	Sports drinks (Gatorade)
Services	
	Overnight air delivery
	ATMs
	Credit cards
	IRAs, annuities
	Internet
	Priceline.com
	Ariba
	LivePerson.com
Durables	
	Microwave ovens
	Room air conditioners
	Dishwashers
	Black-and-white TVs
Industrial products	
	Nylon
	Semiconductors
	Nuclear power reactors
	Printing presses

FIGURE 9.8   Analysis and Programs for New versus Old Products

Analysis	Existing Product, Mature Market	Existing Product, Dynamic Growing Market	Slightly New Product	Quite/Really New Product
Competitor identification and focus	Current (same as last year) (Product form, category)	Current plus likely entrants (Category, generic)	Current producers of product category (Category)	Possible entrants with similar products and competing technologies (Generic, budget)
Customer analysis	Current customers Competitors' customers	Current customers Potential new customers Competitors' customers	Competitors' customers Current customers (cannibalization, upgrading)	Potential new customers Users of alternative technologies
Potential and forecasting	Extrapolation from past results	New uses and users	Survey data; controlled experiments	Potential analysis Epidemic models (e.g., Bass)
Objective	Profit Share Customer retention	Sales Customer acquisition, expansion	Share Profit Customer acquisition	Sales Learning Keeping options open Customer acquisition
Programs:				
Price	Competitively based	Competition Experience curve	Competitively based Value for added feature (lemon scent)	EVC* based Portion of value—cost difference to give to customers to cover risk, dislocation (incompatibility)
Advertising	Reminder/repeat Comparative	New uses	New feature	Awareness and trial Information on use
Promotions	Retain current users Induce switching	Increase use New users	Trial	Awareness/interest Trial
Sales and services	Delivery	Gaining distribution	Gaining distribution	Technical support Training Gaining distribution

*Economic value to the customer.

as product newness increases. For a really new product there is no industry to analyze and the competitive set is undefined. While potential customers can indicate their satisfaction level with current offerings, it is often hard to directly assess the likelihood that they will buy a new offering.

While more mature products tend to be managed to maximize some combination of profits and shares, really new ones can be pursued to learn from the experience and/or keep the option open to participate in a potentially large market. In terms of marketing programs, less emphasis is placed on competitors and gaining share and more on primary demand (sales). Advertising and sales shift from an emphasis on current customers and customers of similar products to new customers and increased awareness, trial, and eventual use by noncustomers.

Getting Ideas for Really New Products

Ideas for really new products come from the same sources discussed earlier. However, really new products have a certain radical quality. Thus, the emphasis may be on

1. Asking (or listening to) *dis*satisfied customers.
2. Asking *non*representative customers.
3. Using open-ended, qualitative (versus structured survey) procedures.
4. Involving customers as co-developers (especially for industrial products).
5. Listening to scientists and newcomers rather than engineers and experts.
6. Scanning the literature (e.g., technology) for interesting possibilities.

Further, the style of search is likely to differ. For lemon-scented new products, the emphasis is on fixing or improving existing products, methodical continuous improvement, and project completion. In contrast, the mind-set for really new products involves taking an outsider's view, doing things differently, disrupting current behavior, and using different technologies. In contrast to well-defined project completion, process reengineering and discovery (à la Franklin, Bell, and Edison) are the models.

Evaluating Really New Products

Really new products tend to take a long time (e.g., 20 years) from conception to development and from initial development to mass sales. Hence, one of the main requirements is patience, something that is in short supply in most corporations.

In considering a new product, it is useful to analyze the characteristics mentioned in Chapter 6 and defined by Rogers (1983) plus the perceived risk dimension of Bauer (1960):

1. *Relative advantage.* Essentially, is it a "better mousetrap"? (versus the benefits of the product it replaces).
2. *Compatibility.* The ability of the consumer to use it in a way consistent with past behavior, which increases the chances of adoption. This includes (*a*) the procedures the user employs (Hint: Don't try to change the location of keys on a keyboard) and (*b*) the ability to use existing "software" and complementary products (e.g., bobbins on sewing machines). Incompatibility is often the major deterrent to adoption.
3. *Risk.* Perceived risk can be broken down into several categories (e.g., financial, physical/health, psychic/social), all of which work against adoption.

Three other dimensions also affect adoption, although generally indirectly (Holak and Lehmann, 1990):

4. *Complexity.*
5. *Observability/communicability.* The ability to explain and see the benefits in simple, clear terms.
6. *Trialability/divisibility.* The ability to sample the product without a major commitment.

In general, complexity works against adoption, and observability and trialability work for it. For slightly new products, the basic emphasis is on relative advantage (e.g., the lemon scent) versus financial risk (cost) as emphasized by economic value calculations.

FIGURE 9.9 Evaluating New Products

| | Constituency | | | | |
Aspect	Customers	Within Company	Suppliers	Channels	Public/ Regulators
Relative advantage					
Compatibility					
Risk					
Complexity					
Communicability					
Trialability					

In contrast, for really new products compatibility and social risk become much more crucial. Human beings, unless desperate, generally resist innovation and change. Incompatibility and social risk thus are major impediments to adoption. While some delay in adoption can be traced to customers waiting for (1) the price to drop and (2) the quality (features, reliability, availability of complementary products) to increase, incompatibility accounts for more of the delay.

Also, for a really new product to succeed, a variety of parties must adopt it (e.g., customers, channels, and suppliers plus both superiors and vital functions such as production and sales within the firm) and infrastructure often needs to be developed (e.g., software for computers, programming content for HDTV and recorded music formats). Evaluating the likelihood of success of a really new product requires considerations such as those in Figure 9.9. Only when all parties benefit from an innovation is it likely to be adopted.

Interestingly, experts appear to be less prone to adopt really new products, at least initially (Moreau, Lehmann, and Markman, 2001). As an example of resistance to innovation, consider plastic plumbing. Lighter in weight and less toxic than metal plumbing (no lead in the solder), it seemed like a natural improvement. Yet it took over 20 years to make major inroads in the U.S. home market. Part of the delay can be traced to resistance by plumbers. Their livelihood was based partly on the skill of sweating joints (joining copper pipe together using flux, solder, and a torch). They also had considerable influence on local building codes, which set standards for construction. As a result, the first widespread use of plastic plumbing was in mobile homes, which were not subject to local building codes.

Perhaps the ultimate examples of resistance to change occur in the military. In spite of the clear objective function and reliable data, tradition has overwhelmed data time after time. From the tradition of marching in close formation through the woods (General Braddock and the Redcoats) through repeating rifles in the U.S. Civil War, continuous aim firing gunnery in the Navy, and air power (General Billy Mitchell), clearly superior technology was actively resisted. Given the life-or-death nature of the consequences, it is less surprising that profits (for industrial firms) or inconvenience or social pressure (for individuals) are insufficient to induce immediate adoption of new things.

Adoption and Expansion

First purchases of a new product are crucial. Still, adoption implies something different, a commitment to using the product in the long run. Basements are full of exercise equipment and other items that are used briefly and then stored (or used as clothes hangers). For that reason, frequently purchased products are considered to be adopted only after second repeat (to exclude novelty-based trial). Other signs of true adoption are (1) "automated" replacement when a product fails ("I never thought I needed a VCR or microwave oven, but now, when mine breaks, I go directly to the store to buy another"), (2) upgrades to better models, and (3) purchases of accessories and complementary products (which also provide an opportunity to increase profits, as sellers of cameras and snowmobiles well know).

Forecasting Really New Products

Forecasting sales of really new products is hazardous at best. Procedurally, one can apply the Bass (1969) model to develop category-level first-purchase estimates, combining past patterns with actual sales data (Sultan, Farley, and Lehmann, 1990) or by picking an analogous product and assuming sales will follow the same pattern. Particularly interesting is the pattern of diffusion across countries (Dekimpe, Parker, and Sarvary, 2000; Talukdar, Sudhir, and Ainslie, 2002; Tellis, Stremersch, and Yin, 2003). One can also use advanced purchase orders (e.g., for a new model from Boeing or Airbus) in conjunction with early sales data and to aid in forecasting (Moe and Fader, 2002).

Direct structured questioning of potential customers either in straight concept evaluation form or through devices such as conjoint analysis is less useful. First, the product itself often is not available, so product tests are not possible. Further, the product often requires a major shift in behavior and may serve a need that is latent (unknown) rather than active (when the customer is actively searching for such a product) or even passive (the customer wasn't searching for it but responds, "Now that you mention it, . . .").

Therefore, methods such as "information acceleration" (developed by Glen Urban and colleagues at MIT and now offered by Mercer Management Consultants) have been developed (Urban, Weinberg, and Hauser, 1996). In essence, these methods attempt to place subjects in a future world and familiarize them with a product (often using multimedia technology) to improve the quality of their responses. However, it remains extremely difficult to have people imagine both a radically new product and the world in 20 to 30 years and then accurately assess likelihood of their using it. Put differently, to forecast really new products you need a really big—and lucky—coin.

Summary

New products are the lifeblood of many companies. Indeed, companies (e.g., 3M, Gillette, HP) often set goals for sales based on new products (e.g., 35 percent from products introduced in the last five years). Like any metric, however, these goals may distort behavior. One suspects that one reason life cycles are often thought to be shortening is the increasing number of lemon-scented products and the decreasing fraction of really new ones.

Little evidence exists that really new products are being adopted faster. Humans' inherent tolerance for innovation is largely unchanged. Indeed, considering the risk taken by those who set out in small wooden boats across a sea and were predicted to fall off the edge of the world, our reluctance to try new things seems almost laughable.

Lemon-scented, slightly new products are relatively easy to forecast and low in risk. Further, they rarely raise messy issues about channels and organization structure. They are also often profitable, even when in a technical sense they are not widely creative, as the new flavors of ice cream introduced by Dreyer's in 2000 demonstrate (Figure 9.10).

FIGURE 9.10 Dreyer's New Flavors for 2000

New Flavors for 2000		
Grand Light Ice Cream	**No Sugar Added Ice Cream**	**Frozen Yogurt**
Chocolate Raspberry Escape™	All About PB™	Caramel Fudge Cosmo™
S'Mores & More	Chips 'N Swirls™	Hokey Pokey™
		Mumbo Jumbo
Homemade	**Fat Free/No Sugar Added Ice Cream**	**Whole Fruit Bars**
All Natural Vanilla	Blueberry Cobbler	Creamy Banana (Chocolate Dipped)
Apple Pie a la Mode		Creamy Strawberry (Chocolate Dipped)
Brownies a la Mode	**Whole Fruit Sorbet**	Lemonade
Caramel Peanut Brittle	Boysenberry	
Chocolate Chip Cookie Jar	Chocolate	
Chocolate Cream Pie	Mango	
Limited Edition Flavors for 2000		

Infinity Divinity™ Grand Light (January)
Chunky Toy Funilla™ (January)
Peach Whole Fruit Bars (January–April)
Girl Scouts™ Thin Mint Cookie (February–May)
Girl Scouts™ Samoas® Cookie (February–May)

Girl Scouts™ Tagalong® Cookie Grand Light (February–May)
Blackberry Pie Grand Light (February–May)
Jeff Gordon Checkered Flag Sundae (February–June)
50/50 Bar Grand Light (June–October)
Peanut Butter Blitz (August–January)

Wild Berry Whole Fruit Bars (September–December)
Pumpkin (September–October)
Halloween Bash™ (September–October)
Gingerbread Man Grand Light (September–December)
Peppermint (November–December)

Source: Dreyer's Ice Cream website, *www.dreyers.com/globals/main_whatsnew.html,* June 28, 2000.

Really new products, in contrast, are hard to forecast, raise numerous tough organizational issues, take a long time to develop, and not infrequently produce profits for later entrants but not for pioneers (or none at all, if a subsequent technology makes them obsolete; Chandy and Tellis, 2000; Robinson and Min, 2002). Because of the time it takes them to reach a mass market (often 20 years or more), really new products require a level of patience unusual for businesses driven by quarterly profits. They are often the equivalent of a lottery ticket or an option: Typically you lose a little, but if you win, you can win big.

This book is focused on managing existing brands and marginal improvements. Really new products, however, involve quantum improvements. The riskiness of new products increases as both the *newness to the company* (in terms of both customer and process knowledge) and *newness to the customer* increase, as does the likelihood that success will disrupt the current organization. It is therefore not surprising that really new products are viewed with suspicion. Still, both for the potential they offer and for the invigorating effect radical change has on an organization, we recommend that some fraction of activity be devoted to them.

Illustration

As an indication of a schedule of the new products introduced by companies, Figure 9.10 shows the 2000 schedule for Dreyer's new product introductions. While many are appealing, they are not really new products. Similarly, Palm's m100, targeted toward women and high school students, was a clear line extension.

SUMMARY

Conceiving of, developing, and evaluating new products is a complex process. Conception can come from many sources, including, importantly, copying others.

Development itself is a topic that needs multiple chapters. One of the major problems is coordination among marketing, design, R&D, and operations. Forming teams across functions and keeping them in touch with customers are clearly beneficial for the systematic development of most new products (cf., Sethi, Smith, and Park, 2001). For the occasionally really new product, however, a visionary (product champion) is usually required.

Evaluation proceeds gradually through the steps shown in Figure 9.1. By way of summary, Figure 9.11 provides criteria (both customer and company based) that underlie the evaluation and inevitable projected sales and P&L statements.

FIGURE 9.11   **Evaluation Criteria for New Products**

Customer Level
1. Do customers like it?
2. Is it unique?
3. Will they buy it?
4. How soon/fast will they buy it?

Firm Level
1. Does it add to our customer base through
   a. Acquisition?
   b. Expansion?
   c. Loyalty/retention?
   d. Enhanced brand equity?
2. Does it detract from our customer base through
   a. Cannibalization?
   b. Customer defections?
   c. Lowered brand equity?
3. Do we have the capabilities to
   a. Develop it?
   b. Produce it?
   c. Distribute and sell it?
   d. Buy or partner to do *a–c?*
4. Will it be profitable
   a. On a stand-alone basis?
   b. Long-run impact on produce line?
5. Are there other benefits associated with it
   a. Learning/capability enhancement?
   b. PR?
6. Are there other costs associated with it
   a. Legal liability?
   b. PR?
7. Can we control the market in the long run?

Most product managers have limited flexibility in changing product composition. Still, small changes can have a major impact. This chapter gave a brief overview of some considerations in deciding whether to change a product, with emphasis on the long-run effects (e.g., the impact on brand value/equity and customer loyalty) as well as the immediate sales impact on current customers, occasional customers, and noncustomers. Although change (even in product labels) can have important and even dramatic positive effects, it has downside risks in terms of costs and potential customer confusion and alienation. Hence, as in the case of any mix decision, long-term consequences must be considered.

References

Aaker, David A., and Kevin L. Keller (1990) "Consumer Evaluations of Brand Extensions," *Journal of Marketing* 54, January, 27–41.

Ahluwalia, Rohini, and Zeynep Gürhan-Canli (2000) "The Effects of Extensions on the Family Brand Name: An Accessibility-Diagnosticity Perspective," *Journal of Consumer Research* 27, December, 371–81.

Assmus, Gert (1975) "NEWPROD: The Design and Implementation of a New Product Model," *Journal of Marketing* 39, January, 16–23.

Balachander, Subramanian, and Sanjoy Ghose (2003) "Reciprocal Spillover Effects: A Strategic Benefit of Brand Extensions," *Journal of Marketing* 67, January, 4–13.

Bass, Frank M. (1969) "A New Product Growth Model for Consumer Durables," *Management Science* 15, January, 215–27.

Bass, Frank M., Trichy V. Krishnan, and Deepak C. Jain (1994) "Why the Bass Model Fits without Decision Variables," *Marketing Science* 13, Summer, 203–23.

Bauer, R. A. (1960) "Consumer Behavior as Risk Taking," in R. S. Hancock, ed., *Dynamic Marketing for a Changing World.* Chicago: American Marketing Association, 389–98.

Blackburn, Joseph D., and Kevin J. Clancy (1980) "LITMUS: A New Product Planning Model," in Robert P. Leone, ed., *Proceedings: Market Measurement and Analysis.* Providence, RI: Institute of Management Sciences, 182–93.

Blattberg, Robert, and John Golanty (1978) "TRACKER: An Early Test Market Forecasting and Diagnostic Model for New Product Planning," *Journal of Marketing Research* 15, May, 192–202.

Bottomley, Paul A., and Stephen J. S. Holden (2001) "Do We Really Know How Consumers Evaluate Brand Extensions? Empirical Generalizations Based on Secondary Analysis of Eight Studies," *Journal of Marketing Research* 38, November, 494–500.

Broniarczyk, Susan M., Wayne D. Hower, and Leigh McAlister (1998) "Consumer Perceptions of the Assortment Offered in a Grocery Store: The Impact of Item Reduction," *Journal of Marketing Research* 35, May, 166–76.

Buchanan, Bruce S., and Pamela W. Henderson (1992) "Assessing the Bias of Preference, Detection, and Identification Measures of Discrimination Ability in Product Design," *Marketing Science* 11, Winter, 64–75.

Chandy, Rajesh K., and Gerard J. Tellis (2000) "The Incumbent's Curse? Incumbency, Size, and Radical Product Innovation," *Journal of Marketing* 64, July, 1–17.

Claycamp, Henry, and Lucien Liddy (1969) "Prediction of New Product Performance: An Analytical Approach," *Journal of Marketing Research* 4, November, 416.

Cooper, Robert G. (1994) "New Products: The Factors That Drive Success," *International Marketing Review* 11, March, 60–76.

Cooper, Robert G. (1993) *Winning New Products,* 2nd ed. Reading, MA: Addison-Wesley.

Day, Ralph (1965) "Systematic Paired Comparisons in Preference Analysis," *Journal of Marketing Research* 2, November, 406–12.

Dekimpe, Marnik G., Philip M. Parker, and Miklos Sarvary (2000) "Global Diffusion of Technological Innovations: A Coupled-Hazard Approach," *Journal of Marketing Research* 37, February, 47–59.

Durge, Jeffrey E., Gina Colarelli O'Connor, and Robert W. Veryzer (1996) "Using Mini-Concepts to Identify Opportunities for Really New Product Functions," MSI Working Paper, #96–105.

Fourt, Louis A., and Joseph W. Woodlock (1960) "Early Prediction of Market Success for New Grocery Products," *Journal of Marketing* 25, October, 31–38.

Goldenberg, Jacob, Donald R. Lehmann, and David Mazursky (2001) "The Idea Itself and the Circumstances of Its Emergence as Predictors of New Product Success," *Management Science* 47:1, January, 69–84.

Goldenberg, Jacob, David Mazursky, and Sorin Solomon (1999) "Toward Identifying the Inventive Templates of New Products: A Channeled Ideation Approach," *Journal of Marketing Research* 36, May, 200–10.

Henard, David H., and David M. Szymanski (2001) "Why Some New Products are More Successful than Others," *Journal of Marketing Research* 38, August, 362–75.

Holak, Susan, and Donald R. Lehmann (1990) "Purchase Intentions and the Dimensions of Innovation: An Exploratory Model," *Journal of Product Innovation Management* 7, March, 59–73.

Johnson, Richard M. (no date) *Simultaneous Measurement of Discrimination and Preference.* Chicago: Market Facts, Inc.

Keller, Kevin L. (2002) *Branding and Brand Equity.* Cambridge, MA: Marketing Science Institute.

Keller, Kevin L., and David A. Aaker (1992) "The Effects of Sequential Introductions of Brand Extensions," *Journal of Marketing Research* 29, February, 35–50.

Kuester, Sabine, Christian Homburg, and Thomas S. Robertson (1999) "Retaliatory Behavior to New Product Entry," *Journal of Marketing* 63, October, 90–106.

Loken, Barbara, and Deborah Roedder-John (1993) "Diluting Brand Beliefs When Brand Extensions Have a Negative Impact," *Journal of Marketing* 57, July, 71–84.

Moe, Wendy W., and Peter S. Fader (2002) "Using Advance Purchase Orders to Forecast New Product Sales," *Marketing Science* 21:3, Summer, 347–64.

Montoya-Weiss, Mitzi M., and Roger Calantone (1994) "Determinants of New Product Performance: A Review and Meta Analysis," *Journal of Product Innovation Management* 11, December, 397–417.

Moore, William L. (1982) "Concept Testing," *Journal of Business Research* 10, June, 279–94.

Moore, William L., and Edgar A. Pessemier (1993) *Product Planning and Management.* New York: McGraw-Hill.

Moreau, C. Page, Donald R. Lehmann, and Arthur B. Markman (2001) "Entrenched Knowledge Structures and Consumer Response to New Products," *Journal of Marketing Research* 38, February, 14–29.

Morgenson, Gretchen (1992) "Is Your Product Your Advocate?" *Forbes,* September 14, 468.

Morrison, Donald G. (1981) "Triangle Tests: Are the Subjects Who Respond Correctly Lucky or Good?" *Journal of Marketing* 45, Summer, 111–19.

Parfitt, J. H., and B. J. K. Collins (1968) "Use of Consumer Panels for Brand-Share Prediction," *Journal of Marketing Research* 5, May, 131–45.

Park, C. Whan, Sung Youl Jun, and Allan D. Shocker (1996) "Composite Branding Alliances: An Investigation of Extension and Feedback Effects," *Journal of Marketing Research* 33, November, 453–66.

Park, C. Whan, Sandra Milberg, and Robert Lawson (1991) "Evaluation of Brand Extensions: The Role of Product Feature Similarity and Brand Concept Consistency," *Journal of Consumer Research* 19, September, 185–93.

Pringle, Lewis R., R. Dale Wilson, and Edward I. Brody (1982) "NEWS: A Decision-Oriented Model for New Product Analysis and Forecasting," *Marketing Science* 1, Winter, 1–29.

Robinson, William T., and Sungwook Min (2002) "Is the First to Market the First to Fail? Empirical Evidence for Industrial Goods Businesses," *Journal of Marketing Research* 39, February, 120–28.

Rogers, Everett M. (1983) *Diffusion Innovations.* New York: The Free Press.

Sethi, Rajesh, Daniel C. Smith, and C. Whan Park (2001) "Cross-Functional Product Development Teams, Creativity, and the Innovativeness of New Consumer Products," *Journal of Marketing Research* 38, February, 73–85.

Silk, Alvin J., and Glen L. Urban (1978) "Pre-Test Market Evaluation of New Packaged Goods: A Model and Measurement Methodology," *Journal of Marketing Research* 15, May, 171–91.

Smith, Daniel C., and C. Whan Park (1992) "The Effects of Brand Extensions on Market Share and Advertising Efficiency," *Journal of Marketing Research* 29, August, 296–313.

Sullivan, Mary W. Sullivan (1992) "Brand Extensions: When to Use Them," *Management Science* 38, June, 793–806.

Sultan, Fareena, John U. Farley, and Donald R. Lehmann (1990) "A Meta-Analysis of Applications of Diffusion Models," *Journal of Marketing Research* 27, February, 70–77.

Swaminathan, Vanitha, Richard J. Fox, and Srinivas K. Reddy (2001) "The Impact of Brand Extension Introduction on Choice," *Journal of Marketing* 65, October, 1–15.

Talukdar, Debabrata, K. Sudhir, and Andrew Ainslie (2002) "Investigating New Product Diffusion Across Products and Countries," *Marketing Science* 21:1, Winter, 97–114.

Tauber, Edward M. (1988) "Brand Leverage: Strategy for Growth in a Cost-Control World," *Journal of Advertising Research* 28, August, 26–30.

Tauber, Edward M. (1972) "HIT: Heuristic Ideation Technique—A Systematic Procedure for New Product Search," *Journal of Marketing* 36, 58–61.

Tellis, Gerard J., Stefan Stremersch, and Eden Yin (2003) "The International Takeoff of New Products: The Role of Economics, Culture, and Country Innovativeness," *Marketing Science* 22:2, Spring, 188–208.

Urban, Glen L., and John R. Hauser (1993) *Design and Marketing of New Products,* 2nd ed. Englewood Cliffs, NJ: Prentice Hall.

Urban, Glen L., John S. Hulland, and Bruce Weinberg (1993) "Pre-Market Forecasting of New Consumer Durables: Categorization, Elimination, and Consideration Phenomena," *Journal of Marketing* 57, April, 47–63.

Urban, Glen L., Bruce D. Weinberg, and John R. Hauser (1996) "Pre-Market Forecasting of Really-New Products," *Journal of Marketing* 60, January, 47–60.

Appendix 9A   Sample Concept Test Formats*

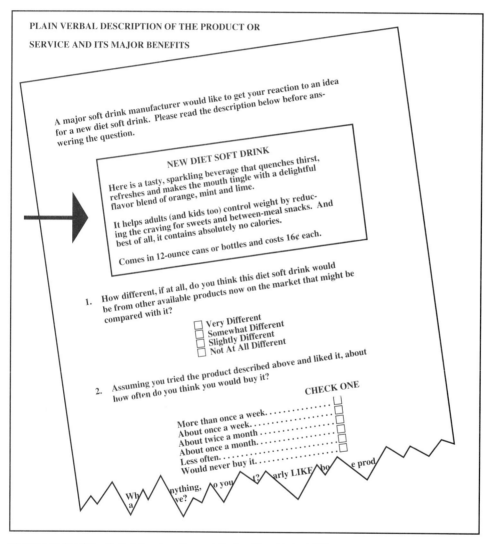

PLAIN VERBAL DESCRIPTION OF THE PRODUCT OR
SERVICE AND ITS MAJOR BENEFITS

A major soft drink manufacturer would like to get your reaction to an idea for a new diet soft drink. Please read the description below before answering the question.

> **NEW DIET SOFT DRINK**
>
> Here is a tasty, sparkling beverage that quenches thirst, refreshes and makes the mouth tingle with a delightful flavor blend of orange, mint and lime.
>
> It helps adults (and kids too) control weight by reducing the craving for sweets and between-meal snacks. And best of all, it contains absolutely no calories.
>
> Comes in 12-ounce cans or bottles and costs 16¢ each.

1. How different, if at all, do you think this diet soft drink would be from other available products now on the market that might be compared with it?

   ☐ Very Different
   ☐ Somewhat Different
   ☐ Slightly Different
   ☐ Not At All Different

2. Assuming you tried the product described above and liked it, about how often do you think you would buy it?

                                                          CHECK ONE

   More than once a week. . . . . ☐
   About once a week. . . . . ☐
   About twice a month . . . . ☐
   About once a month. . . . . ☐
   Less often. . . . . ☐
   Would never buy it. . . . . ☐

*Source: National Family Opinion, Inc., *Concept Testing* (New York, 1975).

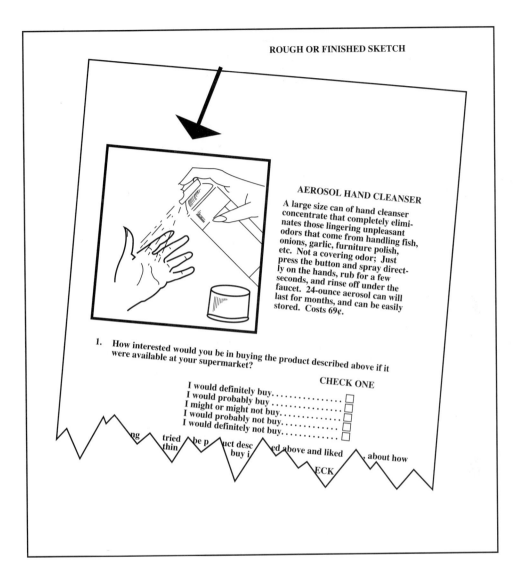

ROUGH OR FINISHED SKETCH

AEROSOL HAND CLEANSER

A large size can of hand cleanser concentrate that completely eliminates those lingering unpleasant odors that come from handling fish, onions, garlic, furniture polish, etc. Not a covering odor; Just press the button and spray directly on the hands, rub for a few seconds, and rinse off under the faucet. 24-ounce aerosol can will last for months, and can be easily stored. Costs 69¢.

1. How interested would you be in buying the product described above if it were available at your supermarket?

CHECK ONE

I would definitely buy. . . . . ☐
I would probably buy . . . . ☐
I might or might not buy. . . . . ☐
I would probably not buy. . . . . ☐
I would definitely not buy. . . . . ☐

ng   tried   be p   uct desc   ed above and liked   about how
thin   buy i   ECK

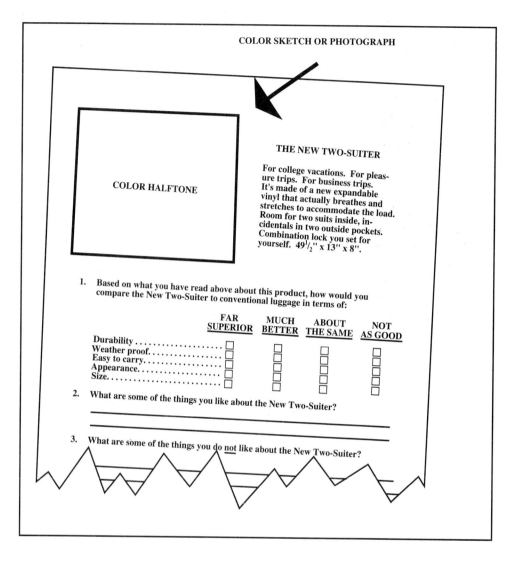

COLOR SKETCH OR PHOTOGRAPH

COLOR HALFTONE

THE NEW TWO-SUITER

For college vacations. For pleasure trips. For business trips. It's made of a new expandable vinyl that actually breathes and stretches to accommodate the load. Room for two suits inside, incidentals in two outside pockets. Combination lock you set for yourself. $49\frac{1}{2}$" x 13" x 8".

1. Based on what you have read above about this product, how would you compare the New Two-Suiter to conventional luggage in terms of:

	FAR SUPERIOR	MUCH BETTER	ABOUT THE SAME	NOT AS GOOD
Durability	☐	☐	☐	☐
Weather proof	☐	☐	☐	☐
Easy to carry	☐	☐	☐	☐
Appearance	☐	☐	☐	☐
Size	☐	☐	☐	☐

2. What are some of the things you like about the New Two-Suiter?

3. What are some of the things you do not like about the New Two-Suiter?

Appendix 9B Assessing Discrimination and Preference

Three approaches can get around the problem of guessing in preference testing. One approach allows for *indifferences;* that is, it allows subjects to indicate that they cannot tell the difference. Unfortunately, because being unable to discriminate is generally not seen as desirable, response to this option often contains considerable error. A more subtle version of allowing for indifference asks, in addition to discrimination and preference judgments, for a rating of confidence in the judgment, thus allowing for low weighting of subjects with low confidence and vice versa.

A second approach to disentangling guessing from true preference involves *multiple preference judgments.* In a single paired comparison, it is impossible to disentangle lucky guessing from true preference. To get a better fix on consumers' ability to discriminate and their preferences, it is common to replicate the paired test. It is also possible to use groups of three products (called *triangles* or *triads,* in which two of the products are identical) to better estimate the ability of consumers to discriminate. To see why a replicated test is useful, consider the following situation (Johnson).

A set of subjects are presented with a pair of products (A and B) on two different occasions. We assume there are three kinds of consumers:

1. Those who can tell the difference and prefer A.
2. Those who can tell the difference and prefer B.
3. Those who cannot distinguish between A and B and indicate preference randomly.

The key is to estimate these three fractions. First, we must observe the actual reported preference table:

| | First Preference | |
Second Preference	A	B
A	48%	15%
B	13%	24%

The naive interpretation is that 48 percent prefer A (because they consistently choose it) and 24 percent prefer B. As we will see, however, this is a bad estimate. Consider the conditional probabilities of test results given true consumer preference shown in the table above. Hence, the expressed percentage is a function of true preference as follows:

$$\%AAe = \%At + 1/4\,(\%\ \text{neither}\ t)$$
$$\%BBe = \%Bt + 1/4\,(\%\ \text{neither}\ t)$$
$$\%\ \text{neither}\ e = 1/2\,(\%\ \text{neither}\ t)$$

where

$\%AAe$ = Expressed percentage who choose A both times.

$\%At$ = True percentage who prefer A.

$\%$ neither t = True percentage of subjects who cannot tell the difference.

Solving this for the true fractions gives

$$\text{\% neither } t = 2 \text{ (\% neither } e)$$

$$\%At = \%AAe - 1/4 \text{ (\% neither } t).$$

$$\%Bt = \%BBe - 1/4 \text{ (\% neither } t).$$

For our example, we get

$$\text{\% neither } t = 2 \text{ (13\% + 15\%)} = 56\%$$

$$\%At = 48\% - 1/4 \text{ (56\%)} = 34\%$$

$$\%Bt = 24\% - 1/4 \text{ (56\%)} = 10\%$$

Thus, the correct interpretation of the results is that most people do not perceive a difference and that B is in trouble.

Paired comparison testing involves a number of concerns. An *order effect* favors the first alternative (Day, 1965). When letters are used to represent brands, the *letters* may not be equally appealing, which can also affect the results. Although this may sound a bit far-fetched, letter preference was once a basis for a lawsuit claiming that ads reporting preference for one beverage over another were unsubstantiated and misleading. Sequential trials also offer the strong possibility of a *carryover effect*. Food tests traditionally involve an intermediate task, such as drinking water or eating a cracker to "cleanse the palate," and reduce the carryover effect.

Another, and in many ways preferable, approach involves comparing more than two alternatives at a time. For example, triangle tests (tests among three alternatives) are a common approach (Morrison, 1981). Using more alternatives makes it less likely that someone can make consistent identification or preference judgments by chance. Someone could make the same (correct) selection in two paired comparisons 25 percent of the time, but only 11 percent of the time if three alternatives are used and only one of the three is the correct choice.

A third approach for dealing with limited discriminatory ability is to *separately assess discrimination and preference* and then weigh the preferences by the customer's discrimination ability. The probability that an individual will correctly identify the different member of a triad containing two identical samples of one brand and one sample of another is assumed to vary. Data on average discriminating ability and individual discrimination performance are used to produce estimates of individual discriminating ability.[1]

The procedures just mentioned generally improve understanding, but at a cost of both respondent effort (which can diminish discriminatory ability and response quality) and dollars. As a consequence, many studies rely on a single comparison. When multiple comparisons are used, they are generally few in number (e.g., three paired comparisons or two triangle tests). A reader interested in the specifics of different forms of comparative product testing should consult other sources.

---

[1] The process, formally known as *empirical Bayes estimation,* increases the estimate of mean ability for individuals who correctly discriminate a substantial portion of the time and decreases it for individuals who fail to correctly discriminate a large portion of the time (Buchanan and Henderson, 1992).

Chapter Ten

Pricing Decisions

Overview

No decision is more critical than the appropriate price to charge customers. Price is an observable component of the product that results in consumers purchasing or not purchasing it, and at the same time it directly affects margin per unit sold. Other components of the marketing mix are important, of course, since they must work together to create a unified brand image and produce sales. However, price is the marketing variable that most often makes or breaks the transaction.

Product managers make decisions about what prices to charge intuitively and routinely, usually based on cost (Monroe, 2002; Nagle and Holden, 1995). If price is such an important decision variable, why does so little science underlie the decision?

Focus on costs as the basis for pricing decisions results because traditionally accountants or financial analysts have done most of the analyses for determining price. It is easy to see why many pricing decisions are cost based. First, adding some kind of markup or profit target to the actual cost reduces setting price to a simple formula. Second, it makes intuitive sense not to charge a price lower than what it costs to make the product or deliver the service. Third, such a pricing mechanism can be implemented quickly because it is generated internally and the only data needed are available within the firm.

To illustrate that cost can be unrelated to price, examine the Web page shown in Figure 10.1 from Buy.com. As can be seen, there are multiple 50-inch plasma TVs being offered: a Panasonic for $10,999.99, a Viewsonic for $7,999.99, and a Sampo for $6,269.99. Although there might be slight differences in features, it is likely in today's global supply markets that all three brands have access to similar sources of products with similar costs. Clearly, in this case, willingness-to-pay is perceived to be different by the marketing managers based upon brand name.

Costs, of course, do matter in setting price. However, *customer value,* what a product or service is worth to the customer in dollars, is much more important. The customer generally does not know or care what your costs are; what is important is whether or not the product delivers an appropriate amount of value for the price being paid. Cost-based pricing mechanisms can produce prices lower than value so the product manager is "leaving money on the table." Alternatively, they can result in prices higher than value, producing lost sales and eventual adjustment downward. Thus, the purpose of price is not to recover costs, but to capture the perceived value of product in the mind of the customer.[1]

---

[1] This quote is adapted from pricing consultant Daniel Nimer.

FIGURE 10.1 Buy.com Website

This short statement represents a different approach to pricing than the cost-based methods. It recognizes that price is determined not by internal company factors alone but also by customers. The often-heard statement "price what the market will bear" is not market-based pricing or useful; different prices produce different levels of demand. What *is* useful is to look at the customer for cues to what prices to set. This chapter therefore places a special emphasis on the role of customer research in making decisions about price.

An excellent illustration of the notion of pricing-to-value was the (failed) attempt by Coke in 1999 to introduce a vending machine that would adjust the prices of the company's soft drinks by the ambient temperature. On a hot day, the prices would rise to capture the increased value customers placed on quenching their thirsts. On cool days, the prices would remain stable. From a theoretical perspective, this idea embodies the ideal notion of capturing customer value. However, the company bungled the implementation by announcing the concept well before they thought out the public relations nightmare that would ensue. Radio stations blared forth the concept and people in other public forums ridiculed it. The idea was quietly withdrawn.

However, prices are not determined by customer value and costs alone. Other elements include the marketing strategy and competitors' prices. In this chapter, we go into more depth about these four factors and other issues that enter into the product manager's pricing decision.

Pricing has become one of the most innovative areas of marketing. For example, the rapid growth of the Internet has had a dramatic impact on pricing. Buyers can easily compare prices using websites like MySimon.com and Shopping.com. Customer value is expressed through "reverse" auctions such as Priceline.com where customers can indicate the maximum prices they are willing to pay for airline tickets, food items, and the like. In addition, companies like Sun Microsystems have developed pricing schemes for products based on the number of employees the customer has, i.e., a pricing scheme based upon how much value Sun can deliver. Although we will discuss these issues at the end of the chapter, there are still some fundamental concepts of pricing that hold no matter how the environment is changing.

THE ROLE OF MARKETING STRATEGY IN PRICING

As discussed in Chapter 8, marketing strategy is first designed and *then* the implementation of that strategy, the marketing mix, is set. Thus, the price must be consistent with the marketing strategy that is developed. As noted in Chapter 8, marketing strategy consists primarily of the market segmentation and core strategy or product positioning decisions. Strategy decisions do not lead to a specific price-setting rule; rather, they give general guidelines for whether a price should be low or high.

For example, a number of years ago, the short-sleeved sport shirts sold under the Izod label were very popular. They were sold in many colors and were extensively distributed in the best department stores, such as Macy's. The marketing strategy and mix were consistent: The target segments were upscale consumers, the product positioning emphasized fashion and color, and the marketing mix supported the strategy through classy advertising, limited distribution, and, of course, high price.

Izod was subsequently bought by packaged goods marketer General Mills. The company believed the brand had substantial growth opportunities beyond the targeted segments. In the words of the strategic framework developed in Chapter 8, it believed there were considerable market development opportunities available. To reach these other segments, the channels of distribution were widened and the price reduced; discount stores began selling the Izod sport shirts. Unfortunately, reaching new market segments produced a mismatch between the strategy (fashion, color, exclusivity) and the marketing mix (discount stores, low price). The upscale segment simply stopped buying the shirts and fled to competitors such as Polo. Eventually, General Mills divested Izod, which recently has begun to go back to its former successful strategy, including opening up its own retail stores.

The target market affects price because prices can vary widely over segments. Economists refer to this as *price discrimination,* that is, charging different prices to segments according to their price elasticity or sensitivity. The brand offerings in most product categories vary in price among market segments, often based on order quantity. Airline ticket prices vary based not just on class of service (first, business, tourist), but also on time of travel and when the ticket is purchased (e.g., 21-day advance). Industrial products often have multitiered pricing depending on whether or not a service contract is purchased, speed of delivery required, and so forth.

Of course, substantial price variation can exist even within a targeted segment. These variations have been referred to as price *bands* (Ross, 1984). Figure 10.2 shows the price band within market segments and price discrimination among segments for the ice cream market. As the movement of the price distributions shows, there is a positive relationship between price and perceived quality. The curves in Figure 10.2 represent distributions of prices within each segment so that the greater the spread in the distribution, the wider the variation in price. The higher perceived quality segments also exhibit greater price variation among brands.

Why do variations exist within segments? First, customers become brand loyal to certain products or suppliers; they tend to rate price relatively low compared to other factors such as reliability, speed of delivery, brand equity, and the like. Second, in some industries, the price charged is less visible than it is at supermarkets or other retailers where the price is marked on the item. For many industrial products, the list price is only

FIGURE 10.2 The Price Band in Ice Cream

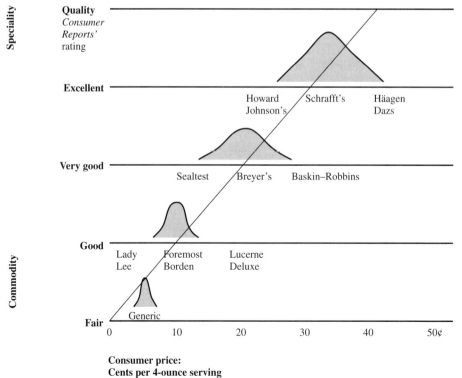

Consumer price:
Cents per 4-ounce serving

a basis from which discounts that vary among customers are given. Third, competitive intensity can vary among segments; the larger the number of suppliers and the more intense the competition, the narrower the price band.

It is critical for the product manager to understand the price sensitivity of the different market segments and, further, how much price flexibility (i.e., the width of the price band) exists in the targeted segments. Thus, the marketing strategy dictates the kind of pricing policies that can be employed at any given point in time.

Along with understanding customers' price sensitivity, the product manager should ask other questions that relate to price (see also the discussion on customer analysis in Chapter 6). A key question is how customers make purchase decisions. How important is price in the overall decision, and how important is it to different individuals in the purchase decision process? Simple surveys will not suffice since respondents often claim price is more important than it really is. Finding out the importance of price takes in-depth knowledge of the customers and perhaps some marketing research such as conjoint analysis. For example, a study of buyers of local area networks (software and hardware used to link personal computers) showed that in terms of importance, price was behind service, the supplier's reputation and technical ability, and product availability. Another aspect of understanding price is determining how important your product is to the customer, who will be less price sensitive for a key component in a high-quality product. For example, Rolls-Royce does not quibble about the cost of the leather it uses for its car interiors.

MEASURING PERCEIVED VALUE AND PRICE

As we noted in the chapter introduction, the key to setting price and understanding why customers react the way they do to prices is perceived value. Whether the product in question is an industrial product for which the customer can calculate the money saved by purchasing it or a consumer product for which the benefits are perceptual, customers have some notion of what constitutes a good or a bad price. This notion is developed (1) by comparing the price being charged to the perceived value or benefits that would be derived through purchasing, and (2) by comparing price to a reference point such as what price has been in the past.

Here we explicitly consider three possible relations among perceived value, price, and variable cost:

1. Perceived value > price > variable cost.
2. Price > perceived value > variable cost.
3. Price > variable cost > perceived value.

Note that in all three situations, we assume price is greater than variable cost.

Perceived Value > Price > Variable Cost

This represents a situation in which the product manager has set a price that covers the cost of making the product (or delivering the service) but less than the customers' true perceived value. This "leaving money on the table" scenario sacrifices profits (either knowingly or unknowingly) by charging less than the producer could obtain. The amount of lost profit is directly related to the dollar value the customer places on the product. Customers react to this by thinking they are getting a "bargain." Interestingly, customers do not usually write letters to the company complaining they are not paying enough. Thus, except for the extreme case of such insufficient production that shortages occur, this situation is difficult for the product manager to discover without using the marketing research methods described later in this chapter.[2] Of course product managers may purposely price well below customer value. This notion of "value pricing" (to be distinguished from "pricing to value," which is a price set equal to customer value) is common in today's price-sensitive marketplace and is discussed later in this chapter.

A good example of value pricing is the Mazda Miata, introduced in 1990. Mazda's objective was to introduce a two-seat convertible with few power options and luxurious details. This throwback to the 1950s was just a simple car with a sporting feel and was introduced at a low price of $16,000 to $18,000. However, demand for the Miata was so high during the first few months after it was introduced that prices of $25,000 in the used-car sections of newspapers were common. Customers were buying the cars and quickly reselling ("flipping") them to make a significant arbitrage profit. Clearly, Mazda could have charged more for the Miata. Perhaps company managers underestimated the demand for the car. However, they probably knew this craze was a short-term aberration and believed the original price was more consistent with their long-term marketing strategy for the car. Also, high initial prices that are later reduced play havoc with the used-car market. Customers who paid the high price and tried to sell the cars later would find no demand for them because people could buy a new car for less than a used one. Interestingly, this low entry price relative to customer value strategy was copied by Porsche and BMW with their own roadster entries, the Boxster and the Z3, as well as Chrysler's PT Cruiser.

Price > Perceived Value > Variable Cost

This represents an unfortunate situation: The price is set higher than the costs *and* higher than the customer's perceived value. In this case, the product is a "bad deal." Unlike in the first scenario, customers *do* let you know when the price is higher than their perceived value; they simply do not buy the product. Waiting for customer reaction is an expensive form of marketing research, however, because the customers may have bought another product and be out of the market for some time. The cure for customers' failure to buy is obvious: Some kind of downward price adjustment or increase in customer value is necessary. However, without knowing what the perceived value is, the product manager does not know how far to lower price and usually uses the competition as the reference point.

Two examples show how companies have had to reduce their prices due to the discovery that perceived value was lower than the price they were charging. Iridium LLC was a company (it went bankrupt) that was formed to provide global cellular phone service

---

[2] This is sometimes referred to as "seller's remorse." For example, a person selling a house who receives several offers immediately at the listing price always believes he or she should have set a higher price.

through a network of 66 low-orbit satellites. It was hoped that the project, managed and 18 percent owned by Motorola, would have 500,000 subscribers by the end of 1999. However, by the middle of 1999, only 15,000 customers had signed up. On July 1, 1999, the company reduced its prices by 65 percent. Unfortunately, even a steep price cut was insufficient to save the company (Hardy, 1999). An additional example is from the video game industry. As of August 2003, Nintendo's GameCube held only 19 percent of the market, well behind Sony's PlayStation 2 and Microsoft's Xbox. In September, Nintendo cut the price of the GameCube to $99 from $149 or about 45–50 percent lower than its competitors. As a result, its share surged to 37 percent putting it in second place behind Sony (Dvorak, 2003).

Price > Variable Cost > Perceived Value

The final scenario represents the case in which price is higher than cost but the perceived value is even lower than the cost. This is clearly a failure scenario. Such products are usually weeded out in the new-product development process. If not, they are ultimately withdrawn from the market. For example, the Yugoslavian-made car, the Yugo, was withdrawn from the U.S. market because it received such negative press in publications such as *Consumer Reports* that consumer value fell even below the manufacturing and marketing costs.

The usefulness of understanding customer value can be shown through Figure 10.3. Assume that the product manager has measured "average" customer value in a particular target market (the top line in Figure 10.3) and that he or she knows the cost to make the product or deliver the service (the bottom line in Figure 10.3). Then the manager makes an informed and strategic decision about how much value to give to the customer and how much to keep. The maximum price the manager can charge is the customer value; the minimum is the variable cost. Anything in between represents sharing value between the product manager and the customer. Price (A) in Figure 10.3 represents a decision to keep most of the value. This might be a reasonable approach if there is little competition or if the product is a one-time purchase. Price (B) represents a decision to give the customer most of the value. In this situation, the manager is interested in building market share, enhancing customer satisfaction, or in some way rewarding the customer.

FIGURE 10.3   **An Illustration of the Gap between Customer Value and Cost**

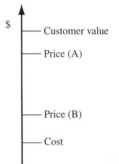

FIGURE 10.4 Methods for Estimating Customer Value

1. Industrial engineering methods
   Internal engineering assessment: Physical laboratory tests within the firm.
   Indirect survey questions: Customer estimates the effects of product changes on firm operations used to infer the value of product attributes.
2. Overall estimates of customer value
   Field value-in-use assessments: Customer interviews determining economic benefits of using the product.
   Focus group value assessment: willingness-to-pay questions in a small-group setting.
   Direct survey questions: willingness-to-pay questions in a survey format.
3. Decomposition approaches
   Conjoint analysis: A method for estimating customer trade-offs of product attributes.
   Benchmarks: Customer indication of willingness to pay for incremental (or fewer) attributes that can be compared to an example from the product category.
4. Compositional approach: Direct customer questions about the value of product attributes.
5. Importance ratings: Customer rank ordering or rating of the importance of product attributes as well as comparisons among competitors.

Measuring Customer Value

Figure 10.4 shows the general types of methods that can be used to estimate customer value (Anderson, Jain, and Chintagunta, 1993). The following sections indicate how to use them.

Calculating Value-in-Use

Particularly for industrial products, a useful way to estimate customer value is through a method called *value-in-use* (referred to as *field value-in-use* in Figure 10.4).[3] The approach is basically the same as the economic value calculation discussed in Appendix 6A. First, the product manager selects a reference product, usually either the product the customer is currently using or a competitor's product. Second, the product manager calculates the *incremental* economic (dollar) benefit to the customer of using the product or brand in question. Assuming it is positive, this incremental economic benefit describes the range of prices obtainable. As in Figure 10.3, pricing equal to the incremental benefit gives all the value to the company, pricing to capture none of the incremental benefit gives it all to the customer, and in-between prices share the economic benefit.

Figure 10.5 shows one approach to the value-in-use calculation (Forbis and Mehta, 1981). The bar on the far left is the reference product, *Y.* Assume the reference product cost (i.e., the initial price) is $300. Also assume that the company that produces it incurs start-up costs of $200 (e.g., training) and postpurchase costs of $500 (e.g., maintenance). Together these costs are referred to as *life cycle costs* and recognize that the cost of buying a product often goes far beyond the acquisition cost.

The product manager's product, *X,* is represented in the next bar on the right. It is assumed product *X* has $100 less in both start-up and postpurchase costs. It is also assumed the product offers approximately $100 more in "value" through some additional features (e.g., energy savings). Therefore, if the customer is willing to pay $300 for product *Y,* then

---

[3] See Anderson and Narus (1998) for a good discussion of customer value in an industrial marketing context.

FIGURE 10.5 **The Economic Value Concept**

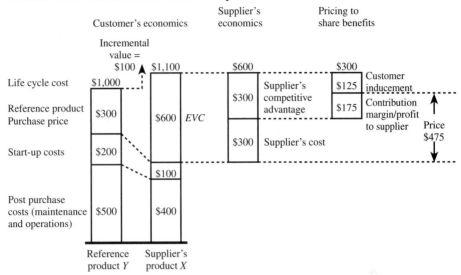

the customer should be willing to pay $300 more ($200 in reduced life cycle costs plus $100 extra value) for product *X*. The third bar to the right assumes the variable cost of product *X* is $300. Thus, we know our pricing range: The variable cost of $300 is the floor; the incremental dollar value to the customer is $600 (the *economic value* to the customer, or EVC, in Figure 10.5). The difference, $300, is the amount the product manager has to "play with" in terms of setting price. This is labeled the "supplier's competitive advantage." The last bar to the right shows one hypothetical split of the $300 pricing range (incremental to the $300 variable cost), which leaves $125 for the customer and $175 for product *X*.

An attractive feature of this approach is that the analysis provides valuable information for a salesperson to use in trying to close the sale. In this case, the salesperson can explicitly quantify the incremental economic benefit to the customer and show that the company is willing to give a "discount" of $125 from the true economic value. Since industrial buyers like to be shown how they can make a greater profit buying one product versus another, this information can be quite persuasive.

It is possible, of course, to apply this method to a case in which the incremental value is lower than the reference product but the customer would be compensated by a lower price. Suppose the reference product is again product *Y* in Figure 10.5. However, let product *X* have $50 higher start-up costs and $75 higher postpurchase costs with no incremental value characteristics. This puts product *X* at a $125 deficit for the EVC, meaning the maximum the customer would pay is $300 − $125 = $175. However, if the cost of making this new product is only $50, the product manager still has a $125 pricing decision range.

Of interest in the first illustration is how the $100 worth of incremental value is calculated. The value-in-use approach attempts to break down the advantages of the product into its components and thus has a decompositional aspect. That is, if the product has advantages over the reference product, these advantages must be quantified in terms of each way the product benefits the customer economically.

Animalens, Inc., which makes vision-blurring lenses for chickens, is an effective if unusual example of this approach (Clarke, 1975). The lenses were developed to reduce cannibalism in egg-laying chickens; reducing their vision makes them less able and willing to fight, thereby increasing their productivity. The reference "product" in this case is debeaking, that is, shortening the chickens' beaks to make it difficult to use them as a weapon. The contact lenses had three main advantages that produced economic benefits to chicken farmers: (1) reduced cannibalism, (2) increased egg production, and (3) reduced feed consumption (actual data have shown that the costs of lens insertion and debeaking are about the same). The economic benefits can be quantified by studying the behavior of two flocks, one using the lenses and the other using debeaking. The comparison establishes the range of prices: The lower limit is the variable cost of producing the lenses, and the upper limit is the sum of the economic benefits of the three components of cost saving or improved productivity plus the cost of the current method, debeaking.

The method shown in Figure 10.5 can be applied to both products and services. A major trend in business is *outsourcing,* purchasing a service from an outside vendor to replace the company's operation. For example, rather than operating copying machines and worrying about how to use them properly, many companies subcontract their copying operations to third parties that assume responsibility for the work. University bookstores subcontract their bookstore operations to companies such as Barnes and Noble with more efficient operations. Other examples include General Motors paying PPG Industries to operate its automobile painting facilities, IBM contracting with Federal Express to act as a warehousing agent around the world, and companies who host software applications (applications service providers, or ASPs) for other companies. In these cases, the agents whose services are purchased can use the cost of the company providing the service itself as a reference product. Even if it is more expensive to pay other companies for these services, benefits such as better utilization of employee time and company capital, increased productivity, and better technology can be quantified and shown to produce value to potential customers.

As you have probably discerned, the value-in-use method works particularly well with many industrial products and services but not as well for those consumer products whose benefits are difficult to quantify in dollar terms. The methods described next are primary research methods that can be applied to all kinds of product categories.

Pricing Experiments

In attempting to understand customer value, particularly in situations where engineering approaches like the one previously described will not work, it is often useful to obtain measures of customer *willingness-to-pay* (WTP) at different price levels in order to better understand not only the maximum people will pay but also how they would react to different intermediate price levels between the maximum and the minimum (cost). Experimentation is useful in this context. In an experiment, the manager manipulates a marketing variable (price) and sees the reaction of customers to the different levels of the variable. Some experiments put their subjects in an artificial environment (laboratory experiments); some use real-world settings such as actual store environments.

A common approach to understanding how customers react to new product concepts or product modifications involves simulating the shopping experience, a laboratory experiment. Marketing research companies often set up laboratories at or near shopping malls where customers are asked to select brands, watch commercials, and the like, in what looks like an actual store (e.g., supermarket) setting. In such experimental settings, marketing mix variables such as price can be manipulated to see if reactions vary to different possible prices for a brand. The reactions are usually measured by purchase intention or selection from a set of choices rather than actual purchase.

Industrial product companies also use such research. For example, Hewlett-Packard (HP) developed a new test instrument and wanted to find an appropriate price. The company realized that asking direct questions about willingness to pay was not likely to produce accurate responses, so it developed a catalog that included competing products and the new product. HP then hired a marketing research firm to conduct the study and disguise who was collecting the data to avoid biasing responses. Potential customers were randomly assigned to different groups, and each group received the same brochure, except that the price for the HP instrument varied. By controlling all other factors, the only difference in response had to be due to price. The customers were then asked to indicate which testing machine they would choose, thus simulating the buying experience. Interestingly, HP managers found that as they increased price, demand went up. They subsequently priced the instrument thousands of dollars higher than they had planned (Kendall, 1990).

A field experiment conducted by a German mobile phone manufacturer examined the sales response over three different regions of the country to automobile installation of the phones. Before the experiment, the price charged was 1,200 DM and the "take" rate was 24 percent. The manufacturer then varied the price by charging 600, 900, and 1,200 DM in the three regions (the regions were chosen due to their similarities on a number of economic variables). The results are shown in Figure 10.6. As can be seen, 45 percent of the buyers installed the phone in their new cars when the price was 600 DM while at 900 DM, the demand declined to 41 percent. These real-world findings give the manager valuable information about the potential demand at different price levels.

FIGURE 10.6 **Price Experiment for a Mobile Phone**

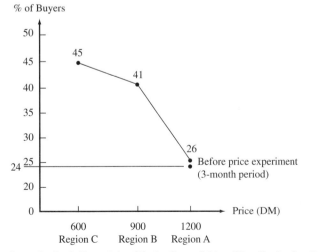

Source: Reprinted with permission of The Free Press, a division of Macmillan, Inc. from *Power Pricing* by Robert J. Dolan and Hermann Simon. Copyright 1996 by Robert J. Dolan.

Using Price Thresholds

Another approach that requires primary marketing research involves customer price thresholds. This approach provides an overall estimate of customer value (Figure 10.4). One important threshold is called the *reservation* price. This is the highest price a customer would pay for a product or service. A second price threshold is a lower boundary, the lowest price someone would pay for a product. It may appear to be common sense that one would pay as little as possible in all instances. However, often customers associate low price with low quality. This relationship between price and perceived quality has been found in many (but not all) product categories (Zeithaml, 1988). Thus, a price level can exist below which a customer would not purchase due to suspicions about the product's quality.

These two thresholds can be used as follows. First, the product manager identifies customers most likely to buy the product category. These respondents are then shown a card with a range of specific prices. For example, if the product is a low-priced good that normally sells for around $5, the range might be from $2 to $8 in 25-cent or 50-cent increments. The respondents are then asked to identify their two price thresholds with the following questions: (1) "Above which price on this card would you not buy this product?" and (2) "Below which price on this card would you not buy this product because of suspicions that the quality is poor?" The product manager can then determine the price to charge by identifying the price most often mentioned as acceptable.

Dollarmetric Scales

Conventional rating scales are often used to assess willingness to pay for a product. For example, a typical survey question offers a series of prices and then asks potential customers to indicate how likely they are to purchase the product on a 1-to-7 scale, with 1 being very unlikely and 7 representing very likely. Among other problems with such an approach, the 1-to-7 ratings give the product manager little information on which to base a pricing decision; it is difficult to know whether a 6 should be counted as a likely buyer or whether only 7s should be used.

An alternative scale puts responses in dollar or other currency terms. Figure 10.7 applies and analyzes a dollarmetric scale for soft drinks. This example includes five brands: Coke, Pepsi, 7UP, Dr Pepper, and Fresca. The question is: What should be the relative prices of the four brands? The respondent first chooses which of two brands she or he prefers. Next, the respondent indicates in dollars and cents how much extra he or she would be willing to pay to get a six-pack of the preferred brand.[4] The product manager then analyzes the data by summing the differences, positive and negative, between each brand compared to each of the others. As the bottom of Figure 10.7 shows, for this customer a six-pack of Coke is worth 2 cents more than Pepsi, 8 cents more than 7UP, 5 cents more than Dr Pepper, and 12 cents more than Fresca. If these results held up over a national sample, the average differences indicate the price differences Coke could maintain over the competing brands (e.g., 2.5 cents versus Pepsi and 6.25 cents versus Dr Pepper).

---

[4] An alternative way to phrase the question is to ask how much the respondent would have to be paid to be indifferent between the preferred brand and the other brand.

FIGURE 10.7 Dollarmetric Example

Data		
Pair of Brands **(more preferred brand underlined)**	**Amount Extra Willing to Pay to Get a Six-Pack** **of the More Preferred Brand** **(cents)**	
Coke, Pepsi	2	
Coke, 7UP	8	
Coke, Dr Pepper	5	
Coke, Fresca	12	
Pepsi, 7UP	6	
Pepsi, Dr Pepper	3	
Pepsi, Fresca	10	
7UP, Dr Pepper	3	
7UP, Fresca	4	
Dr Pepper, Fresca	7	

	Analysis		**Sum**	**Average** **Difference**
Coke:	+2 (versus Pepsi) + 8 (versus 7UP) + 5 (versus Dr Pepper) + 12 (versus Fresca)		= 27	+6.75
Pepsi:	−2 + 6 + 3 + 10		= 17	+4.25
7UP:	−8 − 6 − 3 + 4		= −13	−3.75
Dr Pepper:	−5 − 3 + 3 + 7		= 2	+0.50
Fresca:	−12 − 10 − 4 − 7		= −33	−8.25

Using the Perceived Value Concept

Consider a functional relationship among market share, perceived value, and price:

$$\text{Market share is proportional to } f\left[\text{perceived value/price}\right]$$

Although there is a potential correlation between the numerator and the denominator, this proportional relationship provides some useful insights into managerial behavior. How can an observed decline in the market share of a product be reversed? The immediate response is usually a decrease in the denominator, that is, a price cut either through list price or a price promotion. Cutting price is certainly one way to bring the relationship between perceived value and price back into balance. However, there is another way: The product manager could also choose to increase the perceived value of the product.

This increase in perceived value can be accomplished in a variety of ways, including the following:

Improve the product itself by increasing actual quality or offering better service or a longer warranty period.

Advertise to enhance the product's image.

Institute value-added services, such as technical support or financing, in the distribution channels.

Improve the sales effort by training the sales force to sell value rather than price.

These are only a sampling of the kinds of things product managers can do to improve value rather than cut price.[5]

Interestingly, while reducing price is a more common way to regain share losses, it is actually much more expensive than adding value since the lower resulting profit margin requires a large increase in unit volume to offset it. A 3 percent price cut by the average Standard & Poor's 1,000 company reduces profits from 8.1 percent to 5.1 percent, a reduction of 37 percent. In addition, McKinsey consultants estimate that the average S&P 1,000 company would need a 12 percent increase in sales volume to offset the 3 percent price cut (Serwer, 1994). Note that the activities designed to raise perceived value can cost considerably less. How much does it cost to improve sales training procedures? How expensive is it to offer improved customer service? Value-enhancing activities are not free, but they often involve fixed costs that can be spread over a large volume as opposed to per-unit reductions in margins.

A good example of a company investing in value rather than cutting price is Toyota's behavior toward pricing the new version of its Sienna minivan in 2003 (Zaun, 2004). U.S. car manufacturers have been "buying" customers using lavish rebate programs. Obviously, this is an alternative way to reduce price as it is nondiscriminatory and thus is in force for all units sold. Instead of reducing price, Toyota kept the price of the Sienna the same while making it bigger with a more powerful engine and adding a number of new standard features such as keyless entry, power mirrors, and tinted glass.

Thus, a key point is that product managers can get considerable leverage from first increasing the perceived value of products rather than immediately reducing price. Although reducing price is usually the gut reaction to a drop in market share, it is worth thinking about the numerator in the value/price relationship. Companies know this: In the automobile industry, executives have long said that they want to stop focusing on price and break the habit of rebates and instead build brand equity—add value. However, with few exceptions, such as Saturn in the early 1990s, the price/promotion wars continue.

Besides adding value, managers have other alternatives for combating a competitor's price pressure (Rao, Bergen, and Davis, 2000). These can be classified into nonprice and price responses. A useful nonprice response is to signal your strategic intentions and capabilities without necessarily changing the price. For example, you can make a public pronouncement that you will match any price cut or emphasize your cost advantage. Price responses that do not result in a cut in the "list" price include using complex price actions such as bundling, quantity discounts, and price promotions and introducing product line extensions that address the more price-sensitive segments.

PSYCHOLOGICAL ASPECTS OF PRICE

Many customers actively process price information; that is, they are not just price "takers" (to use the conventional term from microeconomics). Customers continually assess the prices charged for products based on prior purchasing experience, formal

---

[5] Since price and perceived value are often correlated, some readers may argue that one way to increase perceived value is to raise price. However, this works only if there is additional investment in the product that also raises value, such as packaging and advertising, and if an appropriate market segment exists that will respond to such a strategy.

communications (e.g., advertising) and informal communications (e.g., friends and neighbors), and point-of-purchase or Web-derived listings of prices, and they use those assessments in the ultimate purchase decision. Two key concepts relating to the psychological aspects of pricing are reference prices and the price–perceived quality relationship.[6]

Reference Prices

A reference price is any standard of comparison against which an observed price is compared. There are two kinds of reference prices: internal and external, also sometimes referred to as *temporal* and *contextual,* respectively (Rajendran and Tellis, 1994; Briesch et al., 1997). External reference prices are usually observed prices that, in a retailing setting, are typically posted at the point of purchase as the "regular retail price." Internal reference prices are mental prices used to assess an observed price. Since the product manager cannot easily manipulate internal reference prices, although they have a strong effect on buying behavior, we discuss them in more detail.

A large number of internal reference prices have been proposed (Winer, 1988), including:

The "fair" price, or what the product ought to cost the customer.

The price frequently charged.

The last price paid.

The upper amount someone would pay (reservation price).

The lower threshold or lowest amount a customer would pay.

The price of the brand usually bought.

The average price charged for similar products.

The expected future price.

The typical discounted price.

Many of these considerations contribute to the concept we call the *perceived* price, the price the customer thinks is the current actual price of the product.

Reference price has a significant impact on brand choice of both durable and non-durable goods (Kalyanaram and Winer, 1995). In particular, when the observed price is higher than the reference price, it can negatively affect purchasing because the consumer perceives this situation as an unpleasant surprise or a bad deal. For example, the large price increases for cars in the 1970s created what became known as a "sticker shock" effect when consumer reference or perceived prices for cars were significantly lower than the prices they saw in the showroom. A happier situation occurs when the observed price is either at or below the reference price. This happens when a brand a consumer might buy anyway is being promoted at a lower price. Interestingly, several studies have found that the unpleasant surprises have a greater impact on purchasing probabilities than the pleasant surprises.

This concept of reference price has important implications for product managers. Consider the situation in which a brand has been on price promotion for several weeks. The customer will begin to replace the normal price with the promoted price as the

---

[6] See Gourville (1999) for a good summary of the behavioral aspects of price.

reference point. Then, when the brand comes off deal and returns to the regular price, the customer may perceive the change as an increase in price, with a resulting positive difference between observed price and reference price, and at least temporarily stop purchasing it.

A second important concept of reference price is expected future price. This is a particularly important concept for any product category that experiences significant price changes over time. Several examples highlight how customers use future price expectations. The airline industry has had protracted fare wars in which the prices of some flights fell rapidly in short periods of time. Some segments of fliers, such as business travelers, are unaffected by changes in fares because they do not have discretion concerning when they fly. However, fliers who have flexible schedules, such as people planning to visit relatives, simply wait for prices to drop further before booking. Price cutting exacerbates the airlines' problems because sales are low while discretionary travelers wait for the fares to drop even further. The same situation results from rebate programs in the automobile industry. In 2003, the average cash rebate from Chevrolet was $3,231 and from Ford, $2,752 (Lundegaard and Freeman, 2004). With programs like those, consumers are going to wait to purchase until some kind of monetary incentive is offered. New consumer durables are also subject to this phenomenon. The prices of personal computers are falling so rapidly that customers are worried they will overpay. Again, discretionary purchasers can simply wait until the prices decrease further. The problem is predictability: Product managers who create predictable pricing patterns may underestimate customers' abilities to process the information and to make decisions based on their personal forecasts of future prices.

The Relationship between Price and Perceived Quality

In some situations, contrary to standard microeconomics, a higher price can lead to higher rather than lower demand. This occurs when price is used as a signal that the product in question is of high quality.

One reason such a relationship exists is for exclusivity or prestige. Pricing a product high means fewer customers can afford it. It is likely that Rolex could charge substantially less for its watches and still make a profit. However, because few consumers can afford thousands of dollars for a watch, few will own a Rolex, imparting a feeling of prestige to the owner.

A second example of a strong price–perceived quality relationship occurs when a product's quality is either difficult to assess before purchasing (sometimes these products are referred to as *experience* goods because you have to actually try the product to know how good it is) or difficult to assess at all. Good examples include wine, perfume, and many professional services such as consulting and legal advice. Perhaps the ultimate example is life insurance; no matter what you pay, you will never use the product.

The major implication for the product manager was stated earlier in this chapter: Price must be consistent with marketing strategy. If customer research shows a significant correlation between price and perceived quality, a core strategy stressing quality or value-added features requires a consistent price. An exotic vodka supported with highly creative advertising stressing exclusivity and prestige cannot be priced at $1.99 a bottle without striking a discordant feeling in the (presumably) upscale consumer.

The Odd-Ending Effect in Prices

One of the more interesting phenomena in marketing is the popularity of "odd" prices, or those ending with nines or other odd numbers. Sometimes these are referred to as "just below" prices as they are often "just below" an even price, for example, $1.99 vs. $2.00. While the real differences in price from even numbers are usually insignificant, odd prices can have an important impact on purchasing behavior. Note that this kind of pricing behavior exists even for expensive goods; houses are often priced at, say, $599,999 rather than $600,000.

Schindler and Kibarian (1996) conducted a field study to examine the effect of odd-ending prices on sales. A split-run field study was conducted using a mail-order catalogue on 90,000 subjects. The first 30,000 subjects were mailed catalogues with prices ending in 00, the next 30,000 got catalogues with 88-ending prices and the last 30,000 were sent catalogues with 99-ending prices. Interestingly, sales generated by 88-ending catalogues were the same as 00-ending catalogues; but the 99-ending catalogues had 10 percent higher sales!

Such effects of odd-ending prices have come to be labeled as image effects (Stiving and Winer, 1997). Image effects explanation suggests that consumers' preference for odd-ending prices is based on the symbolic significance of odd-ending digits. This explanation posits that odd endings (e.g., using $2.89 instead of $2.80 or $3.00) provide cues about price and quality of the product. Based on a survey of published material and informal conversations with consumers and retailers, Schindler (1991) proposed a list of 14 meanings that price endings are likely to communicate to consumers. These meanings can be broadly classified into two groups: price-related meanings (such as "low price," "discount price") or meanings concerning nonprice attributes of the product or retailer (such as "low quality"). The psychological process that underlies odd-ending effects continues to be unclear. "What can we conclude about odd pricing? The effect seems to vary across purchase situations from none to quite significant. At this time, we do not know exactly why this variation occurs" (Nagle and Holden, 1995).

COMPETITION AND PRICING

So far our discussion about setting price has described two key elements of the product manager's thinking: the marketing strategy and the value customers place on the product relative to other available options. The first is obviously an internal factor because the product manager has control over the marketing strategy. The second dimension accounts for one of the external elements affecting all decisions: customers.

A third critical element in pricing decisions is the competition. The competitors' prices act as a reference point, either explicitly as shown in the value computations earlier, or implicitly as a way to assess the price of the product in question. Competitors' prices do not necessarily represent willingness to pay because the set of possible prices or marketing strategies may have been limited. In other words, just because the major competitors' prices hover around 50 cents does not mean customers would not pay more for a product delivering superior value, either real or perceived. However, the 50-cent price level does represent a reference point; a price of $1 may appear to customers to be out of the reasonable range, even when the product manager believes it is reasonable from a value perspective.

Two factors that are key to understanding the role of competition in the pricing decision are the competitors' costs and the historical pricing behavior in the category.

Competitors' Costs

In Chapter 5, we discussed the importance of studying the competition to make better strategic decisions. Product managers cannot make intelligent pricing decisions without having some estimate of the relative cost positions held by competitors in the product category. Even better are estimates of the actual costs. An understanding of the cost structure of the category provides at least two types of guidance. First, assuming no brand would be priced below variable cost for an extended period, cost estimates provide the product manager with an idea of how low some competitors can price. This can be very useful in a price war. Second, cost estimates give the product manager some idea of the margins in the category. Coupled with data on sales volume, which are usually relatively easy to obtain, and information on marketing program costs, total profits can then be estimated. This can be important information in forecasting the likelihood that a product will stay in the market and the amount of money a competitor has to put behind its brand strategy.

Costs can be estimated in several ways. A common approach for manufactured products, described in Chapter 5, is to use reverse engineering for a detailed analysis of the cost structure. Product managers should purchase competitors' products and take them apart, studying the costs of the components and packaging. For many products, managers can readily identify components and their costs in the market. If a component is proprietary, such as a custom microprocessor in a computer, engineers or other personnel can estimate the cost.

Another way to estimate costs, or at least margins, is to use publicly available data on the competitors. Based on annual reports, 10Ks, and the like, average margins can be ascertained. These margins can be assumed to directly apply, especially if the product is a big component of total sales or if, as is often the case, the company tends to follow a cost plus percent markup strategy. Alternatively, the overall average can be adjusted (either subjectively or via analysis) to account for such factors as the category average, the relative number and strength of competitors in the category, and production experience.

Particularly for manufactured products, it is possible to both understand current costs and forecast future costs through the use of the experience curve (Abell and Hammond, 1979). The experience curve phenomenon applies to products for which repetitive production of larger and larger amounts and concomitant investment in new manufacturing equipment systematically reduce costs over time. The conventional functional relationship assumed in experience curve economics is that costs (adjusted for inflation) are a decreasing function of accumulated "experience" or production volume. Figure 10.8 shows an example of the experience curve phenomenon. In this case, experience is approximated by market share. Costs (and concomitant prices) are shown to be correlated with market share: The larger the share, the lower the costs.[7] If the product manager can

---

[7] This is discussed at length in Buzzell and Gale (1987). Their analysis is based on the Profit Impact of Market Strategies (PIMS) database composed of cross-sectional time-series data across different firms and industries. The difference between using experience and share is that the former measures volume over time whereas the latter is more closely related to economies of scale or current production values.

FIGURE 10.8 **Market Share versus Price/Costs**

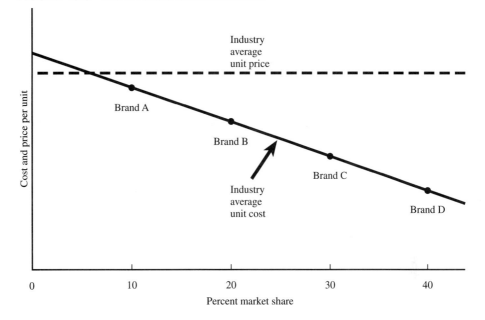

construct a plot such as that in Figure 10.8 and statistically estimate the implied relationship between share and costs, she or he can forecast future relative cost positions under different assumptions of brand shares.

The costs of delivering services are more difficult to estimate. Because the costs associated with service products, such as labor, office buildings, and the like, are largely fixed, the manager can estimate relative cost positions by examining the number of employees, looking at efficiency ratios such as sales per employee, and assessing other, similar measures. Again, it is particularly useful to understand the cost structure by becoming a customer of a competitor's service.

Historical Pricing Behavior

As noted at the beginning of the chapter, the product manager makes pricing decisions in two contexts. First, the decision can be *proactive:* During a period of relative price stability, the product manager can choose to be the first to either raise or lower price. In this situation, the product manager wonders what the reaction will be to the price change. Second, the decision can be *reactive* when a competitor has taken the lead and the product manager has to decide whether to match the price, keep it the same, or reduce the price more or less than the competitors. If prices are being adjusted in a category, most product managers prefer to be proactive because that forces competitors to make difficult decisions at a time and in circumstances not of their choosing; in other words, the product manager is setting the rules of the game.

To understand price changes, it is useful to examine historical behavior. Individual product managers may change over time, but there are often companywide or institutional reasons certain brands consistently tend to be proactive and others reactive. For example, U.S. Steel (before it was USX) was consistently the price leader in the U.S.

steel industry: It would change prices first and competitors would follow. Similarly, predicting future reactions of competitors can be partially related to historical price competition in the category for many products.

More important, the competitor analysis gives clues to the pricing behavior in the product category. What are some noncost characteristics to look for? The most important is the competitor's operating objective. Clearly, if the objective seems to be profit oriented, that brand will not be an aggressive price cutter. Alternatively, if the objective is to increase market share, lower price might be used as a weapon. Thus, as noted in Chapter 5, understanding competitors' objectives is key to anticipating pricing moves in the category. Other factors are the financial health of the product or parent company, its capacity (undercapacity is a warning that price might be cut), and a new product's or a senior manager's historical behavior in other markets.

The Role of Own Costs

We suggested earlier in this chapter that costs should have little to do with the pricing decision other than to act as a floor or lower limit for price.[8] In a non-market-driven firm, full costs (variable costs plus some allocation for overhead) plus some target margin is used to set price. This approach totally ignores the customer: The resulting price may be either above or below what the customer is willing to pay for the product. Yet this is a very common approach to setting price.

Other problems exist with using costs to set price. First, there are at least four different kinds of costs to consider.[9] First, development costs are expenses involved in bringing new products to market. These costs are often spread out over many years and sometimes products. Should price be set to recover these costs and if so, in what time period? In some industries, such as pharmaceuticals, patent protection allows setting the prices of prescription drugs high initially to recover development costs and then reducing them when the drugs come off patent and generics enter the category. However, if there is no legal way to keep competitors out, these costs must be viewed as sunk costs that do not affect decision making after the product is introduced into the market. A second kind of costs is overhead costs such as the president's salary, the corporate jet, and the exercise club at headquarters. These costs must ultimately be covered by revenues from individual products, but they are not associated with any one product. The mechanism used to allocate these overhead costs among products is often arbitrary and bears no relationship to how individual products utilize overhead or whether they would change if the product were not produced. A third kind of costs is direct fixed. These costs, such as the product manager's salary, product advertising and promotion, and so on, are associated with individual products but do not vary with volume. Finally, there are variable costs, the per-unit costs of making the product or delivering the service. These, of course, must be recovered with price. Therefore, one problem with using "costs" to set price is that several kinds of costs are related in different ways to an individual product. Included in this category are the costs of plant, inventory, receivables, and the like, that are tied to the product. Many companies now attempt to account for

---

[8] In fact, Drucker (1993) refers to cost-driven pricing as a "deadly sin."

[9] We cover financial analysis for product management more completely in Chapter 15.

these by calculating the opportunity cost of the resources committed to the product by multiplying the amount of resources by either the firm's average cost of capital or return on investment. By subtracting these from revenues, the so-called direct product profitability (DPP) is calculated.

A second problem with using costs to set price, particularly variable or unit costs, is that they may be a function of volume and therefore difficult to know in advance when developing marketing plans. Even if this is not the case, unit costs may be related to the utilization of capacity. Therefore, when developing marketing plans, product managers should simulate profits and sales volume using a number of possible prices and costs.

Ultimately, in most instances customers do not really care what the firm's costs are; as Drucker (1993) puts it, "Customers do not see it as their job to ensure manufacturers a profit." Using cost increases to justify raising price generates limited sympathy (which of course is better than none in the case of increases that appear to be opportunistic gouging) from customers, particularly industrial customers, because the price increase (justified by a cost increase) has just raised their costs, which they may not be able to pass along in their market segments. The price increase may stick, but only if there is value behind the product that justifies the higher price.

DECIDING HOW MUCH OF THE VALUE–COST GAP TO CAPTURE: PRICING OBJECTIVES

The decision about how much of the customer value minus cost gap to keep or give away is manifested first in the general pricing policy the product manager pursues. This setting of the pricing policy or objective(s) is captured by Figure 10.9. General pricing objectives are set after the three major background analyses described earlier in the book—category, customer, and competitor—are performed and the marketing strategy is determined. Like brand or product objectives, a price objective is a guide for more precise decision making. For example, if a penetration or low price objective is selected, the product manager considers a range of prices at the low end of the cost–value gap.

Penetration Pricing

Penetration, or market share, pricing is employed when the product manager purposely gives most of the value to the customer and keeps a small margin. It is often used as an entry strategy for a new product and is particularly useful for discouraging competitive entry. The objective of penetration pricing is to build or keep market share. For example, many instances of low prices found on the Internet are due to the businesses' need to build customer volume. Penetration pricing is appropriate when experience or scale effects lead to a volume–cost relationship, and it is necessary for price-sensitive market segments. Penetration pricing generally should not be used with products or services subject to a price-perceived quality relationship (see the further discussion that follows) or when the product has a strong competitive advantage. Another limitation of penetration pricing is that it is always more acceptable to customers to drop price than it is to raise it, which limits the flexibility of penetration pricing for some situations (Farrell and Schiller, 1993).

FIGURE 10.9 **Influences on Pricing Decisions**

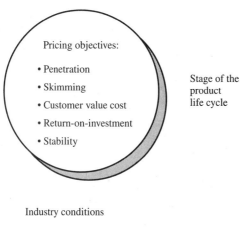

Psychological aspects:

- Reference prices

- Price/Perceived quality

Pricing objectives:

- Penetration
- Skimming
- Customer value cost
- Return-on-investment
- Stability

Stage of the product life cycle

Industry conditions

- Threat of new entrants

- Power of buyers/suppliers

- Rivalry

- Substitutes

- Capacity situation

Return on Sales/Investment Pricing

This objective has fairly limited usefulness. It implies that the product manager can set a price that delivers the rate of return demanded by the senior managers in the company. Of course, investment pricing ignores customer value and competition. It is therefore useful only when the product has a monopoly or near-monopoly position so that the market will produce the needed sales volume at the price set by the product manager. This was typical of the pricing of regulated utilities such as gas and electricity before they were deregulated.

Pricing for Stability

Sometimes customers for industrial products are more concerned about price stability than levels. It is difficult to develop profit forecasts and long-range plans when prices for products that make up a substantial portion of the buyer's costs fluctuate dramatically. Telephone rates for large users such as telemarketing firms and banks fall into this category as do oil and other commodity prices. Such customers expect rates to rise over time. However, significant price hikes at random intervals play havoc with their planning processes. As a result, these firms would rather pay a somewhat higher average rate than be subjected to constant fluctuations. Forward contracts on raw materials play this role in many manufacturing industries.

Skimming

The opposite of penetration pricing is skimming, or prestige pricing. Skimming returns more of the value to the producer rather than the customer. This is appropriate in a variety of situations. If there is a strong price–perceived quality relationship (e.g., wine) and the core strategy is to position the product at the high end of the market, this objective makes sense. It is also a reasonable objective when there is little chance of competition in the near future; however, the higher the price, the higher the margins and thus the greater the chance that competition will enter. Skimming is also a good objective when costs are not related to volume and managers thus are less concerned about building significant market share.

Competitive Pricing

Competitive pricing describes a situation in which the product manager tries to maintain a "competitive" price by either pricing at the category average or mimicking a particular competitor. This is appropriate when customers have not been persuaded that significant differences exist among the competitors and view the market as a commodity category. It may also be necessary in a product category with high fixed costs.

OTHER FACTORS AFFECTING PRICE

The previous section focused on pricing objectives, implying that the product manager has full discretion about how much of the value–variable cost gap she or he could obtain at any given point in time. However, other factors outside the control of the product manager also affect available pricing flexibility.

Stage of the Product Life Cycle

As with many decisions discussed in this book, the way prices are set also changes over the product life cycle. Figure 10.10 illustrates how DuPont has traditionally approached pricing with the life cycle in mind. As can be seen, DuPont simplifies the life cycle to three generic stages: sole supplier (introductory phase); competitive penetration (early and late growth); and shared stability, commodity competition, and withdrawal (maturity and decline). Particularly interesting is the focus for pricing decisions over the life cycle. When little competition exists, focus is on the customer and value is stressed. Notice that there is no mention of either variable or investment costs that must be recovered.

FIGURE 10.10   DuPont Pricing over the Product Life Cycle

Competitive Cycle Stage	Focus of Attention	Pricing Method
Sole supplier	Customers	Value-in-use Perceived value
Competitive penetration	Customers Competitors	Reaction analysis
Shared stability	Competition and costs	Profitability analysis
Commodity competition		
Withdrawal		

When competition enters, the focus is on both customers and competitors. Customer value is still important but, as discussed earlier in this chapter, how competitors will react is also addressed. Finally, in the late stages of the product category, the focus shifts toward competitors and costs to determine whether remaining in the market makes economic sense. There profitability analysis is the key.

Another way to look at the life cycle impact is through experience curve pricing. Product managers have flexibility in pricing decisions when the product tends to adhere to the experience curve. Figure 10.11 shows three different pricing scenarios. Increases in industry cumulative volume represent movement along the product life cycle. One possible pricing pattern, C, acknowledges little competition and assumes increased customer value through consistent lowering of prices over time. In pattern B, the product manager

FIGURE 10.11 **Experience Curve–Based Pricing Patterns over the Product Life Cycle**

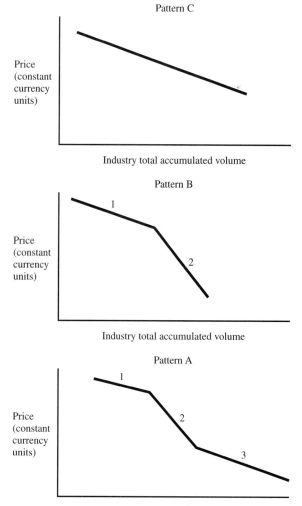

keeps margins up for a period of time because there is little competition (segment 1 of the curve is flatter than segment 2) and then drops price more rapidly as competition enters later in the life cycle. In pattern A, the product manager reacts twice: first when competition enters (segment 2 is again steeper than segment 1) and again when competition drops out (segment 3 is flatter than segment 2). Thus, under this last pricing pattern, margins are high in the early phase of the life cycle, drop due to competition, and then rise again after a category shakeout occurs.

Category Conditions

The category factors discussed in Chapter 4 also give product managers some ideas about the kind of pricing environment there is in the product category.

Threat of New Entrants

The likelihood of new entrants into a category has an important effect on price. If the likelihood is low (barriers to entry are high), higher price levels can be sustained. If new entrants are possible either from within the industry or from outside, lower prices help to protect the market position from potential erosion and make the profit potential of the market look worse for new product entries.

Power of Buyers/Suppliers

High buyer power obviously tends to depress prices, as it puts more pressure on the product to deliver a good value/price ratio. If suppliers have power, they will often charge higher prices for goods or services supplied, whether raw materials, labor, or anything else. High supplier power thus raises the floor beneath which prices cannot be set.

Rivalry

This concept is also relatively straightforward: High industry rivalry tends to be manifested in strong price competition. One industry factor that should be examined in this context is the level of exit barriers, that is, how difficult it is to withdraw a product from the market. Substantial investment in plant and equipment is one example of an exit barrier. Sometimes the exit barrier is emotional, such as when the product has a long history in the company. When exit barriers are high for some or all of the category participants, price competition is likely to be fierce.

Pressure from Substitutes

As with the threat of entry, the more potential substitute technologies or solutions to customer problems are available and the more value they offer, the greater the chance that price competition will exist.

Unused Capacity

Capacity is particularly important in a high-fixed-cost, high-contribution-margin (price less variable cost) product category. These markets are characterized by some of the most vicious price battles (e.g., airlines) because there is plenty of margin over variable cost to give and the products need to generate revenues to cover fixed costs. When economies of scale are important (e.g., in automobile manufacturing), overcapacity also leads to price wars because the degree of capacity utilization directly affects unit costs.

SOME SPECIFIC PRICING TACTICS

Product Line Pricing

One common pricing task facing product managers is setting prices for a closely related set of products or for a product line. The products can differ in small ways, such as features (e.g., a 17-inch versus a 21-inch color TV), or they can be complementary (e.g., razors and blades). We assume that one product manager has the authority to price the line or that the decision is made in tandem with another manager. Different elements of the line can be used to appeal to different segments of the market. The low end of a product line can be used as either a low-priced option for the price-sensitive segments or as a way to introduce customers to a brand with the hopes of getting them to trade up. This is the way Mercedes uses its C-class cars; as can be seen in Figure 10.12, the nine models in the product line range in price from $25,000 to nearly $140,000 with the C-class being the entry-level.

Price Bundling

One approach is price bundling, which takes a set of products, offers them to customers in a package, and then usually (but not always) prices the package lower than the sum of the individual components. For example, home stereo systems are commonly offered in a "rack" system consisting of an amplifier, a tuner, a CD player, and perhaps a DVD player, hopefully in an attractive case. This bundle of items, often consisting of models that

FIGURE 10.12 **Mercedes Product Line**

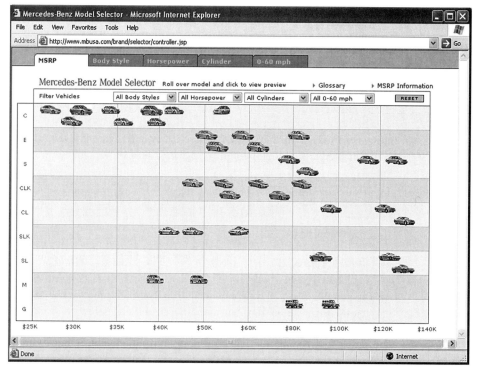

are slow sellers, is usually specially priced to eliminate inventory. A similar example is packages of options in automobiles.

An alternative approach takes the opposite view: Sometimes the bundle can be priced *higher* than the sum of the components because it is attractive or convenient. A good example is McDonald's Happy Meals, which are targeted toward children. Any parent who computed the sum of the hamburger, french fries, and drink could find that he or she is paying a considerable sum for the toy and the package. Clearly, such a bundle provides extra value to customers and can be priced accordingly.

A different way to look at the issue is by unbundling. Some companies offer pre-designed packages of features and services that include components some market segments do not need. For example, a telecommunications system might come with a standard service contract some customers may not find attractive because they already have considerable on-site technical help, or a value meal may come with unwanted fries. In such cases, the product manager could seek ways to unbundle the product package to allow customers to choose what they want to pay for.

For example, San Luis Sourdough Company sells 1-pound loaves of sourdough bread to supermarkets using a three-tier pricing policy. Level 1 prices the bread at 97 cents per loaf for supermarkets that are happy to have the bread simply dropped off. If the store wants to be able to return day-old bread for credit—level 2—the cost is $1.02 per loaf. If the store wants the company to accept returns, stock the shelves, and place bar codes on the packages, this level 3 service costs $1.05 per loaf. Thus, the company has cleverly unbundled its service levels so customers can choose the level that fits their needs.[10]

Complementary Pricing

This applies to products that are used together when one of the products fills a sustainable need. Two good examples are razors and blades and videogame boxes and the games. Gillette prices razors rather modestly but makes huge margins on the blades. Similarly, the prices for videogame machines as we have seen from the example earlier in the chapter are rather modest; the prices of a few games equal the price of the machine. A similar pattern exists for HP printers and printer cartridges. This kind of pricing is useful only when there is limited competition for the sustainable component. For example, it does not apply to autos and replacement parts because of the huge aftermarket composed of companies that do not manufacture cars themselves.

Complementary pricing is also used for services that have fixed and variable components to price. Two examples are private golf clubs and telephone service. Both have a fixed monthly fee and a variable usage fee. Such complementary pricing can be a creative way to keep the marginal costs to customers low ("pennies per day") and retain a continuous stream of revenue.

Value Pricing

Although the term has never really been defined, value pricing has been used by airlines, hotels, rental cars, supermarkets, and various other (usually consumer) categories. The originator of the concept may have been Taco Bell. In 1990, Taco Bell developed a value menu that offered several entries, such as tacos, for very low prices, around 29 to 39 cents.

---

[10] For a good review of bundling, see Simon, Fassnacht, and Wubker, 1995.

The company was very successful in making inroads against other fast-food chains, which subsequently caused McDonald's and others to offer value-priced menu entries (which they still offer today). The sustained recession of the early 1990s caused other products to pick up the concept and it has continued in the early 2000s.

It is important to clarify the distinction between value pricing and pricing to value. Pricing to value relies on estimates of the dollar value customers place on products and, when coupled with an estimate of the variable costs of producing a product or delivering a service, determines the range of possible prices that can be charged. Value pricing gives the customer most of the value–cost difference, that is, a "good deal." However, the term *value pricing* is not the same as penetration pricing, described earlier. Penetration pricing implies low price alone. Value pricing is related to customer expectations: It gives customers more than they expect for the price paid. This does *not* necessarily imply low price. Thus, value pricing is consistent with pricing at less than customer value, but is accompanied by communications, packaging, and other elements of the marketing mix that indicate a reasonably high level of quality.

A good example of a product that was value priced when introduced is the Lexus 400. The car cost around $40,000, which is not at the low end of the market. However, the brand was very successful because it offered the kinds of luxury, features, and service for which some European manufacturers charged much more. Again, value pricing does not imply inexpensive, only that what you get represents more net value than other available options. At about $50,000 today, the Lexus is less value priced and represents Toyota's ability to capture more of the customer value due to its prior success in the market.

There are several other good examples of successful value pricing. Seagram's gin captured 30 percent of the gin category and was the third-place spirit brand because the product was priced at half the level of the premium brands such as Beefeater and Tanqueray. However, the product is not "cheap"; the Seagram name connotes quality, and the bottle has an upscale look. Sara Lee Corporation markets L'Eggs hosiery, a brand with a well-established quality reputation and a relatively low price. JetBlue has low prices but an excellent on-time record, leather seats, in-flight satellite TV, and soaring revenues.

Everyday Low Pricing

At the time the first edition of this book was written, an important phenomenon in retailing was everyday low pricing, or EDLP. Both consumers and regulators had become more suspicious of high "regular" prices and frequent "sales" sponsored by retailers, sometimes referred to as "high–low" pricing. In addition, many companies were tiring of the enormous levels of spending required for promotions to get retailers to stock and promote products and get customers to buy, and the effect of uneven demand on the costs of producing and distributing the product. Therefore, a simpler approach was advanced that would lower prices permanently and significantly reduce both trade and consumer promotions. EDLP has, in fact, been adopted by successful chains such as Wal-Mart (now, the largest company in the world), Home Depot, and Toys "R" Us. In a well-publicized move, Sears attempted an EDLP policy in 1989, although it was ultimately unsuccessful and rescinded. Sears's experience showed there are risks in switching to an EDLP policy. Some of the problems are peculiar to Sears. Given its high cost structure, its price reductions were not sufficiently significant to produce a large consumer response, particularly when compared with its competitors. Because the prices were not low enough, Sears continued to run sales, thus confusing customers. Two other problems exist in shifting abruptly to EDLP policies. First, reference prices and pricing policies are conditioned by past prices and are hard to change in the short run. Second, an aggressive adoption of EDLP can create a pricing environment in which competitors engage in cutthroat pricing. EDLP is also unstable in terms of competitive reaction; if all but one firm is EDLP, then the firm that prices high–low will capture a substantial share of the market.

Extremely damaging to EDLP prospects was an extensive field experiment conducted in the Chicago area in a supermarket environment across 19 very disparate product categories (Hoch, Dreze, and Purk, 1994). The experiment showed that while retail EDLP policies increased sales volume relative to high–low pricing, the increased volume did not nearly compensate for the lower margins. The result was lost profits in every category. The problem is one alluded to earlier in the chapter: The price elasticities of demand at the retail level in most supermarket categories (and probably many other consumer product categories) are simply too small to support significant price cuts. Perhaps the most famous move to EDLP was that instituted by Procter & Gamble in the early 1990s (Ailawadi, Lehmann, and Neslin, 2000). They simultaneously increased advertising and price and decreased promotions. While this appeared to have increased profits, it did so at a cost of market share as competitors did not match their decrease in promotions.

Hidden Price Increases

Whether due to competition keeping the lid on prices or restricted customer budgets, during periods of recession, it is often difficult for product managers to raise prices. As a result, managers often look for ways to raise prices without explicitly increasing the posted price. For example, Kimberly-Clark tried to sneak in a 5 percent price increase by cutting the number of diapers in each package of its Huggies brand of disposable diapers (Ellison, 2003). Hotels often tack on charges/fees for cleaning your room, retailers charge "restocking" fees for returned goods, long-distance companies charge "regulatory assessment" fees, Broadway shows add to the price of a ticket for refurbishing a theater (Thornton, 2003).

Price Discrimination

Price discrimination to end customers, while unpopular with consumer advocacy groups, is not always illegal, and it is done all the time (Nagle and Holden, 1995, Chapter 14). Witness the senior citizen discounts given at movie theaters or the quantity discounts on personal computers given to large customers. The theory is that price discrimination maximizes products' profits by charging each market segment the price that maximizes profit. However, in practice, it is difficult to implement a price discrimination policy, particularly in consumer markets, due to the fragmentation of the customer base and the existence of firms that buy at one segment's low prices and resell to others (such as consolidators in airline tickets).

One way to implement price discrimination is through targeted delivery of coupons or other discount mechanisms. Given the quality of databases available today, it is relatively easy to determine those households that have the highest probability of buying the product *and* need a price inducement. These households can then be targeted by direct mail, magazine delivery of coupons, or in real-time on the Internet. In fact, the amount of the discount can be varied if managers find multiple levels of price sensitivity. Customers who are brand loyal apparently should receive no inducement, because that would merely give them a discount for a product they would have purchased at full price. Still, great disparity in price erodes brand equity and loyalty. For example, many magazine subscribers realize they should not renew early since better offers follow.

The Internet has made it much easier to price discriminate in real time. Online retailers have detailed information on their customers and can entice different customers with different prices depending upon their loyalty to the retailer. If you are a steady customer of, say, Lands End, you may receive special discounts from time to time that others do not. Some airlines offer Internet-only specials to frequent flier program members. This policy of giving preferred prices to Internet users has been copied by other industries. For example, a study by Brown and Goolsbee (2002) showed that Internet shoppers for term life insurance could result in savings of 8–15 percent from "offline" prices. Prices can also change dynamically according to demand-supply conditions. Software companies like Zilliant provide online merchants with this capability by setting up controlled testing of different prices to different customers, a real-time version of the pricing experiment described earlier in this chapter.

However, this kind of price discrimination is not without risks. In September 2000, Amazon.com DVD shoppers found that orders for the *Planet of the Apes* DVD could result in price differences by as much as $10 despite being placed at approximately the same time. Variations were due to which browser was being used, whether a customer was new or repeat, and which Internet service provider a customer was using. While the company said that it was only running an experiment on its pricing policies, a considerable amount of negative publicity ensued.[11]

Second-Market Discounting

A useful pricing strategy when excess production exists is called *second-market discounting*. This policy sells the extra production at a discount to a market separate from the main market. As long as the product is sold at a price greater than variable cost, the contribution margin produced can help cover corporate overhead. Some examples of secondary markets are generic drugs, private-label brands, and foreign markets. The difficulty with generics and private labels, however, is that you go into competition against yourself if the target customers are not completely different than your main segments or if the equivalence of the products is widely recognized. It also is widely criticized in international trade as "dumping."

Periodic Discounting

This pricing strategy varies price over time. It is appropriate when some customers are willing to pay a higher price to have the product or service during a particular time period. For example, utilities such as electricity and telephone service use peak load pricing policies that charge more during the heaviest usage periods, partly to encourage off-peak usage. Clothing retailers mark down items that are slow sellers; those who want an item when it is first introduced pay a higher price. Theater tickets are more expensive on weekends, and movie tickets cost more in the evenings.

---

[11] Linda Rosencrance (2000), *Computerworld, http://www.computerworld.com/industrytopics/retail/story/0,10801,49569,00.html.*

Auctions

As we have seen, the increased penetration of the Internet and its emphasis on personalization have created a new pricing environment for marketing managers. The notion of a fixed price charged to all customers has virtually disappeared in the e-commerce world in favor of "personalized" pricing. This is a very price-competitive world in which shopping agents check for the lowest price and customers specify the prices they are willing to pay.

Nowhere is this more evident than with the tremendous growth in the use of auctions on the Web. This is, of course, best represented with the astounding success of EBay, which is not only the most heavily used Internet auction but also a key distribution channel for many small businesses that sell most of their goods on Ebay. The company generated over $15 billion in revenues in 2002 from the percentage that it takes from each sale.[12] On the business-to-business side, companies like DoveBid auction off goods and companies. The reverse-auction king, Priceline, generated over $900 million in sales revenues from its travel services. Product managers clearly have more pricing options than ever and need to be aware of the impact of the Internet on their decisions.

ETHICAL ISSUES

For certain kinds of products, the pricing decision can have implications far beyond generating revenue (or recovering value). A good example of this is the high-priced basketball shoes produced by Nike, Reebok, and other manufacturers and endorsed by NBA stars such as LeBron James and Allen Iverson. Most of these shoes are priced over $125, and their desirability, due to exclusivity and peer pressure, has led to several highly publicized incidents in public schools in which owners of the shoes were assaulted and the shoes stolen. One can argue that Nike bears no responsibility for what is essentially a U.S. social problem. However, the fact that the high price and resulting image of exclusivity may have had some influence on the school incidents cannot be easily dismissed.

A somewhat different ethical problem involved the pricing of the Wellcome PLC drug AZT, a treatment for AIDS. When the drug was introduced, a year-long treatment cost $10,000. The company argued that the investment in such a drug, which had a relatively small market, required a high price. In addition, the analysis provided earlier in this chapter shows that the customer value for a drug that could substantially ameliorate AIDS symptoms would be enormous. However, the reaction to AZT's price was so negative that the company eventually reduced it. Despite the price reduction, the company's image and reputation suffered some damage.

As a result, in addition to the aspects involved in setting price discussed in this chapter, price may have some social implications far beyond what is expected. Further, this issue is not relevant only to products such as drugs that clearly can generate negative public reaction if priced too high. For example, the issue of the "digital divide" is where upper-income and educated individuals have greater access to the Internet. Since the Internet tends to be characterized by more price competition, this exacerbates the problem of lower-income, and less-educated people paying higher prices on average.

---

[12] Interestingly, as of 2003, more than 25 percent of the offerings on EBay are at fixed prices for companies like Sears and Walt Disney.

SUMMARY

In this chapter, we have argued that, as shown in Figure 10.9, the price objective and subsequent decision cannot be made without adequate analysis of the market and a consideration of the marketing strategy being employed. Customers (e.g., their value for the product and your brand), competitors and your company (e.g., costs, their pricing actions), and category conditions (e.g., stage of the product life cycle) all impact the product manager's selection of what price to charge. We particularly emphasized the importance of customers, as past pricing practices have focused on the other factors without paying sufficient attention to measuring how much customers are willing to pay. The product manager's job is to decide where the price should be in the range between cost and the value customers place on the product. The Internet has changed the rules of pricing, and any pricing decision made today must consider the options afforded through that medium.

References

Abell, Derek F., and John S. Hammond (1979) *Strategic Market Planning.* Englewood Cliffs, NJ: Prentice Hall.

Ailawadi, Kusum, Donald R. Lehmann, and Scott Neslin (2000) "The Impact of P&G's Policy Change to EDLP." Working paper, Columbia University.

Anderson, James C., Dipak C. Jain, and Pradeep K. Chintagunta (1993) "Customer Value Assessment in Business Markets: A State-of-Practice Study," *Journal of Business-to-Business Marketing,* 1.

Anderson, James C., and James Narus (1998) "Business Marketing: Understand What Customers Value," *Harvard Business Review,* November–December, 53–65.

Briesch, Richard A., Lakshman Krishnamurthi, Tridib Mazumdar, and S. P. Raj (1997) "A Comparative Analysis of Reference Price Models," *Journal of Consumer Research,* September, 202–14.

Brown, Jeffrey, and Austan Goolsby (2002) "Does the Internet Make Markets More Competitive? Evidence from the Life Insurance Industry," *Journal of Political Economy* 110, no. 3, pp. 481–507.

Buzzell, Robert D., and Bradley T. Gale (1987) *The PIMS Principles.* New York: The Free Press.

Clarke, Darral G. (1975) "Optical Distortion, Inc. (A)," Harvard Business School case #9-575-072.

Dolan, Robert J., and Hermann Simon (1996) *Power Pricing.* New York: The Free Press.

Drucker, Peter (1993) "The Five Deadly Business Sins," *The Wall Street Journal,* October 21, A16.

Dvorak, Phred (2003) "Nintendo's GameCube Sales Surge After Price Cut," *The Wall Street Journal,* November 4, B4.

Ellison, Sarah (2003) "In Lean Times, Big Companies Make a Grab for Market Share" *The Wall Street Journal,* September 5, A1.

Farrell, Christopher, and Zachary Schiller (1993) "Stuck! How Companies Cope When They Can't Raise Prices," *Business Week,* November 15, 146–55.

Forbis, John L., and Nitin T. Mehta (1981) "Value-Based Strategies for Industrial Products," *Business Horizons,* May–June, 32–42.

Gourville, John T. (1999) "Note on Behavioral Pricing," Harvard Business School case #9-599-114.

Hamilton, Joan C. (1990) "Genentech: A Textbook Case of Medical Marketing," *Business Week,* August 13, 96–7.

Hardy, Quentin (1999) "Iridium to Cut Prices, Alter Marketing Strategy," *The Wall Street Journal,* June 22, B9.

Hoch, Stephen J., Xavier Dreze, and Mary E. Purk (1994) "EDLP, Hi-Lo, and Margin Arithmetic," *Journal of Marketing,* October, 16–27.

Industry Standard (2000) April 24, 189.

Kalyanaram, Gurumurthy, and Russell S. Winer (1995) "Empirical Generalizations from Reference Price Research," *Marketing Science* 14, no. 3, part 2 of 2, G161–169.

Kendall, Tim (1980) "And the Survey Says . . . ," *The Marketer,* September, 47–48.

Lundegaard, Karen, and Sholnn Freeman (2004) "Detroit's Challenge: Weaning Buyers From Years of Deals" *The Wall Street Journal,* January 6, A1.

Monroe, Kent B. (2002) *Making Profitable Decisions,* 3rd ed. New York: McGraw-Hill.

Nagle, Thomas T., and Reed K. Holden (1995) *The Strategy and Tactics of Pricing,* 2nd ed. Englewood Cliffs, NJ: Prentice Hall.

Rajendran, K. N., and Gerard J. Tellis (1994) "Contextual and Temporal Components of Reference Price," *Journal of Marketing,* January, 22–34.

Rao, Akshay R., Mark E. Bergen, and Scott Davis (2000) "How to Fight a Price War," *Harvard Business Review,* March–April, 107–16.

Ross, Elliot B. (1984) "Making Money with Proactive Pricing," *Harvard Business Review,* November–December, 145–55.

Schindler, Robert M. (1991), "Symbolic Meaning of a Price Ending," in *Advances in Consumer Research,* Vol 18, eds. Rebecca H. Holman and Michael R. Solomon. Provo, UT; Association of Consumer Research, 794–801.

Schindler, Robert M., and Thomas Kibarian (1996) "Increased Sales Response through the Use of Nine Ending Prices," *Journal of Retailing,* 72 (2), 187–199.

Serwer, Andrew E. (1994) "How to Escape a Price War," *Fortune,* June 13, 82–90.

Simon, Hermann, Marin Fassnacht, and Georg Wubker (1995) "Price Bundling," *Pricing Strategy & Practice* 3, no. 1, 34–44.

Stiving, Mark, and Russell S. Winer (1997), "An Emprical Analysis of Price Endings with Scanner Data," *Journal of Consumer Research* 24, June, 57–67.

Thornton, Emily (2003) "Fees! Fees! Fees!" *BusinessWeek,* September 29, 99.

Winer, Russell S. (1988) "Behavioral Perspectives on Pricing." In Timothy M. Devinney, ed., *Issues in Pricing: Theory and Research.* Lexington. MA: Lexington Books.

Zaun, Todd (2004) "Japanese Battle U.S. Discounts with Extras" *The Wall Street Journal,* January 6, B1.

Zeithaml, Valarie A. (1988) "Consumer Perceptions of Price, Quality, and Value: A Means–End Model and Synthesis of Evidence," *Journal of Marketing,* July, 2–22.

Chapter **Eleven**

Advertising Decisions

Overview

Advertising is highly visible and can be an event in its own right (think of the ads at the Super Bowl). While clever, creative copy is aesthetically appealing, however, the real measure of success is whether it generates sales and profits in the short and/or long run (e.g., through building brand equity).

Figure 11.1 shows the communications mix a company uses. As the figure indicates, the different elements of the mix are advertising, public relations (PR), sales promotion, direct marketing, and packaging and graphics. (While personal selling obviously has an important communications role, it is usually considered separately or as part of distribution channels decision-making.) One would hope that these elements work together to effectively communicate the product's features and benefits to the target customers. However, decisions about these communications mix elements are often made independently by different people and organizations. Under this silo-type communications organization, advertising is handled largely by the advertising agency, public relations by the PR department or agency, direct marketing by an outside agent, and packaging and graphics by either in-house specialists or consultants. Only sales promotion might be handled directly by the product manager.

A coherent communications mix is usually referred to as *integrated marketing communications* (Schultz, 1998). In an integrated marketing communications approach, the manager specifies the problem to be solved (e.g., increase the repeat purchasing rate) and coordinates the necessary communications rather than using a predetermined set of communications tools (i.e., those that the company always uses). An integrated approach also assumes that a combination of activities does better than any one alone and that they should be consistent rather than at cross purposes. For example, in an integrated communications campaign, a point-of-purchase (POP) display might use the same display theme or a character used in a TV ad. Figure 11.2 outlines some parts of an integrated communications program. The objective of the communications is common to all elements of the overall program. Specific targets might vary over the different programs depending on how the marketing manager viewed the different strengths and weaknesses of, say, advertising versus promotion for a particular campaign. Still, the communications themes and personality the campaign exhibits are common across the mix elements.

FIGURE 11.1 **The Communications Mix**

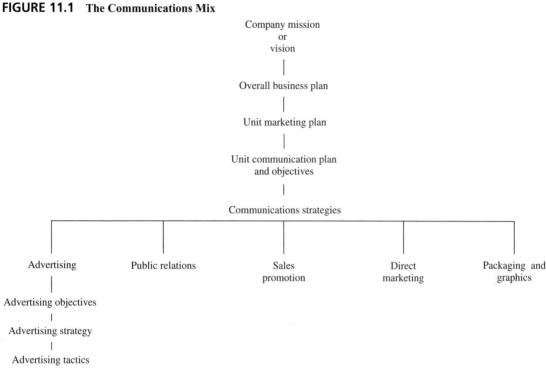

Source: Don E. Schultz and Beth E. Barnes, *Strategic Advertising Campaigns,* 4th ed., NTC Business Books, 1995. Reprinted by permission of the McGraw-Hill Companies.

Figure 11.3 shows how allocations for specific communications mix elements vary between consumer and industrial or business-to-business products. Not surprisingly, consumer product managers emphasize television, print advertising, and promotional events while industrial product managers use print advertising, direct mail, catalogs, and trade shows. The large amount industrial product managers spend on direct mail has been increasing with the overall trend toward greater use of direct marketing. Direct mail is an excellent support program to aid the direct sales force as well as to sell lower-priced items and aid in customer retention. Perhaps most intriguing, Figure 11.3 shows that as late as 1996, the Internet played virtually no role in communications spending. By 2002, Internet advertising spending was about $4.9 billion in the United States, still a very small part of the over $237 billion spent on advertising that year. The impact the Internet has had on advertising is disproportionate to the amount of money being spent on banner and other advertising forms. The direct response nature of banner ads and their concomitant measurability has led to substantial attention paid to metrics such as "click-through" rates (the percentage of people clicking on a banner ad), which have been trending downward. In this book, we emphasize three elements of the integrated mix that are most often the responsibility of the product manager: advertising (this chapter), sales promotion (Chapter 12), and direct marketing (Chapter 14). Much of PR involves divisional or corporate-level promotions designed to improve the general image or equity of the company and hence is not within the control of the product manager. As a consequence,

FIGURE 11.2 American Cancer Society Integrated Communications Strategy

Health objective	To encourage the target to avoid sunburn		
Purpose	To encourage the target to protect their skin from the cancer-causing rays of the sun by using a sunscreen with a sun protection factor (SPF) of 15+ instead of other tanning lotions or oils		
Target	Adult "sun worshippers"	*Primary* Adult "sun worshippers"	*Secondary* Cosmetic, Toiletry and Fragrance Association Physicians Pharmacists
Promise	When I use a sunscreen with an SPF of 15+. I will feel in control of my health because sunscreen with SPF 15+ helps protect me from the deadly, cancer-causing rays of the sun while allowing me to obtain an attractive "light" tan.	*Primary* Same as for advertising	*Secondary* CTF Assn.: "I will feel satisfied that I am helping to create a favorable sales environment." Physicians, pharmacists: "I will feel satisfied that I am doing the best job possible for my patients'/customers' preventive health maintenance."
Support	Studies show that unprotected sun exposure is closely related to all types of skin cancer, including those that can kill you. Doctors advise moderate exposure to sun and to use sunscreen. Sunscreen with SPF of 15+ gives 15 times your natural defenses against the sun's rays.		
Personality	Warm; caring; foremost authority; professional; renowned.		

	General Advertising	**Public Relations**	**Sales Promotion**	**Direct Response**
Media	National TV MTV (cooperative program) Pop radio Print magazine ads Billboards	Program with CTF Assn. to help with visibility, reach, materials distribution, and costs Collateral materials: educational brochure (with coupon to purchase any SPF 15+ product) Poster (professionals only) Spokesperson	Work with CTF Assn. to develop and implement system to code (via symbols and/or colors) grades of protection for sunscreen products to include packaging and POP chart coordinated with packaging Coupon	Direct-response offer

Source: Don E. Schultz and Beth E. Barnes, *Strategic Advertising Campaigns*, 4th ed., NTC Business Books, 1995. Reprinted by permission of the McGraw-Hill Companies.

we have chosen not to focus on public relations. Still, some elements of public relations, such as event sponsorship (e.g., NASCAR's Winston Cup, which now is sponsored by Nextel), are product or product-line focused. Similarly, while packaging and graphics are specialized activities best left to experts, the product manager should be the final decision maker about what is and is not appropriate.

FIGURE 11.3 **Marketing Communications Expenditures: Consumer versus Business-to-Business Products**

Category of Expenditures	Percentage of Communications Budget	
	Consumer	**Business-to-Business**
Television	45.1%	2.7%
Print advertising	14.5	27.4
Literature, coupons, POP	16.2	9.3
Direct mail	6.4	27.1
Radio	5.6	0.8
Catalogs	4.1	10.7
Public relations	3.1	5.3
Trade shows	2.0	12.9
Out-of-home media	1.7	0.5
Dealer/distributor materials	1.3	3.3

Source: Cyndee Miller, "Marketing Industry Report: Who's Spending What on Biz-to-Biz Marketing?" *Marketing News,* January 1, 1996, p. 1; "Marketing Industry Report: Consumer Marketers Spend Most of Their Money on Communications," *Marketing News,* March 11, 1996, p. 1.

Figure 11.4 shows the advertising planning process and the product manager's role in it (Eechembadi, 1994). While we advocate a different ordering of the steps, particularly setting the advertising budget (which we think depends on the strategy and likely effectiveness of the advertising), the figure highlights the important steps. Besides development of the overall marketing plan, the product manager's major responsibilities

FIGURE 11.4 **The Advertising Planning Process**

Stage	Primary Players	End Product
Developing the marketing plan and budget	Product manager	Budget Spending guidelines Profit projections
Planning the advertising	Product manager Advertising manager Ad agency Corporate advertising department	Identification of target market Allocation of spending Statement of advertising strategy and message
Copy development and approval	Ad agency Copy research company Product manager Advertising manager Senior management	Finished copy Media plan (with reach and frequency projections)
Execution	Ad agency or media buying company	Actual placement
Monitoring response	Market research manager Product manager Ad agency (research)	Awareness, recognition, and perception tracking Perceptual maps Sales/share tracking

Source: Naras V. Eechembadi, "Does Advertising Work?" *The McKinsey Quarterly,* no. 3 (1994), pp. 117–29.

include setting the budget, planning the advertising (identifying the target audience, developing the general advertising strategy and message), working with the ad agency to test different advertising copy and the media plan, and monitoring the response to the advertising. The product manager typically does not develop advertising copy, nor does he or she execute the media plan by buying specific media for placing the advertising. Thus, in this chapter we focus on those areas that are most critical for a product manager to manage: the target audience, advertising objectives, budget, copy, and media plan. The ultimate goal is to fill out Figures 11.18, 11.19, and 11.20 in order to optimize advertising spending.

THE TARGET AUDIENCE

In deciding who the target audience is (sometimes divided into primary and secondary audiences), the obvious starting point is the target customers in the overall marketing strategy (see Chapter 8). Consider a company selling a CD-ROM software product, targeted toward children, that has both play value and educational value. In this case, several decision makers and possible influencers may be relevant, including children, parents, and other friends or relatives searching for gift ideas. The choice of the primary target audience (see Figure 11.5) depends to a large extent on (*a*) who is most influential in the decision process and (*b*) who you think you can influence. You can focus on the children, emphasize fun, and hope that they will use their own financial resources, which in the United States are substantial, or that they "pull" the purchase through the channels of parents, friends, and relatives. On the other hand, you may want to address the parents, possibly trying to convince them that their children will be at an educational disadvantage if they do not have the software.

The "kids versus parents" issue arises in many product categories, illustrating the "buying center" concept developed in Chapter 6. Industrial goods offer myriad cases of multiple parties involved in decisions. Most technical products can be directed to either technical people (e.g., engineers, who tend to set specifications), operational people (e.g., production supervisors or workers), or managers (who tend to focus more on some bottom line or, in the case of product managers, on the top line, than on operational

FIGURE 11.5 Educational Toy: Advertising Choices

Target Audience	Objective	Copy Focus
Children	Buy on their own	Fun
	Ask for it by name	Popular
Parents	Buy it for their children	Educational benefits
Friends, other relatives	Buy it as "just the right gift"	Fun to play

	Sample "Logical" Media	
	Print	**TV**
Children	*Scholastic Magazine*	*The Simpsons*
Parents	*Better Homes & Gardens*	*60 Minutes*
Friends, other relatives	*U.S. News and World Report*	*Law and Order*

FIGURE 11.6 New Personal Computer Microprocessor: Advertising Choices

Target Audience	Objective	Copy Focus
Engineers	Get them to write it into specifications	Improved performance
Production supervisors	Get them to put/request it in their budget	No downtime problems
Production workers	Get them to lobby for it	Easy to install
Managers	Get them to pressure operations to include it in their budget	Improved profit

details). Thus, the advertising target audience could be broader than the target markets or market segments identified by the product manager in the product strategy.

Of course, it is perfectly reasonable, albeit expensive, to target all relevant groups, but it is generally best to have one primary focus. Figure 11.6 shows a generic example for selecting a target audience for a new microprocessor for a personal computer. In this case, there are at least four target audiences: the engineers, who probably have the final say because they write the PC specifications; the production supervisors, who are responsible for efficient production; the production workers, who install the new microprocessor; and the managers, who are responsible for sales of the end product. (Note that we are ignoring for the present final customers who can be addressed with "Intel inside" style promotions.) The product manager for the microprocessor has different objectives for each party to the decision and may select both the sales message and choice of media differently for each party.

In summary, even when multiple parties are involved, it is important to specify the primary target audience. This depends mainly on an assessment of the relative importance of the different target audiences, susceptibility of the audiences to advertising, and cost to reach them. Often the target audience is described in product category terms (e.g., heavy users, nonusers) or in terms of current product usage (e.g., users of product X, users of our product). This is often less useful for selecting media vehicles that tend to be described in terms of demographic characteristics. Consequently, in describing target audiences, it is useful to describe them both in terms of product behavior (e.g., current customers, competitors' customers, or noncustomers) and in specific terms (e.g., demographics) that facilitate media planning.

The Internet permits a very direct form of targeting based upon a variety of descriptive and behavioral variables. Figure 11.7 shows how the Web advertising network, DoubleClick, allowed advertisers to target potential customers:

- *Content targeting:* This targets viewers based on what sites they are visiting. This approach would be analogous to choosing different print or TV media.
- *Behavioral targeting:* This approach targets viewers based on, for example, their past purchase or browsing behavior, including the time of day they are likely to use the Web.
- *User targeting:* This targeting is based on demographics or other descriptive variables.
- *Tech targeting:* Advertisers can target customers based on their PC operating system, Internet service provider (ISP), or browser type (e.g., Netscape versus Internet Explorer).

FIGURE 11.7 **Doubleclick Targeting**

Source: DoubleClick.net's website, *http://www.doubleclick.com...reisers/automotive/targeting_filters.html,* July 31, 2000.

SETTING ADVERTISING OBJECTIVES

A product manager can choose from several types of objectives.

Customer-Focused Objectives

The most obvious objective, of course, is to increase sales and profits. For industrial products, an alternative measure is leads generated for the sales force. Advertisers spend large amounts of money and expect to get a return of increased customer demand. Unfortunately it is often difficult to measure the impact of advertising. Two common difficulties are the following:

> Advertising can take some time to create an effect, which may not coincide with the planning cycle or data collection period.

> It is difficult to separate the effects of advertising from the other marketing mix variables or the quality of the strategy. The advertising could be great, but the strategy or price could be inappropriate.

As a result, the operational objective of advertising is frequently to make the customer aware of the product and create interest, positive attitudes, or intention to buy the product since other marketing and communications mix elements (e.g., price, channels, promotion, and sales force) are needed to close the deal.

However, sales is a good criterion for *direct-response* advertising. This includes infomercials or other advertisements where the goal is to persuade the customer to call a phone number to order a product or to send in a card requesting further information.

FIGURE 11.8   Strategic Advertising Objectives

Central/High Involvement/Thinking Route	Peripheral/Low Involvement/Feeling Route
Awareness/recall	Awareness
(Emotional) arousal/interest	Arousal
Information search	
Comprehension	
Attitude	
Intention	Intention
Trial/purchase	Purchase
Reevaluation	Evaluation

Banner ads on the Internet are another form of direct-response advertising. While they also have communications content (e.g., image, awareness), the intent is to get a customer to click on the banner and be routed to the sponsor's website. With clickthrough rates at less than 1 percent, many advertisers question the long-term prospects for banner ads.

A crucial distinction in customer decision processes is between so-called high-involvement and low-involvement decisions. High-involvement decisions involve thought ("cognitive effort") to evaluate the pluses and minuses of a product and their net benefit. This evaluation then leads to a positive (or negative) purchase decision. In the low-involvement situation, exposure to an ad or a product leads more or less directly to purchase, with evaluation occurring only after use. These two different approaches have been called the central and peripheral routes to persuasion (Petty, Cacioppo, and Schumann, 1983). Foote, Cone, and Belding (FCB), a major advertising agency, classified products into "thinking" and "feeling" products and then used a 2-times-2 table (high versus low involvement, feeling versus thinking) to help direct advertising design (Vaughn, 1980).

Figure 11.8 presents an abbreviated hierarchical model of the central route decision process (which is more prevalent for high-involvement, "thinking" products). In the high-involvement hierarchy, in many cases individuals proceed through the stages sequentially. For an unknown product, it may be important to first establish awareness and interest, then convey specific information (e.g., product benefits), and finally convert the benefits into attitude, action plans (intention), and actual behavior. Hence, awareness objectives are often appropriate. In contrast, for a well-established product (assuming major repositioning is under way), it may be more appropriate to define objectives in terms of attitude, shopping, or purchase. Some research suggests that mere exposure to ads is enough to improve attitude. Interestingly, research has also found that a relation may exist between exposure and perceived quality, suggesting that awareness leads to better quality ratings as consumers infer quality from advertising expenditures. Also a long delay (several months) often occurs between deciding to buy a particular consumer good and actually making a purchase. As a consequence, shortening this cycle might be a reasonable objective (Greenleaf and Lehmann, 1991).

On the other hand, sometimes (e.g., in the case of new food or fashion products) the process is almost reversed: The decision to try precedes "formal" consideration of benefits. In these situations, objectives tend to focus on either generating awareness and interest (and hence trial) *or* increasing positive reinforcement. Reinforcement can be especially important in the case of products such as life insurance, which has annual premiums (and hence requires renewed commitment on the part of the customer) but no feedback to indicate whether the choice of policy was a good one.

Exposure-Oriented Objectives

Exposure-oriented objectives are generally quantitative measures of exposure, typically in terms of reach (the number or percentage who receive at least one exposure), frequency (the average number of exposures a potential customer receives), or gross rating points (GRPs, the total number of advertising exposures received), which is reach times frequency (or in Internet terms, hits times visits). When feasible, these objectives should be defined in terms of a target audience rather than just customers or people in general.

The choice between reach and frequency depends on how many exposures are needed for the advertising to be effective. One intriguing rule of thumb, developed many years ago, suggests that customers need three exposures for an ad to have an impact (Krugman, 1965). In general, the clearer the message in the ad and the more involved the customer, the fewer ad impressions are needed before a customer responds. Thus, an industrial product advertising a new feature that increases output 30 percent probably needs fewer exposures than a laundry detergent with no obvious distinguishing feature.

Because these operational objectives have such direct budget implications, we turn to a discussion of budget setting, leaving the choice of exact reach, frequency, and GRP objectives to be constrained by the overall budget decision.

Objective Specificity

Like product objectives, advertising objectives should be operational and specific in nature. Examples include increasing awareness from 45 to 60 percent, improving attitude toward a brand one point on a seven-point scale, increasing average usage from 1.7 to 2 units per household per year, and generating 6,000 shopping visits or inquiries from potential customers.[1] Exposure objectives are used partly because they are easier to assess and partly because other measures, such as awareness, attitude, and store visits, are influenced by a number of factors, so the impact of advertising on them is not clear. A reasonable exposure objective might be to reach 80 percent of a target audience (e.g., females age 13 to 30) at least once during a three-month period and to reach 30 percent of them at least three times. In many cases, it makes sense to have both exposure objectives (to guide media selection) and customer objectives (to aid in the development and evaluation of copy).

SETTING ADVERTISING BUDGETS

As noted earlier in this chapter, advertising is a big business. In 2002, the main media for U.S. ad spending were broadcast and cable TV ($58 billion), print (newspapers plus magazines, $56 billion), direct mail ($46 billion), radio ($19 billion), and yellow pages

---

[1] For some research on the importance of usage-based advertising objectives, see Wansink and Ray (1996).

FIGURE 11.9   Top Spending Megabrands by Category

Rank	Category/Megabrand	U.S. Measured Advertising Spending in 2002 ($)
1.	Automotive	16,365
	Ford vehicle	834
2.	Retail	13,528
	Sears stores	535
3.	Movies, media, and advertising	6,024
	Sony movies	550
4.	Food, beverages, and confectionery	6,015
	General Mills cereals	215
5.	Medicines and proprietary remedies	5,445
	Nexium heartburn Rx	192
6.	Financial services	4,658
	Visa credit cards	278
7.	Telecommunications	4,297
	Verizon telecommunications	1,022
8.	Toiletries, cosmetics, and personal care	4,200
	L'Oreal beauty products	270
9.	Airline travel, hotels, and resorts	3,800
	Southwest airlines	133
10.	Restaurants	3,741
	McDonald's restaurants	548

Source: *Ad Age* analysis of data from TNS Media Intelligence/CMR.

($14 billion). Internet was $4.9 billion, behind billboards ($5.2 billion) as well as event sponsorship, which included $6.5 billion on sporting events alone in North America (*Marketing News,* 2003).

To give the reader some idea of how large advertising budgets are, Figure 11.9 shows the 10 largest advertising spenders by category for 2002 and Figure 11.10 shows the 10 largest B-to-B advertisers for 2002.[2] Because of the large amounts involved and the importance of advertising to the success of many products, setting advertising budgets has an immediate impact on costs and longer-term effects on sales. Consequently, advertising is in many ways an investment (sometimes called "consumer franchise building") in much the same way spending on R&D is, albeit with a both less distant and, at least in a technical sense, less dramatic breakthrough potential. Like spending on R&D, spending on advertising has a long history and a relatively weak record for measuring effectiveness precisely. Unlike R&D, it tends to be expensed rather than capitalized as an investment.

A crucial distinction exists between viewing advertising spending as an investment versus an expense. Investments are expected to generate returns over a long period of time. Often, when advertising is used as an expense, the budget is cut near the end of the quarter or fiscal year to achieve a profit target. In contrast, marketing-oriented firms

[2] There could be some overlap in the data; in particular, the Figure 11.10 numbers probably contain some advertising targeted toward consumers.

FIGURE 11.10 Top 10 B-to-B Advertisers

Rank '02	'01	Company	Total ($ thousands)	% Change	Business Publications	Internet	Consumer Magazines	Sunday Magazines	Local Newspapers	National Newspapers	Outdoor	Network TV	Spot TV	Syndicated TV	Cable TV Networks	Spanish Language TV	Network Radio	National Spot Radio
1	1	Verizon Communications	$319,986	13.2%	$1,285	$4,952	$6,687	$0	$149,000	$12,007	$7,406	$64,198	$32,057	$4,506	$15,156	$6,484	$1,009	$15,240
2	5	Sprint Corp.	263,613	38.7	6,243	3,397	8,032	22	145,665	16,377	1,059	57,274	17,874	198	3,670	0	59	3,745
3	6	SBC Communications	233,485	29.5	1,876	2,797	2,426	52	122,845	5,359	3,850	25,383	41,598	86	7,256	1,812	124	18,022
4	3	Hewlett-Packard Co.	233,355	11.0	59,520	25,359	63,126	756	30,753	22,535	99	21,900	1,237	98	7,119	0	0	852
5	4	AT&T Wireless Services	213,229	5.8	886	8,496	3,652	0	130,662	10,195	3,924	14,187	21,752	1,192	6,724	4	523	11,033
6	7	IBM Corp.	198,856	16.3	80,133	9,632	32,200	604	9,795	26,610	1,099	19,312	121	2,240	17,021	0	0	88
7	2	Microsoft Corp.	197,858	-25.1	80,012	24,962	36,686	87	1,445	9,291	1,530	35,766	626	5	7,362	0	0	88
8	18	United Parcel Service	144,260	104.9	2,974	1,887	21,047	0	976	3,625	87	83,408	5,120	190	11,345	0	0	13,601
9	8	Visa International	110,234	-4.5	2,884	10,134	10,018	0	1,189	740	1,340	64,733	1,970	3,160	11,870	15	1,534	647
10	12	Bank of America Corp.	103,819	21.9	1,591	4,768	8,282	332	18,355	1,832	2,179	38,181	5,080	76	12,124	2,675	95	8,249

Source: B-to-B analysis of data from TNS Media Intelligence/CMR.

FIGURE 11.11   The Relationship between Cumulative Advertising Spending and Market Share
Tobacco Industry

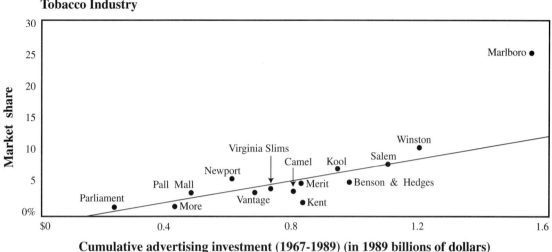

Cumulative advertising investment (1967-1989) (in 1989 billions of dollars)

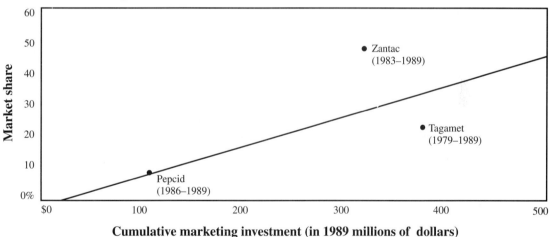

Cumulative marketing investment (in 1989 millions of dollars)

Source: *IMS America, Ltd, and CDI estimates.*

view advertising as a long-term investment in the brand (see, for example, Slywotzky and Shapiro, 1993).

Figure 11.11 shows a positive relationship between advertising investment measured as cumulative advertising spending and market share for the tobacco and antiulcer drug categories. While the direction of causality is ambiguous and firms with higher sales can afford to spend more on advertising, consistent investment in advertising for products can lead to a superior market position.

Clearly the "right" way to set budgets is to first develop a model that quantitatively estimates the impact of advertising (as well as the rest of the product offering *and* the impact of competitors and environmental changes) on sales and profits. Then the product manager need only determine optimal spending levels either analytically for a simple model or, for more complicated models, numerically or by trial and error. Unfortunately, though later in this chapter we briefly discuss some promising model-building and data analysis methods for improving advertising effectiveness, current models have neither been perfected nor are universally used. The most widely considered methods are described next.

Objective and Task

Budgeting by objectives and tasks is a logically appealing approach in which the product manager first determines the advertising objectives (e.g., target audience, reach, and frequency goals), and then chooses an advertising plan (and consequently budget) to achieve the objectives. When the objective-and-task method is followed, objectives lead to a budget and determine reach and frequency. Criteria such as reach and frequency are more often objectives within budget constraints. For example, an operational objective might be to maximize reach subject to a $10 million budget cap.

Percentage-of-Sales

The percentage-of-sales method seems to turn normal causal thinking—that advertising causes sales—on its head. One argument for this approach is based on a form of the efficient-market hypothesis developed in finance: Firms that survive tend to be those with more optimal budgets, so the survivors' budgets may offer an estimate of the optimal level in a competitive market. Alternatively, you can view the ad/sales ratio as the cooperative (agreed-to) solution in a multiperson game. Basically, however, the percentage-of-sales method is used because it is convenient and safer than committing to nontraditional spending levels. Figure 11.12 shows advertising-to-sales ratios in 2002 for the 200 largest advertising spending industries. Although not all the companies in these industries use the percentage-of-sales method for setting ad budgets, the ratio for a product's industry category or SIC code is a useful starting point for trying to put together a budget from scratch. The range of the ratios is quite large; the highest advertising-to-sales ratios are for loan brokers (38 percent) and health services (33 percent), while the smallest ones include petroleum refining (0.1 percent) and wholesale groceries (0.2 percent).

Competitive Parity

The competitive parity approach considers share of advertising dollars spent (also known as *share of voice*) rather than absolute advertising dollars to determine sales per share point and to set budgets accordingly. One approach to competitive parity is to compare share of voice to actual or desired brand share. Small-share brands tend to focus on profit taking and large-share brands on investing in future profits (Jones, 1990). Moreover, the average share of voice tends to be higher for low-share brands and lower for high-share

FIGURE 11.12 2003 Advertising-to-Sales Ratios for 200 Largest Ad Spending Industries

Industry	SIC Code	Advertising as % of sales	Advertising as % of margin
Accident & health insurance	6321	1.1	8.5
Agricultural chemicals	2870	3.0	7.4
Agriculture production-crops	100	0.3	0.5
Air courier services	4513	1.2	10.7
Air transport, scheduled	4512	1.2	24.2
Air-cond, heating, refrig eq	3585	1.6	6.3
Amusement parks	7996	10.7	20.9
Apparel & other finished pds	2300	4.7	11.4
Apparel and accessory stores	5600	3.6	9.4
Auto and home supply stores	5531	1.2	2.6
Auto dealers, gas stations	5500	0.9	5.8
Auto rent & lease, no drivers	7510	2.3	6.9
Bakery products	2050	1.7	3.4
Beverages	2080	9.2	14.3
Biological pds, ex diagnstics	2836	1.8	2.2
Blankbooks, binders, bookbind	2780	5.7	9.0
Bldg matl, hardwr, garden-retl	5200	3.2	7.3
Books: pubg, pubg & printing	2731	4.5	8.6
Btld & can soft drinks, water	2086	3.0	6.5
Business services, nec	7389	3.6	11.1
Cable and other pay tv svcs	4841	7.7	15.4
Caculate, acct mach, ex comp	3578	0.8	2.3
Can fruit, veg, presrv, jam, jel	2033	1.5	8.7
Can, frozn, presrv fruit & veg	2030	4.5	13.1
Catalog, mail-order houses	5961	6.4	23.8
Chemicals & allied products	2800	3.3	6.1
Cigarettes	2111	1.8	4.4
Cmp integrated sys design	7373	1.6	4.4
Cmp processing, data prep svc	7374	1.8	4.9
Cmp programming, data process	7370	4.8	13.3
Commercial printing	2750	0.2	0.8
Communications equip, nec	3669	1.3	3.2
Communications services, nec	4899	3.7	9.2
Computer & office equipment	3570	0.8	3.4
Computer communication equip	3576	1.1	1.7
Computer peripheral eq, nec	3577	2.7	5.5
Computer storage devices	3572	0.3	1.0
Computers & software-whsl	5045	1.1	1.9
Conglomerate	9997	0.5	1.2
Construction machinery & eq	3531	0.5	1.7
Construction-special Trade	1700	2.8	9.3
Convrt papr, paprbrd, ex boxes	2670	2.7	5.4
Cutlery, handtools, gen hrdwr	3420	3.3	6.4
Dairy products	2020	1.2	5.5

continued

FIGURE 11.12 2003 Advertising-to-Sales Ratios for 200 Largest Ad Spending Industries—*continued*

Industry	SIC Code	Advertising as % of sales	Advertising as % of margin
Dental equipment & supplies	3843	2.1	3.9
Department stores	5311	3.6	10.6
Distilled and blended liquor	2085	14.9	43.7
Dolls and stuffed toys	3942	7.8	14.7
Drug & proprietary stores	5912	0.8	3.3
Drugs and proprietary-whsl	5122	0.3	5.1
Eating places	5812	3.2	14.5
Educational services	8200	6.2	15.0
Elec meas & test instruments	3825	1.6	3.3
Electr, oth elec eq, ex cmp	3600	3.3	10.1
Electric & other serv comb	4931	0.5	5.1
Electric housewares and fans	3634	7.5	18.2
Electric lighting, wiring eq	3640	0.9	2.8
Electrical indl apparatus	3620	3.0	9.1
Electromedical apparatus	3845	0.8	1.2
Electronic computers	3571	1.4	6.6
Electronic parts, eq-whsl, nec	5065	1.6	11.8
Employment Agencies	7361	4.1	20.8
Engines and Turbines	3510	1.3	6.0
Equip rental & leasing, nec	7359	3.2	5.8
Fabricated plate work	3443	3.7	11.0
Family clothing stores	5651	2.4	7.4
Farm machinery and equipment	3523	0.8	3.3
Finance Lessors	6172	2.5	7.0
Food and kindred products	2000	10.2	21.5
Footwear, except rubber	3140	4.1	10.0
Functions rel to dep bkg, nec	6099	2.8	8.8
Furniture stores	5712	5.9	15.5
Games, toys, chld veh, ex dolls	3944	8.2	16.7
Gen bldg contractor-residntl	1520	2.9	11.4
General indl mach & eq, nec	3569	1.7	3.5
General industrial mach & eq	3560	0.8	1.8
Grain mill products	2040	4.3	16.7
Greeting cards	2771	2.0	2.8
Groceries & related pds-whsl	5140	2.3	10.7
Groceries, general line-whsl	5141	0.2	2.2.
Grocery stores	5411	1.0	4.2
Hardwr, plumb, heat eq-whsl	5070	0.6	5.3
Health services	8000	32.5	83.6
Heating eq, plumbing fixture	3430	8.4	18.8
Help supply services	7363	0.3	1.8
Hobby, toy, and game shops	5945	1.8	5.4
Home furniture & equip store	5700	2.5	6.0
Hospital & medical svc plans	6324	0.4	1.7

FIGURE 11.12 2003 Advertising-to-Sales Ratios for 200 Largest Ad Spending Industries—*continued*

Industry	SIC Code	Advertising as % of sales	Advertising as % of margin
Hotels and motels	7011	2.3	9.7
Household appliances	3630	1.5	6.3
Household audio & video eq	3651	6.9	44.9
Household furniture	2510	4.3	15.2
In vitro, in vivo diagnostics	2835	3.0	13.4
Indl inorganic chemicals	2810	0.4	1.3
Industrial measurement instr	3823	0.7	2.2
Industrial organic chemicals	2860	5.5	26.8
Ins agents, brokers & service	6411	1.1	1.7
Investment advice	6282	1.9	3.6
Iron and steel foundries	3320	1.0	4.0
Jewelry stores	5944	5.1	11.5
Knit outerwear mills	2253	3.9	10.4
Knitting mills	2250	9.6	26.8
Lab analytical instruments	3826	0.8	1.5
Leather and leather products	3100	3.9	5.6
Life insurance	6311	0.6	8.3
Loan brokers	6163	38.4	43.2
Lumber & oth bldg matl-retl	5211	1.1	3.4
Malt beverages	2082	8.5	18.2
Management consulting svcs	8742	0.7	1.7
Manifold business forms	2761	5.1	15.8
Meat packing plants	2011	2.0	18.1
Med, dental, hosp eq-whsl	5047	0.7	3.2
Membership sport & rec clubs	7997	5.8	28.1
Mens, boys frnsh, work clthng	2320	3.6	8.8
Metalworking machinery & eq	3540	3.7	10.2
Misc amusement & rec service	7990	1.3	3.3
Misc business services	7380	0.9	1.8
Misc chemical products	2890	5.3	15.9
Misc elec machy, eq, supplies	3690	3.0	9.6
Misc equip rental & leasing	7350	1.1	2.6
Misc fabricated metal prods	3490	1.5	8.8
Misc fabricated textile pds	2390	1.8	27.2
Misc food preps, kindred pds	2090	4.9	9.7
Misc manufacturing industries	3990	1.0	2.1
Misc nondurable goods-whsl	5190	0.4	2.8
Misc shopping goods stores	5940	3.2	10.4
Misc transportation equip	3790	2.7	13.3
Miscellaneous publishing	2741	12.9	17.5
Miscellaneous retail	5900	1.1	3.6
Mobile homes	2451	1.4	4.7
Mortgage bankers & loan corr	6162	1.2	3.0
Motion pic, videotape prodtn	7812	8.4	15.8

continued

FIGURE 11.12 2003 Advertising-to-Sales Ratios for 200 Largest Ad Spending
Industries—*continued*

Industry	SIC Code	Advertising as % of sales	Advertising as % of margin
Motion picture theaters	7830	1.5	5.3
Motor vehicle part, accessory	3714	0.4	2.6
Motor vehicles & car bodies	3711	2.4	11.1
Motorcycles, bicycles & parts	3751	1.4	3.0
Newspaper: pubg, pubg & print	2711	1.3	3.2
Operative builders	1531	1.1	4.8
Ophthalmic goods	3851	4.9	6.7
Ortho, prosth, surg appl, suply	3842	2.5	4.0
Paints, varnishes, lacquers	2851	1.2	3.1
Paper and allied products	2600	1.0	4.3
Paper mills	2621	7.6	32.3
Patent owners and lessors	6794	6.0	11.3
Perfume, cosmetic, toilet prep	2844	7.4	16.1
Periodical: pubg, pubg & print	2721	6.7	15.6
Personal credit institutions	6141	1.2	2.8
Personal services	7200	3.3	10.6
Petroleum refining	2911	0.1	0.6
Pharmaceutical preparations	2834	4.9	7.1
Phone comm ex radiotelephone	4813	2.5	5.7
Photographic equip & supply	3861	4.7	12.1
Plastic, foil, coatd papr bags	2673	0.9	3.1
Plastics products, nec	3089	1.8	5.9
Plastics, resins, elastomers	2821	0.5	2.4
Pottery and related products	3260	2.9	7.3
Poultry slaughter & process	2015	2.4	5.7
Prepackaged software	7372	3.5	4.7
Prof & coml eq & supply-whsl	5040	0.5	1.3
Pwr, distr, specl transformers	3612	0.8	2.4
Racing, incl track operations	7948	2.8	7.9
Radio broadcasting stations	4832	1.2	3.8
Radio, tv broadcast, comm eq	3663	0.9	2.3
Radio, tv, cons electr stores	5731	3.2	12.4
Radiotelephone communication	4812	2.9	5.0
Real estate agents & mgrs	6531	4.6	20.1
Real estate investment trust	6798	2.2	5.8
Record and tape stores	5735	1.7	5.0
Refuse systems	4953	0.3	0.8
Retail stores, nec	5990	4.9	11.2
Rubber and plastics footwear	3021	8.4	20.9
Security brokers & dealers	6211	3.8	15.3
Semiconductor, related device	3674	2.5	4.9
Shoe stores	5661	2.5	7.7
Soap, detergent, toilet preps	2840	11.3	21.8
Special clean, polish preps	2842	9.7	20.0

FIGURE 11.12 2003 Advertising-to-Sales Ratios for 200 Largest Ad Spending
Industries—*continued*

Industry	SIC Code	Advertising as % of sales	Advertising as % of margin
Special industry machy, nec	3559	0.5	1.7
Sporting & athletic gds, nec	3949	7.6	17.5
Srch, det, nav, guid, aero sys	3812	4.0	7.2
Steel works & blast furnaces	3312	0.3	1.2
Subdivide, dev, ex cemetery	6552	2.2	16.1
Sugar & confectionery prods	2060	11.7	23.3
Surgical, med instr, apparatus	3841	3.9	7.0
Tele & telegraph apparatus	3661	1.2	3.1
Television broadcast station	4833	9.3	36.2
Textile mill products	2200	3.6	15.7
Tires and inner tubes	3011	2.0	8.2
Tobacco products	2100	4.0	4.8
Transportation services	4700	7.2	16.0
Trucking, except local	4213	0.4	3.4
Trucking, courier svc, ex air	4210	0.1	3.4
Variety stores	5331	0.9	3.8
Video tape rental	7841	3.5	6.6
Watches, clocks and parts	3873	7.4	11.3
Water transportation	4400	8.8	24.1
Wine, brandy & brandy spirits	2084	3.9	12.4
Wmns, miss, chld, infnt undgrmt	2340	4.2	11.5
Women's clothing stores	5621	2.8	6.7
Womens, misses, jrs outerwear	2330	4.1	7.6
Wood hshld furn, ex upholsrd	2511	3.0	9.4

Notes: Ad dollars as % of sales: Ad spending divided by net sales. Ad dollars as % of margin: Ad spending divided by (net sales minus cost of goods sold).

Source: Schonfeld & Associates (www.saibooks.com) Copyright © 2003, Crain Communications Inc. -Privacy Statement Chaffee Interactive, Inc.: Programming, Technology & Hosting Services

brands relative to their market shares (see Figure 11.13). This suggests that large, well-known brands (or products with over a 13 percent market share) can underinvest in advertising relative to their market share. In focusing on brands with at least a 13 percent market share, it was found that brands with rising trends underinvested by 1 percent on average (their share of voice was 1 percent less than their share of the market), brands with constant share had share of voice 3 percent less than their market share, and brands with declining trends had share of voice 4 percent less than their market share. While the direction of causality in these data is unclear (Did they spend less on advertising because they knew share was going down, or did spending less on advertising contribute to decreasing share?), it does suggest that market share is a good starting point for choosing advertising share and hence budget.

Affordable

The affordable method is the ultimate in "advertising is a cost of doing business" thinking. It selects an advertising budget that, together with projected sales, price, and other costs, results in an "acceptable" income statement and profit level. Unfortunately, as

FIGURE 11.13 Market Share versus Share of Voice

Market Share	Share of Voice−Market Share
1–3%	+5%
4–6	+4
7–9	+2
10–12	+4
13–14	+1
16–18	+2
19–21	0
22–24	−3
25–27	−5
28–30	−5

Source: Reprinted by permission of *Harvard Business Review.* An exhibit from "Ad Spending: Maintaining Market Share," by John Phillip Jones, January–February 1990. Copyright © 1990 by the President and Fellows of Harvard College, all rights reserved.

advertising becomes less affordable because a brand is doing poorly, the role of advertising may become more important, thus leading to a vicious cycle of poor results, less advertising money, poorer results, even less advertising money, and so on.

Experimentation

In the experimentation approach, the manager tries different levels of spending, either in different regions or in more controlled settings, and monitors the results. The manager then uses the results to select among different advertising budgets and plans. With up to 20 percent of companies reporting using this method, it is increasing in popularity and represents a step toward developing optimizing models. The case of Equal highlights the use of experimentation in helping to set advertising budgets (Clarke, 1985). Product managers for Equal used information from Information Resources, Inc. (IRI), to determine advertising spending. IRI operated what it called BehaviorScan markets, geographically distinct markets in which the company installs electronic scanners in retail outlets in the city to track purchase behavior, and "split cable," two different TV cables running through the city with some households on cable A and others on cable B, to test different advertising strategies and budget levels. Companies can run extra commercials on one cable—say, A—when public service spots run on B for comparison. The household purchasing data indicate if the extra advertising created additional purchasing in the households on cable A. In the case of Equal, when the brand was introduced, the brand manager tried two levels of media spending: $3.8 million and $5.7 million (extrapolated to national levels). After a 20-week test, there was no significant difference between Equal purchasing rates from households on the two cables; thus, the lower spending level was reasonable.

Decision Calculus

Computerized decision support systems (DSSs) such as ADBUDG (Little, 1970) help structure budget decisions systematically. Managers provide subjective inputs about, for example, the expected impact of increasing or decreasing advertising spending by 50 percent. The computer program then estimates consumer response and solves for optimal spending. Although using solely subjective data produces results that are hard to sell to others, DSSs that combine judgment with data have facilitated decision making and promise to be more useful in the future.

Summary

Studies on what methods are used in practice have covered the United States and abroad (see the review by Bigné, 1995). The general findings are the following:

- Most companies use multiple methods for setting budgets.
- Overall, methods have evolved from the rather simple percentage-of-sales method to an increased use of the more sophisticated objective-and-task method. The latter is particularly true in larger companies and those manufacturing consumer products.
- Percentage of sales and the affordable methods are still popular, particularly among industrial and smaller firms.
- Competitive parity approaches are generally not the main method but are more complementary to others.
- A small but noticeable trend toward more experimentation has been discerned. This is particularly easy to do on the Internet.

How to improve the advertising budgeting process remains an important area for research as organizations such as the Marketing Science Institute have commissioned studies investigating how more progress can be made (Greyser and Root, 1999). Some reasonable guidelines to setting advertising budgets beyond the convenience/affordable approaches are the following (Lamons, 1995):

Market share is important; the higher your share, the more you should spend to protect it.

New products require higher advertising support than established ones.

Markets growing 10 percent or more annually require a higher-than-average advertising investment.

If your production is at less than two-thirds capacity, you should think about increasing the ad budget.

Products with low unit prices (under $10,000) require higher advertising support than ones with high unit prices. Premium-priced and heavily discounted products should receive more support than "average" priced products.

Higher-quality products generally require higher advertising spending.

Broader product lines require more support.

Standard, off-the-shelf products need more support than customized products.

EVALUATING AD COPY: LABORATORY-BASED MEASURES

As noted earlier in this chapter, product managers get involved only infrequently with the development of the actual advertising copy; that task is delegated to either in-house or agency creative specialists. However, the product manager should be involved with testing the advertising campaign before a substantial amount of money is committed to it. A large number of variables are usually testable: the spokesperson, the message itself (copy), the execution (e.g., humor versus other approaches), media, and other factors.

FIGURE 11.14 **Classification of Advertising Copy-Testing Methods**

	Advertising-related test (reception or response to the message itself and its contents)	Product-related test (impact of message on product awareness, liking, intention to buy, or use)

Laboratory measures (respondent aware of testing and measurement process)	**Cell I**
	
	Pretesting procedures
	  1. Consumer jury
	  2. Portfolio test
	  3. Readability tests
	  4. Physiological measures
	     Eye camera
	     GSR/EDR
		Cell II
		
		Pretesting procedures
		  1. Theater tests
		  2. Trailer tests
		  3. Laboratory stores

Real-world measures (respondent unaware of testing and measurement process)	**Cell III**
	
	Pretesting procedures
	  1. Dummy advertising
	     vehicles
	  2. Inquiry tests
	  3. On-the-air tests
	Posttesting procedures
	  1. Recognition tests
	  2. Recall tests
	  3. Association measures
	  4. Combination measures
		Cell IV
		
		Pretesting and posttesting procedures
		  1. Pre- and posttests
		  2. Sales tests
		  3. Minimarket tests

Source: George E. Belch and Michael A. Belch, *Advertising and Promotion: An Integrated Marketing Communications Perspective,* 4th ed., Homewood, IL: Richard D. Irwin, 1997, Chapter 20. p. 687.

Figure 11.14 is a typology of the different methods used for both pretesting and posttesting advertising (Belch and Belch, 1993; Batra, Myers, and Aaker, 1996). Laboratory tests bring people to a particular location where they are shown ads and asked to respond to them. The advantage of lab tests is that the researcher can carefully control the environment without distractions to the respondent and manipulate several different aspects of the advertising; that is, the test has very high *internal validity*. The disadvantage is that the situation is not realistic; the respondent provides answers in an unnatural environment (i.e., *external validity* is low). Field tests provide real-world measures because they are conducted under natural viewing conditions. Their advantages and disadvantages are the mirror image of lab tests: The environment is realistic, but the researcher cannot control other variables that might affect the response to the ad, such as a competitor's ad, noise from children, and so on. Thus, field tests have high external but low internal validity.

Consumer Jury

A common form of advertising testing uses focus groups, a small group of customers who are led in a discussion of the advertising by a moderator. Advertising concepts are often in the form of what are called *storyboards* for TV ads, rough pictures showing the idea behind the "story" that will be told (obviously for radio ads, words instead of pictures are used). For magazine or other print formats, actual executions are shown; multimedia technology allows for the use of more realistic ads.

Portfolio Tests

In this approach, a group of respondents are shown both control and test ads. After viewing a portfolio of ads, respondents are asked what information they recall from the ads and which they liked best. The ads with the highest recall and liking are considered to be the most effective.

Readability Tests

Readability of the copy of a print ad can be determined through the use of methods that, for example, count the number of syllables per 100 words, the length of sentences, and other structural aspects of the copy. The results provide an assessment of the reading skill needed to comprehend an ad that should match the target audience (you don't talk to third graders the same way you talk to Ph.D.'s—it is simpler and often more enjoyable to deal with third graders) and can be compared to norms obtained from successful ads.

Physiological Methods

A "weird science" approach to assessing advertisements involves a set of techniques that measure involuntary physical responses to the ad. These include

Pupil dilation. Pupilometers measure dilation (an activity related to action or arousal) and constriction (conservation of energy).

Galvanic skin response/electrodermal response (GSR/EDR). Response to a stimulus activates sweat glands; this activity can be measured using electrodes attached to the skin.

Eye tracking. Viewers are asked to watch or read an ad while a sensor beams infrared light at their eyes. This can measure how much of an ad is being read, what part of the ad is attracting attention, and the sequence of reading and attention.

Brain scans. Tracking brain activity indicates which parts of the brain are active and hence the level of involvement, affect, etc.

Theater Tests

This method is used for pretesting TV commercials. The service is sold by companies such as Advertising Research Services and Advertising Control for Television. Participants for theater tests are recruited by phone, shopping mall intercepts, direct mail, or via the Internet. A television show or some other entertainment is provided in a movie theater–like facility with commercial breaks ("trailer" tests use smaller, mobile facilities near shopping malls). The show is used so the respondents do not focus solely on the commercials; a cover story might inform them that the TV show is a pilot for a new network or cable series. After viewing the ads, the participants are asked questions about recall, attitude, interest, etc.

Laboratory Stores

In this testing procedure, the researcher attempts to simulate a shopping environment by setting up, for example, a supermarket-like shopping shelf with real brands. Respondents are shown advertising copy and make actual brand choices. A popular supplier of this kind of testing is Research Systems Corporation with its ARS Persuasion copy-testing system. Virtual stores on the Web are another and relatively new option.

REAL-WORLD MEASURES

Dummy Advertising Vehicles

Researchers construct "dummy" magazines with regular editorial matter, regular ads, and a set of test ads. The magazines are distributed to a random sample of homes in a predetermined geographic area. After being asked to read the magazine as they normally would, the consumers in the sample are interviewed on the editorial content as well as the test ads.

Inquiry Tests

A product manager and/or ad agency can track the number of inquiries generated from an ad that has a direct-response Internet site, toll free phone number, or a reader inquiry card attached. In B to B marketing, the use of "bingo" cards, response cards that have numbered holes corresponding to the numbered ads in the magazine, is very common.

On-the-Air/Recall Tests

IRI, Burke Marketing Research, ASI Market Research, Gallup & Robinson, and Nielsen all sell this kind of service. Essentially, a real TV ad (one of perhaps several executions being tested) is inserted in a TV program in one or more test markets. Consumers are then contacted and asked if they saw the ad; if so, they are asked further questions about recall of copy points, brand, and the like. The services differ somewhat in the questions asked and how the sample is recruited. Gallup & Robinson, for example, prerecruits a sample of people who are asked in advance to watch the particular show on which the test ad is being run.

Recognition Tests

This is the most widely used method for posttesting print ads and is closely associated with Starch INRA Hooper's "through the book" method. With this approach, a researcher interviews respondents at home by first asking if they have read a particular issue of a magazine and then going through the issue to obtain information about whether the respondents have seen the ad, how much of it they have read, and how much they recall. The Starch method and the resulting Starch "scores" are used to track and evaluate complete campaigns.

Sales/Minimarket Tests

The Information Resources, Inc. (IRI) BehaviorScan markets described in the section on advertising budgeting are also used to test ad copy. Using the split-cable methodology rather than testing a pure increase in advertising dollars, households on the two cables receive different advertising copy. By comparing purchasing behavior at the stores where the households shop, the product manager can determine if one copy platform is more effective than the other. However, as noted elsewhere in this chapter, short-term sales are not necessarily the only appropriate criterion for advertising.

Internet advertising is relatively easy to test. Different banner ads can be run by the time of day, week, by type of site, and so on. In addition, as we have discussed earlier in the chapter, the direct response nature of Internet advertising makes it straightforward to evaluate in terms of clickthroughs and ultimate purchase.

MEDIA SELECTION

Media planning is a field in itself and typically is a specialty within advertising agencies. Therefore, the media plan is often left up to the "experts." However, both to help product managers understand some aspects of media planning and to provide an approach to follow when no help is available, we provide a skeletal discussion of media planning. More detailed treatments are available that are well beyond the scope of this book (e.g., Sissors and Bumba, eds., 1996).

The basic media plan defines *where* (in what vehicles, e.g., TV, magazines, radio, the Internet) and *when* (time of year, day, etc.) advertising will appear. These decisions, which effectively determine how often an ad is seen and by how many people, are in turn heavily influenced both by earlier decisions on advertising strategy, message, and target audience and by issues such as the rate of ad wearout (which in turn is influenced by the amount of "clutter" anticipated in general and in competitive ads in particular). For ease of explanation, we discuss the *where* and *when* issues separately.

Where

The decision of where to advertise has three basic components: match to target audience, contextual fit, and duplication and wearout.

Efficient Audience Selection

Trying to match target audiences typically leads to a comparison of vehicles in terms of efficiency in reaching desirable audiences. Some measures, such as cost per thousand (CPM), become the yardstick for comparing different vehicles. CPM measures how much it costs the advertiser to reach 1,000 customers by using a particular medium. For example, according to the data on circulation and advertising rates from the website *www.MediaStart.com,* the 2000 CPM for *Business Week* for a four-color print ad was $97.14, whereas for *People* it was $44.31. Ratings and circulation data (such as Arbitron's radio audience ratings, Nielsen's TV ratings, Standard Rate and Data Services, Audit Bureau of Circulations, and Simmons's magazine audience measurements) are vital inputs to decisions and consequently are hotly contested measures. The focus should be (and increasingly is) on cost per thousand of "relevant" readers, listeners, or viewers, that is, the cost per thousand in the target market. This is what leads to so many beer and car ads on sports shows, for example. All this said, much of the industry still relies on maximizing GRPs as a criterion for media selection. It is important to recognize that CPM or GRP numbers may badly overstate actual ad readers or viewers. Most people do not read the many pages of ads that fill the fronts of magazines, study inserts in newspapers, or even stay in the room during TV ads (preferring instead to read, get food, go to the bathroom, sleep, etc.). Hence adjusting total audience to likely readership or viewership levels is very important.

One important aspect of targeting is product use. A number of services (e.g., MRI) rate media vehicles by average product usage. Therefore, cost per thousand can be weighted by product usage.

Another important aspect of a media plan is regional differentiation. Not only does product usage vary by region; so do features desired and cultural preferences. Therefore, even though regional vehicles may cost more in a CPM sense, it is often desirable to focus on certain regions (especially if your share or distribution level varies regionally) and use somewhat different messages and media by region.

Contextual Fit

Contextual fit falls into two subcategories, general media fit and program and ad context. The media level fit issues are fairly obvious: It is difficult to demonstrate operation of a machine on the radio, incorporate music or other sounds in print media, or provide detailed information that will be recalled in radio or TV ads.

A more subtle level of fit involves the context of the ad, including both the program and other ads. Product fit involves the interaction between the product image and the image of the vehicle. For example, even if professional wrestling delivers upscale viewers at a competitive CPM, does it make sense to advertise upscale products (e.g., Tiffany glass, imported fine wine) between bouts? This issue is magnified if a vehicle airs controversial topics that can lead to a backlash or even a boycott against advertisers (as the quick withdrawal of ads from controversial shows or shows with controversial spokespersons demonstrates).

The interaction of ad image and its immediate context is also relevant. For example, a humorous ad may lose its effect if placed in the context of a comedy show or a series of eight other humorous ads. In a serious vehicle, it may even be perceived as tasteless. Although it is impossible to control or predict exactly what story will appear on the facing page for a print ad or exactly which other commercials will run during a particular TV commercial break, educated guesses are both possible and recommended. Competitive effects are serious when many products in the same category advertise close together, with the result that many consumers cannot distinguish the claims from one another. (We know after watching sports we should buy beer, sneakers, and cars, but we rarely remember why or which ones.)

Duplication and Wearout

Depending on the goal, duplication (multiple exposures to the same ad) may be either desirable (e.g., for a subtle message, a complicated concept or benefit, or a message that is soon forgotten) or wasted (e.g., for a simple message). Apparently competing vehicles commonly duplicate audiences; for example, tremendous overlap occurs among readers of *Fortune, Business Week,* and *Forbes.* There is also evidence that customers tire of exactly the same message fairly quickly, though less so for complex messages than simple ones. In contrast, some evidence suggests that varying copy slightly, though somewhat expensive due to the multiple executions necessary, slows ad wearout (Unnava and Burnkrant, 1991). Although the number of possible combinations of vehicles makes thorough analysis difficult (though not impossible given increased computer power), a reasonable sense can be achieved by estimating the unduplicated audience of each vehicle and, when reach is the objective, concentrating on vehicles with large unduplicated audiences.

When

Issues involving when to advertise directly affect the evaluation of where to advertise. For example, readership and product consumption vary by season or issue and viewership or listenership by program, time of day, day of week, and so on. For this discussion, we assume most of these are accounted for in the *where* analysis and address here two issues: seasonality and spending pattern.

As discussed earlier in the book, seasonality exists for many products, both consumer and industrial. The question of when to advertise is affected strongly by the target

FIGURE 11.15   Media Vehicle Evaluation Form

		Contact			Impact			Effective CPM
Vehicle	Cost	Size of target audience	Duplication with other vehicles	Target CPM (T)	Impact/ product vehicle fit	Copy, context fit	Overall effectiveness (E)	T/E

audience—for example, retail stores versus consumers for skis and dealers versus customers for industrial goods, because retailers and dealers make decisions well before most customers do. In addition, issues of immediate relevance (which suggests advertising during the buying season) and clutter (which may argue for off-season advertising) have an impact on timing. Alternatively, for some products such as cold remedies, a "leading" spending pattern is sometimes used that delivers messages prior to the major usage season (e.g., the cold/flu season) to get consumers to stock up on a brand and simultaneously take them out of the market for competing brands.

One issue in setting the spending pattern is when during the life cycle to advertise. One study found that advertising is more effective early in the life cycle and hence should be heaviest during introduction and growth (Parsons, 1975). Also important is the question of whether spending should be level throughout the relevant time period or heavily bunched in a short span of time. A number of studies suggest that an uneven spending pattern (pulsing) is more effective than a level pattern.

Other Considerations

In addition to the complexities already discussed, decisions concerning media schedules are influenced by various pricing deals and promotions offered by the media. For example, large advertisers get a much better rate for TV than small advertisers because they buy large blocks of time "upfront," such as before the fall TV season begins. Consequently, as mentioned earlier in the chapter, the media decision is typically left to specialists who have the best information on current rates and the negotiating ability to get the best media prices. Nonetheless, it is still sometimes useful to have a worksheet for evaluating various vehicles. The worksheet in Figure 11.15 has been found helpful in this regard.

EVALUATING ADVERTISING EFFECTS

Given the amount of money spent on advertising, it is surprising how little effort is spent assessing whether or not it is working. Volumes have been written on topics such as copy testing with focus groups and in theater settings; however, as we discussed earlier in this chapter, these two methods tend to be used for making decisions about different copy strategies rather than for postimplementation assessment. In this section, we focus on quantitative assessment of the impact of advertising expenditures after the finished campaign has run.

Tracking Studies

Conventional tracking studies are relatively simple surveys that ask respondents two kinds of questions. One type is "top of mind" or, more technically, unaided recall in which the respondent is asked if he or she can recall seeing an ad for the brand. For example, the respondent might be asked, "Have you seen the advertising campaign with famous actors and actresses with milk on their lips?" If the answer is *yes,* this technique follows up the question with a request to repeat the main copy points to determine comprehension. If the respondent indicates that the campaign is "Got Milk?" the campaign gets higher marks. Attitudinal questions might also be asked. The second type of survey uses aided recall: "Have you seen the 'Got Milk?' advertising campaign?" This method detects information not actively in memory that can be important when primed at point-of-purchase. Not surprisingly, the recall numbers produced by aided recall are much larger than those by unaided recall.

These studies then track responses over time, often at constant time intervals, using either the same sample of respondents (a panel) or a different, randomly selected group. The product manager can then view how awareness, comprehension, or interest builds, plateaus, or never gets off the ground. The percentages obtained from these studies are often compared to norms derived from previous advertising campaigns.

Tracking studies also use recognition tests. As mentioned earlier, Starch uses what are called "through the book" methods. These aided recall situations show respondents a magazine (or other media vehicle). For each ad, they ask questions pertaining to whether the person had seen the ad, how much she or he had read, and so on. Tracking studies such as these tend not to ask questions about purchasing because the focus is more on objectives such as those shown in Figure 11.8.

Past Sales and Advertising

Most early studies of historical advertising effects were at the aggregate level (that is, they assessed the impact of annual budgets on annual sales). Essentially they involved observing the relation between past advertising spending and past sales either across different geographical areas (cross-sectionally) or over different time periods. These methods continue to be used, albeit less often than the tracking studies.

Figure 11.16 shows two possible nonlinear relationships between advertising spending and market response (sales, share, etc.) The solid curve is S shaped and assumes there is an interval in which advertising delivers increasing returns: The next dollar spent is actually more effective than some previous dollars were. This occurs between points *a* and *b.* Past point *b,* advertising delivers decreasing returns. The dotted curve shows a relationship delivering decreasing returns over the whole range of advertising expenditures.

These methods use actual market data to assess the impact of sales on advertising: $S = f(\text{Adv})$, that is, to estimate the curves shown in Figure 11.16. Mathematically, these tend to follow three different forms:

1. Linear: $S = B_0 + B_1 \, \text{Adv}$
2. Decreasing marginal returns:
   (*a*) $S = B_0 + B_1 \log(\text{Adv})$
   (*b*) $S = B_0 + B_1 \, \text{Adv} - B_2 \, (\text{Adv})^2$
3. S shaped: $S = \exp[B_0 - B_1 \, \text{Adv}]$,

FIGURE 11.16 **The Impact of Advertising Spending**

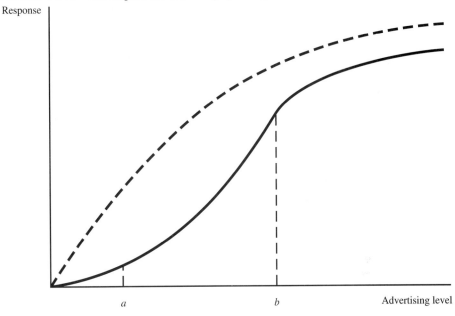

where "exp" is "exponentiation," that is, raising the mathematical constant e to the $[B_0 - B_1 \text{ Adv}]$ power. Generally, these models are estimated using standard regression analysis programs. Though generalizations are difficult, support for the S-shaped model seems strongest (Simon and Arndt, 1980).

One serious problem with the previous models is that they are incomplete (technically *misspecified*); that is, other variables that affect sales (e.g., price, quality, distribution, inertia/past sales, competition) are excluded from the model. Hence the estimates of the effects of advertising may be inaccurate (typically they are overstated) due to confounding with the effects of the other (omitted) variables. This suggests that attempts to assess the effect of advertising also need to assess simultaneously (control for) the effects of other relevant variables. For example, this converts the linear model into

$$\text{Sales} = B_0 + B_1 \text{ Adv} + B_2 \text{ Price} + B_3 \text{ Quality} + B_4 \text{ Distribution} + B_5 \text{ Past sales} + \ldots$$

Here B_5 represents the carryover effect of past sales (and hence prior advertising, etc.) on current sales. Models of this type are often referred to as *Koyck* models.

A number of studies done in this tradition have yielded some generalizable results (Assmus, Farley, and Lehmann, 1984). Across 128 studies, the average effect (elasticity) of current advertising on current sales is about .22 (that is, a 100 percent increase in advertising leads to a 22 percent change in sales), and the carryover effect, the elasticity of impact of current advertising on future sales through the inertia effect of past sales on current sales is about .47, indicating that the long-run impact is as important as its immediate effect. Also, small but interesting differences seem to occur across products and markets; for example, food products had slightly higher elasticities. However, other researchers suggest lower impacts for advertising. Consequently, a reasonable starting point for estimating the impact of advertising is that doubling the advertising budget (a 100 percent increase) is likely to generate between a 1 and 30 percent increase in sales, ceterus paribus.[3]

Given our earlier discussion about the investment value of advertising, it is worth describing some further results about its long-run impact. Rather than simply looking at the long-run elasticity, an interesting perspective is how long $1 of advertising lasts. Several studies have examined this issue (Clarke, 1976; Leone, 1995). They have found consistent evidence that 90 percent of the impact of advertising for consumer goods occurs within the first six to nine months, implying that any benefits due to "mere exposure" are gone within a year and that advertising and other communication efforts must be continually employed.

Another weakness of these econometric models is that they ignore the effect of competition. Competition can be incorporated simply by using relative values for the predictor variables such as share of advertising, price relative to average category price, and so on. An alternative approach is to consider the following starting point, assuming a mature market with constant primary demand:

Our share = Our effort/(Our effort + Sum of their efforts)

Mathematically, this is typically represented by the following (logit) model:

Market share of brand i = $\exp[B_{i0} + B_{i1} \text{Adv}_i + \ldots]/\Sigma \exp[B_{j0} + B_{j1} \text{Adv}_j + \ldots]$

There is also evidence that advertising interacts with other variables such as price. Two hypotheses suggest how advertising can affect price sensitivity. One is the *market power* hypothesis that increased levels of advertising build brand loyalty and therefore decrease price sensitivity. The other is the *advertising as information* hypothesis, which suggests that advertising provides more information about brands in a category, which consumers will then use to switch based on price and other factors; that is, advertising increases price sensitivity. (This led to predictions of dramatically falling prices due to the Internet which generally have failed to materialize.) Not surprisingly, the empirical evidence supports both hypotheses (Mitra and Lynch, 1995). Still, it generally appears that advertising decreases price sensitivity (Jedidi, Mela, and Gupta, 1999; Mela, Gupta, and Lehmann, 1997).

This kind of analysis can be used to help set budgets as well as to diagnose the effects of advertising spending. An example of the application of econometric methods to budget setting involved the General Foods powdered orange drink, Tang (DeBruicker, 1974). The model used in that application was

$$S_t = B_0 + B_1 L[1 - \exp(-bA_t)] + B_2 P_t + B_3 S_{t-1},$$

where the dependent variable, sales, was measured over time for different sales territories; the L term shows differences in advertising effects due to distribution coverage, demographics, and existing sales levels among sales territories; P is promotion expense; and the lagged sales term shows carryover effects. The exponential advertising term creates a nonlinear response between advertising and sales with both a ceiling and a lower bound.

---

[3] The vast majority of empirical research in this area has focused on consumer products and services. Thus, generalizing these findings to industrial products should be done with caution.

After estimating advertising spending effects with actual data, the parameters of the model (the *B*s) were used to determine optimal spending levels of advertising.

The other main approach to estimating the impact of advertising on sales uses individual customer purchase data. These data became widely available with the introduction of supermarket scanners in some categories (frequently purchased consumer goods) and are also available in many company records (e.g., utilities and phone companies). Essentially, the model forms parallel those discussed before, but the data are analyzed at the individual household (or at least segment) level. While start-up costs (e.g., getting data in form for analysis) are high, this type of data is beginning to provide more precise estimates of the impact of advertising, especially when "single-source" data, data that also have advertising exposure at the individual level, are used (Tellis, 1988; Winer, 1993).

Perhaps the most detailed study of advertising effectiveness is due to Lodish et al. (1995). Their conclusion, based on 389 advertising weight (budget) tests, was that advertising spending creates notable increases in sales only when the ads convey some new benefits or uses (as in the case with new products). This finding has been replicated by others, including Eastlack and Rao (1989) and Vakratsas and Ambler (1999). What it means is that the effect of doubling a budget is likely to be a 2 percent or less increase in sales for a mature product with no new information whereas it can be in the neighborhood of 30 percent for a new product or application. The low impacts for mature products are partly due to competitive reaction: If Coke increases advertising, so does Pepsi, so that sales increases come either from other (smaller) competitors or by increasing category sales (primary demand).[4] Still, some research (MacInnis, Rao, and Weiss, 2002) suggests that affect-based copy can be effective for frequently purchased brands.

Experimentation

In addition to its use in setting budgets and evaluating potential advertising copy described earlier in this chapter, experimentation as a means of assessing advertising effectiveness has a long tradition in marketing. Early examples involved examining different advertising timing policies (Zielske, 1959) and alternative amounts of advertising spending (Ackoff and Emshoff, 1975). Unfortunately, field experiments—using real products in an actual setting—are costly and time-consuming. Still they do provide evidence that ads work, for example, in stimulating calls to an advertised number (Tellis, Chandy, and Thaivanich, 2000). Field experiments involve manipulating different levels of marketing variables in different sales territories, different stores, or to different groups of customers for an extended period of time to detect any effects of the manipulated variable. Moreover, field experiments are politically difficult, for while it is easy to get a regional manager to accept an increased advertising budget (or price cut), it is hard to obtain acceptance for a cut in advertising (or an increase in price), both at the regional and corporate levels.

Linking Objectives to Incremental Contribution

Evaluating advertising effectiveness often requires a link from the advertising objectives to the (hopefully) increased contribution resulting from the advertising (Eechembadi, 1994). An illustration of the approach for a luxury sports sedan appears in Figure 11.17.

---

[4] An interesting study by Tellis, Chandy, and Thaivanich (2000) examines the effectiveness of direct TV advertising according to creative execution, TV station, and the interaction of station by time of day.

FIGURE 11.17 **From Objectives to Incremental Contribution**

Example: Luxury Sports Sedan			
Changes in perceptions		6.7%	
Impact on consideration	× 1.5	10.0%	Increase in consideration
Conversion to showroom visits	× 0.5	5.0%	Increased probability of showroom visit
Closing rate on showroom visits	× 0.10	0.5%	Increased probability of purchase
Size of segment	× 500,000	2,500	Incremental cars sold
Marginal contribution per car	× $5,000	$12.5m	Net incremental contribution from advertising to segment

Suppose the product manager has goals of a 10 percent improvement in the perception of style, 5 percent in performance, and 5 percent in sportiness, for an average improvement of 6.7 percent over the three dimensions. Prior research has shown that there is a multiplier of 1.5 from perception improvement to increase in the number of buyers who will consider buying the car, hence the 10 percent increase in consideration. Also, experience tells us that 50 percent of the increase in consideration actually results in a showroom visit and 10 percent of those cases result in a sale (these assumptions can be continually monitored in the marketplace). Thus, the advertising has increased probability of purchase 0.5 percent. If the segment size is 500,000 people and the profit contribution per car is $5,000, the incremental contribution from the advertising is $12.5 million. This figure can then be compared to the cost of the advertising for evaluation purposes.

Evaluating Ad Budgets

It is not uncommon for a budget to request an increase in ad spending which in a pro-forma P&L leads to an increase in sales. A critical, but not always addressed, question is whether it is reasonable to expect the implied increase based on the increased spending. Consider the following budget increase:

	Current	Proposed
Sales	30,000,000	39,000,000
Gross margin (50%)	15,000,000	19,500,000
Advertising	5,000,000	8,000,000
Profit	10,000,000	11,500,000

Would you propose (as a product manager) or accept (as a more senior manager) the budget?

One way to deal with this is to run a test, but this takes both time and money. A simple alternative is to see what similar budget increases have generated in the past. Fortunately a number of meta-analyses (summaries of past studies) have been done in this area (Assmus, Farley, and Lehmann, 1984; Eastlack and Rao, 1989; Lodish et al., 1995). The basic (over-simplified) conclusion is that simply increasing the amount spent on advertising on a mature product with no new information produces elasticities of 1 percent, whereas money spent on new products or real information about new uses of old products can generate elasticities of about 30 percent. The present budget suggests a 50 percent increase in ad spending will result in a 30 percent sales increase, an elasticity of 60 percent. While the campaign may be creative (which of course many of the other campaigns in the meta-analyses tried to be also), it is probably not that "special." Prudence suggests rejecting the budget unless something else is going on to justify the increase.

SUMMARY

This chapter delineated advertising decisions to be made, provided a set of worksheets to facilitate the process, and suggested what we have learned about the effects of advertising. Having developed the advertising plan, it is important to concisely summarize it. Here we suggest three summary charts.

The first chart, Figure 11.18, succinctly summarizes the general strategy in three parts. It defines the target audience (both primary and, when applicable, secondary), both generally (e.g., children) and in terms of specific descriptors used for selecting among media vehicles (e.g., children age 11 to 14 in homes with over $20,000 per year annual income). It specifies operational goals in terms of impact (e.g., increase awareness from 20 to 40 percent) and exposure (reach 80 percent of the target audience at least three times from January through March). Finally, it states the basic message (selling point in terms of benefit).

The second chart, Figure 11.19, summarizes the spending plan. Basically, it divides the budget among the costs of the media vehicles selected, production cost, and testing both before and after the ads are run. Production costs vary widely depending on, among other things, the use of a celebrity endorser, the length of the ad (e.g., quarter page, full page, multiple page; 15 seconds, 30 seconds, 60 seconds in TV), and the general slickness of the presentation. Similarly, testing costs vary depending on the sample used (size, ease of locating), what is asked of respondents, and sampling method. The main point here is that the spending plan should include adequate resources to conduct production and testing well *and* allow for the time needed to accomplish these activities.

The third chart, Figure 11.20, provides a timetable detailing when spending will occur. This chart also provides a standard against which to compare actual spending throughout the year. Remember that production is not instantaneous; for example, TV ads often require four to six months to prepare and finalize.

FIGURE 11.18 Advertising Strategy Summary

	General Description	Specific Targeting Characteristics (e.g., demographics)
1. Target audience		
Primary		
Secondary		
2. Operational objectives		
Impact		
Exposure		
3. Message/copy		
Primary		
Secondary		

FIGURE 11.19   **Advertising Spending Plan and Budget**

Media	Specific Vehicles and Frequency	Production and Testing Budget	Space/Time Budget	Total Budget
Newspaper				
National				
Regional/local				
Magazine				
National				
Regional/local				
TV				
Network				
Spot				
Regional/local				
Radio				
Network				
Regional/local				
Internet				
Other				
(Billboard)				
Public relations				
Research and monitoring				

Of course, a number of parties need to approve an advertising budget, including divisional and corporate managers and the legal department. Moreover, as the year unfolds, various events may (and often do) occur that lead to a revision of the plan. Thus, the advertising plans developed, like any other plans, need to be viewed as something to be sold internally and modified as needed rather than something to be inflexibly implemented.

FIGURE 11.20   **Detailed Monthly Advertising Spending Plan: Production and Placement**

Media	January Ads	January Cost	February Ads	February Cost	. . .
Newspaper					
National					
Regional/local					
Magazine					
National					
Regional/local					
TV					
Network					
Spot					
Regional/local					
Radio					
Network					
Regional/local					
Internet					
Other					
(Billboard)					

References

Ackoff, Russell, and James R. Emshoff (1975) "Advertising Research at Anheuser-Busch," *Sloan Management Review,* Winter, 1–15.

Assmus, Gert, John U. Farley, and Donald R. Lehmann (1984) "How Advertising Affects Sales: Meta-Analysis of Econometric Results," *Journal of Marketing Research* 21, February, 65–74.

Batra, Rajeev, John G. Myers, and David A. Aaker (1996) *Advertising Management,* 5th ed. Upper Saddle River, NJ: Prentice Hall.

Belch, George E., and Michael A. Belch (1997) *Advertising and Promotion: An Integrated Marketing Communications Perspective,* 4th ed. Homewood, IL: Richard D. Irwin.

Bigné, J. Enrique (1995) "Advertising Budget Practices: A Review," *Journal of Current Issues and Research in Advertising* 17, Fall, 17–31.

Clarke, Darral G. (1976) "Econometric Measurement of the Duration of Advertising Effect on Sales," *Journal of Marketing Research* 13, (November), 345–57.

Clarke, Darral G. (1985) "G.D. Searle & Co.: Equal Low-Calorie Sweetener (A)." Harvard Business School case #9-585-010.

DeBruicker, F. Stewart (1974) "General Foods Corporation: Tang Instant Breakfast Drink (A)." Harvard Business School case #9-575-063.

Eastlack, Joseph O., Jr., and Ambar G. Rao (1989) "Advertising Experiments at Campbell Soup Company," *Marketing Science* 8, Winter, 57–71.

Eechembadi, Naras V. (1994) "Does Advertising Work?" *The McKinsey Quarterly,* 117–29.

Greenleaf, Eric, and Donald R. Lehmann (1991) "Causes of Delay in Consumer Decision-Making," *Advances in Consumer Research* 18, 470–75.

Greyser, Stephen A., and H. Paul Root, eds. (1999) "Improving Advertising Budgeting," Marketing Science Institute report #99–126.

Jedidi, Kamel, Carl F. Mela, and Sunil Gupta (1999) "Managing Advertising and Promotion for Long-Run Profitability," *Marketing Science* 18, 45–47.

Jones, John Philip (1990) "Ad Spending: Maintaining Market Share," *Harvard Business Review,* 68, January–February, 38–48.

Krugman, Herbert (1965) "The Impact of Television Advertising: Learning without Involvement," *Public Opinion Quarterly* 29, 349–56.

Lamons, Bob (1995) "How to Set Politically Correct Ad Budgets," *Marketing News,* December 4,5.

Leone, Robert P. (1995) "Generalizing What Is Known about Temporal Aggregation and Advertising Carryover," *Marketing Science* 14, G141–150.

Little, John D. C. (1970) "Models and Managers: The Concept of a Decision Calculus," *Management Science* 16, B466–85.

Lodish, Leonard M., Magid Abraham, Stuart Kalmenson, Jeanne Livelsberger, Beth Lubetkin, Bruce Richardson, and Mary Ellen Stevens (1995) "How T.V. Advertising Works: A Meta-Analysis of 389 Real World Split Cable T.V. Advertising Experiments," *Journal of Marketing Research* 32, May, 125–39.

MacInnis, Deborah J., Ambar G. Rao, and Allen M. Weiss (2002) "Assessing When Increased Media Weight of Real-World Advertisements Helps Sales," *Journal of Marketing Research* 39, November, 391–407.

Marketing News (2003), July 7, 16–24.

Mela, Carl, Sunil Gupta, and Donald R. Lehmann (1997) "The Long Term Impact of Promotion and Advertising on Consumer Brand Choice," *Journal of Marketing Research* 34, May, 248–61.

Mitra, Anusree, and John G. Lynch, Jr. (1995) "Toward a Reconciliation of Market Power and Information Theories of Advertising Effects on Price Elasticity," *Journal of Consumer Research* 21, 644–59.

Parsons, Leonard J. (1975) "The Product Life Cycle and Time-Varying Advertising Elasticities," *Journal of Marketing Research* 12, November, 476–80.

Petty, Richard E., John T. Cacioppo, and David W. Schumann (1983) "Central and Peripheral Routes to Advertising Effectiveness: The Moderating Role of Involvement," *Journal of Consumer Research* 10, 134–48.

Schultz, Don E. (1998) *Strategic Advertising Campaigns,* 4th ed. Lincolnwood, IL: NTC Business Books.

Simon, Julian L., and Johan Arndt (1980) "The Shape of the Advertising Function," *Journal of Advertising Research* 20, 11–28.

Sissors, Jack Z., and Lincoln Bumba, eds. (1996) *Advertising Media Planning,* 5th ed. Lincolnwood, IL: NTC Business Books.

Slywotzky, Adrian J., and Benson P. Shapiro (1993) "Leveraging to Beat the Odds: The New Marketing Mind-Set," *Harvard Business Review* 71, September–October, 97–107.

Tellis, Gerard J. (1988) "Advertising Exposure, Loyalty, and Brand Purchase: A Two-Stage Model of Choice," *Journal of Marketing Research* 25, May, 134–44.

Tellis, Gerard J., Rajesh K. Chandy, and Pattana Thaivanich (2000) "Which Ad Works, When, Where, and How Often? Modeling the Effects of Direct Television Advertising," *Journal of Marketing Research* 37, February, 32–46.

Unnava, H. Rao, and Robert E. Burnkrant (1991) "Effects of Repeating Varied Ad Executions on Brand Name Memory," *Journal of Marketing Research* 28, November, 406–16.

Vakratsas, Demetrios, and Tim Ambler (1999) "How Advertising Works: What We Really Know," *Journal of Marketing* 63, January, 26–43.

Vaughn, Richard (1980) "How Advertising Works—A Planning Model," *Journal of Advertising Research* 20, October, 27–33.

Wansink, Brian, and Michael L. Ray (1996) "Advertising Strategies to Increase Usage Frequency," *Journal of Marketing* 60, January, 31–46.

Winer, Russell S. (1993) "Using Single-Source Scanner Data as a Natural Experiment for Evaluating Advertising Effects," *Journal of Marketing Science* (Japan) 2, 15–31.

Zielske, Hubert A. (1959) "The Remembering and Forgetting of Advertising," *Journal of Marketing* 23, 239–43.

Chapter **Twelve**

Promotions

Overview

Sales promotion (hereafter referred to as *promotion*) consists of a collection of devices aimed at generating active customer response within a short period of time (Blattberg and Neslin, 1990; Totten and Block, 1994). Interestingly, most of the effort has been directed at channel customers; Procter & Gamble (P&G) refers to retail stores and chains as customers (not the individuals who eventually buy Crest, etc.). As Figure 12.1 shows, it has been receiving an increasingly large share of the advertising/promotion budget, particularly for promotions oriented toward the trade (distribution channels). One factor favoring promotions is the easy-to-track and often-dramatic short-run increase in sales during a promotion, which makes them appear to be "accountable/justifiable." Food product manufacturers spent $25 billion per year on trade promotion in 2000 (Schoenberger, 2000). In 1990 25 percent of sales time and 30 percent of brand management time were spent on promotions (Buzzell, Quelch, and Salmon, 1990), and it has increased since then.

Coupons and promotions play a large role on the Web as well. Over 50 percent of both first time and repeat buyers were influenced by either coupons or free shipping during summer 2000 (Williamson, 2000).

At the same time, the use of promotions is a hotly debated topic. For example, in the early 1990s Procter & Gamble attempted to reduce its use of coupons by focusing on everyday low pricing (EDLP) partly due to the inefficiency (only 2 percent are redeemed) and costs of printing, distribution, and processing coupons (Schiller, 1996), and much more because of their impact on increasing costs of production and distribution. Similarly, Heinz tried to reduce its dependence on price-focused communications activities (e.g., trade-oriented promotion), and increased investment in advertising (Spethmann, 1995).

FIGURE 12.1 **Changes in Advertising and Promotion Spending***

	1981	1986	1991	1994	1998
Advertising	43%	34%	25%	26%	22%
Consumer promotion	23	26	25	25	20
Trade promotion	34	40	50	49	58

*Expressed as percentage of the total amount of dollars spent on advertising and promotion.

Sources: "Category Management: Marketing for the 90's," *Marketing News,* September 14, 1992; Donnelly Marketing Inc., *17th Annual Survey of Promotional Practice,* 1995; A.C. Nielsen.

FIGURE 12.2 IRI Data on Instant Coffee Purchasing

Brands purchased by 0.5% or More of All Households	Category Volume Share	Type Volume Share	% of Households Buying	Volume per Purchase	Purchase per Buyer	Purchase Cycle (days)
Category—coffee	5,647.4*	100.0%	76.1%	1.1	6.9	60
Type—soluble	9.6	100.0	31.9	0.5	3.5	81
Flavored	5.1	53.2	17.9	0.5	3.3	76
Nestlé S.A. (Switzerland)	0.7	7.7	5.6	0.4	1.9	84
Nescafé	0.2	2.5	3.0	0.3	1.5	72
Nescafé Mountain Blend	0.2	2.6	1.4	0.5	2.2	87
Tasters Choice	0.1	0.7	1.3	0.2	1.5	88
Philip Morris Co. Inc.	4.2	43.0	14.3	0.5	3.2	75
General Foods International Coffee	3.1	32.2	9.0	0.6	3.2	71
Maxwell House	1.0	10.8	7.2	0.3	2.5	75
Caffeinated	3.2	33.1	13.9	0.5	2.8	82
Nestlé S.A. (Switzerland)	0.5	5.3	2.7	0.5	2.0	85
Nescafé Classic	0.5	5.2	2.5	0.5	2.1	85
Philip Morris Co. Inc.	0.8	8.5	3.5	0.5	2.6	81
Maxwell House	0.8	8.5	3.4	0.5	2.6	81
Procter & Gamble	1.4	14.1	7.3	0.4	2.4	83
Folgers	1.4	14.1	7.3	0.4	2.4	83
Private Label	0.4	3.9	2.5	0.4	2.3	79
Private Label	0.4	3.9	2.5	0.4	2.3	79
Decaffeinated	1.3	13.7	6.8	0.5	2.4	90
Nestlé S.A. (Switzerland)	0.2	1.9	1.3	0.5	1.7	102
Nescafé Decaf	0.1	1.1	0.8	0.5	1.5	125
Philip Morris Co. Inc.	0.5	5.5	2.2	0.5	2.6	91
Sanka	0.5	5.2	2.1	0.5	2.6	91
Procter & Gamble	0.6	6.2	3.9	0.4	2.0	83
Folgers	0.6	6.2	3.9	0.4	2.0	83

Data reflect grocery store purchases only.
*Category volume per 1,000 households.

Source: IRI Market Fact Book, 1994.

Competitors, however, did not follow suit and while profits may have increased, shares apparently have decreased (Ailawadi, Lehmann, and Neslin, 2001).

To give an idea of how strongly promotions affect consumer behavior, Figure 12.2 displays some descriptive data for the soluble (instant) coffee category. The data are from IRI's 1994 edition of *The Marketing Fact Book,* which reports on purchases of households in supermarkets where the products' universal product codes (UPCs) are electronically scanned. The column definitions are as follows:

- Category Volume Share: share of all coffee sales.
- Type Volume Share: share of subcategory (e.g., flavored, caffeinated).

Share Category Requirements	Price Per Volume	% Volume with the Specified Deal						Average % Off on Price Deals
		Any Trade Deal	Print Ad Feature	In-Store Display	Shelf Price Reduction	Store Coupon	Manufacturer Coupon	
100%	3.75	42%	20%	17%	31%	3%	18%	24%
27	7.91	18	6	3	14	1	25	23
22	6.90	18	4	4	13	1	31	27
11	7.84	18	2	1	18	0	26	29
6	6.39	19	3	3	17	0	36	38
17	8.62	19	1	0	19	0	25	19
5	18.23	12	1	0	12	0	62	23
21	6.68	18	5	4	13	1	33	26
25	6.29	17	5	5	11	1	32	23
10	7.82	23	4	3	18	1	37	30
23	8.76	22	11	4	16	1	15	18
17	7.50	39	27	13	26	4	31	23
17	7.50	40	27	13	26	4	31	23
24	8.22	27	13	5	20	1	25	16
24	8.22	27	13	5	20	1	25	16
19	9.39	16	7	1	12	1	8	16
19	9.39	16	7	1	12	1	8	16
13	7.96	12	2	0	11	2	1	16
13	7.96	12	2	0	11	2	1	16
20	9.75	13	5	1	11	1	29	17
13	9.27	12	7	5	7	5	21	21
12	9.34	16	12	8	8	9	36	22
26	9.41	14	8	1	11	1	46	16
26	9.40	15	8	1	12	1	47	16
16	10.19	12	2	0	12	0	17	17
16	10.19	12	2	0	12	0	17	17

- % of Households Buying: percentage of all households that purchased the category at least once during the period.
- Volume per Purchase: average volume purchased on a single purchase occasion in pounds.
- Purchases per Buyer: average number of times the item was purchased by each buyer.
- Purchase Cycle: average interpurchase time in days between purchases of the item.
- Share of Category Requirements: total proportion of category volume that the item represents among its buyers (a measure of brand loyalty).
- Price per Volume: average price paid per equivalent volume (not necessarily the price per unit or package).

- Any Trade Deal: percentage of volume purchased using an advertising feature (newspaper), in-store display, shelf price reduction, store coupon, manufacturer coupon, or a combination of these.
- Average Percent Off on Price Deals: the average percentage price reduction the consumer obtained when a price deal is used.

The notable features about Figure 12.2 are the percentages of purchases made with some kinds of promotion. Overall (the top row of the figure), 31 percent of all coffee purchases were made with some shelf price reduction, 18 percent used a manufacturer coupon, and the average price reduction was 24 percent. Interestingly, a whopping 62 percent of purchases of Tasters Choice flavored instant coffees were made with a coupon. Also, Maxwell House used trade deals and coupons much more than Folgers in the caffeinated subcategory; 27 percent of Maxwell House purchases were made using some kind of trade deal, and 25 percent were made using a coupon. Promotion competes with advertising for budget; it also provides a different approach to influencing sales. In the case of advertising, the basic approach is to create or increase a desire on the part of the customer for the product itself. In contrast, most promotions implicitly assume the level of desire for the product is fixed and try to "close the deal" by providing incentives to purchase. This is, of course, an oversimplification. A "get them while supplies last" ad focuses on immediate response, and promotions involving free samples aim at generating repeat business. Nonetheless, promotions, many of which involve temporary price reductions, are generally a form of marketing effort that is more aggressive and oriented toward immediate results. In reality, one of the few ways product managers can obtain a short-run increase in sales or market share is to use sales promotion, i.e. cut price.

Figure 12.3 shows a simplified channel structure in which the manufacturer sells to a channel customer (here a retailer), which in turn sells to the final customer (the consumer) as well as directly to the final customer. In this situation, promotion falls into three main categories:

1. Final customer promotion.
2. Manufacturer promotion to the channels/trade promotion.
3. Channel-originated promotion/retailer promotion.

FIGURE 12.3 **Simplified Channel and Promotion Structure**

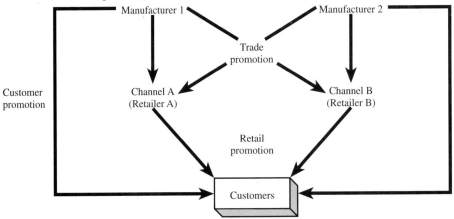

Final customer promotion comes directly to the customer from the manufacturer. Trade promotion, in contrast, is directed at intermediate channels of distribution in an attempt both to get them to buy more of a product and to commit their own efforts (e.g., sales force) to "pushing" the product through the next channel and ultimately to the final customer. Channel-originated promotions are run by the channel itself to either the next channel in the distribution chain or to final customers.

For consumer packaged goods sold through supermarkets, retailer promotions are an especially visible form of promotion. Displays, feature advertising, and price deals (price cuts, free merchandise, retailer-issued coupons) all affect sales and profits and either augment or detract from manufacturers' direct customer promotions. In general, the purpose of channel promotions is to increase sales of all products to the customer. Hence, a promotion of Pepsi by a retail store may be designed to increase store traffic and total sales or profits, not to increase Pepsi sales alone (e.g., in Figure 12.3, promotion by retailer A is designed to increase store sales and profits, typically at the expense of retailer B). However, a manufacturer may have limited (or no) control over retail promotions; in fact, in the United States, retailers of consumer goods now have considerable control over manufacturers' trade promotions. Therefore, this chapter focuses on promotions, both direct and trade, that originate with the manufacturer.

Promotion objectives and programs may be either *offensive* or *defensive.* Offensive promotions attempt to gain an advantage through exclusivity: being the only company to offer a particular promotion or level of promotional support. In most markets, however, competitors quickly match (provide defensive) promotions (e.g., airline frequent flyer programs). On top of that, in some areas, notably consumer packaged goods, the channels (e.g., Wal-Mart) have become sufficiently powerful to both demand and schedule promotions. The result is that companies, including those with household brand names and dominant market shares, are promoting due more to a perceived necessity to match competition and satisfy the channels than to a conviction that promotions benefit the manufacturer.

Although many of the examples and references in this chapter relate to consumer products, services and industrial products use sales promotional devices extensively. Short-term price discounts to customers are very common in industrial markets. In addition, farm equipment and office products manufacturers, for example, frequently target channel members for promotions, which may or may not be passed on to the customers.

As in the previous chapter, the goal here is to decide on the best combination of final customer and trade promotions. Operationally, this means producing Figures 12.16, 12.17, and 12.18 to provide budget and time schedules for promotions.

PROMOTION OBJECTIVES

Final Customer Promotions

As noted earlier, final customer promotion, at least for existing or mature products, typically takes a short-run view. Even when the focus is long run, such as to generate trial, the operational objective of most promotion is to generate immediate response in the form of sales. The possible advertising objectives in Figure 11.7 range from generating awareness to increasing product understanding to improving attitude toward purchase. In principle, promotion can be directed toward any of these goals as well as to those shown in Figure 12.4.

For example, if awareness is a problem, a company can run a promotion such as a game or sweepstakes designed to increase awareness of a product rather than to increase

FIGURE 12.4 Customer Promotion Objectives

Objective	Typical Programs
I. Long-run (relationship building)	
A. Awareness enhancement	Sweepstakes, contests, tie-ins
B. Image enhancement	Sponsorships
II. Short-run (transactional)	
A. Current customers	
1. Buy more	Volume discount/special "value" packages
2. Be more loyal	"In pak" coupons, premiums, frequent buyer programs
3. Buy now	Rebates, coupons
B. Occasional customers (deal prone; brand switchers)	
Capture next purchase	Coupons, displays, rebates
C. Noncustomers	
Trial	Trial sizes, sampling

immediate sales. For example, Nike used a 3-on-3 soccer tournament to build interest in its line of soccer shoes. Similarly, a company can run a tie-in promotion (e.g., giving a certain percentage of sales revenues to a worthy cause) that may, in addition to raising current sales, have a residual positive impact on brand image. Such relationship-building sponsorships, however, account for only a small percentage of the promotion dollar.

By far the most common objective of a consumer promotion is to generate more transactions (sales) in a short period of time. The objective is usually stated in specific terms, such as "to increase sales 20 percent in the March–April time period." This statement should be qualified in two ways. First, we need to specify from what level sales should increase. The easiest benchmark is last year or last period; the more difficult measure, but one from which the true success of the program should be gauged, is what sales would be, absent the promotion. Later in the chapter we address building baselines against which to evaluate promotion. Second, we must select the target customer and define desired behavior. Basically, you can focus on getting current customers to buy more (customer expansion), capturing occasional but not loyal customers (customer retention), or generating sales from current noncustomers (customer acquisition). Many promotions focus on current customers, attempting to get them to buy more through a volume discount, to be more loyal (using coupons or frequent user programs), or to accelerate their purchases and buy sooner (rebate-type promotions). Attracting occasional customers, typically through temporary price cuts such as coupons and rebates, is effective but also expensive. This not only produces lower margins on the sales to occasional customers but may also lower margins on sales that would have been made in the absence of the promotion to either occasional or regular customers. Hence, a major concern is how to target promotions to competitors' customers alone. Promotions to noncustomers are generally used when a product is new (or "new and improved") to generate trial. In a sense, targeting noncustomers implies a long-run relationship-building objective. In addition to their sales-generating role, selectively distributed promotions provide a legal means of price discrimination. Special airline fares requiring Saturday night stayovers are designed to lure pleasure travelers with the lower fares and exclude business travelers, who then pay a higher fare. Special coupons may act as price discriminators as much as sales promoters, which we discuss further later in the

FIGURE 12.5 Trade Promotion Objectives

Objective	Typical Programs
Transactional: increase stocking levels	Volume allowances
	Financing terms
	Discount/price cuts
	Slotting allowances
Transactional: increase sales efforts	Advertising allowances
	Display allowances
	Premiums
	Contests
	Sales force incentives (not all dealers allow these)
Relationship building	Free goods

chapter. Similarly, different sale prices can be offered to target groups in catalogs (or individuals via the Internet) based on their past purchasing behavior.[1]

Trade Promotions

Trade promotions objectives fall into three main categories (Figure 12.5). The first category focuses on getting the trade to buy or stock the product in greater quantities by offering various financial incentives. One version of this which aligns both parties' objectives is to pay the channel based on final customer sales, measured by scanner data (Drèze and Bell, 2003). The second category tries to increase the level of trade support given to the product by means other than increasing their inventories. A variety of allowances and direct incentives relate to this task. The final set of objectives involves relationship building. One example of relationship building is to give extra product to a channel with no explicit strings attached.

Required Promotion

While it sounds strange, lots of promotion is actually required (demanded) by channel members (Bloom, Gundlach, and Cannon, 2000). That is, it is essentially a fixed cost of doing business more than a decision variable. For example, many retailers charge a fee for each shelf space "slot," which can run up to $25,000 per item per retail chain for food products (Schoenberger, 2000). Similarly a catalog company often charges for including a product in its catalog. Similarly volume discounts are as much demanded by powerful channel members as initiated by manufacturers. In other words, many promotions are not optional (i.e., not really decision variables for the product manager).

An interesting study examined the reasons for conducting trade and consumer promotions (Narasimhan, 1990) of 65 brand managers. The results in Figure 12.6 show that introduction of a new product was, not surprisingly, the most important reason, and neither reducing inventories nor collecting market research information was at all important.

---

[1] Interestingly, this ability to price discriminate though direct-mail pieces such as catalogs is being challenged. In 1996, several recipients of Victoria's Secret catalogs noticed they were being offered different discounts on merchandise and filed a lawsuit. (At the time, legal experts opined that as long as Victoria's Secret was not discriminating on the basis of sex, race, and other groups protected by U.S. law, the case had little substance.) Targeted promotions in general can lead to negative reactions from those who were not targeted (Feinberg, Krishna, and Zhang, 2002).

FIGURE 12.6 Survey Results: Why Trade and Consumer Promotion Are Used

Importance Ratings: Trade Promotions*		
Variable	**Mean (standard deviation)**	**Rank**
1. Introducing a new product	8.16 (2.43)	1
2. Getting more retailer push	7.92 (1.98)	2
3. Achieving sales/contribution targets	7.58 (2.08)	3
4. Maintaining shelf space	6.98 (2.50)	4
5. Meeting competition	6.78 (2.23)	5
6. Increasing consumer usage rate	6.53 (2.65)	6
7. Motivating the sales force	6.02 (2.21)	7
8. Reducing inventory	3.56 (2.43)	8

Importance Ratings: Consumer Promotions†		
Variable	**Mean (standard deviation)**	**Rank**
1. Introducing a new product	8.86 (1.83)	1
2. Increasing sales	8.12 (2.03)	2
3. Inducing brand switching	8.02 (1.68)	3
4. Increasing consumer usage rate	6.68 (2.72)	4
5. Achieving sales/contribution targets	6.51 (2.39)	5
6. Lower price to more price-sensitive consumers	6.50 (2.31)	6
7. Retaining loyal consumers	6.29 (2.34)	7
8. Meeting competition	6.28 (2.25)	8
9. Expanding category volume	4.60 (2.54)	9
10. Increasing total shelf space	4.35 (2.70)	10
11. Conducting marketing research	2.75 (1.98)	11

*$N = 65$ †$N = 65$

Source: Chakravarti Narasimhan, "Managerial Perspectives on Trade and Consumer Promotions," *Marketing Letters* 1 (November 1990), p. 241.

An important type of trade promotion involves participating in trade shows. One major purpose of trade shows is to entice current and potential channel members to carry a product. Trade shows are a multi-billion-dollar business in their own right. Participants have multiple objectives, including image enhancement, new product introduction (see Figure 12.7), and competitor monitoring.

FIGURE 12.7 Purposes of Trade Show Participation

	Mean Importance
Enhancing corporate image	5.32
Introducing new products	5.14
Identifying new prospects	5.08
Getting competitor information	4.94
Servicing current customers	4.69
Enhancing corporate morale	3.75
Selling at the show	2.79
New-product testing	2.17

Source: Roger A. Kerin and William L. Cron, "Assessing Trade Show Functions and Performance: An Exploratory Study," *Journal of Marketing* 51 (July 1987), pp. 87–94.

PROMOTION BUDGETING

Overview

Deciding on a promotion budget generally follows the same approaches discussed for setting advertising budgets (see Chapter 11). Again, the major distinction is between analytical methods (e.g., objective and task, optimization) and convenient rules of thumb (e.g., percentage of sales, competitive parity). However, two questions must be considered: (1) How much money should be spent on the total advertising and promotion budget, and (2) given the answer to the first question, how much should be spent on promotion?

The Total Advertising and Promotion Budget

Seven factors have been found to affect the total budget for advertising and sales promotion for manufactured products (Farris and Buzzell, 1979). Companies spend more on advertising and promotion relative to sales when

1. The product is relatively standardized (as opposed to when the product is produced or supplied to order).
2. There are many end users.
3. The typical purchase amount is small.
4. Sales are made through channel intermediaries rather than directly to end users.
5. The product is premium priced.
6. The product has a high contribution margin.
7. The product or service has a small market share.

Most of these conditions, mainly 1 through 4, are consistent with the data shown in Figure 11.3, which indicate that managers of consumer products and services spend much more money on advertising and promotion than do their counterparts managing business-to-business products and services.

Allocating Money between Advertising and Promotion

Several factors affect this allocation decision. First, the total amount of resources (budget) available has a major impact. If the marketing budget is small, extensive media advertising is usually not worthwhile unless the target market is local and can be reached by media such as radio and newspapers, because advertising usually needs a minimum or threshold amount to have any impact. Beneath the threshold value, the money is virtually wasted. In such cases, spending the budget on sales promotion produces a greater impact than advertising.

Second, customer factors affect allocation decisions. One relevant aspect of customer behavior is the degree of brand loyalty. Promotion money spent on a product or service exhibiting high levels of loyalty primarily rewards existing customers. Although this may be what the product manager wants (i.e., to increase customer retention), it may not be the best way to spend money. If customers are not very loyal, there may be an opportunity to attract brand switchers with promotions. It is also possible, however, that the product manager has created nonloyal customers through frequent, price-based promotions, and thus all that happens is a temporary swapping of customers.

A second relevant aspect of consumer behavior is the type of decision required of them. If the product is complex and therefore requires a fair amount of information processing, more dollars should generally be spent on advertising because it is a better communications device. Most sales promotion dollars are spent on product categories in which decision making is routine and involves little processing of information about the product.

The third factor affecting allocation decisions is whether advertising and promotion dollars highlight the unique *consumer franchise building* (CFB) aspects of the product (Prentice, 1977). CFB activities are those that build brand equity, including advertising, sampling, couponing, and product demonstrations. Non-CFB activities focus on price alone and include trade promotions, short-term price deals, and refunds. This suggests that the product manager track the following ratio:

$$\text{CFB ratio} = \text{CFB \$}/(\text{CFB \$} + \text{non-CFB \$})$$

One rule of thumb is that the CFB ratio should stay above 50 to 55 percent for a brand to remain healthy.

FINAL CUSTOMER PROMOTIONS

Deciding on which promotion elements to employ in many ways parallels the media selection process in advertising. Although we discuss promotion evaluation later in this chapter, basically the product manager should attempt to calculate the return (i.e., incremental sales and profits) from various options and then select those with the biggest "bang for the buck."

This section briefly describes several types of customer promotions. The number of different promotions is limited only by the promoter's imagination. Nonetheless, it is possible to classify most customer promotions into five main categories (see Figure 12.8).

Product-Based Promotions

One obvious category of promotions is to give away the product itself. Extra-volume packages are common in consumer products (e.g., "get a sixth candy bar free," "28 percent more . . ."). Even more dramatic are completely free products. One year Ford reportedly placed certificates good for one free month's use of a car under chairs at business meetings; of those who used the certificate, 25 percent ended up buying the car. In 1992, Pepsi planned to ship 1 million cases of Diet Pepsi to confirmed Diet Coke drinkers. Coupons for free goods show up in the mail, on or in packages of the good, or in media vehicles (e.g., newspapers, magazines). Computer hardware and software companies often give free copies of their products to select customers as "beta" test sites to help get any bugs out and stimulate (hopefully favorable) early word of mouth. Who hasn't received a disk and offer of hours of free Internet use from AOL? Or free calling minutes to switch from AT&T to Verizon or one of the Baby Bells? It is not surprising that the Internet has been filled with promotions at sites like *yourfreestuff.com.*

Sampling has the obvious benefit of stimulating product trial because it gives the customer the opportunity to try the product for free. However, it has some serious shortcomings. First, it can be very expensive. Second, it may not target the right potential customers; people who distribute free samples in supermarkets or on street corners are

FIGURE 12.8 Final Customer Promotions

I. Product based
   A. Additional volume/bonus pack
   B. Samples
      1. Central location
      2. Direct (e.g., mail)
      3. Attachment (in-/on-pack coupons)
      4. Media placed (clip-and-send coupons)
II. Price based
   A. Sale price
   B. Coupons
      1. Central location (e.g., in-store)
      2. Direct (mail)
      3. Attachment (in-/on-pack)
      4. In media (e.g., websites)
   C. Refunds/rebates
   D. Financing terms
   E. Frequent users
III. Premiums
IV. Place-based promotions (physical displays; Internet site based)
V. Games (sweepstakes, contests)

not very discriminating about to whom they give the product. (The Gatorade and Power Bars consumed at the conclusion of road races rarely go to nonusers.) This is a particular problem for tobacco companies because trial packs could be given illegally to teenagers under 18 years old.

Price-Based Promotions

Another obvious type of promotion involves price. The use of sale prices is understated if we describe them as being "widespread." As Figure 12.2 shows, 31 percent of the purchases in the coffee category in 1994 were accompanied by a shelf price reduction. Unfortunately, most short-term price reductions are not narrowly targeted because all buyers, including extremely brand-loyal ones, have access to in-store price reductions.

Many targeted price reductions that require at least some effort on the part of the consumer involve coupons. Coupons are one of the very few ways to legally price discriminate, that is, charge different prices to different people. Billions of coupons are delivered each year, many from Wednesday editions of local newspapers (P&G sponsors its own set of coupons in Sunday papers), and others from mass mailings such as Carol Wright. The use of attachment coupons (either in or on the package of a good) allows a more focused price cut, though outright theft and trading of coupons are common. One interesting use of coupons is by Quaker Oats, which provided coupons for its products to its own shareholders. Similarly IBM makes special offers to its shareholders. The Internet has numerous examples of price promotions such as Netcentives and MyPoints.

As just noted, one advantage of coupons is that they can be delivered by mail, at the cash register, or through the Internet to carefully targeted audiences. In addition, because they normally have to be cut out and physically carried to the point of transaction, coupons require more commitment to purchase the product, and thus may engender more repeat purchases. They are also flexible because they can be designated for larger package sizes, a new flavor extension, and the like. However, the redemption rates are appallingly low, often around 2 percent, and discounts given for the wrong brands at checkouts are a significant (misredemption) problem. Other price-based consumer promotions are also options. Refunds and rebates are common and effective, though the long-run effects may be negative. For example, car rebates may speed up sales volume initially but lead to lower profits and lower sales immediately after the rebates end and have in the long run mainly succeeded in creating a customer expectation of large discounts. Frequent-user programs such as those offered by airlines, supermarkets, hair salons, restaurants, and sporting goods stores are useful for encouraging brand loyalty and allow consumers to buy products at a discount (or get them for free) after they have accumulated a sufficient number of "points." Interestingly, the way a deal is presented can have a substantial effect on its impact in unexpected ways. For example, restrictions such as "limit three per customer" can increase sales (Inman, Peter, and Raghubir, 1997).

Other Customer Promotions

In addition to product- and price-based promotions, other elements of the marketing mix can be used to meet company objectives. Point-of-purchase displays ("place" based) are common; notice the checkout and end-of-aisle displays at any supermarket. The L'eggs pantyhose display trees were an effective example of the power of display (and the source of plastic eggs to play with for a generation of children). One popular form of place-based promotion is expositions at which manufacturers congregate to display and sell their wares, such as annual car and boat shows, ski expositions, and computer expos. Another inducement to purchase is free service (e.g., free oil changes for one year). In addition, various premiums have proven effective. The use of free glasses or packaging to promote beverage sales (e.g., Coke's reuse of its classic glass bottle) is widespread. It is amazing how many cereal boxes have been bought for the "prize" inside or how many stupid acts have been performed for trinkets, including a large number by otherwise intelligent people who recognize how they are being manipulated. Games, sweepstakes, and contests, both those that require proof of purchase and those that are open to the general public, such as Publishers' Clearing House Sweepstakes, are other types of promotions. One classic example was *Scientific American*'s contest that gave prizes for the paper airplane that flew the farthest and longest. Not only did the contest attract both top engineers and "normal" people, it also generated substantial publicity for the magazine itself. Premiums are big business in their own right, as evidenced by the Annual Premium Incentive Show held at the massive Javits Convention Center in New York each spring.

Summary

One interesting study of many consumer packaged goods categories (Fader and Lodish, 1990) found that overall, 27.1 percent of volume was purchased on deal. Not surprisingly, the use of newspaper features, in-store displays, price cuts, and store coupons were all highly correlated, ranging from .39 (display, store coupon) to .92 (feature, price cut), with manufacturer's coupons slightly negatively correlated to the other four variables ($-.04$ to $-.07$).

The study also grouped 331 grocery product categories into four clusters based on the percentage of volume purchased on various deals (see Figure 12.9). The first cluster

FIGURE 12.9 Dealing Patterns in Grocery Products

	Cluster				Overall
	1 (N = 80)	2 (28)	3 (77)	4 (146)	N = 331
Features	16.8	21.6	7.7	5.6	13.9%
Display	8.4	26.4	7.1	3.4	11.0
Manufacturer coupon	7.3	6.7	26.1	4.2	9.7
Store coupon	1.3	1.9	0.5	0.3	1.1
Price cut	20.3	25.1	10.9	7.9	17.9
Penetration	58.1	70.9	22.6	15.1	
Purchase cycle (days)	65.9	61.4	83.4	97.9	
Purchase/household	5.6	7.6	3.2	1.9	
Private label share	16.9	17.8	9.5	7.6	
Price	1.9	10.0	2.0	2.0	

Source: Peter S. Fader and Leonard M. Lodish, "A Cross-Category Analysis of Category Structure and Promotional Activity for Grocery Products," *Journal of Marketing* 54, pp. 52–65.

contained product categories dominated by features and price cuts. This cluster was the second highest in purchase frequency and private label share. The second cluster was highest in terms of purchase frequency, private label share, and all forms of store promotion. The third cluster was dominated by manufacturer couponing. The final cluster was the most infrequently purchased and least promoted. This suggests that different types of promotions may be appropriate in different situations. By matching a product category with one of the clusters, a product manager can estimate the level and type of promotion necessary to achieve competitive parity.

TRADE PROMOTIONS

Trade promotions are directed not to the final customer but to the channels through which the goods are sold. Like consumer promotions, they can be broken into five categories (Figure 12.10).

Product-based promotions include free goods and generous returns policies. Returns policies allow the channel to return unsold merchandise for a full or partial refund, reducing the risk of carrying the product. Price deals include various volume discounts and allowances, as well as financing terms such as a long period of time before payment is due or below-market interest rates.

Place-based allowances are especially important for consumer packaged goods. Slotting allowances, which are basically payments for placing a product on the shelf, have become increasingly important as power has shifted from manufacturers to retailers. These fees charged to manufacturers have had a negative effect on the number of competitors in many product categories and have been particularly hard on small companies, for which the fees can become prohibitive. Display allowances compensate retailers for prominent display of goods. Other promotions involve reducing inventory and transportation costs by either warehousing the goods for the channel (as in just-in-time inventory) or paying all or part of delivery charges. Providing selling assistance is also common. In addition to selling aids (brochures, etc.), companies often provide cooperative advertising, sharing the channel's advertising expense. One problem with this approach is the possibility of

FIGURE 12.10 Trade Promotions

I. Product based
   A. Free goods
   B. Consignment/returns policy
II. Price based
   A. Buying allowances
   B. Financial terms
III. Place based
   A. Slotting allowances
   B. Display allowances
   C. Warehousing/delivery assistance
IV. Advertising and promotion based
   A. Co-op advertising
   B. Selling aids
   C. Co-op selling
V. Sales based
   A. Bonuses and incentives
   B. Contests and prizes

fraudulent charges, so monitoring becomes an advisable part of such arrangements. Manufacturers can also provide cooperative selling, in which their sales forces back up or refer leads to the channel's sales force. Probably the most extensive form of this involves category management, where one manufacturer effectively manages the category (their brand and competitors) for the retailer as, for example, P&G and Colgate have done.

Finally, there are sales-based incentives, for example, bonuses to the company for meeting or exceeding a quota. Sales incentives can also take the more controversial (and in some cases forbidden) form of direct prizes, bonuses, and the like, to the channel's own sales force.

EVALUATING CUSTOMER PROMOTIONS

Overview

The easiest way to evaluate customer promotions is to simply look at incremental results (sales, share, profits) during the period of promotion. This method provides a useful starting point, but may lead to an overestimate of the benefit of promotion because it ignores both where the sales come from and the long-term consequences of promotion.

As with evaluating advertising effects, a standard approach to measuring the impact of a sales promotion is tracking. Figure 12.11 shows a typical tracking study with point A on the horizontal axis representing the time when the promotion—say, a price reduction—is given to end customers. The effects of a sales promotion often show up quickly.

Unfortunately, product managers tend to look at the shaded area above point A in Figure 12.11 as a measure of the impact of the promotion. This kind of simplistic analysis has many limitations:

> The gain could be offset by the crosshatched "dip" at point B, representing the possibility that consumers have increased their inventories at home, thus negating the need to rebuy soon.

FIGURE 12.11 **Evaluating Sales Promotions: Tracking Studies**

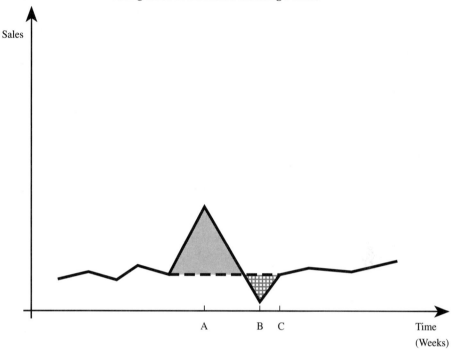

The gain must be evaluated relative to a base amount: the amount of sales that would have been generated had the promotion not run. The baseline is difficult to calculate because it can change depending on time of year, competitive conditions, and so on. Further, past promotions decrease the baseline (Kopalle, Mela, and Marsh, 1999).

The analysis does not account for other factors in the marketplace, including actions by both the product in question (e.g., an advertising change) and the competition.

Product managers must carefully examine point C in Figure 12.11, the point at which sales seem to return to "normal"; it could be higher than the base for some period of time, representing a positive long-run effect (see further discussion below).

If products have several promotions running simultaneously, it is difficult to separate the effects of one promotion from another.

Thus, although it appears to be easy to measure the effect on sales or share from a sales promotion, it is actually complicated.

An appropriate approach, of course, is to evaluate the promotion against its objectives (Figures 12.4 and 12.5). A price promotion that increases sales 30 percent but fails to attract a substantial number of new customers may be a failure because it basically gave a discount to current customers who may have simply stocked up, thus depressing future sales. The following section provides a more extensive approach for evaluating the sales impact of promotion.

Short-Run Evaluation

Sales increases from promotions may be generated by accelerating purchasing by loyal buyers. Many coupon redeemers, for example, may be customers who would have bought the product anyway and simply used the coupon as "found money" or, at best, bought the product somewhat sooner than they would have in the absence of a promotion.

Basically, a coupon can have several incremental impacts (Neslin and Shoemaker, 1983):

1. *Accelerated regular purchases*—that is, regular buyers of the brand simply buy sooner.
2. *Accelerated captured purchases*—purchasers who neither would have bought at the time nor bought the promoted brand but are persuaded to do both by the promotion.
3. *Unaccelerated regular purchases*—regular buyers who use the coupon as a "bonus" price cut.
4. *Unaccelerated captured purchases*—purchasers of other brands who switch to the promoted brand because of the promotion.

Obviously, categories 2 and 4 are pluses and category 1 also represents incremental sales, albeit borrowed ones. Category 3 is basically a negative, with the amount of the coupon (plus redemption costs) coming out of revenues. Category 1 is potentially but not necessarily negative. If subsequent sales are depressed as a result of increased inventory, there is no benefit (except a slight time value of money advantage) and a clear cost (the coupon value). Of course, one possible benefit of promotion is that "captured" buyers will remain loyal and repeat purchase the promoted brand on a subsequent purchase occasion (i.e., the promotion leads to customer acquisition). However, evidence suggests that sales typically soon return to normal and no permanent effect occurs (Pauwels, Hanssens, and Siddarth, 2002; Nijs, Dekimpe, Steenkanp, and Hanssens, 2001). It is also possible that promotion increases category purchase quantity, either with or without depressing future purchase quantity. Interestingly, considerable evidence suggests that increased quantity due to promotion is neither preceded nor followed by decreased quantity purchased, which is the opposite of the normally expected trough effect shown in Figure 12.11 (Neslin and Stone, 1996). However, a recent study found a dip of between 4 and 25 percent for tuna and toilet tissue, two readily stockpileable items (van Heerde, Leeflang, and Wittink, 2000).

To assess the value of a promotion, then, it is necessary to estimate both the source of additional sales (accelerated or not, increased quantity or not, loyal buyers or non-regular/captured buyers) and its overall magnitude. In addition, the profit consequences of each need to be considered. Figure 12.12 provides a framework for such an evaluation.

In Figure 12.12, the promotion decision appears to be nontrivial, as it should. Of course, some of the complication disappears if you are willing to make certain assumptions (e.g., that no share changes occur). On the other hand, this analysis does not explicitly include competitor reactions (e.g., matching promotional deals in either the promotion period or a subsequent period) or the impact of promotion on brand equity (e.g., loyal buyers could perceive their brand to be cheapened by promotion and hence become less loyal). Second, for many segments, generally available promotions hurt long-run profits. This is especially true of loyal segments 1 and 3. In fact, Figure 12.12

FIGURE 12.12 Profit Impact of Customer Promotion

Buyer Segment	Category Quantity		Sales Impact	
	Promotion Period	Subsequent Period	Promotion Period	Subsequent Period
1. Loyal	No change	No change	0	0
2. Loyal	Increase	No change	ΔQ_p	0
3. Loyal	Increase	Decrease	ΔQ_p	ΔQ_s
4. Switchers	No change	No change	$\Delta M_p Q$	$\Delta M_s Q$
5. Switchers	Increase	No change	$\Delta M_p Q + (M + \Delta M_p)\Delta Q_p$	$\Delta M_s Q$
6. Switchers	Increase	Decrease	$\Delta M_p Q + (M + \Delta M_p)\Delta Q_p$	$(M + \Delta M_s)\Delta Q_s + \Delta M_s Q$
7. Nonbuyers of category	No change	No change	0	0
8. Nonbuyers of category	Increase	No change (return to 0 consumption)	$\Delta M_p \Delta Q_p$	0
9. Nonbuyers of category	Increase	Increase (continue to purchase)	$\Delta M_p \Delta Q_p$	$\Delta M_s \Delta Q_s$

Profit Impact

Promotion Period	Subsequent Period
1. $-QDR$	0
2. $-QDR + \Delta Q_p(P - C - DR)$	0
3. $-QDR + \Delta Q_p(P - C - DR)$	$\Delta Q_s(P - C)$
4. $-MQDR + \Delta M_p Q(P - C - DR)$	$\Delta M_s Q(P - C)$
5. $-MQDR + (\Delta M_p Q + \Delta M_p\Delta Q_p + M\Delta Q_p)(P - C - DR)$	$\Delta M_s Q(P - C)$
6. $-MQDR + (\Delta M_p Q + \Delta M_p\Delta Q_p + M\Delta Q_p)(P - C - DR)$	$(M\Delta Q_s + \Delta M_s Q + \Delta M_s\Delta Q_s(P - C)$
7. 0	0
8. $\Delta M_p\Delta Q_p(P - C - DR)$	0
9. $\Delta M_p\Delta Q_p(P - C - DR)$	$\Delta M_s\Delta Q_s(P - C)$

Net Profit* Impact per Segment Member	Total Impact: Segment Size	Size × Profit Impact
1. $-QDR$	N_1	
2. $-(Q + \Delta Q_p)DR + \Delta Q_p(P - C)$	N_2	
3. $-(Q + \Delta Q_p)DR$	N_3	
4. $-(M + \Delta M_p)(QDR + \Delta M_p Q(P - C) + \Delta M_s Q(P - C)$	N_4	
5. $-(M + \Delta M_p)(Q + \Delta Q_p)DR + (\Delta M_p Q + \Delta M_p\Delta Q_p + M\Delta Q_p(P - C)$ $+ \Delta M_s Q(P - C)$	N_5	
6. $-(M + \Delta M_p)(Q + \Delta Q_p)DR + (\Delta M_p Q + \Delta M_p\Delta Q_p + s\,M_p\Delta Q_p)$ $(P - C) + (\Delta M_s Q + \Delta M_s\Delta Q_s + M_s\Delta Q_s(P - C)$	N_6	
7. 0	N_7	
8. $\Delta M_p\Delta Q_p(P - C - DR)$	N_8	
9. $(\Delta M_p\Delta Q_p + \Delta M_s\Delta Q_s(P - C) - \Delta M_p\Delta Q_p DR$	N_9	

Q = Typical purchase quantity P = Price C = Variable cost
D = Cost of promotion (i.e., face value of coupon plus redemption cost)
R = Redemption rate of the promotion for those who buy the brand
ΔQ_p, ΔQ_s = change in quantity due to promotion in the promotion and subsequent period
M = typical share among switchers (M = 0 for nonbuyers. 1 for loyals)
ΔM_p, ΔM_s = change in share due to promotion in the promotion and subsequent periods
*This means members forward buy, stockpiling the good when it is on promotion. Since nonbuyers can't go below their current 0 level of sales, stockpiling is not considered for segments 7–9.

tediously but correctly suggests that unless segments 8 and 9 and, under some circumstances, 2, 4, 5, and 6 are large, promotions hurt profits. Put differently, if promotions primarily cannibalize existing sales, they harm profits. Because segments 8 and 9 tend to be small in mature markets, this suggests that promotions need to capture a large number of switchers to make up for lost profits due to deal redemption by current customers. Notice that some promotions have lower redemption rates than others, for example, freestanding insert coupons (low) versus on-pack or register price discounts (high), which lessens their negative impact on profit margins but at the same time decreases their impact on quantity. The main point here, then, is that it is possible to estimate the impact of a promotion through systematic analysis and that the results of such analysis are often quite sobering. Not surprisingly, small-share brands may benefit more from promotions than large-share brands, mainly because promotions cannibalize fewer sales to regular customers, although evidence suggests their promotions have less impact.

In addition to the direct effects of manufacturer promotions on customers, the promotion has an indirect impact on channel (retailer) behavior. For example, retailers may increase stocking of the good or run their own promotions in conjunction with the manufacturer. Inasmuch as these generate benefits beyond immediate customer sales, they need to be considered as well.

Notice that a major factor affecting the profitability of promotions is whether or not a good is easily stockpiled. Perishable goods and services (e.g., seats on an airplane) cannot be stockpiled; paper towels can be. Hence, paper towel promotions tend to result in stockpiling and, if competitors match the promotion, lead to lower profits. In contrast, promotions on underused services or perishable goods may produce increased profits.

Long-Run Concerns

Promotion also has two important long-run impacts. First is the impact of promotion on customer perceptions of the brand. Brands bought on promotion may be seen as lower in quality (i.e., "If they were really good, they wouldn't have to put them on sale") and, in the extreme, something it makes sense to buy only on deal. Recent evidence has documented a negative long-run impact of promotions (Mela, Gupta, and Lehmann, 1997). A recent study suggests when long-run negative impacts are considered, the total impact of a promotion is positive but only one-third its short-run (apparent) impact (Jedidi, Mela, and Gupta, 1999). Moreover, as mentioned in Chapter 10, customers may anticipate promotions and delay purchase until a deal occurs. This is particularly a problem when the deals are run at regular intervals, such as January white sales on linens and bedding. However, delaying purchases has also been a problem when the deals were frequent but irregular; for example, auto rebates and airline fare wars tend to cause discretionary buyers to wait until a better deal comes along. After a promotion ends, consumers may view the return to normal prices as a price increase and suffer "sticker shock."

Competitive Reaction

There is also concern about the impact of promotions on competitors. Most markets are oligopolies, and hence decisions need to take likely competitive reactions into account. Not surprisingly, competitors often match promotions quickly, thus negating many of the possible benefits while increasing costs. A promotion spiral can ensue with great benefit to customers and harm to companies' profits. One classic example of this occurred at the retail level when Miracle Whip was promoted at well below its cost to the retailer ($1.09 versus $1.60) after a series of reactions to competitors' promotions.

Obviously then, there is a question of whether it is in a company's best interest to engage in heavy promotion spending. Promotion spending is another example of the decision problem referred to as the "prisoner's dilemma." In the prisoner's dilemma, two criminals are apprehended and questioned separately, with no communication between them. Both are separately told that the law will go easier on them if they confess, which is true. They are not told, however, that the evidence is mainly circumstantial and hence if neither confesses, they may get off free or at most face a reduced charge. The dilemma is that each prisoner is always better off by confessing regardless of what the other prisoner does, but both are collectively better off if neither confesses.

The "promotion dilemma" can be similar. If category sales are fixed—that is, marketing expenditures do not increase primary demand and dropping expenditures do not cause them to decrease to the benefit of other product categories—and no objectives exist to increase market share, all companies are better off at a low level of expenditure, with the difference between a high and a low level being increased profits. Short of collusion (which is illegal in the United States), however, cooperating is risky. In fact, playing a "martyr" strategy (always keeping expenditures low) turns out to be a strategy that performs poorly. Rather, a so-called provocable strategy that retaliates against competitors with high promotion expenditures has often proven most effective in simulated markets.

Findings about Promotion Effects

A comprehensive review of the impact of sales promotion is given by Neslin (2002). We know consumers use coupons extensively. Further, some accelerate purchases and stockpile goods in response to promotions. Overall, many different reactions to promotions have been identified (Currim and Schneider, 1991). One particularly interesting issue concerning promotions is their impact on both a brand's equity (overall evaluation) and its reservation price, that is, the most a consumer is willing to pay for it.

Given the prevalence of scanner data for supermarket and drugstore products, it is not surprising that a large number of models have been developed to use them to assess the impact of marketing variables such as promotion or assuming primary demand (market size) is constant on share. The models generally assess the value of each brand to an individual customer as a function of several components (Guadagni and Little, 1983):

1. The inherent value of a brand-size combination (e.g., Ragu 16 ounces plain spaghetti sauce). This is either treated holistically (with a dummy variable and a unique value for each brand) or further decomposed into product attributes (plain, chunky, etc.).
2. The nonproduct marketing mix elements: price, promotion, the amount of the promotion, and advertising.
3. Carryover effects of past purchases.
4. Customer loyalty or inertia.

Mathematically, this becomes

$$\text{Value} = B_i(\text{if brand size } i) + B_p(\text{price}) + B_{pr}(\text{if promotion})$$
$$+ B_{\text{deal}}(\text{if promotion})(\text{amount of promotion}) + B_A(\text{advertising})$$
$$+ B_C(\text{value last period}) + B_R(\text{if same brand was bought last time})$$

Share is then typically specified via a logit model:

$$\text{Share}_i = \exp[\text{Value}_i]/\Sigma_j \exp[\text{Value}_j]$$

This model is then estimated with a procedure to maximize predictive accuracy by varying the model's parameters. An alternative model form involves a multiplicative relation among the determinants, that is,

$$\text{Value} = (\text{Brand})^{B_1}(\text{Price})^{B_2}, \text{ and so forth}$$

Scanner data are not a perfect means for assessing the impact of promotions. They generally include only household-level (as opposed to individual) data, do not cover purchases at nonscanned stores, and exclude many potential influences on sales (e.g., magazine ads). They are, however, a useful and unobtrusive means for evaluating both natural and controlled experiments (see the discussion that follows). Scanner data are increasingly being used to compare different promotions and provide directional guidance (e.g., whether to raise or lower advertising spending) to managers.

Most of our knowledge of the impact of promotion is based on analysis of consumer packaged goods. Following is a summary of what we have found from these analyses (Blattberg, Briesch, and Fox, 1996):

1. Temporary retail price reductions substantially increase sales.
2. Higher market share brands are less deal elastic.
3. The frequency of deals changes the consumer's reference price (see also Chapter 10).
4. The greater the frequency of deals, the lower the height of the deal "spike."
5. Cross-promotional effects are asymmetric, and promoting higher-quality brands affects weaker brands (and private label products) disproportionately.
6. Retailers pass through less than 100 percent of trade deals.
7. Display and feature advertising have strong effects on item sales.
8. Advertised promotions can result in increased store traffic.
9. Promotions affect sales in complementary and competitive categories.

Some other findings include:

1. Past research on the demographics of coupon users has found contradictory results. While one might think that coupons would appeal mainly to low-income consumers who could benefit most from them, some research has found the opposite. One study found that demographics cannot explain coupon redemption rates; product managers also have to understand cost/benefit perceptions, shopping-related person traits, and nondemographic general consumer characteristics (e.g., loyalty, psychographics; Mittal, 1994).
2. An important issue concerning promotions is whether or not they have any long-term effects after the promotion period. Most early studies found that deals had a negative

effect on subsequent attitudes and repeat purchase rates (Dodson, Tybout, and Sternthal, 1978). More recent research has softened this position, suggesting that repeat purchasing depends on brand knowledge or loyalty, and the negative effect of deals decreases for knowledgeable, loyal customers (Davis, Inman, and McAlister, 1992). Other work on the long-term effects of coupons shows that increased purchases using coupons erode brand loyalty and increase price sensitivity (Papatla and Krishnamurthi, 1996). Promotion retraction often leads to a decreased repeat purchasing rate due to the fact that promotions attract buyers who value the brand itself less and hence are naturally less likely to repeat buy it (Neslin and Shoemaker, 1989). Finally, it appears that consumers anticipate deals (Krishna, 1991, 1994) and hence may delay purchase until the next deal.

3. Promotional response appears to depend upon characteristics of the product category (Narasimhan, Neslin, and Sen, 1996). Promotional response is higher for categories with fewer brands, higher category penetration, shorter interpurchase times, and higher consumer propensity to stockpile.

TEST MARKETS

Test markets are as useful for evaluating different sales promotions as they are for advertising copy or pricing experiments. A product manager can attempt different combinations of free samples, end-of-aisle displays, coupons, and special price promotions over a period of time, using some stores as the experimental group and others with no promotional activity as the "control" group.

Figure 12.13 shows an illustrative result of a special display experiment run in a BehaviorScan market. As can be seen, a significant spike in unit sales occurred around

FIGURE 12.13 A BehaviorScan Display Experiment

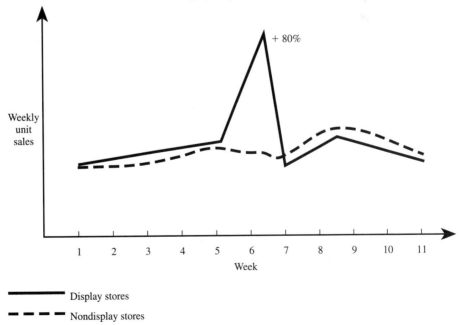

the date when all of the special displays were installed. The dotted line is the sales volume from the control stores where there were no special displays. The figure shows an 80 percent change at the peak of the sales increase. An interesting result is that although the sales in the experimental stores were lower than those in the control stores, after the experimental period there was no large "trough," thus implying that the net effect was quite positive. Notice that Figure 12.13 indicates a significant effect of the displays on sales, not necessarily profits, since the cost of the displays has not been accounted for.

EVALUATING TRADE PROMOTIONS

As discussed earlier, many users of consumer promotion would have bought the product anyway, so they simply pocket the value of the promotion and stock up at the low price. A similar problem exists for trade promotions, the issue of "gray markets." Gray markets involve authorized dealers or retailers that buy the product from the producer and then resell it to other, unauthorized dealers. This practice is common when a company offers a volume discount and multiple dealers in effect pool their orders to obtain it. Various Internet-enabled consortia have sprung up to take advantage of these discounts. Gray markets often account for 20 to 30 percent of sales, so their impact is substantial. Consequently, the lost revenue due to gray market activity is an important component of calculating the effectiveness of a trade price promotion. Evaluated as profit-enhancing devices, trade promotions are often failures. According to one estimate (Abraham and Lodish, 1990), only 16 percent of trade promotions directed at supermarkets are profitable. Further, although many trade promotions involve implied cooperation on the part of the channel (e.g., to pass along at least 40 percent of the price discount to the customer and advertise the sale price), these provisions are hard to monitor and enforce. Put differently, although the manufacturer's objectives are best served when promotions are passed through to consumers, channels' profits are often increased by retaining all or a substantial amount of a promotion allowance as profit. One way to evaluate trade promotions is as a necessary cost of doing business, an explicit recognition of the growing power of mass merchandisers in consumer packaged goods marketing in the United States. Slotting allowances of over $200 per slot (shelf keeping unit, or SKU) per store to introduce a new product indicate the power of retailers over manufacturers.

Trade promotions now account for more of the promotion budget than either advertising or consumer promotions. One reason is that trade support is a key to increased volume. For example, the results of IRI studies of 2,400 products showed that although price reductions produced increases of 25 to 60 percent in five categories (English muffins, toilet tissue, cough drops, yogurt, and sausage), adding a newspaper feature raised the increase to between 103 and 440 percent, adding a display increased sales by 109 to 708 percent, and adding both a feature and a display increased sales by 181 to a whopping 1,008 percent (Williams, 1990). Unfortunately, such strong support rarely occurs. Another study examined 992 promotions and found that only 7.3 percent were coupled with major displays and 15.2 percent with minor displays, meaning over 77 percent received no additional display. Similarly, while 827 of the 992 promoted products were advertised, most (500) received only a single line in the store ad, 29 percent received one column inch, and only 4 percent received more than two column inches (Chevalier and Curhan, 1976).

One approach to modeling the impact of trade promotions develops a model to trace the effects through channel inventories and retailer promotions to consumer sales (Blattberg and Levin, 1987). The model consists of four equations:

Manufacturer shipments $(t) = f_1$ (channel inventory $(t - 1)$, trade promotions (t), other factors (t))

Retailer promotions $(t) = f_2$ (trade promotions (t), channel inventories $(t - 1)$)

Consumer sales $(t) = f_3$ (trade promotions (t), retailer promotions $(t - 1)$, other factors (t), other factors $(t - 1)$)

Inventories $(t) = f_4$ (inventories $(t - 1)$, shipments (t), consumer sales (t))
$$= \text{Inventory } (t - 1) + \text{ shipments } (t) - \text{consumer sales } (t)$$

In an application of this model, data on retailer promotions were not available, so the retailer promotion equation was dropped and the consumer sales equation was simplified to

Consumer sales $(t) = f_3$ (inventories $(t - 1)$, other factors (t))

Trade promotions consisted of three basic types—off-invoice discounts, sales drive discounts, and special fall premiums—and their effects were treated separately. The model included an "end-of-deal" variable to account for orders placed during the deal period but not shipped until the next period. The sales drive consisted of a percentage payment to the channel when it sold units to the retailer. The special fall premium was direct payment to the manufacturer's own sales force. To remove the impact of the direction sales were headed on their own (i.e., to establish a baseline), the model also used a time trend term.

The shipment and consumer sales equations were fit to 10 items in 10 markets. The overall fits were good, with average adjusted R^2s of .66 (range .23 to .95) and .57 (range .15 to .94) for the shipment and sales equations, respectively. The signs of the coefficients were overwhelming (over 90 percent) as expected. Figure 12.14 gives a sample result. Shipments responded significantly and positively to off-invoice price reductions in both markets and to the sales drive and price reduction in market 1 as well. Also interesting were wide swings in manufacturer shipments (up at the beginning and at the end of the promotion, then down) and little change in consumer sales. This suggests that most of the impact was on channel stockpiling and that relatively little led to increased sales to customers.

A different approach uses an expert system style modeling method (PROMOTER) based on the results of many past promotions (Abraham and Lodish, 1987). This approach begins by developing a baseline sales level based on trend and seasonality plus any unusual factors that may have affected sales. Essentially, baseline estimation relies on periods when promotion is zero. Incremental sales are computed as the difference between baseline and actual sales, and this figure is used to evaluate a promotion. Thus, in contrast to the multiple-equation approach shown in Figure 12.14, PROMOTER does

FIGURE 12.14 Impact of Trade Promotions on Shipments and Consumer Sales

	Coefficient Estimates for Two Markets and One Size				
	Shipments Equation				
	Market 1/Size 2			Market 2/Size 2	
Variable	Coefficient	t-Ratio		Coefficient	t-Ratio
Lagged inventory	-3.29×10^{-5}	-2.94		-4.26×10^{-5}	-3.15
Trend	-5.964×10^{-3}	-0.72		7.24×10^{-3}	0.88
Off-invoice	36.9071	6.51		25.6119	4.93
End of deal	3.4142	0.75		4.2845	0.99
Sales drive	21.4402	3.27		3.4890	0.55
Price change	13.5317	2.31		4.6786	0.89
Fall premium	0.2029	1.34		0.2290	1.61
Constant	8.8366	45.32		8.7882	45.54
	$\bar{R}^2 = 0.845$			$\bar{R}^2 = 0.611$	
	Number of observations = 35			Number of observations = 35	
	Consumer Sales Equation				
Lagged inventory	3.295×10^{-6}	2.10		4.880×10^{-7}	0.17
Seasonality	0.0127	2.69		0.0270	4.60
Trend	-0.0005	-2.01		1.737×10^{-3}	0.92
Lagged advertising	0.0005	0.33		1.990×10^{-3}	1.08
Constant	7.89	16.45		6.2365	10.65
	$\bar{R}^2 = 0.446$			$\bar{R}^2 = 0.511$	
	Number of observations = 35			Number of observations = 35	

Source: Robert C. Blattberg and Alan Levin, "Modeling the Effectiveness and Profitability of Trade Promotions," *Marketing Science* (Spring 1987), p. 134.

not assess the process by which a promotion works; rather, it concentrates on estimating its magnitude. The general findings from PROMOTER are the following:

Trade deals tend to have lower "pass-through"; that is, savings by the retailer are passed along to consumers less often than manufacturers hope.

Retailers tend to forward-buy when they are offered promotions, allowing them to stock up and ultimately making the promotion unprofitable for the manufacturer.

The effectiveness of trade deals varies greatly across sizes of products and markets.

THE RETAILER'S PERSPECTIVE

Although this book focuses on the product manager rather than on the retailer, the effectiveness of both consumer and trade promotions clearly relies on the cooperation of the retailers involved. In addition, given the trend toward category management described in Chapter 1, the product manager should view the retailer as an ally to work with for the profitability of the entire category. The product manager becomes successful only if the retailer is successful, that is, if the product generates sufficient contribution margin to warrant the shelf space allocated to it. When this perspective is lost, the product manager–retailer relationship becomes more adversarial than cooperative.

Why does the product manager need this cooperation? As noted earlier, many trade deals simply provide additional profit for the retailer, who forward-buys goods at a lower price without passing the lower price along to the end customer. The product manager must demonstrate that the retailer can enhance total profits over a period of time by passing the promotion through. In addition, manufacturers often need the cooperation of retailers to implement various promotions. For example, "shelf talkers," signs at point of purchase indicating reduced prices, must be installed. Sometimes on-pack coupons must be physically placed on the packages by the retailer. Of course, manufacturers rely on the accurate redemption of coupons by the checkout personnel, which, as noted earlier in the chapter, can be a major problem. The important point for a product manager is that most product categories are highly competitive and consumers do not have substantial brand loyalty. It is therefore easy for a retailer to give the space currently allotted to the products of an "uncooperative" product manager to a competing brand.

SUMMARY

Promotions are a big business, representing $234 billion of expenditure in a wide variety of venues (Figure 12.15). Deciding how much to spend, and what vehicles to use, is a difficult task. To summarize promotion plans, both budget and time schedule tables similar to those developed for advertising are useful. For example, an ice cream Promotion Plan could include these elements:

- Budget: $10 million.
- Sampling in supermarkets, more theaters.

FIGURE 12.15 **Promotion Industry Spending by Segment (figures in millions of U.S. dollars)**

Segment	2001	2002	% change
Premiums/promotions	$42,265	$44,100	▲ 4.34%
POP displays	$15,500	$15,500	0.00%
Sponsorships	$9,300	$9,393	▲ 1.00%
Coupons	$6,500	$6,800	▲ 4.62%
Specialty printing	$5,900	$5,770	▼ −2.20%
Licensing	$5,800	$6,000	▲ 3.45%
Fulfillment	$3,230	$3,666	▲ 13.50%
Agency net revenues	$2,845	$3,266	▲ 14.80%
Interactive marketing (Internet)	$1,500	$1,700	▲ 13.33%
Games, contests, sweeps	$1,650	$1,800	▲ 9.09%
Research	$1,475	$1,497	▲ 1.49%
Product sampling	$1,230	$1,340	▲ 8.94%
In-store services	$850	$867	▲ 2.00%
SUBTOTAL	$98,045	$101,699	▲ 3.73%
Event marketing	$115,000	$132,000	▲ 14.78%
REVISED TOTAL	$213,045	$233,699	▲ 9.69%

Source: PROMO Magazine and Promotion Marketing Association, Inc., New York.

FIGURE 12.16 Consumer Promotional Budget

Promotion Category	Production Cost	Distribution Cost	Redemption Cost	Total Cost
Product based				
Price based				
Premiums				
Place based				
Games				

- Mobile Ice Cream Trucks in high-population-density areas.
- Contests for design of parking for new products.
- Web-based referrals (postcards).

For consumer promotions (Figure 12.16), three basic cost categories are relevant: the cost of "producing" the promotion (e.g., coupon printing or premium buying), the incremental cost of distributing the promotion (e.g., mailing or newspaper ad or insert costs), and the cost of "redeeming" the promotion (e.g., sending out rebates) including the cost of misredemption. For trade promotions (Figure 12.17), redemption costs also include the cost of monitoring trade performance, for example, in the case of cooperative advertising. Both trade and consumer promotions are put together into a promotion schedule or calendar as shown in Figure 12.18. Promotions in general and price promotions in particular are the elements of the marketing mix that have the most dramatic impact on short-term sales. Used sparingly and strategically by a weak brand or in connection with new-product introductions, they can be powerful and useful tools. When used extensively and matched by competition, however, they damage profits (Jones, 1990). While "ruinous" competition may suit the objective of driving less well-capitalized competitors out of a market (or discourage entry), it does so at a high cost.

FIGURE 12.17 Trade Promotion Budget

Promotion Category	Production Cost	Distribution Cost	Redemption Cost	Total Cost
Product based				
Price based				
Place based				
Advertising and promotion based				
Sales based				

FIGURE 12.18 Detailed Promotion Schedule

Promotion Category	January	February	March	. . .
Trade promotions				
.				
.				
.				
Consumer promotions				
.				
.				

References   Abraham, Magid M., and Leonard M. Lodish (1990) "Getting the Most out of Advertising and Promotion," *Harvard Business Review* 68, 50–60.

Abraham, Magid M., and Leonard M. Lodish (1987) "PROMOTER: An Automated Promotion Evaluation System," *Marketing Science* 6, 101–23.

Ailawadi, Kusum, Donald R. Lehmann, and Scott Neslin (2001) "Market Response to a Major Policy Change in the Marketing Mix: Learning from Procter & Gamble's Value Pricing Strategy," *Journal of Marketing* 65, January, 44–61.

Blattberg, Robert C., Richard Briesch, and Edward J. Fox (1996) "How Promotions Work," *Marketing Science* 14:3, Part 2 of 2, G122–G132.

Blattberg, Robert C., and Alan Levin (1987) "Modeling the Effectiveness and Profitability of Trade Promotions," *Marketing Science,* Spring, 124–46.

Blattberg, Robert C., and Scott A. Neslin (1990) *Sales Promotion: Concepts, Methods, and Strategies.* Englewood Cliffs, N.J.: Prentice Hall.

Bloom, Paul N., Gregory T. Gundlach, and Joseph P. Cannon (2000) "Slotting Allowances and Fees: Schools of Thought and the Views of Practicing Managers," *Journal of Marketing* 64, April, 92–108.

Buzzell, Robert D., John A. Quelch, and Walter J. Salmon (1990) "The Costly Bargain of Sales Promotion," *Harvard Business Review* 68, March–April, 141–49.

Chevalier, Michel, and Ronald C. Curhan (1976) "Retail Promotions as a Function of Trade Promotions: A Descriptive Analysis," *Sloan Management Review* 18:1, Fall 19–32.

Currim, Imran S., and Linda G. Schneider (1991) "A Taxonomy of Consumer Purchase Strategies in a Promotion Intensive Environment," *Marketing Science* 10, 91–110.

Davis, Scott, J. Jeffrey Inman, and Leigh McAlister (1992) "Promotion Has a Negative Effect on Brand Evaluations—or Does It?" *Journal of Marketing Research* 29, 143–48.

Dodson, Joe A., Alice M. Tybout, and Brian Sternthal (1978) "Impact of Deals and Deal Retraction on Brand Switching," *Journal of Marketing Research* 15, 72–81.

Drèze, Xavier, and David R. Bell (2003) "Creating Win–Win Trade Promotions: Theory and Empirical Analysis of Scan-Back Trade Deals," *Marketing Science* 22:1, Winter, 16–39.

Fader, Peter S., and Leonard M. Lodish (1990) "A Cross-Category Analysis of Category Structure and Promotional Activity for Grocery Products," *Journal of Marketing* 54, 52–65.

Farris, Paul W., and Robert D. Buzzell (1979) "Why Advertising and Promotional Costs Vary: Some Cross-Sectional Analyses," *Journal of Marketing* 43, Fall, 112–22.

Feinberg, Fred M., Aradhna Krishna, and Z. John Zhang (2002) "Do We Care What Others Get? A Behaviorist Approach to Targeted Promotions," *Journal of Marketing Research* 39, August, 277–91.

Guadagni, Peter M., and John D. C. Little. "A Logit Model of Brand Choice Calibrated on Scanner Data," *Marketing Science* 2, 203–38.

Inman, J. Jeffrey, Anil C. Peter, and Priya Raghubir (1997) "Framing the Deal: The Role of Restrictions in Accentuating Deal Value," *Journal of Consumer Research* 24, June, 68–79.

Jedidi, Kamel, Carl F. Mela, and Sunil Gupta (1999) "Managing Advertising and Promotion for Long-Run Profitability," *Marketing Science* 18:1, 1–22.

Jones, John Philip (1990) "The Double Jeopardy of Sales Promotions," *Harvard Business Review* 68, September–October, 145–52.

Kopalle, Praveen K., Carl F. Mela, and Lawrence Marsh (1999) "The Dynamic Effect of Discounting on Sales: Empirical Analysis and Normative Pricing Implications," *Marketing Science* 18:3, 317–32.

Krishna, Aradhna (1994) "The Effect of Deal Knowledge on Consumer Purchase Behavior," *Journal of Marketing Research* 31, 76–91.

Krishna, Aradhna (1991) "Effect of Dealing Patterns on Consumer Perceptions of Deal Frequency and Willingness to Pay," *Journal of Marketing Research* 28, 441–51.

Kerin, Roger A., and William L. Cron (1987) "Assessing Trade Show Functions and Performance: An Exploratory Study," *Journal of Marketing* 51, July, 87–94.

Mela, Carl, Sunil Gupta, and Donald R. Lehmann (1997) "The Long-Term Impact of Promotion and Advertising on Consumer Brand Choice," *Journal of Marketing Research* 34, May, 248–61.

Mittal, Banwari (1994) "An Integrated Framework for Relating Diverse Consumer Characteristics to Supermarket Coupon Redemption," *Journal of Marketing Research* 31, 533–44.

Narasimhan, Chakravarti (1990) "Managerial Perspectives on Trade and Consumer Promotions," *Marketing Letters* 1, November, 239–51.

Narasimhan, Chakravarthi, Scott A. Neslin, and Subrata K. Sen (1996) "Promotional Elasticities and Category Characteristics," *Journal of Marketing* 60, 17–30.

Neslin, Scott A. (2002) *Sales Promotion.* Cambridge, MA: Marketing Science Institute.

Neslin, Scott A., and Robert W. Shoemaker (1989) "An Alternative Explanation for Lower Repeat Rates after Promotion Purchases," *Journal of Marketing Research* 26, 205–13.

Neslin, Scott A., and Robert W. Shoemaker (1983) "A Model For Evaluating the Profitability of Coupon Promotions," *Marketing Science* 2, 361–88.

Neslin, Scott A., and Linda G. Schneider Stone (1996) "Consumer Inventory Sensitivity and the Postpromotion Dip," *Marketing Letters* 7, January, 77–94.

Nijs, Vincent R., Marnik G. Dekimpe, Jan-Benedict E.M. Steenkamp, and Dominique M. Hanssens (2001) "The Category-Demand Effects of Price Promotions," *Marketing Science* 20:1, Winter, 1–22.

Papatla, Purushottam, and Lakshman Krishnamurthi (1996) "Measuring the Dynamic Effects of Promotions on Brand Choice," *Journal of Marketing Research* 33, 20–35.

Pauwels, Koen, Dominique M. Hanssens, and S. Siddarth (2002) "The Long-Term Effects of Price Promotions on Category Incidence, Brand Choice, and Purchase Quantity," *Journal of Marketing Research* 39, November, 421–39.

Prentice, Robert M. (1977) "How to Split Your Marketing Funds between Advertising and Promotion," *Advertising Age,* January 10, 41.

Schiller, Zachary (1996) "First, Green Stamps. Now, Coupons?" *Business Week,* April 22, 68.

Schoenberger, Chana R. (2000) "Ca-Ching!" *Forbes,* June 12, 165:14, 84–85.

Spethmann, Betsy (1995). "Heinz Moves to Balance Ads vs. Trade Spending," *Brandweek,* June 26, 3.

Totten, John C., and Martin P. Block (1994) *Analyzing Sales Promotion,* 2nd ed. Chicago: The Dartnell Corporation.

van Heerde, Harald J., Peter S. H. Leeflang, and Dick R. Wittink (2000) "The Estimation of Pre- and Postpromotion Dips with Store-Level Scanner Data," *Journal of Marketing Research* 37, August, 383–95.

Williams, Monci Jo (1990) "Trade Promotion Junkies," *The Marketer,* October, 30–33.

Williamson, Debra Aho (2000) "E-tailers Missing the Mark with Flood of Web Coupons," *Advertising Age,* September 25, 104.

Chapter **Thirteen**

Channel Management

Overview

This chapter covers distribution channels for two important reasons. First, while distribution structure is difficult to change within a short time frame, it is still critical for the product manager to maintain good channel relations. Even when the product uses "direct" distribution through a sales force, the product manager must depend on others in the distribution system. Second, for many product categories, the distribution system has changed dramatically. As with other aspects of the marketing mix, innovation in distribution offers opportunities for differential advantage.

The personal computer (PC) category is a good example (see Figure 13.1). Traditionally, mainframes and minicomputers were sold directly via a company's own sales force or some other third party such as independent agents. Particularly for minicomputers, an additional channel evolved: the original equipment manufacturer (OEM) or value-added reseller (VAR), which was composed of companies that bought computers from major firms such as DEC, added proprietary software, and sold the resulting systems to banks, hotels, and others with particular needs. Computer retailers also became widespread, dominated initially by companies such as ComputerLand and Businessland. These retailers targeted both households and small businesses, sold products as well as software, and gave service and instruction to novice users.

A critical change in the market occurred in the mid-1980s: Customer knowledge about PCs grew as the novelty wore off, and increased numbers of competitors made price and availability the most highly valued product attributes. The change in the market resulted in four major changes in distribution channels for PCs (Figure 13.2). First, a new channel developed consisting of mass resellers, companies that buy large quantities from manufacturers and resell them at quantity discounts to large companies, such as Merrill Lynch. Second, direct sales became a large and important channel. By 1995, Dell was selling $2.9 billion worth of computers in the United States, mainly through direct mail. Third, we have seen the growth of computer "supermarkets," such as CompUSA and Soft Warehouse. Finally, today (2004), the growth of the Internet as a retail "site," particularly spurred by Dell's success, has resulted in the Internet becoming a major rival to bricks and mortar retailers. While the Internet only accounted for 8 percent of PC purchases in 1999, some forecasts suggest it could reach 40 percent by the end of 2004.

Is the personal computer category unique? Hardly. Witness the shift from small stores with personalized service to large superstores such as Circuit City in consumer electronics. Allstate's decision to begin Web-based sales and airlines' moves to reduce commissions to and sales through travel agents while increasing direct sales further highlight

FIGURE 13.1　**Personal Computer Distribution Channels**

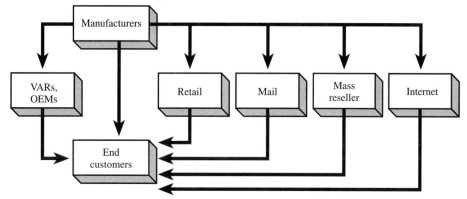

the fluidity of channels. Likewise, large office equipment retailers such as Staples and Office Depot have grown dramatically. Other businesses have prospered based on their use of direct marketing, including Harry and David in fruits, Calyx and Corolla and PC Flowers in flowers, Netflix in DVD rentals, and Franklin Mint in collectibles. The key point is that for many product categories, channels change.

Direct-distribution consumer packaged goods companies, such as Avon in cosmetics and Amway in household cleaning products, gained differentiation through the channel decision. Competitors of these companies used conventional retailers such as supermarkets and drugstores. In fact, almost any economic analysis shows how expensive it is to sell lipstick door to door. However, these companies found that some segments of the population enjoy their personal approach to selling these low-priced products, and they have created very large niches for themselves not only in the United States but in Europe, Asia, and other parts of the world as well.

Changing relationships complicate the channel issue. For example, Wal-Mart now completely dominates retailing, particularly for hard goods, and is attempting the same in foods. In 2003, 7.5 cents of every retail dollar spent in the United States other than for automobile parts went to Wal-Mart and it represented 2.3 percent of GDP. With respect to channel relationships, a large number of companies have become highly

FIGURE 13.2　**PC Sales Volumes by Channel (% of units shipped)**

	Direct Sales	Direct Response	VARs[1]	Dealers	Computer Superstores	Mass Merchants	Consumer Electronics
1984	15.0	10.0	10.0	60.0	0	2.0	3.0
1987	10.4	13.1	12.3	56.8	0	3.4	4.1
1988	9.5	14.2	13.4	55.1	0	3.6	4.1
1990	8.3	14.6	14.9	51.2	1.5	5.0	4.5
1992	5.1	16.1	15.5	44.7	4.9	8.6	5.1
1994	3.9	14.2	16.2	42.0	8.5	9.6	5.6

[1]Value-added resellers

FIGURE 13.3 **Percentage of Company Sales to Wal-Mart**

Tandy Brands:	39%
Mattel:	23%
Clorox:	23%
Hershey:	21%
Revlon:	20%
RJR Tobacco:	20%
P&G:	17%
Kraft Foods:	12%

Source: Jerry Useem (2003), "One Nation under Wal-Mart," *Fortune,* March 3, pp. 65–78.

dependent upon Wal-Mart's business. Figure 13.3 shows that sales to Wal-Mart account for over 20 percent of the sales of six very large companies.

This chapter emphasizes the two major aspects of channel decision making that are relevant for product managers: the channel selection problem and channel management. In addition, we will cover perhaps the fastest growing channel used by product managers: direct marketing. While many consumers have a negative perception of direct marketing, referring to direct mail as "junk" mail and expressing irritation at telemarketers, the fact is that it is a huge business. In 2001, sales attributable to direct marketing were nearly $2 trillion, with telemarketing leading the way with sales of $669 billion and direct mail next with $580 billion.[1] Although more precise statistics will be reported later in the chapter, it is interesting to note that while most people associate direct marketing with consumer products and services, nearly half of the $2 trillion was from B-to-B products and services. What makes the direct marketing field particularly relevant today is the rapid growth of direct e-mails for both communications and sales. About $1 billion was spent on e-mail marketing in 2001 and this amount was expected to rise rapidly due to rising mailing costs and anthrax scares (*Smartbusinessmag.com,* 2002).

CHANNEL SELECTION

Direct versus Indirect Channels

Channel selection is often thought of as two sequential decisions (see Figure 13.4). First, the product manager has to decide whether to use direct or indirect customer contact. Then the manager must select particular channels (e.g., representatives or distributors).

The choice between direct and indirect channels, like any other decision, ultimately rests on the relative profitability of the two methods. How much is it worth (in terms of margin) to use distributors to get products and services to customers? Studies point to some general guidelines. Direct appears to be better than indirect when:

1. Information needs (often due to technical complexity) are high.
2. Product customization is important.
3. Quality assurance matters.
4. Purchase orders are large.
5. Transportation and storage are complex (Rangan, Menezes, and Maier, 1992).

[1] *www.the-dma.org/cgi/registered/research/charts/dmsales_medium_market.shtml.*

FIGURE 13.4 **Company-to-Company Contacts**

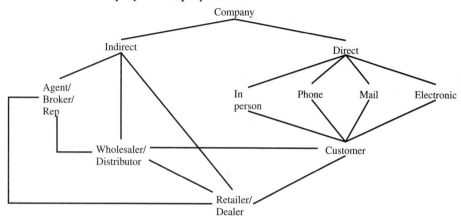

In contrast, the following factors tend to point to indirect channels:

1. One-stop shopping for many products is important.
2. Availability is important.
3. After-sales service is important.

There are numerous counterexamples to these general guidelines. As mentioned before, Dell has been very successful with a direct marketing strategy even though availability and service are important for PCs. Similarly Avon, Mary Kay, and Tupperware have done well with direct strategies even though information needs, customization, and purchase order levels are low. This suggests that both direct and indirect channels are often useful.

Another factor to consider in choosing between direct and indirect channels is the level of commitment from the potential intermediaries. Channel members must be motivated to sell your product when they have multiple products to sell. Figure 13.5 gives some conceptual idea of why levels of commitment can vary. From the product manager's perspective (shown in the top part of the figure), different channel entities can be utilized to get the product or deliver the service to the customer. However, from the channel member's perspective, multiple products must be distributed, some that sell better than others and some that do a better job of giving the channel services and incentives to sell the product. Thus, as we noted in Chapter 1, this has led to the emphasis on "category management" by retailers, that is, trying to optimize profits from soft drinks as a whole. As a consequence, manufacturers (including big ones such as Pepsi) are required to present a plan to retailers for selling not only their own brands but competing ones as well.

The product manager can implement a variety of means to get high levels of commitment from channel members. Of course, higher margins are important. Giving the channel member the exclusive rights to distribute or sell the product in a particular geographic area is another approach. Providing sales training programs, promotions such as cooperative advertising plans, and "pull" support through customer-targeted advertising are other ways to gain channel commitment.

Sometimes the choice between direct and indirect channels is based on the likelihood that the channel member will compete with your product. Store brands or private labels are examples of channel-manufacturer competition, and during the early 1990s they gained

FIGURE 13.5 **Differing Perspectives between Manufacturers and Channel Members**

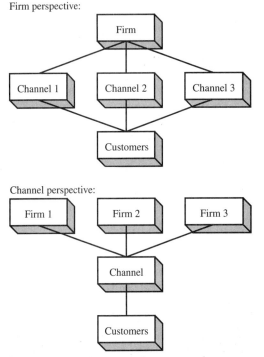

Firm perspective:

Channel perspective:

share at the expense of national brands. The Gap started by selling Levi's jeans and other products. Eventually, The Gap switched to selling its own brand of jeans and dropped Levi Strauss as a supplier.

Another factor in the decision between direct and indirect channels is customer loyalty. For some kinds of products, the customer builds loyalty to the channel member rather than to the manufacturer. This loyalty can pose a long-term problem if the channel member drops the product. For example, customers are often more loyal to their stockbrokers than to the brokerage firm. As a result, if the broker leaves, say, Merrill Lynch and goes to UBS Financial Services, the customer may shift his or her business along with the broker.

Finally, advances in information technology disrupt the channel structure of many industries. Not only are more channels, such as electronic shopping services and telemarketing, being added to the channel mix, but in some circumstances existing channels are bypassed. For example, Wal-Mart's deliveries come directly from manufacturers rather than through a wholesaler because its suppliers are tied in directly to Wal-Mart's central computers which track sales by item.

INDIRECT CHANNELS

While no general statement about channels is always true (and innovative solutions are available), the following represent general tendencies of the various channels. The main choices among indirect channels are representatives, wholesalers, and retailers.

FIGURE 13.6 The Distribution/Value-Added Chain

Representatives

Representatives/agents (reps) sell the product or service but carry no inventory and merely refer orders back to the manufacturer. Reps are common for many industrial goods as well as for personal insurance and real estate. Representatives (agents, etc.) are often a low-cost way to reach a large number of intermediate (e.g., stores) or final customers and sometimes the only way to get to difficult-to-reach target populations (e.g., entertainers, athletes, politicians). Unfortunately since many are nonexclusive (handle many products and/or clients), the product manager's control is limited.

Wholesalers

Wholesalers/brokers physically take possession of the product and then resell it to retailers. Wholesalers (distributors, etc.) provide an efficient way to reach multiple small retailers (stores). While under tremendous pressure from direct purchase initiatives by large retailers such as Wal-Mart, they still represent a major channel for small retail outlets.

Retailers

Retailers take possession of the product and resell it to final customers (who, of course, may use it as a component in their own products). Direct selling to final retailers moves inventory (and depending on the returns policy, financial burden and risk) to the stores. Home Depot, Office Depot, and the like, represent major customers for many companies. They are good at moving lots of popular merchandise at low margins; selling less popular products (e.g., backlisted books) requires smaller, specialized outlets.

Channel Members as Value-Added Intermediaries

A distribution system can be thought of as a value-added chain (see Figure 13.6). In this system, firms supply the product manager with the raw material for the product or service in question (with services, the raw material might be primarily people and the "suppliers" would be the labor market). The channel options between the product and the end customer are intermediaries that may or may not take title to or possession of the product. For example, travel service firms such as Expedia and Orbitz do not buy the seats on the airplanes they are selling; instead, they act as agents on behalf of the airlines. (There are, of course, travel service firms that actually buy airline seats in bulk and resell them to customers.) Oil brokers take title to large quantities of the product but usually do not take physical possession of it.

The intermediaries in Figure 13.6 survive in a free market only if they add value to the product. These intermediaries are compensated through margins based on the value of the services delivered. If no services that add value can be delivered, there is no economic rationale for having a particular intermediary.

What kinds of services do channel members normally provide? Figure 13.7 lists many of them. Some services are particularly valuable to the product manager and are

FIGURE 13.7 Services Provided by Channel Members

- *Marketing research:* Gathering information necessary for planning and facilitating interactions with customers
- *Communications:* Developing and executing communications about the product or service
- *Contact:* Seeking out and interacting with prospective customers
- *Matching:* Shaping and fitting (customizing) the product or service to the customer's requirements
- *Negotiation:* Reaching final agreement on price and other terms of the transaction
- *Physical distribution:* Transporting and storing goods (inventory)
- *Financing:* Providing credit or funds to facilitate the transaction
- *Risk taking:* Assuming risks associated with getting the product or service from firm to customer
- *Service:* Developing and executing ongoing relationships with customers, including maintenance and repair

clearly worthy of compensation. Physical distribution is often very important, particularly when customers are geographically dispersed. Distributors often can also promote the product very efficiently. Auto dealers, electronics stores, and farm equipment dealers all do the actual selling. Matching customers to specific products can be particularly important for complex products. For example, the local area network supplier Novell used regional Bell operating companies to determine the exact needs of new office buildings for computer interconnections.

In the design of a distribution (supply) chain, it is important to make sure all the functions in Figure 13.8 are covered. Unless you can put a "check" in each row indicating that one part of the supply chain is dealing with each activity for each key segment, the supply chain is probably inadequate.

The product manager can also use the services channel members provide to help identify which ones are attractive at any given time. For example, the product manager can assign a set of weights that sum to 1 to represent the relative importance of the different

FIGURE 13.8 Channel Function Analysis

	Channel			Internal	
	Representative	**Wholesaler**	**Retailer**	**Sales Force**	**Direct (phone, mail, Internet)**
Research information					
Communication					
Contact					
Matching/customizing					
Negotiating					
Physical distribution					
Financing					
Risk taking					
Product service					
Relationship management					
Overall attractiveness					

FIGURE 13.9 A Hybrid Marketing Channel System

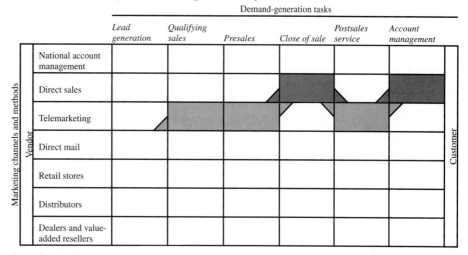

Source: Reprinted by permission of Harvard Business Review. An exhibit from "The Hybrid Grid: The Elements of a Hybrid Marketing System," by Rowland R. Moriarity and Ursula Moran, November–December 1990. Copyright © 1990 by the President and Fellows of Harvard College. All rights reserved.

functions provided. The product manager then rates each channel option on, say, a 1-to-7 scale, evaluating the ability of the option to provide the function. By multiplying the importance weight of the function by the channel evaluation and adding across all the functions, each channel receives a score that can be compared against the other options. Although you should not rely solely on a mechanical scoring procedure such as this for making important decisions such as which channel(s) to use, the process of thinking about the importance weights and how the different channel options perform the functions is very useful.

Hybrid Channels

Product managers often use combinations of channels. For example, a common approach is to use direct sales to large accounts (either final users or discounters) and a wholesaler to smaller accounts (for which direct sales are not cost-effective).

Figure 13.9 shows an example of a hybrid marketing system (Moriarity and Moran, 1990) utilizing different channel options. The channels vary by the tasks they perform for the product manager. These tasks include lead generation, qualifying sales leads, pre-sale marketing activity, closing the sale, postsales service, and account management, that is, maintaining relations with an existing account. The various methods and channels that can be used to accomplish these tasks are listed down the side of the figure. In this example, direct mail is used to generate leads, telemarketing to qualify leads and for presale activity and postsales service, and direct sales to close the deal and manage the account once the sale is made. The grid in Figure 13.9 can be useful for identifying points of overlap and conflict in a marketing system. It can also be useful for designing a system for a new target group of customers who may require a different marketing approach than prior customers. Although it was designed prior to the widespread use of the Internet, the latter can be easily added to the scheme. The Web is particularly good for lead generation, for example.

Summary

Why not select and utilize all possible channels of distribution? There are two obvious reasons: cost and conflict.

1. *Cost.* Each channel requires an additional fixed cost (establishing accounts, hiring and providing benefits for sales staff, or building and maintaining a website).

2. *Channel incentives and conflict.* A channel's enthusiasm to support a product decreases when other channels compete in the same market, in part because high-quality outlets resent being used as an information source for customers who later price-buy at other sites (e.g., discounters, factory outlet stores, websites). Franchises traditionally resist the location of other franchisees in their trading area since the synergy (demand stimulation) effect is usually less positive than the cannibalization effect. Similarly, when Goodyear placed its tires in Sears, it had major resistence from its franchised stores.

At some level, then, channel selection involves selecting a portfolio of approaches that is neither too large (so that it is inefficient, gives little incentive to any channel member to promote the product, and leads to conflict among the channels) nor too small (leaving important customer segments or activities uncovered).

Examples

For Odwalla energy bars, in order to maintain above-industry growth, it must increase its national distribution in mainstream supermarket, drug store, and mass merchandising channels as well as the growing food channels like Wal-Mart and Target. In targeting supermarkets, Odwalla's managers should continue to leverage its equity from the juice brand to encourage produce managers to place Odwalla Bars near juice coolers in produce departments. In addition, Odwalla should leverage its rapid category growth and its corporate relationships with Minute Maid and Coca-Cola to secure multiple stocking sites within the store.

For the Handspring Visor, the emphasis could be on cost-efficient direct sales (phone via toll-free number plus website). As the year progresses, major retailers would be targeted. These include Computer Electronics, Best Buy, Radio Shack, The Good Guys, Circuit City, and Office Depot.

INDIRECT CHANNEL MANAGEMENT

Channel management is easiest when the incentives of the manufacturer and the channel are consistent, and consistent goals are another useful basis for channel selection. At some point, however, a manufacturer generally wants to exert some direct control over the channel. The degree of control a company has through an intermediary depends on three basic components of the relationship: contractual/legal provisions, self-interest, and human contact.

Contractual/Legal Provisions

A naive view of control is to spell out required behaviors (e.g., the amount and type of marketing support given to the product such as number of feature ads run) and outcomes (primarily sales volume) through written contracts. Although some level of written agreement is often useful for setting expectations and delineating roles, the view that it guarantees coordination and control is naive for several reasons. First, it implies that all conditions can be foreseen and specified unambiguously, which rarely is the case. Second,

FIGURE 13.10   Good Stuff, Inc., Sales by Channel

Channel	Dollar Volume (000s)	Percent of Channel's Total Sales
Sears	62	0.12
Home Depot	20	1.02
Cost Cutters	6	0.63
Pro Hardware	<u>12</u>	21.17
	100	

Source: Mark Bergen, Shantanu Dutta, and Orville C. Walker, Jr., "Agency Relationships in Marketing: A Review of the Implications and Applications of Agency and Related Theories," *Journal of Marketing* 56 (1992), pp. 1–24.

it assumes the behavior specified will be adhered to. Not only is it difficult and costly to monitor behavior, but enforcement is difficult and expensive, as anyone involved in litigation in the United States knows.

At one time price maintenance (that is, selling at a price set by the manufacturer) was legal in the United States. In the early 1960s, Head Ski introduced the metal ski, which it sold only through specific specialty retailers, which were required to feature the skis and sell them at a set price. Head dropped retailers that did not follow the policy. The company had this degree of control largely because of its technological strength and the equity of the brand. However, as other competitors began producing skis of high quality and retailers grew larger and hence less dependent on a particular product line, manufacturer control of the channel decreased. Decreased control, coupled with the abolition of "fair trade" laws (which allowed a manufacturer to set the retail price), effectively ended Head's control over the channel.

Self-Interest

A good starting point for understanding the behavior of people or organizations is their own utility function. Put more bluntly, most people act largely, if not exclusively, in their own best interests. In business dealings, self-interest is largely coincident with economic interest. In other words, channels act to maximize their profits.

The term *agency theory,* borrowed from economics, refers to the behavior of an agent (channel) in response to the needs or demands of a principal (manufacturer). Considerable effort has been expended to relate this concept to sales force compensation, channel selection and control, and consumer promotion, and an excellent review of its use in marketing is available (Bergen, Dutta, and Walker, 1992). Basically, agency theory formalizes the explicit consideration of self-interest.

Consider the example of a manufacturer (Good Stuff, Inc.) of hardware items (hammers, screwdrivers, etc.) selling through four retailers in a concentrated geographic region (see Figure 13.10). From which channel would you like the most cooperation, and from which channel would you expect the most cooperation? Obviously, Sears represents the most volume (62 percent of your sales) and hence is most critical to you, followed by Home Depot and Pro Hardware. On the other hand, as a percentage of Sears's total sales (and profits), you represent very little. Hence, you depend on Sears far more than it depends on you (unless, of course, your hammer has impact as a traffic builder or an image creator, which seems highly unlikely for an unknown company called Good Stuff). Consequently, you will have little control over Sears. Since it already carries Craftsman (its own brand) and Stanley Works tools, you are likely to be a price brand (and have very poor margins) at Sears. In contrast, you are somewhat more important to Pro Hardware than it is to you (at least in terms of volume), so you will tend to have more control over it. This means not only that you could enforce contract provisions with Pro Hardware for marketing support (e.g., newspaper advertising) but also that Pro Hardware will tend to display and promote your product on its own. Hence, it is important to assess the (economic) importance of manufacturers to channels, and vice versa, before structuring formal arrangements and behavioral expectations.

Channel conflict often arises when a manufacturer uses multiple channels. Goodyear dealers were upset when Goodyear began distributing through Sears, and the use of direct marketing and owner-operated retail sites by computer manufacturers proved problematic for companies such as IBM and Apple. In fact, the objections of J. C. Penney caused Levi Strauss to change its website's focus to information rather than sales.

Company policy often dictates using a shared company sales force. Using a company sales force is similar to using other channels such as representatives. The sales staff has multiple products and the attention it can pay to yours is limited. Although you can try to get management to single out your product for extra effort, other product managers are likely to be doing the same thing. Hence the best approach to getting attention is the same for any channel: Make it easy to sell the product and thus earn commissions or bonuses, provide incentives (in addition to cash, prizes and other incentives have impact), and maintain simple human contact. Put bluntly, selling the sales force is an important job of the product manager, and the company sales force is best treated as a potential channel to be encouraged rather than as a dedicated staff.

Human Contact

A final source of control in any kind of relationship is human contact. How often have you done something (given a donation, bought a product) just because someone asked you nicely? Most people respond positively to friendly, reasonable requests. Hence, regular contacts by competent company personnel are likely to encourage desirable behavior above and beyond that driven by contracts and economic self-interest. In contrast, standoffish, bureaucratic treatment will decrease support. It is hard to say *please* and *thank you* too often.

Power in Channel Relationships

How different parties in a channel relationship ultimately get along relates to the balance of power among them. The party with the most power generally calls the shots and dominates the relationship. As noted earlier in this chapter, in many consumer product categories power has drifted more and more toward large retailers.

What factors affect this balance of power? Channel members are likely to have significant bargaining power with the product manager if

- The channel's volume of sales of the product is large relative to the product's total sales volume.
- The product is not well differentiated from competitors (having brand equity leads to power over the channels).
- The channel has low switching costs; that is, it is relatively easy to find an alternative to replace the product.

- The channel poses a credible threat of backward integration or competing with the product.
- The channel member has better information than the product manager about market conditions. (Note that with scanner data, retailers now know the profitability of various products and hence are less easily influenced by manufacturer claims.)

As noted previously, the product manager–channel relationship need not be adversarial; that is, it is mutually beneficial for all parties in the channel structure to be successful. Still, the party with incremental power (or the perception of power) is often able to take aggressive actions. For example, a product manager could allocate less product to a retailer, or a channel member could drop a supplier capriciously.

Figure 13.3 portrays the dominance of Wal-Mart with some of its suppliers. Some ways product managers can deal with "power retailers" such as Wal-Mart, CompUSA, Target and others are the following (Schiller et al., 1992):

- Protect the brand name. If customers come to a store and ask for the product by brand, the retailer's power is diluted. This implies spending money on the consumer franchise building activities.
- Customize products and promotions. This involves treating each retailing chain as a separate market segment and developing a unique approach for each, such as separate brand names or model numbers.
- Innovate constantly, since commodities are sold based on price.
- Organize around the customers, in this case the retailers, as mentioned in Chapter 1.
- Invest in technology. Large retailers demand that their suppliers be as sophisticated as they are in managing inventory and monitoring sales performance.
- Cut costs to keep prices down.
- Support smaller retailers as well; they may grow and help you survive sometime in the future!

Channel Arrangements

Exactly what duties channels perform and how they are compensated is open to negotiation. Many channels have patterns and hence expectations of treatments (e.g., a set markup to retail for wholesalers). Thus, a practical starting point is the industry standard.

Among the important areas of arrangement is (1) *service.* When a customer finds that a product does not perform according to expectations, he or she often returns to the place of purchase. An important issue, therefore, is who is responsible for service and at what level (e.g., replacement or repair, training, timeliness). Other issues include (2) *delivery* (timing, speed), (3) *price,* (4) *returns and allowances* policy (e.g., can the channel return unused product for a full refund up to a certain date?), and (5) *support level* given the product by the channel (e.g., display) and the channel by the company (e.g., advertising). Another important issue is (6) *the degree of exclusivity* afforded the channel and product (e.g., may an auto dealer sell multiple nameplates/brands?). Further, (7) the *compensation* expected for a sale when direct company sales effort and a channel's region and customers overlap (see Figure 13.11) is important. Even if a product manager has little control over these arrangements, the manager still benefits from a clear understanding of what they are.

FIGURE 13.11   **Channel Arrangements**

Inventory	Who holds it; who pays for it
Service	Who does what—repair, replacement, training—and who pays for it Quality expectations Timeliness
Delivery	Time frame Minimum order size Customization

Price	Wholesalers/brokers:
	    Basic price
	    Discount schedule
	    Payment (e.g., terms)
	Reps/agents: Commissions/fees

Returns and allowances	What is allowed to be returned and at what price by customer, channel
Support level: channel	Sales effort Advertising Display prominence
Support level: company	Sales effort Advertising Stocking
Exclusivity	Overlapping channels Overlapping product lines
Credit for sales	When direct contact occurs in a channel's region or customer list, how much does the channel get

MONITORING PROFITABILITY BY CHANNEL

Obviously, many aspects of a channel are worth monitoring, including effort, specific support programs (e.g., advertising), and the quality level of the channel (cleanliness, intelligence of personnel, etc.). Here we focus on one important aspect: profitability by channel, with the implicit goal of considering when to add or delete a channel. Basically, this is an exercise in cost accounting, with cost allocation being the key decision. (We cover more accounting-related issues in product management in Chapter 15.) The same basic approach that applies to evaluating products (e.g., direct product profitability, or DPP) or territories applies here: Assign revenues and costs to subunits (channels, products, territories) and then ask whether other considerations (e.g., future trends, image, contracts) affect current profit-based decisions.

Consider the hypothetical Surefoot Company, which makes a line of running shoes. As product manager of the Master, a training shoe, you are interested in the profitability of the three channels you use:

- Specialty outdoor and running stores.
- General sporting goods stores (e.g., Sport's Authority).
- Discount stores (e.g., Kmart, Wal-Mart).

FIGURE 13.12   **Overall Surefoot Master Contribution**

Sales	$900,000	
COGS	450,000	
Gross margin		$450,000
Salaries	150,000	
Lease	75,000	
Supplies	40,000	
Advertising	90,000	
		355,000
Net profit		$ 95,000

You have the following data:

1. Sales are $150,000 for specialty stores, $450,000 for general stores, and $300,000 for discount stores.
2. Gross margin is 50 percent.
3. Salaries and fringes for the people working on the Master (manager, salespeople, warehouse, clerical) are $150,000.
4. The lease on the building where offices and warehouse facilities are located is $75,000 per year.
5. Purchases of supplies total $40,000.
6. The co-op advertising budget is $90,000 per year.

Notice that this example includes no fixed assets. If such assets existed, you might also consider their opportunity cost (e.g., a $1 million building in a company that earns a 10 percent return on capital has a $100,000 implicit cost, and unless you cover that you might be better off dropping the particular product/channel). Here the overall profitability, given in Figure 13.12, is $95,000, a 10.6 percent return on sales. However, as in many cases, the aggregate picture may obscure problems (or opportunities). (This is referred to as the "iceberg" principle in Chapter 15.) Here we assess the profitability of the three main channels (specialty, sporting goods, and discount stores). To do that, we need to allocate costs to represent activities. We could allocate costs based on percent of sales, but this approach does not recognize differential expenses and would make all channels appear profitable.

Instead, we allocate costs in two steps. First, we allocate the basic expenses (salaries, etc.) to functions (selling, advertising, etc.). For salaries, allocation often is based on the percentage of time spent on the activities. For leases, allocation can be based on the amount of space allocated to each activity. For supplies, allocation can be based on purchase orders. In this case, assume the allocation was as shown in Figure 13.13.

Next, we allocate functional costs to the channels based on activity level. That is, we can allocate selling expense per sales call, advertising based on actual billings (here we use a per-ad basis), and shipping and billing per order (which will slightly understate the cost of large orders). This leads to the breakdown given in Figure 13.14.

FIGURE 13.13 Allocation of Costs by Function

	Function		
	Sales	Advertising	Shipping & Billing
Salaries	$60,000	$ 30,000	$ 60,000
Lease	10,000	20,000	45,000
Supplies	10,000	20,000	10,000
Advertising		90,000	
	$80,000	$160,000	$115,000

Using the results in Figure 13.14, we now restructure the profit statement of Figure 13.12 into three separate statements in Figure 13.15. For example, allocating selling expense per call leads to a selling expense for specialty channels of 5,000 calls $\times$ $8/call = $40,000. Notice that the picture is now quite different: Discount stores appear to be most profitable, followed by sporting goods stores, with specialty stores apparently unprofitable. This analysis reflects the economies of scale in dealing with large customers.

The obvious next question is what to do about these findings. The obvious, naive, and usually incorrect answer is to drop specialty channels. This response ignores both the still aggregate (e.g., across all specialty stores) nature of the analysis and the possibility that costs would not go down as a result of dropping a channel. Hence, although channel deletion may be worth considering, a number of issues must be addressed:

1. Does appearance in specialty stores enhance brand equity? Do people see the shoes there, then look for them on sale at sporting goods or discount stores? Conversely, does the shoes' presence in discount stores detract from brand equity?
2. Is selling expense an allocated part of a shared sales force and hence fixed?
3. Is the lease breakable? Would the same space be used even if a channel (e.g., specialty) were dropped?
4. Is the shoe part of a product line that enhances the sale of other Surefoot products (e.g., the Novice)?
5. Should the company change the allocation of sales calls by channel?
6. Should the company use distributors rather than sell directly to the specialty stores (thereby decreasing both sales and shipping and handling expenses)?
7. Are there some specialty stores that are profitable (and some discount stores that are not)?

FIGURE 13.14 Allocation of Functional Costs to Channels

Basis for Allocation	Selling (number of sales calls)	Advertising (number of ads)	Shipping and Billing (number of orders)
Specialty stores	5,000	800	13,000
Sporting goods stores	4,000	1,600	4,000
Discount stores	1,000	600	3,000
Total	10,000	3,000	20,000
Expense to allocate	$80,000	$150,000	$115,000
Expense per activity	$8	$53.33	$5.75

FIGURE 13.15 **Profit by Channel for Master Shoes**

	Channel		
	Specialty	**Sporting Goods**	**Discount**
Sales	$150,000	$450,000	$300,000
COGS	75,000	225,000	150,000
Gross margin	75,000	225,000	150,000
Selling	40,000	32,000	8,000
Advertising	42,667	85,333	32,000
Shipping and billing	74,750	23,000	17,250
	157,417	140,333	57,250
Net profit	$(82,417)	$85,667	$92,750
Return on sales	(54.9%)	19.0%	30.9%

In short, the product manager should assess the profitability of channels carefully and not jump to hasty conclusions.

DIRECT CHANNELS

As the name implies, direct channels provide more control over the channel for the company designing the channel system. A variety of direct options exist.

Own Store Maintaining your own stores (either wholly owned or franchised) is an important option. Gateway Stores for its consumer electronics lines (e.g., plasma TVs) and the ubiquitous outlet stores represent an important option. The key is to have sufficient volume to justify operation and yet not to overly cannibalize other channels. Of course publicity and exposure, rather than simply sales, are justifications for having your own store. As an example, Niketown sells only Nike products, separated by activities (e.g., basketball, tennis). Niketown is a minimall in itself. Not only does the store expose shoppers to the entire Nike line, it also does a fairly good retail business. Also, by selling at full price, the store establishes a reference point that makes purchases at discount seem like a great deal, thus increasing their likelihood. Perhaps most fascinating is a room where Nike TV commercials are shown continuously on a wide screen. The room always seems to contain at least 10 to 15 people, which is perhaps the ultimate compliment: People come to your store to watch your ads.

Sales Force Salespeople play a major role in both marketing and literature (e.g., *Death of a Salesman*). They are excellent at establishing personal relationships, but it is not easy to make them cost-effective (i.e., full-time ones have a fixed-cost component) and align their interests (i.e., compensation) with the goals of the firm.

The Internet as a Channel

Despite the rise (and fall) of the stock prices of Internet "pure play" companies, quite clearly, the reduction in the cost of the technology and its widespread use in marketing has made the Web a standard part of the direct channel toolkit of product managers rather than something unique as it was in the late 1990s. In addition, as we have discussed already in this book, the Web has significant implications for pricing, communications, and almost all aspects of product management.

A few comments about the Web as a channel are the following:

1. It is not the first new communication technology. Earlier information technologies, including the printing press, radio, and TV, all "revolutionized" marketing (among other aspects of life). Further, it is not the first interactive technology: Mail, the telegraph, the telephone, railway and highway systems, and fax all provide for two-way communication that can be initiated by either party and all (except perhaps the telegraph or pony express) still have important roles to play. Indeed, new communications technologies have rarely made the earlier forms obsolete.

2. For most products, it is not a sufficient channel. The Internet moves information, not physical products. With exceptions (software, music, etc.), it does not provide delivery or after-sales repair service. Thus, for most products, it must be part of a hybrid system, relying on either other channels or third parties (e.g., UPS or FedEx, which were building and operating inventory and shipping centers well before the Internet was a significant factor).

3. Its "widespread availability" is limited. Many of the Internet users in the world are in the United States and even there less than half the households are regular users. Its audience makeup of upscale, educated U.S. citizens raises marketing as well as social issues.

The point, therefore, is that as important as the Internet is—and it is very important—it is not in general "the answer" (as the difficulties encountered by the grocery Internet retailers have found). The issue thus becomes to understand its role amid the existence of other channels (i.e., to put it in its place).

What are the primary benefits of the Internet? Compared to other communication devices, its benefits are principally fourfold:

1. *It is interactive.* While this does not make it unique, it does differentiate it from newspapers, broadcast (but not citizens band [CB] or ham) radio, cable TV, etc. Notice, however, that even these allow for interactivity (i.e., letters to the editor), albeit at a much slower and more selective pace.

2. *It is inexpensive.* At least at present, the cost is low in the United States (less than $20 per month or even free, ignoring the cost of hardware and phone access charges) for basic telephone modem service (broadband is, of course, higher, closer to $50 per month). Further, although this may change in the near future and varies by retailer, goods sold via the Web have not been subject to taxes, both a practical and a psychological advantage.

3. *It has broad scope.* Subject to the limits of who is "on the Web," it crosses geographic borders.

4. *It is fast.* Responses are essentially instantaneous and available 24 hours per day.

What can't it do?

1. *Provide physical product.* Despite advances in simulating the fit of clothing, for example, this means that both inspection (e.g., for feel of fabric and fit) and distribution require other channels.

2. *Provide human contact.* This is changing with the diffusion of interactive, real-time customer service capabilities and the development of brand communities.

Internet Metrics

The most obvious metric is product sales. However, as mentioned before, a channel can contribute more (or less) than its sales level suggests. Customers may initially visit bricks-and-mortar stores and then purchase via the Internet or search for information about a product on the Web and then purchase it at a physical store. Further, early websites attracted attention (and hence potential advertisers) separate from their sales role. For that reason, firms like ComScore MediaMetrix have collected a variety of data, including:

1. Hits—total contacts with the website.
2. Clickthroughs—those hits that are followed by opening a subsequent page.
3. Unique hits—the number of people who have hit on the site.
4. Time spent per hit.

Trade Shows

An often overlooked but also often critical direct channel is trade shows. This multi-billion-dollar industry plays a key role in many categories. Boat shows, computer expos, and the like are a constant activity. Trade show spending in 2003 was over \$8 billion[2] and is important for both channel and final-customer contact.

Trade shows provide a way to generate publicity and sales leads as well as actual sales. They also serve as a way to get customer feedback (from a nonrandom sample of potential customers) and competitor information. The negative side of trade shows is that competitors get (early) information about your products as well. Still, for many products, trade shows are make-or-break activities, especially in terms of press coverage. A number of factors influence performance, including preshow promotion booth space, attention-getting techniques, competition, and the number and training of salespeople (Gopalakrishna and Lilien, 1995). Even placement within a show matters; the Alcort Sailfish got a major boost when its booth happened to be placed next to the largest boat at the New York Boat Show. Thus, especially for durable goods, a product manager needs to consider when and how to include trade shows in the channel strategy/marketing mix.

DIRECT MARKETING

One of the strongest trends in marketing has been toward increasing use of *direct marketing,* one of the most important direct channels. Direct marketing is most often associated with traditional methods such as direct mail (often called junk mail) and telemarketing. However, it also includes Internet-based marketing as well as radio, TV (e.g., "infomercials"), and teleconferencing. In general, direct marketing includes any method of distribution that gives the customer access to the firm's products and services without any other intermediaries (generally, direct marketing excludes the sales force). Thus, like personal selling, direct marketing is a hybrid of a channel and communication device.

---

[2] *Folio,* December 1, 2003, *http://foliomag.com/ar/marketing_trade_show_tell/.*

FIGURE 13.16   Direct Marketing Statistics and Projections

	1995	1999	2000	2001	2005	Compound Annual Growth	
						95–00	00–05
Direct Mail	$338.2	$482.1	$528.5	$580.3	$820.1	9.3%	9.2%
Consumer	216.8	299.9	326.6	355.2	484.8	8.5	8.2
Business-to-Business	121.5	182.3	201.9	225.0	335.3	10.7	10.7
Telephone Marketing	367.2	553.6	611.7	668.8	939.5	10.7	9.0
Consumer	167.0	236.0	256.9	276.6	373.3	9.0	7.8
Business-to-Business	200.2	317.6	354.7	392.2	566.3	12.1	9.8
Newspaper	150.7	219.6	239.0	261.0	356.8	9.7	8.3
Consumer	100.0	142.0	153.7	166.3	219.6	9.0	7.4
Business-to-Business	50.7	77.6	85.3	94.7	137.3	11.0	10.0
Magazine	56.5	83.4	91.3	99.8	135.3	10.1	8.2
Consumer	30.7	43.8	47.5	51.4	66.8	9.1	7.1
Business-to-Business	25.8	39.6	43.8	48.4	68.6	11.2	9.4
Television	68.5	105.4	117.6	128.9	178.9	11.4	8.8
Consumer	42.1	63.0	69.8	75.9	101.8	10.6	7.8
Business-to-Business	26.4	42.3	47.7	53.0	77.1	12.6	10.1
Radio	26.0	44.0	50.4	56.4	83.0	14.2	10.5
Consumer	15.1	24.8	28.3	31.5	45.2	13.4	9.8
Business-to-Business	10.9	19.1	22.1	24.9	37.9	15.2	11.4
Other	50.6	78.2	92.0	111.7	224.0	12.7	19.5
Consumer	33.9	49.3	54.8	62.3	105.5	10.1	14.0
Business-to-Business	16.7	28.9	37.2	49.5	118.5	17.4	26.1
Total	$1,057.7	$1,566.3	$1,730.4	$1,906.9	$2,737.7	10.3%	9.6%
Consumer	605.3	858.8	937.7	1,019.2	1,396.8	9.1	8.3
Business-to-Business	452.2	707.5	792.8	887.7	1,340.9	11.9	11.1

Source: Direct Marketing Association (2002). *www.the-dma.org.*

The definition of direct marketing is the following:[3]

Direct marketing is an interactive marketing system that uses one or more advertising media to effect a measurable response and/or transaction at any location.

Two key parts of this definition are the word *interactive* and the phrase *measurable response*. Direct marketing is a one-to-one activity and targets individual people or organizations. In addition, it is engaged to deliver a short-run response (much like sales promotion) that is easily measurable by the sponsoring organization.

In the introduction to this chapter, some overall numbers on the size of the direct marketing business were given. Figure 13.16 gives more details about the size of the market by medium and by consumer versus B-to-B. Direct marketing sales grew 10.3 percent

---

[3] The Direct Marketing Association, *www.the-dma.org.*

from 1995 to 2000 and were projected to grow another 10 percent from 2000 through 2005. Why has there been such an increase in the use of direct response methods? Two events, occurring simultaneously, have driven this trend. First, in an era where cost control is of paramount importance, direct marketing can be used to make the channel system more efficient. For example, direct mail can be used to reach prospects that would be too expensive to reach with a sales force because of their disparate geographic locations or low purchase rates. As we discussed earlier in this chapter, mail or phone also can be used to complement other channel activities in a hybrid channel system. Second, an effective direct marketing operation relies heavily on an excellent database of customer names, addresses, and phone numbers, and companies have been making significant investments in such databases for direct marketing and for building and maintaining customer relationships. Improvements in computer technology and data mining software (programs that sift through vast amounts of customer information) have made it easier to use direct marketing and have resulted in greater efficiency of this channel and higher profits.

THE DIRECT MARKETING PROCESS

Developing a direct marketing campaign entails a systematic approach with the following steps:

1. Set an objective. Because of the measurability of the impact of direct marketing, you can set a goal in terms of sales, number of new customers, etc.

2. Determine the target market. Like the marketing strategy described in Chapter 8, a direct marketing campaign requires that you determine which customers are the targets. Most direct marketing methods are too expensive to use a "shotgun" approach.

3. Choose the medium/media. As noted above and in Figure 13.16, you can select from a variety of media for the campaign. The pros and cons of the major types will be discussed later in this chapter.

4. Get a list. Because of the targeted nature of direct marketing, a list of members of the targeted customers is required. There are two basic sources of lists: internal lists from customer records and externally purchased lists. With respect to the latter, lists can be purchased from list brokers or companies (e.g., publishers) that sell their own customer lists. Companies such as Dun & Bradstreet and Donnelly (which compile lists of prospects with particular characteristics) and InfoUSA.com (see Fig. 11.13) are sources for mail and telephone, while Yesmail is a source for e-mail lists. Some companies such as Yahoo! have come under fire for selling their lists to companies launching direct marketing programs without the permission of their customers or registered members. The cost of renting a mailing or e-mail list is about $110–$125 per 1,000 names.

5. Analyze the list. For companies that keep sufficiently good internal records of customer purchasing behavior, significant effort is made to constantly analyze their lists to see who are the best prospects for the target audience. This is particularly a major priority for catalogue companies such as Lands End. A particularly popular model that has been used for many years is called the *R* (Recency) *F* (Frequency) *M* (Monetary value) model. Companies using this model develop a scoring method for each customer

on its internal list, with higher scores given for customers who have most recently purchased, who purchase the most often, and who spend the most.[4]

6. Develop the offer. The "offer" is the text of the direct marketing message. This is obviously tailored to the particular circumstances.

7. Test the offer. A unique characteristic of direct marketing is that it is relatively easy and inexpensive to test alternative offers. Thus, Lands End will often experiment with different catalogs to test different layouts and product mixes. Testing the offer is particularly easy and cheap with direct e-mails.

8. Analyze the results. The "bottom line," of course, is how the campaign performed relative to the objective. It is also important to measure response rate and cost per customer acquired.

DIRECT MARKETING METHODS

Telemarketing

As can be seen from Figure 13.16, despite what people might think, telemarketing works for many companies. Clearly, the human interaction aspect is a plus in that (at least in principle) the telemarketer can tailor the presentation to the customer. However, it is expensive ($1–$3 per message) and intrusive. With respect to the latter, telemarketing engenders a considerable amount of negative publicity and bad-will toward the direct marketing channel and the industry.

The three keys to successful telemarketing are:[5]

- The list. Demographic targeting, beginning with a good list of prospects, can increase the success rate by as much as 60 percent.

- The offer. There must be a compelling reason for the customer to buy over the phone. The reason can be a significant discount from the normal price or, more often, the offer of a product or service that cannot be purchased elsewhere. This offer must be stated early in the conversation and communicated clearly.

- Integrity. There is considerable perceived risk when buying over the phone. The telemarketer must reduce this risk through devices such as money-back guarantees or a well-known brand name.

Direct Mail

Direct mail is cheaper than telemarketing ($0.75–$2 per message) and, despite people complaining about too much "junk" mail, it does not generate the bad-will that telemarketing does as it is less intrusive. It is, of course, easy to ignore direct mail by quick disposal and, for B-to-B markets, it is very difficult to get the mail piece to the customer target in an organization.

---

[4] For more details on other approaches to analyzing lists see Füsun F. Gönül, Byung-Do Kim, and Mengze Shi (2000), "Mailing Smarter to Catalog Customers," *Journal of Interactive Marketing*, Spring, pp. 2–16, and Nissan Levin and Jacob Zahavi (2001), "Predictive Modeling Using Segmentation," *Journal of Interactive Marketing*, Spring, pp. 2–22.

[5] Laura Hansen (1997), "Dialing for dollars," *Marketing Tools,* January/February, pp. 47–53.

For a successful direct mail effort, the following guidelines apply beyond the tele-marketing guidelines above (Throckmorton, 1996):

- Copy. In general, longer copy (the text of the direct mail letter) is better because it gives you the opportunity to inform and persuade. The letter should be as long as it takes to communicate your product's benefits. However, you have about four minutes to convince the reader that the offer is worth buying. Words, sentences, and paragraphs should be kept short, with a friendly tone.
- Layout/design. Decisions about typeface, colors, graphic elements, personalized addressing, and other visual elements should be considered carefully. Format is very important because direct mail is often screened, particularly in a business-to-business context.

E-mail

Much of the excitement in the direct marketing field has come from the explosion of the use of e-mails as a direct marketing medium. This can be readily seen by a simple examination of your e-mail in-box every day. Companies have discovered that e-mails are inexpensive ($.20 per message, including creative and list generation, but only $.005 to deliver) and flexible as they can deliver text, HTML, and streaming video and audio. As noted in the introduction to this chapter, the total amount spent on direct e-mail marketing was about $1 billion in 2001. E-mails are also very easy to test, are highly trackable, and unlike the other media, can be part of an overall customer relationship program due to the high level of interactivity offered by the Web. Companies like Kana Communications, Digital Impact, e-Dialog, and others offer services to companies looking to use this relatively new direct marketing medium.

The downside of e-mail is that, like telemarketing, unsolicited or "spam" e-mails have proliferated. An estimate is that in 2004, over half of the e-mails received in the United States are spam.

One analysis has compared direct e-mail to direct mail to get a better idea of their strengths and weaknesses (Nail, 2000). Figure 13.17 compares the economics of the two media on cost per sale using costs per 1,000. In addition, a distinction is made between

FIGURE 13.17   **Direct Mail vs. Direct E-mail**

	Customer Acquisition		Customer Retention	
	Direct Mail to Rented List	**E-mail to Rented List**	**Direct Mail to House List**	**E-mail to House List**
Cost per 1,000:				
Production	$462	N/A	$462	N/A
Media	$118	$200	N/A	N/A
Delivery	$270	N/A*	$270	$5
Total	$850	$200	$686	$5
Clickthrough rate	N/A	3.5%	N/A	10%
Purchase rate	1.2%	2.0%	3.9%	2.5%
Cost per sale	$71	$286	$18	$2

*Delivery cost for rented lists are incorporated into list media costs. Direct-mail costs and response rates sourced from the "Direct Marketing Association Statistical Fact Book 1999." Banner costs and response rates are Forrester estimates.

Source: Jim Nail (2000), "The E-mail Marketing Dialogue," *The Forrester Report* (January), Forrester Research.

customer acquisition performance (using a list purchased from an outside source) versus customer retention (using your own or "house" list). Direct mail to a rented list results in an estimated cost per sale of $71 (1.2 percent purchase rate $\times$ 1,000 or 12 purchasers divided into $850 in expense). E-mails using a rented list resulted in a $286 cost per sale (3.5 percent clickthrough rate $\times$ 2 percent purchase rate or .7 purchasers divided into $200 cost), much higher than the direct mail cost per sale. Even though the cost of the e-mail campaign is lower, there are two points of customer defection, the clickthrough and the purchase incidence once a customer goes to the appropriate website. Thus, although direct mail has a low response rate, it has only one "gate" through which a customer must pass. Note that the situation reverses, however, with respect to customer retention. When using a "house" list consisting of past customers, direct e-mails become much more efficient with a low $2 customer acquisition cost. The economics of e-mail have deteriorated, however, as clickthrough rates dropped from over 3 percent shown in Table 11.4 to under 2 percent in 2002 due to the proliferation of such messages (O'Connell, 2002).

PRIVACY ISSUES

Of the three direct marketing channels described in this section, telemarketing and e-mail have received the most attention from regulators, particularly the latter. In 2003, the U.S. Federal Trade Commission established a national "do not call" registry where consumers supplied their home phone numbers and the wish to not be disturbed. Telemarketers ignoring this registry could be fined up to $11,000. Although telemarketing does provide a service that many consumers and businesses utilize, it is reasonable to permit those who do not want to receive telephone calls to be able to block them.

A livelier battle is shaping up over Internet privacy in general and, specifically, with respect to the direct e-mail industry. As noted earlier, people dislike junk mail but seem to dislike spam even more. A book titled *Permission Marketing* (Godin, 1999) introduced the notion that marketers would receive greater response rates to direct e-mails if they sent them only to customers who had agreed in advance to receive such contact. These are called "opt-in" programs. Although there is debate about whether permission should be obtained by customers actively checking a box that indicates they are willing to receive e-mails versus "unchecking" a prechecked box indicating such willingness ("opting out"), the current P3P, or Platform for Privacy Preferences, standard on the Internet mandates that websites offer either opportunity to customers. Unfortunately, despite these safeguards, most readers undoubtedly still find it much easier to get on an e-mail list than to remove themselves from it.

A potential larger battle looms over Internet privacy. This goes beyond the e-mail issue to include how companies assemble lists of e-mail addresses and what other information they are sharing.[6] The largest uproar in this area occurred in February 2000 when the online advertising placement company DoubleClick announced that it was going to merge

---

[6] Other issues such as security of financial information are part of the discussion but beyond the scope of this book.

FIGURE 13.18 Direct Marketing Planning

A. Solicitation

Method	Direct Marketing Plan			Response		Profitability	
	Target Group	Method of Solicitation	Number of Contacts	Expected	Actual	Expected	Actual
In-person sales force							
Mail							
Phone							
Internet							

B. Relationship Maintenance

Method	Direct Marketing Plan			Response		Profitability	
	Target Group	Method of Solicitation	Number of Contacts	Expected	Actual	Expected	Actual
In-person sales force							
Mail							
Phone							
Internet							

its information on the browsing habits of Internet users with offline purchasing information owned by Abacus Direct, a company in which it had a significant strategic investment. Abacus Direct was the leader in collecting information from catalogue purchases and using that data to target advertising to consumers. The company had five-year buying information on 88 million households including name, address, phone number, credit card numbers, income, and purchases. DoubleClick realized that the value of targeted online advertising, including direct e-mails, would be substantially increased if information from online browsing activities was merged with these data.[7] Although DoubleClick quickly abandoned its plans, many consumer advocacy groups are concerned about how online companies are assembling their lists for direct e-mails and how much information they have about consumers. As a result, the United States is moving toward the European Union Directive on Data Protection that was established in 1998 which stipulates that:

1. A company must obtain permission from a customer for personal information and explain its purpose, and
2. Promise not to use it for anything else other than the stated purpose without consent.

Figure 13.18 provides a summary of, and format for, the basic decisions regarding direct marketing.

---

[7] For more information on the DoubleClick/Abacus Direct incident, see David P. Baron (2001), "DoubleClick and Internet Privacy," Graduate School of Business, Stanford University case #P-32.

SUMMARY

A product manager has to determine some approach for getting products and services to customers. As noted in this chapter, this involves first choosing among or selecting a combination of indirect and direct channels. Using indirect channels means selecting which indirect channels to utilize and deciding (jointly with the channels) what is expected of them and how to compensate them. The other issue regarding indirect channels is to monitor both current volume and profit and trends in volume and profit, and, to the extent possible, to control them. Product managers should carefully monitor channels used by competitors lest an important innovation be overlooked. Product managers should also monitor sales through channels neither they nor the competition have chosen. So-called gray markets (unauthorized dealers) often account for a large fraction (e.g., 30 percent) of actual sales.

Another major area concerning channel options involves direct solicitation. Besides selecting an approach (in-person sales force, mail, Internet, etc.), the product manager must specify target groups and method of solicitation, as well as the number of solicitations per member of the target group. Of course, expected response rates and profits must be calculated to check for the reasonableness of the plan and for comparison with actual results. Notice that unlike for advertising and even promotion, it is fairly easy to assess the profit impact of direct solicitation methods such as direct mail. Hence, this area lends itself to analytical supervision. It is important to remember that not all customer contacts are equal. Merely finding them is insufficient; they must be satisfied with the interaction. One definition of customer contact is the interaction of communication time (length of contact), the richness of information, and the level of "intimacy"/personal customization (Kellogg and Chase, 1995), essentially so-called quality time.

An important caveat with respect to direct solicitation has to do with invasion of privacy. Public sentiment in the United States does not necessarily favor direct solicitation; many view it as unfair and wasteful. Hence, caution and good taste are recommended, as is attention to current and future laws governing its use (Bloom, Milne, and Adler, 1994).

The choice of channel involves division of effort and profits. From the company's point of view, an ideal channel does all the work (incurs all the cost) at a high level of quality and incurs all the demand uncertainty while making a minimal profit. Obviously, from the channel's point of view, the opposite is true. Choice of channel therefore implies trade-offs, with the stronger party gaining the greater share of available profits.

Channel image can also have an impact on the product, and vice versa. High-quality channels enhance the appeal of a product; low-quality channels often decrease the value of a product, as Izod found out when it started selling its once-famed crocodile shirt through discounters. In other words, being featured at "blue light specials" may increase volume at the cost of brand equity and profits. As an example of this, in 2000 Calvin Klein sued Warnaco (which makes their jeans under a licensing agreement) for cheapening the brand by selling to K mart and similar low-end stores. Sometimes the reverse can occur; Martha Stewart's well-publicized legal battles in 2003–2004 have hurt Kmart's chances of recovering from bankruptcy since her branded goods are sold there.

Perhaps the most important task is to keep the various channels focused on your product working together rather than focused on each other and warring among themselves and with you. This involves, hopefully, an increasing pie (meaning more for everyone), minimal cannibalization, incentives for cooperation (e.g., the local dealer gets some credit for an Internet sale), and considerable human contact and explanation.

References

Bergen, Mark, Shantanu Dutta, and Orville C. Walker, Jr. (1992) "Agency Relationships in Marketing: A Review of the Implications and Applications of Agency and Related Theories," *Journal of Marketing* 56, 1–24.

Bloom, Paul N., George R. Milne, and Robert Adler (1994) "Avoiding Misuse of New Information Technologies: Legal and Societal Considerations," *Journal of Marketing* 58, January, 98–110.

Godin, Seth (1999) *Permission Marketing*. New York: Simon & Schuster.

Gönül, Füsun F., Byung-Do Kim, and Mengze Shi (2000) "Mailing Smarter to Catalog Customers," *Journal of Interactive Marketing,* Spring, 2–16.

Gopalakrishna, Srinath, and Gary L. Lilien (1995) "A Three-Stage Model of Industrial Trade Show Performance," *Marketing Science* 14, Winter, 22–29.

Kellogg, Deborah L., and Richard B. Chase (1995) "Constructing an Empirically Derived Measure for Customer Contact," *Management Science* 41, November, 1734–49.

Levin, Nissan, and Jacob Zahavi (2001) "Predictive Modeling Using Segmentation," *Journal of Interactive Marketing,* Spring, 2–22.

Moriarity, Rowland T., and Ursula Moran (1990) "Managing Hybrid Marketing Systems," *Harvard Business Review* 68, 146–55.

Nail, Jim (2000) "The Email Marketing Dialogue," *The Forrester Report,* Forrester Research, January.

O'Connell, Vanessa (2002) "E-Mail Ads Just Don't Click With Consumers," *The Wall Street Journal,* July 2, B2.

Rangan, V. Kasturi, Melvyn A. J. Menezes, and E. P. Maier (1992) "Channel Selection for New Industrial Products: A Framework, Method, and Application," *Journal of Marketing* 56:1, July, 69–81.

Schiller, Zachary, Wendy Zellner, Ron Stodghill II, and Mark Maremont (1992) "Clout! More and More, Retail Giants Rule the Marketplace," *Business Week,* December 21, 66–73.

Smartbusinessmag.com (2002) March, 30.

Throckmorton, Joan (1996) "Discovering DM," *Marketing Tools,* November/December, 51–57.

Chapter **Fourteen**

Customer Relationship Management

Overview

A product manager, unsurprisingly and appropriately, focuses on selling a product. Yet both the thrust of this book and the trend in marketing is toward customer-focused activities (i.e, being market versus product focused). As we saw in Chapter 13, direct marketing and the Internet in particular allow for tailored relations at the individual-customer level. The focus thus shifts from transaction-based activities (get the sale/customer acquisition) to long-term relationship building (satisfy the customer/customer retention).

However, most companies spend the vast majority of their marketing resources on customer acquisition. A marketing manager at Bristol-Myers Squibb, the pharmaceutical company, reported that his company spends about 85 percent of its marketing dollars on acquisition.[1] A study conducted by the Boston Consulting Group in 1999 showed that Internet companies spent 33 percent of their resources on building awareness, 55 percent on customer acquisition, and only 12 percent on retention. This is particularly noteworthy given that one of the main advantages the Internet brings to marketing is customer retention through improved relationship building.

The previous chapters of this book focused on what might be called customer acquisition, or the ways marketing is normally used to obtain customers. Companies spend considerable sums acquiring customers; how much does your company or ones that you know spend on retaining customers? More and more companies are spending money on computer systems and marketing programs on what is called *customer relationship management,* or CRM for short. CRM is often used in the context of relationships that are long-term in nature. However, a true CRM strategy develops programs that match the kind of relationship the customer wants with the company whether it is relational or transactional. In this chapter, the focus is on how to develop a CRM program for customer retention, or how to keep customers over the long term for different customer types. This is the challenge facing many companies like Odwalla and PalmOne/Handspring. In many ways, CRM is a throwback to old-fashioned country store type retailing where the store owner knew his or her customers by name and knew their shopping habits well enough to make product recommendations. Today, we often use technology to accomplish this goal.

---

[1] James Masterson in a speech given at the Marketing Science Institute's Marketing Metrics conference, October 2000.

As noted in Chapter 1, the separation of a product manager's job into the components of acquisition and retention has led to the consideration of hiring separate people to concentrate on customer acquisition and retention. Even without separate managers, it is useful to conceptualize customer strategy in this way and to consider the different marketing activities necessary to be successful at each.

All companies face this problem. Providers of frequently purchased products and services, from retail gasoline as well as less frequently purchased durable and industrial goods, have attempted to build higher levels of customer satisfaction through the development of better relationships with their customers. Many of these relationships are intended to increase repeat purchasing rates and therefore increase long-term sales and profits. Some relationships are not long-term in nature; however, so it is important for the marketing manager to understand what kind of relationship the customer wishes to have with your company and its brands. This chapter discusses the necessary steps to creating programs that achieve higher customer satisfaction through this matching process.

What is the impact of high switching rates between products? The cellular industry is an excellent example. Consider the huge expense of getting customers to switch cellular suppliers in the United States. It has been estimated that it costs a cellular company $350–$475 in discounts, promotions, and advertising expenditures to sign up each subscriber; each percentage point increase in churn costs enough to reduce the total market value of the cellular companies by $150 million (Peterson and Harris, 2002). However, the data shown in Figure 14.1 illustrate that the amount of money that Verizon, Nextel, Cingular, and others have spent have largely attracted switchers. As can be seen from Figure 14.1, in 2003, the annual churn rate of customers is about 25–30 percent.

Different perspectives on the buyer–seller relationship are shown in Fig. 14.2. In the situation represented by panel A, the seller figures out a way to make the sale to the buyer,

FIGURE 14.1 Cellular Service Customer Churn

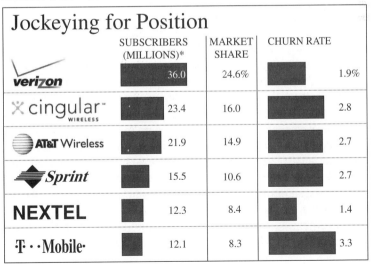

Jockeying for Position	SUBSCRIBERS (MILLIONS)*	MARKET SHARE	CHURN RATE
verizon	36.0	24.6%	1.9%
cingular WIRELESS	23.4	16.0	2.8
AT&T Wireless	21.9	14.9	2.7
Sprint	15.5	10.6	2.7
NEXTEL	12.3	8.4	1.4
T··Mobile·	12.1	8.3	3.3

*As of third quarter 2003.

Source: *The New York Times,* November 24, 2003, p. C4.

FIGURE 14.2 **Buyer-Seller Relationships**

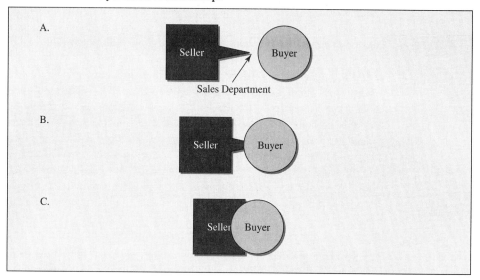

Source: Theodore Levitt (1986), *The Marketing Imagination* (New York: Free Press), pp. 113–14.

but the relationship between the two is at a distance because the seller has done little to try to understand the buyer's motivations and needs. The salesperson has used his or her creativity or personality to make the sale, not an understanding of the customer.

In panel B, the company selling the product or service has done a better job understanding the customer by getting "into" the buyer, determining enough about his or her needs to make the sale. This is the more traditional marketing concept of customer orientation. A panel B company spends money on marketing research, segments its markets appropriately, and has developed a marketing strategy on the basis that the value proposition fairly represents what its target segment wants.

However, while both panel A and B relationships are necessary to be successful, neither concept is sufficient in today's globally competitive environment. Both can be characterized by the following: For the seller, the sale is the end of the process; for the buyer, it's the beginning (Levitt, 1986).

In today's competitive environment, where long-term relationships are critical to marketing and general business success, it takes more than the execution of the marketing concept to satisfy customers over a long period of time. Panel C illustrates the new model of relationship marketing. Here, the buyer and seller have become interdependent. Each party to the relationship depends on the other in some way. The sale therefore is no longer the end of the process.

A distinction has been made between different kinds of industrial buyer–seller relationships (Jackson, 1985). This distinction is applicable for all kinds of goods and services. Transaction buyers are those who are interested only in the purchase at hand. They may not be interested in a long-term relationship at all, or the sellers in the market may not have done a good job showing the customer the benefits of such a relationship. The former situation exists when a company sees the benefit in sharing the business between a number of suppliers. Relationship customers see the benefits of the interdependency shown in panel C of Fig. 14.2. Both kinds of customers can be loyal, but the nature of the loyalty is different.

THE ECONOMICS OF LOYALTY

A simple example demonstrates the economic power and importance of loyalty. A number of years ago, a passenger flying on a British Airways (BA) flight from London to San Francisco complained about being seated near the smoking rows in the coach section. Although there is no in-flight smoking today, many readers will identify with this traveler's complaint; being one or two rows from the smoking area on a 10-hour flight was more than annoying. The coach section was full and the dissatisfied customer was (or at least claimed to be) a regular BA customer. A simple solution would have been to move the customer to business class in an unobtrusive way (so other passengers do not get the same idea) because there were unoccupied seats in that section. Our guess is that such a move would have gained a strongly loyal customer at a very low marginal cost (for business class food). However, the BA personnel declined to move the passenger, who very loudly indicated that he would never fly BA again.

This example illustrates a very important concept: lifetime customer value. Compare the amount of revenue and profits that would be derived from the customer to the small incremental cost of moving him to business class. When you lose a customer for life, you are actually losing the (discounted) stream of income that would have been produced over the customer's lifetime. In addition, how many other potential customers will he tell about it?

Clearly, no company is going to have a 100 percent loyalty rate. As noted earlier, some customers have multiple vendors as company policy. Other customers do not want to feel any kind of obligation to purchase from the same vendor. In addition, if many customers are involved, it is impossible to satisfy all of them. However, the economic reasons for increasing the retention rate are compelling. Figure 14.3 shows the impact of a 5-percentage-point increase in retention on the net present value of a customer revenue stream for a variety of industries. For example, in the advertising agency industry, increasing its client retention rate from, say, 80 to 85 percent results in an increase of 95 percent in the net present value of the average customer's billings. This occurs for two reasons. First, what looks like a small difference in retention rates is greatly magnified over a long period of time. Second, retained customers are much more profitable than switchers.

Figure 14.4 breaks down the difference in profits. Loyal customers are more profitable because they stimulate revenue growth, are less expensive to serve, refer new customers to the company, and are often willing to pay a price premium. Let us look in more detail at the components of Fig. 14.4.

Acquisition Cost

Obviously, any new customer involves some incremental costs, called acquisition costs. For example, American Express must send a number of direct mail pieces or make telemarketing pitches to obtain new customers. New customers of industrial equipment require more sales calls than existing ones. Thus, acquisition costs represent an initial investment in a customer.

FIGURE 14.3 Impact of a Five-Percentage-Point Increase in Retention Rate on Customer Net Present Value

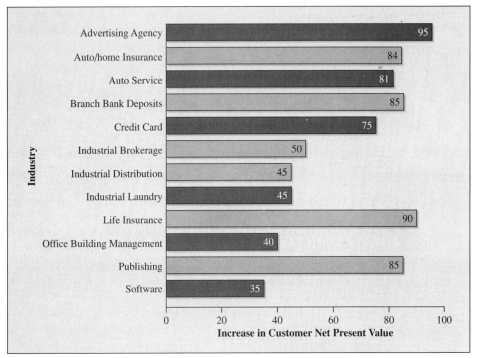

Source: Frederick F. Reichheld (1996), *The Loyalty Effect* (Boston: Harvard Business School Press), p. 37.

FIGURE 14.4 Why Loyal Customers Are More Profitable

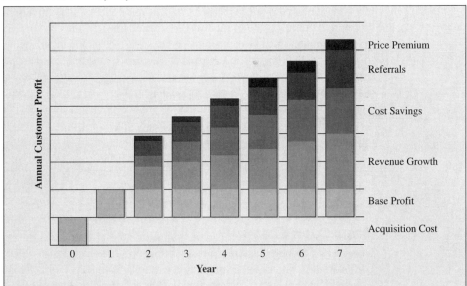

Source: Frederick F. Reichheld (1996), *The Loyalty Effect* (Boston: Harvard Business School Press), p. 39.

Base Profit

This is simply the profit margin a company earns from an average customer. The longer a customer is retained, the longer the base profit is earned.

Revenue Growth

Retained customers often have been found to increase their purchase quantities over time. This is an intuitive finding. Think about a store to which you have become more loyal over a period of time. It is likely that you not only shop there regularly, but that you also buy more items there. Alternatively, you might purchase life or home insurance from the company from which you purchase auto insurance.

Operating Costs

Existing customers also frequently cost less to serve than new customers. The former have a better knowledge of the company's systems and procedures. For example, if you are a good customer of the direct mail clothing company Lands' End, you undoubtedly know how to fill out the form (fewer mistakes for the company to follow up on) and how to read the product descriptions (less time on the phone for customer service representatives).

Referrals

Good customers also talk to their friends and neighbors about your company. Additional business comes from favorable word of mouth by satisfied customers. This is a particularly good source of new business for service companies; as we will see in the next chapter, service quality is more difficult to ascertain before purchasing, so advice from someone who has tried the service and is satisfied with it is particularly important.

Price Premium

Loyal customers are often more price insensitive than customers who need a price inducement to switch or to become a new customer. When was the last time you checked the price of your favorite brand of toothpaste? Such loyal customers are getting significant customer value from using the product or service and are not concerned about price.

Thus, although there is some evidence to the contrary (Dowling and Uncles, 1997; Reinartz and Kumar, 2000), building and sustaining long-term relationships can be both strategically sound and profitable.

A FRAMEWORK FOR CUSTOMER RELATIONSHIP MANAGEMENT

CRM has come to mean different things to different people. For some managers, CRM means sales force contact software like the products sold by salesforce.com. For others, it means telephone call centers for contact management. Additionally, many focus their attention on loyalty programs such as Harrah's Total Rewards program, which provides incentives for players to repeat their visits to their casinos.

FIGURE 14.5 Customer Relationship Management Model

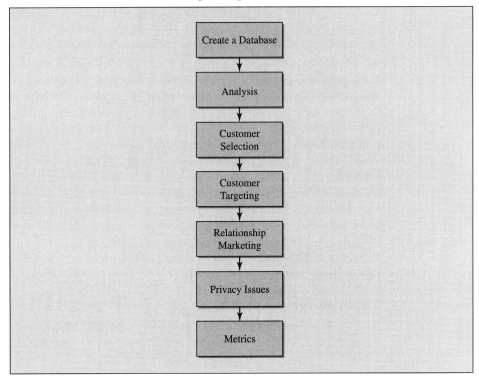

A systematic view of CRM that integrates these perspectives is shown in Figure 14.5. As can be seen, major components of a complete framework are the following:

1. Constructing a customer database.
2. Analyzing the database.
3. Based on the analysis, selecting customers to target.
4. Targeting the selected customers.
5. Developing relationship programs with the customers in the target group(s).
6. Considering privacy issues.
7. Measuring the impact of the CRM program.

These steps in the comprehensive approach to CRM will be covered in more detail below.

CREATING THE DATABASE

The core of a CRM program is a customer database, sometimes referred to as a customer information file or CIF (Glazer, 1999). The CIF is the repository of information about the customer and serves as the basis for identifying and targeting both current and potential customers. The basic idea behind a CRM program is to assess the value to the

FIGURE 14.6 Customer Information File

Customer	Characteristics	Purchase History	Contacts	Response	Value
1					
.					
.					
.					
.					
n					

firm of each customer in the CIF and then develop relationship programs that will be customized in both content and intensity depending upon that value. The optimal contents of this CIF are shown in Figure 14.6.

As can be seen, there are five major areas of content in the CIF:

1. Basic customer descriptors. These are the kinds of variables described in Chapter 6 in terms of consumer and firm demographics and contact names and addresses.

2. Purchase history. Like descriptors, the customer's purchase history is considered to be a basic part of the CIF. This information should be as detailed as possible, including products bought, the channels utilized, and prices paid. If possible, the margin made on each purchase should be recorded as well.

3. Contact history. Part of a customer's history with you is any recordable contact they have had through, say, customer service. For example, any time a customer calls you with questions about your product or service, this should be noted. Similarly, sales call information would be part of this area of the CIF.

4. Response information. Particularly valuable is information about how customers have responded to prior direct marketing activities, promotional offers, or other traceable marketing activity.[2] This provides information about potential responsiveness to such future programs.

5. The value of the customer. This number is an estimate of the monetary value of the customer to the firm which will be discussed in more detail later.

The CIF shown in Figure 14.6 appears to be two-dimensional. However, there is an important third dimension that is difficult to show: time. It is critical that the CIF contain information on these dimensions over time so that you can spot trends in terms of which customers are becoming better and those whose relationship with the firm is becoming worse.

---

[2] "Traceable" activity would be any marketing program where the response can be directly related to the program. An example would be a catalogue mailing. Mass advertising would not be included, for example.

FIGURE 14.7 **Getting More Customer Interaction**

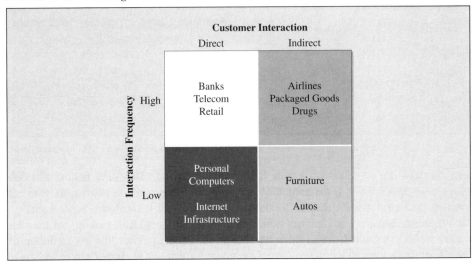

Many companies view their CIFs as a key source of competitive advantage. For example, UPS does not want to be known as a package shipping company. The company views itself as an information technology company. From all of the information it collects about shipping, it compiles a database that is useful to its customers in terms of the products purchased, geographical locations, addresses, and other parts of the CIF. This is only part of the information UPS collects that is useful to its customers (Schonfeld, 2001).

The challenge for many companies is to create the kind of CIF shown in Figure 14.7. Figure 14.7 characterizes the ease with which the CIF can be created by conceptualizing the problem as a 2 × 2 matrix defined by the kind of interaction the company has with the customer (direct versus indirect) and the frequency of that interaction (high or often versus low or infrequent).[3] Companies in the upper-left quadrant are able to develop most of a CIF relatively easily. Banks, telecommunications firms, and retailers have direct and frequent contact with customers, which results in those types of firms having generally excellent CIFs (at least in terms of customer and purchase information). However, firms with indirect customer contact have to work much harder to collect such information. For example, Odwalla, Clif Bar, and the other energy bar manufacturers have to rely on their distribution network to provide customer information back to them. This is not the most reliable way to collect accurate data. Consumer durable companies such as Sony and the PDA manufacturers rely heavily on warranty information from either cards or online registration; however, the completion rate is only about 30 percent.

---

[3] This framework is due to Professor Florian Zettelmeyer.

As a result, many companies have to create special programs or events to collect as much customer information as they can. Some of this comes through loyalty or frequent-shopper programs. Some of these special programs can be quite creative. For example, Kellogg's developed a program called "EET and ERN" (eat and earn) where the company put 15-digit encrypted codes inside of cereal boxes and a website URL. After going to the site, inserting the code, and registering, participants (mainly kids) can receive free toys. Loewe's Theaters invites people to visit a website and provide some personal contact information in order to enter a sweepstakes to win free movie tickets for a year. The idea is to create a database of the company's best customers. Professional services firms such as management consultants often host free seminars in specialized topic areas where the goal is to develop a list of, and information about, prospective clients.

Another challenge to creating databases is the fact that, as we saw in Chapter 13, with the expansion in the number of possible channels or "touchpoints" where customers can have contact with the company, it is becoming increasingly difficult to track behavior. Some companies, such as Acxiom, have developed software that is part of an overall CRM strategy where customer purchases and preference from brick-and-mortar stores, catalogues, and the Web are tracked and pulled into one centralized database.

It should be noted that building the database with customer information is only part of the challenge. To fully reap the benefits of CRM, the company must collect all the information shown in Figure 14.6 and be prepared to continually update the database. Thus, it requires a considerable investment of time and money and a strong customer orientation to fully implement this stage of the process.

ANALYZING THE DATABASE

Many types of analyses can be performed on a CIF once it has been assembled. The general name given to such analysis is *data mining*. People with significant statistical skills use computer software and large computer resources to troll through the CIF to find segments, purchasing patterns, trends, and other useful outputs.[4] Large companies like Siebel Systems, Oracle, e.Piphany, and others provide such software to its corporate customers.

A particularly important analysis that provides the information in the last column of the CIF shown in Figure 14.6 is estimating lifetime customer value (LCV). This analysis takes the purchase information and, together with information about profit margins on each product purchased, projects the profit implications of each customer or row in the CIF. While not an exact science due to the difficulties of making projections far into the future, the goal is to ultimately place a monetary value on each customer that the firm can use to make resource allocation decisions.

While there are a number of formulas that can be used to estimate LCV (Berger and Nasr, 1998), one way to start is with a relatively simple formula that utilizes only the available purchase information in the CIF to calculate each customer's cumulative

---

[4] See, for example, Michael J. A. Berry and Gordon S. Linoff (2000), *Mastering Data Mining* (New York: Wiley).

profitability in the past:

$$\text{Customer profitability} = \sum_t \left[\sum_j (P_j - C_j) - \sum_k MC_k \right]$$

where

t = the number of past and current time periods measured

j = the number of products purchased in a time period

k = the number of marketing tools used in a time period

P = price

C = cost

MC = cost of marketing tool (e.g., direct mail).

Basically, the formula computes the total profits generated by a customer by taking the total margin generated by the customer $(P - C)$ in each time period from all products and services purchased, subtracting off the traceable marketing costs attributable to each customer, and then summing over all time periods in the database.

The formula above is useful for purposes other than computing customer profitability. An examination of its components shows the levers for increasing individual customer profitability. Profits can be increased by

- Increasing P and j by cross-selling (purchasing more products) and/or up-selling (purchasing more expensive products).
- Reducing the marketing costs MC over time as customer loyalty is better established.
- Increasing the number of time periods t that the customer purchases.

To compute the LCV, you have to project customer's generated margins and marketing costs into the future and discount back. This involves a number of very heroic assumptions about the nature of a customer's purchasing pattern in the future. A back-of-the-envelope approach to calculating LCV is a margin "multiple" which can be used to multiply the current margin generated by each customer to estimate the LCV (Gupta and Lehmann, 2003). This multiple, assuming constant yearly margin, is

$$r/(1 + i - r).$$

In this formula, r is the retention (loyalty) rate for your product and i is the discount or cost of capital rate used by your company. Some sample multiples are shown in Figure 14.8.

FIGURE 14.8 **Margin Multiple***

Retention Rate	Discount Rate			
	10%	12%	14%	16%
60%	1.20	1.15	1.11	**1.07**
70%	1.75	1.67	1.59	1.52
80%	2.67	2.50	2.35	2.22
90%	**4.50**	4.09	3.75	3.46

*Multiple is $\dfrac{r}{1 + i - r}$.

Source: Sunil Gupta and Donald R. Lehmann (2003), "Customers as Assets," *Journal of Interactive Marketing,* Winter, pp. 9–24.

FIGURE 14.9 **Customer Life Cycle Profit Pattern in the Credit-Card Industry**

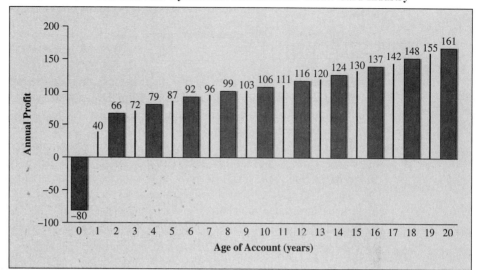

Source: Frederick F. Reichheld (1996), *The Loyalty Effect* (Boston: Harvard Business School Press), p. 39.

Thus, for a product whose retention rate is 70 percent and a discount rate of 12 percent, take the margin generated by each customer and multiply it by 1.67. This approximates the LCV for that customer. For those that are interested in more details, further details about this approach are given in Appendix A.[5]

A different way to look at LCV is from the perspective of customer acquisition costs. Figure 14.9 is an illustration from the credit card industry showing the increase in value of an active account over 20 years. For example, the value of a customer who stays for three years is $98 ($178 in profit minus the $80 acquisition cost); if a credit card issuer can retain a customer for five years, the net profit is $264.

An interesting question is how much you would pay today to acquire an account, given the kind of information shown in Figure 14.9. Suppose we knew that the average account remained active for five years. You should not be willing to pay $264 for that account today because the cash flows occur in the future and those dollars are worth less today because of the time value of money. The present value of a five-year customer, assuming a 10 percent discount rate, is $40/(1 + .10) + $66/(1 + .10)^2 + $72/(1 + .10)^3 + $79/(1 + .10)^4 + $87/(1 + .10)^5 − $80, or $172.98. In other words, you should not pay more than $173 to acquire an account that you expect to retain for five years. Another way to look at these numbers is from a retention perspective. If a credit card customer in the third year indicates that he or she is thinking about switching, the present value of the incremental profit for years 4 and 5 is $79/(1.10) + $87/(1.10)^2 (recall that we are in year 3 already), or $143.72. This gives you an idea of how much you would spend

[5] For an examination of LCV in a channels context, see Rakesh Niraj, Mahendra Gupta, and Chakravarthi Narasimhan (2001), "Customer Profitability in a Supply Chain," *Journal of Marketing*, July, pp. 1–16.

to retain that customer (for example, using a reduction in the interest rate on the card or adding benefits such as life insurance or lost card protection).[6]

CUSTOMER SELECTION

The customer profitability analysis just described can be used to separate the customers who will provide long-term value to the firm from those that are likely to be unprofitable. The venerable 80-20 rule in marketing often applies (if only approximately) in that 80 percent of the company's profits are provided by 20 percent of its customers. There is nothing in the "rules" of marketing indicating that every customer must be served; marketing is not supposed to be inconsistent with making a profit. Thus, a major benefit of the LCV and profitability analyses previously described is to permit the marketing manager to make informed decisions about (1) which customers to keep, and (2) for those kept, how much money to spend keeping them.

An example of the result of a profitability analysis is shown in Figure 14.10 (Mulhern, 1999). This analysis was performed by a pharmaceutical company on all prescription products sold by the firm in three sales territories. The customer unit was physicians. The analysis covered 1.5 years of prescriptions so it is profitability analysis rather than a full LCV analysis. The margins were calculated on the prescriptions written and the marketing costs (*MC* in the profit formula above) included sales calls, product samples, and direct mail. As can be (approximately) seen from Figure 14.10, of the 834 physicians covered, the profitability was highly variable, ranging from a high of $62,407.20 to a low of −$12,814.12. There are some very-high-profit physicians, generating over $20,000 in profits for the firm, and a very large number of low-profit customers with over 50 being unprofitable. Clearly, a large percentage of the profits result from a relatively low number of the doctors.[7]

As a result of analyses such as these, the marketing manager has relevant information to help select which customers to keep or "fire." Criteria include

- Current profitability.
- Future profitability (LCV).
- Similarity of the customer's profile to other customers who are currently profitable.

However, you should be wary about indiscriminately "firing" unprofitable customers. As noted earlier, LCV calculations are based on assumptions that are often difficult to validate. For example, it is difficult to know which small customers will grow into large ones. It would not have been smart for a supplier to have cut off Microsoft as a customer back in the late 1970s. In addition, some customers may be particularly vocal in the community. While it may look like a sound financial decision to cut off an unprofitable doctor using the data in Figure 14.10, one of those doctors could be influential in the physician community.

---

[6] For a more detailed look at this acquisition/retention decision, see Robert C. Blattberg and John Deighton (1996), "Manage Marketing by the Customer Equity Test," *Harvard Business Review,* July–August, pp. 136–144.

[7] For a similar result in customer profitability being concentrated among a few customers, see Niraj, Gupta, and Narasimhan, 2001, in note 5.

FIGURE 14.10   **Customer Profit Ordering for Physicians: Highest to Lowest**

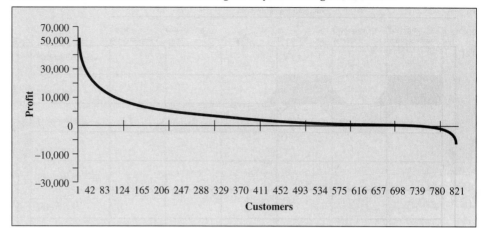

Source: Frederick F. Reichheld (1996), *The Loyalty Effect* (Boston: Harvard Business School Press), p. 39.

However, there is also no doubt that many companies continue to serve unprofitable customers simply because they lack the CIF to perform a customer-level profitability analysis.

CUSTOMER TARGETING

Once the customers that you wish to target have been selected, conventional direct marketing approaches are then used to keep them. In the context of CRM, these direct marketing channels are often referred to as 1-to-1 marketing. Special promotions, prices, perks, products, and other offers are made through telemarketing, direct mail (surface, fax, e-mail), and personal sales calls. More details on these kinds of programs are given in Chapter 13.

RELATIONSHIP MARKETING PROGRAMS

Given the preceding discussion concerning customer targeting, it is important to describe marketing programs beyond discounts and other special perks that are part of the normal arsenal of product managers and that have been described elsewhere in this book. Thus, this section of the chapter describes programs that have been specifically designed for retaining customers.

Customer Satisfaction

Clearly, one of the requirements of customer loyalty is satisfaction. Satisfied customers are much more likely to repurchase and become good customers than dissatisfied customers. Many studies have shown a positive relationship between satisfaction, loyalty, and profitability (Anderson, Fornell, and Lehmann, 1993).

Spurred by the quality movement of the 1980s, the introduction of several very public competitions such as the Malcolm Baldrige Award for Quality, and well-publicized

FIGURE 14.11 **Customer Satisfaction Model**

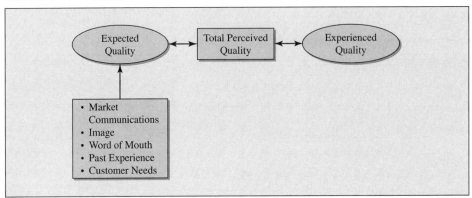

satisfaction surveys such as the one done by J. D. Power for automobiles, many companies around the world are investing substantial sums in measuring customer satisfaction
and exploring its impact on their businesses. As a result, this has become a big business
for research firms. By one estimate, up to one-third of all revenues generated by U.S.
marketing research firms are from customer satisfaction surveys and analyses.

The basic customer satisfaction model is shown in Fig. 14.11. The model is often
called an *expectation confirmation/disconfirmation* model because it presumes that levels of customer satisfaction with a product or service are determined by how well the
product performs relative to what the customer expected. In the center of the figure is
perceived customer satisfaction. The circle on the right is experienced quality, or how
the product or service actually performed. To the left, the customer is assumed to form
an expectation or prediction about the product's performance. This expectation is formed
from a variety of sources of information, including advertising, word-of-mouth information from friends and relatives, and past experience with the product or product category. If the product meets or exceeds expectations, the customer is satisfied to different
degrees. Obviously, if the product just meets expectations, satisfaction is less than if the
product goes well beyond expectations. Any performance below expectations results in
a dissatisfied customer.

Satisfaction can be measured in a number of ways. As in the multiattribute model shown
in Chapter 6, the most common approach is to use a scale to compare satisfaction, along
a number of product dimensions, with competition and expectations. Figure 14.12 shows
several common scale types. Federal Express has been known to use the 101-point scale,
General Electric uses the 10-point scale, and most other companies use a 4- or 5-point
scale. For example, a satisfaction question for an airline might look like the following:

"How satisfied were you with the food (relative to your expectations)?"

Very Dissatisfied				Very Satisfied
1	2	3	4	5

FIGURE 14.12 **Customer Satisfaction Scales**

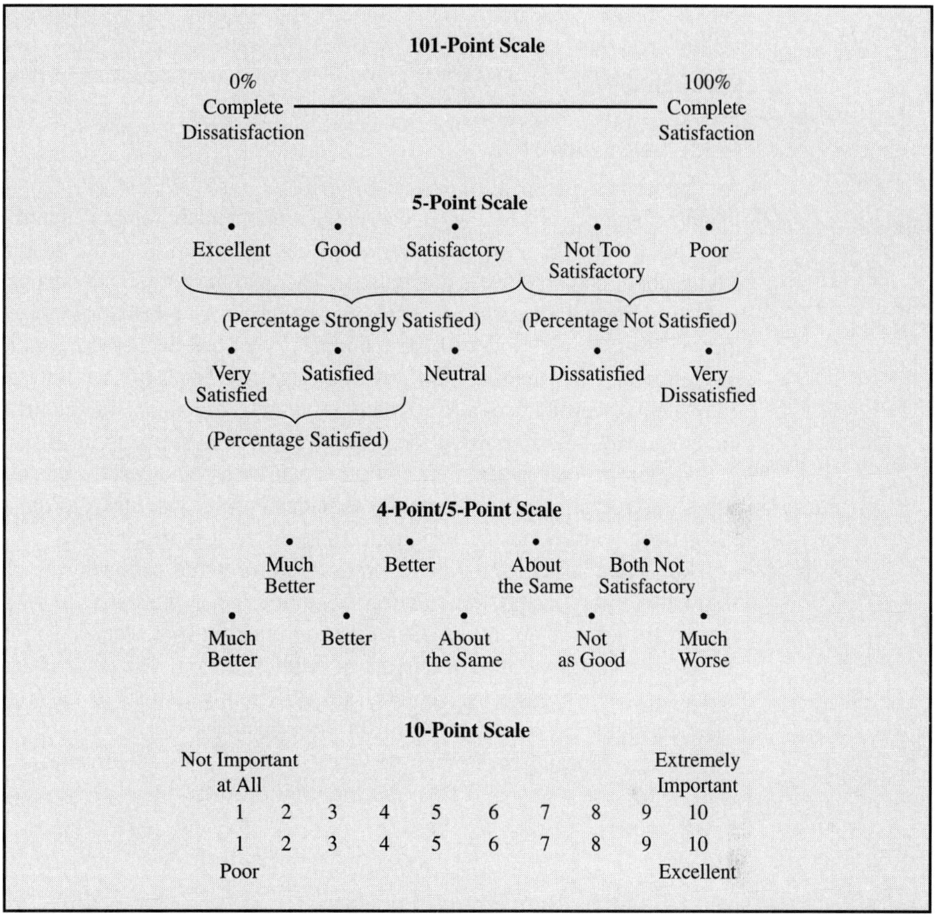

101-Point Scale

0%   100%
Complete ———————————————— Complete
Dissatisfaction   Satisfaction

5-Point Scale

| Excellent | Good | Satisfactory | Not Too Satisfactory | Poor |

(Percentage Strongly Satisfied)   (Percentage Not Satisfied)

| Very Satisfied | Satisfied | Neutral | Dissatisfied | Very Dissatisfied |

(Percentage Satisfied)

4-Point/5-Point Scale

| | Much Better | Better | About the Same | Both Not Satisfactory |

| Much Better | Better | About the Same | Not as Good | Much Worse |

10-Point Scale

Not Important   Extremely
at All   Important

1   2   3   4   5   6   7   8   9   10

1   2   3   4   5   6   7   8   9   10

Poor   Excellent

Source: Mack Hanan and Peter Karp (1989), *Customer Satisfaction* (New York: AMACOM), p. 104.

After obtaining satisfaction measures on specific attributes, the survey always contains an overall satisfaction question:

"Overall, how satisfied were you with the flight today?"

Very Dissatisfied				Very Satisfied
1	2	3	4	5

Most companies track these satisfaction measures over time and relative to competition in order to determine trends in different market segments or product areas.

Customer satisfaction surveys for products and services sold via the Web can be conducted quickly and easily using software from companies such as Customersat.com and Zoomerang.com. The website operator first designs the survey using a variety of questionnaire options provided. The survey is then distributed by a pop-up window at the client's website. The frequency of the pop-up window can be adjusted to appear to every visitor or as few as 1 out of 100 visitors for sites that have heavy traffic. Reports based on the answers to the survey questions are generated and updated in real time for the client.

Customer Service

An important component of customer satisfaction is *customer service*. All products, whether manufactured or services, have a service component. Automobiles and computers must be repaired. Customers have questions about how to set up a VCR. Machinists need technical advice about how to operate a new lathe. The quality of these encounters can make or break a relationship with a customer. How many times have you sworn not to return to a restaurant or not to buy a product from a company that has delivered poor customer service?

Companies that market services know that the level of customer service delivered is equivalent to product quality. However, many companies in manufacturing businesses underestimate how important these service encounters are to customer loyalty. Although it is important that a personal computer works as advertised, for some consumers it is equally important that the company provides helpful responses to questions and does not leave them waiting on the telephone to speak to a representative.

Thus, regardless of the type of product, as we noted earlier in the chapter, the relationship between buyer and seller is only beginning when the purchase is made. The points of contact between buyer and seller are not all equal in importance. Those that are critical to the relationship are called moments of truth (Carlzon, 1987). It is important for you to understand which customer contacts are sufficiently critical to the long-term relationship to be considered moments of truth for your business.

The key to using customer service to develop these long-term relationships is to view service as a way of differentiating your product from the competition. Figure 14.13

FIGURE 14.13 **The Augmented Product**

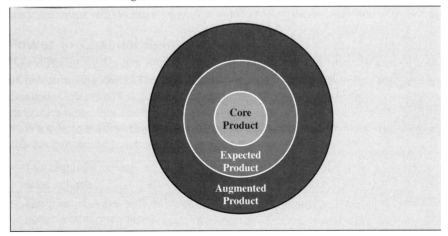

Source: Theodore Levitt (1980), "Marketing Success through Differentiation—of Anything," *Harvard Business Review,* January–February, pp. 83–91.

illustrates this differentiation effort. Consider the core product to be the basic attributes of the product or service. For a manufactured product, these would be the physical characteristics. For example, for a car, color, weight, gas mileage, and similar characteristics constitute the core product. The expected product is the core product plus any expectations about the product or service held by the target segment. Thus, the expected car would also feature a certain level of reliability, service from the dealer, prestige obtained from driving it, and so on.

How, then, do you use customer service to differentiate your products? Usually, whether you are in a high-tech or low-tech business, all competitors in a market either offer or have the potential to offer equivalent core products. Thus, it is difficult to achieve differentiation based on product features and attributes. Also, simply meeting expectations is insufficient for maintaining buyer loyalty over an extended period of time. To differentiate, you need to reach a third level (shown in Fig. 14.13): the augmented product. In other words, you have to go beyond expectations by offering levels of customer service that competitors cannot match.

One way to differentiate through customer service is with service guarantees (Heskett, Sasser, and Hart, 1990). Guarantees not only offer the customer some assurance about product quality but also reinforce the brand image at the same time. Some examples are Domino's Pizza's promise that you will get your pizza delivered in 30 minutes or you do not have to pay for it (now you receive a reduced-price coupon) and Lucky Supermarkets' offer of "Three's a Crowd" service that guarantees the opening of a new checkout station when any line has more than three people. Although their effectiveness varies, such guarantees can differentiate a product from the competition.

Another way to demonstrate excellence in customer service is through service recovery. Unfortunately, products do break down and there are often tense moments as services are delivered (e.g., the waiter spills soup on your dress). Thus, a critical moment for a company is when the product or service does not perform up to expectations or fails to work properly. How you react in such situations is crucial for maintaining customer relationships.

Effective service recovery demands significant training and the right people to do the job. When service recovery is necessary, customers are typically unhappy because some aspect of the product or service has failed. The people dealing with the situation must be compassionate and good listeners, as well as effective problem solvers. In 1997, because of its highly selective screening process focusing on interpersonal and empathy skills, Southwest Airlines sorted through 105,583 job applications to fill 3,006 positions (Kaydo, 1998).

Turning around a potential disaster can be a tremendous boost to loyalty. The British Airways anecdote earlier in this chapter was a lost opportunity. In a more positive vein, an IBM account team was having difficulty overcoming the hostility of a potential major buyer of mainframe processors. Although the potential buyer did own several IBM processors, the company was not interested in buying any more or in buying peripheral equipment such as tape and disk drives. The account team's basic strategy was to build a new level of confidence from the lower levels of the company's organization that were key influences in the buying decision. Although they were having some success with this approach, one of the breakthrough events that turned the account around was how they handled a failure of one of the installed IBM processors. A large number of IBM personnel worked around the clock to restore the system. Their efforts prompted a laudatory letter from the director

FIGURE 14.14 **LivePerson.com Application**

of the company's information systems group and went a long way toward improving the relationship. Eventually, the team's efforts resulted in a larger order.[8]

Web-based customer service has improved substantially with the advent of live chat and other similar services. An example of a company that provides such services is LivePerson.com. Figure 14.14 shows a typical LivePerson application, in this case, for the TechnoScout website. A visitor to the site can choose between three different modes of customer service: a telephone number, e-mail, and live chat. If you choose the latter, the pop-up screen shown in the figure appears and the dialogue begins. The software firm Intuit also employs LivePerson's software on its site. The company claims that 67 percent of all of its online purchases are handled through its live chat service, and that visitors who chat are three times more likely to purchase from the site than those who do not. Also, order size is 50 percent higher for people who chatted (Fuller, 2002).

[8] "International Business Machines (B): Applitronics Account Strategy," Harvard Business School case #9-581-052.

Loyalty Programs

One of the major trends in marketing is the ubiquity of loyalty programs or, in general, frequency marketing. These are programs like Harrah's Total Rewards program, mentioned earlier in this chapter, that encourage repeat purchasing through a formal program enrollment process and the distribution of benefits. The best example of such programs are the frequent-flier programs offered by every major airline in the world, where miles are accumulated and then exchanged for free travel or merchandise. The innovator was American Airlines, which started its AAdvantage program in 1981. A newsletter that follows loyalty programs is *Colloquy, www.colloquy.com.*

These programs have migrated to many different industries. Some examples are the following:

- Cracker Barrel, a restaurant chain with a country flavor, has its Cracker Barrel Old Country Store Neighborhood program where you earn one "neighborhood" point for every dollar spent at its stores. The points are redeemable at the stores.
- The retailer Pier 1 Imports has a Preferred Card program with three levels of benefits: basic (under $500 in annual spending), Gold ($500–$1,000), and Platinum (over $1,000 spent annually).
- Hallmark's Gold Crown Card program is targeted to customers of their Gold Crown retail stores. Customers receive points for money spent and greeting card purchases, which are redeemable for certificates of different monetary value. These certificates are spendable only in the Gold Crown stores.
- A British pharmacy retailer or "chemist" has its Advantage card program, which it launched in 1997, which enables shoppers to earn points toward free goods.
- A small Spanish grocery chain, Plus, differentiates itself from other grocery chains through its loyalty card program; over 80 percent of its customers use the card.

Technology is changing the way these programs can operate. Most of them currently involve a special-purpose membership card or a co-branded Visa or MasterCard. The magnetic strip on the back of the card forwards data from the transactions to a separate information system, which tracks behavior and issues rewards. So-called smart cards have microprocessors built into them. These cards can store points accumulated from loyalty programs, which allows for more sophisticated multiple retailer programs to be developed. For example, in the United Kingdom, Shell has a program whereby points collected at Shell service stations can be converted into free gifts, flights, or movie tickets.

Frequency or loyalty programs can have several problems (Dowling and Uncles, 1997):

- Making the reward too high. Restaurant chain Chart House's program, the Aloha Club, offered free around-the-world trips to any member who ate in all 65 Chart House restaurants. Unfortunately, the company underestimated the zeal of its 300,000 members; 41 members qualified, costing the company a considerable sum of money. Although the value of the program to the customer should exceed the cost of being a member, the programs should also be cost-effective.

- Ubiquity. There are so many programs that customers are rebelling against carrying all the cards. You should target your best customers with these programs and provide a compelling reason for joining.
- What kind of loyal customers are you actually getting? As we have noted in this chapter, it is possible to confuse loyalty with repeat purchasing. United Airlines has many repeat-purchasing customers in the San Francisco Bay Area because of its Premier frequent-flier program. At the same time, because United is the major carrier in the region, these customers are also "hostages" and are not necessarily attitudinally loyal to the company. Compare the failure of United's shuttle services in California with Southwest Airlines' tremendous success (although Southwest's frequent-flier program is less attractive than United's).
- Lack of inspiration. Many programs are simply copies of other programs. To be successful, the program must have a differential advantage over competitors' programs.
- Lack of communication with customers. Loyalty/frequency programs need to have a significant communication component to retain customer satisfaction.
- Insufficient analysis of the database. A large amount of information is produced from these programs about customer behavior. To maximize the value of these programs, these data must be mined for better market segmentation, targeting, and new product development. This is particularly a problem for supermarkets. Only a few of the chains with frequent shopper programs have gone beyond offering discounts at the cash register to cardholders.

In general, loyalty programs seem to work best when

- The program supports and is consistent with the brand's value proposition.
- The program adds value to the product or service.
- Lifetime customer value is high.

MASS CUSTOMIZATION

Customer retention and loyalty are also being affected by a marketing process called mass customization. This is a process whereby a company takes a product or service that is widely marketed and perhaps offered in many different configurations and develops a system for customizing (or nearly customizing) it to each customer's specifications. This imparts a feeling that the product was made especially for the customer, an important affective (attitudinal) component of a buyer–seller relationship (Pine II, 1993). Because services can be and often are tailored to each customer, most of the attention on mass customization has been in the manufacturing sector, where a combination of information and flexible manufacturing technologies have enabled companies to personalize their products for customers.

One writer has characterized the mass customization process as a choiceboard (Slywotzky and Morrison, 2000). Choiceboards are online, interactive systems that permit customers to design their own products by choosing from a menu of attributes, components, prices, and delivery options. This information is transmitted electronically to the

FIGURE 14.15 Nike Choiceboard

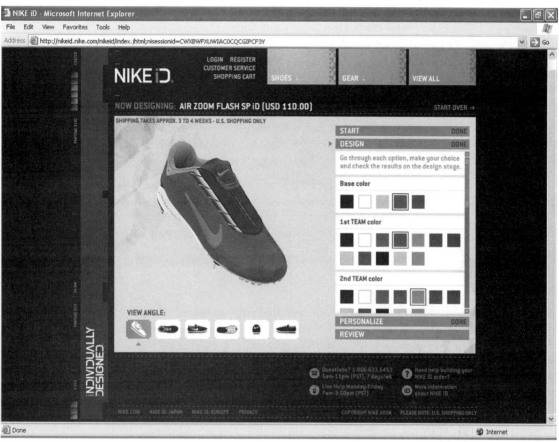

company's supply, assembly, and delivery operations. The fundamental shift implied is one where customers are moving from product "takers" to product "makers."

Perhaps the most well-known example of a choiceboard is Dell's online ordering system. A customer has over 25 attributes from which to choose and multiple options within each attribute. Another example of a choiceboard is at the site where you can custom-build a pair of Nike running shoes (*nikeid.nike.com*). Part of this site is shown in Figure 14.15. Note that in both cases, customers are not offered an unlimited number of combinations. However, these two examples show how customization can work in a manufacturing environment to deliver products that meet individual customer specifications.

There are four different approaches to mass customization:

- Collaborative customizers talk to individual customers to help determine their needs, identify the exact product meeting those needs, and then make the customized product for them. This is the typical concept of mass customization represented by the examples just cited.

- Adaptive customizers offer one standard but customizable product that is designed so users can alter it to their own specifications. This would be appropriate when customers want the product to perform differently on different occasions.
- Cosmetic customizers present a standard product differently to different customers. An example would be a company that sells a product to different retail chains, each of which wants its own packaging, sizes, and other features.
- Transparent customizers provide each customer with unique products or services without telling them that the products have been customized for them. This is most useful when customers do not want to restate their needs repeatedly. Internet services such as Amazon.com produce customized recommendations for books to customers based on past purchases. These recommendations are sent via e-mail.

The commonality between the four kinds of mass customizers is that they all realize that customers are heterogeneous and want different combinations of product features and benefits. This recognition goes beyond market segmentation as mass customization engenders a feeling among customers that the company cares enough for them to develop products that precisely fit their needs. The desired outcome is a longer-term relationship than would be obtained using conventional marketing and manufacturing approaches.

A version of mass customization that is used to customize websites is called *personalization*. Every time you visit a website, information about you is collected by that site and can be ultimately used to target specific messages. Some of this information is collected by what is called a cookie, a small tag of data inserted into your Web browser files that can identify you as a unique entity every time your return to the site that issued it.

Community Building

A challenge for marketing managers is to create a sense of affinity to their companies and brands in their customers. Even customers that are brand loyal do not necessarily feel a sense of "belonging" to the brand, a more emotional, dedicated sense of a relationship in the human sense. In such a situation, it may not take a significant activity on the part of a competitor to induce a brand switch.

As a result, many managers seek to create more than simply a set of customers who purchase their product but a *community* of customers who share information between themselves and the company about their experiences with the product or service. The concept of a community is not new; high-tech products have formed user groups for years where groups give the company feedback and give each other tips on how to better use the product. These user groups can be sponsored by the company or formed independently. Figure 14.16 shows the community-building page of palmOne (Handspring's parent company). As can be seen, the site is the locus for a number of interactions with the company, including a newsletter, discussion board, user-to-user information, and so on.

Particularly since the expansion of the Internet, community building is normally high on the list of goals for the construction and enhancement of a website for all kinds of products and services due to the ease of interacting. Successful communities on the Internet offer participants the following (McWilliam, 2000; Muniz, Jr., and O'Guinn, 2001;

FIGURE 14.16   PalmOne Website

McAlexander, Schouten, and Koenig, 2002):

- A forum for exchange of common interests.
- A sense of place with codes of behavior.
- The development of congenial and stimulating dialogues leading to relationships based on trust.
- Encouragement for active participation by more than an exclusive few.

Such online communities offer real opportunities for enhancing the brand and creating long-term relationships because of the increased involvement offered. Customers do not feel simply like they are buying a product—they are also purchasing entry into and participation with a similar group of people. In fact, with respect to Internet behavior, a study found that the more a person uses the community features of a site, the more that person tends to visit it and make purchases there. Users who contribute product reviews or post messages remain twice as loyal and buy almost twice as often as those who do not (Brown, Tilton, and Woodside, 2002).

Other Ideas

The notion of building relationships with customers is often thought of as the job of the sales force or other personnel related to marketing. From the customer's perspective, the concept of customer service does not necessarily imply marketing; in many cases, it may simply be the need to communicate with the company, to personalize it.

A successful program built on this idea was launched by Southwestern Bell Telephone Company in 1995 (Long, 1997). The company began the Volunteer Ambassador program in which employees volunteer to establish relationships with designated customers. The objective was to put a face on the company and to let each customer know that Southwestern Bell cares about him or her and values the business. The ambassadors were drawn from a pool of nonsales employees, and each was assigned 5–10 customers whom they were expected to visit quarterly. The program started with 1,300 volunteers and expanded to 3,500 in two years.

A good source of information about how to improve customer loyalty is to examine customers who defect. Marketing research studies often focus on your customers or potential customers; rarely are ex-customers analyzed. However, there may be more to learn from customers who have been lost than those who are loyal because the former can provide a number of ideas on how to improve the product or service, based on actual performance levels they deemed too low to continue as a customer (Reichheld, 1996).

PRIVACY ISSUES

Because of the importance of detailed customer information (the CIF in Figure 14.6) to an effective CRM strategy, the issue of privacy again looms important. All of the issues raised at the end of Chapter 13 in the context of direct marketing are obviously relevant here.

The issue of privacy is particularly important in online communities. Not only do you have to register to join, but many of the communities host chat rooms where product users communicate with each other creating personal contact. Thus, online communities should post links to the company's privacy policies. All of the communities noted above explicitly list their privacy policies. In addition, for example, both the Microsoft Xbox and Adobe software Web-based communities are certified by TRUSTe, an independent initiative to build user confidence in joining communities and using the Web in general.

METRICS

Traditional metrics for measuring the effectiveness of marketing programs are market share, sales volume, ROI, and similar aggregate measures. However, the whole concept of CRM is based on the idea of 1-to-1 customer relationships. Thus, while aggregate metrics are important and should always be collected, CRM demands that customer-level measures should be taken as well.

Examples of these kinds of metrics include (see also the discussion in Chapter 16):

- Customer acquisition costs.
- If an e-commerce site, customer conversion rates, that is, the percentage of visitors who are converted into customers

- Customer retention rates.
- Customer profitability.
- Same customer sales by period.

While this is not an exhaustive list, the point is that marketing managers must move from a world where market share, volume, and profits are the only important measures to the CRM world where measures based on customer activity are crucial to understanding the impact of relationship programs on the customer base.

SUMMARY

The marketing environment in the early part of the 21st century places a greater premium on customer retention and loyalty than has been the case in the past. The basic idea is that the buyer–seller relationship does not end when a sale is made; buyers expect sellers to deliver services after the sale. If you do not, the customer can easily move to a competitor. While brand loyalty has always been important, the rapid improvements and reduced costs of information technology have made the creation of customer databases and their subsequent analysis much easier to do and amenable to businesses of all sizes.

The economic advantages of customer loyalty through long-term relationships are clear: increased profits derived from profit margins produced over the term of the relationship, increased revenues from greater purchase volume, lower costs of serving loyal customers, referrals to new customers, and price premiums (because loyal customers tend to be more insensitive to price).

A complete CRM program consists of building a customer database, analyzing the database, selecting which customers to pursue and allocating resources to them, developing the specific relationship marketing programs, being concerned about customer privacy, and establishing appropriate customer-based metrics for evaluating the program's success. While we did not get into the specifics of the kinds of computer software and hardware that are often necessary to fully implement a CRM program, we feel that the key is understanding what you want to accomplish with the program and assessing your company's current efforts on CRM versus the goals.

We also feel that the current pressure marketing managers feel to deliver high levels of return on investment (ROI) with CRM systems, particularly in the short-run, are misguided. While the lack of such an ROI has led to widespread dissatisfaction with CRM, investments in customer loyalty must be evaluated in the long term, much like investments in advertising are. Looked at another way, the cost of not spending sufficient funds on CRM activities is high rates of customer churn. Would you like to be a product manager in an industry facing the kinds of customer turnover shown in Figure 14.1?

References

Anderson, Eugene W., Claes Fornell, and Donald R. Lehmann (1993) "Economic Consequences of Providing Quality and Customer Satisfaction," *Marketing Science Institute Report #93-112*, Cambridge, MA.

Berger, Paul D., and Nada I. Nasr (1998) "Customer Lifetime Value: Marketing Models and Applications," *Journal of Interactive Marketing*, Winter, pp. 17–30.

Brown, Shona L., Andrew Tilton, and Dennis M. Woodside (2002) "The Case for Online Communities," *The McKinsey Quarterly,* January, *www.mckinseyquarterly.com.*

Carlzon, Jan (1987) *Moments of Truth.* Cambridge, MA: Ballinger.

Dowling, Grahame R., and Mark Uncles (1997) "Do Loyalty Programs Really Work?" *Sloan Management Review,* Summer, pp. 71–82.

Fuller, Peter (2002) "A Two-Way Conversation," *Brandweek,* February 25, pp. 21–27.

Gilmore, James H., and B. Joseph Pine II (1997) "The Four Faces of Customization," *Harvard Business Review,* January–February, pp. 91–101.

Glazer, Rashi (1999) "Winning in Smart Markets," *Sloan Management Review,* Summer, pp. 59–69.

Gupta, Sunil, and Donald R. Lehmann (2003) "Customers as Assets," *Journal of Interactive Marketing* 17, Winter, 9–24.

Heskett, James L., W. Earl Sasser, and Christopher W. L. Hart (1990) *Service Breakthroughs: Changing the Rules of the Game.* New York: Free Press.

Jackson, Barbara Bund (1985) "Build Customer Relationships That Last," *Harvard Business Review,* November–December, pp. 120–28.

Kaydo, Chad (1998) "Riding High," *Sales & Marketing Management,* July, pp. 64–69.

Levitt, Theodore (1986) "Relationship Management," in *The Marketing Imagination.* New York: Free Press, Chapter 6.

Long, Pat (1997) "Customer loyalty, one customer at a time," *Marketing News,* February 3, p. 8.

McWilliam, Gil (2000) "Building Stronger Brands through Online Communities," *Sloan Management Review,* Spring, pp. 43–54.

McAlexander, James H., John W. Schouten, and Harold F. Koenig (2002) "Building Brand Community," *Journal of Marketing,* January, pp. 38–54.

Mulhern, Francis J. (1999) "Customer Profitability Analysis: Measurement, Concentration, and Research Directions," *Journal of Interactive Marketing,* Winter, pp. 25–40.

Muniz, Jr., Albert, and Thomas C. O'Guinn (2001) "Brand Community," *Journal of Consumer Research,* pp. 412–32.

Peterson, Andrea, and Nicole Harris (2002) "Chaos, Confusion and Perks Bedevil Wireless Users," *The Wall Street Journal,* April 17, p. A1.

Pine II, B. Joseph (1993) *Mass Customization: The New Frontier in Business Competition.* Boston: Harvard Business School Press.

Reichheld, Frederick F. (1996) "Learning from Customer Defections," *Harvard Business Review,* March–April, pp. 56–69.

Reinartz, Werner J., and V. Kumar (2000) "On the Profitability of Long-Life Customers in a Noncontractual Setting: An Empirical Investigation and Implications for Marketing," *Journal of Marketing,* October, pp. 17–35.

Schonfeld, Erik (2001) "The Total Package," *Ecompany,* June, pp. 91–96.

Slywotzky, Adrian J., and David J. Morrison (2000) *How Digital is Your Business?* New York: Crown Publishers.

Chapter **Fifteen**

Financial Analysis for Product Management

Overview

In today's business environment, product managers need to be knowledgeable about the financial dimensions of their jobs as well as the marketing portion. As we noted in Chapter 1, in many companies product managers assume the role of mini-CEOs in that they have complete profit and loss responsibility for their products. In such cases, the product manager must be familiar with *all* aspects of business, including operations management, human resources, and so on. However, besides the analyses marketing managers perform to better understand customers, competitors, and the rest of the external market environment, several other analyses related to the financial aspects of the product's performance are also necessary. As a result, to be part of a firm's overall decision making, product managers must understand the financial implications of their decisions.

Financial decision making is closely related to product strategy. The top part of Figure 8.2 shows that the ultimate objective of product managers is profitability, whether or not the short-term objective in the marketing plan is oriented toward share or profits. The left-hand side of the diagram includes marketing-oriented activities, such as the decision of whether to seek new segments or to pursue existing customers. However, the right side of the figure includes activities that are primarily financial, including decisions about cost cutting, improving the sales mix to emphasize products with higher margins, and the like.

Two key kinds of information are important to marketing decision making and strategy development. First, if the product manager is to have profit and loss responsibility or set short- and long-term profit objectives, he or she must have a good understanding of how profits are computed. As any financially oriented manager knows, computing profits is not a straightforward issue. Later in this chapter, we show that there is no such concept as *the* bottom line; in fact, there are at least three ways to calculate the "profitability" of a product. The second kind of information that is critical to a product manager's understanding of financial performance is relevant if there is a product line or many product variants (e.g., different sizes, colors) because it analyzes the performance of different product variants. This is called a *sales* analysis and is also discussed later in this chapter.

The financial analyses described in this chapter can be used in a variety of ways. One way to use either profitability or sales analyses is for planning purposes. As noted in the outline in the appendix to Chapter 2, budgeted, or *ex ante,* profitability needs to be reported in a marketing plan. In addition, analysis of the relative sales performances of different product variants can lead to a new marketing strategy or the pruning of a product line.

These analyses can also be used *ex post,* or after the planning period, and at specific intervals within the planning period. Such a use of financial analyses would be for *control* purposes. Obviously, it is important to measure how the company has done or how it is doing, the latter being particularly important for making adjustments during the execution of the plan.

In this chapter, we take a detailed look at several kinds of financial analyses that are important for product management. Besides the sales and profitability analyses just mentioned, we describe a strategic approach to control that explicitly links financial to marketing analysis. We also discuss capital budgeting from a marketing perspective.

SALES ANALYSIS

Overview

Consider the advertisement shown in Figure 15.1. Although it undoubtedly overstates the case just a bit, the point made by the graph and the text is clear: In many cases, it is impossible to determine how successful a product or service really is without digging deeper into its sales records. The overall picture can be quite rosy while some real problems can exist in certain channels, regions of the world, sizes, and so on.

This realization leads to the *iceberg principle.*[1] Many of the real problems facing a product manager lie "beneath the water." Like the tip of an iceberg, total sales or profits are the small amount of the mass that is readily visible. However, if the product manager wishes to avoid the fate of many passengers of the *Titanic,* the large amount of mass that is invisible should also be taken into account.

A simple example illustrates the iceberg principle. Suppose the planning horizon coincides with the calendar year and for control purposes, the product manager analyzes her product's sales performance for the first six months, January through June. She finds that sales are $400,000 below objective. Now suppose further that the product is sold in four sizes, and after digging a bit deeper, you find that sales versus objective vary by size:

Size	Over Objective	Under Objective
1	$200,000	
2	160,000	
3	20,000	
4		$780,000
Total	$380,000	$780,000

Thus, the $400,000 figure is a *net* figure that combines $380,000 over objective with $780,000 below objective. Clearly, the problem is severe for size 4. Taking the analysis

[1] The term apparently originated in Crisp (1961).

FIGURE 15.1 Why Sales Analyses are Needed

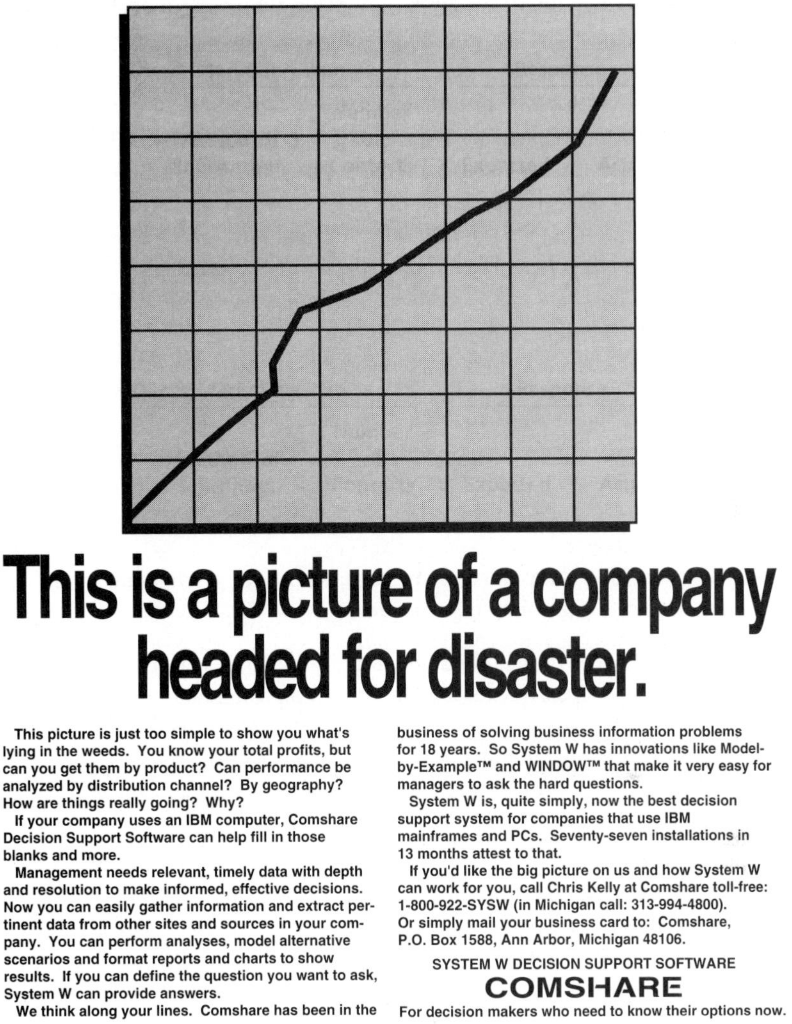

This is a picture of a company headed for disaster.

This picture is just too simple to show you what's lying in the weeds. You know your total profits, but can you get them by product? Can performance be analyzed by distribution channel? By geography? How are things really going? Why?

If your company uses an IBM computer, Comshare Decision Support Software can help fill in those blanks and more.

Management needs relevant, timely data with depth and resolution to make informed, effective decisions. Now you can easily gather information and extract pertinent data from other sites and sources in your company. You can perform analyses, model alternative scenarios and format reports and charts to show results. If you can define the question you want to ask, System W can provide answers.

We think along your lines. Comshare has been in the business of solving business information problems for 18 years. So System W has innovations like Model-by-Example™ and WINDOW™ that make it very easy for managers to ask the hard questions.

System W is, quite simply, now the best decision support system for companies that use IBM mainframes and PCs. Seventy-seven installations in 13 months attest to that.

If you'd like the big picture on us and how System W can work for you, call Chris Kelly at Comshare toll-free: 1-800-922-SYSW (in Michigan call: 313-994-4800). Or simply mail your business card to: Comshare, P.O. Box 1588, Ann Arbor, Michigan 48106.

SYSTEM W DECISION SUPPORT SOFTWARE
COMSHARE
For decision makers who need to know their options now.

Source: Courtesy of Comshare, Inc.

one step further by decomposing the sales for size 4 into different geographic regions produces the following:

Region	Over Objective	Under Objective
East		$1,200,000
Central	$260,000	
South	60,000	
Pacific	100,000	
Total	$420,000	$1,200,000

Again, the problem has now grown into a much bigger one than the initial $400,000 below objective indicated.

This simple analysis provides two clear benefits. First, the product manager better understands the true magnitude of any problems that exist. Second, potential problem areas are identified. For example, the product manager should focus efforts on size 4 and the East region to attempt to understand why the product is unsuccessful in that size and region and not the others. This evaluation could lead to eliminating the size, the region, or both, or to revamping the marketing strategy in those product and geographic segments. However, sales analysis does not explain *why* there are problems; it only pinpoints their location.

The Value of Sales Analysis

In general, sales analysis can be defined as "the gathering, classifying, comparing, and studying of company sales data" (Wotruba, 1971). Obviously, all firms do the gathering part as a way to measure the performance of their products. However, most companies do not study their sales records systematically. In fact, the advertisement in Figure 15.1 illustrates a common belief that companies fail to analyze their own sales records. As the simple analysis above shows, when compared to some standard of performance (in this case, the stated objective), sales analysis can be a powerful tool in the hands of a product manager.

Figure 15.2 shows the major components of a sales analysis. The four major parts correspond to the following questions.

1. How are sales defined? As noted in Figure 15.2, sales can be defined in terms of orders, shipments, or cash receipts. The definition can matter a great deal, particularly for manufactured products. Some companies book sales when the product is shipped, for example, prior to receiving payment for them. Overly zealous managers who are short of sales goals have been known to ship product to themselves to achieve quotas!

2. In what units can sales be analyzed? Sales can be measured in terms of currency, units, or percentage of company sales, among other measures. Currency is useful, particularly when the product can be purchased in a large number of sizes. However, increases in sales in currency terms mask price increases. (Units do not have that problem.) Even when the product is available in different forms (e.g., a cold remedy that is available in both tablet and liquid forms) or sizes, the industry can develop norms of measurement (such as a standard dosage size).

3. In what categories or classifications can the sales data be placed? There are many possibilities here. In the example above, we used geographical area and product size. Figure 15.2 shows some other categories. Other common bases of classification are product types, customer types, markets or channels, order sizes, and time periods. Order size is a particularly useful way to break down sales, as shown in Figure 15.3. A situation in which 20 percent of the orders constitute over 80 percent of the sales dollars is not uncommon. In that case, a profitability analysis would show that the small orders not only produce a small percentage of total sales but are also unprofitable to fill.

4. What are the appropriate standards against which the sales can be compared? As Figure 15.2 shows, some of these standards include historical results, current results from another category in the same time period, some predetermined standard such as an objective or quota, averages across the company or some other business unit, and sales relative to market share (such as the share of voice concept discussed in Chapter 11).

FIGURE 15.2   **Components of Sales Analysis**

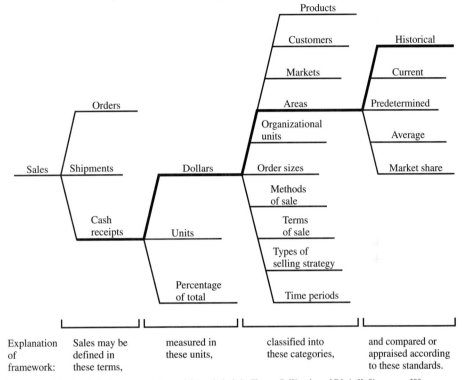

Explanation of framework:	Sales may be defined in these terms,	measured in these units,	classified into these categories,	and compared or appraised according to these standards.

Source: Reprinted from *Sales Management: Text and Cases,* 2nd ed., by Thomas R. Wotruba and Edwin K. Simpson, p. 589.
© PWS-KENT Publishing Company, by South-Western Publishing Company, a Division of International Thomson Publishing, Inc.

Each kind of sales analysis can be denoted by using Figure 15.2 and drawing a line beneath the construct used. As shown, one such analysis could compare historical cash receipts from geographical areas. Naturally, the particular analysis used should be consistent with company record keeping, the particular product being analyzed, and the markets in which it is sold.

FIGURE 15.3   **Sales Analysis Example**

Size of Order	Number of Orders	Percentage of Total Orders	Sales Value	Percentage of Total Sales	Average Sales Value per Order	
Under $10.00	477	17.2	$ 2,599	0.3	$ 5.45	
$10–$24.99	462	16.8	8,607	1.0	18.63	
$25–$49.99	558	20.3	21,059	2.4	37.74	
$50–$99.99	388	14.1	29,798	3.4	76.80	
$100–$199.99	151	5.5	23,450	2.7	155.30	
$200–$499.99	156	5.7	50,039	5.7	320.76	
$500–$1,000.00	209	7.6	163,559	18.7	782.58	
Over $1,000.00	352	12.8	576,588	65.8	1,638.03	
	2,753	100.0	$875,699	100.0	$ 318.09	overall average

Source: Thomas R. Wotruba, *Sales Management: Planning, Accomplishment, and Evaluation* (New York: Holt, Rinehart, & Winston, 1971), p. 478.

A good example of the value of sales analysis is Reebok's experience in the late 1990s (Lefton, 1999). The brand had fallen from the success it had in the 1980s, and one of the areas that senior managers felt needed improvement was a reduction in the number of stock-keeping units (SKUs) generated by the large number of model/color/size combinations, what the company refers to as styles. An analysis of the sales by style found that of the 2,200 existing styles, 1,000 of them generated only .003 percent of Reebok's volume. An immediate action was to reduce the number of styles to the 600 generating most of the sales volume, which permitted a greater ability to focus marketing dollars where they counted.

Roadblocks

If this analysis is so simple yet so valuable, why is it not used more by companies and their product managers? We have identified three reasons.

First, information systems often are not designed with product management in mind. Finance, accounting, manufacturing, operations, and human resource personnel are often key informants about the development of an information system. However, to be useful to a product manager, the system must collect the detailed receipt information and make it available for analysis. If marketing personnel are not queried for their needs when developing the system, the system is not likely to have the characteristics necessary for performing sales analyses.

Second, and related to the first point, financial or accounting personnel have quite different mindsets and perspectives than marketing personnel. Their information needs, training, and background are quite different. The differences can lead to inadequate information and a less-than-helpful perspective on the value of the information to the company.

Finally, one reason for failing to conduct sales analysis is a lack of internal marketing on the part of product management. A strong internal marketing program is necessary to induce any kind of change within an organization. It is important that marketing personnel be proactive in convincing senior managers who influence information system design that the detailed sales data are important and have value. Otherwise, the different mindsets and backgrounds will continue to dominate the way such systems are designed.

In retailing environments, these kinds of barriers are being broken down with the increasing penetration of optical scanners, point-of-sale (POS) systems, and other technology-based systems that generate detailed sales data. Because each product variant is labeled with a different code, excellent data for sales analyses are being produced for products sold through food, drug, and many discount stores. However, many consumer products and almost all business-to-business products do not benefit from such technology at the present time.

PROFITABILITY ANALYSIS

Conventional Product Profit Accounting

A good way to begin this discussion is to use an illustration of an actual financial statement. Figure 15.4 shows an income statement for a hypothetical telecommunications service, referred to as NewCall. The top line indicates that 2 million units of the service were sold during the fiscal year at $5 each for total revenues of $10 million. Subtracted from

FIGURE 15.4 Typical Income Statement

Product: NewCall Income Statement, December 31, 2005 (000's)		
Revenues (2M units @ $5)		$10,000
Less: Direct labor		2,500
Direct supervision/clerical		500
Social Security		255
Materials		5
Operations overhead (plant, etc.)		840
Expenses from operations		4,100
Operating or gross margin		5,900
Less: Advertising	$ 700	
Promotion	200	
Field sales	1,700	
Product management	25	
Marketing management	250	
Product development	150	
Marketing research	175	
Customer service	1,500	
Testing	300	
General and administrative	1,000	
Total expenses		6,000
Operating profit		(100)

this revenue figure are expenses related directly to operations such as labor, materials, and certain kinds of operations overhead (utilities, for example). This gives a gross or operating margin of $5.9 million. Finally, all other expenses are subtracted, giving a total profit (loss) of ($100,000).

This approach to computing profits is called a *full-costing approach,* in which all costs associated with a product or service, including corporate overhead, are subtracted from revenues. This is the most popular approach to product profitability accounting. The strength of the full-costing approach is that it guarantees that all the costs of the corporation are covered by the products. Another way to say this is that the corporation will be profitable by ensuring that each product is profitable.

However, this approach has some weaknesses that will become apparent as we work through the example. First, given that the product is losing money, is the company better off by dropping NewCall? At first glance, it appears the company would be $100,000 more profitable by eliminating the product. In reality, this turns out not to be the case; the company could actually be worse off.[2] Second, it is difficult to use the full-costing approach to obtain answers to relatively straightforward questions. For example, if revenues increase by 10 percent, what happens to profitability? We develop the ability to address these questions later in the chapter.

---

[2] This assertion and the later analysis assume there are no opportunity costs of continuing to invest in a product that may generate a lower return on investment than other projects.

Alternative Accounting Systems

We can classify accounting reporting systems into three groups. First, one kind of system is referred to as "financial" or "custodial." Figure 15.4 shows an example of such a system. These systems are good for looking at historical financial results—"how we did." In addition, they are useful for external constituents, such as investors, who may care only about the aggregate or overall financial performance of a company.

Financial reporting systems based on full costing have several problems. First, full-costing methods are inherently unable to link costs, volumes, and profits because different kinds of costs, some of which affect a product's true profitability and some of which do not, are not categorized. The full-cost approach also tends to allocate fixed costs arbitrarily. For example, a common way to allocate overhead costs such as electricity is by sales volume. Clearly, such costs become difficult to plan for because they are almost always variable (as sales volume changes, so do the charges for power). In addition, this approach gives managers a disincentive to raise sales levels because more and more costs are piled on, making the product look less profitable. Finally, these custodial systems fail to draw a distinction between costs that are under the control of the product manager and those that are not. From the product manager's perspective, it is entirely fair to be required to generate more revenues than costs directly attributable to his or her product. However, should a product's profitability, and therefore the manager's evaluation, be a function of how many corporate jets are in the hangar?

A second type of system is performance based. This kind of system is primarily control oriented: It looks at today's performance based on variances from budgets. These variances are useful to pinpoint problems but, like sales analysis, do not provide any answers.

A third kind of system is contribution based. As we show in the next section, its emphasis is on costs the product manager can control, and it makes a clear distinction between fixed and variable costs. Contribution-based systems are designed for operating managers, and are decision oriented. They permit the manager to look toward the future by being able to generate answers to "what if" kinds of questions.

Our point is not that one system should be used to the exclusion of another but that several kinds of reporting systems are important to provide full information to all levels of management. Corporate jets may be necessary to conduct business, and their costs must be covered by the firm's products. However, should the health of an individual product be damaged by being saddled with a high overhead charge? Another kind of profitability thus indicates how much revenue is generated in excess of costs directly related to marketing an individual product. The more a product manager knows about how profits are calculated, the better equipped she or he is to battle with more senior managers over resource allocation decisions.

Contribution-Oriented Systems

The earlier discussion of Figure 15.4 illustrates one of the "bottom lines" that provides useful information (although with some important limitations) to product managers. A second notion of profitability is called *contribution margin*. Basically, contribution margin is the amount of money left over after accounting for variable costs that goes toward covering fixed costs. At this point, it is critical to be clear on the different categories of costs.

FIGURE 15.5 Cost Classification

Category	Total Cost	Components Variable	Components Fixed
Operating expenses ($000)			
Direct labor	$ 2,500	2,500	
Direct supervision	500	500	
Social Security	255	255	
Materials	5	5	
Operations overhead	840	200	640
Subtotal:	$ 4,100	3,460	640
Nonoperating expenses ($000)			
Advertising	$ 700		700
Promotion	200		200
Field sales	1,700	200	1,500
Product management	25		25
Marketing management	250		250
Marketing research	175		175
Customer service	1,500	240	1,260
Testing	300		300
General and administrative	1,000		1,000
Subtotal:	$ 6,000	$ 440	$5,560
Total	$10,100	3,900	6,200

Figure 15.5 categorizes different kinds of costs that will be useful in our discussion. Variable costs are those that vary directly with total volume of sales or production. Such costs normally include materials (for manufactured products) and direct labor (hourly), but they can also include supplies such as packaging. We assume the variable cost per unit remains constant as volume changes.[3]

Fixed costs are more complicated. In general, a cost is fixed if it does not vary in amount with the volume of sales or production. Fixed costs tend to be items such as advertising, customer service, corporate jets, and the like. However, at some level of sales, all costs become variable. That is, rather than being level for any amount of sales, fixed costs often follow a step pattern: They can increase with a large jump in sales but remain level at this new plateau. For example, if the product sells better than expected, additional customer service representatives may have to be hired. Fixed costs can be direct, that is, directly associated with a given product (e.g., advertising), or indirect (e.g., the corporate jet). In addition, programmed fixed costs are highly flexible because they can be increased or decreased at will. Standby fixed costs are difficult to adjust in the short run.

Using these definitions, one can take the numbers in Figure 15.4 and classify them into variable and fixed categories (we will be concerned later with the different categories of

[3] This is not always the case, particularly if the product exhibits *experience curve* effects where costs per unit decline with cumulative volume. However, variable costs per unit are usually fixed within a reasonable range of sales or production.

FIGURE 15.6 Classifying Costs: Fixed versus Variable

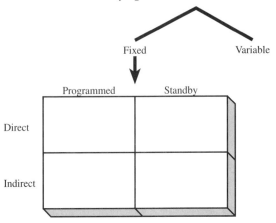

Source: *Nation's Restaurant News.*

fixed costs).[4] Figure 15.6 shows a suggested classification scheme. Examining the operating expenses first (the top part of Figure 15.4), direct labor, Social Security (a fixed percentage of direct labor), and materials are clearly variable because they depend on sales volume. We assume operations overhead has fixed and variable components. For example, utility bills can vary with production volume and hence may be variable, whereas depreciation of plant and equipment is fixed. Much of the nonoperating expense is fixed except for field sales, which have some commission (fixed percentage of sales) and customer service (on-site service expense is a percentage of the number of units sold).

These newly classified costs can be assembled into a new financial statement, shown in Figure 15.7, called a *contribution margin* statement. The revenues remain the same at $10 million. However, we first subtract the variable costs of $3.9 million, leaving $6.1 million in contribution margin. This is the amount of money left after direct costs of making the product or delivering the service that will go toward covering fixed costs. What is called the contribution or variable margin *rate* is the contribution margin divided by the total sales revenue—in this case, $6.1 million divided by $10 million, or 61 percent. Another way to look at this number is that 61 cents of every dollar of sales goes to covering fixed costs. On a per-unit basis, this translates to $3.05 (61 percent times $5). These are important numbers for answering some key questions.

All we have done is reallocate the costs into categories different from those used in the income statement shown in Figure 15.4. Although we have not shown yet how this new scheme helps make better decisions, it should already be clear that Figure 15.7 is somewhat easier to interpret. In fact, now we can easily answer the question posed earlier concerning the profit impact of a 10 percent increase in revenues. If revenues increase to $11 million, variable costs also increase by 10 percent to $4.29 million. Since fixed costs remain the same at $6.2 million, the new profit figure would be $510,000, or an increase of $610,000. This would not have been easy to calculate from the statement shown in Figure 15.4.

---

[4] Obviously, the exact classification will vary across individual situations. Figure 15.4 is meant as an illustration only.

FIGURE 15.7 Contribution Margin Statement

Product: NewCall Income Statement, December 31, 2005 (000's)		
Revenues (2M units @ $5)		$10,000
Variable costs		
Direct labor	$2,500	
Direct supervision/clerical	500	
Social Security	255	
Sales force commission	200	
Customer service	240	
Materials	5	
Operations overhead (plant, etc.)	200	
Total variable costs		3,900
Contribution margin (61%)		6,100
Fixed costs		
Operations overhead	640	
Advertising	700	
Promotion	200	
Field sales	1,500	
Product management	25	
Marketing management	250	
Product development	150	
Marketing research	175	
Customer service	1,260	
Testing	300	
General and administrative	1,000	
Total fixed costs		6,200
Operating profit (loss)		(100)

Using the Contribution Margin Rate

Three basic calculations make use of the contribution margin concept. First, most product managers need to know their *break-even* volume in both units and dollars. This is the amount they need to sell to cover fixed costs. The formulae are:

Breakeven in units = Fixed costs/variable margin per unit

Breakeven in dollars = Fixed costs/variable margin rate

One other important concept is the *safety factor,* which is the amount over (or under) the break-even volume currently being sold:

Safety factor = (Current sales volume − Break-even volume)/Current volume

Using the information from Figure 15.7, the break-even volume in units is the fixed-cost figure of $6.2 million divided by $3.05 (the contribution margin per unit), or 2,032,787 units. The break-even volume in dollars is $6.2 million divided by 61 percent, or $10,163,934. Clearly, NewCall is operating below its break-even level. As a result, the safety factor is negative: 21.6 percent.

A word of warning about break-even analyses is that they are very short-run oriented because the calculations are based on only one year's results. Even though NewCall is below breakeven, it may be a new product and therefore need additional time to establish itself in the marketplace. Overreliance on break-even analyses can result in the company making myopic decisions on products that have considerable promise. However, they are useful benchmarks when used conservatively.

Break-even analysis can also be applied to any incremental change in fixed costs. Suppose the NewCall product manager wishes to hire two additional salespeople at a total cost of $200,000 per year. The sales volume that would have to be generated to cover their salaries (assuming no commission) would be $200,000 divided by .61, or $327,869. Alternatively, if the product manager wishes to spend an additional $100,000 on advertising, $163,934 will have to be generated to break even, assuming no long-term effects of the advertising.

An additional use of the contribution margin information is in profit planning. Suppose the NewCall product manager was given a target of $500,000 profit. The dollar revenues needed would be computed using the following formula:

$$\text{Target profit breakeven} = (\text{Target} + \text{Fixed costs})/\text{Contribution rate}$$

Thus, the target profit acts as an additional hurdle to overcome in addition to fixed costs. In dollars, the necessary revenue would be ($500,000 + $6.2 million)/.61, or $10,983,607. In units, the break-even amount would be $6.7 million/$3.05, or 2,196,721 units.

As noted earlier, it is relatively straightforward to calculate the profit impact of increases or decreases in revenues. An increase in revenues of 10 percent increased profits by $610,000. However, the reverse is also true: A decrease in revenues of 10 percent increases the loss by $610,000. It turns out that more fixed cost–intensive businesses suffer when sales drop because there is less revenue to cover the fixed costs. A good example of this problem is the airline industry (and most service businesses in general). The airline industry is characterized by low variable costs (e.g., fuel, food) and extremely high fixed costs (e.g., flight attendants, interest payments on airplanes). This results in price wars for passengers because any empty seats mean lost revenue that can cover fixed costs. Although revenues per passenger drop, the drop can hopefully be offset by greater total revenues per flight. Recessionary periods and products with inherently slow growth rates exacerbate the problem.

In general, products characterized by different variable margin rates have quite different strategic problems. When variable costs are high (contribution margin rates are low), it is important to keep prices high because profit is made on each item sold. That is, with relatively low fixed costs to cover, profitability is determined by the profit margin on each unit. When fixed costs are high and variable costs are low, sales volume to generate contribution margin to cover the fixed costs becomes critical.

This conclusion is borne out by the figures shown in Figure 15.8. The horizontal dimension is the variable margin rate. Fixed costs increase from left to right. The vertical dimension reflects alternative price changes. The entries in the table are the percentage of new-unit sales to old-unit sales required to break even for a given price change and associated contribution margin rate. Thus, if a product has a 35 percent margin rate and the product manager is thinking of cutting price by 10 percent, sales would have to increase by 40 percent to break even. This occurs because if the price drops, the variable margin rate also drops and less money is left to cover fixed costs. What is alarming is the

FIGURE 15.8   Break-Even Analysis Table

Percentage Change in Price	Variable Margin Rate (percent)								
	10	**15**	**20**	**25**	**30**	**35**	**40**	**45**	**50**
+25	29	38	45	50	55	58	62	64	66
+20	33	43	50	56	60	64	67	69	72
+15	40	50	53	57	59	70	73	75	77
+10	50	60	67	72	73	78	80	82	83
+5	67	75	80	83	86	88	89	90	91
0	100	100	100	100	100	100	100	100	100
−5	200	150	133	125	123	117	114	113	111
−10		300	200	167	150	140	133	129	125
−15			400	280	200	175	160	150	143
−20				500	300	233	200	180	167
−25					600	350	267	225	200

Divide each table entry by 100. Entries represent the ratio of new unit sales to old unit sales required to break even on a price change for products with various current variable margin rates.

amount of additional sales needed to break even for even relatively modest price cuts *for any contribution margin rate!* You can see that the airlines benefit to some extent by having contribution margin rates to the right end (or even off) the scale because the higher the margin rate, the less a price cut hurts contribution margin and the lower the incremental volume that has to be generated to break even for any price cut.

Fixed Costs

As we noted earlier, there are different kinds of fixed costs. Programmed direct fixed costs are the kind product managers control and are usually expended for a specific planning period. In other words, they are discretionary. Examples of this kind of costs are advertising, promotion, and the like. Programmed indirect fixed costs are controlled by management but cover several products. Corporate umbrella advertising would fall into this category. Standby direct fixed costs do not change significantly without a major change in operations and are generally not controlled by the product manager in the short run. An example would be costs associated with a production facility that is dedicated to a specific product. Standby indirect fixed costs are typically corporate overhead—the jet, the CEO's salary, and so on. They are not directly related to any specific product, nor are they controlled by the product manager.

The reason for making these distinctions goes back to the notion of profitability and the evaluation of the product manager. For what costs should the manager be responsible? We could argue that the product manager has a primary responsibility to make a profit by generating revenues in excess of variable costs that cover the fixed costs attributable to his or her product—the direct costs, both standby and programmed. In other words, the product manager should be responsible for making a profit based on costs that would exist *only* if the product existed. Any costs that would not disappear if the product were

FIGURE 15.9 Income Statement: Direct versus Indirect Fixed Costs

Product: NewCall Income Statement, December 31, 2005 (000's)		
Revenues (2M units @ $5)		$10,000
Variable costs		
Direct labor	$2,500	
Direct supervision	500	
Social Security	255	
Sales force commissions	200	
Customer service	240	
Materials	5	
Operations overhead	200	
Total		3,900
Contribution margin (61%)		6,100
Fixed costs		
Programmed direct:		
Advertising	500	
Promotion	200	
Field sales	1,500	
Product management	25	
Marketing management	200	
Product development	50	
Marketing research	150	
Customer service	400	
Total	3,025	3,075
Standby direct:		
Operations overhead	640	
Testing	300	
General and administrative	300	
Total	1,240	1,835
Programmed indirect:		
Advertising	200	
Marketing management	50	
Product development	100	
Marketing research	25	
Customer service	860	
Standby indirect:		
General and administrative	700	
Total indirect costs	1,935	
Operating profit		(100)

dropped are not the responsibility of the product manager. This is, in fact, a conservative approach because some of the direct standby costs might not disappear at all if the product were dropped. A manufacturing plant, for example, could be adapted for producing another product made by the company.

Figure 15.9 illustrates (based on some assumptions) how these fixed-cost categories can affect the profit picture for a product. The fully allocated cost bottom line is the same, of course (a loss of $100,000), as is the contribution margin bottom line of $6.1 million. However, look at the third "bottom line," that is, the profit picture after subtracting all direct fixed costs. After conservatively subtracting both programmed *and* standby direct fixed costs, NewCall shows a "profit" of $1.835 million! Only after subtracting costs over which the product manager has no control does the product show a loss. We can now answer a question stated earlier in this chapter: In fact, the company would be *worse* off by dropping this money-"losing" product because it is generating $1.835 million that is going toward covering indirect fixed costs.[5] Thus, it is not always clear what profits and losses mean.

In sum, each of the three notions of profit developed in this chapter have pluses and minuses. The full-costing statement (Figure 15.4) is of most interest to top management and external constituents. In addition, ultimately *all* costs of the business must be covered. The contribution margin statement (Figure 15.7) is easy to read and gives a quick idea of how much money is being generated to cover fixed costs. However, it does not make a distinction between indirect and direct fixed costs. Finally, the statement breaking down fixed costs (Figure 15.9) is the most relevant for product management because it clearly states how the product is performing. It also reflects that it is becoming more important to relate product costs to actual activity as opposed to arbitrary allocation methods (Cooper and Kaplan, 1991). However, it is also true that all products sold by a company could be profitable by this measure, but the company would go out of business because the excess funds generated beyond direct costs do not cover indirect costs. To repeat a point we made earlier, product managers must equip themselves with information about the different kinds of profit concepts discussed here to make a better case for an increased share of corporate resources.

A STRATEGIC FRAMEWORK FOR CONTROL

The two financial analyses described thus far can be used both for ex ante budgeting (while the plan is being developed) and for ex post (or after the planning period) control purposes. However, a specific kind of analysis called *variance* analysis is used for control only. In this context, a variance is a discrepancy between a planned figure or objective and the actual outcome. Typically, control in a marketing planning context is limited to some simple variances such as comparing actual advertising expenditures to historical averages or market share (using advertising share) or expected versus actual levels of profit or sales. Variance analysis was developed to integrate accounting with concepts from marketing strategy and planning (Hulbert and Toy, 1977). Like the sales analysis presented earlier, the major benefit of variance analysis is identification of potential problem areas, not diagnosing the causes of the problems.

Figure 15.10 presents possible market results for a hypothetical product, Alpha. As is typical with a variance analysis, the three columns refer to the planned amount, the

---

[5] This assumes that there are no product substitutes for NewCall in the short run.

FIGURE 15.10 **Example of Variance Analysis: Product Alpha**

Item	Planned	Actual	Variance
Revenues			
Sales (lbs.)	20,000,000	22,000,000	2,000,000
Price per lb. ($)	0.50	.4773	0.227
Revenues	$10,000,000	$10,500,000	$500,000
Total market (lbs.)	40,000,000	50,000,000	10,000,000
Share of market	50%	44%	(6%)
Costs			
Variable cost per lb. ($)	.30	.30	—
Contribution			
Per lb. ($)	.20	.1773	.0227
Total ($)	4,000,000	3,900,000	(100,000)

Source: James H. Hulbert and Norman E. Toy, "A Strategic Framework for Marketing Control," *Journal of Marketing*, April 1977, p. 13.

actual amount, and the difference or variance. The rows describe different quantities of interest. Of particular note are market size and share that link to well-known models of strategic marketing planning, such as the Boston Consulting Group's growth-share matrix.

Figure 15.10 shows an unfavorable contribution variance of $100,000. Assuming the variances are due to marketing-related activities alone, the $100,000 variance could be due to volume variance, that is, selling a different amount than that planned, or a contribution variance. The volume variance is due to variances between planned and actual figures for market size and market share, the two key strategic variables. By decomposing the results in this way, the product manager has a more complete view of where the problems in the product's performance may lie.

Price–Quantity Decomposition

The following terms are used below:

S = Share.

M = Total market size.

Q = Quantity sold in units.

C = Contribution margin per unit.

An a subscript denotes actual values, and p denotes planned values. The variance is given by a v subscript.

The price/cost variance is

$$(C_a - C_p) \times Q_a = (.1773 - .20) \times 22,000,000 = -\$500,000$$

This comes from selling too much at a low margin. In other words, the product is penalized heavily for missing the contribution target. The volume variance is

$$(Q_a - Q_p) \times C_p = (22,000,000 - 20,000,000) \times .20 = \$400,000$$

The sum of these variances is the $-\$100,000$ shown in Figure 15.10.

Penetration–Market Size Decomposition

The next stage of the analysis decomposes the volume variance into components due to penetration (market share) and market size. The difference in quantity sold is $Q_a - Q_p$. However, we know that actual quantity is actual share times actual market size, or $Q_a = (M_a \times S_a)$. Likewise, planned quantity $Q_p = (M_p \times S_p)$. Thus, the key to understanding the quantity or volume variance is to understand the variances in share and market size.

The variance in contribution due to market share can be expressed by

$$(S_a - S_p) \times M_a \times C_p,$$

which is

$$(.44 - .50) \times 50{,}000{,}000 \times .2 = -\$600{,}000$$

This is offset by the gain from the increased size of the market:

$$(M_a - M_p) \times S_p \times C_p,$$

which is

$$(50{,}000{,}000 - 40{,}000{,}000) \times .5 \times .2 = \$1{,}000{,}000$$

Thus, the sum of the two variances, share and market size, nets out to $400,000, which is the quantity variance noted above.

A summary of this analysis is the following:

Planned profit contribution		$4,000,000
Volume variance		
Share variance	($600,000)	
Market size variance	1,000,000	
		400,000
Price/cost variance		(500,000)
Actual profit contribution		$3,900,000

Summary

Who has responsibility for these variances? The market size variance is due to under-forecasting the size of the market. In some companies, this is the responsibility of the product manager. However, there are numerous explanations for why the forecast is low. One explanation could be that insufficient exogenous factors, such as population growth, government spending, interest rates, and the like, were considered. Many times, the forecast is off due to unexpected changes in competitive strategy. In this case, product Alpha's price was lower than planned. The low price can be due to increased price competition, which, if total market demand is price elastic, can cause the market size to increase. This would be difficult to forecast. No matter what the source of the error was, the under-forecast resulted in a $1 million favorable variance. However, this is not entirely positive. Market growth greater than expected may have contributed to a set of actions by the product manager that led to loss of competitive position. As the (former) market leader in a fast-growing market, this is a serious loss.

In addition, market share was substantially lower than planned. This also can be due to a large number of factors, but it is usually due less to forecasting errors than to actions by the relevant product managers. In the case of product Alpha, it is possible that the product manager reacted late with a price cut, enabling competitors to gain share. Alternatively, a competitor may have launched a particularly creative advertising campaign. In other words, the market share variance is due more to operational problems than to poor forecasting. This error was particularly damaging, however, costing $600,000 in lost profits.

Clearly, decomposing the $400,000 volume variance into the two components, share and market size, provides more information to the product manager. Like the sales analysis, the $400,000 figure is aggregate and masks substantial underlying numbers. Understanding how market share and size variances contribute to the overall volume variance pinpoints areas for further examination, perhaps organizationally (How do we do our forecasting?) and operationally (How should we react to a competitor's price cut?).

The price/cost variance of −$500,000 is also quite large. However, this variance, although calculated separately, is clearly not independent of the volume variance and its decomposition. The drop in price may well have led to the increased market size. Perhaps the drop in share to 44 percent would have been greater without the lower contribution achieved.

Finally, while the example illustrates the use of this strategic framework for control of a product after the end of the planning period, one major potential application of the approach is for control *during* the execution of the plan. It would clearly be better to understand the variances after 6 months than after 12. Appropriate corrective action could take place and reduce some of the negative variances before the end of the year.

CAPITAL BUDGETING

Overview

Product managers often have to weigh alternatives when making incremental changes in a product or deciding whether or not to introduce a new variant. For example, a workstation product manager may have several options for making product improvements, such as a larger hard disk, a new configuration of the case for a smaller "footprint" on a manager's desk, a better monitor, and so on. These alternative projects have different degrees of potential for expanding sales, market share, or both and thus have different potential financial impacts.

The same kind of reasoning can be applied to other kinds of investments made by the product manager. For example, marketing mix expenditures, such as advertising, promotion, sales force, and so on, can be viewed as projects in the sense that they are investments intended to produce some future cash flow to the firm. Thus, an increase of $1 million in advertising must be weighed against expanding the sales force or adopting product improvements.

The same mechanism operates at the firm level. Different new product ideas come from research and development, each with alternative degrees of potential financial success. Like the product manager, senior managers must develop an approach to prioritize investments in new products or major reformulations.

Capital budgeting is an area of finance that deals with this prioritization of projects within a firm.[6] Many readers will already be familiar with the basics of capital budgeting. However, there is rarely any link between what transpires in finance courses and what actually happens in marketing on this topic. For example:

> Marketers and finance people seldom see eye to eye. The marketers say, "This product will open up a whole new market segment." Finance people respond, "It's a bad investment. The IRR (internal rate of return) is only 8%." Why are they so often in opposition?[7]

This section briefly describes the main approaches to rationing resources among a set of risky projects and discusses how marketing issues are heavily related to capital budgeting.

The Basics

Capital budgeting involves five discrete steps:

1. Generating investment proposals.
2. Estimating cash flows for the proposals.
3. Evaluating the cash flows.
4. Selecting projects based on an acceptance criterion.
5. Reevaluating the projects after their acceptance.

We focus on the first three steps in this chapter.

Although a detailed discussion is outside the scope of this book, it is clear that marketing management has great influence on alternative investment proposals (Crawford and DiBenedetto, 2000). New product concepts come from contacts with customers such as focus groups, internally from product management, and from a large variety of other sources besides research and development.

Marketing management also generates estimates of cash flows. Product managers or staff personnel develop sales forecasts. They obtain estimates of penetration rates over time from simulated test marketing laboratories, intention-to-buy surveys, and other marketing research sources.

Given that cash flows (after tax) have been estimated, the third step is to evaluate the attractiveness of the different proposals. Again, these could be new products, refinements, or even investments in advertising. The five major methods used to perform this evaluation are

1. Average rate of return.
2. Payback.

---

[6] A good reference on capital budgeting is Van Horne (2001).

[7] For an extended commentary on this issue, see Barwise, Marsh, and Wensley (1989).

3. Internal rate of return.

4. Present value.

5. Economic value added.

Average Rate of Return

This accounting method takes the ratio of the average annual profits after taxes to the average investment in the project. For example, if the average annual profits are $5,000 and the average investment per year in the project is $20,000, the average rate of return is 25 percent. A variant of this method divides the average annual profits by the original investment rather than by the average. The return rate can be compared to hurdles used by the firm or other standards. The obvious advantage of this method is that it is simple. However, it ignores the timing of the profits since it values the income from the last year as much as income from the first year.

Payback

This method calculates the number of years it will take to recover the initial investment in the project. It is the ratio of the initial investment over the annual cash flows (not profits as in the average rate of return method). Thus, if the initial investment is $100,000 and the annual cash flow is $20,000, the payback period is five years. If the annual cash flows are not equal, you can still easily calculate the payback period by simply adding the yearly flows up to the point where the initial investment is recovered. The calculated payback period is then compared to a threshold level; if it is less, it is accepted. A major problem with this method is that it ignores cash flows after the payback period. It also does not account for the timing of the cash flows.

Internal Rate of Return (IRR)

Most analysts use some kind of discounted cash flow analysis to evaluate projects. The key point is that an equivalent amount of money in the future is not worth as much as it is today. This method and the present value method take account both the size and the timing of the cash flows returned by a project.

Let r be a rate of interest. Assuming the initial investment in the project occurs at time 0 and n is the last period when cash flows (A) can be expected, the internal rate of return is calculated from the following formula:

$$A_0 = A_1/(1 + r) + A_2/(1 + r)^2 + \cdots + A_n/(1 + r)^n$$

Therefore, r is the rate that discounts the future cash flows from the project to equal the initial investment (r is the number that equates the right side of the equation with the initial investment, A_0). As with the other methods, r must be compared to an internal hurdle rate or requirement set by management for a project to be accepted. Obviously, this rate should be higher than what is called the risk-free rate, the rate the company could get by putting the money in the bank.[8] Unfortunately, in many cases companies probably could do better by doing just that!

---

[8] Investors usually demand higher rates of the return than the risk-free rate. This depends on industry and market characteristics.

Present Value

The net present value of a proposal is

$$\text{NPV} = \sum A_t/(1 + k)^t$$

where k is the rate of return the company requires. This is often referred to as the *discount rate* or the firm's *opportunity cost of capital*. Note that when $t = 0$, A is the initial investment and is thus a large negative number. The present value method states that if NPV is greater than 0, the project should be accepted. In other words, you should accept the project if the present value of cash received from it is greater than the present value of cash spent. As might be expected, the internal rate of return and present value methods usually lead to the same decision. However, the NPV method is often favored from a theoretical perspective.

Economic Value Added (EVA)

EVA is a financial performance measure based on operating income after taxes, the investment in assets required to generate that income, and the cost of the investments in those assets (cost of capital) (Ehrbar, 1998). It has become a very popular financial metric since the mid-1990s when it was popularized by the consulting firm Stern Stewart & Company.

The EVA formula is the following:

$$\text{EVA} = \text{After-tax operating income} - (\text{Investment in assets} \times \text{Weighted average cost of capital})$$

EVA is thus a monetary amount. If the amount is positive, the company has earned more after-tax operating income than the cost of the assets employed to generate that income. In other words, the company has created wealth. If EVA is negative, the company is consuming capital. In a capital budgeting context, the manager would therefore accept any project that had a positive EVA.[9]

SUMMARY

Clearly, finance and marketing have much to say to each other concerning capital budgeting.[10] Not only are marketing personnel involved with generating projects and projecting cash flow, but the very concept of what makes a good investment is entirely consistent between the two functions. For a new or reformulated product to generate NPV in excess of the investment costs, it must have inherent value to customers and it must satisfy customer needs better than competitive offerings. The capital budgeting process is much more than simply crunching numbers; the sources of the cash flow must be based on the quality of the marketing strategy and the firm's ability to execute the strategy. Unfortunately, it is often difficult to quantify many of the factors that make a new product or other project attractive to marketing management but unattractive to financial executives.

[9] A more sophisticated approach to assessing investments is to use the notion of a financial option which incorporates uncertainty into the calculations. This has been termed *real option theory*. Although it is beyond the scope of this book, the interested reader is referred to Dixit and Pindyck (1995) and Copeland and Keenan (1998) for good descriptions of this approach.

[10] The material in this section is based on Barwise, Marsh, and Wensley (1989).

Some ways marketing managers can make project evaluation more responsive to strategic concerns are the following:

1. *Use the right base case.* When evaluating a project, the NPV or internal rate of return is normally compared to some reference point. This is usually an implicit *status quo* option. For example, a new product might cannibalize sales of an existing product. The analysis cannot simply consider the new product as incremental revenue and analyze it that way; it must also consider the lost sales of the old product. This is particularly important for investments in marketing mix variables, which often have the intent of stifling a competitor's move. For example, sales promotions often cost more money than they generate. A capital budgeting analysis would probably advise not making such expenditures. However, it is possible that without the promotion, market share and profits would have dropped even more. While base cases are difficult to quantify, they are important for evaluation.

2. *Select the appropriate time horizon.* In the methods described earlier, the time horizon issue was purposely left vague. Clearly, in attempting to implement all the methods except the payback method, it is necessary to have some estimate of *n*, the useful life of the project. In many traditional applications of capital budgeting, the project is a piece of capital equipment whose useful life is typically known. Sometimes the time horizon is set arbitrarily. The size of *n* can affect the NPV or IRR dramatically. For a new product, the stage of the product life cycle would be an important determinant of *n*. In addition, if a new brand name is being established, the value of the name can linger longer than the exact product or service being launched through extensions and modifications. For a marketing mix variable such as advertising, it is difficult to estimate the useful life of additional expenditure; estimating the carryover effects of advertising has been the topic of much discussion for the past 30 years.[11]

3. *Look at other benefits of the investment.* Often investments create other opportunities. An example mentioned earlier is the creation of a brand name that can be utilized by other products. For example, Arm & Hammer has been successful with its brand of toothpaste. It is possible that the company will eventually design a line of toothbrushes. This spinoff value is difficult to quantify in a conventional capital budgeting process.

4. *Unbundle the costs and benefits.* When Procter & Gamble first introduced disposable diapers, it really made several subinvestments. One major investment was in the marketing of the product because advertising, trade and consumer promotion, packaging, and similar components had to be developed. However, the company also had to develop a proprietary production process to efficiently manufacture the diapers. These are really two separate projects that could have separate NPVs or IRRs.

Thus, it is clear that capital budgeting processes need to include strategic considerations that are relevant to product managers. Performing simple financial analyses does not account for these kinds of considerations, which can significantly alter the way a company allocates resources.

---

[11] In fact, from an accounting perspective, advertising is expensed rather than capitalized because the useful life of $1 of advertising is generally unknown. However, viewing advertising as a possible "project" in a capital budgeting sense still captures the essential trade-offs a product manager has to make among various budgets.

References

Barwise, Patrick, Paul R. Marsh, and Robin Wensley (1989) "Must Finance and Strategy Clash?" *Harvard Business Review,* September–October, 85–90.

Cooper, Robin, and Robert S. Kaplan (1991) "Profit Priorities from Activity-Based Costing" *Harvard Business Review,* May–June, 130–35.

Copeland, Thomas E., and Philip T. Keenan (1998) "Making Options Real," *The McKinsey Quarterly* 3, 128–41.

Crawford, C. Merle, and C. Anthony DiBenedetto (2000) *New Products Management,* 6th ed. Burr Ridge, IL: Irwin/McGraw-Hill.

Crisp, Richard D. (1961) *Sales Planning and Control.* New York: McGraw-Hill.

Dixit, Avinash K., and Robert S. Pindyck (1995) "The Options Approach to Capital Investment" *Harvard Business Review,* May–June, 105–15.

Ehrbar, Al (1998) *EVA: The Real Key to Creating Wealth.* New York: John Wiley & Sons.

Hulbert, James M., and Norman E. Toy (1977) "A Strategic Framework For Marketing Control," *Journal of Marketing,* April, 12–20.

Lefton, Terry. (1999) "Bok in the Saddle Again," *Brandweek,* February 8, 26–31.

Van Horne, James C. (2001) *Financial Management and Policy,* 12th ed. Upper Saddle River, NJ: Prentice Hall.

Wotruba, Thomas R. (1971) *Sales Management: Planning, Accomplishment, and Evaluation.* New York: Holt, Rinehart & Winston.

Chapter **Sixteen**

Marketing Metrics

Overview

The marketing plan outline in the appendix to Chapter 2 has a section titled "Monitors and Controls" (Section VII). The major purpose of this section is to ensure that the objectives of the marketing plan are monitored over the course of the period in which the plan is being implemented. For example, if the company does semiannual planning and the product manager has set the marketing objective to be 25 percent of the unit sales of the category, it is not prudent to wait six months to see if the objective is being met. Data should be collected sufficiently frequently in order to make adjustments if necessary during the course of a plan.

In addition to an overall marketing objective such as share or sales, product managers often set goals for the marketing mix and other programs (e.g., customer service). For example, as discussed in Chapter 11, specific advertising objectives such as awareness, attitude change, and so forth are often established. If a website is being used to complement other channels of distribution or is acting as a stand-alone channel, measures such as site visitors, revenue generated, and the like are required to determine if the site is performing adequately. It is thus also useful to monitor progress toward such specific objectives.

Worrying about metrics is not the favorite task of most marketers. Using a baseball (or cricket) analogy, Ambler (2000, p. 11) puts it in the following way: "Marketers are more interested in making runs than scoring." Even casual observers of human nature recognize that product managers have more interest in developing strategies and marketing programs than determining how well these have performed in the market. Metrics can help refocus attention both on specific program outcomes and on results (e.g., ROI) relevant outside of marketing.

Senior managers are placing increasing pressure on product managers to show that programs result in observable, measurable results. This is at least partly due to the Internet, which is a medium (or channel, depending on your perspective) that produces highly measurable results. General financial pressures from the stock market, global competitors, and other aspects of the quickly changing marketplace have also led senior managers to make product and other lower-level managers more accountable for money being spent. This is such an important area that the Marketing Science Institute (MSI), a nonprofit corporate-sponsored research organization with over 60 member companies, has made marketing metrics and assessing the productivity of marketing spending as its leading research priority for the last three two-year priority-setting periods.

In this final chapter, we describe marketing metrics that are used by a variety of organizations. We also describe a conceptual model for guiding a product manager's thinking in this important area. In addition, possible sources of information for the metrics are given.

A FRAMEWORK FOR MARKETING METRICS

While marketers and their annual plans naturally focus on the first two, it is important to recognize that those evaluating the budget (e.g., financial types, CMOs, CEOs) are primarily interested in financial results. Put bluntly, they don't care about awareness or attitude, they only care about the bottom line.

What Needs to Be Measured

What needs to be measured follows a natural progression from customer perceptions to product-market performance, financial returns, the value of marketing assets, and eventually stock market value (Figure 16.1). The first two categories, customer and product-market measures, then, are primarily used as diagnostic tools (to see how you are doing in terms of sales, etc., and why you are getting those results).

The next two categories, financial metrics/program effectiveness and the value of marketing assets, relate to performance assessment (i.e., Are you doing well enough?). Increasingly expenditures are required to have projected ROIs (which better be achieved) associated with them. Valuation of marketing assets has not yet "caught on" as a requirement but it is critical. Often more than half of the value of a company cannot be explained by traditional financial measures (e.g., cash flow, capital assets). Since stewardship of key assets is clearly an important task, it seems only prudent to measure these. Finally, for a publicly traded company, market capitalization is the gold standard in spite of recent irregularities. While the link from most products to market cap is hard to estimate, and product managers rarely even try, remembering what the standard is helps marketers communicate with others in the organization.

While many core measures do not vary by product type (e.g., sales), the unique characteristics of some markets may create correspondingly unique measures. As an example, Figure 16.2 shows some of the metrics for commonly monitored pharmaceuticals versus sports versus food industries. In food-related industries, product/brand managers are interested in how free standing insert (FSI) promotions perform, the "lift," or increased sales, from end-of-aisle displays, and how their marketing strategies affect the interpurchase times of the category and the brand. Pharmaceutical product managers are interested in which doctors are prescribing their drugs, share of prescriptions, and data on diagnoses and new medical procedures. Sports-related marketing managers measure stadium

FIGURE 16.1   The Metrics Value Chain

1. What Customers Think of You (Customer Metrics)
2. How Well You Do in the Product Market
3. Financial Consequences
   - Program Effectiveness/ROI
   - The Value of Marketing Assets (Brands, Customers)
   - (Stock) Market Value

FIGURE 16.2 Key Metrics by Industry

Food	Pharmaceuticals	Sports
Sales	$ Volume	Attendance
Volume	Doctor surveys	TV ratings
Share	Doctor profiling	Licensing sales
Features	Prescription data	Fan base
Displays	Procedure data	Favorite team
FSI	Diagnostic data	Favorite players
Penetration		Fan demographics
Purchase cycle		Share of market
Switching		
Loyalty		
Lift		
Coupons		
Bonus packs		

Source: Presentation given by James W. Masterson, Marketing Science Institute Conference on Marketing Metrics, October 5, 2000.

attendance, revenues from licensing logos, and share of market relative to other entertainment products. Recognizing such differences, we focus on measures likely to be relevant across a broad spectrum of products.

Customer-Based Metrics

Figure 16.3 gives some customer-based metrics. Several of these are particularly interesting. "Share of generic competition" is based on the discussion in Chapter 3 about considering competition to be those products and services that satisfy the same (generic) need and goes beyond the normal definition of market share. This concept can be tailored to an individual product category. For example, a product manager for Sears's Discover Card might expand the set of credit cards to include department store cards, debit cards, American Express cards that do not permit revolving balances, and cash. Thus, "share of wallet" would be an indicator of the percentage of times the Discover Card is used for any payment. Trial is particularly relevant for new products because a new product will rarely be successful unless a sufficient number of households or companies try it. Lifetime customer value (see Chapter 14) is a figure that can be used

FIGURE 16.3 Customer-Based Metrics

Metric	Sources of Information
Share of generic competition	Surveys, focus groups
Penetration	Syndicated sources, internal, sales force, surveys
Trial	Syndicated sources, surveys
Perceived quality	Surveys
Customer satisfaction	Surveys
Complaints	Internal
Customer defections	Sales force
Loyalty	Surveys, syndicated sources
Same customer sales	Internal
Lifetime customer value	Internal

FIGURE 16.4 Brand/Product Level Metrics

Metric	Sources of Information
Brand equity measures	Surveys
Brand "health"	Syndicated sources, surveys
Price premium	Internal

to place a value on a company such as Amazon. Customer defections are monitored by many companies as they point out possible weaknesses in the product line or aspects of the marketing strategy. Satisfaction is a particularly important measure, although overreliance on it leads to nonoptimal decisions (i.e., having a small number of ecstatic customers).

Product-Market Metrics

A key group of metrics attempt to measure brand equity or strength (Figure 16.4). One set of measures focuses on estimating brand equity or the perceived value of a brand. As discussed in Chapter 8, a number of commercial efforts exist. The advertising agency Young & Rubicam has its own proprietary measure called the Brand Asset Valuator. Landor Associates and Millward Brown, both consulting firms, have their own measures as well. Companies interested in developing their own surveys can follow conceptual models developed by Aaker (1995) and Keller (2002). Brand strength can also be estimated using the price premium obtainable in the market relative to a competitor. Brand "health" (Bhattacharya and Lodish, 2000) can be thought of as a combination of the current "well-being" of a brand (e.g., its market share) and its resistance to "disease," such as how loyal its customer base is to a promotional onslaught by a competitor.

While there are a number of possible measures, two predominate: sales and share. These "topline" measures were for a long time the goal of marketing (i.e., before the current emphasis on profits and profitable growth).

Financial Metrics

These metrics (Figure 16.5) range from sales revenue to profits, margin, etc. They are the critical results for budget evaluation. Put bluntly: no profits, no approval. One simple approach to assessing the financial value (to the firm) of a brand is to calculate the extra revenue generated by a brand versus a generic competitor (Ailawadi, Lehmann, and Neslin, 2003).

FIGURE 16.5 Financial Metrics

Metric	Sources of Information
Sales	Syndicated sources, internal, sales force
Profit	Internal
Margins	Internal
Productivity	Internal
ROI	Internal
Marketing investment	Internal

FIGURE 16.6 **Marketing Mix Metrics**

Metric	Sources of Information
Advertising:	
Awareness	Surveys
Recall	Surveys
Attitude	Surveys
Elasticity	Internal
Size of consideration set	Surveys
ROI	Internal
Brand image	Surveys
Media (GRPs, SOV)	Syndicated
Lead generation	Internal
Incremental sales	Internal
Promotion:	
Incremental sales	Syndicated, internal
Trial	Syndicated, surveys
Repeat	Syndicated, surveys
ROI	Internal
Long-term vs. short-term	Syndicated, internal
Distribution:	
Sales	Internal
Cost	Internal
% of ACV	Syndicated
Facings	Internal
Number of distributors	Internal
Sales per store/SKU	Syndicated, internal
Price:	
Sales	Syndicated, internal
Relative price	Syndicated, internal
Elasticity	Internal
% list obtained	Internal
Sales force:	
Productivity (effort)	Internal
Sales vs. goals	Internal
Customer satisfaction	Surveys
Won/lost	Internal
Customer service:	
Time to service	Internal
% resolved on first try	Internal
Perceived performance	Surveys
Costs	Internal

Marketing Mix Metrics

Each of the program elements has its own direct outcomes that in turn lead to customer, product-marketing, and financial results. Some measures used by product managers to evaluate the marketing mix are shown in Figure 16.6. In each case, cost is also needed to assess net, versus gross, impact.

Advertising

The most common metrics by which product managers measure the effectiveness of advertising are awareness, recall, change in attitudes, and incremental sales. The first three are typically measured using either commercial or company-sponsored surveys. Of particular interest is *incremental* sales, that is, the gap between observed sales and what sales would have been without either the change in advertising copy or increase in spending (commonly referred to as *weight*). Incremental-sales analyses can be conducted using internal sales and advertising data. Calculating advertising elasticities, the percentage change in sales due to a 1 percent change in advertising, requires some form of statistical analysis of sales and price data.

In addition to sales response and awareness/recall/attitude measures, product managers often measure advertising by traditional media measures, which do not measure customer response. These include gross ratings points (GRPs), which are a combination of reach (number of people reached by the advertising) multiplied by frequency (the average number of theoretical exposures based on the number of ads placed). Similarly, share-of-voice (SOV), as described in Chapter 11, measures spending relative to that of the competition and is often compared to market shares. The data necessary for these metrics are usually collected by commercial firms specializing in tracking media such as Competitive Media Reporting.

Several other interesting advertising metrics exist. Some companies track the average size and composition of what are called *consideration sets*. A consideration set is the set of brands a customer normally considers when making a purchase. Clearly, the more consideration sets you are in, the greater the sales that will result (and the converse). Since brands enter and leave consideration sets, tracking is an important activity. Survey data, including focus groups, are necessary for this metric. For expensive industrial products, advertisements in trade and other magazines do not normally result in sales but rather often produce *leads* or inquiries that are followed up by a sales call.

Sales Promotion

Normal metrics for sales promotions are incremental sales, trial, repeat, and ROI. Typically, these are estimated using syndicated data sources, but they can also be measured using surveys and internal analyses.

A particularly interesting distinction can be drawn between the short- and long-term effects of promotions. While promotions are normally used for short-term "bumps" in sales, it has been found that they can have long-term effects (Mela, Gupta, and Lehmann, 1997). The existence of long-term effects can be determined with statistical analysis of either syndicated or internal data.

Distribution

Channel metrics include sales and costs of the distribution structure. For products sold through retail channels, percentage of all commodity volume (ACV) is used. This is the percentage of the category volume in a retail trading area that is represented by the stores in which your brand is distributed. For example, if your brand has an ACV metric of 80 percent, it is in stores that represent 80 percent of the volume of that category. Specific in-store metrics such as the number of shelf facings and shelf height are also used. Related measures focus on sales per store or shelf facings.

Price

Price metrics include the obvious measures of sales and elasticity. Product managers are also interested in price relative to competitors. Particularly for industrial products, a good measure of the brand, selling efforts, and other marketing programs is the average percentage of list price obtained (or alternatively the percent sold on deal). Low percentages indicate that steep discounts are often given to win business.

Sales Force

Figure 16.6 lists four common metrics used to evaluate the effort of the sales force. The productivity measure (sales revenue per employee) is a standard financial measure. It is also normal to analyze accounts won and lost and derive statistics for their trends. Measuring the sales force against goals or quotas is usually part of the compensation program. Finally, it is becoming more common to measure and compensate the sales force based on customer satisfaction measures.

Customer Service

All products, both physical and services, have important customer service components. Customer service can be the attempted resolution of any customer problem ranging from repair to product usage questions. Some key measures are performance based, such as the average time to obtaining the service, the percentage of problems solved on the first attempt, and service costs. Unsurprisingly, an important customer-based measure is the perceived quality of the service provided by the company.

WEB METRICS

Although the marketing plan outline shown in the Appendix to Chapter 2 places the website as part of marketing programs, the Internet has generated its own set of metrics, some of which are different from those previously discussed (see Figure 16.7).

Many of the Web metrics focus on the e-commerce aspect; that is, they assume that purchases can be made. Many sites are, of course, for information purposes only. However, a major attractiveness of doing business on the Web is that results are obtained easily

FIGURE 16.7 Web Metrics

Metric	Sources of Information
Sales	Internal
Hits/visits	Syndicated, internal
Repeat visits	Syndicated, internal
"Stickiness"	Internal
Conversion rates	Internal
Revenue/customer	Internal
Profit/customer	Internal
Customer acquisition cost	Internal
% revenue from repeaters	Internal
Abandoned shopping carts	Internal
Digital/Total sales	Internal
Pageviews	Syndicated, internal

FIGURE 16.8   Top 10 Web Properties: January 2001

Weekend of January 21, 2001, U.S.			
Property	Unique Audience	Reach %	Time per Person
1. AOL Websites	28,337,785	43.09	16: 19
2. Yahoo!	23,448,157	35.66	27: 46
3. MSN	21,831,983	33.20	21: 04
4. Lycos Network	7,300,923	11.10	06: 56
5. Excite@Home	7,122,291	10.83	16: 34
6. Microsoft	6,981,513	10.62	06: 22
7. Walt Disney Internet Group	5,523,766	8.40	14: 52
8. eBay	5,364,633	8.16	43: 10
9. Time Warner	4,760,548	7.24	10: 22
10. eUniverse Network	4,249,666	6.46	09: 05

The reported Internet usage estimates are based on a sample of households that have access to the Internet and use the following platforms: Windows 95/98/NT, and MacOS 8 or higher.
The Nielsen//NetRatings Internet universe is defined as all members (two years of age or older) of U.S. households which currently have access to the Internet.
Copyright 2001 NetRatings, Inc.

and quickly. Most of the metrics can be determined by the company running the site or by its site hosting company (both are referred to here as internal sources of information).

Therefore, sales volume is an obvious metric. Similarly, site "hits" or visits and repeat visits are always measured. Besides internal measures, companies like Mediametrix and Nielsen's NetRatings supply industry data on site visits. Additionally, site sponsors are interested in the site's "stickiness," how long a visitor stays at a site and the number of pageviews, how many pages within a site a potential customer visits.

For example, Figure 16.8 shows some sample data from January 2001 for the top 10 websites in terms of their unique audience.[1] As can be seen, AOL, Yahoo! and MSN dominated in terms of both "unique" audience and reach (the percentage of Web-enabled households using the site). However, eBay dominated in terms of stickiness with an average time spent of almost 50 minutes.

With the severe slump in Internet company stocks in 2000, potential investors and analysts began paying more attention to a site's profitability. Therefore, many of the metrics in Figure 16.7 are intended to give a "bottom line" perspective on the website. A key notion is the site's *conversion rate,* the percentage of visitors who are "converted" into buyers. Revenue and profit per customer are self-explanatory. With many websites spending large amounts of money acquiring customers, analysts are interested in average customer acquisition costs. As many as two-thirds of all Web shoppers put items in their virtual shopping cart but never check out. This varies between sites and is obviously useful to track.

Many companies such as Wal-Mart offer both online and off-line opportunities to shop. This so-called "clicks-and-mortar" strategy is emerging as the dominant approach as retailers view the Web as a way to draw in new customers and create a competitive advantage over "pure play" sites by allowing customers to return unwanted items to stores rather than by mail. Therefore, one useful metric in this context is the ratio of digital to total sales.

---

[1] Usually, Mediametrix counts only "unique" visitors within a period of time, say, a month. Unique visitors are unduplicated; that is, you are only counted once if you visit the site several times.

FIGURE 16.9 Percent of Firms Reporting Metric to Board

Marketing Metric	U.S. (n = 224)	Japan (n = 117)	Germany (n = 120)	U.K. (n = 120)	France (n = 116)	Overall
Market share	73	57	97	80	90	79
Perceived product/service quality	77	68	84	·71	75	77
Customer loyalty/retention	67	56	69	58	65	64
Customer/segment profitability	73	40	74	65	59	64
Relative price	65	48	84	53	63	63
Actual/potential customer/segment lifetime value	32	35	51	32	58	40
Average	64	51	77	60	68	

Source: Barwise and Styler (2002)

SUMMARY

Marketing impacts more than sales transactions. In particular, it influences the long-term viability of the business through its impact on the important intangible assets of brands and customers. While most plans do not explicitly consider impact on brand equity and lifetime customer value, they should, since these factors determine future income and hence the financial (stock market) value of the business. Investments in brand equity or customer acquisition rarely pay off in a year, and requiring them to do so means treating expenditures on them as expenses rather than investments. The result can be serious underinvestment.

What does marketing report to the rest of the organization? A survey in five countries of CMOs (Barwise and Farley, 2003) indicates that share is, with the exception of Japan, the most likely metric to reach the board (Figure 16.9).

Of course most product managers do not report to the board. Therefore, they apparently concentrate on customer and product market measures for diagnostic purposes and financial measures for evaluating programs and justifying budgets. While monitoring metrics may be less exciting than designing ad copy, it is critical. As many, including Deming, have suggested, if you don't measure it, you won't manage it.

References

Aaker, David A (1995) *Building Strong Brands*. New York: The Free Press.

Ailawadi, Kusum L., Donald R. Lehmann, and Scott A. Neslin (2003) "Revenue Premium as an Outcome Measure of Brand Equity," *Journal of Marketing*, October, 1–17.

Ambler, Tim (2000) *Marketing and the Bottom Line*. London: Financial Times/Prentice Hall.

Barwise, Patrick, and John U. Farley (2003) "Which Marketing Metrics Are Used and Where?" *Marketing Reports*, Issue 2, 105–7.

Barwise, Patrick, and Alan Styler (2002) *Marketing Expenditure Trends*. London, U.K.: London Business School.

Bhattacharya, C. B., and Leonard M. Lodish (2000) "Brand Health: Basic Concepts and a Store Scanner Data Application." Working paper, Boston University.

Keller, Kevin Lane (2002) *Strategic Brand Management,* 2nd ed. Upper Saddle River, NJ: Prentice Hall.

Mela, Carl F., Sunil Gupta, and Donald R. Lehmann (1997) "The Long-Term Impact of Promotion and Advertising on Consumer Brand Choice," *Journal of Marketing Research,* May, 248–61.

Appendix A

Measuring the Value of Customers

Consistent with the view of a customer as an asset, the value of an individual customer is simply the net discounted margin over time derived from that customer. The expected value depends on the retention probability (r) and margin (m) over time as well as the annual cost to maintain that customer as an account (A). This can easily be set up as a standard spreadsheet (Figure A.1) and the value calculated accordingly.

In addition to the direct value of customers relationship to a firm, of course, there is value in simply having customers (who serve as an ad, in particular when they are celebrities) and in what customers communicate to other customers (word-of-mouth and, now, critically, word-of-web) and to influentials (e.g., government regulators, watchdog groups). These can overwhelm the direct impact of a particular company–customer relationship. For this section, however, we focus on the direct value customers.

The aggregate value of customers is simply the value of an average customer multiplied by the number of customers. More generally, the net aggregate value is

Value of customers = Sum over time of:

$$\begin{pmatrix} \text{Number of} \\ \text{customers} \\ \text{in time t} \end{pmatrix} \begin{pmatrix} \text{Average net} \\ \text{margin} \\ \text{in time t} \end{pmatrix} - \begin{pmatrix} \text{Acquisition} \\ \text{costs}_t \end{pmatrix} - \begin{pmatrix} \text{Retention} \\ \text{costs}_t \end{pmatrix} - \begin{pmatrix} \text{Expansion} \\ \text{costs}_t \end{pmatrix}$$

In a *very* special case, the value of a customer can be reduced to a simple formula. Specifically, if (1) the retention rate is constant over time and (2) the growth/expansion rate is constant over time (a generally untenable assumption if the growth rate is positive since growth eventually slows), the value of a customer reduces to a formula.

For an infinite time horizon[1].

$$\text{VOC} = \sum_{K=1}^{\infty} \frac{(M - A)r^{K-1}(1 + g)^{K-1}}{(1 + d)^{K-1}} = \frac{(M - A)}{1 - \dfrac{r(1 + g)}{1 + d}} = \frac{(M - A)(1 + d)}{1 + d - r(1 + g)}$$

---

[1] Note: These formulas only work when $\dfrac{r(1 + g)}{1 + d}$ is less than 1.

FIGURE A.1 Calculating the Value of a Customer: Spreadsheet Format

	Value in Year					
	1 (current)	2	3	4	...	n
Retention probability (r)	1	r_2	$r_2 r_3$	$r_2 r_3 r_4$	...	$r_2 r_3 \ldots r_n$
Gross margin (m)	m_1	m_2	m_3	m_4	...	m_n
Expected margin (r)(m)	m_1	$r_2 m_2$	$r_2 r_3 m_3$	$r_2 r_3 r_4 m_4$	...	$r_2 r_3 \ldots r_n m_n$
Annual account maintenance cost	A_1	A_2	A_3	A_4	...	A_n
Net margin	$m_1 - A_1$	$r_2(m_2 - A_2)$	...			
Discount factor	1	$\dfrac{1}{1+d}$	$\left(\dfrac{1}{1+d}\right)^2$	$\left(\dfrac{1}{1+d}\right)^3$	...	$\left(\dfrac{1}{1+d}\right)^{n-1}$
Discounted value						

where:

M = Margin.

A = Constant annual account maintenance (retention) cost.

r = (Constant) retention rate.

g = (Constant) growth in margin rate.

d = Constant discount rate.

For a finite time horizon (n years) this becomes:

$$\text{VOC} = \sum_{K=1}^{n} \frac{(M-A)r^{K-1}(1+g)^{K-1}}{(1+d)^{K-1}} = (M-A)\frac{1 - \left[\dfrac{r(1+g)}{1+d}\right]^K}{1 - \left[\dfrac{r(1+g)}{1+d}\right]}$$

In the case when the growth rate is 0 (i.e., margin is constant over time) over an infinite horizon, this reduces to the simple formula for an annuity:

$$\text{Value of a customer} = \frac{(M-A)(1+d)}{1+d-r}$$

EXAMPLE

For an interesting example, consider Federal Express when they began introducing Courier-Pak (Lovelock, 1976). In the dark old days of 1976, they sold Courier-Paks

FIGURE A.2 Value of Advertising Account: Spreadsheet Approach

	Margin	Retention	Discount Factor $\left(\frac{1}{1.12}\right)$	Present Value
1	1,617	1	1	1,617
2	1,617	.9	.89	1,299
3	1,617	.81	.80	1,037
4	1,617	.729	.71	840
5	1,617	. . .	. . .	. . .
6	1,617			
7	1,617			
8	1,617			
9	1,617			
10	1,617	.387	.360	225
Total				

for $12.50 and had a variable cost of $4.00 for a margin per pak of $8.50. One type of account was firms in the advertising business. Specifically, 140 advertising accounts accounted for 2,285 paks per month. To these facts we add the following assumptions:

1. Margin remains constant (i.e., the number of paks per account times the margin per pak stays the same).
2. The retention rate is 90 percent (which seems reasonable for satisfied customers).
3. The appropriate discount rate is 12 percent.

The typical advertising account thus generates $2{,}285/140 = 16.32$ paks per month or $(16.32)(12) = 196$ paks per year. This translates into a margin per year of $(196)(8.50) = \$1{,}617$. Using the spreadsheet approach and a 10-year horizon would then produce Figure A.2, and thus a value of about $7,200. Of course we could use an infinite horizon, but since the margin is constant, this will add little to the total discounted value as the following shows:

1. Infinite horizon: $\text{VOC} = \left(\dfrac{1{,}617}{1 - \dfrac{0.9}{1.12}}\right) = \$8{,}085$

2. 10-year horizon: $\text{VOC} = 1{,}617 \dfrac{1 - \left(\dfrac{0.19}{1.12}\right)^{10}}{\left(1 - \dfrac{0.9}{1.12}\right)} = 1{,}617 \left(\dfrac{1 - .11}{.20}\right) = \$7{,}196$

DRIVERS OF VALUE

The key drivers of the value of a particular customer are (1) the retention rate and (2) expansion (i.e., the growth rate). In the previous example, assume the retention rate was 80 percent instead of 90 percent. Using an infinite horizon, the value decreases to

$$\frac{1,617}{1 - \dfrac{0.8}{1.12}} = \$5,660$$

or 70 percent of the value at a 90 percent retention rate. Similarly if retention could be increased to 95 percent, the value becomes:

$$\frac{1,617}{1 - \dfrac{0.95}{1.12}} = \$10,653$$

which is 32 percent greater than its former value. Thus the value of a customer is very sensitive to the retention rate.

The expansion (or contraction) rate similarly has a major impact on the value of the customer. For example, if we assume a negative 10 percent growth rate, the infinite horizon value becomes

$$\frac{1,617}{1 - \dfrac{(.9)(.9)}{1.12}} = \$5,842$$

or 28 percent less. Similarly at the aggregate (firm) level, expansion comes from a combination of new customer acquisitions and expansion of same-customers' sales (margin).

There is both good news and bad news in these sensitivities. The good news is that it is clear what can be done to improve value: increase retention (e.g., through satisfaction if not barriers to exit) and expand relations with customers (e.g., cross-sell or improve the product mix). Further, small changes make a big difference, thus potentially justifying marketing activity as cost effective. On the other hand, the bad news is that since small changes in the parameters lead to big changes in valuation, there is an obvious opportunity to alter the numbers to justify a particular decision.

Name Index

Subject Index